Macroeconomic Linkage

NBER–East Asia Seminar on Economics
Volume 3

National Bureau of Economic Research
Korea Development Institute
Chung-Hua Institution for Economic Research
Tokyo Center of Economic Research

Macroeconomic Linkage

Savings, Exchange Rates, and Capital Flows

Edited by Takatoshi Ito and Anne O. Krueger

The University of Chicago Press

Chicago and London

TAKATOSHI ITO is professor of economics at Hitotsubashi University and visiting professor of economics at Harvard University. ANNE O. KRUEGER is professor of economics at Stanford University. Both are research associates of the National Bureau of Economic Research.

The University of Chicago Press, Chicago 60637
The University of Chicago Press, Ltd., London

Printed in the United States of America
03 02 01 00 99 98 97 96 95 94 1 2 3 4 5
ISBN: 0-226-38669-4 (cloth)

Library of Congress Cataloging-in-Publication Data

Macroeconomic linkage : savings, exchange rates, and capital flows / edited by Takatoshi Ito and Anne O. Krueger.
p. cm. — (NBER–East Asia seminar on economics ; v. 3)
Includes bibliographical references and index.
1. Saving and investment—East Asia—Congresses. 2. Foreign exchange rates—East Asia—Congresses. 3. Capital movements—East Asia—Congresses. I. Ito, Takatoshi, 1950– . II. Krueger, Anne O. III. Series.
HG5770.5.A3M33 1994
339.4′3′095—dc20 93-30295
CIP

⊗ The paper used in this publication meets the minimum requirements of the American National Standard for Information Sciences—Permanence of Paper for Printed Library Materials, ANSI Z39.48–1984.

Since this volume is a record of conference proceedings, it has been exempted from the rules governing critical review of manuscripts by the Board of Directors of the National Bureau (resolution adopted 8 June 1948, as revised 21 November 1949 and 20 April 1968).

Contents

Acknowledgments

The editors and participants in the Third East Asia Seminar on Economics wish to acknowledge support received to make the conference possible. Four research institutions—the National Bureau of Economic Research, Tokyo Center of Economic Research, Korea Development Institute, and Chung-Hua Institute for Economic Research—have jointly funded each of the first three seminars. We are grateful to them and believe that the contents of this volume, and others in the series, provide an indication of the productivity of that support.

In turn, TCER received support from the Mitsubishi International Fund, and NBER from the Starr Foundation. Their support is acknowledged with thanks.

The Third East Asia Seminar on Economics was held in Sapporo. All participants agreed that the seminar was unusual for the warm hospitality and atmosphere of the conference. The local organizing committee, the EASE 92 Sapporo Local Committee, was responsible for local arrangements and local financial support. The local committee's efforts were essential in providing conference participants with a congenial atmosphere and, in addition, a marvelous introduction to the lovely city of Sapporo.

The EASE 92 Sapporo Local Committee was chaired by Tomoo Nakano. We are deeply indebted to him, and to the other members of the committee and the staff, for warm memories of the conference. Members of the committee and their positions at the time of the conference were:

Committee chairman	Tomoo Nakano, chairman, Hokkaido Economic Federation, and chairman, Hokkaido Electric Power Co., Inc.
Committee vice chairman	Hiroshi Yamauchi, chairman, Hokkaido Community for Economic Development, and president, Hokkaido Taku-Choku Bank, Ltd.

Committee vice chairman	Yasuaki Kashihara, chairman, Northern Regions Center, and chairman, Itogumi Co., Ltd.
Member	Hiroshi Hori, president, Hokkaido Bank, Ltd.
Member and auditor	Masanao Takei, president, North Pacific Bank, Ltd.
Member and auditor	Takashi Shioda, president, Sapporo Bank, Ltd.
Member	Hideji Kitagawa, president, Hokkaido Shinbun Press
Member	Takeshi Itagaki, president, Sapporo International Communication Plaza
Member	Kiyo Akiyama, president, Akiyama Inc.
Member	Hiroshi Yamauchi, chairman, Hokkaido Northern Regions Economic Exchange Association
Member	Arihiro Hayasaka, president, Sapporo Junior Chamber Incorporated
Member	Masao Morimoto, vice chairman, North Pacific Region Advanced Research Center

In addition to the local organizing committee, a number of other individuals contributed to the success of the conference. They include: Kazuo Nojima, Yasuro Ikeshiro, Tetsuo Shimokawa, Hiroaki Doi, Kazuo Yoshida, Kenichi Oosawa. We also wish to thank All Nippon Airways, which provided priority reservations for conference participants with fare discounts.

In addition, Satomi Yanagisawa (Akiyama Inc.), Julie Cairns, Wilson Alley, Takao Chiba, and Tsutomu Kida provided assistance during the conference. Masao Satake (Otaru University of Commerce) and Yoshihiro Kobayashi (Hokkaido University) provided helpful advice on organizing the conference. Mr. Sagara was an excellent research assistant.

Finally, but far from last, we are indebted to Akio Matsue (North Pacific Region Research Center), Machiko Maruyama (Akiyama Inc.), Mitsuhiro Kuramasu (Junior Chamber), and Norio Takayama (Junior Chamber), whose support of the conference was invaluable.

Introduction

Takatoshi Ito and Anne O. Krueger

This volume contains the papers presented at the third annual East Asia Seminar, held in Sapporo from June 17 to June 19, 1992. The theme of the conference was the macroeconomic linkages between the global economy and the East Asian and North American countries.

The world economy has become so highly integrated that almost anything that happens in one country affects all others. But the key macroeconomic variables that strongly affect the global environment include savings and investment behavior, exchange rates, monetary and fiscal policies (including interest rate determination) and the resulting capital flows, and of course, trade. In the 1980s, the macroeconomic experience of the East Asian countries was important for their own economies and also strongly affected North America and the rest of the world. Real exchange rate swings of the yen, the won, the NT dollar, and the U.S. dollar were pronounced. The large U.S. current account deficit was offset, at least in part, by large Japanese capital flows to the United States. In the 1980s, Japan, and later Korea and Taiwan, recorded large current account surpluses which triggered U.S. political pressure on these countries.

These events led to a closer examination of the key macroeconomic linkages between countries. The papers in this volume examine some important aspects of these relationships, and increase our understanding of the extent of interdependence, and the ways in which economic events in one country are transmitted to, and affected by, events in the rest of the world.

The papers presented here are organized around four themes: the overall determinants of growth and trading relations, monetary policies in relation to

Takatoshi Ito is professor of economics at Hitotsubashi University and visiting professor of economics at Harvard University. Anne O. Krueger is professor of economics at Stanford University. Both are research associates of the National Bureau of Economic Research.

capital controls and capital account, the impact of exchange rate behavior on industrial structure, and, finally, the potential for greater regional integration.

Overall growth has been an important phenomenon in itself, but in addition, the rapidly growing East Asian countries have also had increasingly strong trade and payments positions. The factors accounting for these phenomena are investigated in four papers. The first of these, by John Helliwell, contains an overview and analysis of the growth performances of the Asian countries. Noting that East Asia has been spectacularly successful in achieving growth, Helliwell attempts through regression analysis to understand the factors that led to that high growth. Frequently given explanations that he tests include the openness of the trade regime, measured by the frequency of nontariff barriers to imports, the appropriateness of the real exchange rate as reflected by the black market exchange premium, and the relative importance of import duty receipts. He also uses an index of the degree of democracy and measures of the extent of human capital. Human capital fails to explain the rapid growth of the East Asian countries or the lower growth of South Asian countries. Helliwell's regression results find more explanatory power in the measures of openness of the economies. In the discussion that follows, other factors contributing to the differentials in growth rates are discussed.

The Japanese current account balance has been particularly important for the international economy, providing sizable net savings to the rest of the world, especially the United States. In the second paper, Takatoshi Ito investigates the determinants of the Japanese current account, analyzing the extent to which underlying factors such as the real exchange rate, and more transitory factors such as the Gulf War contributions, have affected its size. Ito concludes that the underlying Japanese surplus was shrinking until 1991, but that even taking into account transitory factors, it began increasing again in that year. Ito points to real exchange rate behavior as a key factor in that reversal and uses estimated export and import functions to simulate the responses to the real exchange rate in the absence of a transitory component. His simulations indicate that, given the real exchange rate, the current account balance in Japan would have begun increasing in 1991 in the absence of transitory factors.

The next paper, by Bon Ho Koo and Won-Am Park, analyzes the large Korean current account surpluses which emerged from 1986 to 1988 and their disappearance starting in 1989. They point to the low oil price, the appreciation of the yen, and lower worldwide interest rates as factors accounting for the emergence of the large surplus. After 1989, won appreciation and domestic demand expansion policies led to a reversal of these surpluses. Just as Ito found for Japan, Koo and Park find that an upturn in the world economy is likely to result in a greater increase in exports of goods and services than in imports and thus in an improvement in Korea's current account balance.

The final paper focussing on determinants of the capital account examines the case of Taiwan. Gee San analyzed the effects on Taiwan's trade flows of fluctuations in the NT dollar exchange rate, estimating export and import functions for Taiwan. He found that the rapid appreciation of the NT dollar against the U.S. dollar in the late 1980s had a major effect on the Taiwanese export structure.

The second group of papers focuses on capital controls and monetary policies. Sung Hee Jwa's analysis investigates the history of Korean capital controls since the early 1980s and contrasts them with the situation in Japan, Taiwan, and Indonesia. Capital controls in Korea were heavily influenced by the current account deficits in the early 1980s, as the authorities were concerned with mounting foreign debt at the time of the world debt crisis. After the Korean current account shifted to surplus in 1986, capital inflows began, which in turn resulted in won appreciation (encouraged by the U.S. government). The net result was greatly increased capital mobility both into and out of Korea by the late 1980s, with consequences for the functioning of domestic monetary policies.

In the next paper, Rachel McCulloch analyzes the contribution of Japanese and other East Asian current accounts to global savings, asking how net demands for international investment and savings will balance in the 1990s. She concludes that there may be a smaller contribution to world savings from Japan than in the past and notes that this could result in smaller flows of foreign direct investment into other countries in the East Asian region. However, McCulloch's data and analysis suggest that the overall magnitude of any shift is not likely to be great and that changes in world real interest rates could accommodate most of any change.

The third paper focusing on capital flows and monetary controls examines Taiwanese price and monetary behavior. Chung-Shu Wu and Jin-Lung Lin begin by noting that Taiwan has had a high rate of monetary growth combined with remarkable price stability. They note, however, that the NT dollar appreciated during the period, so that there was a change in relative prices; simultaneously, output was growing rapidly. As a result of exchange rate appreciation, prices of Taiwanese goods became more expensive, but that was offset in the price index by the falling (in NT dollars) price of traded goods. Meanwhile, rapid growth of output also absorbed some of the monetary growth. In a quantity-of-money framework, the increased quantity of goods and the falling price of foreign goods enabled the overall price level to remain stable. In the ensuing discussion, Wu and Lin note that the decline in oil prices was a factor contributing to the remarkable growth and stability experienced not only by Taiwan but also by other East Asian countries.

The last two papers in this section focus on the theoretical properties of exchange rates, real money balances, and foreign borrowing as possible explanatory variables important in explaining East Asian performance in the 1980s. Shin-ichi Fukuda investigates the dynamic properties of exchange rates and real money balances in a small open economy in which the representative agent has real money balances in his utility function. He shows that, under a floating exchange rate regime, there are circumstances in which there can be endogenous cycles in the exchange rate. One interesting question raised in the discussion is whether such exchange rate behavior could be distinguished from that under a random walk.

One of the key features of the 1980s in the international economic arena was the fluctuation in real exchange rates. The third group of papers examines the effects of these fluctuations on industrial structures of countries in the region. Pochih Chen, Chi Shive, and Cheng Chung Chu first examine the change in the commodity composition of Taiwan's exports as the NT dollar appreciated toward the end of the 1980s. As real appreciation took place, Taiwan's exports of labor-intensive commodities diminished as capital-intensive industries' exports expanded. By the end of the decade, Taiwan's comparative advantage appeared to lie in products with a medium degree of both labor and capital intensity, compared to the United States and Japan. Human capital appears to have emerged as a major factor affecting Taiwan's comparative advantage.

Bih Jane Liu also examines the effects of NT dollar appreciation, focusing on more short-run factors. She investigates why the pass-through effects of NT dollar appreciation to the U.S. dollar–denominated price of Taiwanese exports was so small. Her first step is to develop a model in which oligopolistic firms produce and export two differentiated products with a cost externality. Liu then shows that the larger the cost externality, the larger the degree of pass through. However, if the externality becomes sufficiently large, the degree of pass through can even turn negative. Empirical tests of this model for Taiwan show that the pass-through ratio (i.e., the elasticity of the export price with respect to the exchange rate) is less than one in most industries and even negative in a few.

In the final paper in the third group, Kazumi Asako and Yoshiyasu Ono investigate the short-run dynamics of inventory adjustment and exports to analyze the extent to which the export-drive hypothesis may be valid. The export-drive hypothesis is that an extra effort is made to push exports when unplanned inventories rise due to sluggish domestic demand. It is assumed that the firm sells in both domestic and foreign markets. When there is inventory accumulation due to an autonomous decrease in domestic demand, it is optimal to increase exports because of production and inventory smoothing. Thereafter, inventories and exports gradually decline to a new steady state. Under these circumstances, one would observe a positive correlation between inventory holdings and exports. For the importing country, if a quota reduces its trade deficit by the same amount as a tariff, the quota improves welfare more by shifting the inventory cost of adjustment to the exporting country.

The last set of papers examines questions that are important regarding regional linkages. All focus on the extent of future regional integration.

Jeffrey Frankel and Shang-Jin Wei analyze the extent to which there are regional linkages that might permit the yen to become a regional currency. There are three ways in which this might happen. First, the yen could become increasingly important over time as a currency with respect to which other

Asian countries set their exchange rate policies. Second, there might be a regional trading bloc centered on Japan. Third, the fact that Japan is a low-inflation country and other countries stabilize their exchange rates by pegging to its yen might increase the role of intraregional trade.

Frankel and Wei regress the various Asian exchange rates on each other and the U.S. dollar and the European currencies. They find that the yen is far from replacing the U.S. dollar in the region. They also find that the share of intra-regional trade in East Asia does not show any upward trend in the 1980s. Turning to bilateral trade flows, they examine these flows with respect to the volatility of exchange rates and find that more volatility does seem to reduce trade flows. All of these findings suggest that there is little evidence of the formation of a yen bloc and that strong trade and other economic ties continue to link East Asian economies to the United States.

Hiroo Taguchi then proceeds to examine the possibility of a yen bloc in a parallel fashion. The three roles that the yen could play would be: (1) a currency used by nonresidents, (2) a currency anchoring a trade bloc of Asian countries, and (3) a nominal anchor for other Asian countries' exchange rates. Taguchi, like Frankel and Wei, finds little basis for the hypothesis that the yen will become a regional currency or that a trade bloc might form. He does conclude, however, that there may be some value to other Asian countries in using the yen increasingly as a nominal anchor for their own currencies.

The final paper is by Junichi Goto and Koichi Hamada, and it considers the necessary preconditions for Asian regional integration. They find more similarities among Asian countries and more interdependence than was present in Europe in the 1950s before the start of the Common Market there. Using principal component analysis, they also find that real disturbances in East Asia are more closely synchronized than in other regions and that the degree of capital and labor mobility is quite high. However, noting the strong trading ties with the United States, they conclude that there is little or no possibility for an Asian free trade area that excludes the United States.

Hence, although Goto and Hamada find more basis for increasing regional integration than do Frankel and Wei or Taguchi, none considers that East Asian regional linkages could come at the expense of global exchange and trade relations. Linkages across the Pacific, and with the global economy, are too valuable and too important for Asian countries to be able to contemplate any regional linkages that would sacrifice integration with the rest of the world.

1 International Growth Linkages: Evidence from Asia and the OECD

John F. Helliwell

Attempts to estimate models of comparative growth applicable to all of the world's economies have found the Asian experience to be different in key respects from that of the Organization for Economic Co-operation and Development (OECD) countries. The faster-growing Asian economies have typically relied on an outward-looking trading strategy and have rapidly adopted, and sometimes leapfrogged, technical advances developed and originally applied in other countries. This paper seeks to link these two issues, by first assessing the extent to which comparative growth models fitted to global and OECD evidence apply to the Asian experience, and then seeing if differing openness among the Asian economies helps to explain their relative growth rates.

The evidence will be presented in stages. The first section will supply some background and results from a model of comparative growth applied to a global sample of countries, with special attention to the extent to which convergence of growth rates is apparent once due allowance is made for differing rates of accumulation of physical and human capital and for differences in average scale. Then the focus will turn to the same model fitted to the industrial countries and to a step-by-step assessment of the reasons why, and extent to which, the model does not explain the comparative growth performance of the Asian economies. This will be followed by some tests of the contribution of other factors to explaining the Asian growth experience, with special attention to the extent to which the Asian countries are economically and politically open to the rest of the world.

Evidence on these issues is of interest far beyond the boundaries of the countries concerned, since more than half of the world's population lives in Asia,

John F. Helliwell is Mackenzie King Visiting Professor of Canadian Studies at Harvard University, professor of economics at the University of British Columbia, and a research associate of the National Bureau of Economic Research.

and what happens in the Asian economies is bound to become ever more important at the global level. This growing importance is due in part to growing international interdependence, whether measured by trade shares or by the shrinking relative costs of transport and communications, and in part to the fact that average growth rates in Asia are likely to remain above those in the rest of the world for decades to come.

1.1 Background and Global Evidence

The initial results reported in this paper are drawn from cross-sectional estimates of a comparative growth model fitted to explain the growth of GDP per adult in 98 countries between 1960 and 1985.[1] The particular equation used is based on an extended form of the Solow (1956, 1957) growth model, as augmented by Mankiw, Romer, and Weil (1992) to include human capital accumulation, with real output determined as a Cobb-Douglas function of physical capital, human capital, and efficiency units of labor:

$$(1) \qquad Y(t) = K(t)^{\alpha} H(t)^{\beta} (A(t)L(t))^{1-\alpha-\beta},$$

where H is the stock of human capital, L the stock of labor (growing at rate n), K the stock of physical capital, depreciating at the rate δ, and A the level of technology, growing at the constant rate g. The coefficients imply constant returns to all factors taken together, and hence diminishing returns to any combination of physical and human capital. If s_k is the fraction of output invested in physical capital and s_h the fraction invested in human capital, then in the steady state the log of output per capita is

$$(2) \quad \ln(Y(t)/L(t)) = \ln A(0) + gt - ((\alpha + \beta)/(1 - \alpha - \beta))\ln(n + g + \delta) \\ + (\alpha/(1 - \alpha - \beta))\ln(s_k) + (\beta/(1 - \alpha - \beta))\ln(s_h).$$

This framework is extended to include the possibility of what Mankiw et al. call "conditional convergence," that if each country starts at some level of output that differs from its steady-state value, there will be convergence toward the steady-state growth path for that country. This need not imply that all countries have the same equilibrium level of income per capita (they argue that the level of A can be different across countries, based on variations in natural resources, institutions, and other factors unrelated to the stocks of human and physical capital) or even the same growth rate, since the equilibrium growth rate for each country will depend on its population growth and investment in human and physical capital. The Solow model augmented for human capital accumulation predicts that the rate of convergence of each country toward its steady-state growth path will be at the proportional rate λ, where

$$(3) \qquad \lambda = (n + g + \delta)(1 - \alpha - \beta).$$

1. The real GDP data are from the Mark IV data sample described in Summers and Heston (1988), as augmented and implemented by Mankiw, Romer, and Weil (1992).

The log difference between current income per effective worker and that in any given earlier period 0 is thus given by

$$(4) \quad \ln(y(t)) - \ln(y(0)) = (1 - e^{-\lambda t})(\alpha/1 - \alpha - \beta))\ln(s_k) + (1 - e^{-\lambda t})(\beta/(1 - \alpha - \beta))\ln(s_h) - (1 - e^{-\lambda t}) ((\alpha + \beta)/(1 - \alpha - \beta))\ln(n + g + \delta) - (1 - e^{-\lambda t})\ln(y(0)).$$

Applied by Mankiw et al. to a cross-sectional sample of the growth experience of 98 countries from 1960 to 1985, this equation seemed to fit the experience of the developing as well as the industrial countries. There was evidence of conditional convergence for the whole sample of countries, as well as for the more restricted sample of industrial countries. Their results also showed that allowing for the accumulation of human capital lowered the estimated coefficient on physical capital to a level that was consistent with capital's share in output, and hence with the Cobb-Douglas assumption of constant returns to scale. Mankiw et al. interpreted their results as a vindication of the augmented Solow model and an implicit rejection of the increasing number of models built on the assumption that knowledge spillovers created the likelihood of increasing returns to scale at the national level.[2] In the light of earlier results finding some significant evidence of modest returns to average scale at the national level,[3] the equations used in this paper augment equation (4) to include scale effects and also impose the coefficient restrictions implied by equation (4), so that the final form for estimation using cross-sectional data for growth in GDP per adult between 1960 and 1985 is

$$(5) \quad \ln(\text{GDPa85}) - \ln(\text{GDPa60}) = a_0 + a_1\ln(\text{scale}) + a_2\ln(\text{GDPa60}) + a_3(\ln(\text{invest}) - \ln(n + g + \delta)) + a_4(\ln(\text{school}) - \ln(n + g + \delta)),$$

where $a_2 = -(1 - e^{-\lambda 25})$,
$a_3 = (1 - e^{-\lambda 25}(\alpha/(1 - \alpha - \beta))$,
$a_4 = (1 - e^{-\lambda 25})(\beta/(1 - \alpha - \beta))$.

In the Mankiw et al. framework, the productivity index may have a different level in each country (to account for resource endowments, etc.), but has the same exogenous growth rate in each country. This may be contrasted with an alternative that I have previously developed and tested with the collaboration

2. For examples, see Romer (1986, 1990a, 1990b) and Lucas (1988, 1990). Alternative endogenous growth models by Grossman and Helpman (1989, 1990a, 1990b) assume economies of scale and knowledge spillovers at the industry level, which has no necessary implications for returns to scale at the national level. See Helpman (1991) for a helpful survey.

3. The evidence for increasing returns is based entirely on the experience of the industrial countries. Increasing the sample to include 98 countries does not overturn the result, but neither does it provide any evidence for returns to scale. Tests for nonlinearity in the scale effect (reported in Helliwell and Chung 1991c) did not find any apparent threshold effects.

of Alan Chung,[4] in which the efficiency indexes initially grow at different rates in each country, with convergence taking place in the rates of growth, and possibly in the levels, of the technology indexes. In this alternative, international transfers of knowledge are given a central role in convergence, with the initially poorer countries able to have efficiency levels that grow faster than those in the richer countries. This is because the initially poorer countries are able to make use of current best practice procedures already in use in the more productive economies. If a large part of convergence takes place through this channel, rather than just by different investment rates and general use of the same technologies, then it offers strong support for models, such as those of Grossman and Helpman (1991), that treat technology transfer as a costly and time-using process that depends on market structure and relative levels of income and education. It also implies that at least part of the convergence may take place without high levels of investment, although it leaves unspecified the conditions that best facilitate international transmission of technical progress. This issue will be the focus of a later section. For the moment, it is sufficient to note that studies of the OECD economies have shown strong convergence in the rates of growth of "Solow residuals," even after allowing for differences in the rates of investment in human capital.[5] These results force the adoption of a different interpretation of the constant term in cross-sectional growth regressions. In the Mankiw et al. framework, the estimated constant term is just the logarithm of the ratio of equilibrium incomes. If convergence of productivity growth is assumed, the estimated constant term in a cross-sectional regression is a function of the equilibrium-level differences, as well as the speed of convergence, of growth rates and the initial level-differences of the productivity indexes.

Figure 1.1 shows the conditional convergence for the 98-country global sample. The curve shows the predicted growth rate[6] for any country as a function of its 1960 real GDP per capita, assuming the country to have global average values for all of the other variables in equation (i) of table 1.1. The two-letter country codes used in the figures are defined in appendix A. The vertical distance between each country's rectangle and the curve is that country's error term in the cross-country regression and, hence, shows the extent to which the

4. In Helliwell, Sturm, and Salou (1985) and Helliwell and Chung (1991b) for the G-7, in Helliwell and Chung (1991a) for 19 industrial counties, and in Helliwell and Chung (1992c) for 19 industrial and 8 Asian economies. The effects of adding variations to human capital are assessed in Helliwell and Chung (1992a).

5. The Solow residuals are obtained by inverting equation (1) to define a measured series for $A(t)$ using actual values for Y and K, and using the number of employees to represent the labor input HL. Tests supporting convergence of the rates of growth of the Solow residuals for the OECD countries are reported in Helliwell and Chung (1991a) and Helliwell (1992b).

6. The predicted values in the figures are presented as average annual proportionate growth rates, obtained by dividing by 25 the estimated growth rates from the equations reported in table 1.1, which estimate the results for growth over a 25-year period. Figure 1.1 is based on the parameter estimates from the global equation (i), while figures 1.2–1.6 are based on the OECD equation (ii).

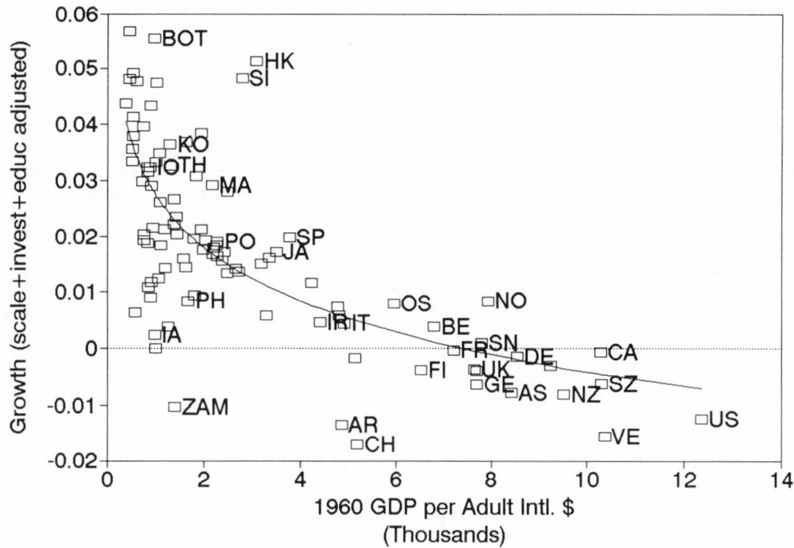

Fig. 1.1 Conditional convergence in the global economy
Note: All country codes in these and the other figures in this chapter are explained in appendix A, with the following exceptions: AR = Argentina; BOT = Botswana; VE = Venezuela; ZAM = Zambia.

global model fits that country's experience. If separate dummy variables are added for continents, growth rates are found to be lower in Africa and South America. There is no significant difference for average growth in Asia, but the model nonetheless does a poor job of explaining the growth experiences of the Asian economies, as can be seen by the rectangles for some of the Asian countries. The model fails to capture either the high growth of Singapore, Hong Kong, and Korea, or the low growth of India and Sri Lanka. To delve further into this, we turn to consider the model's predictions for each of the key factors it uses to explain growth differences. This will be done using parameter estimates for the OECD countries, which do not differ dramatically from those in the global sample and permit a closer inspection of actual and predicted growth rates for each of the Asian and OECD countries.

1.2 Comparing Growth in Asia and the OECD

Figure 1.2 is somewhat akin to figure 1.1, in that growth is on the vertical axis and initial real GDP is on the horizontal axis. There are three key differences. Here the rectangles show each country's actual average annual growth rate of real GDP per adult over the 1960–85 period, while the plus signs vertically above or below each rectangle show what that country's growth rate is

Table 1.1 **Cross-Country Growth Equations**

	Equation					
	(i)	(ii)	(iii)	(iv)	(v)	(vi)
N	98	22	13	11	11	11
Sample	Global	OECD	Asia	Asia	Asia	Asia
Constant	1.758	1.579	0.271	2.10	1.087	1.318
	(3.28)	(2.98)	(2.80)	(4.54)	(6.95)	(7.30)
Coefficients						
scale	.062	.061	−.093			
	(2.53)	(2.79)	(1.02)			
1960GDPa	−.343	−.442	.175			
	(5.60)	(7.29)	(0.66)			
invest − $(n + g + d)$	.502	.467	1.070			
	(6.26)	(3.54)	(3.14)			
school − $(n + g + d)$	.197	.237	−.418			
	(3.31)	(1.95)	(1.33)			
ln(NTB)				−.365		
				(2.80)		
ln(1.0 + .01*BLACK)					−1.505	
					(2.39)	
ln(1.0 + .01*TARIFF)						−4.308
						(3.20)
$\bar{R}^2$	.495	.752	.563	.406	.320	.481
SEE	.317	.123	.317	.371	.397	.347

Source: Series for NTB, BLACK, and TARIFF from World Bank (1991).

Notes: Absolute values of *t*-statistics are in parentheses. The dependent variable in all equations is the growth in real GDP per adult from 1960 to 1985, i.e., ln(GDPa85) − ln(GDPa60).

NTB is the total number of nontariff barriers; BLACK the average percentage black market exchange premium, 1971–85; and TARIFF total tariff revenues, as a percentage of total imports, average over 1971–85.

predicted to be, using the parameters based on OECD data[7] and each country's own actual values for each of the model variables.[8]

The distance by which the rectangle is above the plus sign is thus the equation error for that country.[9] The curve in figure 1.2 shows the predicted growth rate for any country that has the initial income recorded on the horizontal axis and average values for the other variables in equation (ii) of table 1.1. The distance between the curve and the plus sign for each country shows how much of its growth is explained by that country's differences from average values for

7. The parameter estimates are shown in equation (ii) of table 1.1.

8. For all of the results reported in this paper, Japan is treated as part of the OECD sample, since it is a member of the OECD and since the OECD model fits the Japanese experience closely enough that the parameter estimates do not depend materially on whether Japan is included.

9. The distance between the rectangle and the plus sign in figure 1.2 is thus analogous to the distance between the rectangles and the curve in figure 1.1, but is not exactly the same because in figure 1.1 the parameters are based on the global sample while the OECD sample is used to estimate the equation used to define the predicted values in figure 1.2.

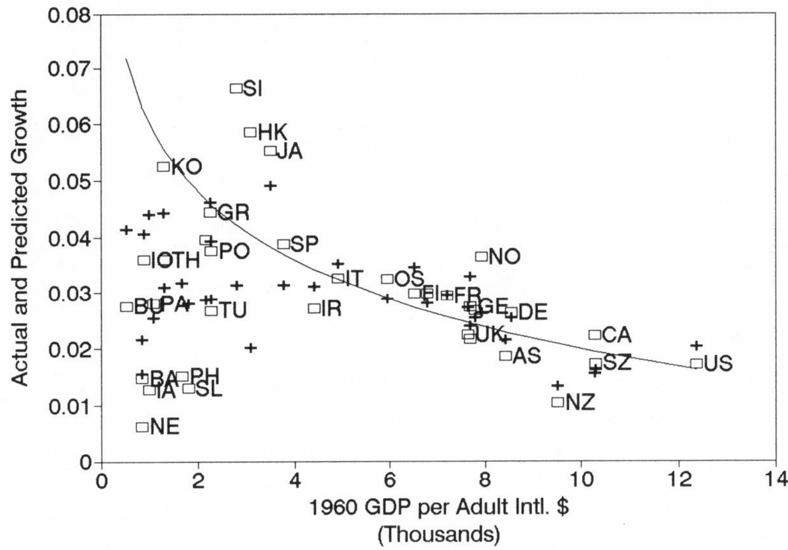

Fig. 1.2 Actual and predicted growth versus 1960 income per adult: OECD and Asia

Note: See note for fig 1.1.

investment rates, schooling, population growth, and scale. The rectangles for the Asian economies, with the exception of Korea, are far from the curve. In some cases, such as that of Japan, most of the distance is explained by the model, while in others, especially Singapore and Hong Kong, the error of the model is even larger than the distance between the curve and the actual growth performance. According to the model, these two economies should have had much lower growth rates, given their relatively high initial incomes (relative to those in most non-OECD countries) and very small size, even given their relatively high investment rates. In fact, there is no evidence of convergence among the Asian economies, with the three richest—Japan, Hong Kong, and Singapore—having the fastest subsequent growth rates, while the two slowest growing—India and Nepal—among those with the lowest initial income levels. Direct estimation of the comparative growth model for Asia, as shown in equation (iii) of table 1.1, shows (insignificant) diseconomies of scale, (insignificant) divergence rather than convergence, a significant investment effect with twice the coefficient estimated for either the global or the OECD samples, and an insignificant negative effect of schooling.

Figures 1.3–1.5 investigate the model results more closely by plotting three of the model's other key partial relationships to show some of the important differences between the Asian and the OECD economies, and among the Asian economies themselves. In all three figures, the curves are drawn using the parameters estimated for the OECD countries. Figure 1.3 shows growth rates

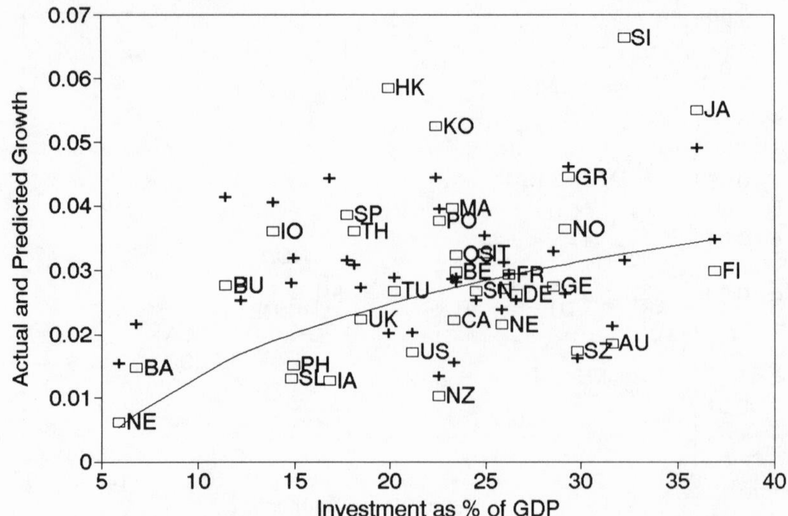

Fig. 1.3 Actual and predicted growth versus investment as percentage of GDP: in OECD and Asia
Note: See note for fig. 1.1.

plotted against investment rates and demonstrates why the investment effect is seen to be so high for the Asian sample on its own (as shown by eq. [iii] in table 1.1), with especially high investment in the faster-growing countries and abnormally low investment in the slow growers. Of course, simultaneous equations bias is likely to be a serious problem in this case, as growth encouraged by other factors would imply higher investment rates in the faster-growing countries to keep the ratios of capital to labor at their cost-minimizing levels.

Figure 1.4 shows the relation between schooling and growth. As shown by the flat curve, the estimated relation is weak for the OECD countries, while equation (iii) in table 1.1 shows that it is even negative for the Asian economies. The variable is significant in the global sample, as shown by equation (i) in table 1.1, because of educational differences among the African countries, and to a lesser extent among the Latin American countries. In Asia, the relation is upset both by the high-growth countries with low schooling rates (Pakistan, Burma, Indonesia, and Thailand) and the slow-growing countries with high schooling ratios (Sri Lanka and the Philippines). To test whether this result was dependent on the use of a particular measure of educational attainment, three alternative variables were also assessed, including the adult literacy rate, the average years of education in the labor force, and estimated years of education of the population of working age.[10] The simple correlations of these three

10. All three of the alternative series are drawn from World Bank (1991), with values equal to the average of the reported observations over the 1960–85 estimation period. The values used are recorded in appendixes.

variables with each other, and with the secondary schooling variable used in the initial regressions, lie between .8 and .9. Each of these three alternative variables attracts an insignificant negative coefficient if used to replace the schooling variable in equation (iii) of table 1.1. Thus the insignificant negative coefficient on schooling in the Asian equation (iii) in table 1.1 is not simply a result of the use of a peculiar measure of educational attainment, leaving open the question of why measures of educational attainment have less cross-sectional explanatory power in Asia than elsewhere among the developing countries.

Figure 1.5 shows the relation between scale and growth, which is significant but of modest size for the OECD (degree of returns to scale at the national level of 1.061) and of the reverse sign for the Asian economies, chiefly because of the influence of small but fast-growing Singapore and Hong Kong and of large but slow-growing India.

Finally, before turning to some attempts to assess the effect of economic openness on relative growth differences among the Asian economies, figure 1.6 shows the relation between growth rates and a measure of political democracy in 1960. Attempts to unravel the complex linkages between political openness and economic growth have generally shown a strong positive relation between a country's level of per capita income and current and subsequent values of several different measures of democracy, including indexes of civil liberties as well as political rights. As for the reverse linkages from democracy to subsequent economic growth, they have proved difficult to measure, in part because of the shortage of data to enable the simultaneous feedbacks from income to

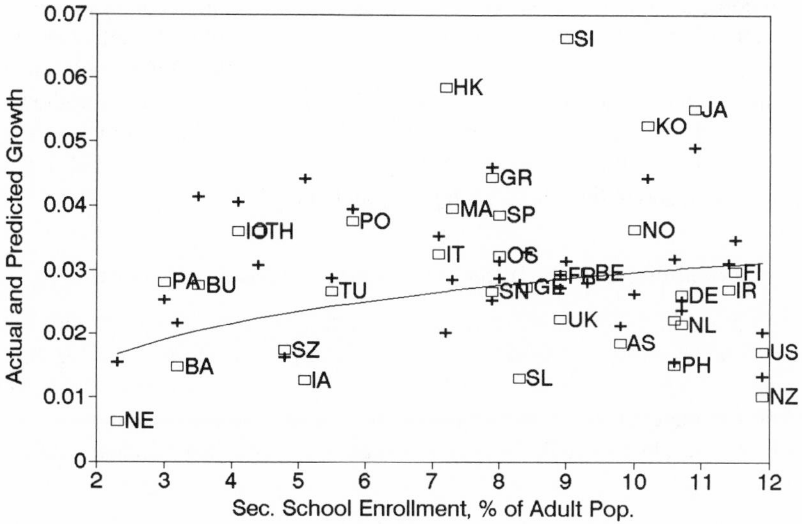

Fig. 1.4 Actual and predicted growth versus secondary school enrollment: OECD and Asia

Note: See note for fig. 1.1.

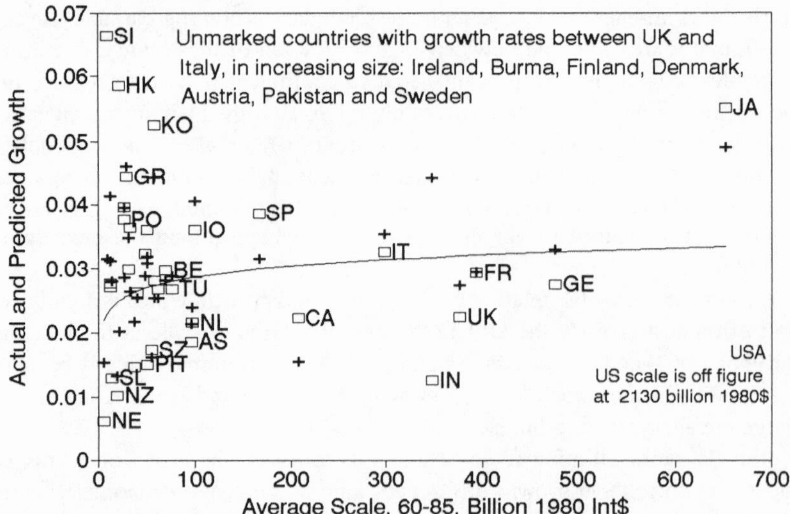

Fig. 1.5 Actual and predicted growth versus scale: OECD and Asia
Note: See note for fig. 1.1.

democracy to be disentangled from the effects of democracy on economic growth.[11] When simultaneous feedbacks are accounted for, as they are by the use of Bollen's (1980, 1990) index of democracy for 1960, the results tend to show a generally negative but very slight effect on subsequent economic growth, for given levels of investment and education. When the positive effects of democracy on education and investment are taken into account, however, the net effect seems to be about zero for the global sample.[12] Simple correlations between the Bollen index and growth, for both the OECD and Asian samples, tend to confirm this result, as does visual inspection of the data shown in figure 1.6. More direct attempts to make use of the Bollen index in explaining growth differences among the Asian economies will be found in the next section and in the equations reported in table 1.2.

1.3 Explaining Growth Differences among the Asian Economies

As noted in the introduction, many of the faster-growing Asian economies have relied heavily on an outward-looking strategy. This section draws together some measures of openness collected and distributed by the World Bank (1991) in the course of research for the bank's 1991 *World Development Report.* The results reported can only be suggestive rather than conclusive, since

11. The substantial but inconclusive empirical literature is surveyed by Sirowy and Inkeles (1990).

12. These results are reported in Helliwell (1992a).

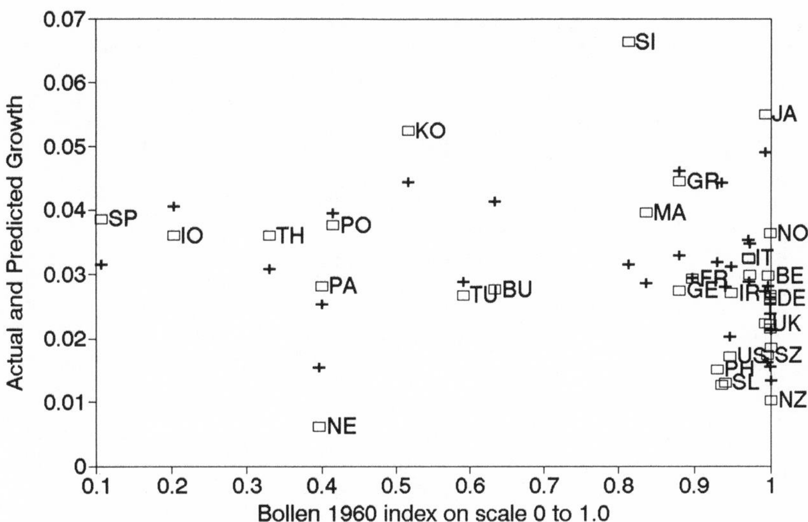

Fig. 1.6 Actual and predicted growth versus 1960 Bollen index of democracy: OECD and Asia
Note: See note for fig. 1.1.

the size of the sample is small and only three measures of economic openness have been assessed. However, as shown by figures 1.7–1.9, and in equations (iv)–(vi) of table 1.1, there is a significant relation between each of the measures of openness and economic growth for the sample of 11 countries for which both types of data are available.[13]

The first of the three measures is the frequency of nontariff barriers (NTBs) applied to all goods, with the total for each country based on total world imports of the products.[14] The regression explains about 40 percent of the cross-sectional variation in growth rates, although the risk of simultaneous equations bias may be serious with an independent variable measured four-fifths of the way through the growth period under review, since countries that succeed in growing quickly for some other reasons may thereafter choose to liberalize their trade. However, figure 1.7 shows that the countries are divided into two distinct groups, with the faster-growing countries generally having fewer nontariff barriers not just in 1981 but over the preceding years as well.

The second measure of openness is the black market exchange premium, which presumably relates to the mobility of capital at least as much as of goods, and is averaged over the period 1971–85, the longest period for which

13. The sample is reduced from 13 to 11 because the measures of openness are not available for Burma and Nepal. The data used are shown in appendix B.

14. The series used here is NTBW5, measured as of 1981, based on UNCTAD (1987) primary data and made available and described in World Bank (1991).

Table 1.2 **Combined Growth Equations for Asia**

	Equation					
	(i)	(ii)	(iii)	(iv)	(v)	(vi)
N	11	11	11	9	9	9
Sample	Asia	Asia	Asia	Asia	Asia	Asia
Constant	1.714	1.579	0.271	3.64	1.512	3.85
	(4.03)	(2.98)	(2.80)	(8.71)	(4.34)	(10.11)
Coefficients						
Bollen 1960				−.823	−.360	−.904
				(4.03)	(0.81)	(4.62)
invest		.532	.607	1.256		1.415
		(0.98)	(2.58)	(5.43)		(7.55)
ln(NTB)	−.129	.002				
	(0.86)	(0.01)				
ln(1.0 + .01*BLACK)	−.874	−0.20				
	(1.60)	(0.23)				
ln(1.0 + .01*TARIFF)	−2.55	−3.029	−3.040	−.947	−3.72	
	(1.55)	(1.76)	(2.61)	(1.13)	(2.33)	
$\bar{R}^2$	.582	.579	.681	.891	.371	.886
SEE	.311	.312	.272	.153	.365	.156

Source: Series for NTB, BLACK, and TARIFF from World Bank (1991).

Notes: Absolute values of *t*-statistics are in parentheses. The dependent variable in all equations is the growth in real GDP per adult from 1960 to 1985, i.e., ln(GDPa85) − ln(GDPa60).

NTB is the total number of nontariff barriers; BLACK the average percentage black market exchange premium, 1971–85; and TARIFF total tariff revenues as a percentage of total imports, average over 1971–85.

The nine countries for which the tariff data and the 1960 Bollen democracy index (from Bollen [1980, app. 2]) are both available include India (.936), Indonesia (.203), Korea (.517), Malaysia (.835), Pakistan (.400), Philippines (.930), Singapore (.812), Sri Lanka (.940), and Thailand (.331); the 1960 values for the Bollen index are shown in parentheses after each country name.

data are available for all 11 countries.[15] It also has a significant correlation with cross-sectional differences in growth rates, with a 1 percentage point increase in the average black market premium being associated with a .06 percentage point decrease in the average annual growth rate over the 1960–85 period.[16] Of the three measures, it contributes the least to explaining differences in growth rates, with one-third of the variance being explained.

The third openness variable is total import duty collected, measured as a percentage of total merchandise imports, averaged over the 1971–85 period. This variable is transformed for estimation, as shown in table 1.1. It has the highest explanatory power of the three variables, with almost half of the cross-sectional variance of growth rates explained by differences in tariff rates. The

15. The data are from the *World Currency Yearbook* and are included in World Bank (1991) under the series title BLACK.

16. To calculate the effect, the coefficient must be divided by 25, since the dependent variable is the 25-year log difference in real GDP per adult.

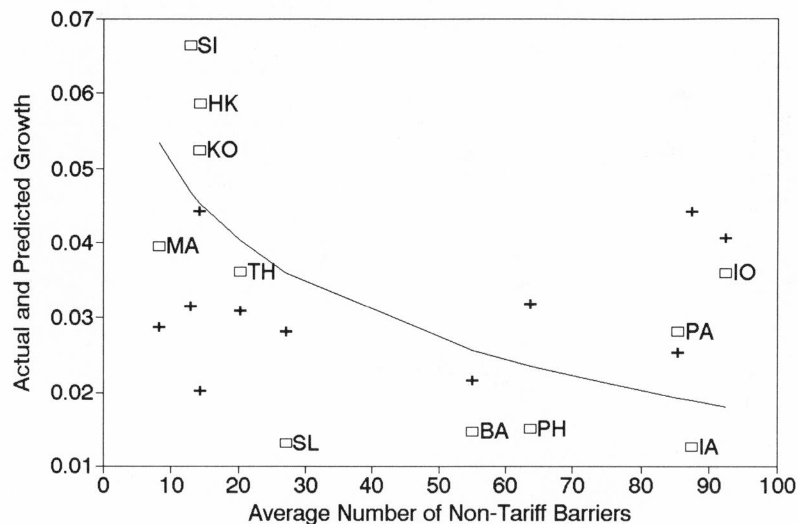

Fig. 1.7 Actual and predicted growth versus number of nontariff barriers
Note: See note for fig. 1.1.

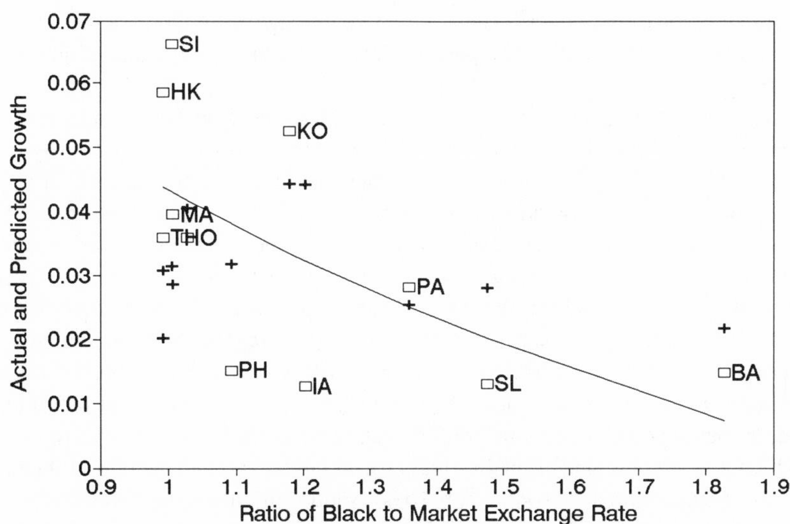

Fig. 1.8 Actual and predicted growth versus black market exchange rate
Note: See note for fig. 1.1.

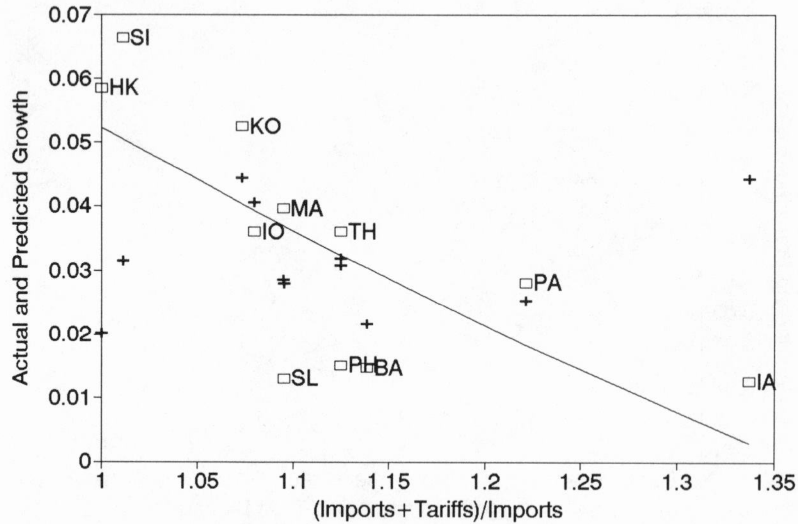

Fig. 1.9 Actual and predicted growth versus import tariffs
Note: See note for fig. 1.1.

estimated size of the effect is such that a 1 percentage point increase in average tariffs is associated with a .17 percent decrease in the average annual growth rate.

To what extent are the three openness variables providing independent information? Their correlations with one another are relatively low, which may be due in part to different errors of measurement and in part to the fact that different countries have adopted different types of trade and capital restrictions.[17] The first equation of table 1.2 attempts to exploit the independent variance in the three measures by including them all in a single equation. Given the small size of the sample and the fact that all three variables are measuring closely related policies, it is not surprising that the significance levels of the individual variables is much reduced. However, the adjusted proportion of the variance explained nonetheless rises to .58, with tariffs and the black market premium being the most important contributors. Equation (ii) adds the investment rate, which was the only one of the original growth model variables to be significant in the Asian estimation for 13 countries. Adding the investment variable has the effect of leaving the overall proportion of variance explained slightly reduced and lowers the effect of the NTBs and the black market exchange premium almost to zero. Removing the latter two variables raises the adjusted R^2 to .68, as shown in equation (iii).

17. For the 11-country sample, the correlations are .37 between the tariff and the black market premium variables, .67 between the tariff and NTB variables, and .41 between the black market premium and NTB variables.

Equations (iv)–(vi) estimate the partial effect of democracy given either investment rates or tariff measures, or both, as basic explanatory variables. When investment rates and the democracy index are both included in the equation, the adjusted R^2 rises to about .89 and is slightly higher when the tariff rate is also included in the equation. The partial effect of democracy is found to be negative, with a coefficient three times as large and more than twice as significant as was earlier found when the Bollen index was added to the global equation.[18] This strong and striking result raises at least two questions of reliability and interpretation. First, the sample size is so small that the result may be heavily dependent on the particularities of one or two countries and on ad hoc choices of functional form and variables. Second, there is a real possibility that although democracy may have a negative partial effect given the level of investment, investment rates themselves may be higher in a democratic system. This latter possibility, which was significant for the global sample, turns out not to be important in the Asian sample, where no significant part of the cross-country variation in investment rates was explained by differences in their 1960 indexes of democracy. Huntington (1991) argues, from the evidence of the successive waves of democratization in the twentieth century, that first attempts often fail, in part because of the lack of previous experience in the successful management of democratic institutions. Asian countries that were in their early stages of democracy, or whose first attempts failed during the data period under study, may well show stronger negative correlations with growth than would be true for the global sample including many countries with more decades of successful operation of democracies. In addition, of course, there is the possibility that for some of the countries studied, the conditions were met for the "conflict perspective" (Huntington 1987; Sirowy and Inkeles 1990) to be applicable, with fledgling democratic institutions being too weak to adopt the policies necessary to foster sustained economic growth.

There is, however, one relationship that is common to the OECD and the Asian economies that is not shared by the other regional groupings of countries. That is the linkage between the real exchange rate and the average level of per capita GDP, as shown in figure 1.10 for 1985. The relationship holds quite strongly among the OECD economies (Hill 1986), among the Asian economies, and between the two groups of economies.[19] It was argued in Helliwell and Chung (1992a) that the failure of the same relationship to hold in Africa and Latin America might well be due to the relative lack of economic and financial openness in those economies. To the extent that this lack of openness led to slower importation of technical progress from abroad or to the extent that it was due to macroeconomic instabilities,[20] then it may have contrib-

18. The coefficient on the Bollen index is −.247, with an absolute value of the t-statistic of 1.61 in the 98-country equation reported in equation (2) of table 3 of Helliwell (1992a).

19. These relationships are more formally estimated and tested in Helliwell and Chung (1992c).

20. The link between macroeconomic instabilities and growth, with macroeconomic instability and high and variable inflation leading to low growth, has been emphasized by Fischer (1991) and Gylfason (1990).

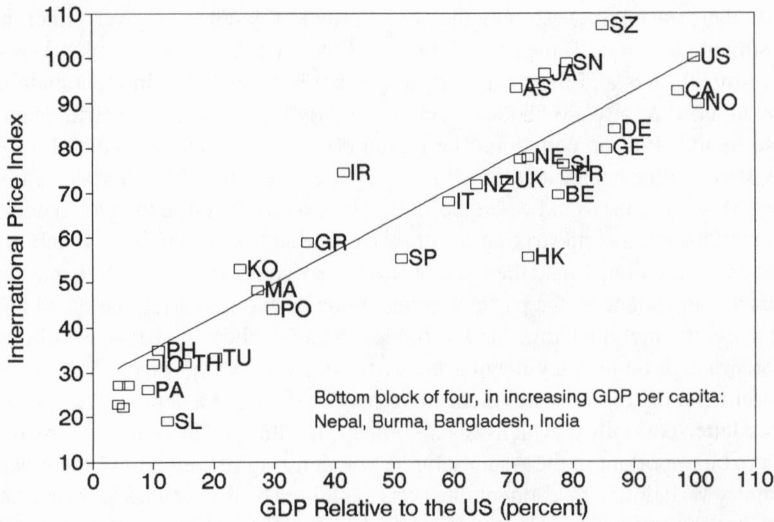

Fig. 1.10 International price indexes and real GDP per capita 1985: OECD and Asia
Note: See note for fig. 1.1.

uted to the lower average growth in Latin America and Africa that appears even after allowance is made for differences in investment in human and physical capital. These intercontinental comparisons, which lack any formal statistical tests at this stage, tend to support the evidence from among the Asian economies that more openness tends to lead to faster growth, presumably by permitting faster flows of ideas from countries where average productivity levels are higher.

1.4 Conclusions

The evidence in this paper has confirmed the general inapplicability to the Asian economies of the same convergence model that has fared rather well for the OECD countries and for several global samples. Growth is not higher in the poorer Asian countries, even after allowing for differences in rates of investment in human and physical capital. Among the OECD countries, by contrast, growth has been higher in those that were initially poorer, whether or not separate allowance is made for other variables influencing cross-country differences in growth rates, and whether the comparison is made using Solow residuals or growth rates of per capita GDP.[21] As for the other variables used

21. The convergence effect applicable to the industrial countries has been reported by Abramovitz (1990), Baumol and Wolff (1988), Dowrick and Gemmell (1991), and Maddison (1982) among others. Helliwell and Chung (1991a) show that convergence is applicable as much to the growth of Solow residuals as to GDP per capita. Levine and Renelt (1992) show that even in

for the global samples of countries, investment in physical capital appears more important in Asia, and education less so.

Growth is faster in those Asian countries that are more open to imports and capital movements. The evidence linking openness and growth for the sample of Asian countries seems even stronger than for developing countries as a whole (Harrison 1991), or for the OECD countries (Helliwell 1992b), although these differences remain to be tested. The relatively small number of Asian countries, and the resulting importance of particular circumstances, may well make general conclusions on this score hard to reach. In any event, there is a clear grouping among the Asian economies under review, with the more open also the faster growing. There are so many other factors distinguishing the two groups of countries that it is clearly premature to make any strong conclusions at this point.

There is also some evidence of a trade-off between more democracy and faster growth for given levels of investment and openness. Whether or not the existence of an Asian trade-off between growth and democracy stands the test of more thorough investigation, such a trade-off relates more to the 1960–85 period than to the next century, since the positive link between incomes and democracy is likely to combine with the high growth rates of most of these economies to put them all into the class of experienced democracies by the time another 25 years have passed.[22] For the countries with lower per capita growth rates and higher population growth rates (Brander and Dowrick 1991), the trade-off, if it is confirmed, may well remain in place for some years to come.

One final qualification is necessary. Easterly et al. (1992) and others have noted that there is substantial variance from one decade to the next in the ranking of growth rates across countries, while there is much more stability in the country characteristics, including the openness measures, used to explain growth rate differences. This suggests that the cross-sectional parameter estimates might be unstable from one period to the next and have little predictive power for future growth. These risks need to be assessed carefully before attaching too much importance to the correlations based on a particular period of previous growth. Nonetheless, the link between openness and growth that is apparent for the Asian countries over the 1960–85 period seems a promising candidate for further investigation.

global samples such as those used by Mankiw et al. (1992) and Barro (1991) there is a robust negative effect running from initial GDP per capita to subsequent growth rates, while noting much less stability in the estimated effects of policy variables, including especially fiscal policies but also some of the openness measures used in this paper.

22. The strong positive linkage from the level of real GDP per capita to democracy is documented in Helliwell (1992a).

Appendix A

Table 1A.1

Country	Code	GDP per Adult 1960	GDP per Adult 1985	Average Growth in Adult Population	Secondary School Enrollment[a]	Average Growth in GDP per Adult	Investment as a Percentage of GDP	Average Scale (billion 1980$)
Hong Kong	HK	3085	13372	3.0	7.2	0.0587	19.92	21.7
Singapore	SI	2793	14678	2.6	9.0	0.0664	32.24	9.2
Malaysia	MA	2154	5788	3.2	7.3	0.0395	23.24	26.9
Sri Lanka	SL	1794	2482	2.4	8.3	0.0130	14.82	14.2
Philippines	PH	1668	2430	3.0	10.6	0.0151	14.93	50.7
Thailand	TH	1308	3220	3.1	4.4	0.0360	18.08	51.3
Korea (ROK)	KO	1285	4775	2.7	10.2	0.0525	22.37	58.4
Pakistan	PA	1077	2175	3.0	3.0	0.0281	12.23	58.6
India	IA	978	1339	2.4	5.1	0.0126	16.82	347.6
Indonesia	IO	879	2159	1.9	4.1	0.0359	13.90	100.2
Bangladesh	BA	846	1221	2.6	3.2	0.0147	6.83	37.1
Nepal	NE	833	974	2.0	2.3	0.0063	5.95	6.2
Burma	BU	517	1031	1.7	3.5	0.0276	11.45	12.4
United States	US	12362	18988	1.5	11.9	0.0172	21.18	2130.1
Switzerland	SZ	10308	15881	0.8	4.8	0.0173	29.79	55.9
Canada	CA	10286	17935	2.0	10.6	0.0222	23.35	207.8

New Zealand	NZ	9523	12308	1.7	11.9	0.0103	22.54	19.9
Denmark	DE	8551	16491	0.6	10.7	0.0263	26.61	40.7
Australia	AS	8440	13409	2.0	9.8	0.0185	31.60	96.3
Norway	NO	7938	19723	0.7	10.0	0.0364	29.19	32.9
Sweden	SN	7802	15237	0.4	7.9	0.0268	24.53	61.8
Germany (FDR)	GE	7695	15297	0.5	8.4	0.0275	28.58	475.7
Netherlands	NL	7689	13177	1.4	10.7	0.0215	25.86	97.4
United Kingdom	UK	7634	13331	0.3	8.9	0.0223	18.44	377.0
France	FR	7215	15027	1.0	8.9	0.0293	26.24	394.1
Belgium	BE	6789	14290	0.5	9.3	0.0298	23.43	70.4
Finland	FI	6527	13779	0.7	11.5	0.0299	36.91	30.8
Austria	OS	5939	13327	0.4	8.0	0.0323	23.45	48.0
Italy	IT	4913	11082	0.6	7.1	0.0325	24.94	298.0
Ireland	IR	4411	8675	1.1	11.4	0.0271	25.98	12.4
Spain	SP	3766	9903	1.0	8.0	0.0387	17.74	166.9
Japan	JA	3493	13893	1.2	10.9	0.0552	36.00	652.9
Turkey	TU	2274	4444	2.5	5.5	0.0268	20.21	76.1
Portugal	PO	2272	5827	0.6	5.8	0.0377	22.56	26.5
Greece	GR	2257	6868	0.7	7.9	0.0445	29.35	29.6

[a]As a percentage of adult population.

Appendix B

Table 1B.1 Openness and Additional Educational Variables for Asia

	Code	Black Market Premium (%)	Import Tariffs (%)	Nontariff Barriers (number)	Adult Literacy (%)	Labor Force Education EDP4 (years)	Labor Force Education EDT (years)
Hong Kong	HK	−0.77	0.00	14.3	77.3	2.40	3.57
Singapore	SI	0.55	1.17	12.9	75.9	3.57	6.10
Malaysia	MA	0.73	9.49	8.2	57.1	1.90	7.39
Sri Lanka	SL	47.77	9.54	27.1	79.8	3.90	7.92
Philippines	PH	9.18	13.45	63.6	79.3	8.00	7.45
Thailand	TH	−0.74	12.45	20.2	78.1	5.00	5.34
Korea (ROK)	KO	18.04	7.33	14.2	79.1	1.20	6.74
Pakistan	PA	35.96	22.15	85.4	21.6	7.00	2.47
India	IA	20.31	33.70	87.4	34.2	5.30	3.35
Indonesia	IO	2.75	8.00	92.5	54.3	6.20	3.48
Bangladesh	BA	82.731	13.80	55.1	24.9	4.10	3.73

Sources: EDP4 is a single observation for each country, based on survey data from Psacharopolous and Arriagada (1986). EDT uses UNESCO data on enrollment, combined with birth and mortality statistics, as initially constructed by Lau, Jamison, and Louat (1991) and subsequently revised by Louat (1991).

References

Abramovitz, M. 1990. The catch-up factor in postwar economic growth. *Economic Inquiry* 28 (1): 1–18.

Barro, R. J. 1991. Economic growth in a cross section of countries. *Quarterly Journal of Economics* 106:407–44.

Baumol, W. J., and E. N. Wolff. 1988. Productivity growth, convergence and welfare: Reply. *American Economic Review* 78: 1155–59.

Bollen, K. A. 1980. Issues in the comparative measurement of political democracy. *American Sociological Review* 45: 370–90.

———. 1990. Political democracy: Conceptual and measurement traps. *Studies in Comparative International Development* 25: 7–24.

Brander, J. A., and S. Dowrick. 1991. The role of fertility and population in economic growth: New results from aggregate cross-national data. Mimeograph.

Dowrick, S., and N. Gemmell. 1991. Industrialisation, catching up and economic growth: A comparative study across the world's capitalist economies. *Economic Journal* 101:263–75.

Easterly, W., M. Kremer, L. Pritchett, and L. Summers. 1992. Good policy or good luck? Country growth performance and temporary shocks. Washington, D.C.: World Bank.

Fischer, S. 1991. Growth, macroeconomics, and development. NBER Working Paper no. 3702. Cambridge, Mass.: National Bureau of Economic Research.

Grossman, G. M., and E. Helpman. 1989. Quality ladders and product cycles. NBER

Working Paper no. 3201. Cambridge, Mass.: National Bureau of Economic Research.

———. 1990a. Trade, innovation, and growth. *American Economic Review* 80 (2): 86–91.

———. 1990b. Comparative advantage and long-run growth. *American Economic Review* 80:796–815.

———. 1991. *Innovation and growth in the global economy.* Cambridge: MIT Press.

Gylfason, T. 1990. Inflation, growth and external debt: A review of the landscape. CEPR Discussion Paper no. 375. London: Centre for Economic Policy Research.

Harrison, A. 1991. Openness and growth: A time-series, cross-country analysis for developing countries. Policy Research Working Paper WPS809. Washington, D.C.: World Bank.

Helliwell, John F. 1992a. Empirical linkages between democracy and economic growth. NBER Working Paper no. 4066. Cambridge, Mass.: National Bureau of Economic Research.

———. 1992b. Trade and technical progress. NBER Working Paper no. 4226. Cambridge, Mass.: National Bureau of Economic Research.

Helliwell, John F., and Alan Chung. 1991a. Macroeconomic convergence: International transmission of growth and technical progress. In *International economic transactions: Issues in measurement and empirical research,* ed. P. Hooper and J. D. Richardson, 388–436. Chicago: University of Chicago Press.

———. 1991b. Globalization, convergence, and the prospects for economic growth. In *The Capitalist Economies: Prospects for the 1990s,* ed. J. Cornwall. London: Elgar.

———. 1991c. Are bigger countries better off? In Economic dimensions of constitutional change, ed. R. Boadway, T. Courchene, and D. Purvis, 345–67. Kingston, Ont.: John Deutsche Institute.

———. 1992a. Convergence and growth linkages between north and south. NBER Working Paper no. 3948. Cambridge, Mass.: National Bureau of Economic Research.

———. 1992b. Aggregate productivity and growth in an international comparative setting. In *International Productivity and Competitiveness,* ed. B. G. Hickman, 49–79. New York: Oxford University Press.

———. 1992c. Tri-polar growth and real exchange rates: How much can be explained by convergence? In *A quest for a more stable world economic system,* ed. L. R. Klein, C. Moriguchi, and A. Amano. New York: Kluwer.

Helliwell, John F., Peter Sturm, and Gerard Salou. 1985. International comparison of the sources of the productivity slowdown 1973–1982. *European Economic Review* 28: 157–91.

Helpman, E. 1991. Endogenous macroeconomic growth theory. NBER Working Paper no. 3869. Cambridge, Mass.: National Bureau of Economic Research.

Hill, P. 1986. International price levels and purchasing power parities. *OECD Economic Studies* 6: 133–59.

Huntington, S. P. 1987. *Understanding political development: An analytic study.* Boston: Little Brown.

———. 1991. *The third wave: Democratization in the late twentieth century.* Norman: University of Oklahoma Press.

Kravis, I. B., and R. E. Lipsey. 1983. *Toward an explanation of national price levels.* Princeton Studies in International Finance, no. 52. Princeton, N.J.: Princeton University, International Finance Section.

Lau, L., D. Jamison, and F. Louat. 1991. Education and productivity in developing countries: An aggregate production function approach. PRE Working Paper 612. Washington, D.C.: World Bank.

Levine, R., and D. Renelt. 1992. A sensitivity analysis of cross-country growth regressions. *American Economic Review* 82 (4): 942–63.
Louat, F. 1991. Time series of educational attainments of the labor force: A cross country data base, 1960–87. World Bank Working Paper. Washington, D.C.: World Bank.
Lucas, R. E. 1988. On the mechanics of economic development. *Journal of Monetary Economics* 22: 3–32.
———. 1990. Why doesn't capital flow from rich to poor countries? *American Economic Review* 90 (2): 92–96.
Maddison, A. 1982. *Phases of capitalist development.* Oxford: Oxford University Press.
Mankiw, G., D. Romer, and D. Weil. 1992. A contribution to the empirics of economic growth. *Quarterly Journal of Economics* 107: 407–37.
Psacharopolous, G., and A. M. Arriagada. 1986. The educational composition of the labor force: An international comparison. International Labor Review 126, no. 5 (September–October).
Romer, P. M. 1986. Increasing returns and long-run growth. *Journal of Political Economy* 94: 1002–37.
———. 1990a. Are non-convexities important for understanding growth? *American Economic Review* 80 (2): 97–103.
———. 1990b. Endogenous technological change. *Journal of Political Economy* 98: S71–S102.
Sirowy, L., and A. Inkeles. 1990. The effects of democracy on economic growth and inequality: A review. *Studies in Comparative International Development* 25: 126–57.
Solow, R. M. 1956. A contribution to the theory of economic growth. *Quarterly Journal of Economics* 70: 65–94.
———. 1957. Technical change and the aggregate production function. *Review of Economics and Statistics* 39: 312–20.
Summers, R., and A. Heston. 1988. A new set of international comparisons of real product and prices: Estimates for 130 countries, 1950 to 1985. *Review of Income and Wealth* 34: 1–25.
UNCTAD (United Nations Conference on Trade and Development). 1987. *Handbook of trade control measures of developing countries.* Supplement, Statistical analysis of trade control measures of developing countries. New York: United Nations.
World Bank. 1991. *World development report 1991: Supplementary data.* Washington, D.C.: World Bank.

Comment Shin-ichi Fukuda

John F. Helliwell has analyzed a very interesting and fashionable issue, international growth linkages in the world economies. Estimating the augmented conditional convergence model, the paper first shows that the conditional convergence model failed to capture either the high rate of growth in Singapore, Hong Kong, and Korea, or the low growth in India and Sri Lanka. The paper then raises the question of why growth in the Asian economies cannot be explained by the conditional convergence model. This question is very important be-

Shin-ichi Fukuda is associate professor of economics at the Institute of Economic Research, Hitotsubashi University.

cause, in recent years, most East Asian countries accomplished remarkable growth, while Latin American and African countries suffered from low growth rates.

I have three comments. My first is on the link between openness and growth. One of the main results in this paper was that openness in East Asian economies led to faster growth. In my view, this is especially true for Singapore and Hong Kong, where openness accelerated economic growth mainly because of their geographical advantage. For example, Hong Kong's neighboring country is mainland China. Since the market of mainland China is closed, openness is very advantageous to Hong Kong. However, when we consider the link between openness and growth for other Asian countries, I think that we need to be more careful. For example, in the case of Japan, it is usually said that the protection of domestic industry by the Ministry of International Trade and Industry (MITI) helped the success of such Japanese companies as Toyota. Similar protection was also successful in Korea. Thus, in these countries, it may be true that some protectionism helped their economic growth. Of course, protectionism in these countries must be distinguished from the inward-oriented import-substitution policies sometimes adopted in Latin American countries. In fact, even under protectionism, the share of exports in GDP was very significant to the economic development of Japan and Korea. However, I think that the Japanese and Korean experience teaches us that it is not always simple-minded openness that leads to successful economic growth.

My second comment is on the role of exports on the demand side of economic development. In the paper, the role of supply-side factors in economic development was stressed. Needless to say, the supply side is important. However, in my view, demand externality or "the big push" was important for East Asian economic development. For the East Asian economies with small domestic markets, export is sometimes the big push and has demand spillover effects. For example, in the case of Japan, it has been said that the special demand for exports during the Korean War was the big push for the Japanese economy. Before this special demand occurred, the Japanese economy was limited by the small size of its market and the small purchasing power of its people. However, special demand was the big push in some industries and generated demand spillover for the products of other industries.

My final comment about the paper is on the sample period of estimation adopted: 1960–85. Although this sample period has been used in most previous studies, it may be somewhat misleading when considering the economic development of East Asian countries. Most East Asian countries achieved remarkable economic development after 1985. For example, in Thailand, GNP in 1990 was more than twice the GNP in 1985, in terms of domestic currency. Even in Korea, which had already achieved high growth rates before 1985, GNP almost doubled from 1985 to 1990, if we measure it in dollars. Since the growth rate of GNP in most Latin American countries was very low after 1985, extending the sample period may change some of the results in the paper.

2 On Recent Movements of Japanese Current Accounts and Capital Flows

Takatoshi Ito

2.1 Introduction

Persistent Japanese current account surpluses have been one of the sources of trade conflict between Japan and the United States. After the 1985 Plaza Agreement, the U.S. dollar overvaluation was corrected, and then the current account imbalance was corrected, with a long lag. Then yen appreciated from 260 yen/dollar in February 1985 to 150 yen/dollar in August 1986. Japan's current account surpluses, and trade surpluses, peaked in 1987 and then gradually declined for the rest of the 1980s. U.S. current account deficits peaked in 1986 and shrank for the rest of the 1980s. However, Japan's current account surpluses appear to have turned upward again in 1991, when their size doubled from the 1990 level and trade surpluses topped $100 billion for the first time. Has the trend of correcting current account imbalance been reversed?

More interesting, (net) long-term capital movement recorded an inflow of capital in 1991. During the 1980s, Japan used dollars earned via trade surpluses for long-term investment. It was said that current account surpluses were "recycled" into the international financial market as Japanese investors purchased sizable shares of U.S. government bonds, acquired "showcase" real estate and golf courses, and built new factories around the world. Now, "Japan money" seems to be in retreat, perhaps to help ease the difficulties in the domestic stock and real estate markets. Will this trend continue? How can it be

Takatoshi Ito is professor of economics at Hitotsubashi University, visiting professor of economics at Harvard University, and a research associate of the National Bureau of Economic Research.

Comments from Maria Gochoco, Yuzo Harada, Anne O. Krueger, Naohiro Yashiro, and Shinichi Yoshikuni were very helpful. Financial support from Kagaku Kenkyuhi (Ministry of Education, Japan) is gratefully acknowledged.

consistent to record large current account surpluses *and* long-term capital inflows?

The rest of this paper analyzes these questions. The next section is an overview of current account and capital movements in the second half of the 1980s. Section 2.3 points out problems in the definition of several items in the data. Section 2.4 examines the argument that current account and capital movements in 1990 and 1991 were affected by several transitory factors, including the Gulf War. I will present a counterfactual estimate of current accounts under the assumption that the Gulf War had not occurred. Section 2.6 discusses policy implications, and section 2.7 concludes with a summary.

2.2 Overview

Movements of current account and capital flows during the second half of the 1980s and in more recent years are summarized in table 2.1.[1] It shows that current accounts (line 1) peaked in 1987 and gradually shrank to a low in 1990. However, it increased again in 1991 and the first quarter of 1992. Trade surpluses recorded an all-time high in 1991. However, the current account/GNP ratio was still about 2 percent in 1991, only half of its 1986–87 level, as shown in figure 2.1.

2.2.1 Capital Account Movements

During the second half of the 1980s, Japan increased its long-term (net) assets (line 2) by more than its current account surpluses. The difference was made up by an inflow of short-term capital (line 3). It was a major characteristic of Japan's capital movement that Japan financed long-term investment by short-term borrowing. In a sense, the startling increase in Japanese investment abroad, or "Japan money," was funded partly by dollars earned by exporting automobiles, machine tools, and semiconductors, but partly by corporate borrowing, through Japanese banks, from the Euro-market.

However, this trend was reversed in 1991. Despite increased current account surpluses, long-term capital movement turned into net inflow. By definition, short-term capital and monetary movement balances (line 4) became a large outflow. This can be seen as "unwinding" the capital movement of the second half of the 1980s. Put differently, Japan as a nation repayed the short-term debt accumulated during the preceding years. Since this unwinding cannot continue indefinitely, long-term capital flow will become outflow sooner or later, provided that current account surpluses continue to exist. This answers our question: it shows how it can be consistent to have current account surpluses and long-term capital inflow.

Note that under short-term capital movement, short-term borrowing and in-

1. For an analysis of current account movement in the first half of the 1980s, see for example Ueda (1988) and Ueda and Fujii (1986).

Table 2.1 **Current Accounts and Capital Flows (billion $ U.S.)**

	1986	1987	1988	1989	1990	1991	1992:1
1. Current accounts	85.8	87.0	79.6	57.2	35.8	72.9	27.4
Trade Balance	92.8	96.4	95.0	76.9	63.5	103.0	31.1
Exports	205.6	224.6	259.8	269.6	280.4	306.6	80.2
Imports	112.8	128.2	164.8	192.7	216.8	203.5	49.1
Service balance	−4.9	−5.7	−11.3	−15.5	−22.3	−17.7	−2.5
Transportation	−2.5	−6.1	−7.4	−7.7	−9.5	−10.5	−2.7
Travel	−5.7	−8.7	−15.8	−19.3	−21.4	−20.5	−5.9
Investment income	9.4	16.7	21.0	23.4	23.2	26.7	9.1
Other	−6.1	−7.6	−9.1	−11.9	−14.6	−13.9	−3.1
Transfers	−2.1	−3.7	−4.1	−4.2	−5.5	−12.5	−1.2
2. Long-term capital	−131.5	−136.5	−130.9	−89.2	−43.6	37.1	13.4
Assets (Japanese capital)	−132.1	−132.8	−149.9	−192.1	−120.8	−121.4	−9.2
Securities	−102.0	−87.8	−86.9	−113.2	−39.7	−74.3	−1.1
Stocks	−7.0	−16.9	−3.0	−17.9	−6.3	−3.6	4.0
Bonds	−93.0	−72.9	−85.8	−94.1	−29.0	−68.2	−4.0
Yen-denominated bonds	−1.9	2.0	1.8	−1.2	−4.5	−2.5	−1.1
Direct investment	−14.5	−19.5	−34.2	−44.1	−48.0	−30.7	−4.0
Trade credits/loans extended	−11.1	−16.7	−22.1	−26.5	−21.5	−9.2	−2.6
Other	−4.5	−8.8	−6.6	−8.3	−11.6	−7.2	−1.2
Liabilities (foreign capital)	0.6	−3.7	19.0	102.9	77.2	158.5	22.6
Securities investment	0.5	−6.1	20.3	85.1	34.7	115.3	14.2
Stocks	−15.8	−42.8	6.8	7.0	−13.3	46.8	7.5
Bonds	−2.1	6.7	−21.6	2.4	17.0	21.2	3.5
External bonds	18.4	30.1	35.1	75.7	30.9	47.3	3.1
Direct investment	0.2	1.2	−0.5	−1.1	1.7	1.4	0.8
Trade credits/loans received	−0.1	−0.1	−0.1	17.8	39.1	38.1	8.2
Other	−0.0	1.3	−0.8	1.0	1.7	3.7	−0.6
3. Short-term capital	−1.6	23.9	19.5	20.8	21.5	−25.8	−21.0
4. Monetary movement balances	44.8	29.5	29.0	33.3	7.3	−76.4	−46.5
Private banks sector	58.5	71.8	44.5	8.6	−13.6	−93.5	−42.1
Official sector	−13.7	−42.3	−15.5	24.7	20.9	17.1	−4.4
Foreign reserves	−15.7	−39.2	−16.2	12.8	7.8	8.1	8.0
5. Errors and omissions[a]	2.5	−3.9	2.8	−22.0	−20.9	−7.8	7.6

Source: Bank of Japan, *Economic Statistic Annual, 1991* (Tokyo).

Note: Negative entries in capital and monetary movement denote outflow of capital from Japan.

[a]Errors and omissions are defined by line 5 = − (line 1 + line 2 + line 3 + line 4).

vestment in short-term assets acquired or sold by investors (not including banks and the government) are included, while under monetary movement balances, any bank transactions with nonresidents, any transactions between bank headquarters and foreign branches, and any government foreign asset transactions are recorded. Hence, a sudden increase in the outflow of short-term capi-

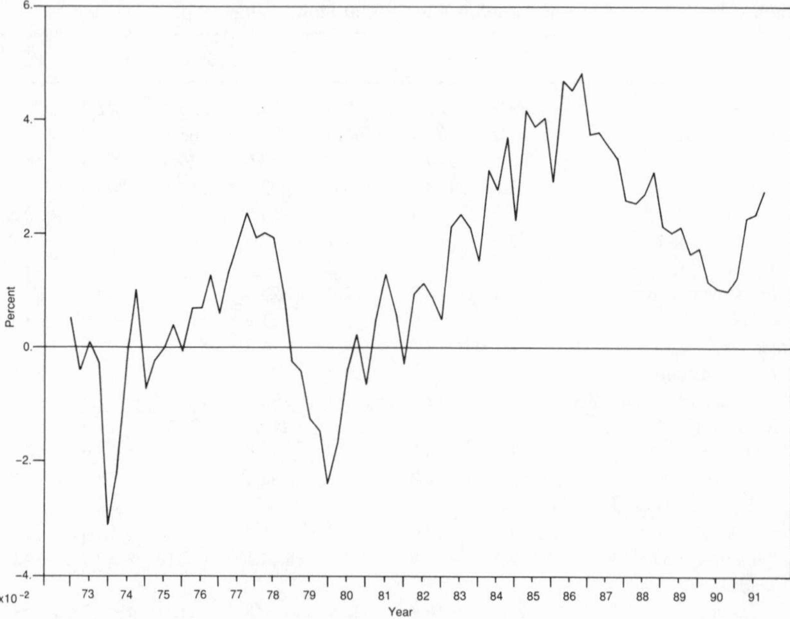

Fig. 2.1 Current account/GNP ratio

tal and monetary movement warrants scrutiny. This will be done in the next section.

Comparing the asset (Japanese capital investment outside Japan) and the liability (foreign capital investment in Japan) sides of long-term capital movement, we see that the change between 1990 and 1991 occurred mainly on the liability side. Namely, foreigners invested in Japanese government bonds and stocks as their portfolio selection. Thus, the switch in long-term capital accounts to net inflow has been caused mainly by the decisions of foreigners, and not by the withdrawal (selling out) of Japanese capital from markets abroad.[2] It is likely that foreigners have decided that Japanese stocks are underpriced (after a more than 50 percent fall in the stock market since its peak in December 1989) and that Japanese bonds have higher yields than some U.S. bonds.

In summary, the inflow shown by long-term capital movement in 1991 was caused partly by the repayment by Japanese capital portfolios of short-term debt from the second half of the 1980s, and partly by foreign portfolio shifts from bank deposits to long-term Japanese assets. Details will be analyzed in section 2.3.

2. This statement, however, may need to be qualified when we look at the figures for the first quarter of 1992. They show a dramatic decrease in Japanese investment abroad. This is partly a seasonal problem, that is, Japanese corporations sold foreign bonds and stocks to help dress up their yearly earnings reports (at the end of March) in the presence of decreasing stock prices.

2.2.2 Current Account Movement

The Japanese current account surplus reached $87 billion (over 4 percent of nominal GNP) in 1987. However, it dropped to only $36 billion (just over 1 percent of nominal GNP) in 1990. This gradual decrease of current accounts has been attributed partly to yen appreciation following the Plaza Agreement and partly to the strong growth of the Japanese economy which increased imports sharply.

Looking at trade statistics, presented in table 2.2, we can see that import volume increased substantially in the second half of the 1980s. It is also noticeable that trade volumes, both exports and imports, were stable through 1990 and 1991.

The trade price index in table 2.2, panel A, comes from customs clearance base. Other export and import price indices are available from the Bank of Japan, as export and import price index statistics; these are shown in panel B.

Table 2.2 **Trade Statistics**

	1985	1986	1987	1988	1989	1990	1991
A. Trade volume and price indices[a]							
Volume index[b]							
Exports	100.0	99.4	99.7	104.8	108.8	114.8	118.2
		(−0.6)	(0.3)	(5.1)	(3.8)	(5.5)	(3.0)
Imports	100.0	109.5	119.7	139.7	150.6	159.3	164.0
		(9.5)	(9.3)	(16.7)	(7.8)	(5.8)	(3.0)
Trade price index[c]							
Exports	100.0	84.6	79.7	77.2	82.8	86.0	85.4
		(−15.4)	(−5.8)	(−3.1)	(7.3)	(3.9)	(−0.7)
Imports	100.0	63.3	58.4	55.3	61.9	68.4	62.6
		(−36.7)	(−7.7)	(−5.3)	(11.9)	(10.5)	(−8.5)
B. Export and import price indices[a]							
Export price index							
In yen	100.0	84.9	80.6	78.8	82.3	84.0	81.1
		(−15.1)	(−5.1)	(−2.2)	(4.4)	(2.1)	(−3.5)
In contract currency	100.0	104.3	108.6	115.7	117.0	113.1	114.8
		(4.3)	(4.1)	(6.5)	(1.1)	(−3.1)	(1.5)
Import price index							
In yen	100.0	64.2	58.9	56.2	60.5	65.7	60.6
		(−35.8)	(−8.3)	(−4.6)	(7.7)	(8.6)	(−7.8)
In contract currency	100.0	83.6	88.2	93.3	96.8	100.3	98.3
		(−16.4)	(5.5)	(5.8)	(3.8)	(3.6)	(−2.0)

Sources: Panel A, Ministry of Finance, *Gaikoku Boeki Gaikyo, 1991* (Tokyo); panel B, Bank of Japan, *Economic Statistics Annual, 1991* (Tokyo).

Note: Numbers in parentheses are percentage change from previous year.

[a]1985 = 100.

[b]Volume index is defined by (value index)/(unit price index).

[c]Trade price index is defined for the contractual currency basis.

From 1985 to 1986, the value of yen doubled and the crude oil price declined by half. This was reflected by a sudden change in price indices: the import price index in yen dropped by 35 percent, while the price index in contract currency base dropped by 16 percent. The latter shows mainly the crude oil price effect, and the former shows both exchange rate and oil price effects. A brief spell of yen depreciation and oil price increase in 1990 is reflected in increased import prices. However, this was corrected in 1991.

The export price index in table 2.2, panel B, also shows characteristics of pricing behavior by Japanese manufacturers. When the yen appreciated sharply, Japanese exporters often lowered the yen-denominated prices of exports, in order to keep moderate the increase in dollar-denominated prices in the retail market in the United States and other countries. This "pricing-to-market" behavior is reflected in the decline in yen-denominated export price and the slight increase in contract-currency-base export price in 1986–1988.[3] This partly explains the long tail of the J-curve.

A major increase occurred in imports of manufactured goods, with the volume of manufactured imports increasing by about 20 percent from 1985 to 1989. Manufactured goods imports as a percentage of total imports (on customs clearance basis) increased from 22.8 percent in 1980, to 31.0 percent in 1985, to 50.2 percent in 1990. Some policymakers in Japan now feel that the criticism that Japan avoids importing manufactured goods is no longer plausible. However, these ratios may be misleading, because they may reflect the decline in prices of agricultural goods, oil, and other raw materials and also the decrease in the weight of nonmanufactured goods in the economy.

Bilateral trade balances by region are shown in table 2.3. From 1990 to 1991 Japan recorded sharply increased trade surpluses mainly against EC and Asian countries. Trade surpluses with the European Community increased because imports from the European Community—mainly expensive automobiles and paintings—decreased, while trade surpluses against Asian countries increased mainly because of parts exports.

Except for investment income, which gradually grew due to increased external assets, service balance deficits also contributed to the decrease in current account surpluses from 1987 to 1990. A sharp increase in Japanese overseas travel contributed to a widening of transportation and travel deficits.[4]

In summary, the gradual decrease in current accounts from 1987 to 1990 was driven mainly by a large increase in manufactured goods import volumes. Imports from the European Community increased most in 1989–90, but dropped sharply in 1991. Exports to East Asian countries increased sharply in 1991. Trade surpluses against the United States decreased in the second half of the 1980s and were stable in 1990–91, despite a sharp increase in overall

3. See Marston (1990, 1991), Ohno (1989), and Ito (1992, 301–5) for theories and empirical research on the pricing-to-market behavior of Japanese firms.

4. The estimation method of travel account was changed in July 1988, which contributed to an increase. See Ito (1992, 293).

Table 2.3 **Bilateral Trade Balance (billion $ U.S.)**

	1986	1987	1988	1989	1990	1991
A. Balance of payments[a]						
United States	54.9	57.1	52.4	49.4	41.9	43.4
European Community	18.0	21.3	24.6	18.8	16.3	33.4
Southeast Asia	—	17.4	22.9	22.6	30.1	43.4
NIES[b]	—	22.0	26.5	26.1	31.4	43.9
B. Customs clearance basis						
United States	51.4	52.1	47.6	44.9	38.0	38.2
European Community	16.7	20.0	22.8	19.8	18.5	27.4
Southeast Asia	12.3	14.4	19.3	20.6	28.1	37.4
Korea	5.2	5.2	3.6	3.6	5.8	7.7
Taiwan	3.2	4.2	5.6	6.4	6.9	8.8

Source: Ministry of Finance, *Zaisei Kinyu Tokei Geppo* (Tokyo, August 1992).
[a]IMF formula.
[b]Newly industrialized economies (NIEs) are Hong Kong, Korea, Singapore, and Taiwan.

current account surpluses. Exports during 1990–91 did not increase due to sharp yen appreciation. Export price measured in yen declined, due partly to decreased costs of imported materials and partly to deliberate efforts to keep down the local prices in destination markets (export yen price × exchange rate) in the face of sharp yen appreciation. However, after five years of the stable yen—between 120 and 160 yen/dollar—the cost structure of the Japanese manufacturing sectors seems to have adjusted to the new exchange rate environment. In 1991, the momentum of import increase seems to have been lost and the volume of exports started to increase.

2.3 Problems in Capital Movement Data

The format used to report Japan's balance of payments contains several kinds of problems in definition.[5] First, statistical distinctions between long-term and short-term capital movements may not actually reflect their implied activities. Stocks, long-term bonds, and long-term loans and credits are classified as long-term investments, while short-term bonds, deposits, and short-term loans and credits are classified as short-term investments. A particular securities investment is classified as long-term if the securities purchased (or sold) are long-term (bonds with an original maturity of more than one year). However, an apparently long-term investment, using long bonds as instruments, may be reversed quite easily. It used to be the case that even repurchase agreements (*gensaki*) were treated as long-term investment, if the instruments were long bonds. However, repurchase agreements have been treated as short-term capital movement since January 1982. A problem that remains is that if an outright

5. This section is based on Bank of Japan (1992, esp. 15–16) and Harada and Ikawa (1992).

purchase of long bonds is followed by an outright sale, this is still classified as a transaction in long-term assets. This practice contributes to large month-to-month fluctuations, but in the long run, purchases and sales should cancel each other out within the category of long-term assets.

Second, nonresident transactions with banks, in terms of deposits and loans, are recorded in "monetary movement balances." Hence, if nonresidents withdraw yen-denominated deposits from banks and purchase Japanese government bonds and stocks, this transaction will cause a capital outflow in "monetary movement balances" and a matching capital inflow in "long-term capital." In fact, this is a plausible explanation for striking simultaneous increases in "liabilities (securities investment)" and "monetary movement balances" in 1991. (But this is only a part of the whole picture, because if only this were happening, the size of current account surpluses would not change.)

Third, Japanese banks take positions in foreign assets with funds borrowed from the Euro-market. This kind of portfolio shift causes outflows in "monetary movement balances (private bank sectors)," simultaneous with inflows in long-term capital. This must have been the case in the second half of the 1980s, though this shift did unwind in 1991.

Fourth, suppose that Japanese firms issue foreign-currency-denominated bonds abroad. If foreign investors purchase these bonds, this creates an inflow of long-term capital (an increase in "liabilities [securities investment, bonds]"). However, if Japanese investors purchase these bonds, it creates an outflow of long-term capital (an increase in "assets, [securities, bonds]").[6] Again, this transaction would increase both assets and liabilities, and hence should on average have a neutral effect on long-term capital movement.

Fifth, suppose Japanese firms borrow Euro-yen impact loans from abroad. This increases "liabilities (loans received)," or the inflow of long-term capital, if loans are classified as long-term, or the inflow of short-term capital if loans are classified as short-term. However, most Euro-yen impact loans are provided by foreign branches of Japanese banks, and their funds come from their headquarters in Japan. This headquarter-branch transaction is recorded in "monetary movement balances." In fact, from April to September 1990—while a restriction on real-estate lending was in effect—Japanese firms (including nonbanks) relied on impact loans from abroad in order to avoid this restriction. This contributed to large simultaneous inflows of long-term capital and outflows of monetary movement (headquarter-branch transactions).

Sixth, direct investment from Japan may not be declining, as it might seem.

6. There are two reasons for Japanese corporations to issue bonds to be purchased by Japanese investors abroad. First, because of overregulation in the Japanese corporate bond market, transaction costs of issuing bonds in the Euro-market are lower than in the domestic market. This is still the case in the 1990s. Second, during the first half of the 1980s, Japanese life insurance companies were, by regulation, not to invest in foreign bonds over a certain ceiling ratio (to their total assets. The ceiling was increased in steps during the 1980s). However, foreign bonds issued by Japanese corporations were exempted from the ceiling, so that investors preferred such bonds. However, as the ceiling was raised high enough in the mid-1980s, this consideration became irrelevant.

After initial direct investments made by moving money abroad from Japanese parent companies (to purchase equities or build factories), additional lending may be done by foreign branches of Japanese banks. Funds are sent from bank headquarters in Japan, hence the transactions again inflate "monetary movement balances" (outflow) but not "direct investment" in long-term capital. Moreover, reinvestment using the profits of subsidiaries set up by direct investment does not show up in the balance of payments.

Overall, these idiosyncrasies in the data imply that the long-term capital "inflow" in 1991 was partly a result of portfolio shifts among nonresidents and banks. The level of underlying (gross) long-term capital exports from Japan did not decline in 1991. Thus, the real picture is far from the often-rumored withdrawal of "Japan money" or sell-off of foreign assets by Japanese investors.

2.4 Transitory Factors

Current account movement, especially the sudden increase in 1992, needs explanation. It has been argued that movements of the current account in 1990–91 were disturbed by transitory factors (Bank of Japan 1991; Harada and Ikawa 1992). According to this argument, a decrease in current account surpluses in 1990 was exaggerated by payments to the Gulf War coffer, a sudden increase in the crude oil price (due to the Gulf War), and the apparent import of gold for a new type of savings account (the gold investment account). After these transitory factors, which reduced current account surpluses in 1990, either disappeared or were reversed, current accounts appear to have increased sharply in 1991. In 1991, gold investment accounts shrank, so that Japan recorded gold exports. The Gulf War (when fighting began) affected Japanese travelers, so that travel account deficits declined in 1991.

It also has been pointed out that export and import volume (as opposed to value) has been stable throughout recent years. This implies that the profit margins (value added) of such Japanese exports as automobiles rose in 1991. In the rest of this section, these arguments will be quantified.

2.4.1 Investment Gold

Toward the end of the 1980s, securities firms introduced a new product—the gold investment account. It is essentially a swap arrangement to buy spot gold and sell gold forward in the international gold market, with exchange rate risk cover (buy spot dollars and sell forward dollars). This arrangement provides a market (yen-denominated) interest rate and allows securities firms to offer an account comparable to a bank deposit.[7] Moreover, the interest rate on

7. Banks also sold the gold investment accounts. However, these accounts were much more vigorously promoted by securities firms.

the gold investment account was slightly higher than a comparable bank deposit (regulated) interest rate.

The net purchase of spot gold for the investment accounts is counted as gold import, in Japan's international balance of payments; however, the gold itself is only registered in the market and not physically transported to Japan. Gold imports for the investment accounts do not show up in the customs clearance statistics.

Hence, when the balances of gold investment accounts increase, Japan appears to import gold, and when the balances decrease, Japan appears to export gold. (To be precise, they are "negative gold imports" as recorded in official statistics. Hence, only imports should be corrected for this effect in what follows.)[8] The amount of apparent gold imports and exports can be estimated from the difference between the gold trade statistics of the balance of payments and those of the customs clearance statistics. Following Harada and Ikawa (1992), apparent imports and exports of gold are estimated as in table 2A.1.

2.4.2 Gulf War

The Gulf War had several transitory effects on Japan's current accounts. First, the war raised the oil price, which in turn contributed to decreasing Japan's current account surpluses. Second, Japan's monetary contribution to the Gulf War amounted to $13 billion, of which $9 billion were paid to the U.S. command of the multicountry forces. Third, because of the Gulf War, international travel decreased for fear of terrorism.

Let us now estimate these effects. The actual oil price (at customs clearance basis) and imported amount (customs clearance basis) for the period August 1990–to April 1991 are shown in table 2.A.2. The oil price, measured at Japanese customs, rose sharply from September 1990 to November 1990. It then gradually declined to its previous level by April 1991. Suppose that the oil price had stayed at the August 1991 level, $16.39, for the following eight months. Then we estimate that Japan's surpluses would have been larger by more than $10 billion.

Monthly statistics of the transfer of the current account show some unusual payments in September and December 1990 and March and July 1991. It is roughly estimated that Japan contributed $2.5 billion in 1990 and $10.5 billion in 1991 as a part of the Gulf war–related transfers (table 2A.3).

The travel account balance was also affected by the Gulf War, because fear of terrorist attack on foreign soil or in the sky reduced the number of Japanese tourists going abroad. In 1989 and 1990, travel account deficits increased, on average, at the rate of 18.3 percent per annum (table 2A.4), while the magnitude of deficits declined significantly in the first quarters of 1991. If these

8. I am indebted to Naohiro Yashiro for pointing this out to me.

Table 2.4 **Effects of Transitory Factors on Current Account Movement (billion $)**

	1990	1991
Investment Gold	−2.4	12.80
Oil price	−7.21	−3.09
Transfer	−2.50	−10.50
Travel	0.00	4.8

Source: See appendix.

deficits had increased in 1991 at their 1989–90 rate, travel account deficits would have been larger by $4.8 billion in 1991 (table 2A.5).

We summarize the effects of the transitory factors outlined above in table 2.4.

2.4.3 Expensive Imports and Exports

Both the Bank of Japan (1991) and Harada and Ikawa (1992) point out that there was a sharp increase in imports of expensive automobiles, paintings, and diamonds in 1989 and 1990 and a subsequent reversal in 1991. (Hence, the logic goes, a decrease in the trade balance in 1990 and an increase in 1991 were both exaggerated by this factor.) These goods were imported due to wealth effects related to a sharp increase in land and stock prices. (Stock prices peaked in December 1989, but profits from capital gains were used with a time lag.) There may be cases in which these goods were used to reduce the tax liabilities, through depreciation, of corporations and wealthy individuals. Because of a crash in the stock market and declining land prices, imports of these luxury goods, presumably through a (reverse) wealth effect, declined sharply in 1991.[9] I will not consider correcting for these expensive imports, however. Shifts in the composition of imports are not particularly interesting in a discussion of the overall trade balance, and there is no hard evidence that these expensive imports are not just a result of substitution for other goods. In other words, a temporary shift in the import function would have to be shown in order to count these expensive imports as a transitory factor.

According to the Bank of Japan (1991) and Harada and Ikawa (1992), a decomposition of exports into price and volume shows that most of the increase in exports (export value) in 1991 is due to upgrading effects. That is, the same export commodity from Japan (say, an automobile) has become more expensively or highly value-added (say, a model shift from small/compact cars to luxurious cars). Again, I will not investigate this change in this paper.

9. Since the stock and land price increases of the second half of the 1980s are considered examples of financial "bubbles," these goods are nicknamed "bubble goods."

2.5 Exchange Rate Effect—Simulation

2.5.1 Export and Import Functions

A last factor, which I consider more structural, is the exchange rate. The yen/dollar exchange rate has essentially stayed in the 120–160 yen/dollar range since the spring of 1986. During the following six years, the productivity increase in the tradable sector was higher in Japan than in the United States, so that the same nominal rate implies the tendency of more exports from Japan.[10]

In order to assess the effect of the yen/dollar exchange rate on Japan's exports and imports, (nominal) export/(nominal) GNP and (nominal) import/(nominal) GNP ratios are regressed on the yen/dollar exchange rate, controlling for the growth rates of Japan and the United States, the inflation (GNP deflator) differential of the two countries, and the oil price. Imports are adjusted, before estimation, for gold investment account effects. Results of these regressions are shown in tables 2.5 and 2.6. Yen appreciation (a decline of LYEN) indeed decreases exports and increases imports, as shown from the sign of the sum of lagged LYEN coefficients. We have obtained in our estimates the expected signs for effects of U.S. growth and the inflation differential on exports; we also obtained the expected signs for effects of Japanese growth, the oil price, and the inflation differential on imports.

2.5.2 Counter-factual Hypothesis

Using these regression results, we first calculate how exports and imports would have been different if the exchange rate had not experienced yen depreciation from 1989 to 1990. Let us assume that the yen/dollar exchange rate stayed at 125 yen/dollar (the average of daily closing rates in the last quarter of 1988) from 1989:1 to the end of 1991. In addition, let us estimate the effect of the oil price increase due to the Gulf War, using the import functions. Let us assume that the spike in the oil price due to the Gulf War had not occurred, so that the oil price stayed about $18 per barrel (the oil price in 1990:3) from 1990:4 to 1991:2.

Tables 2.7 and 2.8 simulate such a case using the estimated coefficients of export and import functions in tables 2.5 and 2.6. Exports would have been uniformly lower than actual statistics in 1989–91. Imports would have been smaller in 1989 and 1990 and higher in 1991.

It is now of interest to derive the hypothetical paths of trade and current account surpluses under a set of assumptions which eliminate the Gulf War effects and exchange rate fluctuations. Effects of gold investment accounts, travel account deficits (in service trade), and the Gulf War contribution effect (transfer), taken from table 2.4, can be considered, in addition to the simulated trade balance, calculated in tables 2.7 and 2.8, namely the exchange rate and

10. It is assumed here that fundamentals suggest that the "equilibrium" level of the Japanese yen appreciate against the U.S. dollar in the long run. See Yoshikawa (1990) for such an analysis.

Table 2.5 Export Function (estimation period, 1975:1–1991:4)

Variable	Coefficient	*t*-statistic
ER (*t*−1)	0.7873	8.828
LYEN (*t*)	0.0619	4.643
LYEN (*t*−1)	−0.0506	−2.384
LYEN (*t*−2)	0.0134	0.629
LYEN (*t*−3)	−0.0017	−0.084
LYEN (*t*−4)	−0.0003	−0.014
LYEN (*t*−5)	−0.0182	−0.819
LYEN (*t*−6)	0.0237	1.094
LYEN (*t*−7)	−0.0069	−0.333
LYEN (*t*−8)	−0.0070	−0.562
LUSYR (*t*−1)	0.1026	1.471
LUSYR (*t*−2)	0.0134	0.119
LUSYR (*t*−3)	−0.0735	−0.675
LUSYR (*t*−4)	−0.0401	−0.556
USJADEF (*t*−1)	0.1600	1.699
USJADEF (*t*−2)	−0.1457	−1.600
CONSTANT	−0.0838	−0.364
QTR2	0.0144	7.558
QTR3	0.0110	6.641
QTR4	0.0139	8.356
Sum of LYEN coefficients	0.0142	
$\bar{R}^2$	0.921	
SSR	0.000957	
SEE	0.004466	
D-W	2.045	

Note: Export Equation is
$ER = a_0{*}ER\ (t-1) + \sum a_i{*}LYEN\ (t-i) + \sum b_i{*}LUSRY\ (t-i) + \sum c_i{*}USJADEF\ (t-i) + d_1 + d_2{*}QTR2\ (t) + d_3{*}QTR3(t) + d_4{*}QTR4(t) + e(t).$

Definition of variables:

ER = exports (trillion yen)/GNP (trillion yen)
LYEN = log yen/dollar rate, average over quarter
LUSYR = log U.S. real GNP (1982 price), proxy for the world demand
USJADEF = log (U.S. GNP deflator) − log (Japan GNP deflator)
QTR2 = dummy variable for the second quarter
QTR3 = dummy variable for the third quarter
QTR4 = dummy variable for the fourth quarter

oil price effects. The "benchmark" column in table 2.9 shows the trade and current account surpluses adjusted for those factors listed above.

Briefly, this exercise can be understood as follows. If the Gulf War had not occurred, the oil price would have been stable through 1990 and 1991, Japanese travel would not have been reduced in 1991, and of course, the monetary contribution to the allied forces and other neighboring countries would not have been necessary. In addition to eliminating the Gulf War effect, suppose

Table 2.6 Import Function (estimation period, 1975:1–1991:4)

Variable	Coefficient	t-statistic
IR ($t-1$)	0.6901	7.047
LYEN (t)	0.0694	6.489
LYEN ($t-1$)	−0.0616	−3.595
LYEN ($t-2$)	0.0275	1.600
LYEN ($t-3$)	−0.0383	−2.309
LYEN ($t-4$)	0.0053	0.327
LYEN ($t-5$)	−0.0083	−0.490
LYEN ($t-6$)	0.0052	0.313
LYEN ($t-7$)	−0.0012	−0.076
LYEN ($t-8$)	−0.0011	−0.118
LOIL (t)	0.0097	3.281
LJAYR ($t-1$)	0.1154	1.574
LJAYR ($t-2$)	−0.0972	−1.122
LJAYR ($t-3$)	0.0252	0.287
LJAYR ($t-4$)	−0.0512	−0.702
USJADEF ($t-1$)	−0.0336	−0.041
USJADEF ($t-2$)	−0.0263	−0.325
CONSTANT	0.0555	0.444
QTR2	0.0030	2.363
QTR3	0.0017	1.388
QTR4	0.0066	4.948
Sum of LYEN coefficients	−0.0032	
$\bar{R}^2$	0.973	
SSR	0.000581	
SEE	0.003517	
D-W	1.545	

Note: Import equation is

$$IR = a_0*IR\ (t-1) + \sum a_i*LYEN\ (t-i) + \sum b_i*LJAYR\ (t-i) + \sum c_i*USJADEF\ (t-i) + c_5*LOIL\ (t-i) + d_1 + d_2*QTR2\ (t) + d_3*QTR3(t) + d_4*QTR4(t) + e(t).$$

Definition of variables:

IR	= imports (trillion yen)/GNP (trillion yen)
LYEN	= log yen/dollar rate, average over quarter
LJAYR	= log Japan real GNP (1985 price)
LOIL	= log oil price ($ per barrel, customs clearance base)
USJADEF	= log (US GNP deflator) − log (Japan GNP deflator)
QTR2	= dummy variable for the second quarter
QTR3	= dummy variable for the third quarter
QTR4	= dummy variable for the fourth quarter

that the yen had stayed at 125.00 yen/dollar in 1989–91 and that gold investment accounts had not been available. The hypothetical current account "benchmark" column in table 2.9 simulates the current account surpluses in such a situation. One may regard this column as the benchmark for Japanese current account surpluses without transitory factors.

Table 2.7 Simulation of Exports

Year and Quarter		EXPORT	Fitted Value		Strong Yen Scenario	
			FEXPORT	EXPR	FEXPORT2	EXP2R
1989	1	66945	65143.5	−2.69	63834.1	−4.65
	2	66560	68701.3	3.22	64311.2	−3.38
	3	68157	69449.2	1.89	63697.6	−6.54
	4	67908	73707.3	8.54	66850.5	−1.56
1990	1	65460	67260.6	2.75	58329.5	−10.89
	2	65510	72776.5	11.09	61827.7	−5.62
	3	70500	74915.8	6.26	66208.3	−6.09
	4	78904	85648.5	8.55	79926.2	1.30
1991	1	71778	75786.3	1.08	68513.2	−8.62
	2	68790	77980.5	8.32	70902.5	−1.51
	3	73734	77337.1	0.52	72384.7	−5.91
	4	79495	84820.8	2.57	81124.4	−1.90

Note: Conditions for simulation were: exchange rate was 125 yen/dollar from 1989:1 to 1991:4, and oil price was at its 1990:3 level from 1990:4 to 1991:2.

Definition of variables:

EXPORT = Actual exports (million $)
FEXPORT = Fitted value of the regression, with actual RHS variables (million $)
FEXPORT2 = Simulated exports (million $)
EXPR = Deviation of FEXPORT from EXPORT (%)
EXPR2 = Deviation of FEXPORT2 from EXPORT (%)

In this benchmark case, it is clear that the Japanese current account did not fluctuate so wildly in 1989–91. However, even in the benchmark case, it is clear that current account surpluses increased in 1991 from their level in 1990, although the change was only 10 percent, as opposed to more than 100 percent in the actual statistics. Hence, transitory factors alone do not explain the reversal. Thus we can conclude that there was a fundamental change in the movement of current account surpluses in 1991. The same observation applies to the trade balance. The most likely cause for the trend reversal was a lack of yen appreciation in recent years and, moreover, some yen depreciation in 1990. We will see the effects of yen/dollar movement on trade and current account surpluses in the next section.

2.6 Policy Implications

If the size of current account surpluses is judged to pose some political problems for Japan, yen appreciation is a potent policy tool.[11] In order to determine

11. Of course, the position that no size of current account surplus/deficit matters is perfectly acceptable from an economist's point of view, because it is just the borrowing/lending (saving-investment balance) of the nation as a whole. When a demographic change makes Japan a society with many retirees (as is predicted to happen in the next two or three decades), the current account will become deficit.

Table 2.8 Simulation of Imports

Year and Quarter		IMPORT	IMPORT − G	Fitted Value		Strong Yen Scenario	
				FIMPORT	IMPR	FIMPORT2	IMPR2
1989	1	44634	44984	44536.3	−1.00	43067.9	−4.26
	2	45766	46116	45987.7	−0.28	41295.4	−10.45
	3	47387	47737	46779.7	−2.00	41066.7	−13.97
	4	50866	51216	52963.7	3.41	46717.5	−8.78
1990	1	50467	50467	50851.9	0.76	44335.1	−12.15
	2	51296	51296	51039.0	−0.50	44109.5	−14.01
	3	52751	52751	49933.7	−5.34	47231.2	−10.46
	4	59932	59932	57947.9	−3.31	56570.4	−5.61
1991	1	54249	57449	54792.3	−4.62	52962.9	−7.81
	2	48638	51838	52247.1	0.79	52281.8	0.86
	3	49095	52295	51026.2	−2.42	51615.9	−1.30
	4	51232	54432	55659.5	2.25	58554.2	7.57

Note: Conditions for simulation were: exchange rate was 125 yen/dollar from 1989:1 to 1991:4, and oil price was at its 1990:3 level from 1990:4 to 1991:2.

Definition of variables:

IMPORT	= Actual imports (million $)
IMPORT − G	= Import − gold investment (when net imports)
FIMPORT	= Fitted value of the regression, with actual RHS variables (million $)
FIMPORT2	= Simulated imports (million $)
IMPR	= Deviation of FIMPORT from IMPORT − G (%)
IMPR2	= Deviation of FIMPORT2 from IMPORT − G (%)

how exchange rate movement would change the trade and current account surpluses, two paths of opposite exchange rate movements are assumed in the next exercise.

In the appreciation scenario, the yen is assumed to have moved from 125 yen/dollar in the first and second quarters of 1989 to 100 yen/dollar in the third and fourth quarters of 1991, with 5-yen/dollar appreciation steps every six months; in the depreciation scenario, the yen is assumed to have moved from 125 yen/dollar in the first and second quarter of 1989 to 150 yen/dollar in the third and fourth quarters of 1991, with 5-yen/dollar steps every six months. The "100 yen" and "150 yen" columns of table 2.9 vividly show how much difference the exchange rate makes in the trade and current accounts. Compared to the benchmark case, the 1991 trade and current account surpluses in the yen appreciation case are about $25 billion less, while the yen depreciation scenario shows just the opposite.

The simulation results show that exports and imports respond to the yen/dollar exchange rate remarkably well, though with lags. If too much surplus is politically unacceptable, a way to cause yen appreciation must be explored. In order to cause yen appreciation, a different domestic policy mix and international policy coordination (or, a second "Plaza Agreement") would be a good idea. The policy mix for yen appreciation should be tighter monetary policy

Table 2.9 Simulations of Trade and Current Accounts for Different Exchange Rate Paths (million $)

		Hypothetical		
Year and Quarter	Actual	100 Yen	Benchmark	150 Yen
Trade account				
1989 1	21,311	20,766	20,766	20,766
2	19,794	23,015	23,015	23,015
3	19,770	22,847	22,630	22,422
4	16,042	20,005	20,133	20,255
1990 1	14,393	14,268	13,994	13,747
2	13,614	16,693	17,718	18,692
3	17,149	17,769	18,977	20,176
4	18,372	20,226	23,355	26,255
1991 1	20,729	11,624	15,550	19,259
2	23,352	12,704	18,620	23,967
3	27,745	13,889	20,768	27,017
4	31,463	12,814	22,570	31,086
Totals				
1989	76,917	86,635	86,546	86,459
1990	63,528	68,958	74,046	78,872
1991	103,289	51,032	77,510	101,330
Current account				
1989 1	16,064	15,519	15,519	15,519
2	14,283	17,504	17,504	17,504
3	14,957	18,034	17,817	17,609
4	11,853	15,816	15,944	16,066
1990 1	12,305	12,180	11,906	11,659
2	7,892	10,971	11,996	12,970
3	7,400	9,120	10,328	11,527
4	8,164	11,418	14,547	17,447
1991 1	10,260	8,391	12,317	16,026
2	18,664	7,128	13,044	18,391
3	19,604	5,810	12,689	18,938
4	24,373	5,068	14,824	23,340
Totals				
1989	57,157	66,875	66,785	66,699
1990	35,761	43,691	48,778	53,605
1991	72,901	26,398	52,875	76,696

Notes: Actual trade account: actual trade balance, reported in balance of payments. Actual current account: actual current account balance, reported in balance of payments.

Hypothetical trade/current account contains corrections for gold investment account, Gulf War–related transfers, and travel decrease. It also assumes oil prices remained at the level of 1990:3. Yen level was assumed as follows: 100-yen scenario: the yen appreciates from 125 yen/dollar in 1981:1 to 100 yen/dollar in 1991:3 by 5 yen/dollar every six months. Benchmark: the yen stays at 125 yen/dollar 1989–91. 150-yen scenario: the yen depreciates from 125 yen/dollar in 1989:1 to 150 yen/dollar in 1991:3 by 5 yen/dollar every six months.

and looser fiscal policy. This mix would enhance a tendency toward strong nonresident demand for Japanese assets as shown in table 2.1. Investigations in earlier sections also show that an increase in nonresident long-term capital investment in Japan was, at least partly, financed by a decrease in short-term yen-denominated assets. When a net inflow of capital, both short-term and long-term, to Japan occurs, the yen will appreciate against other currencies and trigger more structural changes in Japan's imports and exports. Our estimation and simulation analysis supports such an idea and provides some quantitative estimates.

2.7 Concluding Remarks

In this paper, I have described factors affecting Japan's current accounts and capital accounts in the second half of the 1980s and up to 1991. Japanese current accounts appear to have experienced a sharp reversal. However, this is due partly to transitory factors, such as the popularity of gold investment accounts and the Gulf War. Simulation shows that the increase in the current account surpluses in 1991 would have been much more modest if transitory factors had been eliminated.

Japanese long-term capital movement became inflow in 1991. This was due partly to strong demand for Japanese assets by nonresidents and partly to reduction in the short-term debt of Japanese residents. This kind of movement cannot continue long, since, sooner or later, short-term debts will be repayed and long-term capital will turn to outflow, given the large size of current account surpluses. Some transitory factors, such as the Gulf War contributions, are purely exogenous to Japan's economic policies, while others, such as the gold investment accounts, are due to (antiquated) regulations on financial products.

With export and import movements corrected for transitory factors, the simulated trend in current account surpluses, which started in 1987, still shows a reversal in 1991, although the magnitude is much less than the official statistics. If the coming increase in current account surpluses is judged to be politically problematic, yen appreciation would be helpful in avoiding the problem in the near future.

Appendix

Decomposition of Changes in Current Accounts, 1988–91

Table 2A.1 Gold Investment Account (billion $)

	1988	1989	1990	1991
Apparent gold export	1.4	−6.1	−2.4	12.8

Source: Harada and Ikawa (1992)

Table 2A.2 Gulf War Effect: Oil Price

	1990					1991			
	Aug	Sep	Oct	Nov	Dec	Jan	Feb	Mar	Apr
1. Oil price (actual; $)	16.39	22.44	30.34	34.16	32.77	28.16	24.73	19.11	17.49
2. Oil import (actual; million barrels)	113	113	119	133	153	119	128	210	54
3. Oil import value (actual; billion $)	1.85	2.54	3.61	4.54	5.01	3.35	3.17	4.01	0.94
4. Oil import (Hypothetical; billion $)	1.85	1.85	1.95	2.18	2.51	1.95	2.10	3.44	0.89
5. Difference (billions $)		0.69	1.66	2.36	2.50	1.40	1.07	0.57	0.05
Sum of differences (billion $)									
Aug–Dec 1990					7.21				
Jan–Apr 1991									3.09

Source: Lines 1 and 2 from Toyo Keizai Shinpo (1991).
Note: Line 3 = line 1 × line 2. Line 4 = 16.39 × line 2. Line 5 = line 3 − line 4.

Table 2A.3 Gulf War Effect-Transfer (billion $)

	1990	1991
Estimated contribution	2.5	10.5

Table 2A.4 Travel Balance, 1989–90 (billion $)

	1989				1990			
	1	2	3	4	1	2	3	4
Actual	−4.458	−4.593	−5.442	−4.854	−4.782	−5.017	−6.005	−5.546
	(63.8)	(13.6)	(17.8)	(10.2)	(7.3)	(9.2)	(10.3)	(14.2)

Note: Numbers in parentheses are percentage change (in deficit) over same quarter of previous year.

Table 2A.5 Gulf War Effect: Travel Balance (billion $)

	1991			
	1	2	3	4
Actual	−3.893	−4.547	−6.166	−5.905
	(−18.6)	(−9.4)	(2.6)	(6.5)
Hypothetical[a]	−5.657	−5.935	−7.104	−6.561
Difference[b]	1.8	1.4	0.9	0.7

Note: Numbers in parentheses are percentage change (in deficit) over same quarter of previous year.

[a]Equals 1.183 × level in same quarter of 1990. Average of deficit growth rate over eight quarters of 1989–90 is 18.3 percent.

[b]Equals actual − hypothetical.

References

Bank of Japan. 1991. Saikin no Taigai Shushi Doko ni tsuite (On recent movement of external balance). *Monthly Bulletin*, November, 19–42.

———. 1992. 1991 nen chu no Tainaigai Shoken Tohi no Doko (Movements of securities investments, inward and outward, in 1991). *Monthly Bulletin*, March, 1–16.

Harada, Yuzo, and Norimichi Ikawa. 1992. Saikin no Kokusai shushi no Ugoki ni tuite (On recent movements of international balance of payments). *Finance* (Ministry of Finance), April, 72–79.

Ito, Takatoshi. 1992. *The Japanese economy.* Cambridge: MIT Press.

Marston, Richard. 1990. Pricing to market in Japanese manufacturing. *Journal of International Economics* 29 (3/4): 217–36.

———. 1991. Price behavior in Japanese and US manufacturing. In *The US and Japan: Trade and investment*, ed. P. Krugman. Chicago: University of Chicago Press.

Ohno, Ken-ichi. 1989. Export pricing behavior of manufacturing: A US–Japan comparison. *International Monetary Fund Staff Papers* 36(3): 550–79.

Toyo Keizai Shinpo. 1991. *Tokei Nenpo (Economic statistic annual).* Tokoy: Toyo Keizai Shinpo.

Ueda, Kazuo. 1988. Perspectives on the Japanese current account surplus. In *NBER Macroeconomic Annual*, vol. 3. Cambridge: MIT Press.

Ueda, Kazuo, and Mariko Fujii. 1986. On recent capital outflow from Japan (in Japanese). Ministry of Finance, *Financial Review,* no. 3.

Yoshikawa, Hiroshi. 1990. On the equilibrium yen-dollar rate. *American Economic Review* 80 (June): 576–83.

Comment Naohiro Yashiro

This paper summarizes well the recent developments in Japan's balance of payments and explains the major factors affecting them. The major points of this paper are as follows: (1) transitory factors were important in aggravating Japan's surplus in both current and capital accounts in 1991; (2) nevertheless, yen depreciation since 1989 has been mainly responsible for the reversal of the declining trend in Japan's current account surplus from 1991 onward; (3) a policy mix consisting of tighter monetary policy and looser fiscal policy would be desirable if the coming increases in current account surpluses are judged to be politically problematic.

While the first section of this paper is quite informative, the second section is not necessarily persuasive. Moreover, I disagree with the author's policy prescription, mainly because the author explains Japan's ratio of total exports to GNP by using U.S. GNP as a proxy for world demand and the yen/dollar exchange rate. There are two obvious problems with this equation. One is the meaning of the export equation. Does the ratio of Japan's exports to its GNP imply the supply function, i.e., the capacity of Japan's manufacturing sector to export? Alternatively, if it is a traditional demand equation, the export denominator needs to be world GNP, not Japan's GNP. Another possibility is the heroic assumption that U.S. demand represents world demand for Japan's exports. This argument is likely to exaggerate the role of exchange rate, as the share of the U.S. market in Japan's total exports has declined from 37.1 percent in 1985 to 28.7 percent in 1991.

Comment Maria S. Gochoco

Japan's current account surplus declined in the 1980s after the yen appreciated but has started to increase dramatically since 1990–91. At the same time, the long-term capital account recorded inflows in 1991. This is in sharp contrast with Japan's record in the 1980s, when it became the world's largest exporter of capital (from $10 billion in 1981, its net long-term capital flow peaked at $137 billion in 1987).

Ito's study discusses possible explanations for an apparent puzzle in the 1990s. The macro accounting identity implies that the current account is the balance between national savings and investment. If a country runs a current account surplus by exporting more goods and services than it imports, it must

Naohiro Yashiro is professor of international economics at Sophia University and a senior economist of the Japan Center for Economic Research.

Maria S. Gochoco is associate professor at the School of Economics of the University of the Philippines.

lend the difference to foreigners by investing and acquiring an equal amount of net claims through its capital account. A current account surplus must have as its counterpart, therefore, a capital outflow, not an inflow as seems to be the case for Japan since 1991.

It is not clear whether the phenomenon being described is a structural or temporary one, or whether the process of adjustment simply takes time. As an example of the latter, we note that the yen appreciation following the Plaza Accord did not immediately correct the current account imbalance. In section 2.2.1 of his study, Ito seems to believe that this is a temporary phenomenon. He says that the "unwinding" cannot go on indefinitely and that long-term capital flows will become outflows *sooner or later* provided that current account surpluses continue to exist.

Ito cites other reasons, mostly having to do with data, that seem to imply that perhaps the problem is not really a problem at all. The current account surplus is not really that large. He says, for example, that the current account surplus in 1990, which amounted to 1 percent of nominal GNP, was much less than that in 1987, which amounted to 4 percent of GNP. Furthermore, the long-term capital "inflows" in 1991 were partly a result of portfolio shifts among nonresidents and banks. Also, the decline in the current account deficit in 1990 was exaggerated by Gulf War payments, an increase in oil prices, etc.—in other words, by unusual exogenous factors. He estimates that without the yen depreciation and the Gulf War effect, the current account surplus would have increased by only 10 percent between 1990 and 1991.

Perhaps greater attention ought to be given to the determinants of capital flows (see Glick 1991). In the 1980s, long-term capital outflows exceeded current account surpluses. This seems to indicate that independent factors related to greater demand for foreign assets by Japanese investors are important. This is in contrast with the view from the macro accounting perspective that the involuntary acquisition of foreign assets by Japanese investors occurred merely to finance unbalanced trade in goods and services.

Both macro and micro factors may also be important. The aging population's effect on savings may reduce outflows. The stock market crash in 1990 and the current recession may, on the other hand, reduce domestic investment. The stance of monetary policy and exchange rate expectations may also explain portfolio shifts. On the micro side, domestic deregulation may affect the amount of foreign borrowing by banks, for example. The greater degree of integration between Japanese and world financial markets may also affect such flows of capital.

Reference

Glick, Reuven. 1991. Japanese Capital Flows in the 1980s. *Federal Reserve Bank of San Francisco Economic Review*, Spring 1991 (2): 18–31.

3 Perspectives on Korea's External Adjustment: Comparison with Japan and Taiwan

Bon Ho Koo and Won-Am Park

3.1 Introduction

Current account imbalances among major countries in the first half of the 1980s were larger than at any time since the early post–World War II period. In the early 1980s, there was concern about the apparent misalignment of currencies, inappropriate monetary and fiscal policies of major countries, and unfair trade practices and exchange rate manipulation by some developing countries. In order to correct these imbalances, the Japanese yen rose rapidly after the Group of Five's Plaza Agreement in September 1985. The decline of the dollar, however, did not significantly reduce current account imbalances. U.S. trade relations with Japan have been the dominant issue in international economic policy. With the yen's appreciation, more attention was paid to movement in the balance of payments of the East Asian newly industrializing countries (NICs)—Korea, Taiwan, Hong Kong, and Singapore. These countries are most often accused of manipulating their exchange rates, taking advantage of the yen's appreciation but not opening up their markets. In particular, U.S.-Korean economic relations have been strained by a growing number of conflicts over trade and macroeconomic policy.

Korea accumulated large current account surpluses during 1986–88, due mostly to "three lows"—low dollar, low oil prices, and low international interest rates. As this good fortune began to disappear after 1989, Korea's current account deteriorated to record a deficit of more than 3 percent of GNP in 1991, compared with a surplus of 8.2 percent of GNP at its peak in 1988. This sharp turnaround in Korea's current account is unique in that it reverted to a large deficit while Japan and Taiwan, the neighboring nations with which Korea is most often compared, maintained their surpluses. The natural question is, Why

Bon Ho Koo is professor of economics at Hanyang University. Won-Am Park is a fellow at the Korea Development Institute.

did Korea's current account turn so sharply and show a huge deficit in 1991? Further questions could be raised: Was such a big turnaround inevitable when the "three lows" disappeared after 1989, and was it foreshadowed by the huge surpluses during 1986–88? Was it the result of policies aimed at reducing the current account surplus in response to foreign pressure and thus avoidable? And was it possibly even desirable for Korea to make such a turnaround and post a current account deficit?

This paper deals with these questions by focusing on Korea's structural adjustment and policy responses after the current account surplus emerged in 1986. It considers various policy responses made by Korean policymakers and accepts the viewpoint that both expenditure-switching and expenditure-expanding policies have worked to reduce the current account surplus. Special attention is paid to the stabilizing feedbacks of assets markets, in particular land and equities, on goods and asset prices and hence on savings and investment.

This paper is organized as follows. In section 3.2, we provide an overview of Korea's current account balance in comparison to those of Japan and Taiwan from the perspectives of export-import balance and saving-investment balance, respectively. Section 3.3 reviews the actual policy responses to emerging surpluses in the current account and attempts to evaluate these policies in comparison to those of Japan and Taiwan. The role of assets markets in the balance of payments adjustment is highlighted in section 3.4. In section 3.5, we estimate the "conventional" export and import equations and assess the importance of adjusting the real exchange rate and domestic and foreign demand. The last section pulls the results together for an overall assessment and derives implications for future policy debates between the United States and Korea.

3.2 An Overview of Korea's Current Account in Comparison with Japan and Taiwan

Fluctuations in the current account can be examined from two different perspectives. One, related to the elasticity of income and relative price, examines export and import behavior. The other, related to the income-expenditure approach, examines savings and investment behavior as a mirror image of the current account. While the former approach takes into account the effect of relative prices on trade, the latter approach attempts to distinguish between permanent and transitory (disposable) income. Since private consumption responds more to changes in permanent income, the latter approach divides private savings into permanent and transitory components. For example, favorable external conditions improve the current account by increasing foreign demand or strengthening external competitiveness. They can also boost domestic savings by increasing transitory income. Whether through improved external demand and competitiveness or through enhanced domestic savings with temporary changes in domestic demand, changing external and internal conditions may explain the behavior of Korea's current account. This section will examine both approaches and review exports and imports on the one hand and savings and investment on the other.

3.2.1 Exports and Imports

Figure 3.1, panel A, presents movements in Korea's current balance for the last two decades. It clearly shows that the oil shocks of 1974 and 1979–80 set back the current account. But despite these shocks, Korea was almost able to balance the current account in 1977 and again in 1985. In order to distin-

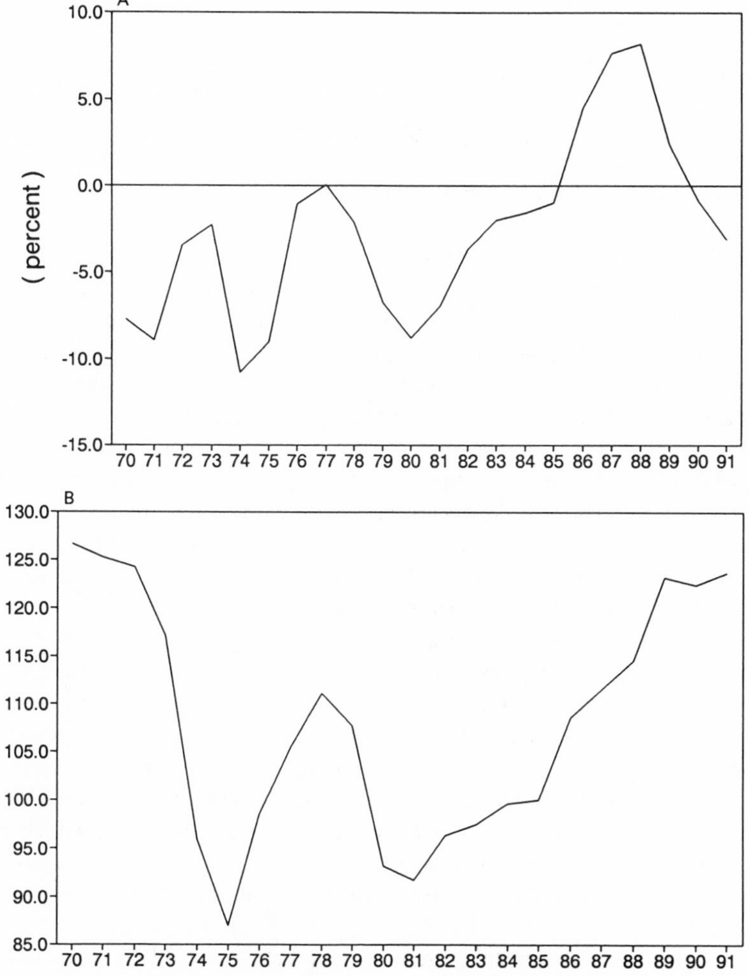

Fig. 3.1 Trade patterns in Korea, 1970–91: A, current account/GNP ratio; B, terms of trade (1985 = 100); C (on p. 56), real trade balance (in 1985 base)
Source: Monthly Bulletin (Seoul: Bank of Korea, various issues).

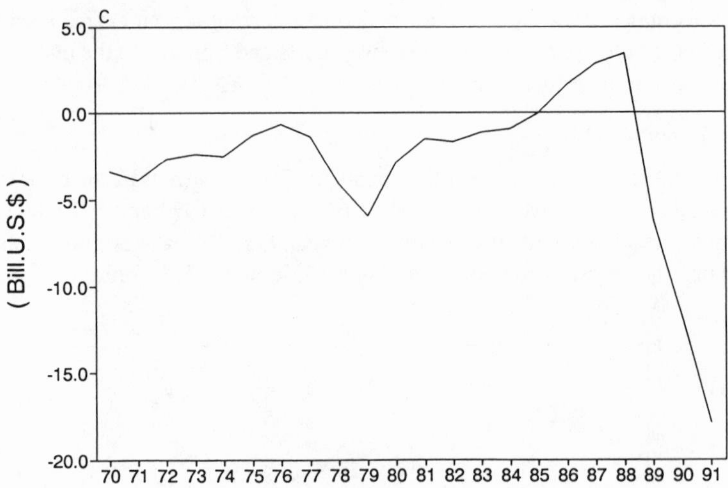

Fig. 3.1 (continued) C, real trade balance (in 1985 base)

guish between nominal and real trade balance, changes in trade account were divided into changes in the terms of trade and in trade volumes in panels B and C. The two oil shocks were associated with drastic deterioration in terms of trade, and the "three lows" with its improvement. The real trade balance, which is equivalent to real exports minus real imports in 1985 dollars, showed a trend of steady improvement up to 1988, except for the years 1977–79. Therefore, it can be concluded that large swings in the terms of trade appear to explain, for the most part, fluctuations in the current account/GNP ratio until 1988. The experiences of Japan and Taiwan are shown in figure 3.2 and figure 3.3, respectively. The adjustment pattern of the current account in each country looks much the same. There was a steady move toward a current account surplus before 1985, though it was interrupted by the two oil shocks.

Movements in the terms of trade, however, differed somewhat among the three countries. Fluctuations were larger in Japan than in Korea and Taiwan. But in all three countries, the terms of trade showed a trend of deterioration in the 1970s and a trend of improvement in the 1980s. Despite the reversed trend in the terms of trade, real trade balance improved quite steadily up to 1985. This trend was more pronounced in Japan and Taiwan than in Korea. Therefore, if there is a secular trend in net real exports due to technological change and other structural reasons that is not captured in the conventional export and import equations, one may find more evidence for it in Japan and Taiwan than in Korea.

The post-1985 adjustment pattern in trade balance could be characterized by a sharp decline in real trade balance with improvement in terms of trade in all three countries. In Japan and Taiwan, terms of trade improved sharply during 1986–87, and the decline in real trade balance began in 1986. In contrast,

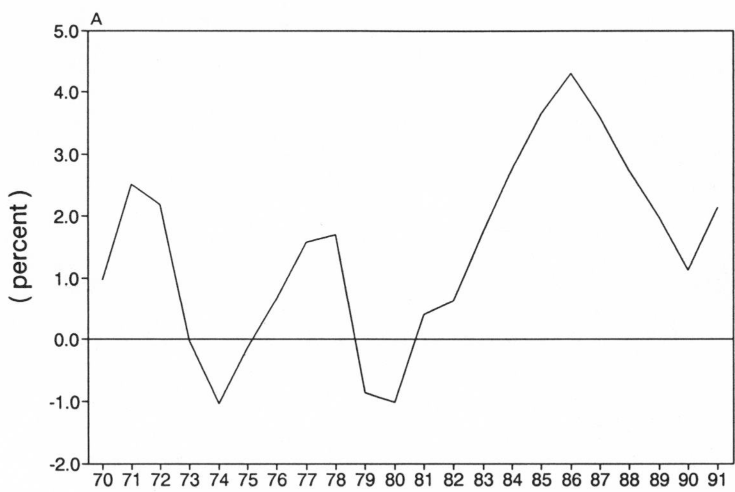

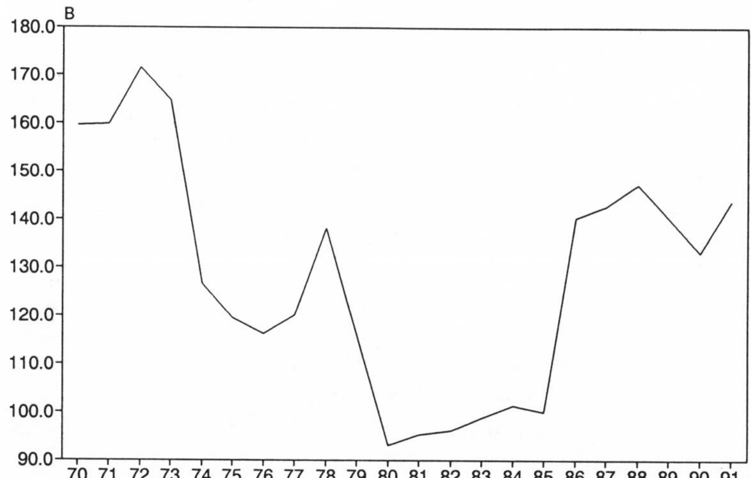

Fig. 3.2 Trade patterns in Japan, 1970–91: A, current account/GNP ratio; B, terms of trade (1985 = 100); C (on p. 58), real trade balance (in 1985 base)
Source: International Financial Statistics (Washington, D.C.: IMF, various issues).

Korea enjoyed gradual improvements in both terms of trade and real trade balance during 1986–88 but experienced a sudden and drastic reduction in real trade balance during 1989–91.

This sharp reduction in real trade balance distinguishes the Korean experience with external adjustment from those of Japan and Taiwan. The decrease in Korea's real trade balance shown in figure 3.1, panel C, is so sharp as to be called excessive, especially when we consider that Korea's improvement in real

Fig. 3.2 (continued) C, real trade balance (in 1985 base)

trade balance during 1970–85 was very slow compared with Japan and Taiwan.

Why did Korea experience such a sharp turnaround in real trade balance during 1988–91? The rest of this paper attempts to find some answers that emphasize both the expenditure-expanding and expenditure-switching polices taken in response to the emerging current account surpluses in Korea.

3.2.2 Savings and Investment

We now turn to the gap between income and expenditure. Figure 3.4 shows the savings and investment behavior of the private and government sectors and the effect of such behavior on Korea's current account. During the past two decades, the current account showed a strong positive correlation with the saving-investment balance of the private sector. The government budget was also positively correlated with the current account, but its correlation was not as strong as that of net private savings (the gap between private savings and investment). Net government savings exhibited a strong increasing trend until 1988.

In Taiwan, the current account also showed a strong positive correlation with the saving-investment balance of the private sector, but a very weak correlation with the government budget (figure 3.5). However, the Taiwanese government budget did not visibly improve or deteriorate, unlike budget trends in Japan and Korea.

The Japanese case is more subtle. While the current account was strongly correlated with private sector savings and investment in Korea and Taiwan, it did not show such a strong correlation with net private savings in Japan, as

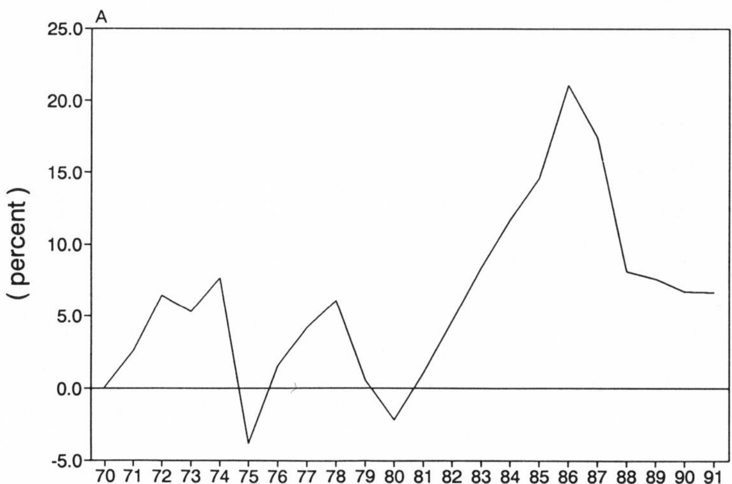

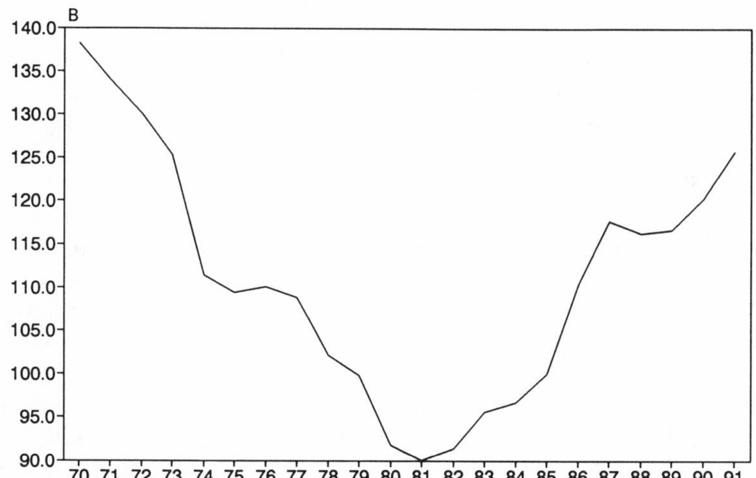

Fig. 3.3 Trade patterns in Taiwan, 1970–91: A, current account/GNP ratio; B, terms of trade (1985 = 100); C (on p. 60), real trade balance (in 1985 base)
Source: Financial Statistics (Taipei: Central Bank of China, various issues).

shown in figure 3.6. The current account was positively correlated with net private savings in the 1970s, while the government budget surplus was negatively correlated with both the current account and net private savings. However, this pattern of correlation among the current account, net private savings, and government budget certainly changed in the first half of the 1980s. During this period, net private savings changed only a little, but the government deficit decreased remarkably. Therefore, increases in the Japanese current account in

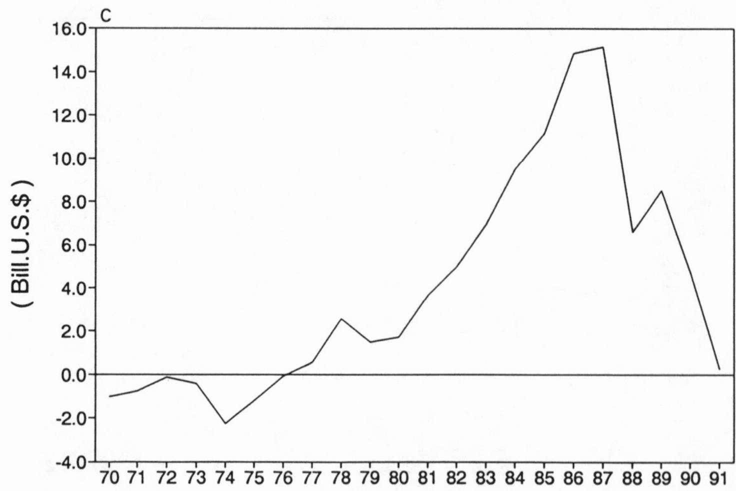

Fig. 3.3 (continued) C, real trade balance (in 1985 base)

the 1980s correspond to Japanese fiscal policy. This well-known trend in the Japanese government budget coupled with the opposite trend in the U.S. budget has been the basis for the Mundell-Fleming view of both the Japanese and U.S. current accounts in the early 1980s (see Sachs and Roubini 1987; Ueda 1988).

The correlation coefficients among net private savings, net government savings, and the current account are reported in table 3.1. They confirm the observations on sectoral net savings and their relationships from figures 3.4–3.6.

While the accounting identity linking budget deficits and the current account cannot be denied, budget deficits need not always be reflected in corresponding changes in the current account. Related to this point may be the two issues of whether budget deficits affect national savings and whether national savings affect the current account. Regarding the first issue, an influential school of "Ricardian equivalence" argues that government deficits will be offset by increases in private savings. According to this view, only temporary changes in government spending will create current account movements, not permanent changes in government spending or any changes in government taxes. Regarding the second issue, the empirical evidence suggests that the link between national savings and the current account has been very weak in OECD countries.

Some very tentative evidence on these two issues is shown in table 3.1. Budget deficits affected national savings in Korea and Japan to a larger extent than in Taiwan. This could imply that if the Ricardian view holds anywhere, it is more likely to hold in Taiwan than in Korea or Japan. On the other hand, national savings spilled over into current accounts in Korea and Taiwan, but not in Japan. Of course, these differing experiences could be explained by the dif-

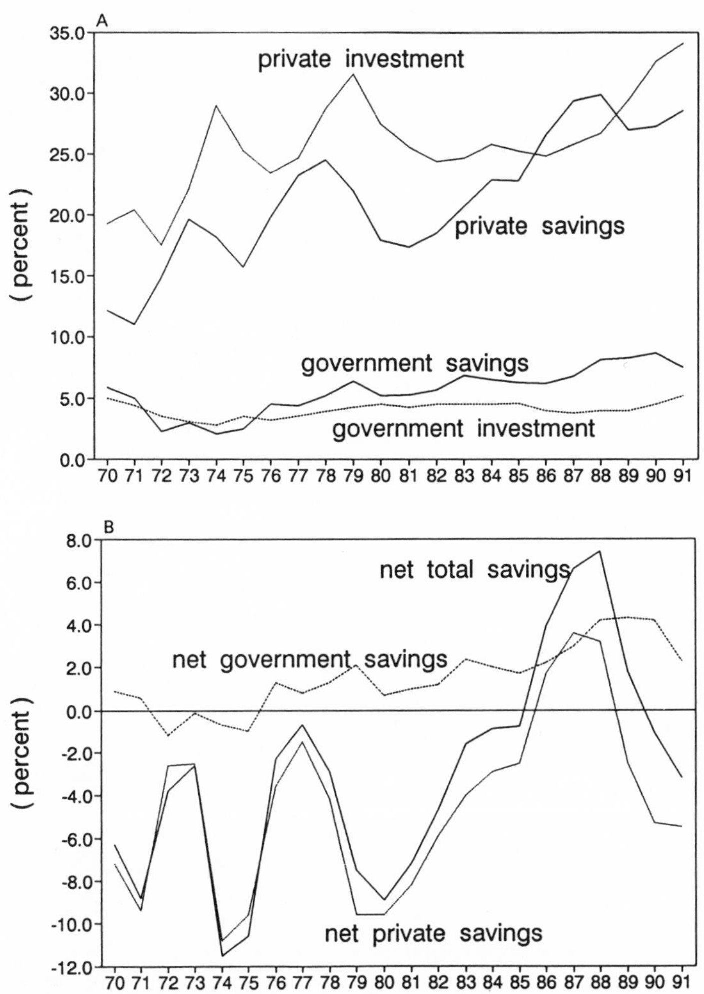

Fig. 3.4 Savings and investment in Korea, 1970–90: A, savings and investment; B, net savings (savings − investment)
Source: National Accounts (Seoul: Bank of Korea, 1991).

ferent investment behavior in each country, particularly its correlation with savings as shown in table 3.1.

If we pay more attention to the post-1985 experience, we can recognize several changes in savings and investment behavior. First, private saving-investment balance played a great role in reducing current account surpluses in all three countries. Even in Japan, the excess of private savings over investment as a ratio of GNP declined by 5 percentage points during 1986–89, while net government savings increased by 3.5 percentage points during the same

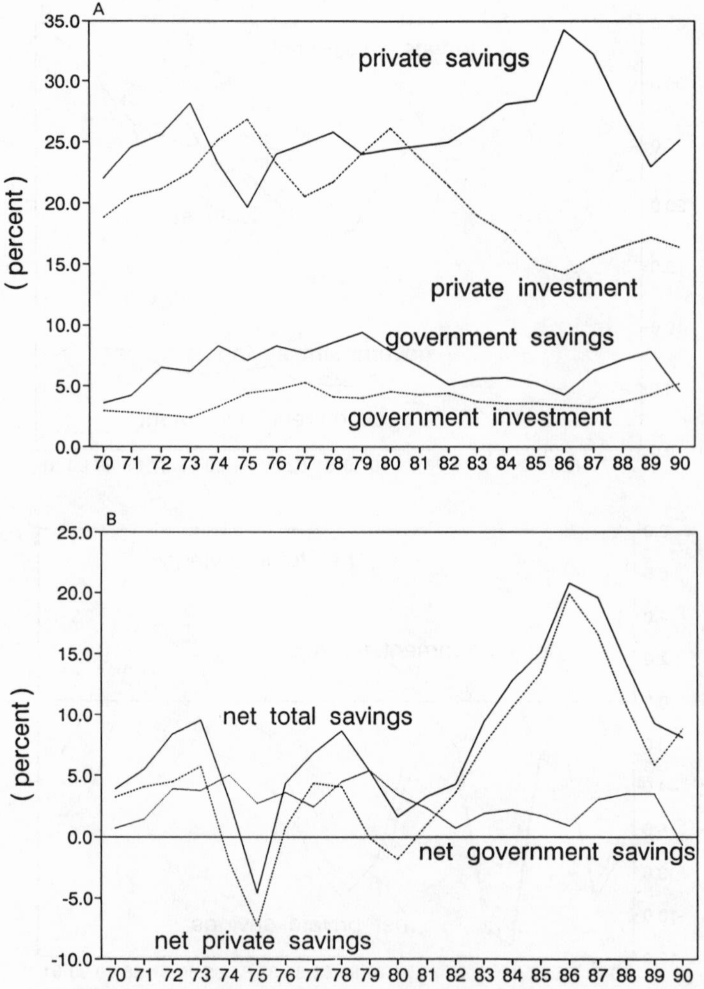

Fig. 3.5 Savings and investment in Taiwan, 1970–90: A, savings and investment; B, net savings (savings − investment)

Source: Taiwan Statistical Data Book (Taipei: Council for Economic Planning and Development, 1991).

period. The increasing role of private savings and investment in the post-1985 period seems to be related to the post-1985 changes in exchange rates and other asset prices. Although no simple model, including the Mundell-Fleming model, could explain their movements after 1985, a number of authors have emphasized the changes in land and stock prices that were triggered by large surpluses in the current account and exchange rate changes. We will return to this topic in section 3.4. Increases in land and stock prices encouraged investment in construction and facilities and consumption via wealth effects.

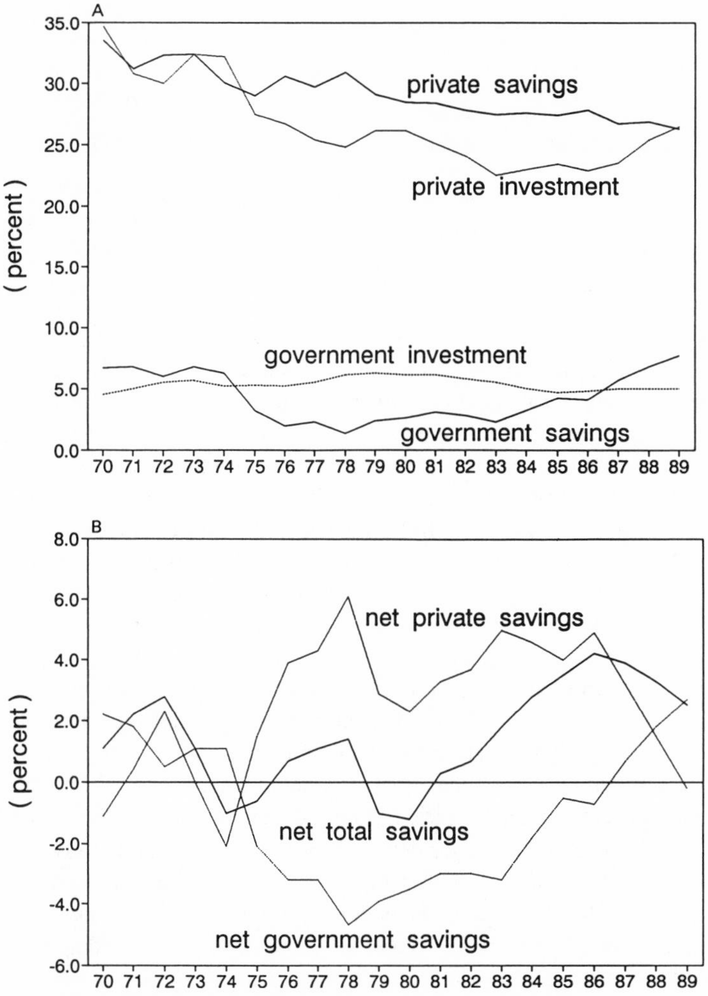

Fig. 3.6 Savings and investment in Japan, 1970–89: A, savings and investment; B, net savings (savings − investment)

Source: Annual Report on National Accounts (Tokyo: Economic Planning Agency, 1991).

Second, fiscal policy played a major role in reducing the current account surplus in Korea and Taiwan, but not in Japan. For instance, in Taiwan net government savings as a ratio of GNP changed little during 1987–89 but declined sharply by more than 4 percentage points in 1990. The Korean case is almost the same: net government savings changed little during 1988–90 and then declined markedly by 2 percentage points in 1991.

Third, we can find differences in the adjustment of private savings and private investment among the three countries. In Taiwan, private savings played a

Table 3.1 Correlation Coefficients for National Savings, Government Budget, and Current Account

	Korea	Taiwan	Japan
Net private savings vs. current account	0.96	0.97	0.28
Net government savings vs. current account	0.71	−0.14	0.44
Net government savings vs. national savings	0.88	0.28	0.72
National savings vs. current account	0.78	0.80	0.03
National savings vs. national investment	0.67	−0.41	0.88

Source: Figs. 3.4–3.6.

greater role in reducing the surplus than private investment. During 1986–90, the private savings ratio declined by 9 percentage points, but the private investment ratio increased by only 2 percentage points. Korea's experience with private savings and investment is in direct contrast with the Taiwanese case in that private investment played a greater role than private savings in Korea. While the current account surplus fell during 1988–91, the private investment ratio increased by about 7.5 percentage points and the private savings ratio decreased by only 1.5 percentage points. In Japan, the private investment ratio began to rise after 1986 whereas private savings has continued to decrease since the early 1970s.

These different patterns of adjustment in private savings and private investment seem to be attributable to different policy responses to a current account surplus. Korea's high investment and high growth policy accounts for its modest decreases in private savings compared to Taiwan, which will be discussed again in the next section. Empirical studies of savings behavior for Korea point to income growth as the major determinant (Collins and Park 1989). Because economic growth in Korea was rapid but variable, the perceived income growth during the external adjustment period, when the surplus was being reduced, could explain modest changes in private savings. According to the permanent income hypothesis of consumption, if income changes are perceived to be transitory, consumption changes little. Thus savings and growth should be highly correlated.[1]

3.3 Korea's Policy Responses to the Current Account Surplus

As shown in figure 3.1, Korea's current account moved steadily toward a surplus during 1970–85. As the current account surplus materialized in 1986 and expanded until 1988, one could have safely said that Korea had a structural surplus in the current account. Although there is no widely accepted definition of a structural surplus, it can be defined as a surplus that can be explained by

1. Collins (1988) compares savings and investment behavior in Korea and Japan using the same reasoning.

a structural model and is expected to persist over a few years unless external and internal conditions change in an unusual fashion. If Korea had a structural surplus, it might have maintained a balance or a small surplus even after the "three lows" disappeared. In fact, the current account turned from a surplus of 8.2 percent of GNP in 1988 to a deficit of 3.1 percent of GNP in 1991. This sharp turnaround in the current account undoubtedly challenges the view that Korea has a structural surplus in the external account.

If policymakers believed that Korea had a structural surplus and that the mounting surpluses after 1986 were transitory, due to unusually favorable external conditions, their response to the current account surplus should not have been to trim it. Only if they believed that the surplus would persist even under the fading of the "three lows," should they have moved to trim it.

3.3.1 How Should Korea Have Adjusted?

It should not be surprising that Korea's current account turned into a deficit. It is natural to have current account deficits after four years of surpluses. Furthermore, some outsiders such as Balassa and Williamson (1990) and some diplomats in the U.S. State Department contended that Korea should eliminate its current account surplus.[2] So, if Korea's extended adjustment is considered to be very surprising, it is because Korea adjusted extremely rapidly, not because its external balance turned into a deficit. The previous section showed how rapid Korea's external adjustment was, particularly in comparison to Japan and Taiwan.

How then should Korea have adjusted to the current account surplus? It is certainly a counterfactual exercise that may hold under a specific set of assumptions on imagined situations. For this reason, we do not carry out counterfactual exercises. Instead, we will recall the policy plans advocated by Korean policymakers in the midst of mounting surpluses in the current account and compare them with the policies that were actually implemented. As Korean Minister of Finance Il SaKong (1989) and Dornbusch and Park (1987) suggested, Korean policymakers seemed to prefer market liberalization to a macroeconomic adjustment centering on the exchange rate and fiscal policy. The case for market liberalization was that it would eliminate market distortions and increase imports. The case for abstaining from appreciating the won was made in light of labor unrest and sharp increases in domestic wages. However, the actual policy responses seemed to be different. We review Korea's actual policy responses in the following subsections, paying special attention to whether the initially asserted priorities were maintained.

2. Balassa and Williamson (1990) argue that Korea would do better to expand investment and consumption, with the current account in deficit, because of its high marginal product of capital, creditworthiness, and low level of consumption. Searching for the optimal level of investment, consumption, and external debt and considering the adjustment costs to negate a simple neoclassical proposition that investment should expand until the marginal product of capital is equal to the interest rate, Park and Anne (1988) found that an external surplus might be optimal for Korea.

3.3.2 Monetary Policies

With the expansion in the money supply through the external surplus, the authorities sought to maintain price stability and appropriate growth by controlling the money supply. Each year, the authorities set the target range of M_2 growth on the basis of their projections of real economic growth, inflation rate, and income velocity of money. Although the M_2 growth rate exceeded the target range in some years, money growth was close to the target. However, this does not indicate that monetary stances have been restrictive.

Table 3.2 compares money growth in Korea with that in Japan and Taiwan. Korea's M_2 growth was maintained well above 18 percent per year during 1987–91 due to the external surplus, after it registered exceptionally low growth of 11.3 percent per year during 1984–85. In contrast, Japan and Taiwan experienced a slight increase in money growth during 1986–88 and a sharp reduction in recent years. Taiwan's M_2 growth dwindled to 11 percent in 1990 and Japan's $M_2 + CD$ growth shrank strikingly to 3.6 percent in 1991.

Table 3.3 shows movements in interest rates that may reflect not only monetary changes but also fiscal changes. Both nominal and real interest rates dropped with monetary expansion during 1986–87 in the three countries. Afterwards, both nominal and real interest rates began to rise with monetary contraction. In Korea, nominal interest rates continued to rise with loose monetary policy, but this reflects heightened inflation since real interest rates had been stabilized.

As was mentioned before, the interesting thing about Korea's monetary management is that the current account's slide into deficit did not bring about a noticeable reduction in money growth. Table 3.4 shows the sectoral increase in Korea's M_2 supply. The money supply through the external sector, reflecting changes in the current account, expanded steadily during 1986–88 and then contracted during 1989–90. Money supply through the external sector decreased in 1991. However, this did not lead to a perceivable reduction in money growth for the following reasons:

First, private sector credit expanded considerably after 1989 to meet the increase in indirect financing by the corporate sector, due to the stock market slump. Second, government credit declined after 1987, but less after 1989. Actually, the government sector contributed to the money supply in 1991, since

Table 3.2 **Money Growth (daily average balance; % per annum)**

	1984–85	1986	1987	1988	1989	1990	1991
Korea (M_2)	11.3	16.8	18.8	18.8	18.4	21.2	18.6
Taiwan (M_2)	22.6	23.2	26.8	22.1	16.9	11.1	15.4
Japan ($M_2 + CD$)	8.1	8.7	10.4	11.2	9.9	11.7	3.6

Sources: Monthly Bulletin (Seoul: Bank of Korea, March 1992); *Economic Statistics Monthly* (Tokyo: Bank of Japan, March 1992); *Financial Statistics Monthly* (Taipei: Central Bank of China, March 1992).

Table 3.3 Interest Rates[a] (% per annum)

	Nominal Interest Rates			Real Interest Rates[b]		
	Korea	Taiwan	Japan	Korea	Taiwan	Japan
1985	14.2	6.3	6.5	11.7	6.2	4.8
1986	12.8	4.0	4.8	10.0	3.6	3.9
1987	12.8	4.1	3.5	8.5	3.3	3.0
1988	14.5	4.9	3.6	9.2	2.8	2.6
1989	15.2	7.3	4.9	8.1	4.0	2.9
1990	16.4	10.5	7.2	8.4	6.4	4.4
1991	18.9	7.4	7.5	—	—	—

Sources: Monthly Bulletin (Seoul: Bank of Korea, march 1992); *Economic Statistics Monthly* (Tokyo: Bank of Japan, March 1992); *Financial Statistics Monthly* (Taipei: Central Bank of China, March 1992).

[a]Corporate bond yields for Korea, interbank call loans for Taiwan, and collateral and unconditional call rates for Japan.

[b]Real interest rates = nominal interest rates − centered 3-year CPI inflation rates.

Table 3.4 Sectoral Increases in Korea's M_2 Supply (end of year; billion won)

	Government Credit	Private Credit	External Sector	Other	Total
1985	40	6,462	−1,595	−1,047	3,860
1986	170	6,765	2,424	−4,091	5,268
1987	−1,656	6,115	9,030	−7,043	6,446
1988	−2,174	8,642	10,212	−8,021	8,659
1989	−1,993	16,871	2,365	−7,543	9,699
1990	−1,458	19,068	118	−7,660	10,070
1991	778	20,840	−3,117	−3,463	15,038

Source: Monthly Bulletin (Seoul: Bank of Korea, February 1992).

the budget has been in deficit since 1990. Finally, the "other" sector's absorption declined substantially in 1991; this was associated with the redemption of the monetary stabilization bonds. Issues of bonds such as the monetary stabilization bonds, bonds for foreign exchange balance fund, and treasury bonds were the primary tools for monetary control. The most conspicuous use of this control was the sharp increase in the issuance of monetary stabilization bonds during 1987–88, which was concentrated in secondary banks. However, the bearish stock market and the consequent shortage of funds for institutional investors necessitated the redemption of these bonds after 1989.

If monetary restraint is needed for Korea to achieve price stability and stable growth, the experiences of Taiwan and Japan suggest that government credit should be curtailed and private credit should grow at a moderate rate. In Taiwan, confronted with stock market slumps as is Korea, private credit increased moderately but government credit diminished in 1990. The external sector absorbed the money supply, but this phenomenon stems from drastic increases in short-term capital outflows rather than from a worsening of the current account. The Japanese monetary contraction in 1991 can also be explained by drastic decreases in government credit and moderate increases in private credit. The external sector did not contribute to the monetary contraction during the same year, as the overall balance turned into a surplus for the first time since 1983.

3.3.3 Fiscal Policies

Fiscal expansion is an effective way of reducing the current account in the absence of Ricardian equivalence. Table 3.5 shows that Korea's fiscal policy became expansionary after 1989. Government revenue as a percentage of GNP increased steadily after 1989. However, government expenditure expanded more, resulting in a budget deficit of almost 1 percent of GNP in 1990. This was expected since Korea's fiscal policy has been countercyclical (Corbo and Nam 1986). With economic setback and increasing demand for national welfare in 1989, the government implemented fiscal expansion.

The importance of fiscal policies can be gathered from Korea's experiences with external adjustment in 1991. As we have seen above, fiscal expansion led to monetary expansion. Also, the current account deterioration in 1991 seems to be attributable mostly to decreases in net government savings, as net private savings changed little in that year.

The external adjustment in Japan and Taiwan offers another example of the importance of fiscal policy. Fiscal policy has been a major determinant of the Japanese current account, as the large budget deficits in the 1970s virtually disappeared in the 1980s. This has been discussed in the previous section. The sharp decline in Taiwan's net government savings in 1990 offset an increase in net private savings. This resulted in a continuous decline in the current account surplus as a percentage of GNP in 1990, although there has been little correlation between the government budget and national savings in Taiwan (see table 3.1).

3.3.4 Exchange Rates and Wages

Exchange rate policy and its impact on the current account have been a focal point of concern for both policymakers and researchers around the world. After a decade of huge swings in exchange rates and trade balances in the G-3 coun-

Table 3.5 **Consolidated Public Sector Budget in Korea (% of GNP)**

	1980–82	1983–85	1986	1987	1988	1989	1990
Revenues	19.8	18.6	17.5	17.8	18.3	18.5	18.9
Expenditure and net lending	23.9	19.9	17.6	17.6	17.0	18.5	19.8
Surplus	−4.1	−1.2	−0.1	0.2	1.3	0.0	−0.9

Source: Government Finance Statistics in Korea (Seoul: Ministry of Finance, 1991).

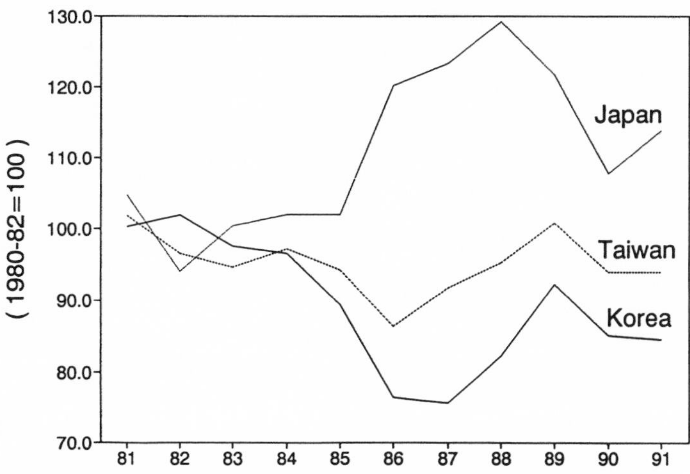

Fig. 3.7 Real effective exchange rates, 1981–91
Source: World Financial Markets (New York: Morgan Guaranty Trust Company, various issues).
Note: The 1991 value is the average up to the third quarter. Higher values mean real appreciation.

tries—the United States, Japan, Germany—the verdict is now that exchange rate changes have worked (Krugman 1991). The same verdict could be reached in the case of Korea.

Figure 3.7 shows the movements in real effective exchange rates of Korea, Taiwan and Japan using data from Morgan Guaranty Trust instead of our own calculations. According to these figures, Japanese real appreciation during 1985–88 was followed by Taiwanese real appreciation during 1986–89 and then by Korean real appreciation during 1987–89. The real effective exchange rates of Korea and Taiwan appreciated by 21 percent and 17 percent during 1986–89 and then returned almost to the 1985 level in 1991. The real effective exchange rate of Japan appreciated by 26 percent during 1985–88 and then depreciated by 11 percent from 1988 until the third quarter of 1991, so that overall it still appreciated compared with the 1985 level.

The above comparison among the three countries based upon gyrations in real effective exchange rates might be misleading once changes in unit labor costs are taken into consideration. Table 3.6 reports the annual percent change in manufacturing unit labor costs. Although the Korean won showed the lowest rate of appreciation vis-à-vis the U.S. dollar, the sharp rise in Korea's wages, stemming from political and social changes since 1987, significantly raised unit labor costs in won terms. As a result, unit labor costs in dollar terms in all three countries rose to almost the same degree in the second half of the 1980s. Thus, it is wrong to say that Korea was slow to appreciate its currency in the face of the yen's appreciation.

In addition, if we consider that Korea relied on real depreciation in the first

Table 3.6 Unit Labor Costs in Manufacturing (annual changes; %)

	1979–90	1979–85	1985–90
Exchange rate (U.S. dollar/ national currency)			
United States	—	—	—
Japan	3.8	−1.5	10.5
Korea	−3.4	−9.3	4.2
Taiwan	2.7	−1.7	8.2
Unit labor cost (dollar basis)			
United States	2.1	3.9	−0.1
Japan	4.1	−0.8	10.3
Korea	3.9	−1.9	11.3
Taiwan	8.0	5.3	11.4

Source: Neef and Kask (1991).

half of the 1980s, it is fair to say that Korea has experienced the sharpest turnaround in external competitiveness and real exchange rates in the second half of the decade. Undoubtedly, this is responsible for the drastic deterioration in the real trade balance shown in figure 3.1.

3.3.5 Market Opening

As stated before, Korean policymakers placed top priority on market liberalization as opposed to rapid appreciation of the won as a means of external adjustment. As far as liberalization is concerned, they emphasized trade liberalization more than financial liberalization, following trade-account-first arguments for opening up the external sector. There is much evidence that Korea accelerated both trade and financial liberalization (Kim 1991; Nam 1992; Lee 1992), although these efforts in the latter half of the 1980s were played down by some writers such as Yoo (1991) and Reisen and Yèches (1991).[3] Table 3.7 shows that import liberalization has been maintained or even accelerated in the latter half of the 1980s. However, trade liberalization does not seem to be the most important reason for the drastic increase in imports in the latter half of the 1980s. In section 3.5, we test whether import liberalization and other policy responses have produced a structural break in import equations after 1985 and reject such a structural-break hypothesis. To preview the conclusions of section 3.5, macroeconomic adjustments through expenditure-expanding and expenditure-switching policies rather than through the microeconomic policy of trade liberalization seemed to play the major role in reducing the current account after 1988.

3. According to Yoo (1991), the apparent consistency in the protection structure seems to indicate that the strength of the government influences on the protection structure was not substantially affected. Reisen aned Yèches (1991), looking at the curb market rates, contend that the degree of financial openness declined during 1985–87 and remained below its 1985 peak up to 1990.

Table 3.7 **Import Liberalization in Korea (%)**

	Average Rate of Legal Tariffs	Degree of Liberalization from Quotas[a]
1970	58.5	46.3
1975	48.1	41.6
1980	34.4	57.4
1985	26.4	78.2
1990	14.1	96.4

Source: Kim (1991).

[a]Represents the degree of import liberalization from quotas according to the trade program and special laws. It is for the second half of each year in 1970 and 1975 and for the second half of the year and the first half of the following year in 1980, 1985, and 1990.

Why did macroeconomic adjustments to reduce the trade surplus take precedence over microeconomic reforms to liberalize trade? This can be explained by the current practice of bilateral negotiations between the United States and Korea. U.S. trade policy has recently been expanded to cover issues such as exchange rate and financial policy in Asian countries. The evolution of U.S.-Korea trade frictions into financial policy talks might be understandable if one reckons with the complementary trade structure between the United States and Korea. Park and Park (1991) among others, by showing that trades among the United States, Japan, and East Asian NICs are complementary rather than substitutable in nature, argue that the East Asian NIC trade imbalances with the United States and Japan will not disappear easily. As U.S. exports to Korea are concentrated in natural-resource-based products and highly capital- and technology-intensive products, bilateral U.S.-Korean trade imbalances may remain significantly unchanged as long as agricultural trade is restricted and modest surpluses in overall trade are maintained.[4] However, as Frankel (1991b) writes, it is unusual for one nation to include such macroeconomic and sovereign matters as financial and exchange rate policy along with standard trade issues when conducting bilateral trade negotiations with another country.

3.3.6 Investment Policy

In addition to the above-mentioned policy responses, Korea's high-growth policy played a dominant role in external adjustment. As shown in table 3.8, facility investment increased sharply during 1986–87 and was followed by sharp increases in construction investment during 1989–90. In the face of economic setbacks in 1989, with sluggish exports and rapid wage hikes, Korea relied once again on a high-growth policy by boosting investments. The government announced the plan for the "new cities" on the outskirts of Seoul. By

4. Sachs and Boone (1988) argue that the Japanese liberalization of agricultural trade could lead to an improvement in the trade balance as Japanese land prices are stabilized, just as the Japanese financial liberalization in the early 1980s led to a higher trade surplus.

Table 3.8 Growth of Fixed Investment (at constant prices; % per annum)

	1985	1986	1987	1988	1989	1990	1991
Korea							
Total fixed investment	4.7	12.0	16.5	13.4	16.9	24.0	11.9
Construction	4.9	3.1	14.0	13.8	18.5	29.1	11.2
Facility	4.5	23.9	19.4	13.0	15.2	18.4	12.8
Taiwan							
Total fixed investment	−5.8	10.1	18.6	14.6	15.3	7.7	9.3
Construction	3.6	7.5	12.3	13.2	10.0	7.5	9.4
Facility	−13.8	12.9	24.6	15.8	19.8	7.8	9.1
Japan							
Total fixed investment	5.3	4.8	9.6	11.9	8.9	—	—
Construction	1.5	4.2	9.1	8.5	4.2	—	—
Facility	11.6	5.6	10.2	16.8	15.3	—	—

Sources: National Accounts (Seoul: Bank of Korea, 1991); *Quarterly National Economic Trends* (Taipei: Directorate-General of Budget, Account and Statistics, February 1992); *Annual Report on National Accounts,* (Tokyo: Economic Planning Agency, 1991).

providing more housing, the government was allegedly attempting to stabilize housing prices. The government also attempted to increase facility investments to expedite structural adjustment and enhance export competitiveness.

The result was rapid growth in both fixed investment, which increased by 24 percent in 1990, and construction investment, which rose by 29 percent in the same year. The rapid rise in construction investment along with real appreciation spurred rapid growth in the production of nontraded goods. This high-growth policy, which was induced by large increases in investment, will lead to a current account deterioration unless it is completely offset by a rise in savings caused by temporary increases in income.

The rapid growth of construction investment in Korea cannot be attributed solely to the government plan for the new cities. The skyrocketing of housing prices would certainly have led to such high growth in construction investment that the role of assets markets in external adjustment would be strengthened. However, since the skyrocketing of housing prices in Taiwan and Japan led to relatively moderate growth in construction investment compared with Korea, the authorities seemed to have played a crucial role in boosting construction investment in Korea.

3.4 Exchange Rates, Assets Markets, and Current Account

In the foregoing, we emphasized the role of exchange rates in external adjustment. Besides the conventional Keynesian income-expenditure mechanism, the effects of real exchange rates on trade flows and of real interest rates on savings and investment are important in external adjustment. If frequent changes in domestic demand and relative prices lead to temporary changes in real growth, this does not change the permanent portion of consumption, so that savings out of increases in income also change frequently.

In addition to the above-mentioned mechanism in external adjustment, similar experiences in the assets markets of Japan, Taiwan, and Korea—for example, the skyrocketing of land and stock prices after 1985—have drawn attention to the role of assets markets and wealth in external adjustment. Table 3.9 shows the movement of land and stock prices in the 1980s. In Korea, stock prices soared almost fivefold during 1985–91, but had risen only 30 percent during 1980–85. Land prices almost tripled during 1985–91, but had risen approximately 60 percent during 1980–85. Japan and Taiwan also witnessed sharp increases in land and stock prices in the second half of the 1980s.

3.4.1 Why Did Land Prices Soar?

There have been different interpretations regarding the recent rise in land and stock prices. Frankel (1991a) attempted to explain high Japanese land and stock prices on the basis of the fundamentals valuation equation. According to this equation, ruling out the possibility of a speculative bubble, the price of land should equal the present discounted value of future rents. If rents are expected to grow at rate *g*, which may be close to the GNP growth rate, then the price/rental ratio should be:

Table 3.9 Increases in Land and Stock Prices[a] (% per annum)

	Land Prices Nation-wide		Stock Prices		
	Korea	Japan[b]	Korea	Japan[c]	Taiwan
1980	11.7	19.3	−9.8	5.4	−2.4
1981	7.5	14.2	16.1	16.5	0.3
1982	5.4	7.0	−3.4	−0.7	−13.0
1983	18.5	2.9	4.7	18.1	37.1
1984	13.2	4.3	3.3	26.0	33.3
1985	7.0	8.2	5.3	22.3	−14.5
1986	7.3	25.8	64.0	32.7	26.7
1987	14.7	33.8	83.3	48.3	126.0
1988	27.5	10.1	66.0	8.7	143.7
1989	32.0	15.8	32.5	20.4	65.6
1990	20.6	—	−18.7	−15.2	−21.4
1991	12.8	—	−11.9	−15.4	−27.3

Sources: Land Price Statistics (Seoul: Ministry of Construction, December 1991); *Annual Report on National Accounts* (Tokyo: Economic Planning Agency, 1991); *Principal Economic Indicators* (Seoul: Bank of Korea, various issues); *Economic Statistics Monthly* (Tokyo: Bank of Japan, March 1992); *Financial Statistics Monthly* (Taipei: Central Bank of China, March 1992).

[a]Annual average.

[b]Value of land.

[c]Tokyo stock price index compiled by Tokyo Stock Exchange.

$$\text{(1)} \qquad \text{price of land/rent} = \frac{1}{r - g},$$

where r is real interest rates. According to this formula, a small percentage change in real interest rates or the rental growth rate can explain sharp changes in the price of land or the land price/rental ratio. However, as Frankel (1991a) admits, the fundamentals valuation equation does not seem to explain the recent rise in Japanese land prices, since expectations of future economic growth are lower and real interest rates are higher than before.

A number of authors point out the possibility of a speculative bubble in the second half of the 1980s. The Japanese economic boom together with the appreciation of the yen was popularly called the "bubble economy." It is possible that the short-term movements of land and stock prices exhibited the properties of a speculative bubble when financial markets were characterized by saddle-path stability. However, adjustments along the saddle path must be distinguished from a speculative bubble, because the former converges into a steady state. To make the bubble story more convincing, one must explain not only short-term movements, but also medium- to long-term movements in land prices. As yet, there seems to be no good model which explains how a speculative bubble gets started and why it collapses.

The more popular view is, as Dekle (1991) points out in his comments on Frankel (1991a), that excess Japanese liquidity raised land and stock prices. The excess liquidity was created by Japan's loose monetary policy intended to prop up the dollar, while the increased exchange rate risk limited capital outflows from Japan. The excess liquidity flowed into the real estate and stock markets, bidding up the prices of these assets.

This explanation for soaring land prices which emphasizes excess liquidity and the public's portfolio choices might even hold for Korea and Taiwan. However, the exchange rate could directly affect land prices in these countries, as liquidity changes cannot account for changes in the exchange rate under the managed float system and capital immobility. Figure 3.8 clearly shows that land price movements are closely related to both money growth and currency appreciation in Korea.

In the following, we construct a simple model for Korea's land prices and current account in the framework of a two-sector general equilibrium portfolio balance model. The roles of both excess liquidity and the exchange rate are highlighted in this model.

3.4.2 A Model for Korea's Land Prices and Current Account

We present a very simple model for Korea's land prices and current account that captures the linkages between assets markets and the real sector. For the sake of simplicity, the model assumes full employment, a fixed exchange rate, purchasing power parity, rational expectations, and only two assets of domestic money and real estate.

The real exchange rate (q) is defined by the relative price of tradable goods

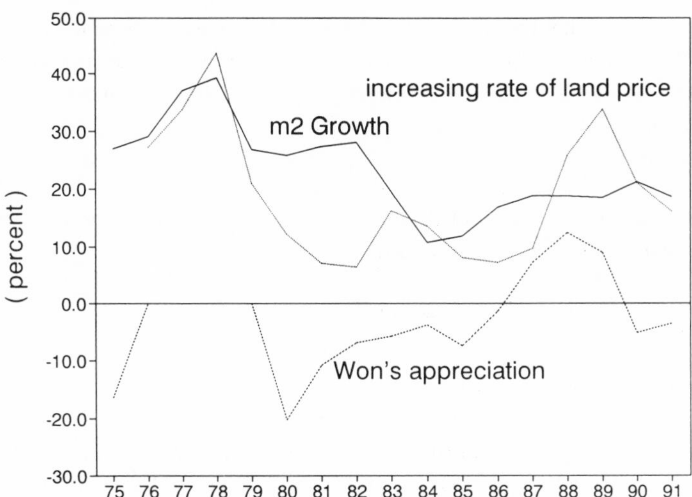

Fig. 3.8 Money (M_2) growth, currency (won) appreciation, and rate of land price change in Korea, 1976–91

Sources: Monthly Bulletin (Seoul: Bank of Korea, various issues); *Land Price Statistics* (Seoul: Ministry of Construction, various issues); *International Financial Statistics* (Washington, D.C.: IMF, April 1992).

Note: Nationwide land prices are used. The won's appreciation refers to its appreciation vis-à-vis the U.S. dollar.

(EP^{T*}, for E the nominal exchange rate and P^{T*} the foreign currency price of traded goods) and home (nontradable) goods (P^H):

(2) $$q = \frac{EP^{T*}}{P^H}.$$

The production (Y) and demand (C) functions for both goods are specified as functions of the real exchange rate (q) and real wealth (a):

(3) $$Y^T = Y^T(q),\ Y^T_q > 0;\ Y^H = Y^H(q),\ Y^H_q < 0,$$

(4) $$C^T = C^T(q,a),\ C^T_q < 0,\ C^T_a > 0;\ C^H = C^H(q,a);\ C^H_q > 0,\ C^H_a > 0,$$

where a subscript denotes differentiation with respect to that variable.

The real wealth of the public, measured in units of tradable goods, is composed of domestic money (M) and real estate (Z), whose physical stock is fixed and whose price is denoted as P^Z.

(5) $$a = \frac{1}{EP^{T*}}(M + P^Z Z).$$

Equilibrium in the market for home goods ($Y^H = C^H$) requires a negative relation between the real wealth of the public and the real exchange rate:

(6) $$a = V(q),\ V_q < 0.$$

It is assumed that the domestic money stock changes only with changes in international reserves, which in turn adjust to the current account under the current Korean practice of concentrating foreign exchange in the vaults of the central bank.

(7) $$\dot{M} = EP^{T*}(Y^T - C^T) = EP^{T*}f(a), f_a < 0.$$

The demand for each asset depends on the expected relative rates of return on the two assets. Thus, when E is fixed,

(8) $$\dot{\rho} = \rho L\left(\frac{m}{\rho Z}\right), \; L' < 0,$$

where $\rho = P^z/E$ and $m = M/E$.

The system can be represented by a set of state variables m and ρ. Figure 3.9 illustrates the phase diagram for two state variables of real balances and a real estate (hereafter referred to as land) premium. When $\dot{m} = 0$, equation (7) determines the unique steady-state value of real wealth at $\bar{a}$. We know from (5) that $P^{T*}\bar{a} = m + \rho Z$. Thus, the $\dot{m} = 0$ locus is downward-sloping. The $\dot{\rho} = 0$ locus should be upward-sloping from (8). Therefore, the saddle path is also upward-sloping in figure 3.9.

3.4.3 Impact of Yen Appreciation, Won Appreciation, and Excess Liquidity

We now consider the impact of changes in liquidity and exchange rates on land prices (more exactly, premiums on the land price) and wealth, which in turn influence savings and the current account.

The yen's appreciation brings about an increase in P^{T*}, which represents the price of foreign goods in dollars. With an increase in P^{T*}, the $\dot{m} = 0$ locus shifts upward in figure 3.9. The land price premium jumps immediately to point B on the new saddle path. As the economy moves toward the new steady state along the saddle path, the land price premium continues to increase and the real balance increases as the current account improves with the yen's appreciation. The land price premium undershoots the steady-state level.

Next consider the appreciation of the won, whose exchange rate vis-à-vis the U.S. dollar was assumed to be fixed. The real balance increases when the won appreciates. The land price premium jumps immediately to point C and then returns to the initial steady-state level, because the steady-state equilibrium is not affected by the won's appreciation. The land price premium overshoots the steady-state level. The real balance declines with the worsening in the current account, as the economy moves along the saddle path.

The impact of won appreciation following yen appreciation that has actually been observed in previous years might be a combination of the two effects mentioned above. When the yen appreciates, Korea's current account improves with rising land prices. However, as yen appreciation is followed by won appreciation, land prices shoot up even further. The consequent increases in the real value of wealth along with real appreciation worsen the current account.

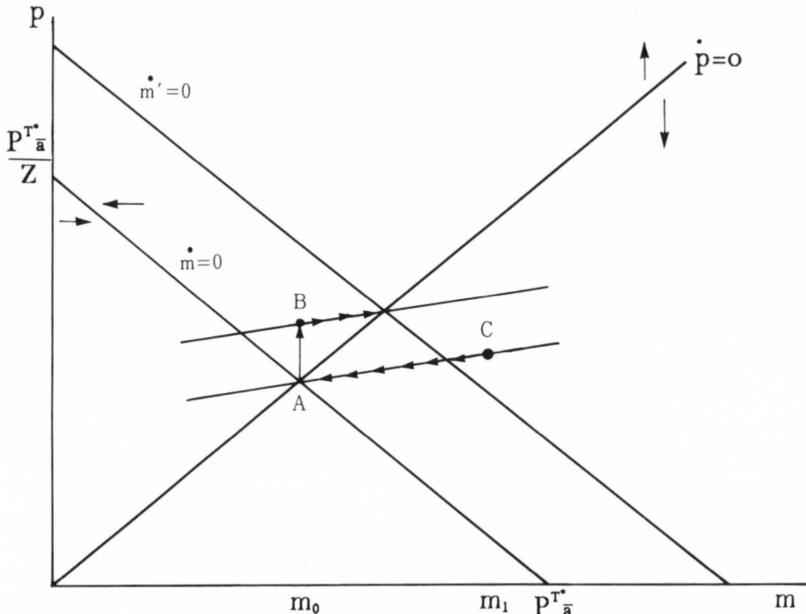

Fig. 3.9 Impact of yen appreciation, won appreciation, and excess liquidity

Short-term movements in land prices characterized by overshooting may look like a speculative bubble, but this overshooting phenomenon of land prices must be distinguished from a speculative bubble since the steady-state equilibrium is not affected.[5]

We can also explain why excess liquidity bids up land prices. In figure 3.9, the impact of the exogenous once-and-for-all increases in money is the same as that of won appreciation. The exogenous increases in domestic money stem from budget deficits, increased private-sector financing, or deterred capital outflows due to exchange rate risk. As we endogenize these money growth mechanisms, we can derive deeper implications. However, we do not elaborate on these various money supply processes.[6]

3.5 The Conventional Econometrics of Korea's Trade Balance

In this section, we offer the "conventional" econometric analysis of exports and imports, which focuses on the role of income and relative prices. Conven-

5. Kim and Suh (1991) detected a growing rational bubble in land prices both in Korea and Japan. However, they only address the question of whether speculation causes the actual price to deviate from a *given* long-run equilibrium price.

6. Park (1992) contains a discussion of the relationship between the exchange rate premium and inflation in dual exchange markets under various money supply processes, which could be extended to our analyses on land prices.

tionally, equations for export and import volume include in the right-hand side foreign and domestic income variables with no lag and a relative price variable with ad hoc lags. There may be caveats about the estimated coefficients for income and price elasticities since the demand and supply sides are not modeled simultaneously (Riedel 1988). Nevertheless, many authors point out that the large estimated income elasticities in the demand equations may reflect supply-side phenomena (Krugman 1989; Muscatelli, Srinivasan, and Vines 1990). These conventional demand equations have displayed accurate forecasting performance and successfully tracked the impact of exchange rates on the trade balance (Krugman and Baldwin 1987).

The equations for export and import volume are estimated from 1973:1 to 1985:4 and then tested for a structural break after 1985:4. The equation for export price is also estimated to examine Korean exporters' pricing to market. Tables 3.10 and 3.11 report the estimation results. The income elasticity of real exports and of real nonoil imports are 2.5 and 1, respectively. The price elasticity of real exports is estimated at 0.3 in the short run (in one quarter) and 2.1 in the long run (within two years). The price elasticity of real nonoil imports is 0.4 in the short run, adding up to 1 within one year. The estimation result for

Table 3.10 Determinants of Export and Nonoil Import Volume in Korea[a]

	Export Volume	Nonoil Import Volume
Income[b]	2.52 (5.43)	0.97 (11.03)
Real exchange rate[c]		
(sum of lags)	2.10	−0.98
Lags: 0	0.34 (2.43)	−0.41 (−3.37)
1	0.34 (3.11)	−0.28 (−6.14)
2	0.34 (3.27)	−0.17 (−3.56)
3	0.31 (3.01)	−0.09 (−1.40)
4	0.29 (2.68)	−0.03 (−0.64)
5	0.23 (2.40)	
6	0.17 (2.18)	
7	0.09 (2.02)	
$\bar{R}^2$	0.99	0.96
D-W	2.02	1.48
ρ	0.86 (17.15)	

Note: Figures in parentheses are *t*-values.

[a]The equations are estimated in logarithmic form for 1973:1–1985:4 using second-degree polynomial distributed lags (PDL), far restrictions. The Cochrane-Orcutt procedures are applied when necessary. Constant and seasonal dummies are included but not reported.

[b]1985 trade-weighted real GNP of the United States, Japan, Germany, and the United Kingdom for the export equation and nonagricultural real GNP for import equation.

[c]1985 trade-weighted WPI of four countries in dollar terms/export unit price in dollar terms for export equation and nonoil import price in won/CPI for import equation.

Table 3.11 Determinants of Export Prices in Korea[a]

	Export Unit Price ($)
Manufacturing wages	0.23 (6.67)
Won's exchange rate with dollar	−0.34 (−7.13)
Import unit price ($)	0.47 (6.10)
$\bar{R}^2$	0.99
D-W	1.49
ρ	0.76 (6.03)

Note: Figures in parentheses are *t*-values.

[a]The equation is estimated in logarithmic form for 1973:1–1985:4 using second-degree PDL, far restrictions. The Cochrane-Orcutt procedures are applied when necessary. Constant and seasonal dummies are included but not reported.

the export price equation shows that the aggregate pass-through rate of exchange rate changes is 34 percent in Korea.

These tables suggest several interesting points. First, in Korea, income elasticity turns out to be quite high for exports and relatively low for imports. This confirms the theory that fast-growing countries show high income elasticities of demand for their exports, while showing low income elasticities of demand for imports.[7] The high income elasticity of exports implies that U.S. budget cuts and the consequent decline in U.S. growth will directly affect Korea's exports and real growth, although the simple Mundell-Fleming transmission channel will not work because of capital controls, the weak response of savings to real interest rates, and the mild response of exports to the real exchange rate.

Second, the price elasticity of exports and imports is not low compared with U.S. and Japanese figures, although the estimated value of price elasticity depends on how the real exchange rate is defined. The long-run price elasticities of 2 and 1 for exports and imports, respectively, are actually higher than the U.S. and Japanese figures reported in Krugman and Baldwin (1987) and Krugman (1991) for the United States, and Ueda (1988) for Japan. This implies that external competitiveness or the real exchange rate is important to Korea's trade and resource allocation.

Finally, Korean exporters pass only 34 percent of exchange rate changes through to the dollar price of exports and only 23 percent of wage changes. The pass-through rate of Korea's major competitors in the U.S. market was estimated to be 60 percent with the presence of a two-year lag (Mann 1986).[8]

7. According to Ueda (1988), Japanese income elasticities for exports and imports are much the same as those in Korea. Krugman and Baldwin (1987) shows that U.S. income elasticity for exports is as high as 2.5, while that for imports is even higher at approximately 2.8. The more or less standard view is that U.S. income elasticity for exports is 1.2 and for imports is 1.8 (Krugman 1991).

8. Other experiments using a more broadly based exchange rate measure and bilateral trade weights produced a long-run pass-through estimate of around 90 percent.

Table 3.12 Likelihood Ratio Tests for Structural Break at 1985:4

	Export Volume	Import Volume[a]		Export Unit Price
		CPI	WPI	
Likelihood Ratio	15.72*	6.99	13.82[b]	20.51**

[a]Real exchange rate in import equation is defined as import unit price in won currency divided by the CPI and WPI, as labeled.

[b]Significance level is 5.5 percent. Thus the hypothesis of no structural break is almost rejected at the 5 percent significance level.

*Hypothesis of no structural break is rejected at the 5 percent significance level.

**Hypothesis of no structural break is rejected at the 1 percent significance level.

Profit margins of foreign firms fall below normal levels as the dollar depreciates and rise above normal levels as it appreciates. To maintain competitiveness in foreign markets, Korean exporters must adjust profit margins more than foreign competitors do.

We now turn to the question of whether Korea's export and import behavior and exchange rate pass-through relationships may have changed after the Plaza Agreement of September 1985. Table 3.12 shows the test for a structural break between the periods 1973:1–1985:4 and 1986:1–1991:4.[9] The hypothesis of no structural break is rejected at the 1 percent significance level in the case of export prices and rejected at the 5 percent significance level in the case of export volume. Interestingly enough, the test results for import behavior turn out to be very sensitive to the choice of domestic price index between CPI and WPI. During the pre-1985 period, the choice between the two price indexes was not important, as both equations tracked the actual performances very well. During the post-1985 period, the tracking ability of the import equation, which includes the WPI, declined markedly. If the CPI is used, however, the hypothesis of no structural break in import behavior is accepted quite well.

Many people in Korea contend that the rapid expansion in imports after 1988 stems from such structural changes as accelerated import liberalization, as evidenced by the sharp increase in consumer goods imports and the greater propensity to import out of increases in income. However, it is very important to note that the simple structural break test does not support such a contention. If we consider the rapid rise in the CPI relative to the WPI in the post-1985 era, the rapid expansion of imports in recent years could be well explained by the import volume equation, which stresses the effects of income expansion

9. The break point at the last quarter of 1985 has been chosen somewhat arbitrarily. We obtained similar results when we chose 1985:3 or 1986:1 as the break point. However, we could not let the data alone determine the break point, because developing countries generally suffered from structural instabilities. Indeed, the break point of each equation was found well before 1985:4, without any relationship to the Plaza Agreement of September 1985.

and real appreciation rather than import liberalization and other structural changes after 1986.

Do the structural breaks in Korea's exports and pricing-to-market behavior imply that Korean firms priced to market more frequently in the post-1985 period than before in order to retain their market position abroad? The answer is no. The out-of-sample static forecasts over the post-1985 period traced remarkably well the actual numbers of export volume and export unit price. Quite contrary to expectations, even the out-of-sample dynamic forecasts underpredicted actual performances.

3.6 Concluding Remarks and Prospects

This paper showed that huge swings in Korea's current account in the post-1985 period could be explained by macroeconomic adjustments rather than microeconomic policy. The conventional adjustment policy of both expenditure-expanding and expenditure-switching did work well in Korea, as Krugman (1991) argued they did for the G-3 countries. Korea's responses to external surpluses, such as investment policy and other domestic demand-expanding policies combined with exchange rate policy, worked remarkably well to reduce the external surplus and finally led to a large deficit. This paper also emphasized the role of assets markets such as the real estate and stock markets, which facilitate adjustments in the real exchange rate. The role played by assets markets supplements the conventional view of external adjustment, which emphasizes either the Keynesian income-expenditure mechanism or the roles played by interest rates and exchange rates in the Mundell-Fleming framework.

What do Korea's past experiences with external adjustment mean for the future? According to our estimates regarding the income elasticity of Korean exports (approximately 2.5), future U.S. budget cuts or sluggish world economic growth would have an enormous impact on Korea's exports. On the other hand, if G-5 growth recovers, a good case can be made for a surplus in Korea's current account aided by adopting policies to reduce domestic demand and depreciate the real exchange rate. Then the impending issue will be whether Korea has a structural surplus with high savings. The related issue will be whether Korea's current account surplus is desirable from the perspectives of welfare maximization and U.S.-Korea trade frictions. Balassa and Williamson (1990) provide some answers to this question, arguing that Korea would do better to expand investment with the current account in deficit because of its high marginal product of capital, creditworthiness, and trade frictions with the United States. In a sense, a model that can completely determine the optimal level of the current account will never exist. Recommendations for high growth are well taken, but there still remains the basic question of why high growth with a modest surplus is not desirable.

Once a current account surplus emerges, the U.S. Treasury will accuse Korea of "manipulating" its exchange rates. What the United States seems to mean by accusations of exchange rate manipulation is that Korea needs to appreciate its currency more rapidly by liberalizing its financial market. However, as Frankel (1991b) asserts, it is perfectly appropriate for a small country to seek exchange rate stability if it so desires.

References

Balassa, Bella, and John Williamson. 1990. *Adjusting to success: Balance of payments policy in the East Asian NICs.* Rev. Washington, D.C.: Institute for International Economics.

Collins, Susan M. 1988. Savings and growth experiences of Korea and Japan. *Journal of the Japanese and International Economies* 2:328–50.

Collins, Susan M. and Won-Am Park. 1989. External debt and macroeconomic performance in Korea (Book 2). In *Developing country debt and economic performance,* ed. J. D. Sachs and S. M. Collins, 151–370. Chicago: University of Chicago Press.

Corbo, V., and S. W. Nam. 1986. The recent macroeconomic evolution of the republic of Korea: An overview. KDI Working Paper no. 8610. Seoul: Korea Development Institute.

Dekle, Robert. 1991. Comment. In *Trade with Japan: Has the door opened wider?* ed. P. R. Krugman, 268–70. Chicago: University of Chicago Press.

Dornbusch, Rudiger, and Yung Chul Park. 1987. Korean growth policy. *Brookings Papers on Economic Activity* 2:5–60.

Frankel, Jeffrey. 1991a. Japanese finance in the 1980s: A survey. In *Trade with Japan: Has the door opened wider?* ed. P. R. Krugman, 225–68. Chicago: University of Chicago Press.

———. 1991b. Liberalization of Korea's foreign exchange markets and the role of U.S. trade relations. Paper presented to a conference on Korean–U.S. economic relations, held at the Hoover Institution, Stanford University, December 5–6.

Kim, Kwang-Suk. 1991. Trade and industrialization policies in Korea: An overview. Manuscript, Kyung Hee University, October.

Kim, Kyung-Hwan, and S. H. Suh. 1991. Speculation and price bubble in the Korean and Japanese real estate markets. Papers for the Third Far Eastern Meeting of the Econometric Society, Seoul.

Krugman, Paul. 1989. Differences in income elasticities and trends in real exchange rates. *European Economic Review* vol. 33, no. 5 (May): 1031–47.

———. 1991. *Has the adjustment process worked?* Washington, D.C.: Institute for International Economics.

Krugman, Paul, and Richard Baldwin. 1987. The persistence of the U.S. trade deficit. *Brookings Papers on Economic Activity* 1:1–43.

Lee, Young Ki. 1992. Korean capital market developments. KDI Working Paper no. 9206. Seoul: Korea Development Institute.

Mann, Catherine. 1986. Prices, profit margins, and exchange rates. *Federal Reserve Bulletin,* June.

Muscatelli, V. A., T. G. Srinivasan, and D. Vines. 1990. The empirical modelling of NIE exports: An evaluation of different approaches. CEPR Discussion Paper no. 426. London: Centre for Economic Policy Research, July.

Nam, Sang-Woo. 1992. Korea's financial reform since the early 1980s. KDI Working Paper no. 9207. Seoul: Korea Development Institute.
Neef, A., and C. Kask. 1991. Manufacturing productivity and labor costs in 14 economies. *Monthly Labor Review.* Bureau of Labor Statistics, U.S. Department of Labor, December.
Park, Won-Am. 1992. Exchange rate dynamics in dual exchange markets. KDI Working Paper no. 9209. Seoul: Korea Development Institute.
Park, Won-Am, and Z. Anne. 1988. Savings, investment and the external debt in Korea. KDI Working Paper no. 8812. Seoul: Korea Development Institute.
Park, Yung Chul, and Won-Am Park. 1991. Changing Japanese trade patterns and the East Asian NICs. In *Trade with Japan: Has the door opened wider?* ed. P. R. Krugman, 85–115. Chicago: University of Chicago Press.
Reisen, Helmut, and H. Yèches. 1991. Time-varying estimates on the openness of the capital account in Korea and Taiwan. OECD Development Centre Technical Paper no. 42. Paris: Organisation for Economic Cooperation and Development, August.
Riedel, J. 1988. The demand for LDC export of manufactures: Estimates for Hong Kong. *Economic Journal* 94:56–73.
Sachs, Jeffrey, and Peter Boone. 1988. Japanese structural adjustment and the balance of payments. *Journal of the Japanese and International Economies* 2(3).
Sachs, Jeffrey, and N. Roubini. 1987. Sources of macroeconomic imbalances in the world economy: A simulation approach. NBER Working Paper no. 2339. Cambridge, Mass.: National Bureau of Economic Research.
SaKong, Il. 1989. The international economic position of Korea. In *Economic relations between the United States and Korea: Conflict or cooperation?* ed. T. O. Bayard and S. Young, 7–17. Washington, D.C.: Institute for International Economics.
Ueda, Kazuo. 1988. Perspectives on the Japanese current account surplus. In *NBER Macroeconomics Annual 1988,* ed. Stanley Fischer, 217–56. Cambridge: MIT Press.
Yoo, Jung-ho. 1991. Political economy of protection structure in Korea. KDI Working Paper no. 9116. Seoul: Korea Development Institute.

Comment Bih Jane Liu

This is a very informative and stimulating paper. It not only studies the different adjustment patterns of current account, real trade balance, and terms of trade among Korea, Japan, and Taiwan, but also develops a theoretical model to explain the sharp increases in land and stock prices in recent years in Korea. I learned a lot from reading this paper. To fulfill my duty as a discussant, I would like to raise some questions and also offer some comments and suggestions.

My first question is related to the study of the changes in the level of current account in this paper. Although the level of current account reflects saving and investment behavior on one hand and export and import behavior on the other and is hence an important indicator of changes in these behaviors, it may be the composition rather than the level of current account that is more crucial in

Bih Jane Liu is professor of economics at National Taiwan University.

determining the dynamic impacts of current account on the domestic economy. For example, the same level of current account but a different composition may create dramatically different impacts on the domestic economy. Therefore, to study the effects of the current account without looking into the details of changes in current account composition may run the risk of missing some important information regarding structural change in the economy.

Another question, which is somewhat related to the first, stems from the authors' apparent preference for Korea to have a modest current account surplus. What is the rationale for such a preference? As pointed out by Kenen (1985) that to pursue a current account surplus may lose efficiency. Moreover, a current account surplus says only that trade in goods and services and flows in investment income contribute more to the national income at home than abroad, but it may not necessarily imply that there is an increase in domestic income. Take the trade balance of Taiwan in 1985 as an example. It increased significantly in 1985, from U.S. $8.5 billion (U.S.) to $10.6 billion (U.S.). This increase in trade surplus was attributed mainly to the decrease in imports, especially those of intermediate materials, capital equipment, and machinery due to the slack demand of domestic investment. Thus, 1985 was also the year that the Taiwanese government worried about the adverse effects of insufficient capital formation on economic growth.

My second observation concerns this paper's examination of the fluctuation of the current account from two perspectives, export versus import behavior and saving versus investment behavior. These two perspectives, in fact, emphasize the ability of country-specific factors to explain the adjustment patterns of the current account. If we look at figures 3.1–3.3, it seems that the adjustment patterns of current account and real balance of trade all look much the same, although the adjustment speeds are rather different for the different countries. Thus, there are really two questions worth discussing here. One main question is, Why do different countries have different adjustment speeds? Or more specifically, Why was the adjustment speed of real trade balance in Japan and Taiwan before 1989 faster than that in Korea, while the opposite trend holds after 1989? This has been discussed in this paper by using country-specific factors. The other question is, Why do these three countries exhibit such similar adjustment patterns? Some common explanatory factors might exist. As we all know, big international events in recent years—the gradual opening of mainland China and Eastern European markets, the Gulf war, the unification of East and West Germany, and the formation of a single European market—have had significant implications not only on politics but also on international trade relations and the direction of foreign direct investment. To what extent and in what way will these factors influence the adjustment pattern of current account? It seems to me that this paper is more concerned with the effects of country-specific factors than with those of common international factors. The paper would be more complete if common factors could also be taken into account.

Third, in section 3.5, the authors use the likelihood ratio to test whether Korea's export and import behavior and exchange rate pass-through relationship have a structural break between the periods 1973–85 and 1986–91. I have several questions about this test.

The first one is why this paper chooses 1985:4 as the break point. It seems that the fact that the real trade balance in Korea turned into surplus in 1985 or that the Plaza Agreement was signed in 1985 could not explain why 1985 was the year that structural change occurred. I suspect that one may probably obtain similar conclusions when choosing 1986:1 or 1985:3 as the break point. That is, instead of choosing the turning point arbitrarily, why not let the data endogenously determine the turning point? In fact, the likelihood ratio test can do this job.

The second question has something to do with the limits of the likelihood ratio test. As Quandt (1960) pointed out, the likelihood ratio test can be used to test the hypothesis that no switch occurs against the single alternative that one switch takes place. In other words, the likelihood ratio test can only test for abrupt changes and not for gradual changes. Moreover, the acceptance of the null hypothesis (i.e., no switch occurs) under the likelihood ratio test may not imply that there is no structural change at all, and the rejection of the null hypothesis may not imply that the break point studied is the only point where structural break has occurred. For these reasons, I would suggest that a CUSUM test or CUSUM square test, introduced by Brown, Durbin, and Evans (1975), may be more suitable because these tests use recursive residuals and thus allow a point-by-point analysis which enables users to see both abrupt and gradual changes. In addition, these tests can be used to investigate the approximate sample periods in which changes occur. And this can let us test whether the structural change in Korea lasted only a short time, say from 1985 to 1989, and then returned to the original pattern after 1990. Although CUSUM and CUSUM Square tests have some limitations too, these tests may give a more complete picture of export and import behavior than the likelihood ratio test does.

Last, in sections 3.4.2 and 3.4.3, this paper concluded that yen appreciation followed by won appreciation caused land prices to soar which in turn worsened the current account. Would this result also hold in the case of flexible exchange rate with or without the sterilization operation by the central bank? And to what extent may the result of this model be used to explain the sharp increase of stock and housing prices in Taiwan during 1988–90?

References

Brown, R. L., J. Durbin, and J. M. Evans. 1975. Techniques for testing the constancy of regression relationships over time. *Journal of the Royal Statistical Society* ser. B, 37: 149–92.

Kenen, Peter B. 1985. *The international economy.* Englewood Cliffs, N.J.: Prentice-Hall.

Quandt, Richard E. 1960. Tests of the hypothesis that a linear regression system obeys two separate regimes. *Journal of the American Statistical Association* 55:324–30.

Comment Hiroo Taguchi

The paper by Koo and Park examines from various perspectives the background of the turnaround of Korea's current account balance. The Korean experience since the mid-1980s, as they describe it, seems to have much in common with that of Japan and, provided my understanding is correct, I agree with most of the authors' basic arguments.

They argue that microeconomic policy played only a relatively modest role in curtailing the current account surplus. This is also true in the Japanese case, although action to make the Japanese market more accessible to foreign exporters is very desirable and may lead to greater horizontal division of labor in the long run.

I also broadly agree with their assessment that the appreciation of the won and the yen played an important role in the adjustment process in their respective countries. In Japan's case, the appreciation of the yen after the Plaza Agreement and resultant change in relative prices worked in favor of increased imports and, with regard to industry, in favor of domestic demand-oriented industries, notably services, which is where the investment boom of the late 1980s in Japan saw its origins. This shift of resources toward domestic demand-oriented industries contributed, at least in the short run, to a decrease in the trade and current account balances. However, the long-term impact is less obvious. While investment in service industries does not directly increase export capacity, it may in the long run have a positive impact on exports by promoting the efficiency of the economy as a whole and, by stabilizing overall price levels, may assist in stabilizing wages.

Another important common feature is that the turnaround in respective current accounts stemmed from increases in overall private investment in the late 1980s. Rises in asset prices are likely to have contributed in both Korea and Japan. However, the similarity between developments in Japan and Korea seems to end there.

As I understand it, in the last several years, there has been quite a difference in the basic strategy of monetary policy in Korea and Japan. Korea, facing a decrease in export growth as a result of the appreciation of the won, relaxed monetary policy in late 1989. The official discount rate was lowered from 8 to

Hiroo Taguchi is chief manager of Research Division I, Institute for Monetary and Economic Studies, Bank of Japan.

7 percent, and while nominal interest remained high, this was due to higher inflation, as Koo and Park rightly point out in their paper.

On the surface, this resembles the now much-criticized monetary policy action in Japan in the aftermath of the substantial appreciation of the yen. However, an important difference is that prices and wages were extremely stable in Japan at that time. Japan's year-on-year CPI inflation rate was actually negative when the Bank of Japan lowered the official discount rate (ODR) in early 1987, and it remained at around zero for quite a long time thereafter. In Korea, the corresponding figure had risen from 5.5 to 6 percent before the ODR was lowered in 1989, and it continued to rise thereafter. Referring to table 3.6, Koo and Park argue that the won's appreciation was not small if the increase in unit labor cost (ULC) is taken into account. They may be right. But I am tempted to read that table in a slightly different way: wages and ULC in Korea maintained a high tempo of increase despite the appreciation of the won. This development, at least to me, seems to have stemmed from easy monetary policy and was the fundamental reason why Korea's current account balance turned around so suddenly.

I do not intend to argue that that was wrong, since I am not able to evaluate Korea's long-term growth potential; neither am I sufficiently informed about the social and political background. The only thing I would like to say is that this reaction to the appreciation of the won resembles Japan's policy reaction to the appreciation of the yen in 1970, when Japan tried to inflate away the current account surplus, which I believe was a serious mistake.

This brings me to the normative aspects regarding current account adjustments. It was not clear, at least not to me, whether the authors believed that adjustment was necessary, or to what degree desirable. Is it not possible to argue that it would have been better for the long-term development of Korea if it had maintained the surplus and avoided accelerated inflation and responded to foreign pressure by liberalizing goods and capital markets more rigorously? Putting a related question from a different angle, in Japan's case it is often maintained, and I have certain sympathy with the view, that it is natural and desirable from a global point of view that Japan is recording current account surpluses at this moment, considering that its population is aging rapidly, a fact which will very likely lead to a considerable drop in net savings in the early twenty-first century. I think it would be very interesting to hear whether similar arguments for the desirability of maintaining a current account surplus exist in Korea and, if so, what Koo and Park's views are.

My final comments pertain to the pricing behavior of firms. In chapter 5 of this volume, which discusses the price elasticity of Korea's trade, Jwa argues that Korean exporters have to adjust profit margins more than foreign competitors do. It was, however, not clear to me why they have to do so. I would like the authors to elaborate somewhat more on this point. Moreover, since a major objective of the paper is to review the Korean experience in comparison with those of Japan and Taiwan, it would enrich the study if they compared Korea's pricing strategy with those in Japan and Taiwan. This should be particularly interesting because industrial structure, especially of export industries, differs quite considerably among these three countries: in Korea, a small number of giant industrial groups dominate the economy, Taiwan is characterized by many small, independent firms, and Japan's industrial structure lies somewhere between.

4 The Effects of NT Dollar Variations on Taiwan's Trade Flows

San Gee

The vast appreciation of the New Taiwan (NT) dollar after the mid-1980s has not only affected the external trade structure of Taiwan but has also had a tremendous impact on internal industrial structural change in Taiwan. For instance, the NT dollar's dramatic appreciation against the U.S. dollar has certainly imposed great difficulties on Taiwanese exporters attempting to sell their products to the United States. In addition, the rising tide of protectionism in the mid-1980s created tremendous pressure for Taiwanese exporters to diversify their markets away from the United States. It is also important to note that, while the NT dollar appreciated considerably against the U.S. dollar, the German mark and Japanese yen appreciated against the U.S. dollar at an even faster pace. As a result, the NT dollar has actually depreciated against the German mark and Japanese yen, despite the fact that it has appreciated by more than 30 percent over the period 1986–90. Furthermore, many Southeast Asian currencies have actually depreciated against the U.S. dollar, which makes it very difficult for Taiwan's exporters to diversify their markets to this region. Consequently, it is not difficult to see that Europe has become the natural and best alternative for Taiwanese exporters to explore, and from the middle of the 1980s there has been a significant trade structure change in Taiwan.

To examine explicitly how the NT dollar appreciation affects Taiwan's external trade structure we have divided this paper into five sections. In sections 4.1 and 4.2 we establish an empirical model to examine how NT dollar fluctuations affect Taiwan's external trade relations, and we report and discuss the model's empirical results. In section 4.3, instead of using the nominal exchange rate to examine the effect of variations of the NT dollar on Taiwan's external trade, we shall calculate the real effective exchange rate (REER) for NT dollars and shall

San Gee is professor of economics at National Central University, Chung-Li, Taiwan.

investigate what kind of REERs are more capable of indicating proper exchange rate levels for the NT dollar and how REERs can explain the export and import behavior of Taiwan's economy. Since REERs are less suitable for explaining bilateral trade activities, in section 4.4 we calculate the price-competition index (PCI) for Taiwan's major trading partners and examine the relationship between PCIs and bilateral trade activities between Taiwan and these partners. Finally, a brief summary of the main findings in this paper is made in section 4.5.

4.1 The Empirical Model

Some studies, for instance, Miles (1979), have tried to determine how a devaluation affects the trade balance or balance of payments. In Miles's model the trade balance is affected by real factors such as the relative growth rate and real output as well as by monetary factors such as the money supply and nominal exchange levels. Miles found that devaluations do not improve the trade balance but do improve the balance of payments. However, Miles's study was criticized by Himarios (1985) for two major reasons: first, Miles uses only nominal exchange rates in his model to examine the effect of exchange rate variations on trade flow. However, as Krueger (1978) pointed out, following devaluation it is the price of tradables *relative* to nontradables that matters. Therefore, Himarios argued, it would be more appropriate to use the real exchange rate, rather than nominal rates, to examine the effect of exchange rate variations on the trade balance. Second, Himarios argued that Miles imposes a priori subtractive linear restrictions and that they produce biased estimates of the coefficients. In light of these studies by Miles and Himarios, we shall undertake a more detailed study by separating Taiwan's trade balance into exports and imports and then examining how these two contrasting trade activities are affected by the nominal and real exchange rates. In addition, a linear, rather than a subtractive linear restrictions, form is employed in order to avoid bias in the estimates.

In light of the above discussion, we shall now specify our empirical model of the effect of changes of the nominal exchange rate on Taiwan's total export (TEXT) as

$$\text{TEXT} = f(\text{INCOME, UST, WAGE, Q1} - \text{Q3, T}), \text{ where}$$

TEXT: Taiwan's total quarterly export value (in million U.S. dollars) from the first quarter of 1972 to the fourth quarter of 1990.

INCOME: the weighted average GNP of Taiwan's five major export destination countries/areas (the United States, Japan, Canada, Singapore, and Hong Kong). The weights are based on their share of exports.

UST: Exchange rate between one NT dollar and the U.S. dollar.

WAGE: Relative real wage ratios between Taiwan's real wages and the weighted average real wages of the above five major exporting countries/regions. The weights are also determined by their share of exports.

Q1 − Q3: Quarterly dummies.

T: Time trend variable.

As for Taiwan's total imports model, it is specified as

$$\text{TIMT} = f(\text{TGNP, UST, WAGE, } Q_1 - Q_3, \text{T}), \text{ where}$$

TIMT: Taiwan's total quarterly import value (in million U.S. dollars) from the first quarter of 1972 to the fourth quarter of 1990.

INCOME: Taiwan's quarterly GNP in billion U.S. dollars.

WAGE: Relative real wage ratios between Taiwan's real wages and the weighted average real wages of Taiwan's five major import-source countries/regions (the United States, Japan, West Germany, Singapore, and Hong Kong).

In the above models we assume that Taiwan's exports (imports) depend on importing countries' (Taiwan's) income levels and terms of trade, which include relative real wages or productivity as well as exchange rates, seasonal factors, and time trends. If we merely wish to examine Taiwan's import and export relationship with the United States, then INCOME will be U.S. GNP, and WAGE will be the relative real wage ratio between Taiwan and the United States.

4.2 Empirical Results for the Nominal Exchange Rate Model

Based on our empirical models of the equations for TEXT and TIMT, we present our empirical results in table 4.1. From this table, we see that when Taiwan's income in terms of GNP value increases, INCOME significantly and positively affects Taiwan's total importing value (TIMT). As for exchange rates, the first two equations of table 4.1 show that an appreciation in the NT dollar (which will lead to an increase in UST by our definition) will lead to an increase in Taiwan's total import value, but this increase will not become significant until after two to three quarters have elapsed. As for the relative real wage ratio between Taiwan and the weighted average of Taiwan's five major import sources, the WAGE variables in equations (1) and (2) confirm that an increase in Taiwan's productivity relative to that of its import sources will lead to a decline in Taiwan's total importing value. Clearly the first two equations of table 4.1 show that an increase in Taiwan's income and/or an appreciation of the NT dollar will lead to an increase in Taiwan's total imports, while an increase in Taiwan's productivity will result in more import substitution and will reduce Taiwan's total imports.

Equations (3) and (4) of table 4.1 report the empirical results for Taiwan's total export value (TEXT). Our empirical results show that an increase in the

Table 4.1 **Determination of Taiwan's Total Exports (TEXT) and Imports (TIMT) (absolute *t*-statistics)**

	TIMT		TEXT	
Variable	(1)	(2)	(3)	(4)
CONSTANT	−6.55 E-3	−9.26 E-3	−1.09 E-4	−1.11 E-4
	(2.68)***	(3.60)***	(9.15)***	(6.55)***
INCOME	171.52	116.49	4.76	4.74
	(2.71)***	(1.70)*	(5.66)***	(5.69)***
UST	1.21 E-5	3.60 E-4	4.86 E-5	5.21 E-5
	(1.47)	(0.41)	(8.19)***	(7.47)***
UST1	7.34 E-4	6.15 E-4	−8.34 E-5	−7.64 E-4
	(1.28)	(1.18)	(1.38)	(1.20)
UST2	9.97 E-4	5.35 E-4	−1.36 E-5	−1.04 E-5
	(1.80)*	(1.01)	(2.36)**	(1.60)
UST3		2.79 E-5		−6.43 E-4
		(3.63)***		(0.70)
WAGE	1225.19	−2103.83	2312.47	−2268.60
	(0.82)	(0.98)	(1.20)	(0.82)
WAGE1	−2450.52	−5841.09	2752.63	3582.72
	(1.32)	(2.53)**	(1.25)	(1.24)
WAGE2	−5420.13	−5151.16	1628.40	924.07
	(3.44)***	(2.13)**	(0.90)	(0.39)
WAGE3		−321.52		−1554.56
		(0.14)		(0.66)
Q1	−157.30	−99.21	−432.68	−464.24
	(1.43)	(0.99)	(3.77)***	(3.84)***
Q2	182.71	246.19	141.89	91.99
	(1.49)	(2.17)**	(1.12)	(0.67)
Q3	56.82	92.98	228.91	195.44
	(0.54)	(0.94)	(2.10)**	(1.65)
T	61.57	86.79	−70.40	−66.68
	(2.76)***	(3.65)***	(1.60)	(1.51)
$\bar{R}^2$	0.93	0.93	0.97	0.98
D-W	1.87	1.94	1.85	1.81
N	78	78	78	78

Notes: Variable INCOME in TIMT equations is Taiwan's GNP level, in TEXT equations, the weighted average GNP of Taiwan's five major export markets. In addition, consult text under eq. (1) and (2) for definitions of WAGE in TIMT and in TEXT equations. UST1, UST2, UST3, WAGE1, WAGE2, and WAGE3 are different time lag variables for variables UST and WAGE, respectively.

*Significant at 10 percent level

**Significant at 5 percent level

***Significant at 1 percent level

weighted average GNP of Taiwan's major export markets (INCOME) will lead to an increase in Taiwan's total exports; the income effect is thus quite clear. As for exchange rates, equations (3) and (4) show that an appreciation in the NT dollar will initially lead to an increase in Taiwan's total exports but will then have an adverse effect on Taiwan's total exports. However, judging from the empirical results in equation (4), this adverse effect may not be very significant. The main reason that an appreciation in the NT dollar will lead to an increase in Taiwan's total exports in the initial period may be that, in light of possible further NT dollar appreciation, Taiwanese exporters are likely to deliver their shipments earlier than they had originally scheduled. Therefore Taiwan's total export value will rise particularly in the initial period of NT appreciation. Although in equation (3) we have confirmed that an appreciation in the NT dollar will adversely affect Taiwan's total exports, this result is not supported by our findings in equation (4). One possible explanation for this may be that an appreciation in the NT dollar against the U.S. dollar may adversely affect Taiwanese exports to the U.S. market. However the NT dollar has actually depreciated against other vastly appreciated currencies such as the German mark and Japanese yen, which will certainly help Taiwan's exporters diversify their markets away from the United States to other major markets, in particular the European market. Consequently, an appreciation in the NT dollar may have no significant impact on Taiwan's total export value.

To support the above argument, we can examine market share statistics in table 4.2. Here, we list Taiwan's export shares for the United States, Japan, and European countries. The statistics show that Taiwan's share of the U.S. market increased dramatically from 34 percent in 1980 to 48 percent in 1985. This is due mainly to the undervaluation of the NT dollar accompanied by the rapid

Table 4.2 **Taiwan Major Export Partners (%)**

Year	United States	Japan	Europe	Great Britain	France	Netherlands	West Germany
1980	34	11	16	2	1	2	5
1981	36	11	13	3	1	2	4
1982	39	11	12	2	1	1	4
1983	45	10	11	2	1	2	3
1984	49	10	10	2	1	1	3
1985	48	11	10	2	1	1	3
1986	48	11	12	2	1	2	3
1987	44	13	15	3	1	2	4
1988	39	14	16	3	2	2	4
1989	36	14	17	3	2	2	4
1990	32	12	18	3	2	3	5
1991	29	12	18	3	2	3	5

Source: Monthly Statistics of Export and Import in Taiwan Area of the ROC (Taipei: Ministry of Finance).

acceleration of the U.S. trade deficit from the early to the mid-1980s. However, as the NT dollar appreciated dramatically after the mid-1980s and as the tide of protectionism in the United States rose, Taiwanese exporters swiftly shifted their markets from the United States to Europe. As a result, Taiwan's U.S. market share declined from 48 percent in 1985 to 32 percent in 1990 and 29 percent in 1991, while Taiwan's European market share increased from 10 percent in 1985 to 18 percent in 1990 and 1991. Clearly, there was a dramatic structural change in Taiwan's trade relationship with the United States and Europe in the 1980s.

In table 4.3, we examine how changes in exchange rates and relative productivities affect Taiwan-U.S. trade. In the first two equations of this table we present the empirical results for Taiwanese imports from the United States (TIMUS). From equation (1) we see that Taiwanese GNP (represented by INCOME) has a significant effect on U.S. exports to Taiwan, while an appreciation in the NT dollar against the U.S. dollar (UST2) and an increase in Taiwan's productivity relative to that of the United States (WAGE2) have significant positive and negative impacts, respectively, on Taiwan's imports from the United States six months later. In equation (2) of table 4.3, we introduce more time lags for exchange rate (UST) and relative productivity (WAGE) variables to examine factors relevant to Taiwanese imports from the United States. The empirical results again confirm the result in equation (1) that an appreciation in the NT dollar will lead to a reduction in import cost and induce more imports from the United States. Conversely, an improvement in Taiwan's productivity relative to that of the United States will promote more import substitution and will reduce Taiwanese imports from the United States.

We also examine relevant factors that affect Taiwanese exports to the United States. The empirical results from equations (3) and (4) show that U.S. GNP levels (INCOME) positively affect Taiwanese exports to the United States. An appreciation in the NT dollar against the U.S. dollar will adversely affect Taiwanese exports to the United States—though it may promote such exports in the first period of NT appreciation. Contrary to our expectations, however, equations (3) and (4) show that an improvement in Taiwan's productivity relative to that of the United States will reduce Taiwanese exports to the United States. This is illustrated by the many negative and highly significant regression coefficients for the WAGE variables. There are several possible explanations for this phenomenon. First, as Taiwan improves its productivity, more and more Taiwanese exporters find it feasible to meet the higher standards demanded by European customers, and therefore an increase in Taiwan's productivity may result in a structural shift in exports away from the U.S. to the European market. Second, the United States introduced more trade protection clauses such as "301" or "super 301" into the U.S. Trade Act in the mid- to late-80s, and this undoubtedly forced Taiwanese exporters to diversify their export market away from the United States. These responses were, in turn, negatively correlated with the faster-rising productivity trend (relative to the

Table 4.3 **Determination of Taiwan's Total Exports (TEXUS) and Imports (TIMUS) with the United States (absolute *t*-statistics)**

	TIMUS		TEXUS	
	(1)	(2)	(3)	(4)
CONSTANT	−2.32 E-3	−4.30 E-3	−3.67 E-3	−5.64 E-3
	(3.90)***	(3.30)***	(2.24)**	(3.62)***
INCOME	35.82	59.09	1.60	2.47
	(2.02)**	(1.39)	(2.26)**	(5.06)***
UST		−7.93 E-4	2.19 E-5	2.98 E-5
		(1.82)*	(6.55)***	(8.47)***
UST1		7.58 E-4	−3.60 E-4	−1.69 E-4
		(2.52)**	(1.15)	(0.51)
UST2	9.67 E-4	5.30 E-4	−9.06 E-4	−6.67 E-4
	(4.18)***	(1.56)	(2.58)***	(1.90)*
UST3		1.51 E-5		−5.73 E-4
		(3.40)***		(1.18)
WAGE		−1471.29	−4493.74	−5514.88
		(0.90)	(3.48)***	(3.48)***
WAGE1		−1459.32	−2422.12	−2869.92
		(0.85)	(1.80)*	(1.54)
WAGE2	−2325.61	−4526.07	1651.16	−914.55
	(1.91)*	(2.29)**	(1.34)	(0.60)
WAGE3		−3777.36		−3644.38
		(2.12)**		(2.60)**
Q1	38.63	14.49	−156.47	−214.71
	(0.75)	(0.27)	(2.95)***	(3.65)***
Q2	132.09	71.29	141.56	93.74
	(2.29)**	(1.17)	(2.32)**	(1.38)
Q3	67.87	53.09	139.93	121.31
	(1.19)	(1.02)	(2.72)***	(2.11)**
T	18.61	30.48	−7.23	−33.52
	(3.00)***	(2.84)***	(0.17)	(1.23)
$\bar{R}^2$	0.87	0.84	0.83	0.95
D-W	1.77	1.72	1.76	1.74
N	78	78	78	78

Notes: Variable WAGE is relative real wages (productivities) between Taiwan and the United States. Variable INCOME in TIMUS equations is Taiwan's GNP level, in TEXUS equations, U.S. GNP level.

*Significant at 10 percent level.

**Significant at 5 percent level.

***Significant at 1 percent level.

United States) in Taiwan. Third, beginning in the mid-1980s Taiwan's outward investment in Southeast Asian countries, as well as in mainland China, increased dramatically. The statistics from the investment authorities of Southeast Asian countries show that in 1989, in Thailand, Malaysia, and the Philippines, Taiwan ranked second only to Japan as the largest foreign direct investment (FDI) source country. Furthermore, it is estimated that the total amount of Taiwanese investment in mainland China increased from $100 million (U.S.) in 1987 to more than $1 billion (U.S.) in 1989. These huge outward investments may be due to such internal factors as the labor shortage together with rising labor cost, the introduction of the Labor Standards Law in 1984 to protect worker's rights, which in turn boosted the cost of labor considerably, the relaxation of foreign exchange control, and the appreciation of the NT dollar. More and more traditional labor-intensive industries have thus moved their operations out of Taiwan. This, in turn, may actually increase Taiwan's overall competitiveness, but it will reduce Taiwanese exports to the United States. Therefore, the negative relationship between a relative improvement in Taiwan's labor productivity and a decline in its export to the United States, as we found in table 4.3, may not be unreasonable at all. From the discussion above we would like to point to the significant trade-structure shift from the United States to Europe after the mid-1980s, which is, in fact, in accordance with the appreciation of the NT dollar and industrial restructuring in Taiwan. To explore this issue more carefully, we shall now turn to the model of Taiwan's trade with Europe in table 4.4.

In table 4.4 we present our empirical results for international trade between Taiwan and Europe. From equations (1) and (2) of this table, we see that Taiwan's income level is the most important factor in determining Taiwan's total import value from Europe. Furthermore, our empirical results also confirm that an appreciation in the NT dollar will also increase Taiwan's imports from Europe. However some possible negative effects also exist. From equations (1) and (2) we also find that an increase in Taiwan's productivity relative to that of the European countries will lead initially to an increase in Taiwan's imports from Europe, but eventually to a decline in such imports. As for Taiwanese exports to Europe, equation (3) in table 4.4 shows that an appreciation in the NT dollar against the U.S. dollar will induce Taiwanese exports to Europe in the initial period. This is likely due to the depreciation of the NT dollar relative to the German mark. As for the relative productivity factor between Taiwan and the European countries, equation (3) suggests that an increase in Taiwan's productivity might induce more Taiwanese exports to Europe (the *t*-statistic for WAGE1 is 1.77). However, the Durbin-Watson (D-W) statistic for equation (3) is still too weak for us to make a strong assertion. In equation (4) we present the empirical results for Taiwanese exports to Europe without correcting for serial correlation. Again, we do find empirical evidence that increased Taiwanese productivity has enhanced Taiwan's diversification to the European market. However the poor D-W statistic keeps us from making any further arguments. Perhaps the basic problem in identifying such a trade structure change is that the relevant change may have occurred only in recent years, too recent to undergo rigorous statistical testing.

In this section of the paper we adopted quarterly data from 1972 to 1990 to examine how a fluctuation in the NT dollar/U.S. dollar exchange rate affects

Table 4.4 **Determination of Taiwan's Total Export to (TEXE) and Import from (TIME) Europe (absolute *t*-statistics)**

	TIME		TEXE	
	(1)	(2)	(3)	(4)
CONSTANT	−486.87	−545.08	−1100.48	−1644.43
	(2.59)**	(2.62)**	(2.18)**	(7.63)***
INCOME	30.63	29.72	0.07	0.37
	(6.01)***	(5.35)***	(0.31)	(3.85)***
UST	2.45 E-4	2.42 E-4	2.33 E-4	6.32 E-4
	(2.52)**	(2.10)**	(2.61)***	(4.91)***
UST1	−1.99 E-4	−1.92 E-4	1.02 E-4	−5.09 E-3
	(1.82)*	(1.74)	(1.17)	(0.31)
UST2	1.56 E-4	6.58 E-3	1.32 E-3	2.96 E-3
	(1.69)	(0.59)	(0.15)	(0.17)
UST3		1.15 E-4		−1.71 E-4
		(1.01)		(1.07)
WAGE	741.30	690.26	157.94	210.52
	(3.14)***	(2.41)**	(0.62)	(0.44)
WAGE1	−115.55	−346.89	559.51	825.53
	(0.52)	(1.26)	(1.77)*	(1.72)*
WAGE2	−769.77	−796.82	236.05	814.55
	(3.37)***	(3.09)***	(0.94)	(2.07)**
WAGE3		156.16		802.50
		(0.57)		(1.91)**
Q1	−32.25	−28.11	−26.40	−19.18
	(1.55)	(1.34)	(1.81)*	(0.62)
Q2	20.44	29.33	−16.67	−5.35
	(0.99)	(1.33)	(1.01)	(0.17)
Q3	18.09	27.34	7.32	7.87
	(0.94)	(1.32)	(0.52)	(0.25)
T	−0.77	−0.34	15.84	−10.32
	(0.45)	(0.17)	(1.04)	(2.02)**
$\bar{R}^2$	0.97	0.97	0.49	0.98
D-W	1.99	1.99	1.50	0.88
N	78	78	78	78

Notes: Variable INCOME in TIME equations is Taiwan's GNP level, in TEXE equations, the weighted average GNP of major European countries. Variable WAGE is relative real wages (productivities) between Taiwan and weighted average of major European countries.

*Significant at the 10 percent level.

**Significant at the 5 percent level.

***Significant at the 1 percent level.

Taiwan's overall international trade, Taiwan's trade with the United States, and Taiwan's trade with European countries. Our empirical results suggest that among various factors affecting international trade, changes in the importing countries' income level is one of the most important in determining Taiwanese exports. Similarly, changes in Taiwan's own income level will also significantly affect Taiwan's import value. Besides income levels, this study also confirms that an appreciation in the NT dollar will increase Taiwan's imports from the United States and Europe as well as Taiwan's overall import value. However, there is a time lag of roughly four quarters for such a stimulation.

Contrary to popular perceptions, we find that an increase in Taiwan's productivity relative to that of importing countries will not have any significant effect on Taiwan's overall level of exports. In addition, this increase in Taiwan's relative productivity may actually reduce Taiwan's exports to the United States. One possible explanation for such a phenomenon is that as Taiwan's productivity improves relative to that of the United States, Taiwanese exporters are more likely and more able to diversify their markets away from the United States to European countries, either because of rising protectionism starting in the mid- to late 1980s in the United States, or because of the depreciation of the NT dollar relative to the German mark, or because of both. As a result, we observe that the share of the U.S. market held by Taiwan's total exports dropped from 48 percent in 1985 to 29 percent in 1991, whereas that share of the European market increased from 10 percent in 1985 to 18 percent in 1991. In this study we also found some empirical evidence for our argument that an increase in Taiwan's productivity relative to that of the European countries will increase Taiwanese exports to those countries. However, because these structural changes have been observed in more recent years, further empirical testing using a longer series of data is needed in order to identify the cause for such changes.

Generally speaking, the role of the NT dollar/U.S. dollar exchange rate is critical to Taiwan's export performance. We find that an appreciation in the NT dollar will adversely affect Taiwan's exports to the United States but that it may have a less adverse affect on Taiwan's exports to Europe. Furthermore, our empirical results show that as the NT dollar appreciates against the U.S. dollar Taiwan's exports are likely to increase, particularly in the initial period of NT dollar appreciation. This is primarily because Taiwanese exporters are likely to advance their delivery ahead of the original schedule in order to minimize their loss from a continuing stronger NT dollar. In the above study, we also found two contradictory results as to the effect of NT dollar appreciation on Taiwan's total exports: one empirical model shows that the vast appreciation of the NT dollar may not necessarily have any significant effect on Taiwan's overall export performance, and the factors discussed above could explain such phenomena. On the other hand, our empirical study does find that NT dollar appreciation can adversely affect Taiwan's overall export performance. To reconcile these differences, further study through differential approaches to the effect of exchange rates on compositional change in Taiwan's overall trade activity is warranted. We turn to this in the next section.

4.3 The Real Effective Exchange Rate and Taiwan's External Trade

In the sections above, we utilized nominal exchange rates to evaluate Taiwan's external trade. The direct advantages of using nominal rates are twofold: namely, the U.S. dollar is the most commonly used currency for international trade, and the adoption of nominal exchange rates between the NT dollar and the U.S. dollar merely reflects this fact. Second, the NT dollar has appreciated considerably against the U.S. dollar since the mid-1980s, and the adoption of nominal exchange rates will thus be able to capture the impact of this appreciation. However, as we discussed in the previous section, both Krueger (1978) and Himarios (1985) argued that it is more appropriate to use the real exchange rate rather than nominal rates to examine the effect of exchange rate variation on trade balance. Furthermore, it is important to note that other major currencies such as the Japanese yen, French franc, and German mark also appreciated considerably against the U.S. dollar in the mid- to late 1980s. In addition, the relative price changes in major trading countries are important in determining comparative advantage for Taiwan's international trade. To properly take all of these factors into consideration, we must evaluate Taiwan's currency on its real effective exchange rate base rather than its nominal value. For this, we shall now try to calculate Taiwan's real effective exchange rates (REER) and try to examine how they will affect Taiwan's external trade.

4.3.1 The Calculation of the Real Effective Exchange Rates

To properly evaluate the real value of the NT dollar, we calculate its real effective exchange rates (REER) from its nominal effective exchange rates (NEER). The formulas for the relevant calculations are:

$$\text{NEER} = \prod_{j=1}^{n}\left(\frac{RT_{j,t}}{RT_{j,0}}\right)^{W_{j,t}*100}, \text{ where}$$

NEER $=$ nominal effective exchange rate for the NT dollar,
$RT_{j,t}$ $=$ exchange rates between one NT dollar and country j's currency at period t,
$RT_{j,0}$ $=$ exchange rate between one NT dollar and country j's currency at period 0, and
$W_{j,t}$ $=$ weights for country j at period t.

$$\text{REER} = \frac{\text{NEER}}{\prod_{j=1}^{n}\left(\frac{P_{j,t}/P_{j,0}}{P_{\text{T},t}/P_{t,0}}\right)W_{j,t}}, \text{ where}$$

REER $=$ real effective exchange rate of NT dollars,
$P_{j,t}$ $=$ wholesale price index of country j at period t,
$P_{j,0}$ $=$ wholesale price index of country j at period 0,
$P_{\text{T},t}$ $=$ wholesale price index of Taiwan (T) at period t, and
$P_{t,0}$ $=$ wholesale price index of Taiwan (T) at period 0.

One may use either Taiwan's bilateral trade value or Taiwan's average export value with country j as the weight for country j in the calculation of NEER and REER. The formula for bilateral-trade weights is

$$W_{j,t}\ (\text{bilateral trade}) = \frac{X_{\mathrm{T}j} + M_{\mathrm{T}j}}{\sum_{j=1}^{n}(X_{\mathrm{T}j} + M_{\mathrm{T}j})},$$

where $X_{\mathrm{T}j}$ = Taiwan's seasonal export value to country j,
$M_{\mathrm{Tt}j}$ = Taiwan's seasonal import value from country j.

The formula for average-export-value weights is

$$W_{j,t}\ (\text{average export value}) = 0.5 * \frac{X_{\mathrm{T}j}}{\sum_{j=1}^{n} x_{\mathrm{T}j}} + 0.5 * \frac{X_j - M_{\mathrm{T}j}}{\sum_{j=1}^{n}(X_j - M_{\mathrm{T}j})},$$

where X_j = country j's seasonal total export value.

It is important to note that in calculating the above NT dollar exchange rate indexes, we have adopted the volume quotation method by calculating the value of country j's currency for one NT dollar. Therefore, if the REER is greater (smaller) than unity, it suggests that the NT dollar is overvalued (undervalued) and that the NT dollar should be devalued (appreciated) so that the real value of the NT dollar is comparable to that in the base period.

In this study we have chosen 1979 and 1980–82 as the two base periods for comparison. The underlying reasons for selecting these two periods are: first, beginning in 1979 Taiwan adopted a floating exchange rate system, and the resulting exchange rate levels are therefore closer to market equilibrium levels. Second, Taiwan's trade surplus in 1980 was only $7.7 million (U.S.), the closest to actual balance over the entire period of the 1970s and 1980s. Consequently, the period 1979–82 has already been adopted by the Central Bank, as well as by many other economic and financial institutions in Taiwan, as the base period for calculating effective exchange rates for the NT dollar.

The trading nations to be included in our calculation are the United States, the United Kingdom, France, (West) Germany, Italy, the Netherlands, Canada, Japan, Australia, Korea, Singapore, Malaysia, Indonesia, Thailand, and Hong Kong. The 15 countries/areas above accounted for 86 percent of Taiwan's total exports in 1991 and 84 percent over the period 1976–91. They also accounted for 83 percent of Taiwan's total trade value in 1991 and 81 percent over the period 1976–91.

Now, we first present our calculations of REERs in table 4.5. From this table it is clear that almost all trade balance statistics for TBUS, TBT, and TB15 are positive over the period 1975–90, which suggests that Taiwan enjoyed a consistent trade surplus over this period. Naturally, the relevant question is then, Does the level of the NT dollar have anything to do with the trade balance? From this table, we see that most of the RE802A statistics are smaller than our base period (1980:1–1982:4) level of 100 except in 1985:1 and

Table 4.5 Real Effective Exchange Rates for the NT Dollar and Taiwan's Trade Balance and Foreign Exchange Reserve (FER) Statistics, 1975–90

Year and Quarter	Rate[a]	Real Effective Exchange Rate				Trade Balance			
		RE802A	RE802B	RE79A	RE79B	TBUS[b]	TBT[b]	TB15[b]	FER[c]
1975 1	38.00	95.39	99.71	103.23	104.05	—	−185	—	1.073
2	38.00	97.37	101.92	105.36	106.36	—	−93	—	1.061
3	38.00	99.48	102.91	107.64	107.40	—	−179	—	1.164
4	38.00	98.50	101.81	106.59	106.25	—	−186	—	1.074
1976 1	38.00	97.96	101.17	105.87	105.30	239	66	153	1.004
2	38.00	97.94	100.73	105.85	104.84	266	72	163	1.301
3	38.00	96.89	99.33	104.70	103.39	422	239	397	1.536
4	38.00	96.01	98.86	103.76	102.89	314	191	284	1.516
1977 1	38.00	94.47	97.01	102.08	100.63	239	47	126	1.259
2	38.00	93.30	95.66	100.81	99.23	363	87	138	1.320
3	38.00	92.30	94.62	99.74	98.15	473	317	372	1.351
4	38.00	89.40	91.23	96.61	94.63	597	400	525	1.345
1978 1	38.00	86.48	88.70	93.54	92.23	493	178	277	1.329
2	38.00	86.15	87.59	93.18	91.07	685	484	505	1.358
3	36.00	88.96	89.71	96.23	93.27	789	587	663	1.447
4	36.00	89.72	91.37	97.05	95.00	667	411	568	1.406
1979 1	35.95	90.38	92.97	97.89	96.87	500	251	381	1.444
2	36.10	92.11	95.37	99.77	99.38	541	254	335	1.448
3	36.03	92.09	95.85	99.74	99.87	689	548	696	1.455
4	36.03	93.29	98.18	101.04	102.30	539	277	442	1.467
1980 1	36.06	96.41	101.18	104.31	105.42	451	26	414	1.509
2	36.01	98.40	102.11	106.47	106.38	508	−246	254	1.489
3	35.93	97.03	100.39	104.99	104.59	524	−29	303	1.836
4	36.01	99.61	101.66	107.78	105.91	604	327	712	2.205

(*continued*)

Table 4.5 (continued)

Year and Quarter	Rate[a]	Real Effective Exchange Rate				Trade Balance			
		RE802A	RE802B	RE79A	RE79B	TBUS[b]	TBT[b]	TB15[b]	FER[c]
1981 1	36.35	100.81	101.26	108.52	105.22	309	−514	−21	2.665
2	36.36	102.74	102.49	110.60	106.50	683	36	516	3.339
3	37.91	102.01	101.27	109.81	105.23	1,303	1,131	1,248	5.216
4	37.84	98.19	98.41	105.70	102.26	1,104	758	1,217	7.235
1982 1	38.13	97.60	97.78	105.00	101.59	702	472	787	7.711
2	39.39	95.81	96.11	103.08	99.85	1,160	674	914	7.525
3	39.87	95.42	95.58	102.66	99.30	1,150	1,128	1,048	7.897
4	39.91	95.79	95.87	103.06	99.61	1,184	1,042	1,287	8.532
1983 1	40.04	92.94	92.67	99.85	96.00	1,031	490	981	9.585
2	40.20	94.23	93.81	101.24	97.18	1,795	1,839	1,827	10.443
3	40.19	95.93	94.98	103.06	98.40	2,044	1,682	2,048	11.446
4	40.27	94.92	93.50	101.98	96.87	1,818	824	1,484	11.859
1984 1	39.92	94.93	93.42	101.76	96.55	2,001	1,669	2,083	12.910
2	39.63	95.75	94.24	102.64	97.40	2,843	2,552	2,875	13.765
3	39.18	98.31	96.20	105.38	99.43	2,689	2,396	2,637	14.571
4	39.47	98.51	95.92	105.60	99.14	2,293	1,880	2,267	15.664
1985 1	39.54	100.52	97.10	107.92	100.38	2,020	2,123	2,461	17.614
2	40.00	96.17	94.05	103.25	97.23	2,723	2,734	3,006	18.557
3	40.40	92.43	91.30	99.23	94.39	2,790	2,938	3,130	20.001
4	39.83	89.38	88.71	95.97	91.71	2,493	2,829	3,002	22.556
1986 1	38.77	87.87	87.76	94.89	91.07	2,781	3,058	3,208	26.027
2	38.09	88.45	88.53	95.52	91.87	3,380	3,820	3,599	30.851

	3	36.72	89.29	89.91	96.42	93.30	3,720	4,209	3,977	38.205
	4	36.29	89.84	90.93	97.02	94.36	3,710	4,597	4,215	46.310
1987	1	34.26	90.59	92.31	98.06	96.18	3,625	4,231	4,012	54.505
	2	31.08	95.30	96.86	103.15	100.91	4,312	4,889	4,610	60.717
	3	30.09	97.61	99.06	105.65	103.21	4,555	5,772	5,602	64.903
	4	28.55	97.98	100.03	106.05	104.22	3,539	3,762	4,118	76.748
1988	1	28.64	94.97	96.64	102.71	100.92	1,965	1,341	1,938	74.756
	2	28.89	94.18	95.63	101.87	99.86	2,111	3,220	3,079	70.326
	3	28.93	97.14	97.60	105.06	101.91	3,306	3,082	3,201	69.005
	4	28.17	96.55	97.37	104.43	101.68	3,078	3,351	3,423	73.897
1989	1	27.17	101.32	101.64	109.46	106.24	2,446	2,773	2,785	75.156
	2	25.91	105.30	105.48	113.75	110.26	3,104	3,449	3,799	74.348
	3	25.60	104.76	105.27	113.17	110.03	3,521	4,288	4,456	73.801
	4	27.17	96.11	97.42	103.82	101.82	2,962	3,528	3,705	73.224
1990	1	26.41	96.82	99.86	104.91	104.62	1,870	1,811	2,200	69.761
	2	27.20	94.22	98.02	102.10	102.70	2,172	3,130	3,180	63.631
	3	27.30	92.29	96.18	100.01	100.76	2,920	4,361	4,524	68.090
	4	27.11	85.34	88.56	92.48	92.79	2,173	3,196	3,688	72.441

Notes: In this table, we have reported four different REERs, which are calculated based on four different assumptions, namely, RE802A—base period is 1980–82 and weights are average export values, RE802B—base period is 1980–82 and weights are total bilateral trade values, RE79A—base period is 1979 and weights are average export values, and RE79B—base period is 1979 and weights are total bilateral trade values.

Trade balance columns report TBUS—Taiwan's trade balance with the United States, TBT—Taiwan's total trade balance, and TB15—Taiwan's trade balance with the 15 major trading countries that we included in the REER calculation. These seasonal trade balance statistics are defined as total seasonal exports minus the corresponding seasonal imports. Therefore, a positive balance is a trade surplus for Taiwan.

Taiwan's foreign exchange reserve statistics are reported as FER.

[a]Nominal exchange rate between 1 U.S. dollar and NT dollar.

[b]In million of U.S. dollars.

[c]In billion U.S. dollars.

1983:3–1989:3. This clearly suggests that the NT dollar was undervalued most of the time, compared to the 1980–82 base period level, and should have been appreciated in order to restore the trade balance situation. Contrary to those for RE802A, however, the statistics of RE79A suggest that the NT was overvalued, especially during the period 1979:4–1985:2, because most of the RE79A statistics are greater than the base level of 100 in 1979; therefore the RE79A index suggests, although not conclusively, that the NT dollar should have been depreciated in order to restore the trade balance. As for the remaining two real exchange rate indexes—RE802B and RE79B, which utilize bilateral trade values, not merely export values, as weights to calculate the real value of the NT dollar—the statistics in table 4.5 show that these two indexes are perhaps more reliable and more reasonable than RE802A and RE79A, discussed above. One can see from table 4.5 that both the RE802B and RE79B indexes suggest that NT dollars were undervalued (the indexes are less than 100) over the period 1982 to early 1987, which is consistent with the rapid growth of the trade surplus as well as with the accumulation of foreign exchange reserves from the early to mid-1980s. In particular, both RE802B and RE79B show that around the first quarter of 1986, REERs of the NT dollar reached an all-time low point (87.76 for RE802B and 91.07 for RE79B), which suggests that the nominal exchange rate level of $1 (U.S.) for NT$38.77 in the first quarter of 1986 was very low. This unbalanced situation persisted, and in the third quarter of 1987 the nominal exchange rate was $1 (U.S.) for NTS$30.09, while RE802B and RE79B registered levels of 99.06 and 103.21, respectively. As a result, all the trade balance statistics in table 4.5 reached high points at that time, namely, $4,555, $5,772, and $5,602 million (U.S.) for TBUS, TBT, and TB15, respectively. Furthermore, the foreign exchange reserve (FER) also increased dramatically from $9.585 billion (U.S.) in the first quarter of 1983 to $64.903 billion (U.S.) in the third quarter of 1987. Obviously, as suggested by both the RE802B and RE79B indexes, the huge trade imbalance and vast accumulation of foreign exchange reserves experienced by Taiwan during the critical 1980–87 period were really due to the consistent undervaluation of the NT dollar. To dramatically cut the enormous accumulation of foreign exchange reserves, the NT dollar began to appreciate sharply from 1987:1 with a rate of $1 (U.S.) for NT$34.26 to $1 (U.S.) for NT$25.60 in 1989:3—a 25.27 percent appreciation within two years. As a result, not only did the RE802B and RE79B indexes increase dramatically, but the accumulation of foreign exchange reserves slowed.

In the discussion above, we found that RE802B and RE79B are more appropriate in explaining the trade balance and foreign exchange reserve problem in Taiwan than the other REERs calculated. To examine the performance of the four different REER indexes more carefully, one can actually compare the correlation coefficients between each of them and the trade balance statistics. As we argued before, when an REER index increases above the base period level of 100, it implies that the NT dollar is overvalued relative to the base period;

this will reduce exports, encourage imports, and therefore worsen Taiwan's trade balance. In contrast, however, when an REER index declines below the base period level of 100 the NT dollar is undervalued relative to the base period; this will encourage exports, discourage imports, and subsequently improve Taiwan's trade balance. Clearly, the correlation coefficient between Taiwan's trade balance and the REER indexes, as defined above, should be negative.

In table 4.6 we report correlation coefficients between different trade balance statistics and the four REER statistics. These results show that RE802B generally has a negative relationship with trade balance statistics, which is in accordance with our argument above. Furthermore, RE802B has larger correlation coefficients when we lag it by two (RE802(−2)) to four (RE803B(−4)) quarters. Similarly, we also find sizable correlation coefficients between various trade balance statistics and the RE79B(−2) and RE79B(−4) indexes. In contrast, however, table 4.6 also clearly shows that the correlation coefficients between trade balance statistics and RE802A or RE79A are very low. Consequently we may conclude that REER indexes weighted by bilateral trade values are more capable of illustrating interaction between trade balance statistics and the real value of the NT dollar.

To examine the relationship between REERs of the NT dollar and Taiwan's external trade activities more closely, in table 4.7 we present the regression results of REER under various definitions and different time lags. For instance, in equation (1) of table 4.7, the REER variable is represented by RE802A, and our empirical results show an increase in REER, representing an overvaluation of the NT dollar. This discouraged Taiwan's total exports (TEXT) for RE802A, and REER lagged by two quarters (REER2) is negative and highly significant

Table 4.6 Correlation Coefficients between Taiwan's Trade Balance Statistics and Real Effective Exchange Rate (REER) Statistics

	Trade Balance Statistics		
REER Statistics	TBUS	TBT	TB15
RE802B	−0.02	−0.12	−0.02
RE802B(−2)	−0.21	−0.20	−0.13
RE802B(−4)	−0.22	−0.16	−0.14
RE79B	−0.02	−0.11	−0.01
RE79B(−2)	−0.21	−0.19	−0.01
RE79B(−4)	−0.24	−0.17	−0.14
RE802A	0.11	−0.001	0.07
RE802A(−2)	−0.03	−0.03	0.02
RE802A(−4)	0.02	0.07	0.09
RE79A	0.11	−0.001	0.08
RE79A(−2)	−0.04	−0.04	0.01
RE79A(−4)	−0.002	0.05	0.07

Table 4.7 Real Effective Exchange Rate (REER) and Taiwan's External Trade (absolute *t*-statistics)

	Equation (REER)					
Variable	(1) TEXT (RE802A)	(2) TIMT (RE802B)	(3) TEXUS (RE79A)	(4) TIMUS (RE79B)	(5) TEXE (RE79A)	(6) TIME (RE802B)
CONSTANT	−5.69 E-3	−6.29 E-3	−3.11 E-3	−1.69 E-3	297.05	19.04
	(1.29)	(1.30)	(1.30)	(0.77)	(0.45)	(0.07)
INCOME	5.03	329.08	1.71	21.32	0.21	45.41
	(2.53)***	(4.89)***	(1.67)	(0.41)	(0.83)	(13.73)***
REER	100.01	−31.77	47.35	−22.64	−2.46	5.12
	(3.75)***	(1.04)	(3.92)***	(1.50)	(0.78)	(1.33)
REER1	−26.96	53.32	−1.66	13.69	−1.32	−5.16
	(1.02)	(2.11)**	(0.14)	(1.20)	(0.43)	(1.04)
REER2	−72.01	11.33	−34.31	2.12	−5.94	−0.28
	(2.71)***	(0.43)	(2.87)***	(0.17)	(1.90)*	(0.05)
REER3	−7.74	48.37	−0.26	19.83	−1.05	0.76
	(0.26)	(1.73)*	(0.02)	(1.62)	(0.30)	(0.20)
WAGE	2.11 E-3	1.50 E-3	−2.63	2.44 E-3	1.23 E-3	989.19
	(0.77)	(0.58)	(1.47)	(1.66)	(2.76)***	(3.25)***
WAGE1	5.29 E-3	−3.75 E-3	−3.06	3.01	1.62 E-3	−215.85
	(1.70)*	(1.27)	(1.48)	(2.47)***	(3.05)***	(0.72)
WAGE2	5.17 E-3	−7.08 E-3	705.70	71.48	1.53 E-3	−956.42
	(1.64)	(2.04)**	(0.34)	(0.04)	(2.62)***	(3.42)***
WAGE3	5.28 E-3	−514.38	346.35	−967.79	1.26 E-3	207.93
	(1.81)*	(0.16)	(0.18)	(0.48)	(2.38)***	(0.68)
Q1	−488.00	−170.84	−181.81	−43.06	−35.64	−36.77
	(3.11)***	(1.22)	(2.29)**	(0.62)	(1.84)*	(1.27)
Q2	160.39	222.49	191.75	32.00	−18.93	17.05
	(0.09)	(1.38)	(2.14)**	(0.39)	(0.87)	(0.57)
Q3	212.83	99.27	175.06	27.80	2.45	19.67
	(1.43)	(0.72)	(2.36)**	(0.41)	(0.13)	(0.69)
T	−89.16	24.58	5.33	10.56	−2.92	−6.07
	(0.77)	(0.69)	(0.07)	(0.69)	(0.16)	(3.79)***
R^2	0.99	0.99	0.99	0.96	0.99	0.98
D-W	1.95	1.84	1.84	1.62	1.36	1.97
N	78	78	78	78	78	78

Note: Consult tables 4.1, 4.3, and 4.4 for definitions of variables INCOME and WAGE.
*Significant at the 10 percent level.
**Significant at the 5 percent level.
***Significant at the 1 percent level.

(the absolute *t*-statistic is 2.71). Clearly, the empirical results in equation (1) reconfirm our previous result that an appreciation of the NT dollar effects Taiwan's total exports and can actually reduce them. Similarly, for Taiwan's total imports (TIMT) model, equation (2) shows that when we use RE802B as the index for REER we find empirical evidence that an increase in REER, or an overvaluation of the NT dollar, will encourage Taiwan's total imports. This is quite consistent with our empirical results in table 4.1. In equations (3) and (4) we examine Taiwan-U.S. trade and our empirical results show that an increase in RE79A can adversely affect TEXUS, because REER2 is negative and highly significant, which is consistent with our empirical results in table 4.3. It is worth noting that in this study we have tried all four REERs but were unable to find one that had any significant impact on Taiwan's imports from the United States. By comparing our results here to those in table 4.3, one can see that REERs are less sensitive than nominal exchange rates in explaining Taiwan's quarterly imports from the United States. In equations (5) and (6) we show the results of how REER affects Taiwan's imports from, and exports to, Europe. We find empirical evidence that REER2 with specification RE79A can adversely affect Taiwan's exports to Europe (TEXE). However, as in TIMUS equation (4), we can find no REER index that had any significant effect on Taiwan's imports from Europe (TIME). Clearly, when we compare the empirical results in table 4.7 and table 4.4, we see that the nominal exchange rate between the NT dollar and the U.S. dollar is also more sensitive to changes in Taiwan's trade with Europe than are the REERs.

Finally, it is interesting to note that in equation (1) of table 4.7 we find new empirical evidence that an increase in Taiwan's productivity relative to that of other countries will enhance Taiwan's export promotion drive, because WAGE1 and WAGE3 are positive and significant in equation (1). Furthermore, equation (2) of table 4.7 reconfirms our earlier findings that an increase in Taiwan's productivity relative to that of other countries enhances Taiwan's import-substitution capability, because WAGE2 is negative and highly significant. In addition, similar to our empirical results in table 4.4, in equation (5) of table 4.7, we find empirical evidence that an increase in Taiwan's labor productivity will help local firms promote their sales in Europe, however, the D-W statistic is still too low to permit us to make a strong assertion. Generally speaking, when we compare the empirical results in sections 4.2 and 4.3, we may conclude that REER indexes seem to be more capable of affecting and explaining Taiwan's overall international trade activities than Taiwan's bilateral trade activities with a specific country or with a specific region.

4.4 Price-Competition Index and Bilateral Trade between Taiwan and Foreign Countries

We have seen that REER indexes are less capable of explaining bilateral trade activities, while the simple nominal exchange rate fails to take into account changes in relative prices. The alternative to REERs for exploring explicitly how changes in exchange rates affect Taiwan's bilateral trade with a specific foreign country is the calculation of a price-competition index (PCI) between the two countries, defined as

$$\mathrm{PCI} = \frac{e_{dt} / P_{dt}}{e_{it} / P_{it}} = \frac{P_{it}}{P_{dt}} \cdot \frac{e_{dt}}{e_{it}}, \text{ where}$$

e_{dt} = exchange rate between \$1 U.S. and NT dollar in period *t*,
e_{it} = exchange rate between \$1 U.S. and country *i*'s currency in period *t*,
P_{dt} = wholesale price index for Taiwan (the domestic country *d*) in period *t*, and
P_{it} = wholesale price index for foreign country *i* in period *t*.

It is clear from the above formula that the PCI is actually the exchange rate between one unit of country *i*'s currency and the NT dollar (e_{dt}/e_{it}) deflated by the relative prices between Taiwan's wholesale price index and country *i*'s wholesale price index (p_{dt}/p_{it}). Therefore, one can easily see that when the NT dollar depreciates with respect to the U.S. dollar and/or Taiwan's wholesale price index decreases relative to that of foreign country *i*, this will induce an increase in the PCI, which suggests stronger competitiveness or an exporting advantage over foreign country *i* for Taiwan. In contrast, an appreciation of the NT dollar with respect to the U.S. dollar and/or a relative increase in Taiwan's wholesale price index will lead to a decrease in the PCI, which suggests weaker competitiveness or an exporting disadvantage compared to foreign country *i*. In addition, due to our different definitions of exchange rate, there is actually a reciprocal relationship between the PCI and REER. As a result, an increase (decrease) in the PCI implies that the NT dollar is undervalued (overvalued), which implies improving (worsening) competitiveness for Taiwan over foreign country *i*.

In the appendixes, we present the relevant PCIs of Taiwan's 15 major trading partners included in this study. In this section, however, we shall focus our attention on selected results. In figure 4.1 we plot the Taiwan-U.S. PCI statistics against Taiwan's trading statistics with the United States. From the figure we can see that during 1980–81, the PCI was substantially lower than 100 and was accompanied by a moderate trade surplus in favor of Taiwan. However beginning in 1982, there was a dramatic increase in PCI until mid-1987. It was during this critical period that a huge trade surplus in favor of Taiwan emerged. As the NT dollar appreciated dramatically against the U.S. dollar from 1987 to 1988, one can also observe a sharp decline in the PCI and in Taiwan's competitiveness, which in turn led to a significant increase in Taiwan's imports from the United States. Although the PCI index after the end of 1988 is still substantially lower than the base period (1980–82) level of 100, its trend is unambiguously upward-sloping, which is certainly consistent with the continuously growing trade surplus in favor of Taiwan after 1988.

One major result that we obtained in the previous section is that there was a tremendous shift in Taiwan's trade composition away from the U.S. to the European market after the mid-1980s. In this section we find that an increase in PCI toward the European market could be one of the important factors that contributed to this structural shift. In figure 4.2, we plot PCIs for Taiwan and Germany, Taiwan and France, Taiwan and the United Kingdom, and Taiwan and the Netherlands. From this figure, it is clear that these PCIs after mid-

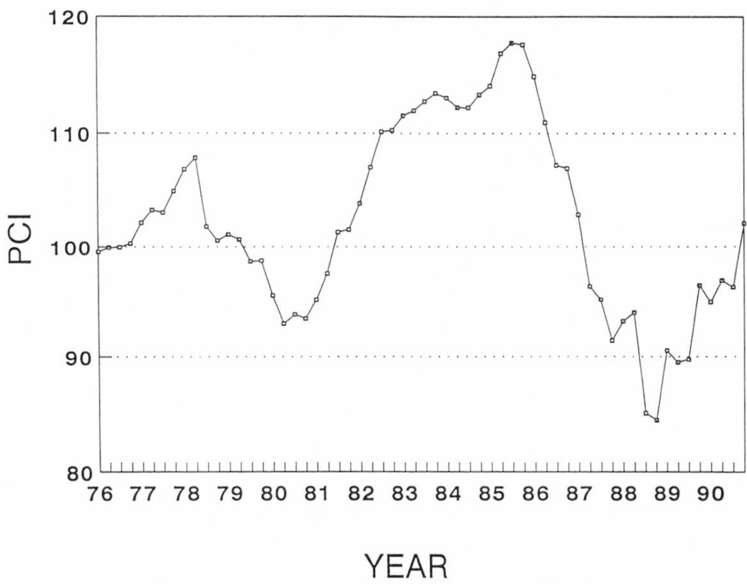

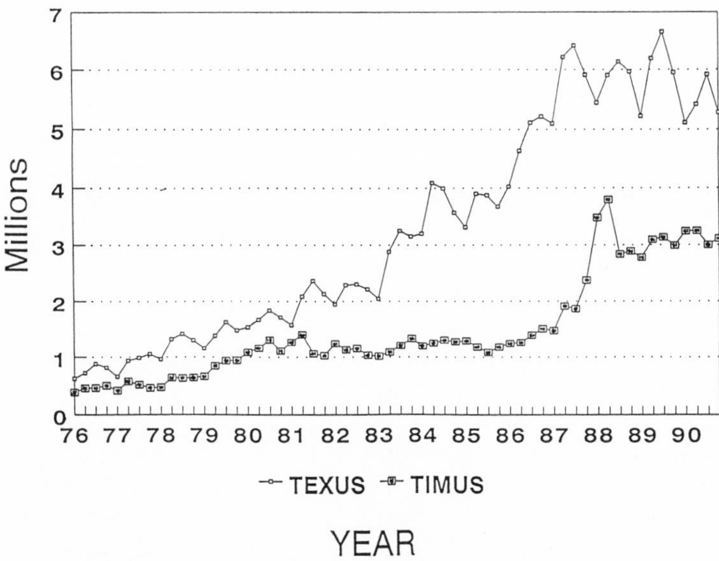

Fig. 4.1 Taiwan-U.S. price competition index (PCI) and trade statistics of Taiwan's exports to (TEXUS) and imports from (TIMUS) the United States (1976:1–1990:4)

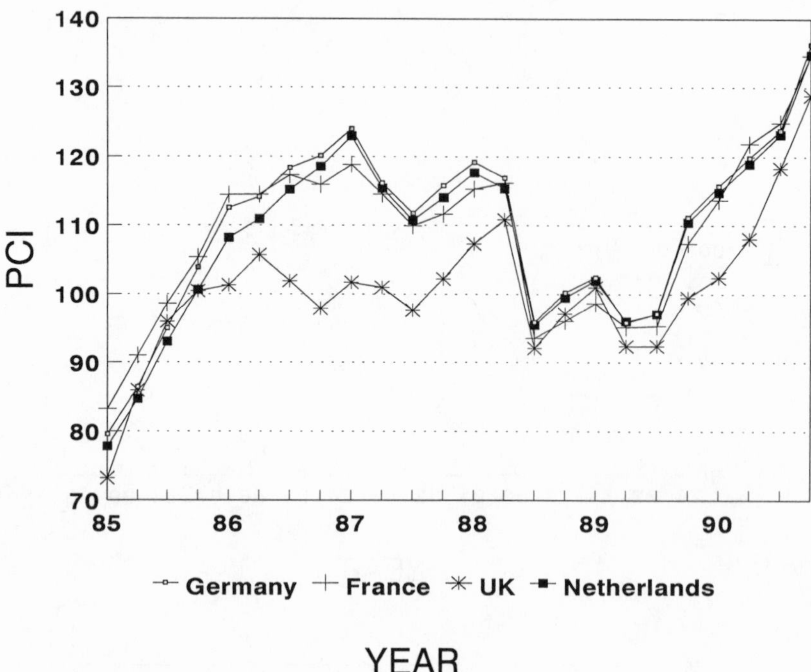

Fig. 4.2 Price competition indexes (PCIs) between Taiwan and its major European trading partners (1985:1–1990:3)

1985 are all substantially greater than 100, which implies stronger Taiwanese competitiveness, and this naturally led to greater Taiwanese emphasis on the European market. As for the basic reasons for an increase in the PCI toward European countries after the mid-1980s, one can examine the data and find that the wholesale price indexes for France, the United Kingdom, Germany, and the Netherlands increased by 7.1, 28.4, 1.9, and 1.7 percent, respectively, from early 1986 to late 1990, while Taiwan actually experienced deflation, and its wholesale price index declined by 10.1 percent over the same period. In addition, we find that the German mark, Dutch guilder, French franc, and British pound appreciated by 36.03, 36.08, 29.92, and 25.98 percent, respectively, against the U.S. dollar from early 1986 to late 1990, while the NT dollar also appreciated against the U.S. dollar by 30.07 percent over the same period. By taking these price and exchange rate factors into consideration, it is clear that Taiwan's competitiveness over European countries after the mid-1980s may have been the result of slowed growth in its wholesale prices relative to those of major European countries, or of a lesser degree of currency appreciation against the U.S. dollar, or both. It is not surprising that this increase in Taiwan's competitiveness with European countries has already translated into a sizable increase in the European share of Taiwan's total exports as we saw in table 4.2.

One phenomenon that the PCI index fails to explain is bilateral trade between Taiwan and Japan. From figure 4.3, we see that after the second quarter of 1985 the PCI increased sharply in favor of Taiwan. However this increase in Taiwan's competitiveness did not help to improve the long-standing trade deficit problem between Taiwan and Japan. On the contrary, the trade deficit between Taiwan and Japan has been widening considerably since 1989. Actually, when one examines figure 4.3 more closely, one can see that as the PCI increases during the period from mid-1985 to early 1988, there is also a considerable increase in Taiwan's exports to Japan. However, Taiwan's imports from Japan also increased at an even faster pace during the same period, resulting in a huge trade deficit problem for Taiwan. The trade imbalance problem between Taiwan and Japan may be beyond factors such as exchange rates and relative prices, which constitute the essence of the PCI. What then are the relevant factors that can enable us to explain the growing trade imbalance between Taiwan and Japan? By examining figures 4.1 and 4.3 simultaneously, one can easily see that there is a great similarity between the variations of TEXUS and the variations of TIMJ. In fact, by calculating the correlation coefficient between TEXUS and TIMJ, we find that it is as high as 0.91125. Furthermore, the correlation coefficients between TIMJ and Taiwan's exports to (West) Germany, France, and the Netherlands are 0.971, 0.986, and 0.983, respectively. Clearly, there is a very close relationship between Taiwan's exports to the U.S. and to Europe and Taiwan's imports from Japan. By examining the relevant customs statistics during this period, we see that machinery, parts, and intermediate industrial products are Taiwan's major import items from Japan. Therefore, the empirical results above seem to suggest that in addition to foreign exchange and other relevant factors, such as labor productivity, Taiwan's international edge is built on its outward sourcing of Japanese industrial equipment and intermediate industrial products. As a result, Taiwan's huge trade deficit with Japan goes hand in hand with Taiwan's growing trade surplus with the West.

Finally, it is interesting to note that the PCIs between Taiwan and Korea and such major Association of Southeast Asian Nations (ASEAN) countries as Thailand, Malaysia, Singapore, and Indonesia worsened substantially after the middle of the 1980s. One of the major reasons for the worsening of PCIs for Taiwan toward these countries is exchange rates. Statistics show that both the Korean won and Thai baht appreciated against the U.S. dollar by 19.39 and 5.24 percent, respectively, between early 1986 and late 1990, while the currencies of Malaysia, Indonesia, and Singapore actually depreciated against the U.S. dollar by about 8.63, 66.16, and 14.79 percent, respectively, for the same period. Clearly, these Asian currency changes are no comparison to the NT dollar's 30.07 percent appreciation against the U.S. dollar, which thus led inevitably to a sharp decline in PCI for Taiwan toward these Asian markets.

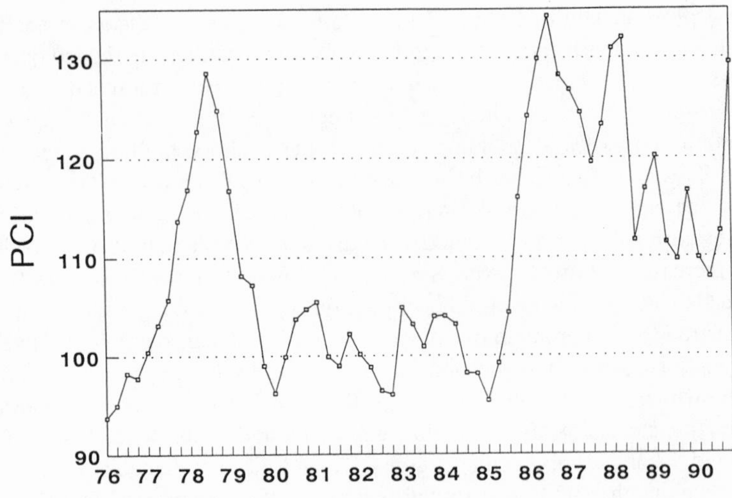

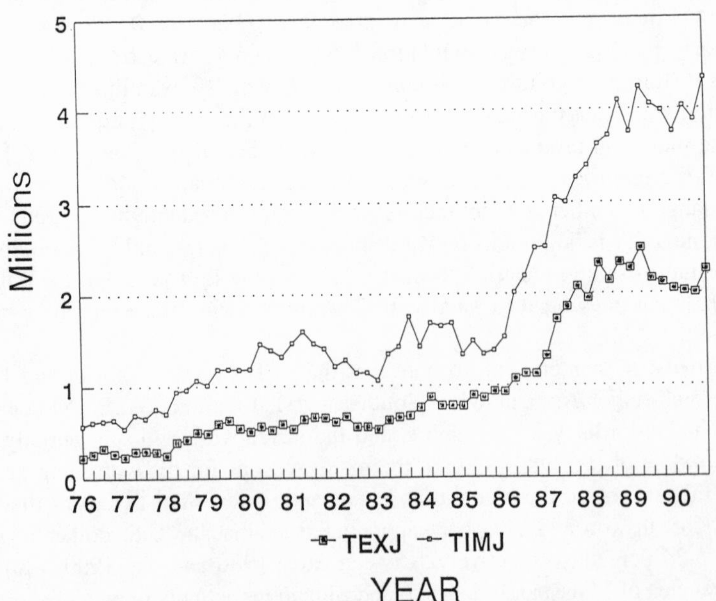

Fig. 4.3 Taiwan-Japan price competition index (PCI) and statistics of Taiwan's exports to (TEXJ) and imports from (TIMJ) Japan (1976:1–1990:4)

4.5 Summary and Conclusion

In this paper we have utilized both nominal and real effective exchange rates to examine Taiwan's external trade activities. In addition, a price-competition index was also calculated to examine Taiwan's bilateral trade activities with its major trading partners. Our empirical results on PCIs and REERs suggest that a sharp increase in Taiwan's competitiveness over the United States was due primarily to the undervaluation of the NT dollar, which inevitably resulted in Taiwan's huge trade surplus over the United States from the early to mid-1980s. This surplus, in turn, not only invited strong protectionism from the United States but also resulted in the rapid accumulation of foreign exchange reserves in Taiwan. How to deal with the enormous resulting inflationary pressure from these reserves then became a major consideration for Taiwan's monetary authorities, and this problem subsequently forced Taiwan to change its low-value-NT export promotion policy into a high-value-NT trade balance policy. As a result, the NT dollar began to appreciate rapidly from early 1987 to 1988, and since mid-1988 the NT dollar has been maintained at about $1 U.S. for less than NT$28, and a new era of a high NT dollar value has thus emerged.

The impact of a vastly appreciated NT dollar on Taiwan's external trade is enormous. From the empirical results in this paper, we found that whether one examines Taiwan's total exports using nominal or real effective exchange rates, the NT dollar will likely have a significant and adverse effect on Taiwan's exports. In addition, a stronger NT dollar was also found to have a significant effect in inducing Taiwan's total imports. Therefore, the rapid appreciation and high value of the NT dollar has become one of the most effective factors for controlling the trade surplus problem in Taiwan. The appreciation of the NT dollar also induced a enormous trade diversification of Taiwan's exports. In this paper we found that the U.S. market accounted for nearly half of Taiwan's exports (49 percent) in the mid-1980s; however in 1991 it accounted for only 29 percent of Taiwan's total exports. One of the major factors that facilitated such a dramatic change was the appreciation of major European currencies such as the German mark, French franc, British pound, and Dutch guilder between the mid-1980s and early 1990. The vast appreciation of the above European currencies, together with relatively low inflation in Taiwan, has helped Taiwan improve its competitiveness over the European market significantly. As a result, the share of the European market held by Taiwan's total exports increased from 10 percent in 1985 to 18 percent in 1991.

In this paper, we also found that it would not be easy for Taiwan to diversify its markets to other areas such as Japan or major ASEAN countries. Our empirical results found that the dramatic increase in Taiwan's PCI with Japan during the period 1985–87 could only help Taiwan control its chronic trade deficit problem with Japan. Between 1987 and mid-1990 there was a downward trend in the PCI that immediately led to a dramatic widening of the trade deficit for Taiwan. Furthermore, our empirical evidence shows that there is a very high correlation between Taiwan's exports to the U.S. and Europe and Taiwan's imports from Japan. Thus the trade imbalance problem between Taiwan and Japan may be less related to exchange rates or relative price changes. Taiwan's overdependence on Japanese parts and intermediate industrial products is perhaps the more relevant factor in this trade imbalance. Finally, this study found that many ASEAN members such as Malaysia, Singapore, and Indonesia have depreciated their currencies considerably against the U.S. dollar, which has certainly dramatically reduced Taiwan's export competitiveness against these countries. Actually, given relative changes in exchange rates between Taiwan and ASEAN countries, as well as the accumulation of huge foreign exchange reserves and the inevitable appreciation of the NT dollar, it is more attractive for Taiwanese enterprises to place more emphasis on outward investment than on exporting. Therefore beginning in the late 1980s Taiwan became one of the major foreign direct investment countries in the region.

Technically speaking, we found that real effective exchange rates can be a fairly good indicator in explaining aggregate trade activities as well as foreign exchange reserve phenomena in Taiwan. Among the various weights and base periods used in calculating real effective exchange rates for the NT dollar, we found that 1980–82 is a better base period than 1979 and bilateral trade values are better than average export values in explaining Taiwan's multilateral trade activities.

Appendix A

Table 4A.1 Price-Competition Indexes (PCIs) between Taiwan and Its Major Western Trading Partners, 1976–90

Year and Quarter	Exchange Rate (NT/US)	United States	Canada	Germany	France	United Kingdom	Netherlands	Italy
1976 1	38.00	99.548	113.067	104.556	118.114	83.255	108.900	98.946
2	38.00	99.953	115.260	105.556	117.534	77.252	107.755	97.118
3	38.00	99.969	115.231	106.484	116.076	77.605	109.669	102.492
4	38.00	100.308	114.056	111.519	114.592	75.570	117.098	105.154
1977 1	38.00	102.164	112.783	112.879	115.720	82.258	118.255	106.617
2	38.00	103.288	112.000	114.118	116.150	85.050	121.723	107.516
3	38.00	103.068	111.186	116.362	116.227	88.354	124.386	109.243
4	38.00	104.975	110.153	121.437	118.212	94.463	127.134	112.735
1978 1	38.00	106.871	111.148	129.763	121.034	102.428	136.943	116.570
2	38.00	107.874	110.505	127.923	124.681	97.569	133.803	116.656
3	36.00	101.819	103.374	123.288	124.199	97.552	127.284	113.564
4	36.00	100.555	100.209	127.719	125.819	98.206	131.077	112.951
1979 1	35.95	101.095	101.115	127.380	128.561	99.334	130.627	113.603
2	36.10	100.658	102.782	122.268	125.012	101.954	122.666	113.261

Table 4A.1 (continued)

Year and Quarter	Exchange Rate (NT/US)	United States	Canada	Germany	France	United Kingdom	Netherlands	Italy
3	36.03	98.661	99.795	123.234	126.315	107.689	122.844	116.249
4	36.03	98.727	99.146	123.982	127.089	103.242	122.208	118.146
1980 1	36.06	95.530	97.055	117.279	120.898	104.218	118.306	115.905
2	36.01	92.945	93.080	112.010	114.498	104.652	112.108	110.776
3	35.93	93.790	94.520	112.286	114.900	108.716	114.051	111.772
4	36.01	93.414	92.967	103.083	108.075	107.508	104.463	105.174
1981 1	36.35	95.136	93.681	95.603	98.568	105.627	96.066	98.791
2	36.36	97.555	95.586	90.060	92.616	98.499	88.737	91.896
3	37.91	101.314	99.548	88.743	92.891	90.865	88.002	91.590
4	37.84	101.538	102.838	97.888	97.812	95.375	97.924	97.026
1982 1	38.13	103.866	104.372	96.585	96.011	97.329	96.439	96.305
2	39.39	107.039	106.361	99.054	96.924	98.179	97.917	96.748
3	39.87	110.117	109.353	98.201	91.470	98.439	98.001	96.821
4	39.91	110.247	111.253	97.741	90.714	95.193	97.837	97.174
1983 1	40.04	111.499	113.519	102.365	96.407	90.554	100.731	102.439
2	40.20	111.928	114.982	99.478	92.511	93.818	96.442	98.646
3	40.19	112.715	115.558	94.020	89.759	91.509	92.673	94.434
4	40.27	113.416	115.524	93.494	90.820	90.356	91.533	94.580
1984 1	39.92	113.017	114.099	92.150	90.967	88.323	90.765	94.009
2	39.63	112.205	110.741	91.364	92.245	86.605	90.167	94.091
3	39.18	112.186	109.809	85.313	87.781	81.095	84.202	88.900
4	39.47	113.279	111.168	83.286	86.389	77.777	81.760	87.345
1985 1	39.54	114.034	110.572	79.559	83.235	73.158	77.771	84.652
2	40.00	116.806	112.393	86.403	90.987	85.937	84.700	90.737
3	40.40	117.708	114.955	94.999	98.612	95.969	92.994	95.729
4	39.83	117.570	113.321	103.891	105.360	100.440	100.618	103.856
1986 1	38.77	114.841	111.519	112.548	114.440	101.305	108.199	112.200
2	38.09	110.911	109.610	114.128	114.466	105.724	110.933	112.600
3	36.72	107.215	106.624	118.350	117.284	101.915	115.172	116.300
4	36.29	106.949	106.712	120.127	115.891	97.919	118.522	120.200
1987 1	34.26	102.865	105.458	124.025	118.825	101.701	122.947	123.500
2	31.08	96.376	98.822	116.134	114.543	100.969	115.380	115.500
3	30.09	95.137	98.679	111.754	109.943	97.641	110.725	111.100
4	28.55	91.444	96.193	115.755	111.652	102.229	114.049	114.500
1988 1	28.64	93.170	101.067	119.199	115.266	107.325	117.651	118.500
2	28.89	93.954	104.680	116.873	116.133	110.835	115.353	116.100
3	28.97	85.025	95.141	95.885	93.526	92.067	95.485	95.800
4	28.13	84.427	95.837	100.208	96.065	97.116	99.479	101.400
1989 1	27.17	90.554	103.298	102.446	98.654	100.968	101.984	105.700
2	25.91	89.503	100.395	95.822	95.175	92.362	96.007	100.300
3	25.60	89.775	101.636	97.144	95.330	92.394	97.103	103.100
4	27.17	96.476	109.407	111.185	107.388	99.477	110.477	116.400
1990 1	26.41	94.914	105.206	115.704	113.665	102.392	114.765	120.100
2	27.20	96.931	108.950	119.874	121.875	108.059	118.935	125.100
3	27.30	96.297	108.011	123.796	124.928	118.331	123.209	127.800
4	27.11	102.114	111.735	136.238	134.625	128.858	134.724	137.400

Appendix B

Appendix B Price-Competition Indexes (PCIs) between Taiwan and Its Major Asian Trading Partners, 1976–90

Year and Quarter	Japan	Korea	Hong Kong	Australia	Singapore	Thailand	Malaysia	Indonesia
1976 1	93.781	92.775	109.107	103.248	91.754	103.534	106.557	88.781
2	95.029	93.529	108.730	103.360	91.878	100.308	105.891	91.033
3	98.258	94.080	111.865	104.829	91.858	100.337	106.657	93.552
4	97.774	95.120	116.147	99.474	93.100	100.684	105.356	96.641
1977 1	100.415	97.627	119.361	96.572	94.524	102.235	110.965	100.791
2	103.115	98.577	117.857	98.657	93.879	105.053	110.620	101.733
3	105.715	100.155	119.589	100.336	94.449	108.306	110.944	102.748
4	113.704	102.521	121.534	104.231	97.309	109.428	114.755	106.141
1978 1	116.860	106.736	123.652	106.797	99.124	110.672	121.654	107.671
2	122.722	107.066	121.711	106.652	98.117	110.506	117.842	105.798
3	128.576	101.905	113.464	102.710	94.902	104.911	112.881	100.304
4	124.819	101.224	109.787	102.029	95.587	102.773	114.694	85.527
1979 1	116.750	101.077	105.365	101.344	95.618	100.049	115.239	83.157
2	108.178	103.998	103.275	99.753	97.504	99.781	110.152	88.001
3	107.217	107.954	104.554	100.012	101.010	101.849	107.637	91.056
4	98.998	107.185	104.624	97.386	99.592	101.979	102.784	94.002
1980 1	96.233	96.379	99.312	93.965	100.447	100.780	100.792	92.363
2	99.890	97.765	99.173	93.384	97.166	100.321	95.621	92.991
3	103.707	96.024	99.198	97.174	99.184	99.547	96.296	93.477
4	104.699	92.803	95.907	97.295	98.261	98.311	92.573	92.511
1981 1	105.466	94.429	96.050	98.094	100.633	100.184	96.435	95.991
2	99.906	98.145	94.698	97.938	99.208	101.545	93.619	97.056
3	98.967	102.903	91.489	102.734	99.733	97.255	95.337	100.564
4	102.178	102.683	102.237	104.263	101.470	97.027	99.532	101.628
1982 1	100.133	102.720	102.744	103.277	100.742	98.043	105.445	105.388
2	98.822	103.399	107.326	105.186	101.813	100.635	107.387	108.204
3	96.464	104.541	105.585	103.779	102.271	102.490	108.455	110.670
4	96.082	104.356	104.308	102.342	100.601	103.628	108.227	109.220
1983 1	104.878	104.684	104.164	104.130	103.969	104.800	117.279	108.204
2	103.148	101.733	100.095	99.389	101.769	105.601	115.975	91.884
3	100.899	99.037	89.754	100.786	100.654	107.322	113.851	92.573
4	103.970	97.991	97.930	105.403	100.865	107.547	114.106	93.602
1984 1	104.003	96.863	97.919	107.505	100.098	102.544	117.903	95.038
2	103.164	95.582	97.807	104.511	99.379	100.199	117.481	94.047
3	98.246	95.090	98.989	98.664	96.732	100.081	115.711	92.377
4	98.174	95.355	100.741	101.680	96.395	90.578	114.021	92.589
1985 1	95.478	93.977	102.878	91.813	95.563	83.890	109.420	91.125
2	99.232	93.117	106.953	86.261	96.420	87.682	114.507	92.383
3	104.338	92.961	109.344	93.207	96.471	91.170	116.523	93.953
4	116.021	91.945	108.035	92.048	98.307	92.600	117.305	94.042
1986 1	124.190	90.724	107.940	94.618	89.1659	91.070	115.088	93.372
2	129.940	87.316	107.600	94.108	78.5748	89.070	107.831	90.078
3	134.290	86.189	105.470	81.761	76.3657	87.600	104.160	78.425
4	128.330	86.250	105.780	86.932	78.5781	87.040	103.921	64.529

Table 4B.1 (continued)

Year and Quarter	Japan	Korea	Hong Kong	Australia	Singapore	Thailand	Malaysia	Indonesia
1987 1	126.840	83.603	101.700	87.087	80.5329	84.180	102.211	66.602
2	124.530	80.559	95.660	86.629	76.4983	80.970	96.413	62.619
3	119.560	80.708	94.530	86.001	75.8724	81.480	92.534	62.119
4	123.300	78.330	92.550	82.523	73.3223	81.330	89.385	60.719
1988 1	130.970	83.514	94.540	87.468	74.6215	84.110	89.286	62.238
2	132.040	87.009	96.210	95.440	75.3461	84.930	88.353	62.178
3	111.670	79.619	87.450	88.734	65.0962	75.730	77.979	55.410
4	116.840	81.708	87.910	93.175	64.8860	76.310	76.516	54.615
1989 1	120.170	88.481	95.280	100.319	71.8691	79.830	79.402	57.520
2	111.450	87.929	95.150	91.643	70.9740	78.450	78.017	56.957
3	109.730	88.212	97.610	92.011	70.0972	80.370	79.688	57.393
4	116.610	94.347	105.950	101.913	76.5826	84.850	85.526	61.779
1990 1	109.840	89.684	105.220	98.181	76.0003	82.650	83.561	60.937
2	107.890	91.110	111.300	102.098	75.6892	84.920	86.201	61.034
3	112.505	89.520	111.470	106.032	82.1603	84.910	84.470	65.763
4	129.500	94.595	117.140	108.563	93.1283	93.500	88.314	69.142

References

Bomhoff, E. J., and K. G. Koedijk. 1988. Bilateral exchange rates and risk premia. *Journal of International Money and Finance* 7(2).

Citrin, D. 1985. Exchange rate changes and exports of selected Japanese industries. *IMF Staff Papers* 32(3).

Corker, R. 1989. External adjustment and the strong Yen—Recent Japanese experience. *IMF Staff Papers* 36(2).

Dornbusch, R., and S. Fischer. 1980. Exchange rates and the current account. *American Economic Review* 70: 960–71.

Gotur, P. 1985. Effects of exchange rate volatility on trade: Some further evidence. *IMF Staff Papers* 32(3).

Grauwe, P. 1988. Exchange rate variability and the slowdown in growth of international trade. *IMF Staff Papers* 35(1).

Himarios, D. 1985. The effects of devaluation on the trade balance: A critical view and reexamination of Miles's "New Results." *Journal of International Money and Finance* 4(4).

Hogan, K., M. Melvin, and D. J. Roberts. 1991. Trade balance news and exchange rates: Is there a policy signal? *Journal of International Money and Finance* 10 (Supplement).

Horne, J. 1983. The asset market model of the balance of payments and the exchange rate: A survey of empirical evidence. *Journal of International Money and Finance* 2(2).

Koedijk, K., and P. Schotman. 1989. Dominant real exchange rate movement. *Journal of International Money and Finance* 8(4).

Krueger, A. O. 1978. *Foreign trade regimes and economic development: Liberalization attempts and consequences.* Cambridge, Mass.: Ballinger.

Lothian, J. R. 1986. Real dollar exchange rates under the Bretton-Woods and floating exchange-rate regimes. *Journal of International Money and Finance* 5(4).

Maciejewski, E. B. 1983. "Real" effective exchange rate indices: A re-examination of the major conceptual and methodological issues. *IMF Staff Papers* 30(3).

Miles, M. A. 1979. The effects of devaluation on the trade balance and the balance of payments: Some new results. *Journal of Political Economy* 87(3).

Spitaller, E. 1980. Short-run effect of exchange rate changes on terms of trade and trade balance. *IMF Staff Papers* 27(2).

Thursby, M. C., and J. G. Thursby. 1985. The uncertainty effect of floating exchange rates—Empirical evidence on international trade flows. In *Exchange rates, trade, and the U.S. economy,* ed. S. W. Arndt, R. J. Sweeney, and T. D. Willett, chap. 10. Cambridge, Mass.: Ballinger.

Veld, J. W. 1991. Fundamental balance and equilibrium exchange rates. *Journal of International Money and Finance* 10(2).

Comment Hideki Funatsu

This paper studies the effects of a change in the NT dollar on Taiwan's aggregate import and export using a simple econometric analysis. A change in the value of import was explained by changes in domestic income level, nominal or real effective exchange rate, and relative wage rate. For the export function, explanatory variables are the weighted average of national incomes of trading partners, nominal or real exchange rate, and relative wage rate. The final section adds a calculation of the price-competition index, defined as the relative wholesale price index multiplied by the relative exchange rate with a trading partner. The author's main argument, based on the empirical results, is that a rapid appreciation of the NT dollar against the U.S. dollar during the mid-1980s caused a shift in Taiwan's exports from the U.S. market to European markets and that the trade imbalance with Japan is not related to exchange rate. I find this paper quite interesting because it touches upon an important policy problem most East Asian countries faced during the 1980s. As a matter of fact, reading this paper reminded me of a 1987 white paper issued by the Japanese Ministry of International Trade and Industry (MITI). At that time, the effect of a rapid appreciation of Japanese yen on the huge trade surplus with the United States was a big issue. That white paper carried out a similar empirical analysis and concluded that Japanese export to the United States is so income-elastic that changing the exchange rate alone cannot correct a trade surplus problem. They advocated diversification of exports to various markets and division of labor with East Asian countries by promoting direct investment. So I can appreciate one of the author's statements in the conclusion that the "trade imbalance problem between Taiwan and Japan may be less related to exchange rates or relative price changes." I also agree with the author on most of his other

Hideki Funatsu is associate professor of economics at Otaru University of Commerce.

points. Nevertheless, in order to sharpen the argument and provide a possible direction in which to extend this interesting research, I would like to make comments on the following four points.

The Interpretation of the Effect of Relative Labor Productivity on Taiwan's Export to the United States

The result reported in equations (3) and (4) of table 4.3 is that relative real wages between Taiwan and the United States have a negative effect on Taiwan's export to the United States. San provides three explanations for this phenomenon, namely, a shift to the European market, protectionism in the United States, and outward direct investments to other East Asian countries. I would like to suggest another explanation: Japanese direct investment. As San states in his conclusion, Taiwan's export relied on Japanese industrial equipment and intermediate industrial products. Therefore, some significant part of the factor content of Taiwan's exports to the United States might be intermediate input imported from Japan and also direct investment made by Japanese firms. If this is the case, an increase in the relative real wage rate in Taiwan reduces its attractiveness as an export site to the U.S. market. Japanese firms will reduce export volume from the high-wage country and move their export base to a lower-wage country. In order to obtain a more convincing result, estimation of a single equation will not be sufficient. We may have to look simultaneously at a change in the direct investment pattern.

In order to analyze such a problem, it would be helpful to use a simple trade model of duopoly. Winston W. Chang and Jae-Cheal Kim (1989) have presented an interesting theoretical model that emphasizes the leader–follower relation of monopoly exports of two countries. Japan is the leader in exporting manufacturing goods to the third market, say, the United States, and Taiwan is the follower in the sense that it must import an important part of the good from the leader. The leader can choose to export directly to the third market or indirectly through the follower. In such a model, exchange rates among the three countries affect trade flow in a manner different from that described by the traditional approach.

Interpretation of the Immediate Effect of a Change in Exchange Rate on Export and Import

An appreciation of the NT dollar was found to lead to an increase in total exports in the initial period. San's explanation is that Taiwanese exporters expect further appreciation so they are likely to deliver their shipments earlier than expected. Can we interpret the result simply in the following way? The immediate effect of appreciation of a domestic currency on the value of export denominated in a foreign currency is positive simply because trade volume cannot adjust so quickly. With some time lags, a higher price in the foreign market will reduce export volume. Generally speaking, the effect of exchange rate on the total value of export or import could be decomposed into two parts:

the effect on the foreign price and the effect on the volume of trade. It will be interesting to see how exchange rate changes affect the volume of Taiwanese trade with the United States and Europe.

Does Exchange Rate Fluctuation Matter?

As economic integration in Europe keeps a rapid pace, European economists are talking about the creation of a new central bank in Europe and a possible movement toward a single currency. The medium-of-exchange role of money is emphasized once again. A stable currency provides externality to a macroeconomy. During the 1980s, most EC members except the United Kingdom participated into the European Exchange Rate Mechanism. Because of the low inflation rate in West Germany before unification, the values of European currencies are much more stable than the U.S. dollar. In addition to the NT dollar's appreciation against the U.S. dollar, this low risk factor in trading with Europe might be another reason for the shift of export from the U.S. market to the European market. If we include the variance of exchange rate fluctuation among the explanatory variables of the estimation equation, we may see whether this risk factor has any effect on the total value of export or not.

Inclusion of a Supply-Side Factor in the Estimation

During the mid-1980s, the price of crude oil fell sharply. Resource-poor countries like Japan and Taiwan certainly benefited from the falling oil price. In the early 1980s, more than 20 percent of the total value of Taiwan's import was the bill for crude oil. This has steadily declined through the 1980s and the ratio was less than 5 percent in 1990. In order to take account of such a factor and carry out a more rigorous estimation of the import and export functions, it would be appropriate to use a simple duality framework. This approach may enable us to include oil price as an explanatory variable in addition to the productivity of labor. Hiroshi Yoshikawa (1990) wrote a short paper which studies the equilibrium yen/dollar exchange rate using such an approach. This approach would also be useful in incorporating the effect of intermediate input import from Japan on the export performance of the Taiwanese economy.

References

Chang, Winston W., and Jae-Cheal Kim. 1989. Competition in quality-differentiated products and optimal trade policy. *Keio Economic Studies* 26 (1).

Yoshikawa, Hiroshi. 1990. On the equilibrium yen-dollar rate. *American Economic Review* 80 (June).

Comment Chong-Hyun Nam

San Gee has given us an excellent paper. One learns a lot from such empirical work. All the econometric work was carefully designed, and the estimation produced powerful results, as one would expect from a casual income-and-price-elasticity model. The highlight of the paper is its confirmation that movement in the relative price variable is crucially important in explaining changes in Taiwan's trade flows. The estimates were consistent whether nominal or real effective exchange rates were used. The price competition index (PCI) also worked very well in explaining movement in bilateral trade flows, except with Japan. I have only three comments on the paper.

First of all, I thought it would have been very useful if San had noted at the outset what kinds of exchange rate systems were at work during his sample period and how they might have influenced his estimation results. What I have in mind is that the type of exchange rate regime could have had an important bearing on the exogeneity of exchange rate movement, leading to the possibility of simultaneous equation bias in the estimation.

According to Chen, Shive, and Chu's paper (chap. 9, this volume), although Taiwan switched to a flexible exchange rate system in 1979, the exchange rate was virtually fixed by Central Bank intervention until 1985. Under a fixed exchange rate regime, Taiwan's trade surplus may be interpreted as driven by an undervalued NT dollar, but under a floating exchange rate regime Taiwan's trade surplus might have been driven by movements in the capital account. Therefore Taiwan's trade flows might have been influenced by variables other than those included in the estimation equation.

My second comment concerns an estimation result that is contrary to a common expectation. That is, an improvement in Taiwan's labor productivity relative to that of the United States leads to a decline, rather than an increase, in Taiwan's exports to the United States. Why?

San proposes a number of possible reasons, including, for example, diversification of export markets into EC countries, rising U.S. nontariff barriers, shifts in production locations of some labor-intensive products to other Asian nations. But I wonder if it is, at least partly, due to some measurement error involved in measuring relative productivity. San seems to use relative productivity and relative real wage rate as perfect substitutes for each other. But I learned from Korea's experience that movement in the real wage rate can be made quite separately from movement in labor productivity, at least in the short run, as in quarterly data. Furthermore, frequent changes in exchange rate may help amplify the short-run discrepancy between real wage and labor productivity. So, I wonder if one might want to try to use a sort of profitability index, like a differential between real wage and physical productivity in the short run, on behalf of real wage or labor productivity.

Chong-Hyun Nam is professor of economics at Korea University.

My final comment involves the possibility of an aggregation problem. I noticed that the PCI works very well in explaining the bilateral trade balance in general, but not for trade with Japan. As San indicated in his paper, the bilateral trade balance between Taiwan and Japan is apparently driven by something other than changes in exchange rates or PCI, and therefore a different model is called for. This suggests that including Japan in the data aggregation may cause an aggregation bias in the estimation. Thus, it may be useful to check the consistency of the estimates by other estimations at a disaggregated level by country, too.

5 Capital Mobility in Korea since the Early 1980s: Comparison with Japan and Taiwan

Sung Hee Jwa

5.1 Introduction

After two decades of rapid economic growth characterized by heavy regulatory intervention in the allocation of financial and physical resources, the Korean government in the early 1980s began to realize the limits of active government intervention and to introduce private sector initiatives in economic management. The active role of the private sector became inevitable for further, sustained economic development.

Government intervention in the 1970s culminated in the policy to promote heavy and chemical industry (HCI) by channeling almost all available resources into this sector. As a part of the HCI policy, the Korean financial sector was treated only as a means of allocating available financial resources to the priority sector. Toward the end of the 1970s, the Korean economy began to show structural weaknesses on many fronts: high inflation, real appreciation of the won, chronic balance of payments deficits, signs of overinvestment in the HCIs, and the dominance of large business groups over small- and medium-size enterprises (SMEs) due to the HCI drive. The second oil price shock further aggravated Korea's worsening economic situation.

Against this background, the government decided to reduce the degree of its intervention in the economy and launched a comprehensive program of economic liberalization and opening in the early 1980s. As a part of this reform plan, financial liberalization and internationalization policies were adopted to invite competition into the domestic financial sector and to improve its efficiency.

Sung Hee Jwa is a fellow at the Korea Development Institute.

The author would like to thank Kazuo Ueda, Pochin Chen, Takatoshi Ito, Anne Krueger, and other conference participants for useful comments. The author also would like to express his appreciation for the research assistance of Junhe Rhee, Jaekyun Yoo, and Steve D. Sun.

Since the early 1980s, the Korean government has tried to relax various controls on capital flows gradually and slowly, so as not to disturb the domestic equilibrium. The controls on inflows and outflows have depended on the balance of payments and debt situation and exchange rate movement and have been given emphasis alternately, consistent with domestic macroeconomic policies. At times, the short-run considerations of macroeconomic management have dominated consideration of the long-run benefits of free capital flows, making it appear that the process of liberalization had been reversed.

Recently, there have been many international as well as domestic discussions on the necessity of capital flow liberalization in Korea. Domestically, a consensus on the need for liberalizing capital flow seems to have been reached, not only to realize the potential gains from the free flow of capital but also to prepare for the Uruguay Round negotiation, to join the OECD in the near future, and to meet the pressure from the United States for further market opening. However, the speed of liberalization is still the subject of lively discussions. Domestic policymakers seem to favor a gradual financial liberalization approach once domestic markets are liberalized.

The purpose of this paper is to provide an overview of Korea's experience of capital control and decontrol since the early 1980s and to quantify the extent of Korea's capital mobility vis-à-vis that of Japan and Taiwan. The paper is structured as follows: In section 5.2, the pattern of Korea's capital account controls will be described, and in section 5.3 the impediments to capital account liberalization will be outlined. Sections 5.2 and 5.3 are meant to be a broad overview of Korea's capital flows and related policies as a preliminary discussion for the in-depth analysis in section 5.4. Section 5.4 will analyze and evaluate the extent of Korea's capital account openness, in comparison with Taiwan and Japan, utilizing various measures and techniques. Section 5.5 will conclude the paper with some observations.

5.2 Pattern of Korea's Capital Control

5.2.1 Development of Korea's Capital Account

The structure of Korea's capital account is illustrated in table 5.1. Concerning the long-term capital transaction on the liability side, public borrowing was the major source of capital inflow in the first half of the 1980s, but in the second half, it switched to become the major source of outflow. The same trend can be observed in commercial borrowings. This trend seems to reflect the stance of capital control policy, which encouraged an inflow during the current account deficit of the former period and an outflow during the current account surplus of the latter period, as will be discussed in the next section.

The role of foreign direct investment (FDI) in Korea increased gradually over the same period and is expected to play a bigger role in the future as further deregulations on FDI are forthcoming. Its role as a source of inflow,

Table 5.1 Accounts of Korea's Capital Transactions (%)

Transactions	1981	1985	1987	1991
Long-term capital transactions				
Liabilities	100	100	−100	100
Public loans	48.7	12.1	−25.3	−10.6
Commercial loans	9.0	−6.2	−18.8	−10.1
Direct investments	3.6	8.8	10.9	20.9
Portfolio investments	2.1	37.1	−2.1	55.4
Long-term trade credits	−0.4	−2.4	0.8	12.2
Bank loans by development institutions	37.8	36.2	−64.4	17.9
Long-term foreign currency borrowings by foreign exchange act; Merchant banking corporation's borrowing; Foreign military sales loans; Long-term foreign currency bills sold; Import by lease under the condition of ownership transfer	−0.8	14.4	−1.2	14.4
Assets	100	−100	−100	−100
Public loans	0	0	0	−0.4
Direct investments	−182.3	−2.2	−57.4	−89.1
Portfolio investments	0	0	0	−2.5
Medium- and long-term trade credits	404.3	−60.9	130.8	54.8
Subscriptions to international institutions	−84.4	−1.3	−8.9	−1.4
Long-term imports prepayments; Long-term lending of development institutions and merchant banking corporations	−37.6	−35.6	−164.4	−61.3
Short-term capital transactions				
Liabilities	−100	−100	−100	100
Short-term trade credit	18.6	−61.5	−401.5	−19.3
Borrowings of crude oil import funds	4.6	−34.4	−92.6	−22.8
Advances under red-clause L/C; Exports on simple remittance basis; Domestic import usance sold; Short-term foreign currency bill sold; Short-term foreign currency borrowings by foreign exchange act; Short-term borrowings of development institutions and merchant banking corporations	−123.2	−4.1	394.1	142.1
Assets	100	−100	−100	−100
Short-term export credits	90.7	−99.3	−300	−18.8
Short-term imports prepayments; Short-term private foreign currency deposit; Short-term lending of development institution; Short-term lending of merchant banking corporations	9.3	−0.7	200	−81.2

Source: Bank of Korea, Monthly Balance of Payments (Seoul, various issues).
Note: Negative entries record outflow.

especially, increased in the second half of the 1980s. Opposite to this trend, the reliance on development institutions for bank loans declined and will be further reduced in the future, while portfolio investment, which has been another source of capital inflow, is expected to continue its rising trend into the next decade. Portfolio investment will become increasingly more important as the opening of the Korean stock market in January 1992 begins to take full effect.

On the asset side, direct overseas investment has been a major source of capital outflow and is currently on a rising trend. It reached 89.1 percent of the total net accumulation in 1991, and further increase is expected as Korea regains its current account balance. Therefore, it will continue to serve as a major source of outflow. However, overseas portfolio investments, which had been almost zero, have begun appearing in recent years. They too are expected to increase as capital flow liberalization proceeds. The repayment receipts of long- and medium-term trade credit has been a source of capital inflow. The long-term lending of development institutions will rise as Korea increases its efforts to supply funds to developing countries.

Concerning short-term capital transactions, short-term trade credit, which was once an important source of import financing, is now a major capital outflow item. In recent years, Korea has been repaying short-term trade credits. On the asset side, Korea has been providing substantial short-term credit to importers of Korean products.

5.2.2 Patterns of Korea's Capital Control

According to an OECD research paper (OECD 1990), the patterns of capital control for all OECD countries in the past 25 years were influenced by the balance of payments situation, exchange rate movements, and the development of monetary management. When countries experienced balance of payments deficits, they tended to rely on restrictions on capital outflow. Also, in the case of monetary management, capital inflows were restricted if they were perceived as making monetary management difficult. Depending on the behavior of these three factors, capital controls were sometimes placed on inflow and at other times on outflow.

The Korean case follows this example. During the 1980s, the pattern of capital control was determined by a consideration of the balance of payments, exchange rate, and monetary management. In the early 1980s, Korea faced balance of payments and foreign debt problems and, thus, restricted capital outflows. In the latter half of the 1980s, when it recorded current account surpluses, Korea had difficulty controlling the monetary aggregate. There were also very strong pressures for capital inflow to appreciate the exchange rate, which in turn would have adversely affected export competitiveness. Thus, Korea placed strong restrictions on capital inflow.

Policies dealing with decontrol of the capital account were strongly influenced by Korea's macroeconomic situation, especially by the current account and debt situation in the first half of the 1980s and by the concern over monetary controls and exchange rate movements in the latter half. In the early 1980s, the government was strictly concerned about accumulating foreign debt and increasing current account deficits, and therefore restricted capital outflow but encouraged capital inflow. On the other hand, in the second half of the decade, the government was concerned about controlling liquidity and avoiding exchange rate appreciation and so restricted capital inflow but encourage capital outflow.

The following section will discuss and evaluate the pattern of Korea's capital control, dividing the 1980s into the two periods of the early and late 1980s.

Early 1980s: Outflow Controlled and Inflow Encouraged

The early 1980s witnessed chronic current account deficits, capital account surpluses, and a continued depreciation of the Korean won (see table 5.2). The international debt crisis disproportionately affected Korea, which had accumulated a large foreign debt (see table 5.3). This foreign debt continued to increase at a rapid pace, reaching its peak, almost 40 percent of GNP, in 1985. However, while the real interest rate differential was favorable to Korea for the period 1981–85, the uncovered interest rate differential was negative on average (see fig. 5.1). Even when the real interest rate was higher, no real incentives existed for foreign capital to come to Korea, because of exchange rate expectations. Despite this, Korea witnessed a large capital inflow during this period, because it had placed very strong regulations on capital outflow, thus leading to the eventual net capital inflow.

Korea has been a net capital importer ever since its economic development process began. The country has relied mainly on foreign borrowing rather than on foreign direct or portfolio investment as a method of financing. During the first half of the 1980s, public borrowing financed more than 50 percent of the total capital account surplus on average. In addition, however, foreign direct investment was also given a fair amount of emphasis as a financing source. In July 1984, the regulators of foreign direct investment adopted a negative list system, which greatly helped activate direct investment by nonresidents. (See app. B for changes in capital flow regulation).

However, the policy mix during this period was very inconsistent. If Korea had really wanted to induce a large capital inflow, the domestic interest rate should have been maintained at a higher level. At the time, the uncovered interest rate parity was unfavorable to Korea. Although the real interest rate was positive, it was smaller than in the latter part of the 1980s. This pattern of real interest rate and uncovered interest rate differentials did not fully match the Korean government's intention to control capital at that time.

Late 1980s: Inflow Controlled and Outflow Decontrolled

From 1986 to 1989, Korea enjoyed the so-called three lows: low international interest rates, low oil prices, and low dollar and won exchange rates vis-

Table 5.2 **Korea's Capital Account and Other Economic Indicators**

	1980	1981	1982	1983	1984	1985	Average 1981–85
Current account balance (million $)	−5,320.70	−4,646.00	−2,649.60	−1,606.00	−1,372.60	−887.40	−2,232.32
(% of GNP)	(−8.8)	(−6.95)	(−3.71)	(−2.02)	(−1.58)	(−0.99)	
Capital account balance	3,801.00	2,759.60	1,233.90	2,163.90	1,309.50	513.30	1,596.04
(% of GNP)	(6.29)	(4.13)	(1.73)	(2.72)	(1.51)	(0.57)	
Long-term capital balance	1,856.50	2,841.90	1,230.30	1,270.40	2,067.40	1,100.80	1,702.16
Liabilities	2,164.30	2,827.80	1,726.70	2,087.50	1,964.70	2,644.20	2,250.18
Public loans	1,261.40	1,378.40	1,493.40	950.40	764.20	319.60	981.20
Commercial loans	588.00	253.30	−128.00	−155.20	−250.00	−163.30	−80.64
Assets[a]	−307.80	14.10	−496.40	−817.10	102.70	−1,543.40	−540.02
Short-term capital balance	1,944.50	−82.30	3.60	893.50	−757.90	−587.50	−106.12
Liabilities	2,033.80	−94.10	−45.00	815.60	−858.60	−485.90	−133.60
Assets[a]	−89.30	11.80	48.60	77.90	100.70	−101.60	27.48
Won/dollar exchange rate	607.40	681.00	731.10	775.80	806.00	870.00	772.78
(rate of depreciation; %)	(25.50)	(12.10)	(7.40)	(6.10)	(3.90)	(7.90)	(7.48)
Real effective exchange rate[b]	82.20	79.40	78.90	84.20	86.90	92.40	84.36
(rate of depreciation; %)	(2.20)	(−3.40)	(−0.70)	(6.80)	(3.10)	(6.40)	(2.44)
Yield to corporate bonds (%)	30.10	24.40	17.30	14.20	14.10	14.20	16.84
Inflation in GNP deflator (%)	24.08	17.38	7.50	5.16	3.64	3.97	7.53
Real interest rate differentials (%)[c]	0.68	−3.65	3.10	4.30	5.19	6.93	3.17
Uncovered interest rate differentials (%)[d]	−15.59	1.69	−3.71	−2.06	0.10	−2.70	−1.34
Capital flows as a percentage of trade (%)[e]							
Overall capital account	21.45	12.88	13.76	7.80	6.50	9.61	10.11

Portfolio investment	0.10	0.14	0.03	0.39	0.62	1.86	0.61
Foreign direct investment	0.05	0.32	0.48	0.41	0.27	0.51	0.40
M_2 (averages; billion won)	10,764.10	13,714.80	17,575.20	21,005.00	23,262.20	26,015.30	20,314.50
Change (%)	25.80	27.40	28.10	19.50	10.70	11.80	19.50
MSBs issued (billion won)	529.70	1,660.40	927.30	3,360.00	4,458.50	1,899.90	2,461.22
(% of M_2)	(4.92)	(12.11)	(5.28)	(16.00)	(19.17)	(7.30)	(12.12)
Net foreign assets (billion won)	−597.10	−2,277.70	−4,326.40	−5,082.30	−6,094.70	−7,696.02	−5,095.46
(% of M_2)	(−5.55)	(−16.61)	(−24.62)	(−24.20)	(−26.20)	(−29.58)	(−25.08)
Real GNP growth rate (%)	−3.70	5.90	7.20	12.60	9.30	7.00	8.40

	1986	1987	1988	1989	1990	Average 1986–90	1991
Current account balance (million $)	4,617.00	9,853.90	14,160.70	5,054.60	−2,179.40	6,301.36	−8,827.2
(% of GNP)	(4.49)	(7.64)	(8.20)	(2.39)	(−0.9)		−3.14
Capital account balance	−2,374.00	−5,842.80	−1,396.50	−3,302.20	3,881.20	−1,806.86	4,711.6
(% of GNP)	(−2.31)	(−4.53)	(−0.81)	(−1.56)	(1.60)		(1.68)
Long-term capital balance	−1,981.90	−5,835.80	−2,732.80	−3,362.50	547.50	−2,673.10	4,185.8
Liabilities	−336.20	−5,517.10	−2,354.80	−1,958.00	1,311.40	−1,770.94	5,708.8
Public loan	−126.30	−1,397.00	−1,129.40	−1,067.30	−816.60	−907.32	−621.4
Commercial loan	94.40	−1,036.20	−1,172.50	−824.70	−764.60	−740.72	−557.6
Assets[a]	−1,645.70	−318.70	−378.00	−1,404.50	−763.90	−902.16	−1,523.0
Short-term capital balance	−392.10	−7.00	1,336.30	60.30	3,333.70	866.24	41.2
Liabilities	−402.60	−6.80	1,544.10	413.40	3,665.40	1,042.70	532.2
Assets[a]	10.50	−0.20	−207.80	−353.10	−331.70	−176.46	−491.0
Won/dollar exchange rate	881.50	822.60	731.50	671.50	707.80	762.98	733.4
(rate of depreciation; %)	(1.30)	(−6.60)	(−11.10)	(−8.20)	(5.40)	(−3.84)	(3.62)
Real effective exchange rate[b]	105.80	106.10	98.80	89.60	93.80	98.82	95.20
(rate of depreciation; %)	(14.40)	(0.40)	(−6.90)	(−9.30)	(4.70)	(0.66)	(1.49)

(continued)

Table 5.2 (continued)

	1980	1981	1982	1983	1984	1985	Average 1981–85
Yield to corporate bonds (%)	12.80	12.80	14.50	15.20	16.40	14.34	18.8
Inflation in GNP deflator (%)	2.83	3.38	5.85	5.12	10.68	5.58	11.23
Real interest rate differentials (%)[c]	5.08	6.25	3.46	5.08	4.93	4.95	7.39
Uncovered interest rate differentials (%)[d]	8.37	12.98	20.12	9.24	1.94	10.73	7.66
Capital flows as a percentage of trade (%)[e]							
Overall capital account	6.40	13.01	12.58	4.86	6.82	8.73	—
Portfolio investment	0.47	0.13	0.45	0.07	0.77	0.38	—
Foreign direct investment	0.86	0.92	0.95	0.90	1.20	0.97	—
M_2 (averages; billion won)	30,396.20	36,119.60	42,893.00	50,793.10	61,576.10	44,355.60	73,024.0
Change (%)	16.80	18.80	18.80	18.40	21.20	18.80	18.6
MSBs issued (billion won)	4,285.20	9,006.70	16,297.20	18,003.10	15,611.50	12,640.74	13,862.3
(% of M_2)	(14.10)	(24.94)	(38.00)	(35.44)	(25.35)	(28.50)	(31.25)
Net foreign assets (billion won)	−6,127.70	−1,605.10	7,251.20	9,104.00	10,139.70	3,752.42	8,075.8
(% of M_2)	(−20.16)	(−4.44)	(16.91)	(17.92)	(16.47)	(8.46)	(11.06)
Real GNP growth rate (%)	12.90	13.00	12.40	6.80	9.30	10.88	8.4

Sources: IMF, *International Financial Statistics* (Washington, D.C.); IMF, *Balance of Payments Statistics Yearbook* (Washington, D.C.); Korea Development Institute database (Seoul).

[a]Negative entry records increase.

[b]Calculated based on a trade-weighted currency basket of Korea's seven major trading partners (United States, Japan, Germany, United Kingdom, France, the Netherlands, Canada) deflated by the wholesale price indices. The base period is 1985:3–86:2. The data is period average.

[c]Real yield to corporate bond minus real LIBOR-on-dollar deposit (deflator: GNP deflator).

[d]Domestic yield to corporate bond minus LIBOR-on-dollar deposit minus actual won depreciation rate.

[e](|outflow| + |inflow|)/(|export| + |import|).

Table 5.3 **Outstanding Foreign Debt and Assets (million $)**

	1981	1982	1983	1984	1985	1986	1987	1988	1989	1990	November 1991
Total foreign debt	32,433	37,083	40,378	43,053	46,762	44,510	35,568	31,169	29,373	31,701	39,054.7
	(5,263)	(4,650)	(3,295)	(2,675)	(3,709)	(−2,252)	(8,942)	(−4,399)	(−1,796)	(2,328)	(7,353.7)
Long-term debt	21,145	23,685	26,353	29,612	33,859	33,568	24,884	20,038	16,421	14,459	16,972.8
(more than 3-year)	(4,105)	(2,540)	(2,668)	(3,259)	(4,247)	(−291)	(−8,684)	(−4,846)	(−3,617)	(−1,962)	(2,513.8)
Medium-term debt	1,061	971	1,910	2,016	2,171	1,686	1,393	1,335	2,004	2,900	4,477.0
(1–3-year)	(307)	(−90)	(939)	(106)	(155)	(−485)	(−293)	(−58)	(669)	(896)	(1,577)
Short-term debt	10,227	12,427	12,115	11,425	10,732	9,256	9,291	9,796	10,948	14,342	17,604.9
(less than 1-year)	(851)	(2,200)	(−312)	(−690)	(−693)	(−1,476)	(35)	(505)	(1,152)	(3,394)	(3,262.9)
Foreign assets	7,963	8,778	9,504	10,108	11,222	12,008	13,155	23,874	26,356	26,845	26,372.5
	(425)	(815)	(726)	(604)	(1,142)	(786)	(1,147)	(10,719)	(2,482)	(489)	(−472.5)
Long-term assets	723	1,101	2,010	1,886	2,839	3,381	2,915	2,735	2,943	2,724	2,596.2
	(32)	(378)	(909)	(−124)	(953)	(542)	(−466)	(−180)	(208)	(−219)	(−127.8)
Short-term assets	7,240	7,677	7,494	8,222	8,383	8,627	10,240	21,139	23,413	24,121	23,776.3
	(393)	(437)	(−183)	(728)	(161)	(244)	(1,613)	(10,899)	(2,274)	(708)	(−344.7)
Net foreign debt	24,470	28,305	30,874	32,945	35,540	32,502	22,413	7,295	3,015	4,856	12,682.2
	(4,839)	(3,835)	(2,569)	(2,071)	(2,595)	(−3,038)	(−10,089)	(−15,118)	(−4,280)	(1,841)	(7,826.2)
Total foreign debt/GNP	48.6	52.0	50.8	49.5	52.1	43.3	27.6	17.8	13.8	13.2	—
Foreign asset/GNP	11.9	12.3	12.0	11.6	12.5	11.7	10.2	13.6	12.4	11.2	—
Net foreign debt/GNP	36.6	39.7	38.8	37.9	39.6	31.6	17.4	4.2	1.4	2.0	—

Source: Ministry of Finance (Seoul).

Note: Numbers in parentheses record change from previous year.

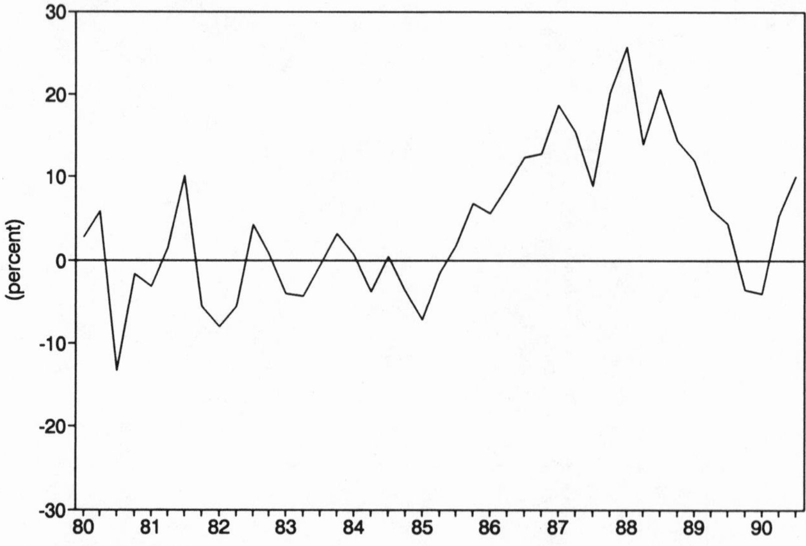

Fig. 5.1 Korea's uncovered interest rate differentials

à-vis the yen. Given this environment and the successful stabilization plan in the first half of the 1980s, Korea was in a position to take full advantage of these conditions. Starting in the latter half of 1986, Korea started recording current account surpluses.

The Korean government then became concerned about the effectiveness of its monetary policy because the current account surplus had automatically brought more liquidity to the economy. With this increased liquidity in the economy, Korea had to sterilize the current account surplus, which peaked at 8.2 percent of GNP in 1988.

Historically, Korea had relied heavily on direct monetary control, instead of indirect monetary management, because the interest rate had been regulated and the short-term money market had not been well developed. Given these structural problems, Korea was not in a position to utilize maximally open market operations. The Korean government issued large stocks of monetary stabilization bonds (MSBs) to sterilize the current account surplus. Instead of selling in the open market at the free market rate, the government allocated certain amounts of MSBs to banks and other nonfinancial institutions. Especially during 1986–89, a huge stock of MSBs was accumulated.

A second concern for the government was the real possibility of further appreciation of the won due to capital inflow in addition to the current account surplus. Strong sentiment existed to continue the current account surpluses, which were the first in Korean history, to resolve the foreign debt problem. To maintain export competitiveness, the Korean won had to remain at a relatively competitive level. Moreover, during this period, international pressure mounted to liberalize imports. This also required a competitive exchange rate to compensate for the adverse impact of import liberalization on the current account. In general, capital account liberalization could be expected to lead to the inflow of capital and the appreciation of the won, given the relatively high Korean interest rates compared with the international rate. The stronger won vis-à-vis other major currencies would have weakened the competitiveness of exports, the driving engine behind Korea's economic growth. This, from the government's viewpoint, has been the main counterargument against the liberalization of the capital account, especially capital inflow. The appreciation of the won has been one of the biggest concerns of the Korean government.

Given the economic situation in the early 1980s, the government pushed very strongly for a policy oriented toward capital outflow during the second half of the 1980s. Regulations governing capital flows were reversed from the early 1980s, during which the Korean government had actively sought to keep capital within the country. The regulations instead were changed to induce capital outflow actively. The deregulations on capital flow during this period seem to have been concentrated on overseas direct and portfolio investments (see appendix B). The Korean government even allowed such transactions as real estate investments in foreign countries, which had been regarded as taboo for a long time.

Analyzing the figures in table 5.2, we find large capital outflows during the 1980s; the largest component was long-term capital outflow, including repayments of commercial as well as public borrowings and accumulation of foreign assets. However, Korea during this period enjoyed a very favorable interest rate differential, much higher than in the early 1980s. The uncovered interest rate differential was also very favorable to Korea, the opposite of the situation in the early 1980s. This interest rate situation provided strong incentives for capital inflow—at a time when the government was actively trying to ship money abroad—and was thus inconsistent with the government intention to encourage capital outflow. Probably as a reflection of this, short-term capital balance, contrary to the case of long-term capital balance, recorded a large surplus led by a huge inflow, through an accumulation of short-term liabilities.

Contrasts with Japan

This pattern of capital control, which is especially conditional on exchange rate movements, is not confined to Korea. It is also interesting to observe that Japan's experience with capital control during the 1970s closely follows this pattern. Fukao (1990, 136) concludes, after a lengthy overview of Japan's pattern of capital control during 1970s that, "foreign exchange controls in the period of the expected appreciation of the yen before mid-1973 worked toward suppressing capital inflows and encouraging capital outflows. But, once the oil crisis occurred, the controls turned 180 degrees toward suppressing capital outflows and encouraging capital inflows. Another volte-face occurred once the yen began to strengthen suddenly in 1977 and 1978 and the direction turned once again toward suppressing capital inflows and encouraging outflows."

Ito (1990, 317) also makes the same observation, noting that, "capital controls were relaxed in several steps during the 1970s. The history of deregulation coincides with the roller-coaster path of the yen/dollar exchange rate. The Japanese monetary authority clearly had the objective of exchange-rate stabilization, so the restrictions on outflow (inflow) were lifted when the monetary authority desired to prevent rapid yen appreciation (depreciation)." In addition, as already mentioned in the beginning of this section, other OECD countries were observed to follow a similar pattern during the period of capital flow liberalization (OECD 1990).

It may be that the effect of government capital control, which works against the economic incentives, tends to be limited concerning private capital flows. The policies to encourage capital inflow against the unfavorable uncovered interest differential during the early 1980s and to encourage capital outflow against the favorable interest rate incentive during the late 1980s both turned out to be ineffective in influencing short-term capital movement in the intended direction. It is also interesting to observe the same phenomenon in Japanese capital control. Fukao (1990, 136) states, "these effects of changing foreign exchange controls can be separated into defensive ones (suppressing capital inflows when the yen was high, and outflows when low) and active ones (such as encouraging capital outflows when the yen was high, and capital inflows when low). The defensive effects were perhaps effective to an extent. . . . However, the active effects are likely to have been limited. Although effective sometimes such as in the expansion of capital outflows in 1972–73, the active effects attempted to work contrary to economic incentives for capital flows on the whole."

Looking at the indicators of interest rate differentials and the importance of capital flow as percentage of total trade in table 5.2, one cannot easily establish any definitive trend for the 1980s. In 1980 the uncovered interest rate differentials exhibited negative values which imply unfavorable conditions for Korea. The value of the differential remained at a relatively low level until 1985, then turned positive in 1986. The differential recorded large positive values for 1987–89 but has gradually declined since then. If one takes the absolute size of the uncovered interest rate differential as the measure of the degree of capital control, it may be concluded that capital flow mobility in the second half of the 1980s was less than in the first half of the 1980s. However, capital flows as a percentage of trade, which could also be taken as a measure of the degree of capital movement, recorded a double digit ratio during the years 1987–88. The years of high interest rate differentials tend to show a high degree of capital movement.

This rather contradictory observation reflects what seems to be an inconsistent capital control policy—policy leaning against the wind—inducing capital outflow under a favorable interest rate condition mainly by repaying public borrowing, but being unsuccessful in reducing the interest rate differentials and, therefore, the pressure on the exchange rate. This case seems to imply that active controls (in this case, encouraging outflow when the won was high and the uncovered interest rate differential was favorable to Korea) were not only ineffective in accomplishing the intended goals, as suggested by Fukao, but rather aggravated the existing real incentives by increasing interest rate differentials, causing private short-term flows in a direction opposite to policy intention. Exporting capital through the early repayment of public borrowing—in the presence of appreciation pressure on the won and defensive controls on capital inflow—have aggravated excess demand for the won, widened interest rate differentials, and produced further pressure for won appreciation, thereby generating further incentive for private short-term capital inflow.

However, it is noteworthy that foreign direct investment led by private investment increased continuously as a percentage of trade during the 1980s, and portfolio investment followed suit, though a little less clearly. Therefore, it seems difficult to come to a conclusion on the trend of capital mobility in Korea by analyzing only traditional indicators. In section 5.4, this issue will be addressed again with additional measurements and also some comparisons with Japan and Taiwan.

5.3 Impediments to Capital Flow Decontrol in Korea

It would be absurd to assume that capital decontrol can be carried out without any financial problems. However, such problems can be minimized by implementing the deregulation in an orderly fashion. As pointed out by the literature on the sequencing of economic liberalization (Fischer and Reisen 1992; Hanson 1992), macroeconomic stability, interest rate deregulation, and flexible exchange rates are the crucial preconditions to a relatively crisis-free transition.

Two different approaches to the liberalization of capital flow were observed among the OECD countries: the rapid and drastic (United Kingdom, Australia, and New Zealand) versus the gradual (Japan, Denmark, and Finland) approach (OECD 1990). Japan, especially, having taken the gradual approach that Korea is taking now, is a possible model for countries newly seeking capital flow deregulation. Starting in 1964 when it joined the OECD, Japan removed its capital controls gradually until 1980. First, foreign direct investment, inward and outward securities investment, and personal capital movement began to be liberalized at the end of 1970. Then, the liberalization of real estate operations and overseas direct investment was initiated in 1971. Restrictions on securities transactions and commercial lending were removed during the period 1975–76. All remaining restrictions were finally lifted in 1980 with the introduction of the new Foreign Exchange and Foreign Trade Control Law (OECD 1990; Fukao 1990; Ito 1991; Fischer and Reisen 1992).

Judging from the experiences of those forerunners, foreign direct investment and trade-related finance seem to be the first areas that could be liberalized since their reform will probably not cause serious problems for the stability and management of the financial sector. Before continuing with liberalization, however, it must be assumed that macroeconomic stabilization will bring down the sustained interest rate differentials, and this drop will probably generate "hot money" or capital flight after capital flow liberalization. Then, deregulation of the domestic interest rate, along with flexible exchange rates, ensures the development of the domestic money market and provides a buffer against hot money flow. Once domestic financial markets deepen and the opportunities for domestic portfolio investment are enlarged, control on capital outflows can be removed.

Following these steps will help lead to interest rates that match international rates. With these mechanisms in place, controls on short-term borrowing for banks and nonbanks and restrictions on nonresident investment in the domestic securities market should be abolished, since the deepened money market enables the authorities to absorb liquidity shocks more effectively and more smoothly.

In Korea, foreign direct investment and trade-related finance have already been mostly liberalized, as discussed in the previous section (see also table 5.1 and app. B). However, it has been observed that Korea has been very slow in liberalizing the flow of portfolio investment and also short-term capital flow. This slowness has been due mainly to concerns about possible disturbances caused by capital flow into the domestic economy induced by financial incentives. Especially in the early 1980s, the Korean government was worried about capital flight because of the negative uncovered interest parity and other factors, both economic and non-economic. However, in the late 1980s, given a regulated interest rate above the international level and an inflexible exchange rate subject to the old double-basket peg regime, rapid capital flow liberalization was thought to induce too large an inflow, which would have made managing domestic monetary policies difficult. Of course, as already mentioned, pressure for won appreciation itself was also one of the government's main concerns.

Therefore, one could argue that the major impediments to capital flow decontrol in Korea are interest rate regulation—which prevents the domestic interest rate from moving consistently with the international rate—the inflexible exchange rate regime based on a basket peg system, and the inefficient monetary control system—which relies on a direct domestic credit control policy that significantly limits the economy's ability to absorb the excess liquidity caused by capital inflow.

5.3.1 The Slow Pace of Interest Rate Deregulation

Before capital account liberalization can be smoothly executed, the domestic interest rate must be liberalized to absorb the shocks from capital flow. However, in Korea, interest rate deregulation has been extremely difficult, and this difficulty has proved a huge hurdle to capital account liberalization.

The Korean government has defended its policy stance of opposing quick interest rate deregulation for several reasons. It has contended that interest rate deregulation will increase funding costs for firms. Korean business firms are characterized by huge debt to equity ratios, and any increase in the interest rate will greatly impact the financial costs of these firms. Second, domestic banks have been burdened by a large portion of nonperforming and policy loans. Interest rate deregulation and more competition in the financial market would put banks in a critically disadvantaged position vis-à-vis nonbank financial intermediaries and foreign banks. The banks, burdened with nonperforming loans, could not compete with other financial institutions that do not have to worry about these bad loans. Deposit rate deregulation in particular would seriously jeopardize the soundness of the banking sector. Therefore, the amount of nonperforming loans makes it extremely difficult to open the banking sector to market competition. Also, policy loans by commercial banks, which are directed by the government, still account for almost half of domestic credit. These include loans to the housing and agricultural sectors, loans to small and medium-sized firms, and foreign currency loans mainly for capital goods imports. Until commercial banks are freed from the obligation of extending policy loans, financial liberalization will be limited.

However, those reasons tell only part of the story. Concerning the problem of funding cost, businesses already pay the market rate because banks, in an effort to evade regulations, employ such techniques as the compensating balance, which asks for a deposit for the loan that is given out, a sort of forced deposit. It has been generally accepted that only a small portion of businesses, mainly big businesses, enjoy access to regulated interest rates, while small and medium-sized firms are exposed to the market rate. Even those businesses that have access to regulated interest rate loans have been known to pay an effective rate near the market rate because of schemes such as the compensating balance. Therefore, the possibility of higher funding costs should not be a great barrier to interest rate deregulation.

On the other hand, the concern has surfaced that the market interest rate itself will rise after interest rate deregulation, so that the industrial sector will be hard hit. However, it is difficult to find a solid and convincing theoretical basis for this argument.

Also, the weight of nonperforming loans has been reduced recently, because the capital base of the banks has been increasing. The Korean banking industry enjoys a deposit and lending rate spread that is very high in comparison to that in Japan or the United States. For all commercial banks in Korea, the spread was 4.53 percent in 1990 and 4.66 percent in 1991, while for Japan it was 1.21 percent in 1989, and for the United States it was 2.38 percent in 1990. This large deposit and lending rate spread has allowed domestic Korean banks bigger profit margins.

The prolonged control of interest rates would result in a vicious circle of interest rate regulation and financial retardation. In spite of the widening gap between regulated and market interest rates in recent years, regulated rates have been adjusted minimally. Because the government hopes to see strong corporate investment that would accelerate the structural adjustment of the Korean industries, it has been reluctant to raise interest rates. The government's desire to borrow cheaply when it issues public debentures must have also affected its interest rate policy.

Therefore, the difficulties outlined by the government do not seem to fully reflect the true nature of the issues at hand. Banks enjoy a large spread buffer, and businesses have already been paying an interest cost that is near the market rate. Therefore, in addition to some of these problems, there seems to be another, deep-rooted reason why a strong push for interest rate deregulation has not been achieved—the political economy of interest rate reform.

In general, during a process of interest rate deregulation, there are always gainers and losers. In the Korean case, the business and banking sectors are likely to be the losers. The business sector, especially big businesses, will lose its privileged position of access to regulated interest rate loans. And the banking sector will lose its monopolistic position protected by the government and the quiet business environment created by interest rate and financial regulation. The Korean banking sector has enjoyed an existence without competition and with high profit margins. Also, interest rate deregulation means that the government or the Central Bank will lose control over the financial sector. If the interdependent relationship between the regulators and the financial sector is scrutinized, it becomes apparent not only that the regulators are concerned about losing their regulatory power but that both are quietly enjoying a mutually beneficial relationship. Moreover, although the major beneficiary of the liberalization is the general public, according to the public choice theory, they are not in a position to effectively mobilize the resources needed to influence current government interest rate policy.[1]

For these reasons, it has been difficult to change the current regulatory environment. In 1988, the Korean government launched an ambitious interest rate deregulation. However, after only about six months, the government reversed its policy when the jumps in the previously regulated interest rate were politically unacceptable. Interest deregulation was tried again for the second time in 1991. The government has tended to back away from its stance when the business sector complains of the higher interest rates. In early 1992, the government intervened again, influencing the interest rate indirectly through moral suasion. The prospect for capital account deregulation in Korea still remains very glum, because without interest rate liberalization, capital account liberalization will remain too difficult for Korea to digest. Continued government intervention in interest rate determination will remain a major impediment.

1. It has been shown that the influence of interest group politics on policymaking is clearly evident in Korea's import liberalization policy during the 1980s. See Jwa (1988). With political democratization after 1986, this force has been reinforced in every area of economic reform including interest rate deregulation.

5.3.2 Exchange Rate Appreciation and an Inflexible Exchange Rate System

Although a system of flexible exchange rates could generate high exchange rate volatility when taken together with the deregulated interest rate, it would be an important buffer against shocks from volatile capital flows and protect, to a large extent, domestic monetary independence.

Korea, especially during the late 1980s, faced the two inconsistent tasks of liberalizing the exchange market and exchange rate systems and avoiding real exchange appreciation—all in the midst of a very favorable interest rate parity. During this period, Korea had been pressed by the United States to liberalize its import regime and exchange rate system, but Korea also saw a strong need for maintaining its current account surpluses and, therefore, a competitive exchange rate level. But at the same time, the won was subject to strong appreciation pressure from market forces, *because* of the current account surplus and favorable interest rate differential, as well as from the U.S. government. However, Korea's exchange rate system during the 1980s, a double-basket system, turned out to be relatively rigid in managing these factors. After all, Korea allowed a gradual appreciation of the won during this period but with strict regulations on capital inflow and encouragement of capital outflow. And finally in 1990, Korea adopted a market-average exchange rate system with the objective of introducing a more flexible exchange rate system in the end.

Korea's exchange rate had been subject to the so-called double-basket system during the 1980s, in which the won/dollar exchange rate was determined as a weighted average of two different nominal effective rates, based on Korea's own basket and the IMF currency basket, respectively. Under this system, ample room existed for the government to influence the exchange rate. But when the won began to appreciate vis-à-vis the U.S. dollar after 1987, because of the current account surplus, and was subject to strong appreciation pressure from capital inflow, the government could not effectively work against the market forces. U.S. pressure to appreciate the won also mounted during the second half of the 1980s. The Korean won appreciated at rates larger that 9 percent in real terms in 1989 and by as much as 11 percent in nominal terms in 1988 (see table 5.2). In the end, Korea adopted the market-average exchange rate system in March 1990, under which the won/dollar exchange rate floats according to market forces within a given narrow band. The central rate under this new system is determined by the quantity-weighted average exchange rate of the previous market day. This is an improvement upon the old double-basket system and is being improved further by gradually widening the band (the band is now ±0.8 percent, which was set in July 1992).

In retrospect, concern over a possible exchange rate appreciation, especially during the late 1980s, turned out to be one of the main impediments to the liberalization of capital flow, especially capital inflow, but with the introduction of a market-average exchange rate system, a more conducive environment has been created for capital flow liberalization.

5.3.3 Monetary Control and the Lack of an Indirect Control Method

The loss of monetary independence, especially the inflationary pressure that will be generated by free capital flow (as in the Korean case), has been a major source of concern for countries implementing capital account liberalization.

Korea has suffered from chronic inflation except for a few years in the mid-1980s. To control inflation, the Korean government employs a direct monetary control method because Korea lacks the environment for market-based monetary management, such as open market operation. The inflow that would result from capital account liberalization may easily lead to inflation, a source of concern for the government. Without effective means to manage the money supply, the Central Bank will experience difficulties in efforts to sterilize the large inflow of capital. An indirect monetary control system allows higher efficiency in absorbing liquidity shocks brought by capital inflow, which would otherwise jeopardize domestic macroeconomic stability. So, unless Korea can develop an indirect management system, it will be difficult to allow large capital inflow.

Currently, Korea is trying to develop an efficient short-term money market by reducing limitations on the operational mechanism of the market and deregulating short-term interest rates, thereby paving the way for efficient open market operation. However, as has already been discussed, the slow pace of interest rate deregulation will hinder rapid financial deepening in the money market. In particular, the reluctance of the government and the Central Bank to deregulate the interest rates of government and monetary stabilization bonds will continue to be a stumbling block to the introduction of an indirect monetary control mechanism and to further capital flow liberalization.

5.4 The Extent of Capital Account Opening: Intercountry Comparison

5.4.1 Capital Flow as a Percentage of Trade

One of the indicators that measure the openness of the capital account is the volume of capital flow as a percentage of trade, measured as exports plus imports. If a country, over time and in comparison with other countries, has an increasing and large volume of capital flow relative to trade volume, it may be stated that this country has increasingly and relatively mobile capital transactions (Gros 1992). Even if a country, in appearance, has numerous regulatory measures against capital flows, the country may be regarded as having a relatively open capital account, depending on the size of the capital flow as a percentage of trade.

When overall capital flows are analyzed as shown in table 5.4 (data for Taiwan were not available), the performance of Korea is poor in comparison with the total flows of Asian developing countries as well as with Japan. We find the same result when we compare foreign direct investment and portfolio in-

Table 5.4 **Capital Flows as a Percentage of Trade (%; period average)**

	Overall Capital Account			Portfolio Investment			Foreign Direct Investment			Other		
Country	1981–85	1986–90	1981–90	1981–85	1986–90	1981–90	1981–85	1986–90	1981–90	1981–85	1986–90	1981–90
Industrial countries[a]	27.29	46.52	36.91	5.76	9.80	7.78	3.23	7.29	5.26	15.18	24.52	19.85
United States	33.34	38.97	36.16	6.25	8.24	7.24	5.14	10.57	7.85	21.01	17.02	19.02
Japan	31.75	117.45	74.60	13.52	28.36	20.94	1.96	7.69	4.83	11.87	71.91	41.89
Germany	13.86	25.18	19.52	4.55	7.22	5.88	1.51	2.87	2.19	5.48	10.78	8.13
Asia (developing countries)[b]	20.10	15.44	17.77	0.73	0.27	0.50	1.34	2.42	1.88	11.93	8.21	10.07
Korea	10.11	8.73	9.42	0.61[c]	0.38	0.49	0.40	0.97	0.68	5.30	4.60	4.95
Singapore	15.12	13.92	14.52	0.69	0.59	0.64	2.92	4.85	3.89	9.20	7.80	8.50
Indonesia	12.51	13.03	12.77	0.42	0.41	0.42	0.67	1.55	1.11	1.34	1.98	1.66

Source: IMF, *Balance of Payments Statistics Yearbook* (Washington, D.C.).

[a]Includes 22 countries: Australia, Austria, Belgium-Luxembourg, Canada, Denmark, Finland, France, Germany, Greece, Iceland, Ireland, Italy, Japan, Netherlands, New Zealand, Norway, Portugal, Spain, Sweden, Switzerland, the United Kingdom, and the United States.

[b]Includes 24 countries: Afghanistan, Bangladesh, China (People's Republic), Fiji, India, Indonesia, Kiribati, Korea, Laos (People's Democratic Republic), Malaysia, Maldives, Myanmar, Nepal, Pakistan, Papua New Guinea, the Philippines, Singapore, the Solomon Islands, Sri Lanka, Thailand, Tonga, Vanuatu, Western Samoa, and Asia not specified.

[c]Includes an extraordinarily high number, 1.86 in 1985. Excluding this gives an average of 0.3 percent.

vestment flows. During the 1980s, while the indices for overall capital and portfolio investment flows seem to suggest a downward trend of capital mobility from the first to the second half of the 1980s, the numbers are slightly misleading because foreign direct investment in 1985 shows an extraordinarily high number, 1.86 percent, which seems to distort the overall picture (see also table 5.2).[2] If 1985 is excluded, the trend for portfolio investment indicates a rise. On the other hand, the index for direct investment, even if still relatively low, suggests a rapidly rising trend of capital mobility. Therefore, it could be the case that the openness of Korea's capital account increased gradually during the 1980s, though it is still very low if the size of the capital account as a percentage of the trade account is taken as a measure of capital mobility.

For Japan, all the indices of capital flow (as a percentage of trade) during the 1980s show a rapidly rising trend over time. And, with the exception of the foreign direct investment index, Japan's indices are higher than those of total flows for industrial countries as well as the flows for the United States and Germany individually. Therefore, one can conclude that the openness of Japan's capital account, according to this measurement, rose rapidly during the 1980s and maintains a very high level.

5.4.2 Interest Rate Differentials

Uncovered as well as covered interest rate differentials have been used as indicators of the extent of capital mobility. The uncovered interest rate differentials, if any, will reflect the exchange risk premium and/or country risk, while the covered interest rate differentials reflect only country risks such as transaction costs, capital controls, taxes, and default risks, since the covered differentials are free of exchange risk by definition. Therefore, one can not definitely know where uncovered interest rate differentials come from, since those differentials could be due to exchange risks, country risks including capital controls, or both. In this sense, covered interest rate differentials could be a better indicator of whether and how strongly capital flows are controlled.[3]

However, for the case of Korea and Taiwan without forward currency markets, only the uncovered interest rate differential can be examined, and it is given as follows:

$$UD_t = R_t - R^f_t - ER_t, \tag{1}$$

where UD_t represents the uncovered interest differential, R_t and R^f_t are the domestic and foreign interest rates measured by the LIBOR-on-dollar deposit,

2. The high percentage of portfolio investment in 1985 seems to reflect the effects of the once-and-for-all nature of such capital decontrol measures as the establishment of the Korea Fund for nonresidents in 1984 and the permission for domestic firms to issue convertible bonds and bonds with subscription warrants or stock depository receipts in 1985. (See app. B for these changes).

3. A lengthy and informative discussion of the usefulness of various concepts of interest rate differentials in quantifying capital mobility can be found in Frankel (1989). Also see Ito (1986) for discussions of the usefulness of covered differentials as an indicator of the degree of capital control.

Table 5.5 **Uncovered Interest Rate Differentials for Korea, Taiwan, and Japan (annualized quarterly average; %)**

Year	Korea	Taiwan	Japan[a]
1981	1.69	−9.6	−0.30
1982	−3.71	−9.62	−0.05
1983	−2.06	−2.44	−0.18
1984	0.10	−1.73	−0.34
1985	−2.70	−3.85	−0.22
1986	8.37	7.42	−0.32
1987	13.98	17.34	−0.75
1988	20.12	0.54	−0.89
1989	9.24	5.74	−0.60
1990	1.94	−6.42	−0.52

[a]Covered interest rate differential.

and ER_t is the expected exchange rate depreciation measured by the actual depreciation rate under the assumption of perfect foresight. On the other hand, for Japan with a well-developed forward yen market, the covered interest rate differential is examined and is defined as follows:

$$CD_t = R_t - R_t^f - fd_t, \quad (2)$$

where CD_t and fd_t represent the covered interest rate differential and forward discount on the yen, respectively, and other variables are the same as in equation (1). However, CD_t is actually measured by utilizing the LIBOR-on-yen deposit as a substitute for $R_t^f + fd_t$ as the covered interest parity rate in equation (2).[4] These data on interest rate differentials are reported in table 5.5 as annual averages and depicted quarterly in figures 5.1, 5.2, and 5.3, for Korea, Taiwan, and Japan, respectively.

For Korea, as illustrated in figure 5.1, the uncovered interest rate differential in the first half of the 1980s was, on average, slightly negative, while in the second half of the 1980s, it was highly positive. Korea faced outflow pressure in the early 1980s, while it faced strong inflow pressure in the second half of the 1980s. In Taiwan, as illustrated in figure 5.2, the pattern of uncovered rate differential was very similar to but more volatile than Korea's. But, on average, Taiwan's differentials are lower than Korea's, especially for the latter half of the 1980s. For Japan in figure 5.3, the covered interest rate differential was very close to zero, denoting almost a full degree of capital mobility. This finding is very similar to what Ito (1986) found by analyzing many different forms of covered interest rate differentials, among which the current form was also ana-

4. One can, instead, use the data on forward discount rate on the yen actually observed in the forward market as fd_t and the data on R_t^f and calculate $R_t^f + fd_t$ as the covered interest parity rate. However, this method is destined to produce larger measurement errors than the method used in this paper.

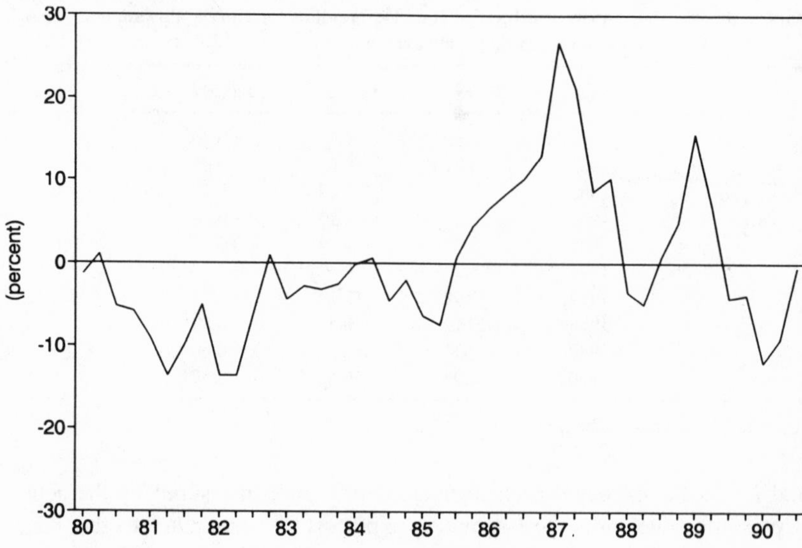

Fig. 5.2 Taiwan's uncovered interest rate differentials

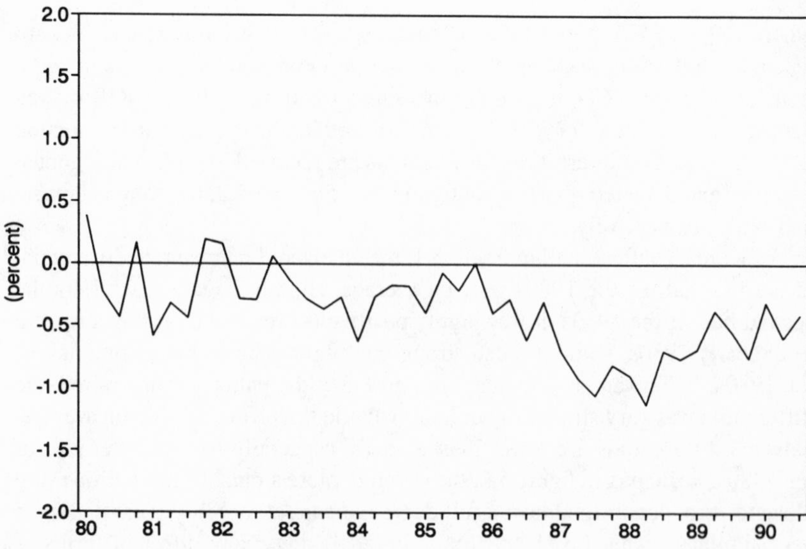

Fig. 5.3 Japan's covered interest rate differentials

lyzed, though he covered the period from the 1970s to the first half of the 1980s. He concluded that Japan's capital controls were almost all lifted in 1980, and the covered interest rate parity was almost perfectly held since then. According to these results, one may conclude that the highest mobility of capital is observed in Japan, while Korea and Taiwan maintain a reasonable, but lower, degree of capital mobility.

5.4.3 Linkages between Domestic and International Interest Rates

Recently, Reisen and Yèches (1991) applied Haque and Montiel's (1990) extended version of Edwards and Khan's (1985) model to Korea and Taiwan and showed an empirical measurement of capital account openness for those countries. In this subsection, Reisen and Yèches's approach is applied to Korea, Taiwan, and Japan. However, for Korea and Taiwan, the data utilized here for money stocks and interest rates are different from those used by Reisen and Yèches (see app. A for the list and sources of variables used in this section).[5]

First, a constant measure of capital account openness is derived, estimating the following equation:

$$R_t - R_t' = \alpha + \psi\,(R_t^* - R_t'),\ 0 \leq \psi \leq 1, \quad (3)$$

where R_t is the domestic nominal market interest rate and R_t^* is the uncovered (covered) interest parity rate defined as international market interest rate plus expected exchange rate depreciation (forward discount rate). Using notation from equations (1) and (2), R_t^* can be written as follows: $R_t^* = R_t^f + ER_t$ for the uncovered parity rate, and $R_t^* = R_t^f + fd_t$ for the covered parity rate. R_t' is defined as the domestic nominal market interest rate that would be observed if the private capital account were completely closed and is derived as follows.[6]

5. The broader concept of money (M_2) is used here instead of the narrow concept (M_1) used by Reisen and Yèches, and the yield to corporate bond for Korea and discount rate for Taiwan are used here as the market interest rate, while they used the curb market rate for Korea and the curb market rate and interbank rate for Taiwan. For Korea, Reisen and Yèches preferred the curb market rate, which is relatively inaccurately measured, to the bond yield because they thought the bond yield—especially the government bond yield in the primary market—was regulated. However, the yield to corporate bonds in the secondary market was pretty much liberalized during the 1980s and so is picked up as an opportunity cost for money holding as well as the market rate. For Taiwan, the discount rate by the central bank was the only available data. In addition, we tried a different measurement for the uncovered interest parity rate by utilizing an univariate ARIMA model for exchange rate forecasting, as will be seen later, in addition to the actual depreciation rate used by Reisen and Yèches for the expected depreciation rate.

6. Equation (3) is derived from Edwards and Khan's (1985) argument that a domestic market-clearing interest rate can be expressed in general as a weighted average of foreign interest rate, i.e., interest rate in a fully open economy, and a domestic interest rate in a completely closed economy, with the weight given to the foreign interest rate being interpreted as the extent of capital mobility: in our notation, "$R_t = \psi R_t^* + (1 - \psi)\,R_t'$" where ψ measures the extent of capital mobility. Then, Haque and Montiel (1990) transformed this form into "$R_t - R_t' = \psi(R_t^* - R_t')$," and Reisen and Yèches (1991) added a constant term, α, to this, as in equation (3) in the text, with the constant term being interpreted as reflecting the interest differential due to the difference in asset quality between foreign and domestic financial assets.

As a first step, a domestic money demand function is estimated in the following simple standard form:

$$\text{(4)} \qquad \ln(M/P)_t = \alpha_0 + \alpha_1 \ln y_t + \alpha_2 R_t + \alpha_3 \ln(M/P)_{t-1} + \varepsilon_t,$$

where M_t, P_t, and y_t are money stock, price level, and real GNP, respectively. Then, estimated equation (4) is solved for R_t, and we introduce $M'_t = M_t - CAP_t$, where CAP_t is private capital movements, as follows:

$$\text{(5)} \qquad R'_t = (\alpha_0/\alpha_2) - (\alpha_1/\alpha_2) \ln y_t - (\alpha_3/\alpha_2) \ln (M/P)_{t-1} + (1/\alpha_2) \ln (M'/P)_t.$$

Now, estimated equation (3) will give ψ as the degree of influence of uncovered or covered interest parity rate on the domestic interest rate, which is to be interpreted as the openness of the capital account.

In addition, for the case of the uncovered parity rate, we measured R^*_t in two different ways alternatively by proxying the expected exchange rate depreciation with the actual depreciation rate under the assumption of perfect foresight (case A) and by forecasting the expected depreciation rate with an univariate ARIMA (1,1,0) exchange rate forecasting model (case B)[7] for Korea and Taiwan, both of which lack a forward currency market. On the other hand, for Japan, with a forward currency market, the LIBOR-on-yen deposit is used as R^*_t, i.e., covered parity rate in this case, as in equation (2) in section 5.4.2.

The estimated results of equations (3) and (4) for Korea, Taiwan, and Japan are reported as follows. Equations (3a) and (3b) are the estimated results of equation (3) cases A and B of R^*_t measurement, respectively. The t-values are in parentheses. The estimated ψ's for these countries are also summarized in table 5.6.

Korea: Sample period, 1980:2–1990:4

$$\text{(3a)} \qquad \underset{(1.155)}{R_t - R'_t = 4.371} + \underset{(22.014)}{0.889}(R^*_t - R'_t),$$

$$\bar{R}^2 = 0.912, \text{RH01} = \underset{(7.237)}{0.759}, \text{D-W} = 2.33.$$

7. Estimation results are as follows with E_t denoting logarithm of exchange rate per dollar at time t and t-value in parentheses:

Korea: Sample period, 1980:1–1990:4

$$E_t - E_{t-1} - \underset{(4.716)}{0.584} (E_{t-1} - E_{t-2}),$$
$$\bar{R}^2 - 0.959, Q(18) = 7.295.$$

Taiwan: Sample period, 1980:2–1990:4

$$E_t - E_{t-1} - \underset{(8.290)}{0.788} (E_{t-1} - E_{t-2}),$$
$$\bar{R}^2 - 0.992, Q(18) - 11.319.$$

Table 5.6 **Measurement of Capital Account Openness: Constant Measure**

Country and Measure	Ψ	t-value	Period
Korea			
Case A	0.89	22.01	1980–90
Case B	0.85	22.23	1980–90
Reisen and Yèches	0.59	7.95	1980–90
Taiwan			
Case A	0.92	17.31	1981–90
Case B	0.96	17.97	1981–90
Reisen and Yèches	0.35	10.20	1980–90
Japan	0.99	315.93	1980–90
Indonesia			
Haque and Montiel	0.87	8.54	1969–87
Malaysia			
Haque and Montiel	0.64	2.93	1967–87

Sources: Reisen and Yèches (1991); Haque and Montiel (1990).

(3b)
$$R_t - R_t' = 5.038 + 0.845(R_t^* - R_t'),$$
$$(5.310)\ (22.234)$$
$$\bar{R}^2 = 0.921,\ \text{D-W} = 1.639.$$

(4)
$$\ln(M/P)_t = -0.29 + 0.086 \ln y_t - 0.002\, R_t + 0.913 \ln (M/P)_{t-1}$$
$$(-2.12)\quad (3.44)\qquad (-3.12)\qquad (36.79)$$
$$\bar{R}^2 = 0.996 \qquad h = -0.302.$$

Taiwan: Sample period, 1981:2–1990:3

(3a)
$$R_t - R_t' = 0.258 + 0.915(R_t^* - R_t'),$$
$$(0.072)\ (17.31)$$
$$\bar{R}^2 = 0.91,\ \text{RH01} = 0.727,\ \text{D-W} = 1.88.$$
$$(6.279)$$

(3b)
$$R_t - R_t' = -3.040 + 0.959\ (R_t^* - R_t'),$$
$$(-2.815)\ (17.974)$$
$$\bar{R}^2 = 0.897,\ \text{D-W} = 1.567.$$

(4)
$$\ln(M/P)_t = 0.215 + 0.374 \ln y_t - 0.022\, R_t + 0.763 \ln (M/P)_{t-1},$$
$$(6.84)\quad (2.36)\qquad (-4.96)\qquad (9.04)$$
$$\bar{R}^2 = 0.99,\ \text{RH01} = -0.25,\ h = -0.324.$$
$$(-2.01)$$

Japan: Sample period, 1980:2–1990:2

(3)
$$R_t - R_t' = -0.348 + 0.993\ (R_t^* - R_t'),$$
$$(-4.528)(315.928)$$

$$\bar{R}^2 = 0.99, \text{RH01} = \underset{(2.674)}{0.366}, \text{D-W} = 1.46.$$

$$(4)\quad \ln(M/P)_t = \underset{(-2.403)}{-2.195} + \underset{(2.365)}{0.272} \ln y_t - \underset{(-1.382)}{0.002} R_t + \underset{(12.213)}{0.848} \ln (M/P)_{t-1}$$

$$\bar{R}^2 = 0.994, \text{RH01} = \underset{(-4.268)}{-0.583}, h = 0.143.$$

If the estimated ψ value from this model turns out to be large, it will be interpreted as implying a high degree of capital account openness. From these results (also see table 5.6), it becomes clear that Korea and Taiwan, both, have relatively high levels of openness. Korea's ψ value is 0.889 for case A and 0.845 for case B, both significantly different from 1. Taiwan's ψ value is 0.915 for case A and 0.959 for case B, which are, however, not all significantly different from 1. These estimates of ψ for Korea and Taiwan are all higher than Reisen and Yèches's estimates of 0.594 and 0.353, respectively. Japan's ψ value is 0.993, implying almost perfectly mobile capital flows, which is, however, significantly different from a value of 1.[8] According to these results, Korea seems to be maintaining a reasonably high openness of capital flows, but to a degree lower than Japan and Taiwan.

On the other hand, the constant term in equation (3) is interpreted as the difference in interest rates due to the difference in asset quality between domestic and international financial assets, but the results are diversified, depending on the different measurement methods of expected exchange depreciation: case A (eqq. [3a]) implies insignificant constant terms, but case B (eqq. [3b]) offers significant terms, both for Korea and Taiwan, even if identical interest rate data are utilized, i.e., asset qualities are not changed for the two cases. For Japan, the constant term turns out to be significant. These results seem to contradict expectations since London interbank yen deposits and Japan's domestic interbank deposits should be more identical in terms of asset quality than London interbank dollar deposits and Korea's corporate bonds or Taiwan's discount lending. Therefore, one must be careful in interpreting the constant term as a measurement of difference in asset quality.

Second, the Kalman filter technique is applied to equation (3), and the time-varying estimates of ψ are derived for the three countries and are plotted in figures 5.4–5.6.[9] To check if the time variation of ψ is significant, i.e., that

8. The estimation result of Japan's money demand equation (4) suggests that interest rate elasticity is relatively less precisely estimated and this may cause larger errors-in-variables problems with the estimated R_t', which could in turn produce a downward bias of the estimated ψ. However, Japan's estimated ψ value seems high enough, and the precision of the estimate is fairly high with a t-value of 315.9. On the other hand, the result that Taiwan's ψ is not significantly different from 1, but that Japan's ψ is, seems inconsistent with the implication of other observations that Japan's openness seems to be higher than Taiwan's, as already seen concerning the degree of capital mobility of these countries. This stems from the fact that the estimate of Taiwan's ψ is least precise among the three countries.

9. See Reisen and Yèches (1991) for the details of this procedure applied specifically to equation (3).

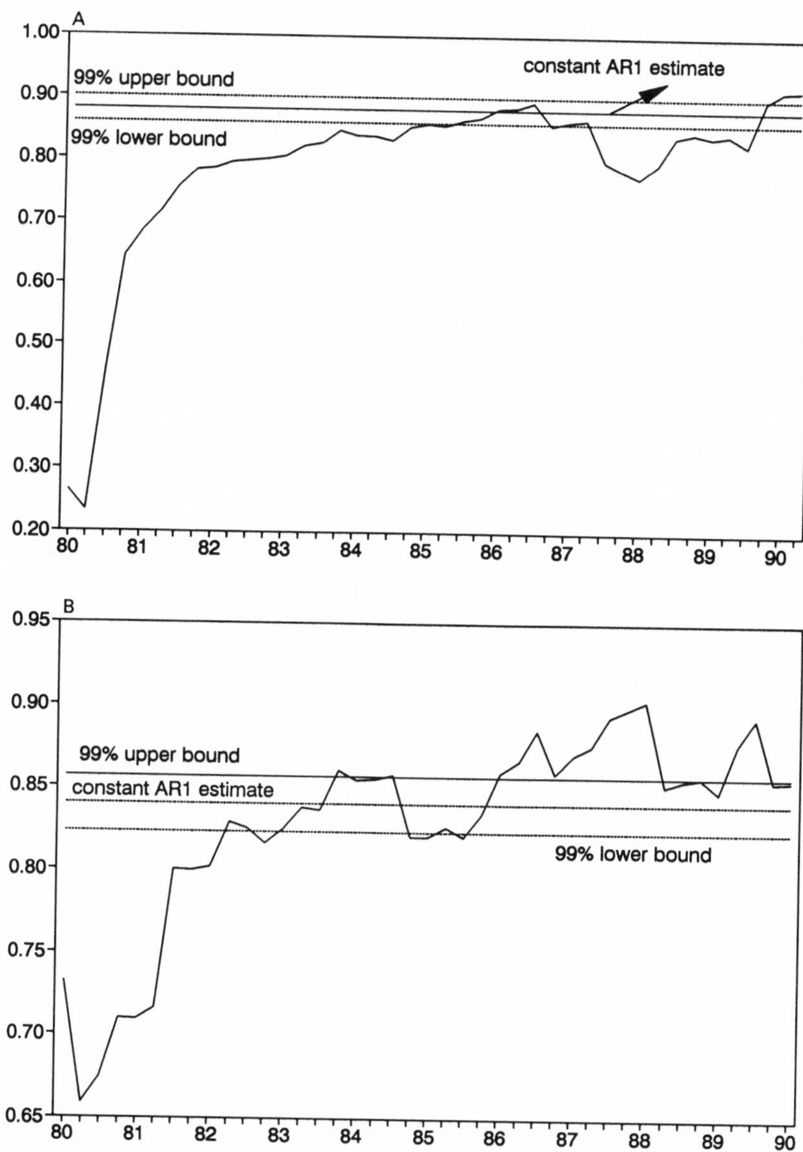

Fig. 5.4 Korea's time-varying estimate of capital account openness (A, Kalman filter, case A; B, Kalman filter, case B)

time-varying estimates of ψ are statistically different from constant estimates of ψ, we also draw the 99 percent confidence interval of the constant estimate. If the time-varying estimate falls outside of this interval, it is significantly different from the constant estimate, and vice versa. First, for case A, Korea's openness has gradually increased from the early 1980s but with a little stagnation during the short interval of late 1987 to early 1988, and time variation

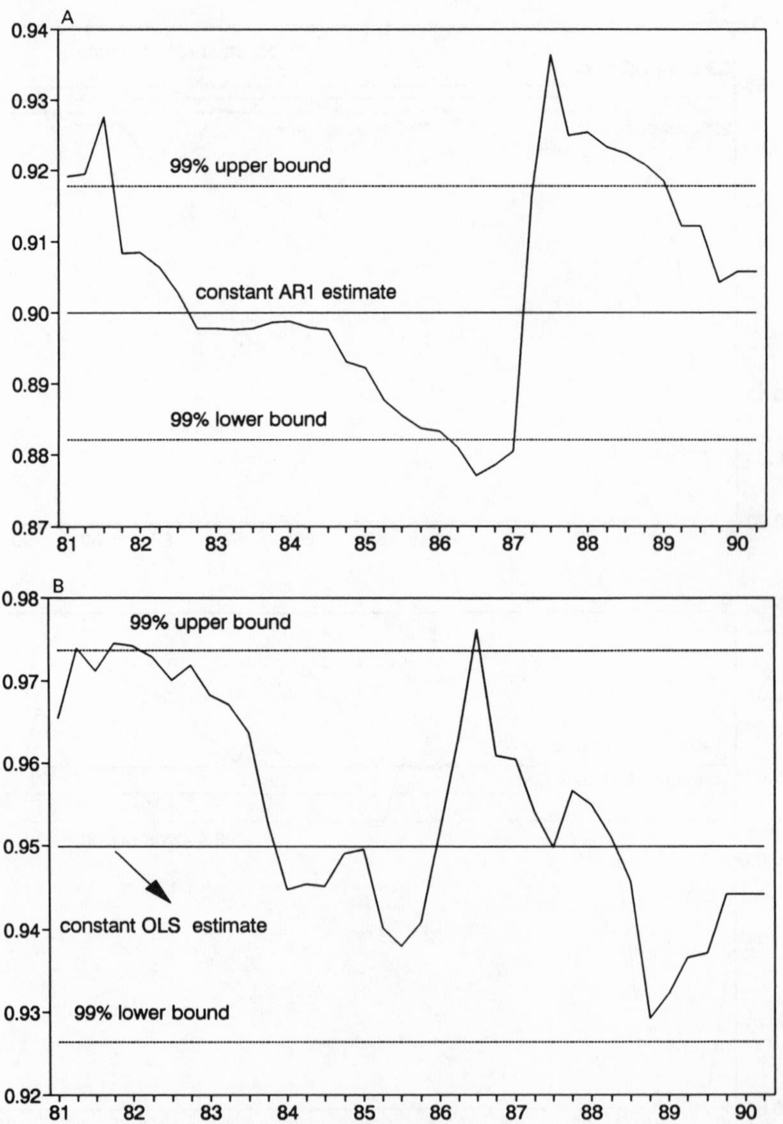

Fig. 5.5 Taiwan's time-varying estimate of capital account openness (A, Kalman filter, case A; B, Kalman filter, case B)

turns out to be significant, implying that Korea achieved a statistically significant improvement in capital account openness. This finding is opposite to the findings of Reisen and Yèches. Their results imply that, in general, Korea's openness gradually declined from the first half to the second half of the 1980s. Taiwan's openness, after staying at low levels until 1986, increased sharply to reach a high level of openness in 1987 but with a slightly declining trend from

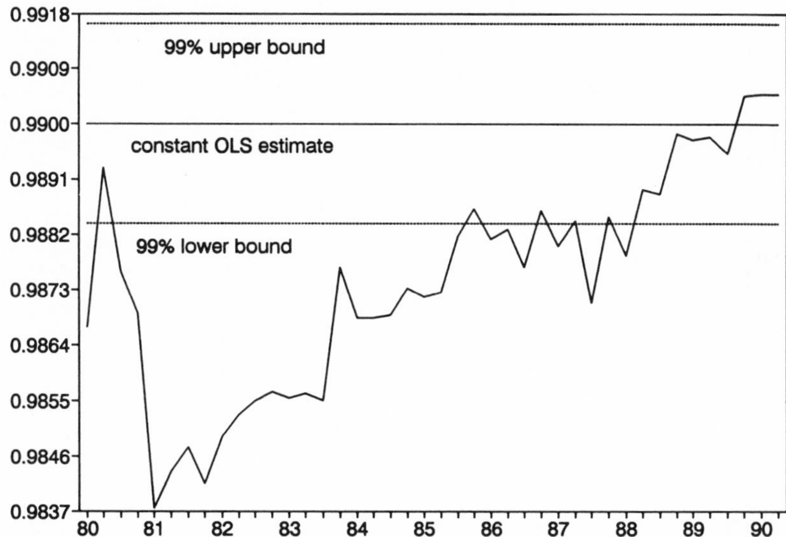

Fig. 5.6 Japan's time-varying estimate of capital account openness (Kalman filter)

then on, and this variation seems significant but much less than for the case of Korea. Second, for case B, Korea's openness has been gradually increasing and the variation is still significant; Taiwan's openness has been fluctuating around a relatively high level but within a narrow band, and so the variation turns out to be mostly insignificant. For Japan, time-varying estimates of ψ, after a short drop in the first quarter of 1981, have been rising continuously, and these changes turn out to be significant, with time-varying estimates of ψ being significantly different from constant estimates.

Finally, to obtain an additional series of time-varying estimates for ψ, a rolling-over regression is applied to equation (3) by adding one more data point at each time, starting from the base regression which utilizes the first 10 data points from the data set used for the estimation of equation (3). The resulting time-varying estimates of ψ are plotted in figures 5.7–5.9 for each country. However, in this case, only case A is reported for Korea and Taiwan. According to this result, Korea displays almost the same trend (illustrated in fig. 5.7) as in the Kalman filter method. In figure 5.8, Taiwan also displays a trend similar to the result of the Kalman filter method. After a sharp rise in openness in the mid-1980s, there was a trend of gradual decrease in the latter part of the 1980s.[10] Japan, in figure 5.9, also shows a trend similar to the result of the Kalman filter estimates.

The evidence presented in this section suggests that Korea has achieved a reasonably high degree of openness, measured by constant estimates. The Kal-

10. Case B both for Korea and Taiwan, not reported here, shows a pattern similar to case A, i.e., that rolling-over regression produces a trend very similar to the Kalman filter method.

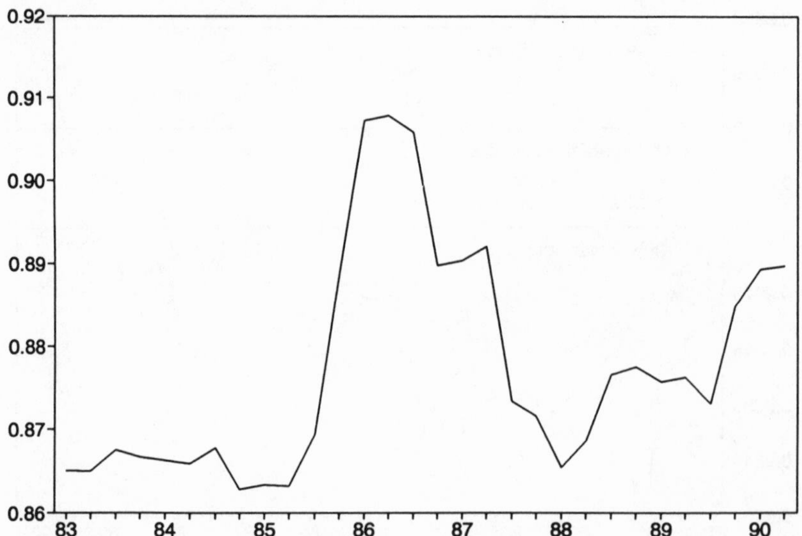

Fig. 5.7 Korea's time-varying estimate of capital account openness (rolling-over, case A)

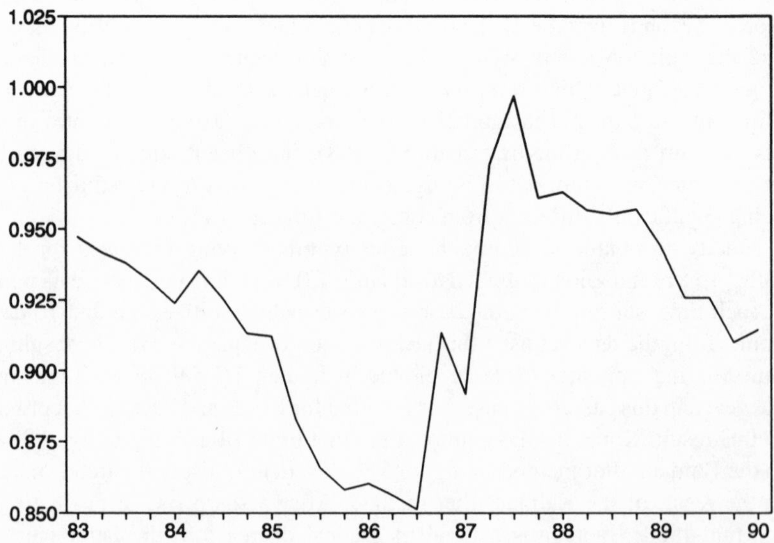

Fig. 5.8 Taiwan's time-varying estimate of capital account openness (rolling-over, case A)

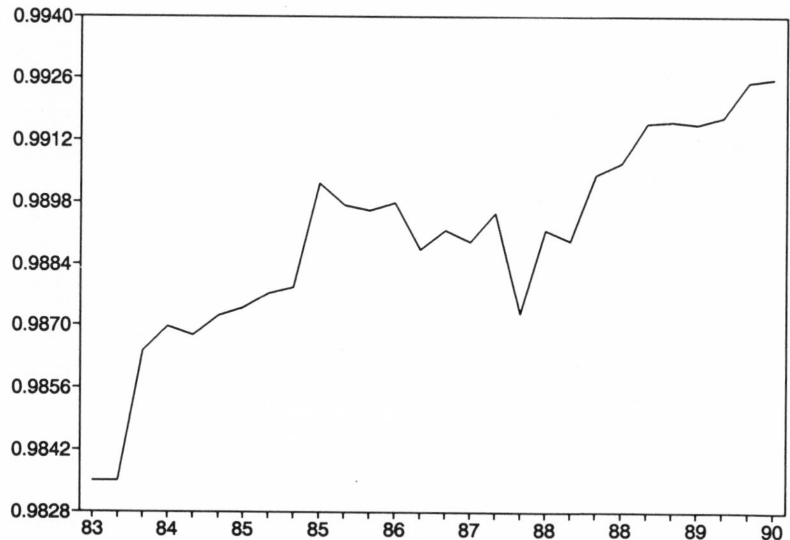

Fig. 5.9 Japan's time-varying estimate of capital account openness (rolling-over)

man filter and the rolling regression show a steady increase in the level of openness during the 1980s, and this increase turns out to be statistically significant. However, it is also interesting to note that time-varying estimates for case A and rolling-over regression both show a relative stagnation of openness during 1987–88, a period which coincides with favorable uncovered interest rate differentials and the rising importance of capital flow as percentage of trade as observed in table 5.2. Again, we find some inconsistency among the implications of various measurements of openness during 1987–88, and it seems still to be the case that the capital control policy of leaning against the wind might have created this situation, as discussed in section 5.2.2. Note that time-varying estimates of ψ in equation (3) crucially depend on and tend to reflect the trend of the data on the uncovered interest parity rate (R_t^*) which are the same data used for the calculation of uncovered interest rate differentials. Therefore, we come to the same situation as in section 5.2.2, where measurements related to uncovered rate differentials suggest a slight stagnation of openness but capital flow as percentage of trade suggests the opposite.[11] However, after this short interval, the extent of openness seems to have returned to its rising trend.

11. This seems to suggest that the time-varying ψ in equation (3) tends to reflect mainly information contained in the data on (un)covered interest rate differentials. In other words, the parameter ψ mirrors mainly the image of (un)covered differentials and, therefore, is somewhat limited in providing additional information on the openness of capital flow. The relationships between the movements of ψ and (un)covered differentials observed for the cases of Japan and Taiwan also lead to the same implication.

On the other hand, Taiwan experienced a sharp increase in openness around 1986, then the trend seems to have declined slightly in the late 1980s, but according to case B, Taiwan's openness turns out to be highly fluctuating even within a narrow band. However, the time variation of openness is not statistically significant, implying that during the 1980s, Taiwan's openness, even if reasonably high, remained stable. In the case of Japan, the openness of the capital account is not only very high but increased during the 1980s, and these changes turn out to be statistically significant.

5.4.4 A Gross Flow Index for Capital Flow

Trading in risky assets contributes to portfolio diversification and leads to a reduction of risk for the overall portfolio. There are gains to be achieved from trading in international financial assets if the prices for bearing certain risks differ for different countries. That is to say, the price differences among financial assets of similar risk for different countries can yield trade gains, as in the international trade of commodities.

"Bringing in the element of risk is thus a major shift from the traditional analysis of capital flows, because it delinks the welfare implications of an open capital account from its effect on investment. Even if saving and investment are unaffected by allowing capital flows, i.e., even if the private capital account were exactly balanced by inflow and outflows of capital, the individual agents of the economy would benefit from trade in risky assets. Moreover, the argument that individuals should be allowed to trade assets internationally, based on differences in preferences, production and evaluation of risk, is, analogously to the trading of commodities, perhaps the strongest argument for open capital markets" (Hanson 1992).

Suppose there could be two types of capital flows as implied in the discussion above: one is a capital flow traditionally perceived to supplement excess savings or investment, and the other exists to take advantage of gains from trade in risky assets. To put the discussion in a simple context, if capital flow is assumed to consist of only the former type, there is no need for two-way trade in capital. Deficient savings compared to investment will require only one-way capital inflow, while excess saving over investment requires only capital outflow. However, once the second type of capital flow is added, the total volume of capital inflow and outflow will tend to increase for a given net flow that will eventually reflect excess savings or investment. Therefore, a relatively larger volume of two-way capital flow, ceteris paribus, could be taken as evidence that capital flow of the second type is more active than otherwise.

Along this line of reasoning, we introduce the concept of the gross flow index for capital flow to measure the degree of capital mobility of this two-way nature. This index measures the importance of two-way trade in capital flow similarly to the so-called intraindustry trade index and is defined as follows:

$$1 - \frac{|\text{ net capital balance }|}{|\text{ capital inflow }| + |\text{ capital outflow }|}.$$

If the index is close to 1, the volume of total capital flow in both directions is very large compared to the net balance required for savings and investment equalization. In this case, we interpret it as saying that capital flow reflects relatively more of the incentive to trade in risky assets. The capital account is more than the simple mirror image of the current account in this situation. If, on the other hand, the index is close to 0, indicating a more one-way flow, capital flow mirrors the current account to a relatively large extent, supplementing deficient domestic savings for investment or encouraging the investment of excess savings abroad.[12]

These gross flow indices for overall capital account, portfolio and direct investment, and other flows for various countries are reported in table 5.7. According to this index, Korea is performing poorly for overall capital and portfolio investment flows, much lower than the Asian (developing) countries' total. But the index shows that Korea has a very high degree of gross flow for foreign direct investment, much higher than the Asian total. However, it is interesting to observe that Japan's indices for all forms of capital flow are lower than the industrial countries' total (recall that Japan's capital flows as a percentage of trade were in all cases higher than the total; table 5.4). In particular, Japan's index for foreign direct investment is much lower than Korea's.

In sum, the openness of Korea's capital flows appears low, whether measured as the importance of capital account in foreign transactions, as in table 5.4, or as intraindustry trade in capital flows. However, the intraindustry trade index, especially for foreign direct investment, is higher vis-à-vis the Asian total than is flow as a percentage of trade. And the trade index, even the one for portfolio investment, rises over time, contrary to the case of the percentage of trade. Therefore, one may conclude that the openness of Korea's capital account is rising and registers higher on the intraindustry trade index than on capital flow as a percentage of trade.

However, in the case of Japan, one can see the reverse: the intraindustry trade indices for portfolio and foreign direct investments declined during the 1980s and were much lower than that of industrial countries' total, while the opposite trend is observed for capital flows as a percentage of trade, as seen in table 5.4. This implies that even if Japan shows a relatively large volume of total capital flow in foreign transactions, the nature of the capital flow is more counteractive, in response to current account surpluses, and less capital flow for its own sake, independent of the current account trend. According to this interpretation, Japan's openness of capital flow, very high by almost all measures, seems to be rather limited.

5.4.5 Evaluation

One may conclude from this section that Korea's capital mobility rose gradually during the 1980s and remains reasonably high, comparable to Taiwan's

12. Gros (1992) also used this index for measuring the effectivenss of capital control in EC countries, but without fully recognizing the importance of this index as a measurement of capital mobility that reflects trade in risky assets.

Table 5.7 **Gross Flow Indices for Capital Flow**

Country	Overall Capital Account[a]			Portfolio Investment			Foreign Direct Investment			Other Long-term Capital			Other Short-term Capital		
	1981–85	1986–90	1981–90	1981–85	1986–90	1981–90	1981–85	1986–90	1981–90	1981–85	1986–90	1981–90	1981–85	1986–90	1981–90
Industrial countries[b]	0.87	0.89	0.88	0.92	0.97	0.94	0.89	0.85	0.87	0.09	0.59	0.34	0.90	0.90	0.90
United States	0.54	0.58	0.56	0.59	0.23	0.41	0.41	0.69	0.55	0.06	0.13	0.10	0.52	0.83	0.68
Japan	0.43	0.56	0.50	0.67	0.44	0.56	0.13	0.04	0.08	0.11	0.14	0.13	0.82	0.79	0.81
Germany	0.50	0.39	0.45	0.78	0.64	0.71	0.34	0.30	0.32	0.00	0.00	0.00	0.45	0.35	0.40
Asia (developing countries)[c]	0.71	0.57	0.64	0.12	0.26	0.19	0.17	0.49	0.33	0.16	0.70	0.51	0.86	0.72	0.79
Korea	0.38	0.29	0.34	0.00	0.17	0.09	0.54	0.53	0.54	0.55	0.33	0.44	0.18	0.23	0.20
Singapore	0.60	0.41	0.50	0.47	0.31	0.39	0.19	0.13	0.16	0.31	0.34	0.32	0.64	0.44	0.54
Indonesia	0.00	0.00	0.00	0.00	0.00	0.00	0.00	0.00	0.00	0.00	0.00	0.00	0.00	0.00	0.00

Source: IMF, *Balance of Payments Statistics Yearbook* (Washington, D.C.).

[a]A weighted average of individual indices of portfolio investment, foreign direct investment, and other long-term and short-term flows with the weight given by the relative size of each category of capital flow in the total capital flow.

[b]See table 5.4, note a.

[c]See table 5.4, note b. Data for Taiwan were not available.

but markedly lower than Japan's. While Taiwan has maintained a higher constant measure of capital mobility than Korea, this estimation is less precise, and time-varying measures show insignificant variations, implying that there has not been much improvement in Taiwan's capital mobility during the 1980s. For Japan, even with its very high degree of capital mobility during the 1980s by almost all measures, the intraindustry trade index for capital flows suggest a relatively limited degree of capital mobility when compared to other measures, such as capital flow as a percentage of trade.

5.5 Concluding Remarks

It has been suggested that stable macroeconomic conditions with low inflation, interest rate deregulation, and a flexible exchange rate system are the prerequisites to successful capital account liberalization. According to the optimal sequencing literature, these conditions should be satisfied before the capital account is opened to any substantial degree.

Korea is now at the threshold of stabilizing its domestic economy, which has been overheated since the late 1980s, and correcting its current account deficit. This is still creating some concern about the possibility that capital inflow may add to inflationary pressure, further aggravating the domestic macroeconomic situation. As mentioned earlier, although official interest rate deregulation policy has been in effect, the pace of deregulation has not developed well, instead becoming entangled with government interventions. The prospect for interest rate liberalization at the moment seems very gloomy. On the other hand, the exchange rate regime is very much liberalized and moving in the right direction.

Because of some of the impediments that still exist in Korea, it may be the case that rapid capital account liberalization is premature at this point. However, now the government as well as the private sector has recognized the need and the inevitability of opening the capital account sector. The business sector in Korea has been eager to expand its access to foreign credit, because the domestic supply of credit is tightly controlled. The government, for its part, is concerned about the effectiveness of its monetary policy and is against too active an inflow of capital initiated by the private sector, though it faces strong U.S. pressure to decontrol capital flow. The U.S. government has been one of the crucial factors in determining the speed of Korea's capital account opening. The United States is pressing the Korean government very hard to open its capital account to allow more freedom to U.S. banks, financial institutions, and businesses that want to invest in Korea. This international pressure will play an integral factor in determining the pace of capital liberalization.

The Korean government, despite the real possibility of rendering domestic monetary policy ineffective, is seriously debating opening the capital account to realize the potentials of free capital movement in the longer policy horizon. Now, the government is preparing a long-term, gradual plan for capital account liberalization[13] and has already enacted a new Exchange Control Law that institutes the negative list system, a great improvement on the old positive list system.

In sum, one can safely say that Korea fares relatively well compared to Japan and Taiwan in terms of international capital mobility. Korea's absolute level of openness is still not very high, but it seems to be moving, even if a little slowly, toward liberalization and institutional and regulatory improvement.

Appendix A

Table 5A.1 Glossary of Variables Used and Their Sources

Variable	Definition and Measurement	Sources
M_t	Money stock (period average): M_2	1
P_t	Price level (period average): consumer price index	1
y_t	Real output: constant GNP	1
CAP_t	Private capital account: direct investment plus portfolio investment plus other capital, plus net errors and omissions	1
R_t	Money market rate: yield to corporate bonds for Korea, discount rate for Taiwan, and short-term interbank rate for Japan	1
R_t'	Domestic market-clearing interest rate that would be observed if private capital account were completely closed	1
R_t*	Uncovered interest parity rate	1, 2, 3
	Case A for Korea and Taiwan: LIBOR on 3-month dollar deposits plus actual exchange depreciation rate	
	Case B for Korea and Taiwan: LIBOR on 3-month dollar deposit plus expected exchange depreciation rate forecasted by ARIMA (1,1,0) model	1, 2, 3
	Covered interest parity rate for Japan: LIBOR on 3-month yen deposit in Euro-market.	1

Data Sources:
1. IMF, *International Financial Statistics,* (Washington, D.C.).
2. Korea Development Institute data base (Seoul).
3. *Financial Statistics Monthly, Taiwan District* (Taipei).

13. In this context, Korea may learn many useful lessons from the gradualist approach to capital account liberalization taken by Japan, Denmark, and Finland. See OECD (1990) for the experience of these countries.

Appendix B

Regulatory Changes in Controls on Capital Transactions during the 1980s.

Direct Investment by Foreigners

84.7.1
- Regulation system transformed from a positive list system to a negative list system.
- Automatic approval system for foreign direct investment adopted for foreign investment in manufacturing businesses with its share under 50 percent and the investment amount under $1 million dollars, unless tax exemption is applied.

87.7.1
- Responsibility of approval for direct investments subject to automatic approval transferred from the Minister of Finance to the Bank of Korea.

  The amount of foreign direct investment subject to automatic approval raised from $1 to $3 million dollars.

90.1.1
- The amount of foreign direct investment subject to automatic approval raised from $3 to $100 million dollars.

91.1.1
- Automatic approval system replaced by a simple reporting system.

Portfolio Investment by Foreigners

81.10.28
- Investment trust companies approved to issue matching funds to foreigners.

84.6.29
- Transaction of domestic securities by foreign investment companies approved. Korea Fund established on July 1, 1984.

85.11.25
- Issuance of convertible bonds and bonds with subscription warrants or stock depository receipts allowed for domestic firms.

87.3.24
- Korea Europe Fund established.

90.6.11
- Issuance of mixed form of matching fund allowed for investment trust companies.

92.1.1
- Portfolio investment in the domestic stock market allowed up to 3 percent of the outstanding shares by a single investor and 10 percent of the outstanding shares by a single company.

Direct Overseas Investment

81.7.21
- Evaluation Committee for Foreign Investment established in the Bank of Korea.
- Prerequisites relaxed for investors from 3 years to 1 year for the experience requirement, and the capital prerequisite relaxed.
- The withdrawal obligation for invested funds and prior approval system for foreign investment project plans abolished.

82.7.19
- The approval procedure simplified for foreign investments: requirement of opinion references of the related authorities abolished in cases of investments less than $100,000 dollars.
- The required ownership ratio for joint ventures alleviated: the required share reduced from over 50 percent to less than 50 percent when real management power can be secured.

83.12.21
- The limit for automatic profit reserve increased.

84.11.16
- Foreign investment prerequisite and evaluation criteria for foreign investments approval enacted.

85.5.24
- Amount of invested money for evaluation by the Inquiry Commission for Foreign Investment Projects adjusted upward from $500,000 dollars to more than $1 million dollars.

85.8.29
- Participation in cooperative projects added to the foreign investment category.

86.12.27
- A system introduced that substitutes authorization by confirmation only of the foreign investment requirements in cases of investments less than $200,000 dollars or an offer of technical service.

87.9.1
- The minimum amount subject to confirmation of foreign investment requirements increased from $200,000 to $500,000 dollars.
- The maximum reserved profit of overseas corporations increased from less than $100,000 dollars to $500,000 dollars.

87.12.28
- Investors' qualifications relaxed, and experience prerequisites abolished.
- A simple reporting system introduced for foreign investments of less than $1 million dollars and foreign investments by reserved profit of less than $1 million dollar.
- Categories of investments subject to approval by the Review Commission for Foreign Investment Projects reduced; the investment amount adjusted upwards from $3 to $5 million dollars, and investment for real estate and agriculture excluded from those categories.

88.3.25
- Export credit deleted from the foreign investment category.
- The limits for voluntary profit reservations abolished for overseas local corporations and an overall reporting system introduced for additional investment by the profit reserves.

  Investment qualification prerequisite relaxed: investment approval by main transaction banks abolished.

  The approval procedure simplified.
- Foreign investments of less than $1 million dollars by individuals liberalized.

88.7.1
- The own-capital requirement removed from the investor qualification.
- Foreign investments by debt-equity swap allowed.

88.9.15
- Providing technical service excluded from the foreign investment category.
- Category of investment expanded for real estate investments.
- Regulation on types of preferred businesses in foreign investment abolished.
- Export-Import Bank of Korea allowed to accept the reporting for foreign investments when projects meet regulatory requirement and are given financial support by the Bank.

88.11.1
- The category of investment subject to the simple reporting obligation expanded from less than \$1 to \$2 million dollars.

89.2.13
- The limit for foreign investments by individuals abolished. The previous limit was \$1 million dollars.
- Gratification requirements for investment relaxed. The ownership share reduced from 50 percent to 20 percent for security investment, and the minimum interest rate requirement (above 6-month Libor rate) abolished.

89.8.10
- The category of investment in foreign real estate expanded.

    Corporations: real estate related to businesses such as facilities for research or training institutes.

    Individuals: overseas acquisition of real estate for business operation and residential houses for workers who work at a foreign branch for a long time period.

90.7.1
- The screening criteria strengthened for the prospect of business for large investments or investments exceeding self-financed capital.

    Large-scale projects: project is larger than \$50 million dollars with Korea's share larger than 50 percent or Korea's share is larger than \$30 million dollars.

    Projects exceeding own capital: the investment exceeds \$5 million dollars and is more than investor's own capital.

Overseas Portfolio Investment

Investment in Foreign Currency Securities by Institutional Investors

85.9.1
- Regulations related to participation in underwriting groups for foreign currency securities enacted.

    Underwriting securities: foreign currency bonds and stock depository receipts that are issued by domestic corporation in foreign markets.

    Scope of underwriting: underwriting limits for each security company set to within 1 percent of the total amount of issuance or less than \$1 million dollars.

    Selling method: sell in foreign countries.

Financial funding for underwriting: the fund raised through selling securities in foreign countries.

87.9.1 • Regulations on investments in foreign currency securities by domestic security companies relaxed.

88.7.1 • Regulation on investments in foreign currency securities by institutional investors relaxed.

Category of investment institutions enlarged to include not only security companies but also investment trust companies and insurance companies.

Limits for investment amount increased to $30 million dollars for security companies and $10 million dollars for insurance companies and investment trust companies.

Investment category expanded to include not only participation in underwriting groups but also in purchasing foreign currency securities in secondary market, depositing foreign currencies, and purchasing certificates of foreign currency deposits issued by financial institutions.

Approval procedure overhauled to report to the Bank of Korea only when participating in underwriting groups, but approvals not required in other cases.

90.3.2 • The limit for investment in foreign currency securities by institutional investors extended.

Security companies: $50 million dollars for securities companies which acquired the dealing license for international businesses; $30 million dollars for others.

Investment trust companies: $30 million dollars for investment trust companies dealing with international businesses; $10 million dollars for others.

Insurance companies: $30 million dollars for insurance companies exceeding $5 trillion won in total assets; $10 million dollars for others.

Acquisition of Main Office Stocks by Korean Employees Who Work for Domestic Branch Offices of Foreign Companies

87.9.7 • Acquisition of main office stocks by Korean employees working for branch offices or offices of foreign banks allowed.

88.3.25 • Regulations on acquiring main office stocks relaxed. Stock acquisition approved for Korean employees who work for foreign direct investment companies or domestic branches of foreign companies in which stocks are allocated specially by the main office.

Short-term Borrowing

81.8.1 • Partial adjustment and relaxation of borrowing conditions.
Borrowing conditions changed from repayment in equal installments to repayment in installments.
Integration of final repayment period from 2 years, 2½ years, or under 3 years, starting on borrowing day to within 3 years.

82.7.29 • Partial relaxation of borrowing conditions.
Equal installment conditions abolished.
Conditions on borrowing interest rates abolished.
In the case of bridge loan, repayment by borrowing from the funds raised with the contract to issue foreign currency bonds allowed.

87.12.28 • The responsibility to review the application for bridge loan shifted from the Bank of Korea to the Minister of Finance.

Local Financing

87.9.1 • The category for local financing expanded to cases related to development of real estates by overseas local construction company.

87.12.28 • The beneficiary of trade related local financing expanded from importers from Korea to importers from Korea and exporters to Korea.

91.1.1 • Specific purpose regulation system replaced by general purpose regulation system.
• Local financing for facility investment and mortgage loan allowed.

91.9.1 • Exemption limit from the procedure of prior approval expanded from less than $1 million to $5 million dollars.
• Limitation of local financing expanded for trade related financing from 30 percent to 50 percent of annual exports.

References

Edwards, Sebastian, and Mohsin S. Khan. 1985. Interest rate determination in developing countries: A conceptual framework. *IMF Staff Papers* 32(3):377–403.

Fischer, Bernhard, and Helmut Reisen. 1992. *Towards capital account convertibility.* OECD Development Centre, Policy Brief no. 4. Paris: Organisation for Economic Cooperation and Development.

Frankel, Jeffrey A. 1989. *Quantifying international capital mobility in the 1990s.* NBER Working Paper no. 2856. Cambridge, Mass.: National Bureau of Economic Research, February.

Fukao, Mitsuhiro, 1990. Liberalization of Japan's foreign exchange controls and structural changes in the balance of payments. *BOJ Monetary and Economic Studies* (Bank of Japan) 8, no. 2 (September).
Gros, Daniel. 1992. Capital controls and capital market liberalization in southern Europe. Paper presented at a joint seminar on Monetary and Financial Policy Reform held by KDI and Friedrich Ebert Stiftung, May 27–28.
Hanson, James A. 1992. An open capital account: A brief survey of the issues and the results. Paper presented at the Conference on the Impact of Financial Reform held at the World Bank, Washington, D.C., April 2–3.
Haque, Nadeem U., and Peter Montiel. 1990. *Capital mobility in developing countries—Some empirical tests*. IMF Working Paper, WP/90/117. Washington, D.C.: International Monetary Fund.
Ito, Takatoshi. 1986. *Capital controls and covered interest parity between the yen and the dollar.* NBER Reprint no. 897. Cambridge, Mass.: National Bureau of Economic Research.
———. 1991. *The Japanese economy.* Cambridge: MIT Press.
Jwa, Sung Hee. 1988. The political economy of market-opening pressure and response: Theory and evidence for the case of Korea and the United States. *Seoul Journal of Economics* 1(4).
OECD (Organisation for Economic Cooperation and Development). 1990. *Liberalization of capital movements and financial services in the OECD area.* Paris: Organisation for Economic Cooperation and Development.
Reisen, Helmut, and Helen Yèches. 1991. *Time-varying estimates on the openness of the capital account in Korea and Taiwan*. Technical Papers no. 42. Paris: Organisation for Economic Cooperation and Development.

Comment Kazuo Ueda

This paper provides a neat summary of Korean capital controls in the 1980s and an interesting econometric analysis of the degree of openness of Korean money and capital markets. In the following, I organize my comments from the perspective of a comparison between the Japanese and Korean experiences.

I was struck by the similarity between the Japanese and Korean experiences with controls on cross-border capital flows. Korean capital controls have responded significantly to balance of payments situations; the same thing happened in Japan in the 1970s. A balance of payments deficit led to more restrictions on capital controls, which were then relaxed as the deficit turned into a surplus.

It may also be interesting to comment on the background of the liberalization of controls in Japan that took place in the early 1980s. First, huge budget deficits in the late 1970s created a need for developing the market for government bonds, which in turn led to the liberalization of the movements of many other interest rates—a precondition for free international capital movements. Second, with the exception of brief periods following the two oil shocks in the

Kazuo Ueda is professor of economics at the University of Tokyo.

1970s, Japan was starting to record large structural current account surpluses, thus relieving the government of its concern about the effects of capital account opening on the balance of payments. Third, there were pressures from the United States to open Japanese markets. These points may provide some interesting lessons for understanding the process of capital account liberalization in Korea.

Jwa also refers to concerns about exchange rate appreciation and the loss of monetary control as impediments to liberalization. These concerns are obviously the two sides of the same coin. If a country wants free capital movements and independent monetary policy, it needs a flexible exchange rate and must forget about exchange rate changes. Japan has moved to a flexible exchange rate since 1973 but has not abandoned exchange rate targets completely, for various reasons. Hence, there have been serious constraints on domestic monetary policy—one good example being the excessive monetary expansion of the late 1980s and the resultant asset price inflation.

I have some reservations about the more technical aspects of the paper. Looking at the ratio of net to gross capital flows as a measure of capital account openness is interesting. Japan is on the liberal side according to this standard. However, this is due to the presence of regulations in the domestic market which have forced Japanese firms to raise funds in foreign markets.

In another test of capital account openness, the estimation of equation (1), Jwa uses actual exchange rate changes in the R^* variable, which creates an errors-in-variables problem, biasing the coefficient estimate toward zero. In the same test, the difference between R and R' depends on the size of private capital movements relative to money supply. This should be small for a country like Japan, which tends to make the coefficient on R' close to zero. A more natural test, though difficult because of the unavailability of data, would be a comparison of Euro-market and domestic interest rates.

Comment Pochih Chen

1. Part of capital flow may hide in trade by reporting false prices and by the practice of lead and lag. Therefore, in addition to the fact that the ratio of trade to GNP may differ from country to country, using the ratio of reported capital flow to trade as an indicator of capital mobility may induce significant measurement errors.

2. Capital flow itself may be a factor affecting money demand, especially in a temporary equilibrium. When someone shifts his money from currency A to currency B in expectation of the future appreciation of currency B, he would keep the funds in the form of money for a while and therefore increase his

Pochih Chen is professor of economics at National Taiwan University.

demand for money in currency B. This is a demand for money similar to the speculative demand for money pointed out by Keynes. If equation (2) of this paper could include this factor the results would be even more convincing.

3. Capital flow may be sterilized by the monetary authority. Capital flow may also influence the credit creation ability of domestic financial institutions. Therefore, the effect of capital flow on money supply may not be as simple as the relation $M' = M - CAP$ used in this paper.

4. Under a floating exchange rate system, money supply will not be affected by capital flow directly. Its indirect effects through exchange rate variations would be very different from what is assumed in this paper.

5. From an econometric point of view, there would be a notable problem caused by measurement error in R_t'. As pointed out above, the method to estimate R_t' is not very delicate, so there would be significant measurement error in R_t'. Because R_t' appears on both sides of equation (1), the estimated value of the coefficient of $(R_t^* - R_t')$ in equation (1) would have a tendency to come closer to one when the measurement error of R_t' increases. This would explain some part of the unacceptable results of the estimations in section 5.4.3.

6. Using the intraindustry trade index to measure the degree of capital mobility induced by the differences in the risk nature of financial assets is an interesting method. However, if the time period for measuring this index is too long, it is possible that there are significant changes in the economic situation so that the relative magnitude of capital inflow and outflow would change drastically within a single period. The direction of net flow may also change. In an extreme case, we may have only capital inflow in one part of the period and only capital outflow in another part. Consequently, intertemporal trade within a period would be misregarded as intraindustry trade, if the length of the period for measuring this index is too long.

6 An Asian Capital Crunch? Implications for East Asia of a Global Capital Shortage

Rachel McCulloch

The strong growth performance of developing countries in East Asia has been fueled by inflows of foreign, especially Japanese, capital. However, dramatic changes in the Japanese economy and elsewhere across the globe are sure to have a major impact on future patterns of saving and investment worldwide. Based on these anticipated changes, many analysts see the threat of a global capital shortage, with dire implications for those areas most dependent on financial inflows from abroad.

This paper reviews the evidence for an impending world shortage of capital and assesses the implications for East Asia of increased competition for international investment. The paper focuses in particular on the role of foreign direct investment, often a potent mechanism for the international transfer of advanced technology and manufacturing organization. One surprising conclusion is that a regime of high capital costs could actually provide further encouragement for the already rapid growth of direct investments from the Asian newly industrialized countries (NICs)—Hong Kong, Korea, Singapore, Taiwan—into other Asian nations.

6.1 What We Mean by a Capital Shortage

The possibility of world "shortage" of capital or savings has clearly become a concern among economic analysts as well as policymakers (Solomon 1991; IMF 1991b). Although the concept is seldom made precise, such a shortage presumably exists when ex ante demand from potential investors exceeds the supply of savings at given terms. If capital transactions are mediated by banks and other market-based private financial institutions, a capital shortage in this

Rachel McCulloch is Rosen Family Professor of Economics at Brandeis University and a research associate of the National Bureau of Economic Research.

sense might be expected to occur at most transiently, with any incipient gap between global savings and global investment quickly eliminated by an induced rise in real rates of interest. One possible interpretation of a capital shortage is thus simply an upward movement in real interest rates.[1] But the history of global capital movements over the past two decades suggests this view is at best incomplete and misses some important features of real-world flows, especially flows to developing countries.

A first crucial omission is the time dimension. Some frequently cited factors underlying the predicted global shortage of capital are secular trends, the most important among these being the decline in private saving in the industrial nations. Others represent large but strictly temporary developments, such as the capital requirements of Kuwait's reconstruction efforts following the 1991 Gulf War. In the early 1990s, a recession in the United States and several other major nations kept private investment in those regions unusually low despite stimulative monetary policy, and the trend in interest rates has been down rather than up.

In the United States, one reason for a very sluggish response to monetary stimulation was that, although short-term interest rates dropped to near-record lows, long rates fell much less. While stickiness of the long rates may have simply reflected lenders' worries about future inflation, an alternative interpretation is that markets anticipated a global capital shortage that would materialize as the industrial nations recovered.

A second problem with the simple story suggested above is the assumption that the market response to changes in supply and demand consists mainly of a movement in price, i.e., interest rate. Even in well-developed financial markets, the reality is far more complex. *Large* long-term changes in supply and demand in a given financial market surely have some impact on interest rates facing those currently in that market, but they also stimulate major shifts of transactors *between* markets and promote the development of new financial instruments and markets. The impact may thus vary according to the type of transaction.

The 1970s offer a graphic illustration of the importance of induced institutional change. Few of the actual consequences of petrodollar recycling in the 1970s could have been predicted by extrapolation from the institutional arrangements already in place in 1973. Indeed, an analysis that focused on the marginal responses of the important pre-1973 players and institutions would have missed almost all of the action. Rather than attempting to increase loans by cutting rates to current borrowers, international bankers literally roamed the world in search of profitable new markets. Thanks to these efforts, by 1981

1. Berner and Sargen (1990) treat a global capital shortage as synonymous with higher real interest rates. Collins and Rodrik (1991) also emphasize estimates of resulting interest-rate increases in their analysis of macroeconomic impact abroad from restructuring in the former Soviet bloc.

Table 6.1 **Funds Raised on International Credit Markets, by Type of Borrower, 1981 and 1989 (% of total)**

	1981	1989
Developed countries	68.4	87.8
Eastern Europe and USSR	0.8	1.3
Developing countries	27.5	6.7
Multilateral institutions	3.3	4.2

Source: Calculated from United Nations (1991, table A-30).

developing nations accounted for more than one-quarter of all funds raised on the international credit markets (see table 6.1). Of course, the debt crisis of the early 1980s led to another major shift, and by 1989 the share of developing nations had dropped to less than 7 percent. For the 1990s, new shifts across markets are already evident. In particular, borrowers in many regions, but most notably Eastern Europe and the former Soviet Union, are shifting away from commercial borrowing in favor of the World Bank and the international Monetary Fund (IMF) as potential sources of new loans, while at the same time a few developing countries are attempting a modest return to bank loans and bond issues as sources of new capital (IMF 1991b).

The final and most important problem with the simple story is that much of the world's international flow of capital, and in particular the flow to developing nations, is not in fact mediated by well-developed, highly integrated, financial markets. In this category are foreign direct investment, some lending and some borrowing by national governments, and most lending by multilateral institutions such as the World Bank and the IMF. In 1987, bilateral and multilateral official development finance (loans and grants) accounted for two-thirds of net resource flows from OECD nations to developing nations, while direct investment accounted for two-thirds of the remainder (see table 6.2). Although these channels differ significantly, an important common element is that in each case a capital shortage is likely to be met through some type of rationing of credit (or of grants) in addition to—or even instead of—a simple rise in its interest cost. An analysis that focuses on interest rates alone assumes that transactors lend or borrow freely at those rates, yet for most types of transactions this assumption is incorrect. Even when financial capital is highly mobile internationally, the terms borrowers face from various alternative sources of credit may be linked only loosely.[2]

2. Frankel's (1991) results indicating a high degree of international capital mobility are based on a comparison across currencies of rates on highly standardized securities (government bonds), a tiny slice of overall capital markets. Mobility in this sense is likely to be much greater than in the Feldstein-Horioka (1980) sense. The breakdown of the Feldstein-Horioka relationship in the 1980s was driven mainly by a surge in U.S. government borrowing and thus may give little indication of the prospects for international flows overall, especially flows to areas in which even government debt cannot be viewed as a riskless asset. The idea of a capital market consisting of loosely

Table 6.2 **Net Resource Flows to Developing Countries, by Type, 1980 and 1987 (% of total)**

	1980	1987
Official development finance	35.2	66.5
Export credits	13.3	−0.8
Private flows	51.6	34.3
Direct investment (OECD only)	8.7	22.5
International bank lending	38.2	5.6
Bond lending	1.2	0.6
Other private	1.6	1.7
Nongovernmental organizations	1.9	3.9

Source: OECD (1988, table III-1).
Note: Details may not add to totals due to rounding.

A second important common characteristic of capital flows to developing nations is the desire on the part of the lenders, and sometimes also on the part of the borrowers, for continuing involvement between the source of capital and the investment activity financed by that capital. For both official development finance and private direct investment, arm's-length transactions are rare exceptions; the prevailing assumption is that the investment's rate of return will be enhanced when the lender also engages in monitoring, training, technology transfer, marketing, and other functions that entail an ongoing multidimensional relationship with the borrower.

The relatively large role of bank credit in the 1970s and early 1980s accommodated the long-standing desire of many developing nations to "unbundle" activities previously carried out through direct investment, i.e., to substitute arm's-length transactions (debt) for ones requiring complex ongoing links with the lender (equity). Had direct investment rather than bank loans been the major vehicle for channeling petrodollars to developing nations, failed projects would have produced disappointing results for corporate stockholders rather than an international debt crisis. In addition, the failure rate for projects undertaken with these funds might well have been lower.

6.2 The Crunch in Bank Credit

A related but different problem from the hypothesized global capital shortage is the credit crunch arising from international banks' attempts to meet the new capital-adequacy standard of the Bank for International Settlements (BIS). This standard, called the Basel standard, requires commercial banks to have $4 of equity capital for each $100 of risk-weighted assets. To meet the standard, many banks have needed to increase capital or to reduce the average riskiness of their asset portfolio. In Japan, the adjustment process has been complicated by the sharp decline in the stock market, because Japanese banks hold stocks as part of their capital base (Murray 1992).

The recent increase in the vigilance of bank regulators in a number of countries provides a second reason to anticipate qualitative change in banking practice. With new regulatory standards in place and old ones enforced with greater zeal, bankers are likely to favor the most conservative lending choices. Since capital adequacy is measured on a risk-adjusted basis, one paradoxical result may have been *lower* bank-lending rates to certain classes of borrowers (e.g., U.S. Treasury bonds; in the early 1990s, market-determined rates on Treasuries fell to their lowest level in decades) as banks attempted to expand their safest investments at the expense of riskier ones (e.g., loans to smaller businesses).

Changes in bank behavior have little or no direct effect on either the supply of savings or the demand for new investment, although they are likely to have important effects on the process by which the two are reconciled. Moreover, because changes in bank behavior affect the money-supply process, regulatory changes have the potential to translate into a significant monetary shock. Thus, the overall impact of regulatory changes in banking may be far from negligible, especially for countries like the United States that are in the early stages of recovery from recession. However, the underlying problem here is not a capital shortage but a disruption in established patterns of financial intermediation.[3]

6.3 Trends in Saving

Since the explosion of international capital flows in the early 1970s, a few supersavers among the world's nations have accounted for the lion's share of net capital inflows to the rest. However, as figure 6.1 and table 6.3 illustrate, the identity of those important few has not remained constant over time. In the 1970s, the major source of new external financing was the recycled current-account surpluses of OPEC nations. In the 1980s, although some OPEC nations continued to show sizable surpluses, Germany and Japan dominated total outflows of surplus national savings (see tables 6.3 and 6.4).[4] But for the 1990s, new circumstances suggest that each of these sources may make a smaller contribution to global flows.

The national savings shortfall relative to domestic investment in the United

linked segments is similar to the preferred habitat analysis used by Modigliani and Sutch (1966) to analyze the term structure of interest rates.

3.There may be a parallel to the late 1980s, when the behavior of asset markets reflected in part the market response to unfamiliar investment opportunities opened up by financial deregulation. Recent regulatory developments have been a response to the unforeseen responses of deregulated markets.

4. Table 6.4 also underscores the extent of error in national current-account statistics. The discrepancy between total world current-account surpluses and the corresponding total deficits probably indicates a large and growing volume of unreported international capital flows.

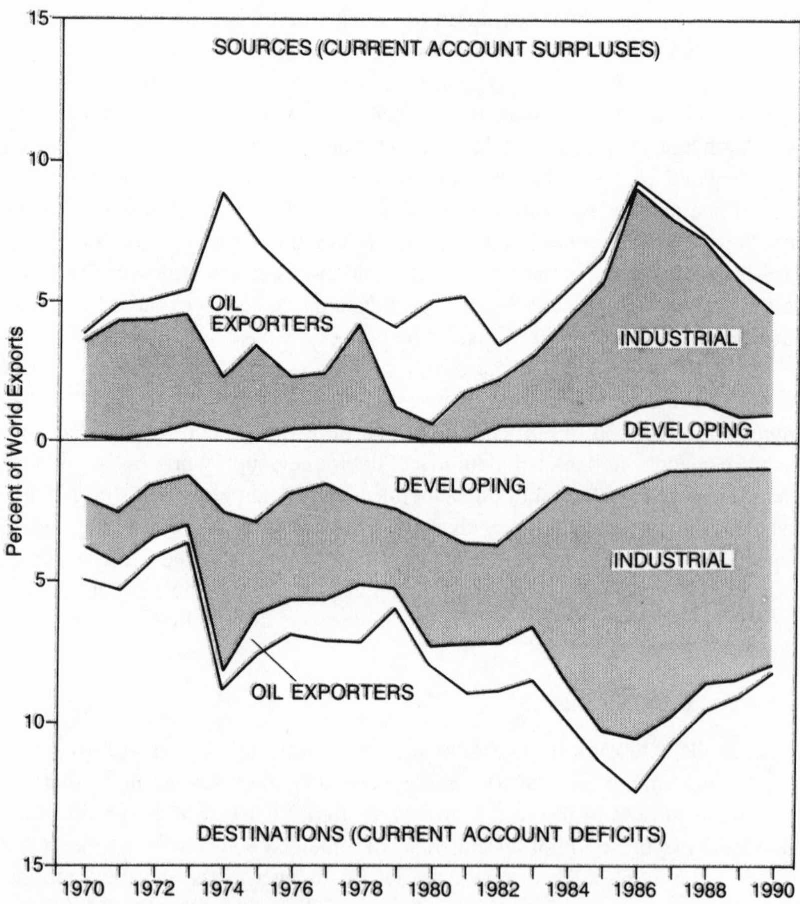

Fig. 6.1 Sources and destinations of world capital flows
Source: McCulloch and Petri (1992).

States has been widely discussed, and widely deplored, both at home and abroad. Less often noted is that the OECD area as a whole has shown evidence of a secular decline in national saving. Analysts explain this reduction, present in many but not all OECD nations, in terms of the slowing of population growth and the associated aging of the population, as well as by reduced government saving—smaller budget surpluses or larger budget deficits—that has not been entirely offset by greater private saving (Dean, Durand, Fallon, and Hoeller 1990). Although Japan continues to save more than its OECD counterparts, it too has experienced a secular decline in the saving rate. However, the effect of this trend on Japan's capital exports has been masked by two other important changes, the integration of Japan's financial markets into world capi-

Table 6.3 **Current Account Positions of Selected Countries, 1974–91 (billion $ U.S.)**

	1974	1980	1986	1990	1991
Oil exporters					
Kuwait	5.9[a]	15.3	5.3	−2.2	—
Saudi Arabia	23.0	42.8	−11.9	−4.1	—
OECD					
Germany	10.6	−14.0	39.9	46.4	−20.6
Japan	−4.7	−10.8	85.8	35.9	72.9
United States	1.9	1.8	−145.4	−92.1	−8.7

Source: IMF (1988, 1992).
[a]Figure for 1975.

Table 6.4 **Current Account Positions by Region and Selected Country, 1990 (billion $ U.S.)**

Region and Country	Current Account
Total	−84.4
International organizations	7.6
Industrial countries[a]	−95.8
United States	−92.2
Japan	35.9
Germany	46.8
United Kingdom	−24.6
Developing Africa	1.4
Developing Asia[a]	−4.1
China (PRC)	12.0
Indonesia	−2.4
Korea	−2.2
Malaysia	−1.6
Philippines	−2.7
Singapore	2.4
Taiwan	10.8
Thailand	−7.1
Central Europe	−7.9
Middle East	16.2
Developing Western Hemisphere	−1.8

Sources: IMF (1991a, table A-1); World Bank (1992, table 18).
[a]Details are for selected countries only and so may not add to totals.

tal markets and a secular decline, albeit from a very high level, in the rate of domestic investment spending.

In the short run, two temporary but important factors could operate in the opposite direction, producing a higher rather than lower OECD saving rate. A sharp decline in real estate prices in many areas, especially in the United States and the United Kingdom, has greatly reduced the ability of households to finance spending through home-equity loans. Negative wealth effects from the fall in real estate and equity prices may also reduce household spending in Japan and some other parts of East Asia.

6.4 The Emergence of Newly Industrializing Supersavers

Most analysts conclude that the likely net effect of the factors summarized above will be to shrink the global supply of savings in the 1990s, at least once the major industrial economies have resumed normal growth. However, the now-standard account omits what may be the most important potential source of international capital flows for the 1990s and beyond: the developing countries themselves, and particularly those in East Asia. While inflows of foreign resources have played a significant role in the development of each of the NICs, their very high rates of domestic capital formation have been financed primarily by very high rates of domestic saving. Moreover, the NICs have already shown their potential as capital exporters, although their current contribution to global capital flows is still small relative to that of Japan. Their high (and in some cases, still rising) saving rates, together with strong growth, suggest these nations cannot be ignored in predicting trends in international capital flows, and especially flows within East Asia.

Ironically, the main pressure to limit potential capital exports from these new sources comes from the world's number one international borrower, the United States. During the 1980s, U.S. policymakers viewed Asian current-account surpluses as the major factor underlying record current-account deficits at home. The root problem was thus seen—at least in Washington—as an excess supply of financial capital in Asia rather than an excess demand for financial capital in America. Accordingly, the U.S. response was to urge (or even demand) adoption of policies in Japan and the Asian NICs to reduce capital exports—domestic expansion and exchange-rate appreciation in Asia, plus direct management of trade flows between Asian nations and the United States. Korea, for example, moved from a peak current-account surplus of more than \$14 billion in 1988, to a 1990 current-account deficit of more than \$2 billion, while Taiwan's current-account surplus fell from nearly \$18 billion in 1987 to less than \$11 billion in 1990 (IMF 1992).

Whether the U.S. approach made sense in the 1980s is open to debate, but its disadvantages are clearly magnified in a period of anticipated global capital shortage. Nonetheless, the same pressures to limit Asian current-account surpluses remain in place in the 1990s. Although the overall U.S. current-account position improved dramatically from 1988 to 1992, at least part of that improvement is expected to be reversed as the economy recovers. The challenge is thus to encourage, or at least not to discourage, Asian capital exports to other nations, while at the same time continuing to reduce politically troublesome U.S. bilateral trade imbalances with Japan and the Asian NICs.

6.5 Trends in Investment

While the prospects for expansion of the global supply of savings are at best clouded even when trends among the Asian NICs are taken into account, there are many new reasons to anticipate an increased overall demand for those savings, especially once the OECD nations have recovered from the current slump.

One major cause of new investment spending is the response to opportunities created by regional economic integration, both ongoing and anticipated. While the peak of investment spurred by the expansion and consolidation of the European market may already be past, the successful conclusion of negotiations to establish a North American Free Trade Area (NAFTA) is expected to accelerate the growth of investment flows to Mexico and to the U.S. border region.

Germany's abrupt turnaround from leading capital exporter to net capital importer (see table 6.3) is the consequence of the unexpectedly high cost of reunification. Although some of this cost reflects the investment required to modernize the capital stock of the former East Germany, a substantial part stems from the needed clean-up of decades of environmental neglect. The high cost of German reunification is thus significant both because of its direct impact on Germany and the world, but also as an indication of the size of likely future financial flows associated with the restructuring of Eastern Europe and the former Soviet Union.

However, any extrapolation from East Germany to the former Soviet bloc must distinguish between the cost of socially desirable restructuring and the cost of the actual restructuring that can be anticipated in the near future. Although it accounts for only a small fraction of the region in terms of population or area, the former East Germany is in a special position that virtually ensures that needed restructuring will actually occur within a relatively brief period. The same presumption cannot be made for the other nations (Collins and Rodrik 1991).

The developing nations as a group illustrate the same distinction between socially desirable restructuring and likely capital flows: the poorest and least-developed nations are unlikely to attract even a proportionate share of total resources flowing to the developing world, and certainly not a share that reflects the extent of needed economic transformation. However, important changes in some of the largest developing nations suggest that the flow of private capital to these regions may be larger in the 1990s than in the 1980s.

Despite some recent setbacks (e.g., Peru, Haiti), the move in Latin America toward democratically elected governments and market-guided development policies has improved the atmosphere for direct foreign investment and for private investment in general; in some countries, notably Mexico, changed political and economic prospects have halted or even reversed the capital flight of the 1980s. In Africa change is also in the wind. A successful political transition in South Africa, for example, could mean a resurgence of foreign investment in a nation that once attracted large amounts of capital from abroad. In Asia, the People's Republic of China (PRC) is once again moving in the direction of market activity, and even India appears to be opening its economy to market forces. At least in the near term, the Middle East is likely to invest more at home, and thus send less capital elsewhere, as Kuwait rebuilds its infrastructure. And across all these regions, greater attention to environmental concerns, especially as they apply to the developing world, will translate into new investment projects encouraged by and financed through multilateral agencies.

As with saving, temporary but important factors may reduce investment demand in some areas. Sharply lower equity prices on the Japanese stock market have led some Japanese multinationals to revise their plans for offshore expansion. Lower prices for real estate, especially commercial real estate, in many OECD nations have led developers to scale back plans for new construction. In either case, the impact is unlikely to be felt only at the margin, i.e., as small reductions across all areas. Rather, each major project still at the planning stage will have to be reevaluated.

6.6 Restoring the Saving-Investment Balance

With the potential for substantially increased investment demand in many regions, some investment plans will have to be scrapped or deferred unless saving also grows. As noted above, there is demonstrated potential for new Asian supersavers to fill at least part of the incipient gap. But an increase in current-account surpluses among the Asian NICs could also create new trade frictions. Moreover, unless their contribution becomes very large, some form of global capital shortage is nonetheless likely to materialize. Another possibility is that governments will choose to save more,[5] i.e., to reduce budget deficits by spending less or increasing tax revenues.[6]

The regional impact of an incipient capital shortage depends critically on the means by which conflicting ex ante plans are reconciled. To the extent that interest rates are pushed upward, there are obvious distributional implications for borrowing and lending nations. Nations with large external debt could feel the kind of pain many developing nations experienced in the early 1980s. This group would include many of the same problem debtors as before, but now

5. This assumes, as evidence from past OECD behavior suggests, that changes in government saving are not fully offset by induced changes in private saving (Dean, Durand, Fallon, and Hoeller 1990).

6. For example, Solomon (1991) concludes his analysis of a coming capital shortage by noting that "the most reliable policy action would be to enlarge government saving. . . . One would hope that the end of the Cold War and the subsequent peace dividend would make this possible without undue political strain." Although recent events make talk of a peace dividend seem premature, the Clinton administration has made defense cuts an important element in efforts to reduce the U.S. budget deficit.

also the United States. Higher interest payments on the huge U.S. government debt would further complicate America's problem of controlling the government deficit, although a large part of the interest payments are to U.S. residents and thus do not represent a net burden to the nation. Net lenders could expect to benefit correspondingly from high real returns on their assets, assuming that borrowers, especially among the developing nations, are not pushed into default. Unfortunately, a new round of debt crisis cannot be ruled out. This would imperil the promising reforms recently implemented in a number of developing nations.

However, as suggested above, rising interest rates would be just one possible consequence of a global capital shortage, and perhaps not even the most important. With capital scarce, most lenders will respond in part by rationing credit rather than simply raising rates. In particular, because of the perceived threat to world peace of economic collapse in the former Soviet Union, lending there is likely to be determined as much by international politics as by market forces. Likewise, political pressure at home will encourage international companies to limit new activities abroad before curtailing planned domestic projects.

6.7 Direct Investment and Firm Strategy

So far this discussion has looked only at prospects for aggregate global flows of capital, ignoring their composition. But the role of private international capital flows in promoting growth in developing nations appears to be tied most closely to the investment activities of businesses, i.e., to foreign direct investments. Moreover, the volume and even the direction of direct investment flows, whether worldwide or between any two regions, is linked only loosely to overall capital flows. Although direct investments do often entail some international transfer of financial capital, this is not their central function.

Foreign direct investment represents the expansion of a firm's business activities into another country. This can mean establishment of a new local subsidiary, but also acquisition of an existing local enterprise or initiation of a joint venture. Direct investors usually possess a competitive advantage such as superior technology, managerial know-how, brand recognition, or efficient channels for product distribution. Foreign direct investment in effect transfers the firm's competitive advantage for use in a new location. This process is fundamentally different from other kinds of investment because the transfer does not leave less of the firm's intangible capital available for use at the other end. The competitive advantage can thus be viewed as having the character of a public good within the enterprise. (Of course, this does not apply to any financial capital, managerial input, or machinery that is also part of the investment package.)

Firms incur the extra expense of establishing production facilities abroad because the location itself confers a substantial advantage. This advantage may reflect the usual elements of comparative advantage as reflected in lower production cost; transport costs, barriers to imports, or host-country policy inducements also play an important role in determining the most advantageous location for production. However, because expansion through direct investment usually means higher cost of management, advantageous location alone is not enough to explain the establishment of foreign subsidiaries. Unless the investor has an advantage over local firms sufficient to offset the higher costs of international coordination, the benefits of location will be captured instead by domestic firms. Moreover, unless the parent firm adds over time to its intangible asset (through new research and development, for example), the relative profitability of foreign control is likely to erode over time. In mature industries, this erosion produces a tendency for control to shift to local entrepreneurs.[7]

6.8 Direct Investment in East Asia

In the 1980s, the scene for an explosion of outward direct investment by firms in Japan and the Asian NICs was set by three related but distinct changes in government policy: elimination of most restrictions on capital outflows, a liberalized regulatory environment toward inward direct investment (in particular, a smaller role for performance requirements), and host-country economic reforms to bring domestic prices into line with world prices (United Nations 1992).

Although in some cases government policies at home gave firms an extra push to expand operations abroad, a large number of direct investments by Asian firms were driven by two location-related factors: exchange rates and trade policy. Japanese direct investment accelerated in the second half of the 1980s, following the sharp rise in the yen relative to the dollar in 1985. Currency revaluations in the late 1980s similarly spurred outward direct investments by firms in Korea and Taiwan (see table 6.5). In all three cases, the exchange rate movement, together with rapidly rising wages at home, provided firms with an incentive to move some manufacturing operations offshore. Other Asian nations became favored locations for labor-intensive manufacturing activities (see table 6.6).

The direct-investment responses to changes in trade policy have been more complex, reflecting the increased use of selective trade restrictions by major importing nations. Production is sometimes moved to the importing country, as in the case of Japanese automobile production for the North American and European markets. Alternatively, it may be shifted to as-yet uncontrolled alternative export sites that offer a significant cost advantage. The Multifibre Agreement and its various precursors thus provided an important impetus for

7. Wells (1992) sees such a shift over time to local ownership in the case of NIC investments in Indonesia. These are typically low-technology manufacturing operations whose relocation is dictated mainly by rising labor costs at home.

Table 6.5 Taiwanese and Korean Direct Investment Abroad, 1985–91 (million $ U.S.)

	1986	1987	1988	1989	1990	1991
Taiwan						
Worldwide total	66	704	4,120	6,951	5,243	1,854
Korea						
Worldwide total (A)	121	300	281	620	1,332	1,368
ASEAN (B)	3	177	57	172	441	273
B/A (%)	2.6	59.1	20.2	27.7	33.1	20.0

Sources: Central Bank of China, *Balance of Payments: Taiwan District, the Republic of China* (Taipei, December 1992); Bank of Korea, *Foreign Investment* (Seoul, various issues [courtesy of Won-Am Park]).

Table 6.6 Direct Investment in Selected East Asian Countries, 1985–91 (billion $ U.S.)

Country	1985	1986	1987	1988	1989	1990	1991
Malaysia	0.7	0.5	0.4	0.7	1.7	2.5	3.5
Indonesia	0.3	0.3	0.4	0.6	0.7	1.1	1.5
Thailand	0.2	0.3	0.2	1.1	1.7	2.3	—
China (PRC)	1.0	1.4	1.7	2.3	2.6	2.7	—

Source: IMF (1992).

the worldwide dispersion of textile and apparel production, and of the associated technology, management skills, and marketing networks, first from Japan to the NICs, and more recently from the NICs to less-developed, lower-cost, and sometimes less-restricted export sites.[8]

Although Japan remains the largest single source of direct investment for most Asian nations, other Asian investors now account for a surprisingly large, and growing, share. This new pattern may reflect the desire of some host nations to avoid excessive dependence on a single source of capital or technology, as well as the location-related motivation of the NIC investors already discussed. In 1988–89, the four NICs together committed almost $8 billion to direct investments in Indonesia, Malaysia, the Philippines, and Thailand, while Hong Kong alone registered $6.6 billion of investments in the PRC over the same period (United Nations 1991). For Indonesia, the anticipated inflow of new direct investment from other Asian source countries has recently exceeded that from Japan (Wells 1992).

8. See Wells (1992) on NIC foreign direct investments in Indonesia and Petri (1992) on investments in Thailand.

6.9 Implications of Scarce Capital for Direct Investment

How will a period of global capital shortage or a shorter-term credit crunch affect direct investment flows from and into East Asia? The surprising answer is that direct investments (and associated transfers of technology and know-how) from the Asian NICs into other Asian nations may be headed for a period of even more rapid expansion. Several related but distinct factors favor the expansion of NIC firms into new Asian locations.

First, for reasons noted above, Japanese firms may scale down their plans for foreign expansion, at least temporarily; indeed, several have already announced their intentions. Thus, host-country competition to attract NIC investments will intensify. While Japanese investments have been especially prized by national planning authorities because of their presumed technological excellence, NIC investments can also offer a welcome technological boost along with the other benefits associated with any new project.

Second, a regime of high capital costs promotes the use of smaller-scale, labor-intensive technologies rather than those requiring large investments in plant and equipment. This favors the types of projects carried out by smaller NIC-based firms over their typically larger and more capital-intensive Japanese, U.S., and European competitors. New investments will be clustered in relatively labor-intensive industries, and within any given industry, in the more labor-intensive production technologies.

Third, the likely expansion of labor-intensive production activities will in turn enhance the location advantage of relatively low-wage Asian nations like Malaysia, Indonesia, Thailand and perhaps the PRC and Vietnam over location sites elsewhere, especially Europe and North America. Although Eastern Europe also offers low labor costs as well as greater proximity to Western markets, problems of property rights, dispute resolution, and worker motivation (all familiar to firms with investments in the PRC) are substantial deterrents. In addition, Asian sites are favored by many smaller investors on account of physical proximity, family ties, or cultural propinquity.

Finally, even if interest rates move upward, there may be reason to expect relatively little impact on capital costs for smaller firms based in the NICs. Much of the investment by these firms is financed either internally or by local partners in the host country, so conditions in global capital markets may play only a remote role in determining the cost of these funds. In Korea, the move toward liberalization of internal capital markets may even have the effect of reducing borrowing costs for smaller firms as government policy attempts to limit chaebol economic dominance.

6.10 Concluding Comments

The review of developments in worldwide patterns of saving and investment suggests that both a short-term credit crunch and a longer-term capital shortage, while by no means assured, may be realistic concerns. However, the examination also underscores that few if any of the important capital-market developments of the past two decades could have been foreseen from a similar exercise of adding up anticipated changes in the supply of savings and demand for investment.

Even in a world of highly integrated capital markets, the consequences of either a crunch or a prolonged shortage are unlikely to materialize mainly as a marginal adjustment to higher interest rates. Rather, any large change in market conditions will promote major shifts across markets, or between market and nonmarket credit sources. Even in market transactions, an important part of the adjustment will come through nonprice mechanisms for allocating credit.

Of course any rise in interest rates will favor lenders. However, in the specific area of foreign direct investment the impact is complex. Direct investors are typically both sources and users of capital. Moreover, high capital costs favor some investments and some investment sites over others. The particular characteristics of direct investment carried out by firms located in the Asian NICs in other Asian nations suggest that a regime of higher capital costs will favor rapid growth of direct investment, and associated transfers of technology and know-how, from the Asian NICs into other Asian nations. An unexpected consequence of a global capital shortage may thus be to reduce the dependence of Asian developing nations on Japan as a source of technology and capital.

References

Berner, Richard B., and Nicholas P. Sargen. 1990. The global capital "shortage": Implications for interest rates. New York: Salomon Brothers, December.

Collins, Susan M., and Dani Rodrik. 1991. *Eastern Europe and the Soviet Union in the world economy.* Washington, D.C.: Institute for International Economics, May.

Dean, Andrew, Martine Durand, John Fallon, and Peter Hoeller. 1990. Saving trends and behavior in OECD countries. *OECD Economic Studies* 14 (Spring): 7–58.

Feldstein, Martin, and Charles Horioka. 1980. Domestic saving and international capital flows. *Economic Journal* 90:314–29.

Frankel, Jeffrey. 1991. Quantifying international capital mobility in the 1980s. In *National saving and economic performance,* ed. B. Douglas Bernheim and John B. Shoven. Chicago: University of Chicago Press.

IMF (International Monetary Fund). 1991a. *Balance of payments statistics yearbook.* Washington, D.C.: International Monetary Fund.

———. 1991b. *International capital markets: Developments and prospects.* Washington, D.C.: International Monetary Fund, May.

———. 1992 and earlier issues. *International financial statistics.* Washington, D.C.: International Monetary Fund.

McCulloch, Rachel, and Peter Petri. 1992. Development finance in an era of capital shortage. Brandeis University Department of Economics Working Paper no. 318.

Modigliani, Franco, and Richard Sutch. 1966. Innovations in interest rate policy. *American Economic Review* 56 (May): 178–97.
Murray, Alan. 1992. Who will finance growth in the '90s? *The Wall Street Journal,* May 4.
OECD (Organisation for Economic Cooperation and Development). 1988. *Development co-operation.* Paris: Organisation for Economic Cooperation and Development, December.
Petri, Peter. 1992. Platforms in the Pacific: The trade effects of direct investment in Thailand. *Journal of Asian Economics* 3:173–96.
Solomon, Robert. 1991. Do we face a global shortage of capital? Brookings Discussion Papers in International Economics, no. 91. Washington, D.C.: Brookings Institution, December.
Wells, Louis T. 1992. Mobile exporters: New foreign investors in East Asia. Paper prepared for the NBER Conference on Foreign Direct Investment Today, May 15–16.
United Nations. 1991. *World economic survey 1991.* New York: Department of International Economic and Social Affairs.
———. 1992. *World investment directory.* Vol. 1, *Asia and the Pacific.* New York: United Nations Centre on Transnational Corporations.
World Bank. 1992 and earlier issues. *World development report.* Oxford: Oxford University Press.

Comment Chong-Hyun Nam

Rachel McCulloch sets out two important propositions in her interesting paper. One is that a short-term credit crunch along with a long-term capital shortage is now becoming a real possibility. The other is that, surprisingly enough, such a global capital shortage is likely to cause Asian NICs to expand, rather than contract, their direct investments into other Asian developing nations. Both propositions are based on careful reviews of surrounding factors. I would like to address my comments to each of these two propositions.

Indeed, I agree with McCulloch's first proposition. As she detailed in her paper, there is ample evidence to believe that global savings will fail to meet global demand for investment in coming years. In most OECD nations, as well as in many OPEC nations, excess savings over domestic investment are not likely to be generated for some time. At the same time, demand for outside sources of funds is expected to rise significantly in many Eastern European countries as well as in the former soviet republics.

The Asian NICs will not be of much help either. Unless the United States changes its trade policy toward the NICs, they are not likely to remain supersavers too much longer. Korea is a good case in point. Of the Asian supersavers, Korea has already become a net capital importer since 1990, after a short period of trade surplus from 1986 to 1989. Of course, many factors contributed to this, but persistent U.S. pressure on the Korean government for

Chong-Hyun Nam is professor of economics at Korea University.

currency revaluation was certainly a major one. As then–U.S. Trade Representative Carla Hills testified before the U.S. Congress, U.S. trade policy toward Korea was most successful on that score. If the United States achieves the same victory over the rest of the Asian NICs, these countries will soon cease to be supersavers, as well.

In addition to such gloomy prospects for regional savings and investment demand, there are now some indications that the world economy is coming out of recession, which is bound to increase investment demand relative to savings capacity.

Now, let me turn to McCulloch's second proposition, that an unexpected consequence of such a global capital shortage may be increased foreign direct investments by Asian NICs in other Asian developing countries, making these nations less dependent on Japan. I have reservations about this proposition on several grounds.

First of all, given the current level of trade surplus in Japan and the prospect that it will be maintained for some time, I wonder where Japan will turn to dump its extra savings. My hunch is that it will keep increasing its portfolio as well as its direct investments abroad. Certainly Asian developing nations will remain attractive sites for Japanese investors. So, in my view, the recent slowdown of Japanese foreign direct investment in Asian developing nations may be only a transitional phenomenon.

Second, of the Asian NIC supersavers, Korea, as I mentioned earlier, has already become a net capital importer, and other Asian NICs may follow suit as long as the United States sticks to its current trade policy. In my view, this policy is likely to continue into the Clinton administration. In other words, given their large dependence on the U.S. market, Asian NICs may choose to ease trade frictions vis-à-vis the United States by increasing domestic investment demand rather than generating excess savings over domestic investments. If this is the case, then, any foreign direct investments they make would need to be financed by foreign savings, which are expected to become increasingly tight.

Finally, I have a hunch that the Asian NICs, as well as Japan, are likely to keep their outward direct investment at a rather high level mainly because their economic growth rate is likely to remain higher than that of the rest of the world, and so they will need to make quicker structural adjustments. Many firms and industries with diminishing comparative advantage may, therefore, wish to relocate their production sites into other Asian developing nations.

An important question is whether their outward direct investment will be encouraged or discouraged as external capital market conditions become more tight. I think this will depend, to a large extent, on the degree of substitutability or complementarity between direct investment and other types of capital movements, especially when the global capital market becomes more tight. I think this is an empirical question yet to be answered.

Comment Kazumi Asako

Rachel McCulloch has presented a very neat and concise paper on worldwide capital markets centering especially on an Asian capital crunch. Many issues are discussed in the paper, and I agree with most of the conclusions. But, in order to play the discussant's role, I will pick up several issues and raise questions.

First, as a general comment, I would like to express a bit of dissatisfaction, as follows: In many places McCulloch states important propositions and observations without referring to the actual data. In other words, her analysis is mostly qualitative in nature and lacks quantitative or statistical foundations. I think McCulloch should include statistical analysis or simulation analysis to improve the persuasiveness of the paper.

Second, I question whether one of the most important conclusions of the paper has quantitative support. That is, I wonder whether the role played by East Asian countries such as Korea and Taiwan as capital exporters to the other Asian countries is large enough to replace the role played by Japan. McCulloch observes that Japan's role as a capital exporter to the Asian countries will decrease in the 1990s partly because stock and land prices have fallen in Japan. But, I think both Korea and Taiwan have also experienced declines in stock and real estate prices. For this reason, I cannot imagine how these countries can afford capital exports large enough to replace Japan's.

Third, I agree that a regime of high capital costs promotes the use of smaller-scale, labor-intensive technologies rather than those requiring large investments in plant and equipment. But, again, I would like to know the quantitative importance of this substitution effect. Without any solid data analysis, the conclusion that the higher the capital costs the larger the direct investments from the Asian NIEs into other Asian nations is not secured.

Fourth and finally, I would like to know how McCulloch assesses the capital flows which are related to environmental protection, which is a hot issue nowadays. Capital flows of Japanese official development aid (ODA) are likely to change because of environmental considerations. How about capital flows between East Asian countries and other Asian countries?

Kazumi Asako is professor of economics at Yokohama National University.

7 Money, Output, Exchange Rate, and Price: The Case of Taiwan

Chung-Shu Wu and Jin-Lung Lin

7.1 Introduction

Does a high growth rate of the money supply necessarily cause a high inflation rate? From table 7.1, it can be shown that from 1981 to 1989, the average annual growth rate of the money supply (M_2) was 22.40 percent. Though the average annual growth rate of real GNP was 8.36% in the same period, there still existed a large gap between the growth rates of nominal GNP and money supply. This puzzling phenomenon was especially apparent during the period 1986–88. Then, the annual growth rates of M_{1b} were extremely high, 33.55, 45.66, and 29.45 percent for each year, respectively. Nevertheless, during the same period, price indexes were either stable or trended downward; among them, the annual growth rates of the CPI were 0.70, 0.51, and 1.29 percent, respectively, and annual growth rates of the WPI were −3.34, −3.25, and −1.56 percent. This strange phenomenon has caused people to wonder whether there *is* a specific relationship between money supply and price.

Many papers have been written on the relationship between money supply and prices. However, the conclusions of these papers are not uniform. For example, Perry (1980) and Saini (1982) find no evidence that money supply has a significant impact on prices. In contrast, Bordo and Choudhri (1982), Burger (1978), Yu (1977), and Wu (1989) do find such evidence. Moreover, little of the existing empirical literature explicitly takes into account the role the exchange rate plays in the relationship between money supply and prices. From

Chung-Shu Wu is research fellow of the Institute of Economics, Academia Sinica. Jin-Lung Lin is associate research fellow of the Institute of Economics, Academia Sinica.

The authors are grateful to Takatoshi Ito for his constructive criticism and helpful suggestions. We are also indebted to two referees, Maria Gochoco and Khee Glap Tan, for clarifying discussions and valuable advice. Finally, we have benefited from comments by Anne Krueger, Koichi Hamada, Rachel McCulloch, and the participants in the conference.

Table 7.1 Annual Growth Rates of Money Supply, Real GNP, and Prices in Taiwan, 1971–91 (percentage change)

Year	*M1B*	*M2*	CPI	WPI	PGDP
1971	—	—	2.79	0.02	—
1972	28.97	28.33	2.97	4.47	5.84
1973	52.12	37.52	8.20	22.85	14.80
1974	20.34	21.07	47.46	40.58	32.70
1975	24.24	31.56	5.23	−5.07	2.27
1976	21.09	21.82	2.49	2.77	5.37
1977	29.63	30.99	7.04	2.76	6.26
1978	36.61	31.14	5.77	3.54	5.26
1979	19.27	17.24	9.75	13.83	11.50
1980	19.42	18.14	19.01	21.54	16.19
1981	14.50	18.89	16.33	7.62	12.14
1982	15.53	23.03	2.96	−0.18	3.47
1983	17.92	26.25	1.36	−1.18	1.95
1984	14.07	23.33	−0.03	0.47	0.86
1985	8.19	21.29	−0.16	−2.59	0.62
1986	33.55	23.31	0.70	−3.34	3.36
1987	45.66	26.57	0.51	−3.25	0.53
1988	29.45	22.06	1.29	−1.56	1.05
1989	12.75	16.83	4.41	−0.37	3.10
1990	−3.31	10.96	4.13	−0.61	3.80
1991	6.62	15.70	3.62	0.17	3.97

Year	RGNP	RX	PM	JUVM1	JUVM2	JUVM 3&4
1971	13.01	0.00	3.61	—	—	—
1972	13.38	0.00	7.07	—	—	—
1973	12.78	−4.47	19.17	45.68	5.47	22.39
1974	1.16	−0.68	49.06	56.49	206.25	33.53
1975	4.44	0.00	−5.58	−13.02	−1.42	−2.09
1976	13.70	0.00	1.16	−4.19	8.32	−3.82
1977	10.25	0.00	7.77	2.53	6.75	9.20
1978	13.99	−2.74	9.19	−2.11	−0.70	17.16
1979	8.45	−2.59	16.35	17.07	27.83	17.05
1980	7.12	−0.01	20.29	66.42	74.57	12.53
1981	5.76	2.35	8.64	−24.38	14.36	9.58
1982	4.05	6.19	−0.70	−10.44	0.66	−2.19
1983	8.65	2.41	−1.47	−6.71	−9.27	−5.70
1984	11.59	−1.17	−0.38	9.90	−4.22	1.78
1985	5.55	0.58	−1.25	−13.51	−2.96	−7.76
1986	12.57	−4.99	−10.06	−13.11	−38.36	−4.11
1987	11.87	−16.12	−7.58	−12.03	−9.6	−8.17
1988	7.84	−9.93	−0.69	6.08	−19.17	4.06
1989	7.33	−7.63	−2.24	−11.13	1.45	−2.40
1990	5.02	1.84	2.87	1.68	21.08	−6.68
1991	7.32	−0.29	−0.85	−1.16	−5.23	−0.61

Notes: M_{1b} = currency in circulation + checking accounts + passbook deposit; $M_2 = M_{1b}$ + quasi money; CPI-consumer price index; WPI-wholesale price index; PGDP-GDP deflator; RGNP = real GNP at 1986 constant prices; RX = exchange rate (*NT/US*); PM = import price index; JUVM1 = import unit value index (agriculture, forestry, fishery, livestock, and hunting products); JUVM2 = import unit value index (minerals); JUVM3&4 = import unit value index (manufacturing products).

the traditional quantity theory of money we know, under the assumption of constant transaction velocity, that the nominal money supply has a positive relationship and real transactions a negative relationship with the price level. With the long-run income elasticity of money demand being 1.6, this high growth rate of real GNP can partly explain why we had only a moderate price fluctuation in the 1970s and early 1980s.[1] However, high growth of real GNP can not explain the case in the late 1980s. Though, in that period growth rates of real GNP were indeed very high, the average inflation rate was much lower than in the 1970s or early 1980s. In addition, if we take a close look at the fluctuation of the exchange rate (see table 7.1) we find that during the period 1985–89, the New Taiwan (NT) dollar appreciated from 39.83 to 26.41 to the U.S. dollar, an appreciation rate of 33.69 percent. Because of this appreciation of the NT dollar, the import price index was decreasing in the late 1980s—during the period 1985–89 the average annual growth rate of the import price index was −4.36 percent—and most of the group import unit value indexes were decreasing as well (see table 7.1).

From these statistics we can see that it may be important to take into account the fluctuation of exchange rates when we discuss the relationship between money supply and inflation rate. If we neglect the impact of the exchange rate as do most traditional empirical studies, we might not be able to explain fully the behavior of price movement and might obtain incorrect predictions of future inflation rates. Therefore, the main purpose of this paper is to reexamine the long-run equilibrium relationship between money supply, output, and price by appropriately taking into account the exchange rate.

Recognizing the importance of stationarity in regression analysis, economists often take the difference of a series to remove the stochastic trend and then proceed with the regression analysis using the differenced series. However, as should be clear from section 7.3, the existence of a long-run equilibrium imposes linear constraints on the long-run components of those variables and taking differences would result in the loss of this precious information. Cointegration analysis—the technique we employ—allows long-run components to obey equilibrium constraints while short-run components have a flex-

1. An equation in Wu (1987) shows that the short-run money demand function of Taiwan can be expressed as

$$\underset{}{m_t} = \underset{(-1.854)}{-1.175} + \underset{(2.105)}{0.393Y_t} - \underset{(-3.825)}{0.092r_t} + \underset{(6.544)}{0.750(M_{t-1}-P_t)} - \underset{(6.948)}{0.879\Delta P_t} + \underset{(3.239)}{0.029Q3}$$

$$+ \underset{(3.180)}{0.035Q4} + \underset{(6.642)}{0.061Q1},$$

$$\rho = 0.252(1.66),\ \bar{R}^2 = 0.993,\ \text{D-W} = 1.996,\ \text{SEE} = 0.022,$$

$$LM1 = 0.0004,\ LM2 = 0.900,\ LM3 = 1.332,$$

where m = real money supply, Y = real GNP, r = interest rate, M = nominal money supply, P = price level, ΔP = change of price, Qi = seasonal dummy, ρ = first order serial correction coefficient, $\bar{R}^2 = R^2$, LM = Lagrangian multiplier jth order serial correlation test. It can be calculated from this equation that the long-run income elasticity of money demand is about 1.6 which is very similar to the results found by Chiu (1992), Chiu and Hou (1992), and Shih (1988).

ible dynamic specification. The estimation method adopted here is Johansen's high-powered maximum likelihood procedure (Johansen 1988; Johansen and Juselius 1990).

The remaining sections of the paper are organized as follows. In section 7.2 we use a simple model to illustrate the relationship between money, output exchange rate, and price. Section 7.3 discusses the statistical method used to analyze the cointegrated systems, section 7.4 offers some empirical results, and section 7.5 contains some concluding remarks.

7.2 Money, Output, Exchange Rate, and Prices

Assuming a two-goods small open economy, the general price index, π, is mainly composed of the domestic price of domestic output, *P*, and the domestic price of the foreign good, *Q*, i.e., the general price index can be defined as

$$\pi_t = \theta p_t + (1 - \theta)q_t, \; 0 \leq \theta \leq 1, \tag{1}$$

where lower-case letters represent the natural logarithm of the values of upper-case letters and θ is the domestic consumption share of the domestic good.[2]

Suppose that the currency of this country can only be used as an exchange medium for domestic transactions and there is no transaction friction in this economy. From the well-known quantity theory of money, the increase of prices of domestic goods would be proportionate to the increase in the domestic money supply. Written in a logarithm form, the old quantity theory can be expressed as

$$m + v = p + y, \tag{2}$$

where *m* is the logarithm of domestic money supply, *v* is the logarithm of the velocity with which domestic money circulates, and *y* is the logarithm of the level of total domestic transaction. If *v* is constant or growing at a steady rate and *y* is also growing at a steady rate, changes in *p* would be directly related to changes in *m*.

If the goods markets are determined through arbitrage, then the domestic price of the foreign good is the foreign price of the foreign good multiplied by the exchange rate. Written in a logarithm form, this relationship can be expressed as

$$q_t = q_t^* + e_t, \tag{3}$$

where q_t^* is the logarithm of the foreign price of the foreign good and e_t is the logarithm of the spot exchange rate (defined as the price of a unit of foreign money in terms of domestic money).

2. The cost of living is best measured by a price index when the utility function is of Cobb-Douglas form.

Combining equations (1), (2), and (3), the relationship among money, total transaction exchange rate, and prices can be stated as

(4) $$\pi_t = \theta(m + v - y) + (1 - \theta)(q_t^* + e_t).$$

For analytical convenience, we assume the velocity of transactions and the foreign-currency price of foreign goods are constant and are normalized to zero. Therefore, it can be seen from (4) that the domestic money supply and the exchange rate should have a positive relation with the domestic general price index, i.e., the increase of domestic money supply and the depreciation of domestic currency would raise the domestic general price index. In contrast, the increase of total transactions would decrease the domestic general price index.

The above deduction might explain why the high growth rates of money supply in Taiwan in the 1980s did not coincide with high inflation rates. From 1981 to 1989, the average annual growth rate of the money supply (M_2) was 22.40 percent. However, the average growth rate of real GNP, which is a proxy for total domestic transaction, was 8.36 percent. In addition, during the same period, the NT dollar appreciated from 37.79 NT/U.S. dollar to 26.12, an appreciation rate of 29.7 percent. The implication is that, though the growth rate of the money supply had a positive effect on inflation rates, high real output growth and the appreciation of the exchange rate resulted in low inflation rates in the 1980s. Thus, we investigate the relationship between money, output, exchange rate, and prices in Taiwan and try to find out whether there is a long-run relationship among them.

7.3 Statistical Analysis of a Cointegrated System

Traditional least squares regression analysis usually suffers the problem of nonstationarity of the time series. Phillips (1986) showed that, in least squares regressions with nonstationary regressors, coefficient estimates might not converge in probability as the sample size increases, and the distribution of *t*-statistics diverge. Therefore, in this paper we adopted Johansen's maximum likelihood cointegration analysis to discuss the relationship between money, output, exchange rate, and prices in Taiwan.

Before we do the empirical analysis, we define the order of integration and cointegration (Granger 1981).

Definition: A series X_t is said to be *integrated of order d*, denoted $X_t \sim I(d)$, if $(1 - B)^d X_t = Z_t$, where $a_p(B)Z_t = b_q(B)\varepsilon_t$, ε_t, is white noise, and the roots of $a_p(B)$ and $b_q(B)$ lie outside the unit circle with no common factor. The components of the vector X_t are said to be *cointegrated of order (d, b)*, denoted $X_t \sim CI(d, b)$ if

(1) all components of $X_t \sim I(d)$, and

(2) there exists a vector β ($\neq 0$) such that $Z_t = \beta' X_t \sim I(d - b)$, where $b > 0$. The vector β is called the cointegrating vector.

The definition states that certain linear combinations of the components of the vector process are integrated of lower order than the process itself. As an immediate consequence, each variable can be nonstationary and can fluctuate rapidly whereas certain linear combinations of them fluctuate smoothly and rarely drift away from the attraction domain.

Granger (1983) and Granger and Weiss (1983) proved that any cointegrated vector system, X_t, has the error correction (EC) representation and vice versa. This result was later coined as the Granger Representation Theorem:

$$A^*(B)(1 - B)X_t = -\alpha\beta' X_{t-k} + \varepsilon_t , \tag{5}$$

where $A^*(0) = I_p$ and α and β are $p \times r$ matrices with $r \leq p$.

It is this representation theorem which endows cointegration with an economic equilibrium interpretation that has attracted economists' attention. To illustrate the main idea, assume $d = b = 1, p = 2$, and $r = 1$. Then after some rearrangement, (5) becomes

$$\begin{aligned} \Delta y_t = {} & a_1 \Delta y_{t-1} + \ldots + a_{k-1} \Delta y_{t-k-1} + b_1 \Delta \chi_{t-1} + \ldots + b_{k-1} \Delta \chi_{t-k-1} \\ & + \alpha(y_{t-k} - \beta \chi_{t-k}) + \varepsilon_t. \end{aligned} \tag{6}$$

Note that all terms in this difference are $I(0)$, and for the equation to be "consistent," the only term in level, $y_{t-k} - \beta\chi_{t-k}$ has to be $I(0)$ too. This term is called the cointegration error and measures the disequilibrium effects of the last k periods on the adjustment path of y_t. All other terms in the difference capture the short-run dynamics of the economic system. When the economy converges to a steady state all terms, including the cointegration error, approach zero. In other words, in equilibrium, y_t and x_t tend to stay in the equilibrium region, a linear line $y = \beta\chi$, in our case.

As the cointegrated system contains integrated regressors, the traditional asymptotic distribution results for regression parameters no longer hold. The t and F statistics do not follow the t and F distributions, respectively, even when the sample size is large. To tackle the estimation and testing issue, Engle and Granger (1987) suggest the two-step regression procedure.[3] Johansen (1988, 1991) makes an important contribution by (1) extending the bivariate system to a multivariate one and (2) deriving the maximum likelihood estimator and the asymptotic distribution of the likelihood ratio statistic, to which we now turn.

A vector autoregressive process is used to model the given series X_t:

$$X_t = \Pi_1 X_{t-1} + \ldots + \Pi_k X_{t-k} + \varepsilon_t, \tag{7}$$

3. This two-step estimator has been investigated by Stock (1987), Phillips (1988a, 1988b), Phillips and Durlauf (1986), Phillips and Park (1988), Phillips and Quliaris (1990), and Stock and Watson (1987).

where $t = 1, \ldots, T$, X_t has p elements, $\varepsilon_1, \ldots, \varepsilon_T$ are *i.i.d.* $N_p(0, \Lambda)$, and $X_{-k+1}, \ldots, X_0$ are given. Denoting the lag operator by B and setting $\Delta = 1 - B$, we rewrite the model as

(8) $$\Delta X_t = \Gamma_1 \Delta X_{t-1} + \ldots + \Gamma_{k-1} \Delta X_{t-k+1} + \Gamma X_{t-k} + \varepsilon_t,$$

where

(9) $$\Gamma_i = -I + \Pi_1 + \ldots + \Pi_i,\ i = 1, \ldots, k-1,$$

and

(10) $$\Gamma = -I + \Pi_1 + \ldots + \Pi_k.$$

Information about the long-run equilibrium is embedded in the coefficient matrix Γ. If the Γ is of full rank, then X_t is stationary. If Γ is the null matrix, then X_t is the traditional p-dimensional multivariate ARIMA(k, 1, 0) process. Finally, if $0 < \text{rank}(\Gamma) = r < p$, then there are r cointegration vectors. That is, there are $p \times r$ matrices α and β such that $\Gamma = \alpha\beta'$ and $\beta' X_t$ is stationary. Thus, the issue of testing a cointegration system is equivalent to testing the rank of Γ. More specifically,

(11) $$H_0\colon \Gamma = \alpha\beta',$$

where α and β are $p \times r$ matrices with full column rank and $r \leq p$.

Johansen (1988, 1991) proved that under the null hypothesis, $\Gamma = \alpha\beta'$, the maximum likelihood estimator of β is the first r eigenvectors, $\hat{v}_1, \ldots, \hat{v}_r$, corresponding to the r largest eigenvalues, $\hat{\lambda}_1 > \ldots > \hat{\lambda}_r$, of $S_{k0}S_{00}^{-1}S_{0k}$ with respect to S_{kk}, where

(12) $$S_{ij} = T^{-1}\sum_{t=1}^{T} R_{it}R_{jt}',\ i,j = 0, k\ ,$$

and R_{0t} and R_{kt} are the regression residuals of ΔX_t and X_{t-1} on lagged differences $\Delta X_{t-1}, \ldots, \Delta X_{t-k-1}$, respectively.

The likelihood ratio test statistic that there are at most r cointegration vectors is

(13) $$-2\ln(Q) = -T \sum_{i=r+1}^{p} \ln(1 - \hat{\lambda}_i)\ ,$$

and its asymptotic distribution is

(14) $$\text{tr}\left[\int_0^1 dBB'\left(\int_0^1 BB'du\right)^{-1}\int_0^1 dB'B\right],$$

where B is a $(p - r)$-dimensional Brownian motion with covariance matrix I.

The likelihood ratio test statistic for testing $H_0(r)$ against $H_0(r + 1)$ is given by

(15) $$-2\ln(Q;r/(r+1)) = -T\ln(1 - \hat{\lambda}_{r+1})\ ,$$

with asymptotic distribution

$$\lambda_{max}\left\{\int_0^1 dBB'\left(\int_0^1 BB'du\right)^{-1}\int_0^1 dBB'\right\}, \tag{16}$$

where $\lambda_{max}\{M\}$ denotes the maximal eigenvalue of M.

Equations (14) and (16) are referred to as trace and λ-max statistics, respectively. However, they are too complicated to have an analytical expression of their critical values, and hence we have to rely on a simulation experiment. The critical values can be found in Johansen and Juselius (1990).

7.4 Empirical Results

The data used in this paper is monthly data from January 1981 to January 1992.[4] Industrial production is used as a proxy for income, which is unavailable on a monthly basis. Money supply is measured by M_2 rather than M_{1b},[5] the exchange rate by the exchange rate of the U.S. dollars in terms of NT dollars, and prices by the CPI.[6] All variables are measured in logarithms and their graphs appear in figure 7.1.

It can be seen from figure 7.1 that the series are either increasing or decreasing through time, i.e., they are not stationary. To investigate the existence of a unit root, Dickey-Fuller (DF) and augmented Dickey-Fuller (ADF) tests with lags set to 4 are used. The t-statistics of ρ in the following regression are compared with the 95 percent quantile, 3.37 for DF and 3.17 for ADF.

$$\text{DF Test: } \Delta Y_t = -\rho Y_{t-1} + \varepsilon_t\,. \tag{17}$$

$$\text{ADF Test: } \Delta Y_t = -\rho Y_{t-1} + \alpha_1 \Delta Y_{t-1} + \ldots \alpha_4 \Delta Y_{t-4} + \varepsilon_t\,. \tag{18}$$

All variables overwhelmingly pass the test and we cannot reject the null hypothesis that each series has a unit root. The results are reported in table 7.2.

Equation (8) including a constant and 11 monthly dummies with $k = 3$ is fitted to the data. The Box-Pierce statistic with 12 degrees of freedom is computed for each equation to check the remaining serial correlation in the residuals. The critical value of chi-square distribution with size 0.05 is 21.026. As is obvious from table 7.3, all equations pass the test of no serial correlation in the residual. As for normality, we compute the Jarque and Bera (1980) statistics. All except money fail the test. However, since all four variables are fairly symmetrically distributed, this nonnormality should not cause serious prob-

4. Though the Taiwanese government adopted the floating exchange rate system in July 1978, it was not until March 1980 that the Central Bank in Taiwan eliminated the fluctuating range limit of the NT dollar.

5. M_2 is a broader definition of the money supply and is more appropriate than M_1 for explaining the fluctuation of prices. In their study of the Danish economy, Johansen and Juselius (1990) also use M_2 to measure the money supply.

6. The source of this data is the Taiwan EPS data bank, Ministry of Education.

Table 7.2 **Unit Root Test of Four Series**

Series	Dickey-Fuller	Augmented Dickey-Fuller
JQIND	2.377	0.632
M_2	1.315	1.835
RX	−1.485	0.055
CPI	−1.098	−1.074

Note: JQIND = industrial production; M_2, RX, and CPI as in Table 7.1.

Table 7.3 **Summary Statistics for Four Residuals**

Series	Skewness	Kurtosis	Normality ($\chi^2(2)$)	B.P.-Q ($\chi^2(12)$)
JQIND	−0.7030	2.460	43.491	8.538
M_2	−0.0756	0.599	2.067	17.352
RX	−0.8480	2.285	43.875	9.357
CPI	0.2400	1.293	10.306	12.380

Note: All series as defined in tables 7.1 and 7.2.

lems. The robustness of the maximum likelihood estimation (MLE) procedure is still an open question.

We have summarized in table 7.4 the estimated eigenvectors and eigenvalues and λ-max and trace test statistics. Using the trace test procedure for the hypothesis $r \leq 1$, the likelihood ratio statistic

$$(19) \qquad -2\ \ln(Q) = -T \sum_{i=2}^{3} \ln(1 - \hat{\lambda}_i) = 30.372$$

is insignificant as compared with the 95 percent quantile, 35.07. For the hypothesis $r = 0$, the test statistic is 58.79, which is greater than the 95 percent quantile, 53.35.

Using the λ-max test procedure for the hypothesis $r \leq 1$, the likelihood ratio statistic

$$(20) \qquad -2\ \ln\ (Q: r = 0|r = 1) = 28.39$$

is barely greater than the 95 percent quantile, 28.17. All these together strongly indicate that the rank of cointegration is 1.

The estimated long-run equilibrium relationship is

$$(21) \qquad \pi_t = -3.771Y_t + 1.277m_t + 0.691e_t\,.$$

All the signs are exactly the same as predicted by the theory: money supply and exchange rate have positive effects on price, and output has a negative effect. The graph of all three cointegration relationships appear in figure 7.2. For comparison, we also include cointegration relationship 4, though it is not statistically significant.

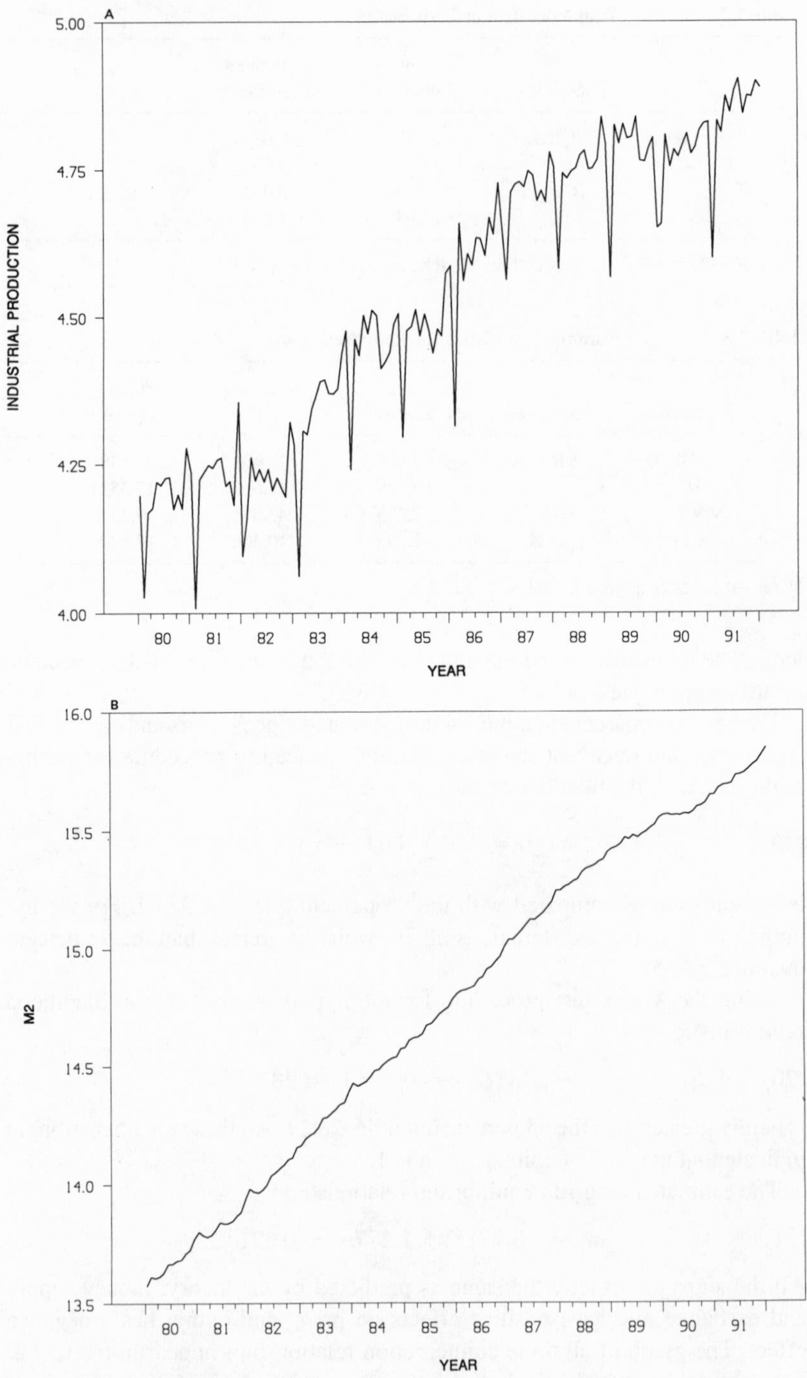

Fig. 7.1 A, Industrial production in Taiwan; B, M2 in Taiwan; C, exchange rate in Taiwan; D, consumer price index in Taiwan

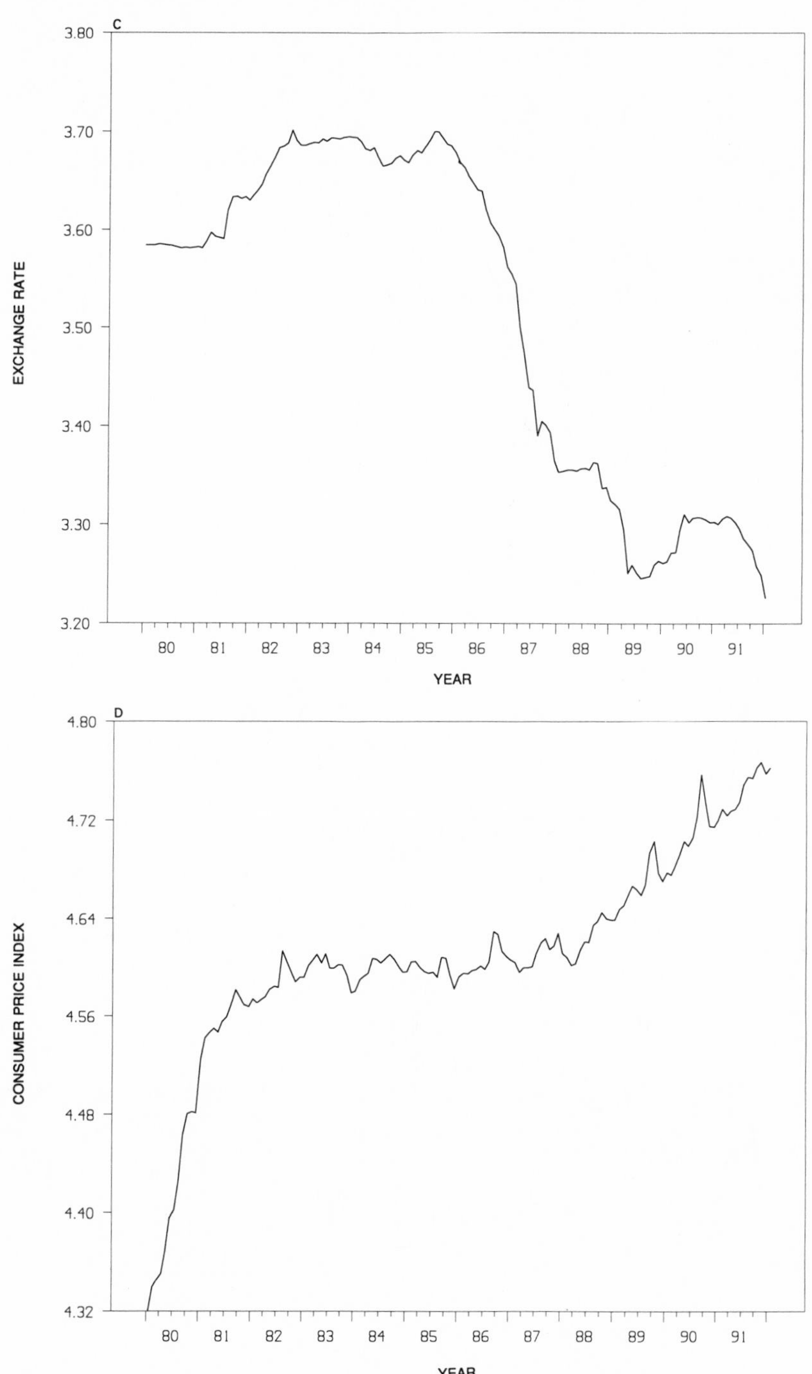

Fig. 7.1 (continued)

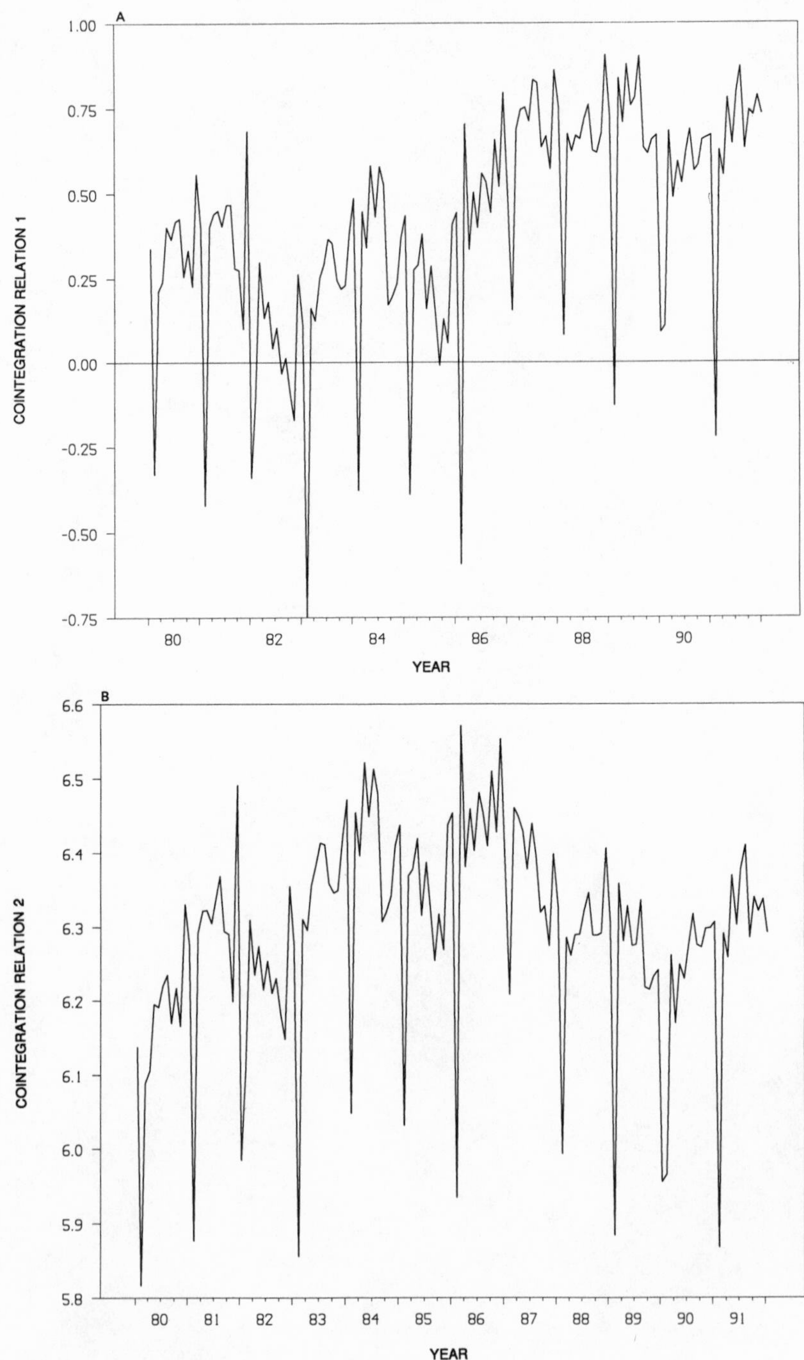

Fig. 7.2 A, Cointegration relation 1; B, cointegration relation 2; C, cointegration relation 3; D, cointegration relation 4

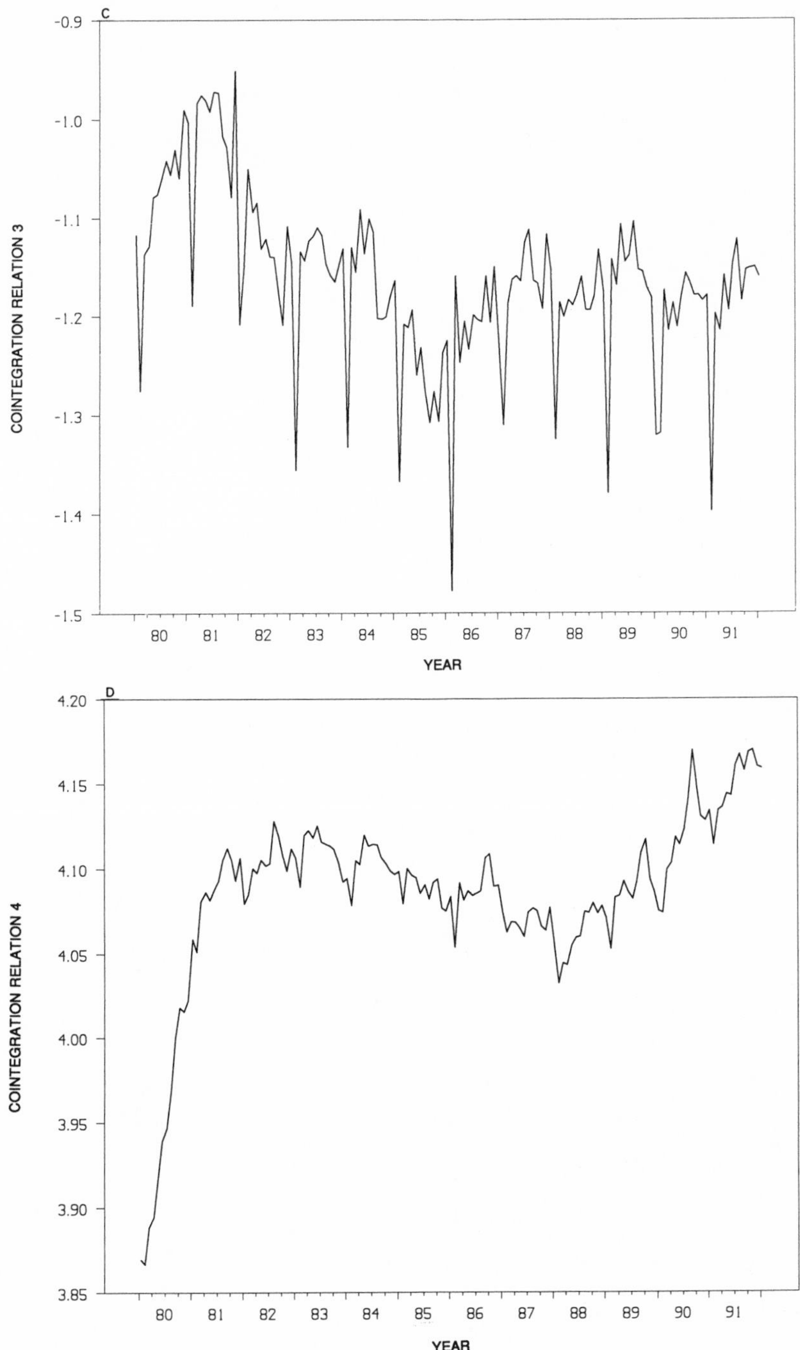

Fig. 7.2 (continued)

Table 7.4 **Estimated Eigenvalues and Eigenvectors, λ-Max Test, and Trace Test.**

Eigenvalues and λ-Max and Trace Test Statistics			
0.19623	0.14667	0.07100	0.00153
28.39719	20.61971	9.57369	0.19917
0.19917	9.77285	30.39257	58.78976
Eigenvectors			
20.842	−30.485	−15.534	4.833
7.057	9.800	9.505	−3.783
−3.819	−9.699	7.609	3.274
5.527	−16.338	−16.776	42.726

Note: In upper half, first row lists eigenvalues in descending order, second row the λ-max test statistics, and third row the trace test statistics. In lower half, each column vector is the eigenvector corresponding to the eigenvalue above in the same column.

For short-run dynamics, the error correction equation for price (monthly dummies not reported here) can be expressed as follows.[7]

$$
\begin{aligned}
\Delta\Pi_t = &- \underset{(-\,0.582)}{0.004} + [\, \underset{(2.155)}{0.015} * (\, \Pi_{t-1} + 0.377\, Y_{t-1} - 1.277\, m_{t-1} \\
&- 0.691\, e_{t-1})] + [\, - \underset{(-\,2.053)}{0.055}\, \Delta Y_{t-1} - \underset{(-\,1.931)}{0.052}\, \Delta Y_{t-2} \\
&- \underset{(-\,2.154)}{0.057}\, \Delta Y_{t-3} - \underset{(-\,2.425)}{0.064}\, \Delta Y_{t-4} - \underset{(-\,2.366)}{0.060}\, \Delta Y_{t-5} - \underset{(-\,2.576)}{0.063}\, \Delta Y_{t-6} \\
&- \underset{(-\,4.645)}{0.106}\, \Delta Y_{t-7} - \underset{(-\,3.919)}{0.093}\, \Delta Y_{t-8} - \underset{(-\,2.278)}{0.048}\, \Delta Y_{t-9} - \underset{(-\,0.771)}{0.011}\, \Delta Y_{t-10} \\
&- \underset{(-\,0.869)}{0.068}\, \Delta m_{t-1} - \underset{(-\,0.206)}{0.015}\, \Delta m_{t-2} - \underset{(-\,2.111)}{0.169}\, \Delta m_{t-3} - \underset{(-\,0.784)}{0.062}\, \Delta m_{t-4} \\
&- \underset{(-\,1.703)}{0.132}\, \Delta m_{t-5} - \underset{(-\,0.293)}{0.022}\, \Delta m_{t-6} + \underset{(1.927)}{0.139}\, \Delta m_{t-7} + \underset{(2.604)}{0.194}\, \Delta m_{t-8} \\
&+ \underset{(1.775)}{0.137}\, \Delta m_{t-9} + \underset{(2.047)}{0.157}\, \Delta m_{t-10} + \underset{(2.542)}{0.198}\, \Delta m_{t-11} - \underset{(-\,0.172)}{0.013}\, \Delta m_{t-12} \\
&+ \underset{(0.168)}{0.014}\, \Delta e_{t-1} + \underset{(0.140)}{0.012}\, \Delta e_{t-2} + \underset{(0.237)}{0.019}\, \Delta e_{t-3} + \underset{(0.080)}{0.007}\, \Delta e_{t-4} \\
&- \underset{(1.050)}{0.086}\, \Delta e_{t-5} + \underset{(0.511)}{0.040}\, \Delta e_{t-6} + \underset{(1.049)}{0.083}\, \Delta e_{t-7} + \underset{(0.477)}{0.037}\, \Delta e_{t-8} \\
&+ \underset{(2.784)}{0.215}\, \Delta e_{t-9} + \underset{(1.487)}{0.120}\, \Delta e_{t-10} - \underset{(-\,2.361)}{0.262}\, \Delta \Pi_{t-1} - \underset{(-\,3.671)}{0.392}\, \Delta \Pi_{t-2}
\end{aligned} \tag{22}
$$

7. We delete terms which are not significant; such elimination does not significantly affect the magnitude or the significance of other coefficients (Leamer 1978).

$$\begin{array}{ll} - 0.254\ \Delta\Pi_{t-3} & - (0.129\ \Delta\Pi_{t-4}] + \varepsilon_t\ , \\ (-\ 2.465) & (-1.248) \end{array}$$

$$\bar{R}^2 = 0.420,\ \text{SEE} = 0.007,\ \text{D-W} = 2.015,\ Q(30)_{S.L.} = 0.981\ .$$

While the term in the first bracket captures the long-run adjustment effect, terms in the second bracket reflect the short-run dynamics. As can be expected, disequilibrium factors push inflation high, and growth of real income has a negative effect on the inflation rate, while an increase in the money supply and a depreciation of the exchange rate have positive effects. We also note that, for short-run adjustment, the negative effect of real output on price can last as long as nine months, and the positive effect of money supply on price may not show up until six months later. Moreover, though the exchange rate has a positive effect on price in the long run, for short-run adjustment, this positive effect becomes significant only eight months later.

7.5 Conclusion

This paper has examined the relationship between money supply, real output, exchange rate, and price using recently developed cointegration techniques. We adopted the maximum likelihood method developed by Johansen. Only by using this sophisticated statistical technique can a multivariate cointegrated system be properly analyzed.

Our empirical results using Taiwan monthly data over the period January 1981 to February 1992 show that money supply (M_2), real output, exchange rate, and price (CPI) are cointegrated with rank one. The estimated equilibrium and the short-run dynamic relationship shows that, as predicted by the theory, an increase in the money supply and a depreciation of the exchange rate have positive effects on price, while increase of real output has a negative effect. This provides a possible explanation of why the high growth rates of money supply during the 1980s in Taiwan did not cause high inflation rates, i.e., during the same period the growth rate of real GNP was relatively high and the exchange rate was appreciating sharply.

One innovation of this paper is examining the relationship between money, output, and price by appropriately taking into account the exchange rate. However, the approach we adopted using aggregate analysis cannot see the impact of exchange rate appreciation on different sectors. It also cannot help us to understand pass-through effects. All these are interesting topics for future research.

References

Bordo, M. D., and E. V. Choudhri. 1982. The link between money and prices in an open economy: The Canadian evidence from 1971 to 1980. *Review* (Federal Reserve Bank of St. Louis) 64 (7): 13–23.

Burger, A. 1978. Is inflation all due to money? *Review* (Federal Reserve Bank of St. Louis) 60 (12): 8–12.

Chiu, P. C. H. 1992. Money and financial markets: The domestic perspective. In *The Taiwan: From developing to mature economy,* ed. G. Ranis, 121–93. Boulder, Colo.: Westview.

Chiu, P. C. H., and T. C. Hou. 1992. Prices, money and monetary policy implementation under financial liberalization: The case of Taiwan. Paper presented at OECD Development Centre Seminar on Financial Opening: Developing Country Policy Issues and Experience.

Engle, R. F., and C. W. J. Granger. 1987. Cointegration and error-correcting: Representation, estimation and testing. *Econometrica* 55:251–76.

———. 1991. *Long-run economic relationships: Reading in cointegration.* Oxford: Oxford University Press.

Gonzalo, J. 1989. Comparison of five alternative methods of estimating long run equilibrium relationships. Discussion Paper 89–55, University of California, San Diego.

Granger, C. W. J. 1981. Some properties of time series data and their use in econometrica model specification. *Journal of Econometrics* 16:121–30.

———. 1983. Co-Integrated variables and error-correcting models. Discussion Paper 83-13, University of California, San Diego.

Granger, C. W. J., and A. A. Weiss. 1983. Time series analysis of error-correcting models. In *Studies in econometrics, time series, and multivariate statistics,* ed. S. Karlin, T. Amemlya, and L. A. Goodman, 255–78. New York: Academic Press.

Jarque, C. M., and A. K. Bera. 1980. Efficient tests for normality, homoscedasticity and serial independence of regression residuals. *Economic Letters* 6:255–59.

Johansen, S. 1988. Statistical analysis of cointegrating vectors. *Journal of Economic Dynamics and Control* 12:231–54.

———. 1991. Estimation and hypothesis testing of cointegration vectors in Gaussian vector regression models. *Econometrica* 59:1551–80.

Johansen, S., and K. Juselius. 1990. Maximum likelihood estimation and inferences on cointegration with applications to demand for money. *Oxford Bulletin of Economics and Statistics* 52:169–210.

Leamer, E. E. 1978. *Specification search: Ad hoc inference with nonexperimental data.* New York: Wiley.

Lin, J. L., and Y. S. Kao. 1992. Long run equilibrium relationship among part-time, full-time female labor force participation rates: An application of cointegration analysis. *Academia Economic Papers* (Taipei: Institute of Economics, Academia Sinica) 20:201–41.

Perry, G. 1980. Inflation in theory and practice. *Brookings Papers on Economic Activity* 1:207–41.

Phillips, P. C. B. 1986. Understanding spurious regressions in econometrics. *Journal of Econometrics* 33:311–40.

———. 1988a. Optimal inference in cointegrated systems. *Cowles Foundation Discussion Paper* 866. New Haven, Conn.: Cowles Foundation, Yale University.

———. 1988b. Spectral regression for cointegrated time series. *Cowles Foundation Discussion Paper* 872. New Haven, Conn.: Cowles Foundation, Yale University.

Phillips, P. C. B., and S. N. Durlauf. 1986. Multiple time series regression with integrated process. *Review of Economic Studies* 53:473–96.

Phillips, P. C. B., and J. Park. 1988. Asymptotic equivalence of ordinary least squares in regression with integrated variables. *Journal of American Statistical Association* 83:111–15.

Phillips, P. C. B., and S. Quliaris. 1990. Asymptotic properties of residual based test for cointegration. *Econometrica* 58:165–93.

Saini, K. G. 1982. The monetarist explanation of inflation: The experience of six Asian countries. *World Development* 10:881–94.

Shih, Yen. 1988. A re-examination of the short-run demand for money in Taiwan. *Quarterly Review* (Taipei: Economic Research Department, Central Bank of China) 10:21–49.

Stock, J. H. 1987. Asymptotic properties of least squares estimators of cointegrated vectors. *Econometrica* 55:1035–56.

Stock, J., and M. Watson. 1988. Testing for common trends. *Journal of the American Statistical Association* 83:1097–1107.

Wu, C. S. 1987. Price expectations, structural change and the specification of Taiwan money demand function. *Academia Economic Papers* (Taipei: Institute of Economics, Academia Sinica) 15:87–113.

———. 1989. The transaction money and prices in Taiwan. Discussion Paper no. 8901. Institute of Economics, Academia Sinica, Taipei.

Yu, Z. S. 1977. An inflation model for Taiwan. *Academia Economic Papers* (Taipei: Institute of Economics, Academia Sinica)5:1–22.

Comment Maria S. Gochoco

Wu and Lin's study examines why there is no apparent proportionate relationship between monetary growth and inflation in Taiwan using monthly data for 1981–92. The reason, as they want to show using cointegration techniques, is that the appreciation by 29.7 percent of the NT dollar between 1981 and 1989 held inflation down to 3.04 percent even as M_2 grew 22.4 percent.

I have several comments: First, on the overall style of the paper, more verbal explanations of the methodology and the empirical results would be useful. For example, the authors could explain why cointegration is a useful procedure by stating that it circumvents the need for each time series in a regression to be stationary—a requirement for standard regression techniques to work.

Second, since cointegration only tells us about the long-run equilibrium relationship between the dependent variable and the independent variables, an error-correction specification can be used to examine their behavior over the short run. Such an error-correction model forces gradual adjustment of the dependent variable toward some long-run values (estimated via cointegration) while explicitly allowing for short-run dynamics.

Third, a better justification for the use of M_2 rather than a narrower monetary aggregate must be made instead of what is stated in footnote 5.

Fourth, the final estimated inflation equation's coefficients have to be explained in light of the theory the paper tests and the statistical significance of these coefficients must also be stated. For example, it does not make sense for the coefficient on monetary growth in the inflation equation to be greater than one.

Fifth, there is hardly any discussion of the conduct of monetary policy in Taiwan. The paper makes no mention of the use by the monetary authorities of

Maria S. Gochoco is an associate professor at the School of Economics of the University of the Philippines.

open market operations, such as the Central Bank's selling its own CDs and savings bonds in 1985 and 1986, changes in the annual rate of domestic credit expansion, the depressing effect on the income velocity of money of the drop in interest rates and price stability between 1974 and 1986, and the liberalization of the foreign exchange market in Taiwan by which capital exports of $1 million to $5 million per year are allowed. These other factors may have had significant roles to play in holding inflation down despite the high rates of growth of money arising from current account surpluses.

8 Endogenous Exchange Rate Fluctuations under the Flexible Exchange Rate Regime

Shin-ichi Fukuda

8.1 Introduction

In the past two decades, we have experienced in the foreign exchange markets significant temporary fluctuations in the exchange rates of major currencies. For example, by plotting the movements of the yen/dollar exchange rate after 1973, we can see a clear downward trend in this exchange rate in the long run. However, we can also see that the trend was not monotonic in the short run and that there were significant temporary fluctuations around the trend (see fig. 8.1). The purpose of this paper is to investigate why the exchange rate shows such significant temporary fluctuations. The model of the following analysis is based on a model of money in the utility function with liquidity-in-advance. Following Fukuda (1990), we investigate the dynamic properties of a small open economy version of this monetary model.

The methodology used in the following analysis is an application of the theory of "chaos." In the previous literature, Benhabib and Day (1982), Day (1982, 1983), and Stutzer (1980) are the first attempts to study chaotic phenomena in economic models. Authors such as Benhabib and Nishimura (1985) derive the competitive equilibrium cycles in a two-sector growth model, while authors such as Grandmont (1985) characterize the chaotic phenomena in overlapping generations models. In addition, Matsuyama (1990, 1991) and Fukuda (1990) find that the model of money in the utility function can produce chaotic dynamic paths.[1] However, throughout these studies there exist few attempts to

Shin-ichi Fukuda is associate professor of economics at the Institute of Economic Research, Hitotsubashi University.

The author would like to thank Michihiro Ohyama, Shang-Jin Wei, and other participants of the Third Annual East Asian Seminar on Economics for their helpful comments on an earlier draft of this paper. This research was supported by the Ministry of Education of Japan.

1. See also Woodford (1988) for related issues.

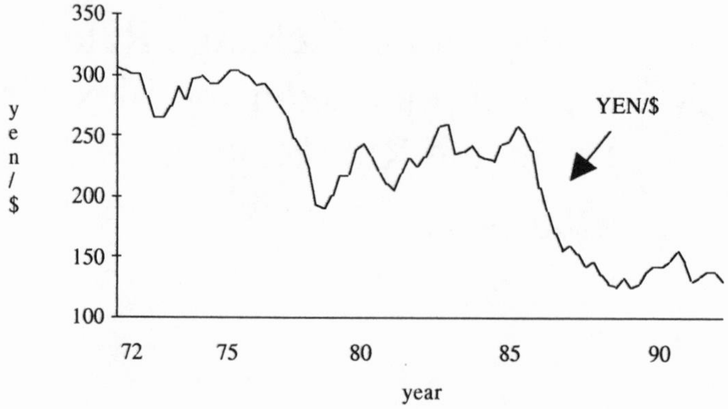

Fig. 8.1 Yen / dollar exchange rate between 1973 and 1991

analyze endogenous periodic dynamic paths in open economy models. Exceptional studies are Nishimura and Yano (1990), Woodford (1990a), King, Wallace, and Weber (1992), and Nishimura and Ohyama (1992). Nishimura and Yano (1990) and Nishimura and Ohyama (1992) have analyzed endogenous periodic dynamic paths in an open economy version of a two-sector growth model. However, since their analysis is based on the model without money, no attention has been paid to the endogenous cycles of exchange rates. The studies of Woodford (1990a) and King et al. (1992) are more related to our analysis because they deal with sunspot equilibria of nominal exchange rates. However, both models are based on cash-in-advance models and a different type of attention has been paid to the dynamic properties of endogenous exchange rate fluctuations.

In the following analysis, we show that a model of money in the utility function can produce periodic and chaotic dynamic paths under the flexible exchange rate regime. In the analysis, the conflict between income and substitution effects plays an important role in producing endogenous business cycles under the flexible exchange rate regime. That is, an expected depreciation of the future exchange rate always has a negative substitution effect on current money demand for the domestic currency. However, since the depreciation requires more money holdings for the future transaction, it always has a positive income effect on current money demand. Hence, the total effect of the change in the future exchange rate on current money demand is always ambiguous, causing the endogenous exchange rate cycles in our model.

Needless to say, our approach is not the only explanation for the temporary fluctuations of the exchange rate. For example, Ito (1987) and Ito and Roley (1987) present evidence that (unanticipated) news may explain most temporary fluctuations of the yen/dollar exchange rate in the 1980s. In addition, Frankel and Froot (1990) and Wei (1991) show that the presence of fundamental traders and chartists can explain the large dollar cycle and chaotic exchange rate movement in the 1980s. This paper does not deny the significance of these earlier studies. Instead, we try to present a supplementary explanation of some temporary fluctuations of exchange rates which these studies do not necessarily explain.

The paper is organized as follows. The next section presents a basic small open economy model of money in the utility function. Following Fukuda (1992), the dynamic properties of the model are analyzed under the flexible exchange rate regime in sections 8.3 and 8.4. Section 8.5 extends the model by introducing the endogenous labor supply. Section 8.6 shows that the fixed exchange rate regime may rule out the possibility of endogenous cycles in the economy. Section 8.7 interprets our results by using a phase diagram, and section 8.8 considers a welfare implication of our analysis. Section 8.9 summarizes our main results.

8.2 The Basic Model

The basic model of the following analysis is based on Fukuda (1992). We consider a small open economy inhabited by identical agents. Until section 8.5, we assume that there is a single, perishable, tradable consumption good in the economy. Each representative agent maximizes the following utility function:

(1) $$U = \sum_{t=0}^{\infty} \beta^t [u(c_t) + v(M_t/p_t)],$$

where c_t is consumption at period t, p_t is the domestic price level at period t, M_t is the amount of domestic currency at the beginning of period t, and β is a discount rate satisfying $0 < \beta < 1$. For all $c_t > 0$ and $M_t/p_t > 0$, we assume that u and v are weakly concave and twice–continuously differentiable (i.e., $u'' \leq$ and $v'' \leq 0$) and are weakly increasing (i.e., $u' \geq$ and $v' \geq 0$).

The budget constraint of the representative agent is

(2) $$b_t = (1 + r)\, b_{t-1} + y_t - c_t - M_{t+1}/p_t + M_t/p_t - T_t,$$

where y_t is exogenous income, T_t is the lump-sum tax (or transfer if negative), r is the world real interest rate, and b_t is the real amount of foreign bonds at period t.

In our representative agent model, the change in the real amount of foreign bonds is equal to the real amount of current account surplus. Furthermore, because of the law of one price, it holds that $p_t = e_t p^*$ (i.e., the purchasing power parity condition) where p^* is foreign price level and e_t is the nominal exchange rate in terms of domestic currency. Since the model is a small open economy, world real interest rate, r, and foreign price, p^*, are exogenously given in our model. In order to rule out extreme consumption behavior in the limit, we assume that world real interest rate, r, is constant and equal to the rate of time preference of the representative agent, that is, $\beta(1 + r) = 1$, in the following analysis.[2] We also normarize foreign price p^* to be one.

Until section 8.5, we assume that exogenous income y_t is constant over time (i.e., $y_t = y$) and is not storable. We also assume that government revenue through money creation is balanced by the exogenous change in the lump-sum transfer. Then, assuming an interior solution, the first-order conditions under perfect foresight are

$$u'(c_t) = \beta(1 + r)\, u'(c_{t+1}), \tag{3}$$

$$(1/p_t)\, u'(c_t) = \beta\, (1/p_{t+1})\, [\, u'(c_{t+1}) + v'(M_{t+1}/p_{t+1})\,]. \tag{4}$$

Since $\beta(1 + r) = 1$, the monotonicity of $u'(c_t)$ implies that c_t is constant over time. Furthermore, since $p^* = 1$, the purchasing power parity condition leads to $p_t = e_t$. Hence, denoting the constant consumption level by c, the dynamic equation (4) is written as

$$1/e_t = \beta\, (1/e_{t+1})\, [\, 1 + (1/u'(c))\, v'(M_{t+1}/e_{t+1}\,)\,]. \tag{5}$$

Equation (5) determines the dynamic system in our model. By using this equation, the following sections investigate whether nominal exchange rate and real money balances may show endogenous cycles under the flexible exchange rate regime. In considering periodic endogenous cycles, we define the iterates of a function h of a set X into itself by $h^1(x) = h(x)$ and $h^i(x) = h(h^{i-1}(x))$ for all integers $i \geq 2$. We then define a periodic orbit (or a cycle) of period k of the backward perfect foresight map h by the sequence $(x_{t+k}, x_{t+k-1}, \ldots, x_t)$ such that (i) x_{t+k} is a fixed point of h^k, i.e., $x_{t+k} = \mathrm{h}^k(\, x_{t+k})$, and (ii) $x_{t+k-1} = h^i(\, x_{t+k}) \neq x_{t+k}$ for all $i = 1, \ldots, k - 1$.

8.3 Endogenous Exchange Rate Cycles

Under the flexible exchange rate regime, the nominal money supply M_t is exogenously determined by the monetary authority. In this paper, we consider the case in which the monetary authority keeps the growth rate of money supply constant as follows:

$$M_t = zM_{t-1} \text{ for all } t. \tag{6}$$

Then, (5) and (6) lead to

$$m_t = (\beta/z)\, m_{t+1}\, [\, 1 + (1/\, u'(c))\, v'(m_{t+1})\,]\,, \tag{7}$$

where $m_t \equiv M_t/\, e_t$.

The dynamic equation (7) determines the dynamic system of real money balances, m_t, in our model under the flexible exchange rate regime. If we define

2. It is well known that $\lim_{t\to\infty} c_t = 0$ when $\beta(1 + r) < 1$ and $\lim_{t\to\infty} c_t = +\infty$ when $\beta(1 + r) > 1$.

$$f(m) = (\beta/z)\, m\, [1 + (1/u'(c))\, v'(m)], \tag{8}$$

equation (7) implies that m_t can be written as a function of m_{t+1} such that $m_t = f(m_{t+1})$ under perfect foresight. That is, our system induces well-defined backward perfect foresight (b.p.f.) dynamics in which the expected future value determines its current value. This b.p.f. map is continuously differentiable.

In order to focus our attention on the well-defined dynamics, the following analysis assumes that $z > \beta$, $\lim_{m\to 0} f'(m) > 1$, and $\lim_{m\to +\infty} f'(m) < 1$. Then, there exists a steady-state equilibrium of real money balances, m^*, such that $[(z - \beta)/\beta]\, u'(c) = v'(m^*)$ under the above assumptions. This steady-state equilibrium m^* is a unique steady-state equilibrium if and only if $\lim_{m\to 0} mv'(m) > 0$. When $\lim_{m\to 0} mv'(m) = 0$, there is another steady-state equilibrium such that $m_t = 0$. However, when $m_t = 0$, the level of nominal exchange rate e_t is infinite (i.e., the domestic currency has no value) because M_t is finite.

In the following analysis, we investigate the possibility that the backward perfect foresight dynamics (7) may have period $k \geq 2$ cycles and local sunspot equilibria even under some economically reasonable conditions. Under the assumption presented above, it is well known that a sufficient condition for period-two cycles and local sunspot equilibria in a one-dimensional map (7) is that $|f'(m)| > 1$ at $m = m^*$ (see, e.g., Grandmont 1985; Blanchard and Kahn 1980). By using this condition, Fukuda (1992) showed the following proposition.

Proposition: A sufficient condition for the existence of period-two cycles and local sunspot equilibria of real money balances is that

$$- m^*\, v''(m^*) \,/\, v'(m^*) > 2\, [z/(z - \beta)], \tag{9}$$

where m^* is the steady-state equilibrium such that $v'(m^*) = [(z - \beta) / \beta]\, u'(c)$.

The proposition states that when the relative risk aversion of the utility on real money balances is large at the steady state m^*, equilibrium real money balances may have period-two cycles and local sunspot equilibria. Furthermore, since the nominal money supply is exogenously given, the proposition implies that the equilibrium nominal exchange rate may also have period-two cycles and local sunspot equilibria.

In general, our model of money in the utility function may have higher-order periodic and aperiodic cycles. However, without specifying the functional form of u and v it is difficult to find the existence of higher-order periodic and aperiodic cycles in our model. Hence, in the next section, we investigate numerically the existence of such higher-order periodic and aperiodic cycles for three specific classes of utility functions.

8.4 Examples

In this section, we investigate the existence of periodic and aperiodic cycles under the flexible exchange rate regime for specific utility functions. We consider the following three classes of utility functions:

(10) $v(m_t) = m_t^{1-R} / (1 - R)$, where $R > 0$;

(11) $v(m_t) = -(b/2)(m_t - k)^2$, where $b > 0$, when $m_t < k$,
$= 0$, when $m_t \geq k$;

(12) $v(m_t) = -(1/a)\exp(-a\, m_t)$, where $a > 0$.

The utility functions are, respectively, a member of the constant relative risk-aversion family, of the quadratic family, and of the constant absolute risk-aversion family. For each utility function, the dynamic equation (7) is written as

(13) $m_t = (\beta/z)\, m_{t+1}\, [1 + (1/u'(c))\, m_{t+1}^{-R}]$;

(14) $m_t = \gamma\, m_{t+1}\, (1 - \delta\, m_{t+1})$, when $m_{t+1} < k$,
$= (\beta/z)\, m_{t+1}$, when $m_{t+1} \geq k$;

(15) $m_t = (\beta/z)\, m_{t+1}\, [1 + (1/u'(c))\exp(-a\, m_{t+1})]$,

where $\gamma = (\beta/z)[1 + (b/u'(c))k]$ and $\delta = (b/u'(c))/[1 + (b/u'(c))\, k]$. Hence, the proposition leads to the following corollary.

Corollary: A sufficient condition for the existence of period-two cycles and local sunspot equilibria under the flexible exchange rate regime is that (i) $R > 2\,[z/(z - \beta)]$ in utility function (10), (ii) $(\beta/z)[1 + (b/u'(c)k] > 3$ under utility function (11), and (iii) $\log[(1/u'(c))(\beta/(z - \beta))] > 2[z/(z - \beta)]$ under utility function (12).

The corollary implies that there exist period-two cycles and local sunspot equilibria under the flexible exchange rate regime (i) when z or R is large enough in utility function (10), (ii) when parameter b, $1/u'(c)$, or k is large enough in utility function (11), and (iii) when $u'(c)$ is small enough in utility function (12). In fact, for parameter values satisfying the sufficiency conditions in the corollary, nominal exchange rate and real money balances may show very complicated dynamic paths around the steady-state equilibrium.

In figures 8.2–8.4, we describe these possibilities for given expected nominal exchange rates (or equivalently real money balances) at time T. In the figures, we depict the dynamics of nominal exchange rate and real money balances for the above three classes of utility functions. The dynamics clearly show that both nominal exchange rate and real money balances follow very complicated fluctuations around the steady-state equilibrium.[3] In particular, although the expected nominal exchange rate at time T is very close to that of the steady state, the transition paths are very different and highly volatile.

8.5 Extensions

The results in the preceding sections were derived from a very simple small open economy model. Thus, in order to derive more realistic implications, the

3. Since the growth rate of money supply is positive (i.e., $z > 1$), nominal exchange rates have trends to the depreciation in the figures.

(i) Exchange rate dynamics

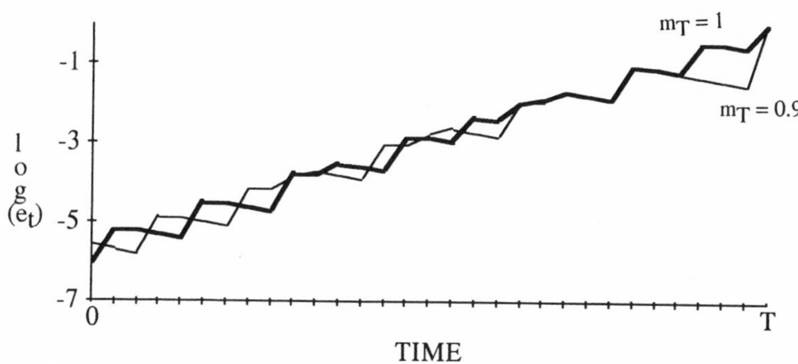

(ii) Dynamics of real money balances

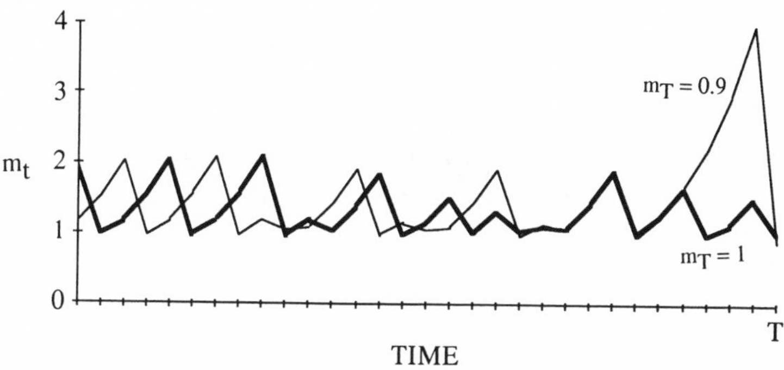

Fig. 8.2 The dynamics of exchange rate and real money balances under utility function (10)

Notes: Parameter set : $\beta = 0.9$, $z = 1.2$, $u'(c) = 1$, $R = 15$, $T = 30$. Terminal values : $m_T = 1$ or 0.9.

model may need to be extended in several directions. We here extend the model by introducing the endogenous labor supply. We consider an economy in which each individual maximizes the following utility function:

$$U = \sum_{t=0}^{\infty} \beta^t \left[u(c_t) + w(L_t, M_t/p_t)\right], \tag{16}$$

where L_t is the amount of leisure at period t. We assume that the utility function $w(L,m)$ satisfies the usual concave assumption. We also allow the possibility that the utilities of leisure and real money balances are not separable.

The budget constraint of the representative agent is

$$b_t = (1 + r)\, b_{t-1} + \omega_t\,(L^0 - L_t) - c_t - M_{t+1}/p_t + M_t/p_t - T_t, \tag{17}$$

where L^0 is the feasible labor hour and ω_t is real wage at period t.

Assuming a linear production function such that $y_t = L_t$, it holds that

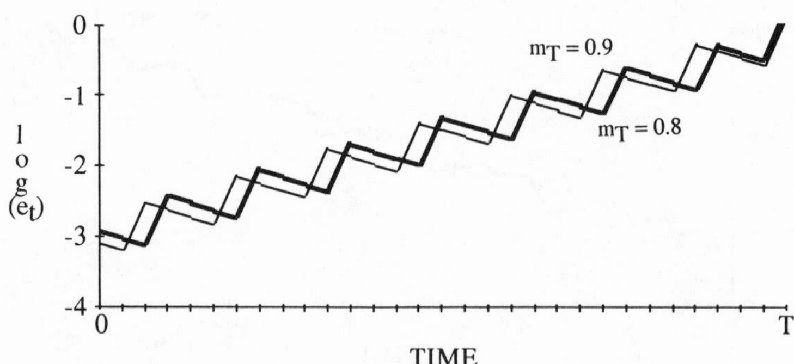

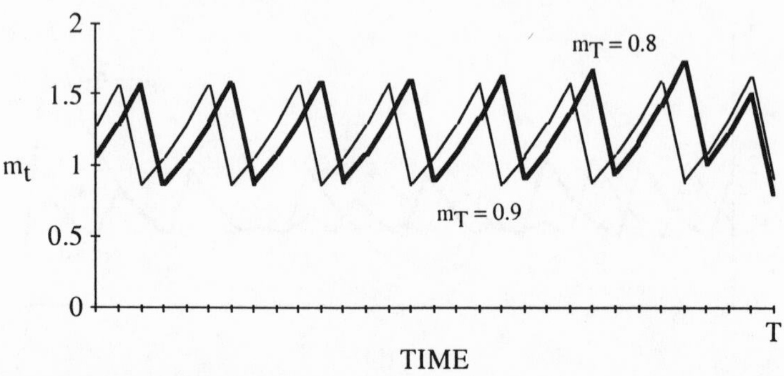

Fig. 8.3 The dynamics of exchange rate and real money balances under utility function (11)

Notes: Parameter set : $\beta = 0.9$, $z = 1.1$, $u'(c) = 1$, $k = 1$, $b = 2$, $T = 30$. Terminal values : $m_T =$ 0.8 or 0.9.

$\omega_t = 1$ in equilibrium. Thus, since $\beta(1 + r) = 1$ and $p_t = e_t$, the first-order conditions for an interior solution are

$$u'(c_t) = u'(c_{t+1}), \tag{18}$$

$$w_1(L_t, m_t) = w_1(L_{t+1}, m_{t+1}), \tag{19}$$

$$(1/e_t)\, u'(c_t) = \beta\, (1/e_{t+1})\, [u'(c_{t+1}) + w_2(L_{t+1}, m_{t+1})]. \tag{20}$$

Condition (19) states that L_t can be written as a function of m_t. Thus, defining a function φ such that $L_t = \varphi(m_t)$ and substituting this function into (20), we obtain

$$(1/e_t)\, u'(c_t) = \beta\, (1/e_{t+1})\, [\, u'(c_{t+1}) + \Psi(m_{t+1})\,], \tag{21}$$

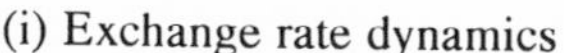

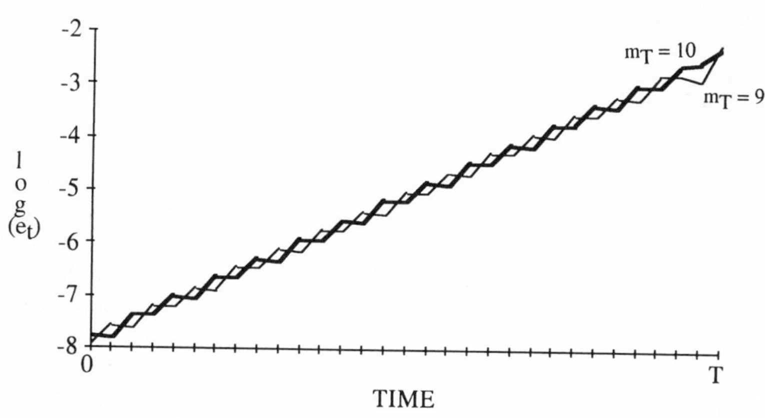

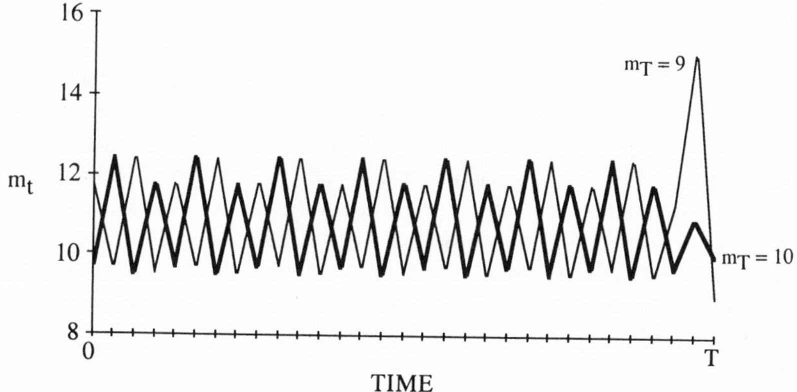

Fig. 8.4 The dynamics of exchange rate and real money balances under utility function (12)

Notes: Parameter set : β =0.9, z = 1.2, $u'(c)$ = 0.0001, a = 1, T = 30. Terminal values : m_T = 10 or 9.

where $\Psi(m_{t+1}) \equiv w_2(\varphi(m_t), m_{t+1})$.

Since condition (18) implies that c_t is constant over time, the dynamic equation (21) is mathematically equivalent to the dynamic equation (7) if we replace $\Psi(m_{t+1})$ by $v(m_{t+1})$. Hence, all results in earlier sections carry through. Thus, we can easily see that the nominal exchange rate and real money balances may have endogenous cycles in the model of endogenous labor supply. In addition, since L_t is a function of m_t, we can also see that labor supply may also fluctuate endogenously unless the utility function $w(L, m)$ is separable in leisure and real money balances. Since the level of consumption is constant over time, this implies the possibility that the current account may also fluctuate endogenously. This result is noteworthy because such endogenous cycles of the current account cannot be derived in the model of previous sections.

8.6 The Optimal Choice of Exchange Rate Regime

The question of optimal exchange rate regime is one of the most extensively debated topics in international macroeconomics. Traditionally, the debate was based mainly on Mundell-Fleming-type open macro models (see, e.g., Boyer 1978; Turnovsky 1984; Fukuda and Hamada 1988; Fukuda 1991). However, the analysis was limited because the models were not necessarily based on individuals' maximizing behavior. In order to overcome this limitation, several authors have recently attempted to investigate the optimal exchange rate regime in models of money with individuals' maximizing behavior. For example, Helpman (1981), Lucas (1982), and Aschauer and Greenwood (1983) have considered models of money with cash-in-advance constraint. They have shown that, without distortions, the choice of exchange rate regime has no real effect on resource allocation but that the existence of distortions introduces the possibility of real effects of exchange rate management. However, their analyses have focused mainly on resource allocation in the steady-state equilibrium and paid little attention to the transition path to the steady-state equilibrium. Hence, it is relatively unknown how the exchange rate regime affects the transition path to the steady-state equilibrium. This has been investigated by Fukuda (1992), however. He showed how the endogenous cycles under the flexible exchange rate regime will be ruled out under the fixed exchange rate regime. This section briefly reviews his main result by considering the dynamic property under the fixed exchange rate regime in our basic model.

Under the fixed exchange rate regime, nominal money supply M_t is endogenously determined by the monetary authority to keep the nominal exchange rate e_t constant. Hence, by noting that $e_t = e_{t+1}$, equation (5) can be written as

$$(22) \qquad [(1 - \beta)/\beta]\, u'(c) = v'(m_{t+1}).$$

Since the left-hand side of equation (22) is constant over time, equation (22) implies that real money balances m_t are constant over time. In particular, since the real money balances that satisfy (22) are equivalent to those of the steady state with constant money supply (i.e., $z = 1$), real money balances stay at their steady-state equilibrium forever under the fixed exchange rate regime without changing the amount of money supply. This result is in marked contrast with that under the flexible exchange rate regime, because real balances under the flexible exchange rate regime may show endogenous fluctuations for some parameter set and terminal condition. That is, once the monetary authority can commit to fixing the exchange rate, real balances (and obviously nominal exchange rate) show no endogenous fluctuations for any parameter set.

One noteworthy point in the above result is that under the fixed exchange rate regime the monetary authority needs to make no intervention in the foreign exchange market to reduce the nominal exchange rate fluctuation. That is, once the initial values of exchange rate and money supply are given, the only necessary condition for the monetary authority to keep the fixed exchange rate regime is to make people believe that the monetary authority will endogenously determine nominal money supply M_t to fix the nominal exchange rate e_t. A crucial point is that, in our model of money in the utility function, periodic cycles or sunspot equilibria may arise when people's expectations diverge from those of the steady-state equilibrium. Thus, once the commitment of the monetary authority to fixing the nominal exchange rate makes people's expectations converge to those of the steady-state equilibrium, deviations of expectations from the steady-state equilibrium are ruled out under the fixed exchange rate regime.

8.7 Diagrammatic Explanation

In order to interpret the results in previous sections, it may be useful to illustrate them by drawing the locus of (7) in the plane (m_t, m_{t+1}). Figure 8.5 shows the locus of (7) under the utility function (11). When the parameter b is small (i.e., the curvature of the utility function is small), the curve is flat and the dynamic path of m_t shows no cyclical fluctuation. However, when the parameter b is large (i.e., the curvature of the utility function is large), the curve is backward bending at some critical point μ. That backward-bending curve arises reflects the conflict between intertemporal substitution and income effects. That is, an expected depreciation of the future exchange rate always has a negative substitution effect on current money demand the domestic currency (or a positive substitution effect on current demand for consumption). However, since the depreciation requires more money holdings for future transactions, it always has a positive income effect on current money demand (or a negative income effect on current demand for consumption). Hence, the total effect of the change in the future exchange rate on current money demand is always ambiguous. This ambiguity through intertemporal substitution and income effects causes the business cycles that were obtained in the above proposition and its corollary.

The only case in which no endogenous fluctuation arises is when real money balances m_t stay at the steady-state equilibrium forever. This special case does not necessarily happen under the flexible exchange rate regime because each individual does not necessarily expect real money balances to stay at the steady-state equilibrium forever. However, under the fixed exchange rate regime, the situation is different: the only self-fulfilling rational expectation is the expectation that the nominal exchange rate (and real money balances) will stay at the steady-state equilibrium forever. As a result, no endogenous fluctuation arises under the fixed exchange rate regime.

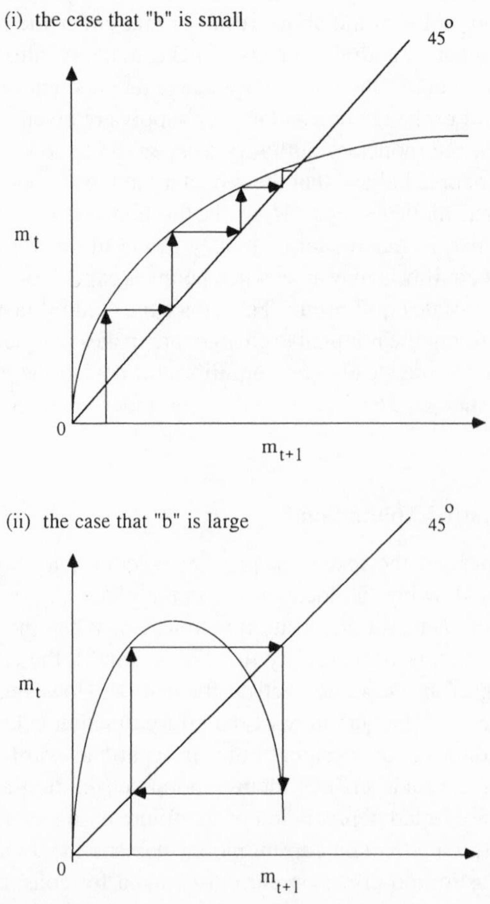

Fig. 8.5 The phase diagram under utility function (11)

8.8 A Welfare Implication

The results in preceding sections have an important welfare implication in determining the optimal exchange rate regime. As we explained in section 8.6, it is well known that if we simply compare the welfare properties of the steady-state equilibria in an economy with some distortions, the optimal exchange rate regime is the flexible exchange rate regime with appropriate money supply growth. In particular, we can show that, in our model of money in the utility function, the optimal rate of money growth is given by Friedman's (1969) rule: the rule which maintains a rate of money growth close to the rate of time preference (see Woodford [1990b] for its proof). However, as we have shown in previous sections, the equilibrium corresponding to a given rate of money growth (say, that specified by Friedman's rule) need not be unique. Since the multiple equilibria are Pareto ranked, it also becomes very important to know under what exchange rate regime nonconvergent paths can be eliminated.

In the previous sections, we have shown that nonconvergent paths can be eliminated under the fixed exchange rate regime. Thus, although the optimal rate of money growth under the fixed exchange rate regime deviates from Friedman's rule, the fixed exchange rate regime can lead to the second-best resource allocation in the sense that nonconvergent paths are eliminated. Of course, we may have the first-best resource allocation under the flexible exchange rate regime with Friedman's rule as long as nonconvergent paths do not arise. However, as we have shown in the previous sections, endogenous periodic dynamic paths can arise even under Friedman's rule. Hence, unless this possibility is ruled out, we may have the less desirable resource allocations of nonconvergent paths under Friedman's rule.

8.9 Concluding Remarks

This paper investigated the dynamic properties in a small open economy model of money in the utility function. Following Fukuda (1990), we have shown that under a flexible exchange rate regime the nominal exchange rate and real money balances may have endogenous periodic dynamic paths for some parameter set and future expectations. We have also shown that if the labor supply is endogenous, the current account may also have endogenous dynamic paths.

Our theoretical results may present one answer to why the empirical relevance of existing classes of exchange rate theories is so poor (see, e.g., Meese and Rogoff [1983] which shows the poor out-of-sample forecasting performance).[4] If a variable follows a chaotic path, its path would be extremely sensitive to the initial value and its forecast would be very difficult by usual statistical procedures. At the current stage, there is very little empirical evidence suggesting the presence of chaos in the exchange rate market. (An exceptional work is by Brock, Hsieh, and LeBaron [1991], which has applied the Brock-Dechert-Scheinkman statistic to the yen/dollar exchange rate with four other major exchange rates.) However, further successful empirical studies may prove the potential importance of a chaotic model of exchange rate.

References

Aschauer, David, and Jeremy Greenwood. 1983. A further exploration in the theory of exchange rate regimes. *Journal of Political Economy* 91:865–75.

Benhabib, Jess, and Richard H. Day. 1982. A characterization of erratic dynamics in

4. The following argument is based partly on comments by Shang-Jin Wei.

the overlapping generations model. *Journal of Economic Dynamics and Control* 4:37–55

Benhabib, Jess, and Kazuo Nishimura. 1985. Competitive equilibrium cycles. *Journal of Economic Theory* 35:284–306.

Blanchard, Olivier J., and Charles M. Kahn. 1980. The solution of linear difference models under rational expectations. *Econometrica* 48:1305–11.

Boyer, Russell S. 1978. Optimal foreign exchange market intervention. *Journal of Political Economy* 86:1045–55.

Brock, William A., David A. Hsieh, and Blake LeBaron. 1991. *Nonlinear dynamics, chaos, and instability: Statistical theory and economic evidence.* Cambridge: MIT Press.

Day, Richard H. 1982. Irregular growth cycles. *American Economic Review* 72:406–14.

———. 1983. The emergence of chaos from classical economic growth. *Quarterly Journal of Economics* 98:201–13.

Frankel, Jeffrey, and Kenneth A. Froot. 1990. Chartists, fundamentalists, and trading in the foreign exchange market. *American Economic Review* 80:181–85.

Friedman, Milton. 1969. The optimum quantity of money. In *The optimum quantity of money and other essays.* Chicago: Aldine.

Fukuda, Shin-ichi. 1990. The emergence of equilibrium cycles in a monetary economy with a separable utility function. Discussion Paper no. 90-3, Yokohama National University.

———. 1991. Exchange market intervention under multiple solutions. *Journal of Economic Dynamics and Control* 15:339–53.

———. 1992. Endogenous exchange rate fluctuations and the desirable exchange rate regime. Discussion Paper no. 92–3, Yokohama National University.

Fukuda, Shin-ichi, and Koichi Hamada. 1988. Towards the implementations of desirable rules of monetary coordination and intervention. In *Toward a world of economic stability,* ed. Y. Suzuki and M. Okabe. Tokyo: University of Tokyo Press.

Grandmont, Jean-Michel. 1985. On endogenous competitive business cycles. *Econometrica* 53:995–1045.

Helpman, Elhanan. 1981. An exploration in the theory of exchange rate regimes. *Journal of Political Economy* 89:865–90.

Ito, Takatoshi. 1987. The Intra-daily exchange rate dynamics and monetary policies after the Group of Five agreement. *Journal of the Japanese and International Economies* 1:275–98.

Ito, Takatoshi, and V. V. Roley. 1987. News from the U.S. and Japan: Which moves the yen/dollar exchange rate? *Journal of Monetary Economics* 19:255–77.

King, Robert G., Neil Wallace, and Warren E. Weber. 1992. Nonfundamental uncertainty and exchange rates. *Journal of International Economics* 32:83–108.

Lucas, Robert E., Jr. 1982. Interest rates and currency prices in a two-country world. *Journal of Monetary Economics* 10:335–60.

Matsuyama, Kiminori. 1990. Sunspot equilibria (rational bubbles) in a model of money-in-the-utility-function. *Journal of Monetary Economics* 25:137–44.

———. 1991. Endogenous price fluctuations in an optimizing model of a monetary economy. *Econometrica* 59:1617–32.

Meese, Richard, and Kenneth Rogoff. 1983. Empirical exchange rate models of the seventies: Do they fit out of sample? *Journal of International Economics* 14:3–24.

Nishimura, Kazuo, and Michihiro Ohyama. 1992. Dynamics of external debt and trade. Paper presented at Third Annual East Asian Seminar on Economics.

Nishimura, Kazuo, and Makoto Yano. 1990. Interlinkage in the endogenous real business cycles of international economies. Discussion Paper no. 90-8, Yokohama National University.

Stutzer, Michael J. 1980. Chaotic dynamics and bifurcation in a macro model. *Journal of Economic Dynamics and Control* 2:353–76.
Turnovsky, Stephen J. 1984. Exchange rate market intervention under alternative forms of exogenous disturbances. *Journal of International Economics* 17:279–97.
Wei, Shang-Jin. 1991. Price volatility without news about fundamentals. *Economics Letters* 37:453–58.
Woodford, Michael. 1988. Expectations, finance, and aggregate instability. In *Finance constraints, expectations, and macroeconomics,* ed. M. Kohn and S. C. Tsiang. New York: Oxford University Press.
———. 1990a. Does competition between currencies lead to price level and exchange rate stability? NBER Working Paper no. 3341. Cambridge, Mass.: National Bureau of Economic Research.
———. 1990b. The optimum quantity of money. In *Handbook of monetary economics,* ed. B. M. Friedman and F. H. Hahn. Amsterdam: North-Holland.

Comment Michihiro Ohyama

This paper constructs a simple but very interesting model of a small open economy with representative agents optimizing under flexible and fixed exchange rates. It shows that under flexible exchange rates, the nominal exchange rate and real money balances may fluctuate periodically, whereas under fixed exchange rates the endogenous cycles of real money balances can be ruled out. In view of this result, the fixed exchange rate regime is said to be desirable in comparison with the flexible exchange rate regime, in the sense that the former eliminates nonconvergent adjustment paths that the latter may have to accommodate.

The analysis of the model seems to be impeccable, and the results are neatly presented and summarized. Thus, all that I can do as a discussant is to reconsider the assumptions of the model and present some comments on their implications.

Balanced Current Account

The paper considers a small open economy with the representative agent maximizing a utility function,

$$U = \Sigma\beta^t[u(c_t) + v(M_t/p_t)]\ ,$$

described in equation (1) in section 8.2. It is said that real money balances, M_t/p_t, held at the beginning of the period yield some utility since money reduces the transaction cost of consumption. If the agent holds money solely for the purpose of reducing transaction cost, however, his or her utility function may not be separable into consumption and real money balance as is presently

Michihiro Ohyama is professor of economics at Keio University.

assumed. The present assumption seems to imply that the agent derives utility from holding money quite independently of his or her consumption of goods.

As is shown in the paper, this assumption of a separable utility function, coupled with another strong assumption that the agent's rate of time preference is equal to the world interest rate, leads to the conclusion that optimal consumption is constant through time. Since output is constant, the budget constraint (2) implies that the economy's current account is always balanced, with its trade account exhibiting a surplus or deficit corresponding to the interest payment arising from the initial (historically given) external debt. This seems to be an overly simplistic setup for a discussion of desirable exchange rate regime.

Needless to say, there are at least two distinct ways out of this trap. One is to modify the separability of the utility function, and the other is to modify the constancy of the rate of time preference. I hope that Fukuda gives some consideration to these modifications.

Transactions Money in Utility Function

The author seems to believe that money must enter the representative agent's utility function along with consumption, separately or otherwise, as long as money is needed to reduce transactions cost. It seems to me, however, that the most direct and purest way of introducing money holding for transactions purposes in the present setup is simply to assume that the real money balance to be held at the beginning of each period is a function of the consumption planned for that period. Under this cash-in-advance approach, the other assumptions of the present model imply constancy of consumption and, therefore, of real money balance. Thus, fixed and flexible exchange rates become virtually indistinguishable.

Despite the interpretation of money in the utility function given in the present paper, I believe that it is necessary to go beyond the simple transactions motive of holding money if one is to investigate the relative desirability of flexible and fixed exchange rates. It may be one's love for money, distinct from one's need for consumption—the motive posited in the paper—or some speculative reason that motivates one's holding money. Paul Krugman, a recent convert to the school of fixed exchange rate regime, argues convincingly in a recent paper that the fatal deficiency of the flexible exchange regime is its vulnerability to an attack of destabilizing speculation.

Some Questions

Finally, let me pose some questions regarding possible extensions of the model. First, the present paper assumes a small open economy facing the rate of interest and terms of trade given in the world. The international monetary system must be designed, however, to meet the needs of countries of comparable size, each with its own monetary authority. It is, therefore, desirable to extend the present analysis to a model comprising at least two countries. The models of Matsuyama (1991) and Fukuda (1990) cited in this paper may provide useful departures.

Second, the fixed exchange rate regime discussed here must be distinguished from the adjustable-peg regime. The latter is vulnerable to speculative attack since the monetary authority's commitment to fixing the exchange rate at a given level is inadequate. The real choice is often between the flexible exchange rate regime and the adjustable-peg regime rather than between the flexible exchange rate regime and the fixed exchange rate regime. Is it possible to construct a model of the adjustable-peg regime along the lines of the model in the present paper?

Third, toward the end of the paper, the author discusses the welfare implications of the present analysis. The discussion is, however, very brief and it is difficult for me to understand the welfare propositions asserted there. For instance, it is asserted that the fixed exchange rate regime can lead to the second-best resource allocation in the sense that nonconvergent paths are eliminated. It seems to me that the author has to expound on this and other welfare propositions in greater detail.

References

Fukuda, Shin-ichi. 1990. The emergence of equilibrium cycles in a monetary economy with a separable utility function. Discussion Paper no. 90-3, Yokohama National University.

Matsuyama, Kiminori. 1991. Endogenous price fluctuations in an optimizing model of a monetary economy. *Econometrica* 59:1617–32.

Comment Shang-Jin Wei

The central aspect of Shin-ichi Fukuda's paper is an interesting demonstration that chaotic movement and sunspot equilibria of exchange rate can arise in a theoretic model. Building on this theoretical possibility of chaos, Fukuda then argues (mostly informally) that a flexible exchange rate system tends to yield lower welfare than a fixed rate regime.

Deriving chaos in an exchange rate model, by itself, is an interesting result. I will focus my comment on this aspect of the paper. Meese and Rogoff (1983) first challenged the empirical relevance of existing classes of exchange rate theories by showing their inferior out-of-sample forecasting performance relative to a simple atheoretical random-walk specification. Many people since then have tried alternative specifications or alternative estimation methods of

Shang-Jin Wei is assistant professor of public policy at the John F. Kennedy School of Government, Harvard University.

exchange rate models in an attempt to outperform the random-walk model. Almost all efforts have failed. It is important to note that the failure of economic models to outperform a random-walk specification does not establish that the (log) exchange rate follows a random walk. In fact, a direct test of the i.i.d. hypothesis for the change in the log exchange rate actually rejects such a null hypothesis (e.g., Brock, Hsieh, and LeBaron 1991).

A chaos model of exchange rate such as the Fukuda model could, in principle, explain these empirical findings. We know that if a variable (which is a well-defined function of other economic fundamentals) follows a chaotic path, its path would be extremely sensitive to the initial value (the so-called butterfly effect). Since the margin of error in measuring usual fundamental variables (e.g., GNP) is not low, we need not be surprised that exchange rate path seems not very forecastable by looking at these fundamentals, even if exchange rate theories have identified correctly that economic fundamentals that matter for exchange rate movement. Second, a deterministic chaos need not be distinguishable from a stochastic (in particular, random-walk) series by usual statistical procedures.

If a chaos model of exchange rate has this appealing potential, how do we get chaos into a model? Fukuda chooses a representative agent approach with money-in-the-utility specification. What initially follows a chaotic path in his model is the domestic price level (and consequently real money balances). A key step to get chaos in the foreign exchange market is the assumption of purchasing power parity (PPP), so that chaos in the domestic price level can be transmitted into chaos in the exchange rate. However, many studies have shown that the PPP does not hold for the short horizons within which erratic exchange rate movement is thought to arise. In addition, a priori, one might think that exchange rates, or other asset prices, may be chaotic for certain time periods. But it appears to be stretching the point to believe domestic price level and real money balance to be erratic or chaotic.

More important, the role of the speculative market itself is missing in Fukuda's model. When people talk about erratic movement in the foreign exchange or any asset market, they have in mind more often than not some aspects of speculative trading itself as the amplifier or the source of short-term erratic fluctuation, which is not necessarily related to economic fundamentals. It seems desirable to have a model of chaotic exchange rate that builds upon speculative trading per se, without relying on the heavy assumption of the PPP.

In the next part of my comment, I will show in a very simple model that this can be done. The source of chaos in my model is the interaction of speculative activities among heterogeneous traders. Chaos is not present all the time, but it occurs for some parameter values. During the times when chaos does arise, the exchange rate movement can be very erratic, including having quantitative breaks even when the fundamentals do not fluctuate. The time path of exchange rate is extremely sensitive to the initial value (or the degree of its precision), which makes it virtually impossible to forecast exchange rates on the basis of economic variables measured with errors. Finally, exchange rate can overreact to "insignificant" news.

Alternative Model Based on Interaction among Heterogenous Agents

This alternative model derives chaotic movement of exchange rate from interaction among heterogenous traders in the market. The presence of heterogenous traders in the foreign exchange market has been recognized before to have important implications. For example, the presence of fundamental traders and chartists has been argued as an explanation for the large dollar cycle in the 1980s (Frankel and Froot 1990).

In the following model, there are two classes of traders. The first class is informed fundamental traders, who believe in economic fundamentals and economic models and have some private but noisy information about the fundamentals. The second class is speculative chartists (similar to the noise trades in Black [1986] or Kyle [1985]). We could have a third class, uninformed fundamental traders, who would complicate the derivations without adding much new insight.

The Environment

To make the story as simple as possible, I will make some drastic assumptions. There are two types of assets. The first is a riskless domestic bond, whose one-period rate of interest is normalized to be zero. The second is a foreign bond, which also has a zero rate of interest when evaluated in the foreign currency. For simplicity, let domestic and foreign markets for foreign bonds be perfectly segregated (for example, a domestic U.S.-dollar bond market and a Euro-yen bond market. A Japanese ban on capital outflow prevents Japanese investors from investing in either of the two markets). Every informed fundamental trader is endowed with one unit of foreign bond, so the total supply of foreign bond in the market is equal to the number of informed traders, Θ.

Informed Fundamental Traders

A representative fundamental trader has a negative exponential utility function with a constant coefficient of absolute risk aversion, δ. We assume that she has a two-period investment horizon (i.e., she will exit the foreign exchange market at the end of next period). She observes a noisy signal, i, about v, the ex post value of next-period exchange rate, $v \equiv S(t+1)$:

$$(1) \qquad i = v + e,$$

where e is a white noise variable. We assume that v and e are independently distributed, v has a normal distribution with mean zero and precision τ_v, and e is also a normal variate with mean zero and precision τ_e. The informed trader's information set contains all the past and present values if i's, the past and present exchange rate, and the behavior rule of the chartists. However, since the informed trader cares only about the value of her wealth at next period, the present value of i is the only relevant information for her. Let $X(t)$ be her demand for foreign bonds. Since she is endowed with one unit of foreign bond, her demand for domestic bonds is $[1 - X(t)]S(t)$, where $S(t)$ is the spot exchange rate at time t. More precisely, the informed fundamental trader solves the following problem:

$$\max \mathbf{E}\{-e^{-\delta W} \mid i(t)\}\,, \tag{2}$$

subject to

$$W = X(t)v + [1 - X(t)]S(t). \tag{3}$$

The solution to this problem is

$$X(t) = \beta i(t) - \pi S(t)\,, \tag{4}$$

where

$$\beta = \frac{\tau_e}{\delta}, \text{ and } \pi = \frac{\tau_v + \tau_e}{\delta}. \tag{3}$$

Chartists

Let $Z(t)$ be the chartists' collective demand for foreign bonds at time t. This demand is assumed to be proportional to the chartists' subjective expectation of the rate of return on the foreign bonds, denoted by $R^{se}{}_{t,t+1}$. Let $u(t)$ be the expectational error made by the chartists. Then,

$$R^{se}_{t,t+1} = \frac{S(t+1) - S(t)}{S(t)} + u(t)\,, \tag{6}$$

and their demand for foreign bonds is

$$Z(t) = \Gamma\, R^{se}_{t,t+1} = \Gamma\frac{S(t+1)}{S(t)} + \Gamma[u(t) - 1]. \tag{7}$$

The chartists here can also represent program traders, or any traders that use exogenous trading rules.

Equilibrium

An equilibrium in the model is defined to be a list $\{X(t), Z(t), S(t)\}$, such that $X(t)$ maximizes the informed fundamental traders' expected utility, $Z(t)$ satisfies the chartists' trading rule, and $S(t)$ clears the market (for foreign bonds).

Applying the definition of an equilibrium, we know that $S(t)$ has to satisfy the following condition

$$\Theta\, X(t) + Z(t) = \Theta\,. \tag{8}$$

With appropriate substitutions, the equilibrium exchange rate path can be characterized by

$$S(t+1) = -\frac{S(t)}{\Gamma}[\Gamma u(t) - \Gamma + \Theta\beta i(t) - \Theta - \Theta\pi S(t)]. \tag{9}$$

This seemingly simple first-order difference equation is, in fact, capable of generating chaotic movement for certain parameter values. To see this, let us first make a simple transformation. Define

$$Y(t) = \frac{\Theta\pi\, S(t)}{\Gamma u(t) - \Gamma + \Theta\beta i(t) - \Theta}. \tag{10}$$

Then, equation (9) can be rewritten as

$$Y(t+1) = \alpha(i,t)\, Y(t)\, [1 - Y(t)]\,, \tag{11}$$

where

$$\alpha(i,t) = \frac{[\Gamma u(t) - \Gamma + \Theta\beta i(t) - \Theta]^2}{\Gamma^2[u(t+1) - 1] + \Gamma\Theta\beta i(t+1) - \Gamma\Theta}. \tag{12}$$

Dynamics of nonlinear equations have been extensively studied recently. The above equation is one of the simplest nonlinear equations that can generate chaos. Let me summarize a relevant result.

Lemma (May 1976): Consider $1 < \alpha(i,t) < 4$. The behavior of equation (11) depends sensitively on the value of $\alpha(\mathrm{i})$:

(1) For $1 < \alpha < 3$, the path of $Y(t)$ converges to some fixed point.
(2) Starting from $\alpha = 3$, the fixed point becomes unstable.
(3) Starting from $\alpha = 3.5700$, the "chaotic" region begins. That is, the accumulation of cycles of period 2^n starts for some integer n.
(4) Starting from $\alpha = 3.6786$, the first odd-period cycle appears.
(5) Starting from $\alpha = 3.8284$, cycles with period 3 appear. By Sarkovsky's theorem, this means that cycles with every integer period are present at the same time.
(6) For $\alpha = 4.0000$, the "chaotic" region ends.
(7) There are stable cycles in the "chaotic" region.

This lemma shows that the time path $Y(t)$ is extremely sensitive to the parameter values. Although chaos is not present at all times, the point is that it can occur for some parameter values.

Note that $\alpha(i, t)$ is a function of the information variable, i. This suggests two possibilities. First, for certain fixed values of i, say $i(t+1) = i(t) =$ some constant (so that there is no fluctuation in the information about fundamentals), the exchange rate could still be very volatile. As is well known from the chaos literature, the exchange rate path in (9) or (11) can have sudden quantitatively large breaks, even with absolutely no shocks to the fundamentals to the market. Second, a slight change in the value of $i(t + 1)$, can dramatically change the dynamics of the exchange rate path. For example, consider a small change in the value of $i(t + 1)$ that changes α from 3.56 to 3.58. For the original value of $i(t + 1)$, the exchange rate is nonchaotic. With this slight change in the news (or rumors) about the fundamentals, the exchange rate suddenly becomes erratic. Therefore, the exchange rate could appear to overreact to "insignificant" news.

What Do We Know Empirically?

Is there empirical evidence suggesting the presence of chaos in the exchange rate market? Since this is a conference on East Asian economies, let me first note that there are no chaotic movements in the bilateral exchange rates of any of the nine East Asian developing countries in terms of the U.S. dollar, since most of them either explicitly peg to or implicitly assign heavy weight in their currency basket to the dollar. The same can be said of many developing countries outside the Pacific region.

What about the yen/dollar rate (or other exchange rates)? Empirical tests on this are very few. One exception is Brock, Hsieh, and LeBaron (1991), who have applied the Brock-Dechert-Scheinkman (BDS) statistic to the yen/dollar rate together with four other major exchange rates. The result from the BDS test is consistent with both a low-dimensional chaos or stochastic nonlinear process. On the other hand, there is a lack of collaborative evidence in support of the chaos hypothesis. If attention is restricted to stochastic nonlinear models, they conclude that nonlinearity in variance is more plausible than nonlinearity in means.[1]

To summarize, a chaotic model of exchange rates has an appealing feature in its potential to explain the empirical failure of many earlier theoretical models of exchange rate determination. Such a chaotic model can be derived in a representative-agent macro model as in Fukuda or in a heterogenous-traders micro model as in this comment. Systematic empirical work is still needed in order to evaluate fully the empirical relevance of the chaos hypothesis of exchange rates.

References

Black, Fischer. 1986. Noise. *Journal of Finance* 41 (July): 529–43.

Brock, Williams A., David A. Hsieh, and Blake LeBaron. 1991. *Nonlinear dynamics, chaos, and instability: Statistical theory and economic evidence.* Cambridge: MIT Press.

1. A successful empirical model of nonlinear dependence in the variance of exchange rate (with no chaos) is Engle, Ito, and Lin (1990).

Engle, Robert, Takatoshi Ito, and Wen-Lin Lin. 1990. Meteor showers or heat waves? Heteroskedastic intra-daily volatility in the foreign exchange market. *Econometrica* 58:525–42.

Frankel, Jeffrey, and Kenneth Froot. 1990. "Chartists, fundamentalists, and trading in the foreign exchange market. *American Economic Review* 80 (May): 181–85.

Kyle, Albert. 1985. Continuous auctions and insider trading. *Econometrica* 53:1315–35.

May, Robert. 1976. Simple mathematical models with very complicated dynamics. *Nature* 261:459–67.

Meese, Richard, and Kenneth Rogoff. 1983. Empirical exchange rate models of the seventies: Do they fit out of sample? *Journal of International Economics* 14:3–24.

Wei, Shang-Jin. 1991. Price volatility without news about fundamentals. *Economics Letters* 37:453–58.

9 Export Structure and Exchange Rate Variation in Taiwan: A Comparison with Japan and the United States

Pochih Chen, Chi Schive, and Cheng Chung Chu

9.1 Introduction

Although Taiwan switched to a flexible exchange rate system in 1979, the New Taiwan (NT) dollar/U.S. dollar exchange rate remained virtually fixed under the Central Bank's firm control until 1985. During this time the macroeconomics situation in Taiwan changed drastically. For instance, Taiwan's trade surplus increased rapidly in the early 1980s, with the trade surplus to GNP ratio increasing from 0.05 percent in 1980 to 17.87 percent in 1985. However, the government made no concrete or immediate efforts to reduce the ever-growing macroeconomic disequilibrium. The major macro policy during this period was large-scale intervention in the monetary market in order to sterilize the effect of the trade surplus on money supply. Nevertheless, the sterilization policy not only restricted the automatic mechanism for reducing the trade surplus through more domestic expenditure and a higher inflation rate, but also aggravated the trade imbalance via less domestic credit creation (Chen 1985). Due partly to the inactive policies in the early 1980s but most importantly to U.S. pressure on Taiwan to reduce its bilateral trade surplus with the United States, the burden of adjustment became formidable for Taiwan after 1985.

This paper analyzes the impact on Taiwan's export structure of the sharply appreciated local currency over the past five to six years, with special reference to Japan and the United States, Taiwan's two major trading partners. Before

Pochih Chen and Chi Schive are professors of economics at National Taiwan University. Cheng Chung Chu is associate research fellow at the Taiwan Institute for Economic Research.

The authors are indebted to Chong Chi Wu, Minshing Kong, and Ya Hui Chou for their helpful discussions, as well to participants of the conference, Shin-ichi Fukuda in particular, for suggestions on revising the paper. Of course, the authors remain responsible for any errors.

analyzing the changes in commodity structure after 1985, in the next section we will offer some background information about Taiwan's trade surplus and exchange rate appreciation in the 1980s. Then in sections 9.3 and 9.4 we will examine the changes in factor intensities and other characteristics of Taiwan's exports. Finally, we will compare the composition of exports from Taiwan, Japan, and the United States with various measures of commodity characteristics. Some inferences can then be drawn about how and at what speed Taiwan's production and export structure will adjust as it approaches the per capita GNP level of a developed country.

9.2 Trade Surplus and Exchange Rate Appreciation

Taiwan's economy was hit by a huge trade surplus in the 1980s—the trade surplus to GDP ratio reached nearly 20 percent in 1986. Since 1985, international pressure on Taiwan to reduce its trade surplus has become so intense that Taiwan has had to rapidly appreciate its currency against the U.S. dollar. The exchange rate appreciated from about 40 NT dollars per U.S. dollar to 26 NT dollars per U.S. dollar between 1985 and 1989. As a result, the rate of appreciation of the NT dollar in the second half of the 1980s was higher than that of most currencies in the world. Table 9.1 shows the price indices of some major currencies in terms of NT dollars. As all indices are set equal to 100 for March 1992, if the NT dollar has appreciated against a certain currency since a specific period, the index of that currency for that period is greater than 100. Conversely an index less than 100 in a period implies that the NT dollar has

Table 9.1 **Price Indices of Major Currencies in Terms of the NT Dollar**

Year	U.S. Dollar	British Pound Sterling	Deutsche Mark	French Franc	Japanese Yen	Korean Won
1980	140.85	192.65	119.10	173.74	92.26	165.42
1981	148.02	163.17	108.43	144.20	89.51	163.76
1982	156.13	146.06	108.11	129.54	88.34	161.59
1983	157.54	132.00	95.38	105.47	90.21	153.48
1984	154.41	103.61	81.16	89.72	81.77	144.63
1985	155.90	129.54	104.49	115.32	103.39	135.72
1986	138.86	117.60	117.42	120.13	116.05	124.93
1987	111.63	120.18	115.80	115.97	119.27	109.20
1988	110.14	115.04	102.62	101.53	116.46	124.78
1989	102.51	94.68	99.45	98.47	93.80	116.90
1990	106.19	117.69	116.90	115.97	103.80	114.87
1991	100.86	108.15	108.82	107.88	106.09	102.74
1992	100.00	100.00	100.00	100.00	100.00	100.00

Sources: International Financial Statistics (Washington, D.C.: IMF, various issues); *Financial Statistics Monthly: The Republic of China* (Taipei: Ministry of Finance, various issues).

Notes: Data refer to the end of each period. Prices in March 1992 are set equal to 100.

depreciated against that currency since that period. As shown in table 9.1, since 1980 the NT dollar has appreciated against all currencies except the Japanese yen.

In addition to the rapid appreciation of the NT dollar, wage rates in Taiwan also rose rapidly in the 1980s due both to the promulgation of the Labor Law in 1983, which tended to raise concern for labor welfare, and to the booming economy, particularly the service sector, in the second half of the 1980s. Consequently, unit labor costs in Taiwan's manufacturing sector as measured in U.S. dollars increased much faster than such costs for all of Taiwan's major competitors, with Japan the only probable exception (see table 9.2). One clear implication is that the international competitiveness of Taiwan's traditional, usually labor-intensive, export products had to have worsened sharply in that period. In order to maintain the same market position as before, Taiwan has had to promptly switch exports from traditional labor-intensive products to those with which Taiwan can rebuild an international comparative, or competitive, advantage.[1]

The pressure for structural change in Taiwan's exports after 1985 was further reinforced by two structural factors, namely the decline of domestic investment after 1980 and the falling share of the manufacturing sector in GDP. Although the appreciation of the NT dollar was caused mainly by Taiwan's huge trade surplus, the surplus before 1985 was not solely the result of the strong international competitiveness of Taiwan's products. Instead, insufficient domestic investment also had a role to play (Chen 1989; Schive 1991).

Since Taiwan is a comparatively open economy, with trade playing an ever-increasing role, the growth rate of GNP and that of exports are usually highly correlated. Even in economically bad years, both indicators have shown the same direction. For example, Taiwan's exports and GNP both grew minimally in 1981 and 1985, as shown in table 9.3. Moreover, a sharp decline in the growth of Taiwan's domestic investment in early 1980s can be detected from table 9.3. The growth rate of gross fixed capital formation in real terms was almost zero between 1981 and 1986, while the growth rate before 1981 averaged about 10 percent. Even without detailed discussion of the sources of Taiwan's trade surplus, data from table 9.3 are probably sufficient to show that the international competitiveness of Taiwan's products was not at its peak in 1985. After 1986, the policy aimed at reducing the trade surplus via exchange rate appreciation put intense pressure on Taiwan's trade sector to adjust.

In addition to the rapid appreciation of the NT dollar, the overexpanded nature of the manufacturing sector compared to that in most developed countries also accentuated the need for structural change in Taiwan after 1985. Kuznets pointed out more than three decades ago that the share of different sectors in

1. Three other papers tackle the same issue from different aspects, including upgrading export products, introducing more automated machinery and equipment, and making outward investment. See Schive (1991, 1992a, 1992b).

Table 9.2 **Unit Labor Cost in U.S. Dollars: 1980–91 (1982=100)**

Year	Taiwan	Japan	Korea	United States	United Kingdom	France	West Germany	Netherlands	Canada	Denmark	Belgium	Norway	Sweden	Italy
1980	87	107	104	87	118	125	124	127	83	126	155	110	130	117
1981	97	114	100	94	112	109	104	103	89	108	126	105	120	103
1982	100	100	100	100	100	100	100	100	100	100	100	100	100	100
1983	97	103	94	98	86	93	95	92	99	93	86	93	84	99
1984	108	99	90	96	77	87	86	77	91	87	79	85	81	89
1985	112	97	88	97	77	88	85	76	88	90	81	86	85	88
1986	127	142	83	97	91	117	120	104	91	128	110	110	109	116
1987	160	157	91	94	103	138	156	130	99	167	129	132	130	138
1988	170	173	112	92	112	138	160	130	111	170	126	141	141	140
1989	192	161	153	93	106	128	150	119	123	160	122	130	146	143
1990	199	—	160	—	—	—	—	—	—	—	—	—	—	—
1991	200	—	163	—	—	—	—	—	—	—	—	—	—	—

Sources: Monthly Labor Review (Washington, D.C.: Department of Labor, Bureau of Labor Statistics, August 1991); *Monthly Bulletin of Earnings and Productivity Statistics* (Taipei: Directorate-General of Budget, Accounting and Statistics (DGBAS], Executive Yuan, April 1992).

Table 9.3 **Growth Rate of Taiwanese GNP, Trade, and Capital Formation (%)**

Year	GNP	Exports of Goods and Services	Imports of Goods and Services	Gross Fixed Capital Formation
1980	24.31	23.03	33.57	35.88
1981	18.51	14.13	7.43	8.24
1982	6.85	−1.80	−10.90	−1.10
1983	9.96	13.14	7.41	−3.34
1984	11.43	21.23	8.24	2.56
1985	5.29	0.88	−8.46	−7.27
1986	16.33	29.73	20.29	10.96
1987	12.41	34.66	44.67	19.83
1988	9.01	13.02	41.99	16.90
1989	10.70	9.29	5.22	17.99
1990	9.02	1.37	4.69	10.78
1991	11.60	13.33	14.89	10.82

Source: Quarterly National Economic Trends Taiwan Area: The Republic of China (Taipei: DGBAS, Executive Yuan, February 1992).

an economy changes over time as the economy moves through different stages of development, a phenomenon also known as the Clark hypothesis. The experiences of many developed countries indicates that the share of manufacturing sector in GDP increases in the early development stage, then decreases in later stages. The turning point seems to be around the per capita GDP level of $5,000 (U.S.; 1985 prices), and the highest level of manufacturing in the major Western countries is about 40 percent of GDP (Chen and Lee 1988).

When Taiwan's per capita GNP was around $5,000 (U.S.) in 1987, the manufacturing sector share of GDP was also around 40 percent. The share of Taiwan's manufacturing sector in GDP has followed the same general pattern over time as other developed economies have experienced. In 1986 Taiwan reached a record share for manufacturing in GDP of 39.70 percent, but this share fell to only 34 percent in 1991. Since the declining ratio means that the manufacturing sector grew much more slowly than the whole economy, certain industries in the manufacturing sector must have encountered mounting pressure and difficulties requiring change. How the manufacturing sector has responded to these challenges should be a major concern.

9.3 Changes in the Factor Intensities of Taiwan's Exports

With the significant rise in Taiwan's labor costs, standard trade theory asserts that Taiwan's international comparative advantage and trade structure should change. However, there are some difficulties involved in measuring structural changes in trade. First, the production factors actually used are more than just capital and labor. A relative decline of labor-intensive products in total trade, thus, may not imply a relative increase in capital-intensive products in total trade. Moreover, trade data are generally classified by commodity or by industry. It is by no means an easy job to examine changes in trade structure in relation to changes in comparative advantages.

Fortunately, a recent study sponsored by the Ministry of Finance (Chen, Schive, and Wu 1991) on the reclassification of tradable commodities provides relevant data and classification criteria to analyze the commodity structure of trade in Taiwan and other countries as well. An input-output table for 1986 and other statistics for Taiwan were used to identify the characteristics of each industry. The characteristics of each commodity in the H.S. classification are then assumed to remain unchanged across different countries for country comparative studies.[2]

Table 9.4 classifies Taiwan's exports according to the factor/input intensities of commodities. The degree of labor intensity of each product was measured by the ratio of domestic labor expenditures embodied in the product to the total domestic factor income that the product contains. Then all industries were divided into three groups—high, medium, and low—according to the level of this measure. The results from table 9.4 show that the share of highly labor-intensive commodities in total trade declined from 47.03 percent in 1986 to 40.10 percent in 1991. In contrast, the share in total trade of commodities with low labor intensities increased from 14.89 percent in 1987 to 21.17 percent in 1991. The direction of the structural change in trade seems to be in line with that expected, but the speed of adjustment may be considered only moderate.

The indicator for capital intensity was measured by the ratio of total domestic capital to labor used directly and indirectly in the production. Note then that the ranking of industries by this measure may not equal the reverse of the ranking according to labor intensity just discussed. The ratio of products with high capital intensities in Taiwan's total exports increased from 22.35 percent in 1987 to 29.81 percent in 1991, and that with low capital intensities dropped from 27.72 percent in 1986 to 19.21 percent in 1991. The directions and speeds of adjustment were similar to those for labor intensities.

When commodities were reclassified by the degree of human capital intensity, the speed of adjustment in trade structure seems to be faster than in the previous two cases. Human capital intensity is measured by the ratio of workers with a college degree or higher educational attainment relative to the total direct and indirect employment of an industry. Table 9.4 shows that the proportion of products with a high degree of human capital intensity in Taiwan's exports increased from 18.37 percent in 1986 to 27.23 percent in 1991, while the proportion of low human-capital-intensity products declined from 47.94 percent in 1986 to 34.26 percent in 1991. The direction of adjustment is consis-

2. The "H.S. classification" refers to the Harmonized Commodity Description and Coding System of the Customs Cooperation Council. We are fully aware that factor intensity may change in different countries. Nevertheless, the reclassification of tradable commodities following each country's own standard would complicate the country comparison to an almost unmanageable degree. Further discussion on this point is addressed in section 9.5 of this paper.

Table 9.4 **Export Structure of Taiwan by Input Intensities, 1985–91 (%)**

	Degree of Labor Intensity			Degree of Capital Intensity			Degree of Human Capital Intensity			Degree of Energy Intensity		
Year	High	Mid	Low	High	Mid	Low	High	Mid	Low	High	Mid	Low
1985	45.93	35.60	18.47	24.48	48.70	26.83	18.75	33.62	47.63	14.14	46.89	38.97
1986	47.03	36.93	16.05	22.91	49.37	27.72	18.37	33.68	47.94	11.82	46.55	41.62
1987	47.93	37.18	14.89	22.35	50.52	27.13	19.30	35.30	45.40	10.84	45.39	43.77
1988	46.27	36.79	16.94	23.49	51.50	25.01	22.55	36.92	40.53	12.37	48.05	44.56
1989	43.44	37.75	18.80	26.59	50.73	22.66	24.25	38.10	37.65	13.07	45.29	41.64
1990	41.02	38.30	20.68	28.95	50.54	20.51	26.73	38.57	34.70	13.78	45.37	40.85
1991	40.10	38.73	21.17	29.81	50.96	19.21	27.23	38.51	34.26	13.89	45.74	40.37

Source: Calculated from tapes of trade statistics of Taiwan (Taipei: Ministry of Finance).
Note: For definitions of measures, see text (also, Chen, Schive, and Wu 1991).

tent again with what one may expect, but the faster adjustment in this classification is of particular interest. More discussions on this point will be presented later.

Commodities were further classified by energy intensity, with the result that the ratios of products with different energy intensities changed only slightly despite significant changes in energy prices during the period of observation. Part of this result is due to the fact that many energy goods are tradable, so that the relative opportunity cost of energy faced by Taiwan and other countries is stable despite wide fluctuations in oil price. Consequently, the main factor determining the international comparative advantage of energy-intensive products would be differences in the efficiency of energy use in different countries rather than the relative factor cost of the countries involved (Caves, Frankel, and Jones 1990, 185–87). It also implies that a relative increase of wage rates or labor costs may not change the comparative advantage of energy-intensive products significantly.

9.4 Other Forms of Structural Change in Taiwan's Exports

Chen, Schive, and Wu (1991) have also applied other criteria to classify trade commodities. Table 9.5 regroups Taiwan's exports into ten categories according to the stages of fabrication or the use of commodities applied in a World Bank study (Balassa 1981). The results shown in table 9.5 indicate further the rapid structural adjustment of Taiwan's exports in the late 1980s.

The shares of primary products and processed food declined steadily as would be expected. Among the categories with increasing shares in Taiwan's exports, type B intermediate products, which are those intermediate products readily usable as final products, replaced consumer nondurable goods as the largest category in Taiwan's exports. The share of type B intermediate products was only 25.98 percent in 1986, but increased sharply to 36.97 percent in 1991. The decline of consumer nondurable goods is even more striking. The share of this category dropped from 35.34 percent in 1986 to 22 percent in 1991. The primary reason behind this drastic change is the change in the relative labor costs between Taiwan and its competing countries explained earlier (table 9.2). However, it is also worth noting that rapid outward investment since 1986 from Taiwan to neighboring countries with low labor costs was another factor behind this drastic change (Schive 1991). Many Taiwanese multinational firms are now importing intermediate products and capital goods from Taiwan to produce final products in neighboring countries. The shares of both intermediate products and capital goods in Taiwan's exports increased while that of consumer goods, both durables and nondurables, declined. Moreover, the share of the U.S. market held by Taiwan's exports decreased from nearly 48 percent in 1986 to 28 percent in 1991, while the share of Taiwanese exports going to neighboring developing countries as well as the share of U.S. imports from these countries have been increasing rapidly to fill the gap (Schive 1992a).

Table 9.5 **Export Structure of Taiwan by Industry and Use, 1985–91 (%)**

Year	Agriculture, Forestry, Livestock, and Hunting Products	Processed Food	Beverage and Tobacco Preparation	Energy and Minerals	Construction Materials	Intermediate Products A	Intermediate Products B	Consumer Nondurable Goods	Consumer Durable Goods	Machinery	Transportation Equipment
1985	1.57	4.28	0.04	0.03	0.55	8.66	26.76	35.54	10.34	10.30	1.71
1986	1.67	4.69	0.03	0.06	0.44	7.40	25.98	35.34	11.68	10.84	1.86
1987	1.40	4.51	0.03	0.11	0.35	6.86	26.51	33.29	11.93	13.14	1.86
1988	1.60	3.73	0.04	0.07	0.35	8.74	27.69	29.67	11.20	15.36	1.54
1989	0.96	3.57	0.03	0.06	0.29	8.98	31.02	27.42	10.30	15.47	1.89
1990	0.84	3.51	0.03	0.05	0.22	9.47	34.92	23.67	8.87	16.31	2.11
1991	0.91	3.63	0.05	0.04	0.23	9.44	36.97	22.00	8.51	16.10	2.12

Source: See table 9.4.

Note: Intermediate products A is defined as products used in the manufacturing process of other intermediate products. Intermediate products B refers to those products which can be used directly in the manufacturing process of final products.

Because outward investment may slow down in the future but not reverse, the resulting impact on the domestic economy is likely to be permanent. In addition, since Taiwan's total exports in U.S. dollars almost doubled from 1986 to 1991, all categories of exports grew during that period. Thus, the structural change in Taiwan's export coincided with a rather high export growth rate and was not attributable to the shrinking of certain categories. A clear implication is that the significant changes in trade structure in the second half of the 1980s were less attributable to Taiwan's short-term business cycle than to long-term structural changes.

The increasing share of producer goods in Taiwan's exports may be regarded as an indication of the upgrading of Taiwan's economy. The rapidly rising shares of less labor-intensive, highly capital-intensive, or highly human-capital-intensive goods also has similar implications. A more traditional and easier way to identify whether there has been industrial upgrading is to look at the share of heavy and chemical industries or the share of high-tech products in total exports. According to table 9.6, the share of heavy and chemical industries in Taiwan's exports increased from 35.63 percent in 1986 to 46.71 percent in 1991. The share of high-tech products jumped from 27.56 percent in 1986 to 36.23 percent in 1991. Both measures indicate a roughly 10 percentage point increase over the short period of five years. Therefore, Taiwan's export structure did change significantly regardless of which indicator is used to measure the change.

9.5 A Comparison between Taiwan, Japan, and the United States

As expected, Taiwan's export structure has been changing rapidly to resemble that of a developed country. Yet it is not clear whether the export structures of developed countries are indeed consistent with what has been gener-

Table 9.6 **Share of Heavy and Chemical and High-Tech Products in Taiwanese Exports, 1985–91 (%)**

Year	Heavy Chemical Industries Products	Non–Heavy Chemical Industries Products	High-Tech Products	Non–High-Tech Products
1985	36.47	63.53	27.03	72.97
1986	35.63	64.37	27.56	72.44
1987	37.89	62.11	30.03	69.97
1988	42.84	57.16	33.70	66.30
1989	44.53	55.47	33.92	66.08
1990	46.67	53.33	35.87	64.13
1991	46.71	53.29	36.23	63.77

Source: See table 9.4.

ally assumed. Moreover, in order to better understand how fast the Taiwanese economic structure has been changing, some information about the current state of the trade structure of developed countries is useful as a reference point for Taiwan. The same classifications used before were applied to calculate the export structures of Japan and the United States. Two minor points should be mentioned. First, because both countries changed their system of commodity classification recently, only data for recent years was analyzed. Second, because the criteria for commodity classification were taken directly from those developed for Taiwan, the results may not correctly reflect the actual export structures of Japan and the United States. Nevertheless, the results turn out to be consistent with both the theory and what has been found before.

Table 9.7 shows the export structures of Japan and the United States by input intensities. The export structure of Japan in table 9.7 was stable over the last four years. Relative to Japan, exports of the United States were more inclined to high labor-intensity, low capital-intensity, and low human-capital-intensity products, yet the gaps between the United States and Japan were much smaller than those between Taiwan and Japan or between Taiwan and the United States. Moreover, the gaps between the United States and Japan and those between Taiwan and the two developed countries have been shrinking in the last few years.

The share of high labor-intensity products in Taiwan's exports in 1991 was 40.10 percent, which was 1.4 percentage points higher than the U.S. level, but the U.S. share was 7.3 percentage points higher than the Japanese level. From this point of view, the export structure of the United States seems to be closer to Taiwan's than to Japan's. However, the share of low labor-intensity products in Taiwan was only 21.17 percent in 1991, while the same figure in the United

Table 9.7 **Export Structure of the United States and Japan by Input Intensities, 1988–91 (%)**

	Degree of Labor Intensity			Degree of Capital Intensity			Degree of Human Capital Intensity			Degree of Energy Intensity		
Year	High	Middle	Low	High	Middle	Low	High	Middle	Low	High	Middle	Low
United States												
1989	41.01	25.26	33.74	38.31	39.26	22.43	63.09	16.88	20.03	15.13	41.72	43.15
1990	39.51	26.08	34.41	38.80	41.35	19.86	62.66	17.43	19.90	14.43	44.44	41.13
1991	38.68	26.02	35.29	39.84	41.61	18.55	63.54	17.46	18.99	14.42	45.77	38.91
Japan												
1988	30.40	29.11	40.50	45.36	40.49	14.15	64.13	30.65	5.22	13.26	49.43	37.31
1989	31.06	29.40	39.54	44.50	41.92	13.58	64.10	30.79	5.11	12.99	49.79	37.23
1990	30.87	29.85	39.28	44.22	42.04	13.74	64.14	30.52	5.34	12.26	49.93	37.81
1991	31.34	29.91	38.75	43.45	42.56	13.99	63.91	30.77	5.33	12.04	49.40	38.56

Source: Calculated from the tapes of trade statistics of the United States and Japan.
Note: For definitions, see discussion in the text, section 9.3 (also, Chen, Schive, and Wu 1991).

Table 9.8 **Export Structure of the United States and Japan by Industry and Use, 1988–91 (%)**

Year	Agriculture, Forestry, Livestock and Hunting Products	Processed Food	Beverage and Tobacco Preparation	Energy and Minerals	Construction Materials	Intermediate Products		Consumer Nondurable Goods	Consumer Durable Goods	Machinery	Transportation Equipment
						A	B				
United States											
1989	8.04	4.15	1.31	2.02	0.13	16.60	29.10	6.48	7.54	15.13	9.50
1990	6.92	4.08	1.62	1.90	0.15	15.87	30.25	7.37	5.72	15.52	10.61
1991	5.85	4.25	1.43	1.80	0.15	15.79	30.12	7.72	5.66	15.71	11.54
Japan											
1988	0.10	0.60	0.05	0.15	0.16	10.82	28.33	3.74	8.04	25.18	22.83
1989	0.10	0.55	0.05	0.16	0.17	10.81	29.44	3.59	7.47	25.58	22.09
1990	0.10	0.51	0.06	0.12	0.16	10.10	29.52	3.91	7.53	25.55	22.45
1991	0.10	0.48	0.07	0.13	0.17	9.78	29.68	3.92	7.22	26.32	22.12

Source: See table 9.7.

Note: See table 9.5 for definitions of intermediate products.

States was 35.29 percent, much closer to the 38.75 percent share in Japan. Similar results also can be found in the classifications by capital intensity. Taiwan and United States were closer in low capital-intensity products while Japan and the United States were closer in high capital-intensity products. As implied, the comparative advantage of Taiwan was concentrated slightly more in products with medium degrees of labor or capital intensity.

The differences among countries in the shares of commodities as classified by human capital intensity are striking. In 1991 the shares of highly human-capital-intensive products in exports were 63.54 and 63.91 percent in the United States and Japan, respectively, while the same measure was only 27.23 percent in Taiwan. Thus, the export structure of Taiwan is still far behind Japan and the United States, while Japan and the United States are similar to each other in their trade structures. As for the shares of low human-capital-intensity products, the 1991 figures for Taiwan, the United States, and Japan are 34.26, 18.99, and 5.33 percent, respectively. Japan seems to concentrate much more on products with a medium-degree of human capital intensity than does the United States.

The shares of products by energy intensities did not differ much among these three countries. This result is interesting but the reasons for it are not yet clear. It is possible that energy and energy-related product prices do not play a major role in determining international comparative advantage for energy-intensive products. The argument of Caves, Frankel, and Jones (1990) applies well in this case.

The results presented in table 9.8 show that the United States enjoyed comparative advantage in primary products, processed food, beverage and tobacco, energy and minerals, intermediate products, and consumer nondurable goods over Japan, while Japan performed better in machinery and transportation equipment. In comparison with its share of Japanese and U.S. exports, consumer nondurable goods was the largest export category in Taiwan recently, although this share has been declining very rapidly. Even so, the share was still 22 percent in 1991, compared with 7.72 and 3.92 percent in the United States and Japan, respectively. The share of machinery in Taiwan's exports was already slightly higher than that of the United States in 1991.

The export shares of heavy and chemical industries and high-tech products shown in tables 9.6 and 9.9 indicate again that the export structure of the United States is between Taiwan's and Japan's, but much closer to Japan's. The shares of heavy and chemical industries in 1991 were 85.76, 65.71, and 46.71 percent in Japan, the United States, and Taiwan, respectively. The shares of high-tech products in these three countries in 1991 were 70.14, 54.39, and 36.23 percent, respectively. Thus, Taiwan still has a long way to go to achieve an export structure similar to that of Japan or the United States.

Before concluding this section, it is worthwhile to point out that the analysis presented here may be affected by the fact that the United States has a richer natural resource endowment so that its export shares of primary products and

Table 9.9 Share of Heavy and Chemical and High-Tech Products in U.S. and Japanese Exports, 1988–91 (%)

Year	Heavy Chemical Industries Products	Non–Heavy Chemical Enterprises Products	High-Tech Products	Non–High-Tech Products
United States				
1989	63.17	36.83	52.39	47.61
1990	64.77	35.23	53.52	46.48
1991	65.71	34.29	54.39	45.61
Japan				
1988	86.27	13.73	70.72	29.58
1989	86.42	13.58	70.64	29.36
1990	85.87	14.13	70.54	29.46
1991	85.76	14.24	70.14	29.86

Source: See table 9.7.

other natural-resource-intensive products are higher. If comparisons are made on the basis of manufacturing goods only, with processed foods also excluded, then the export structure of the United States may be similar to that of Japan. However, Japan's export structure would probably still be slightly ahead of that of the United States according to some measures such as human capital. The use of Taiwan's production characteristics in this study is another factor that should be considered a source of bias.

9.6 Concluding Remarks

Using different factor intensities and other measures to reclassify export data, this paper showed that the export structure of Taiwan has been changing rapidly toward that of a developed country in the last few years. This paper also found that the export structure of the United States generally lies between the structures of Taiwan and Japan, but much closer to Japan's. However, the gaps between Taiwan and Japan and between Taiwan and the United States are still significant for many product categories. Therefore it is still too early to predict when Taiwan can achieve an export structure similar to that of Japan or the United States.

An interesting question is whether, since Japan is a major competitor of Taiwan's in high-tech and human-capital-intensive products in the international market, the greater strength of the Japanese yen relative to the NT dollar in the mid-1980s was a factor in the structural change of Taiwan's exports.[3] The answer is probably yes, but the degree of the yen's impact should not be exaggerated. First, even though the rise of the yen pushed Taiwan's real effective ex-

3. This question was raised at the conference.

change rate down in 1986 (Schive 1992a) and thereby helped to boost exports by 30 percent that year, structural changes in Taiwan's exports did not take place until 1987. Thus, even if a very strong yen in 1985 and 1986 did facilitate Taiwan's export of high-end products, it also helped promote Taiwan's exports in general, so that the effect on overall trade structure, at least in the short run, was not significant. Moreover, the expansion of exports of Taiwan's intermediate and capital goods beginning in 1987 was, to a significant extent, directly attributable to Taiwan's active outward investment that began that year and was therefore mostly unrelated to the yen's value. It may be fair then to conclude that Taiwan's export structure probably would not have changed as quickly as it did had the Japanese yen not appreciated to its present level, but that the value of the yen was not a decisive factor in the change.

Another interesting finding of this paper is that the speed of adjustment in Taiwan as well as the gaps among Taiwan, Japan, and the United States are significant when exports were classified by human capital intensity. This result implies that human capital may play a key role in determining international comparative advantage between semideveloped and developed countries. If this proposition is true, human-capital-intensive industries should be targeted for Taiwan's future development. An adequate supply of human capital will be vital to Taiwan's success in the later stages of economic development.

Highly human-capital-intensive industries have been developing quite well in Taiwan recently. Table 9.10 classifies Taiwan's manufacturing sector by capital intensity and human capital intensity. The production indices of these industry groups with high, middle, and low capital intensities have shown only minor differences. Roughly speaking, between 1971 and 1986, industries with low capital intensity grew at about the same rate as those with high capital intensity, but the former lagged behind in the second half of the 1980s. Although the growth rate in the second half of the 1980s was relatively high for industries with high capital intensity, industries with high human capital intensities grew at an even higher rate. Moreover, industries with low human capital content recorded a negative growth rate between 1986 and 1991. Therefore, changes in the production structure in Taiwan were similar to those in the export structure, and human capital seems to be the dominant factor in Taiwan's international competitiveness.

In view of both the theoretical arguments and empirical findings, human-capital-intensive products are also likely to be the products with which advanced countries may have comparative advantage. Although advanced countries are usually more affluent in capital, human capital, and technology, the degree of international mobility of human capital seems to be lower than that of capital and technology. Consequently, capital-intensive products may be easier to transplant and produce in less-developed countries than human-capital-intensive products. Therefore, human capital would be the dominant factor in determining a country's comparative advantage. Further study along this line is clearly warranted.

Table 9.10 Industrial Production Indices by Capital and Human Capital Intensities: Taiwan, 1971–91 (1986 = 100)

	Capital Intensity			Human Capital Intensity		
Year	High	Medium	Low	High	Medium	Low
1971	17.23	19.69	16.95	17.57	13.86	22.10
1972	21.89	25.19	18.81	21.19	17.49	26.54
1973	25.97	29.10	23.12	25.25	21.19	31.09
1974	24.56	24.68	19.74	22.92	17.51	27.69
1975	25.89	26.35	24.06	22.87	21.62	31.69
1976	40.98	36.49	35.17	32.20	34.43	46.15
1977	46.67	40.86	39.99	38.24	40.93	48.43
1978	55.74	50.85	49.55	47.14	51.38	57.85
1979	58.88	55.35	50.85	51.08	53.56	60.24
1980	63.05	55.16	54.28	52.78	57.15	62.68
1981	69.35	67.27	59.16	66.14	62.71	65.72
1982	69.73	67.09	59.60	63.74	62.87	68.99
1983	79.74	75.26	71.25	76.47	73.66	75.22
1984	85.08	84.11	83.92	84.15	84.68	84.28
1985	89.92	87.41	82.49	86.51	84.94	87.65
1986	100.00	100.00	100.00	100.00	100.00	100.00
1987	109.12	111.70	112.29	113.92	112.56	106.53
1988	115.70	116.65	113.90	122.95	120.00	102.37
1989	108.58	120.63	116.34	120.94	124.08	100.55
1990	123.49	119.11	107.87	135.33	118.93	92.52
1991	132.53	127.19	117.32	145.19	131.38	96.97

Source: Strategies for the Development of Manufacturing Sector (Taipei: Taiwan Institute for Economic Research, 1992).

References

Balassa, B. 1981. *Development strategies in semi-industrialized countries*. Baltimore: John Hopkins University Press.

Caves, R. E., J. A. Frankel, and R. W., Jones. 1990. *World trade and payments,* 5th ed. London: Scott, Foresman–Little Brown.

Chen, Pochih. 1985. The current state and limitation of monetary policy in Taiwan (in Chinese). *Chinese Economic Association Annual Conference Proceedings* (Taipei): 1–34.

———. 1989. Policies and structural adjustment in Taiwan in the 1980s. Paper presented at the Second Conference on Asia-Pacific Relation. Foundation for Advanced Information and Research, Fukuoka, August 28–29.

Chen, Pochih, and H. C. Lee. 1988. *Report on the development and strategies for the manufacturing sector* (in Chinese). Taipei: Taiwan Institute for Economic Research.

Chen, Pochih, Chi Schive, and Chung Chi Wu. 1991. *Report on the multi-classifications of tradable commodities of the Republic of China* (in Chinese). Taipei: Graduate Institute of Economics, National Taiwan University.

Schive, Chi. 1991. How did Taiwan solve its Dutch disease? Paper presented at the Fifth Biennial Conference on U.S.-Asia Economic Relations, Tokyo. Forthcoming in *Journal of Asian Economics*.

———. 1992a. Taiwan's emerging position in the international division of labor. In *Taiwan, beyond the economic miracle,* ed. Denis F. Simon and Michael Y. M. Kau. New York: M. E. Sharpe.

———. 1992b. Micro adjustment to macro imbalance in Taiwan. Paper presented at the First Special Conference on APEC: ASEAN / SAARC, Bangkok.

Comment Rachel McCulloch

From 1980 until 1985, the Central Bank of Taiwan maintained a fixed exchange rate between the NT dollar and the U.S. dollar despite a soaring trade surplus and a politically troublesome bilateral trade imbalance with the United States. In 1985, Taiwan yielded to U.S. pressure to allow the NT dollar to appreciate as a means of reducing the large bilateral imbalance. This paper analyzes changes in Taiwan's export structure during the subsequent period.

Post-1985 changes in Taiwan's exports reflect the rise in the value of the NT dollar relative to the currencies of most of its trading partners (although not Japan), as well as the rapid increase in NT dollar wage rates that began early in the 1980s when Taiwan moved into an era of tight labor markets. Over the period 1980–88, the rise in the value of the NT dollar and in NT dollar wage rates together produced a larger rise in unit labor costs (measured in U.S. dollars) than was experienced by any of Taiwan's trade competitors, including even Japan. However, a third potent agent of change is not mentioned by the authors: U.S. trade policy, which in 1985 shifted abruptly from a largely laissez-faire approach to an active stance emphasizing reduction of bilateral trade imbalances.

Using an input-output table for 1986, Chen, Schive, and Chu classify Taiwan's exports into broad groups according to their production characteristics: labor intensity, capital intensity, and human capital intensity. As one might expect given the rapidly rising unit labor costs, the share of high labor-intensity products in Taiwan's exports fell from 47 percent in 1986 to 40 percent in 1991, while the share of exports with low labor intensities rose from 15 percent to 21 percent over the same period. The authors term the speed of adjustment "only moderate," implicitly raising the interesting question of how to judge the speed of adjustment to changing circumstances. In fact, Taiwan's exports of some high labor-intensity products, apparel in particular, had been constrained by trade policies abroad to levels below those justified by comparative advantage alone. Thus, one hidden effect of the rapidly rising unit labor costs was to reduce the inconsistency between the constrained export levels and domestic costs of production.

Rachel McCulloch is Rosen Family Professor of Economics at Brandeis University and a research associate of the National Bureau of Economic Research

Other likely changes in the manufacturing sector to reduce the impact of increased labor costs cannot be assessed from the methodology used by the authors. Because they rely on a single year's input-output structure, the adjustment measured includes only the part achieved through changes in export mix, not the part achieved through changes in the way any given product was manufactured. Therefore, to the extent firms economized on labor through increased mechanization of production, the authors' approach understates the true response. Problems of interpretation also arise in the case of direct investment in neighboring (presumably lower-wage) countries, because intermediate products previously used in domestic production of exports may now become exports to subsidiaries abroad. Such export increases do not represent new demand for domestic output. Finally, even in the absence of changing unit labor costs, quantitative trade restrictions such as voluntary export restraints are likely to induce upgrading of the restricted exports over time, which often also means changes in the production characteristics of these exports.

The authors go on to compare Taiwan's export structure with those of Japan and the United States. They find Taiwan's export structure has become more like that of these two highly developed countries, with the United States lying between Taiwan and Japan, but closer to Japan, on most dimensions of export structure. The authors conclude their comparison with the observation that "Taiwan still has a long way to go to achieve an export structure similar to that of Japan or the United States." This statement seems to imply that all wealthy countries can be expected to have similar export structures. Should Taiwan's success, or lack of success, in economic development be judged on the basis of its export structure? In fact, rich countries with similar levels of GDP per capita differ widely in the structure of their merchandise exports. As the authors note, the United States is more abundant than Japan in land and natural resources, an element of comparative advantage reflected in the two countries' very different extent of primary-commodity exports. A more interesting comparison is of Japan and Germany. Like Japan, Germany has small primary exports and very large manufactured exports, but the composition of Germany's manufactured exports is quite different from that of Japan. While machinery and transport equipment accounted for two-thirds of Japan's 1990 exports, this category made up less than one-half of German exports.

The aggregate data presented by Chen, Schive, and Chu hint at a fascinating story to be told at the industry level. The authors' discussion focuses entirely on broad commodity groups, yielding such information as that "heavy and chemical industries" generated 86 percent of exports from Japan in 1991 but only 47 percent of Taiwan's exports, and that "type B intermediate products, which are those intermediate products readily usable as final products" have replaced "consumer nondurable goods" as Taiwan's biggest export category. Apparel and semiconductors are never mentioned. Augmenting the analysis of broad trends with some detail on the commodity composition of Taiwan's exports, or even case studies of adjustment by individual firms, could provide a more complete picture of the nation's recent economic transformation.

Comment Shin-ichi Fukuda

This paper gives very interesting information about the Taiwanese economy in the 1980s. Focusing on export structure, the authors describe the drastic structural change that took place in the Taiwanese economy around 1985. Such analysis is very important because Taiwan achieved remarkable economic growth in the 1980s. Although the paper is clearly written, I have four comments.

My first comment is on the comparison of the export structures of Taiwan, Japan, and the United States. The authors show that the export structure of the United States lies between those of Taiwan and Japan. However, this result seems strange to me because I can find no reason for the export structure of the United States to be less developed than that of Japan. Furthermore, the export to GNP ratio in Taiwan is more than 50 percent, while the export to GNP ratios in Japan and the United States are less than 20 percent. This implies that the role of exports in Taiwan is not simply comparable to that in Japan or the United States.

My second comment is on the data sample. The paper focuses on the sample period of the 1980s, especially the late 1980s. I agree that this was the most noteworthy period for Taiwanese economic growth. However, in general, ten years or five years is too short a span over which to discuss economic development. For such a short period, it is difficult to distinguish economic growth from business cycles. For example, the authors stress the very rapid structural change after 1985. However it is possible that this change reflects the temporary boom of business cycles in the Taiwanese economy.

My third comment is on the factors that caused structural change in the Taiwanese economy after 1985. As the authors stress, the main force behind the structural change was the drastic appreciation of the NT dollar after 1985. This appreciation made labor in Taiwan more expensive and led to a less labor-intensive and more capital-intensive industry structure. However, in my view, another important factor was the drastic appreciation of the Japanese yen. As we can see in table 9.1, the appreciation of the Japanese yen was even more drastic than that of the NT dollar. Since Japan is one of Taiwan's main competitors in the less labor-intensive and more capital-intensive industries, it is quite possible that appreciation of the Japanese yen accelerated structural change in Taiwan.

My final comment is on the trade balance in the Taiwanese economy. I am quite interested in how this was affected by the structural change in the late 1980s. If we look at data on the Taiwanese trade balance, we find a surplus throughout the 1980s. However the total trade balance of Taiwan was decreasing in the late 1980s because of the rapid increase in imports after 1985. According to a standard theory of the stages of economic development, the trade

Shin-ichi Fukuda is associate professor of economics at the Institute of Economic Research, Hitotsubashi University

balance is deficit in the first stage, becomes surplus in the second stage, and goes back to deficit in the third stage. It is usually said that Japan with its large trade surplus is in the second stage and the United States with its large trade deficit is in the third stage. Is it then appropriate to say that the recently decreasing trade surplus in Taiwan can be interpreted as foretelling the end of Taiwan's second stage of economic development?

10 Cost Externality and Exchange Rate Pass-Through: Some Evidence from Taiwan

Bih Jane Liu

10.1 Introduction

The depreciation of U.S. dollars relative to New Taiwan (NT) dollars during the second half of 1980s did not seem to solve the U.S. trade deficit problem with Taiwan. Failure by Taiwanese exporters to pass exchange rate changes through to export prices, i.e., incomplete exchange rate pass-through, is often mentioned as one of the main reasons for sluggish adjustment in the trade balance between the two countries. Recently, a number of papers have tried to explain incomplete pass-through from both theoretical and empirical perspectives. However, different studies used different models and thus obtained different conclusions.

Some attributed this incompleteness to the contract relationship prevailing in international trade, under which delivery lags behind the time when a contract is signed (e.g., Moffett 1989). Demand and supply elasticities were shown to be another main determinant of the degree of exchange rate pass-through (e.g., Feenstra 1987; Knetter 1989). Mann (1986) and Froot and Klemperer (1989) argued that in order to maintain foreign market share while domestic currency appreciates, exporters may absorb part of the appreciation by reducing their profit margins. Similarly, if exporters must incur sunk costs in order to open foreign markets and cannot recoup these costs once they exit, they tend to be reluctant to raise their prices abroad when foreign currency depreciates (e.g., Dixit 1989). However, since profit margins can be reduced only when market structure is imperfectly competitive, Krugman (1987), Dornbusch (1987), and Fisher (1989b) further showed how market structure affects the degree of exchange rate pass-through. In addition to market structure, the num-

Bih Jane Liu is professor of economics at National Taiwan University.

The author thanks Serguey Braguinsky, John Helliwell, Rachel McCulloch, and Won-Am Park for their helpful comments.

ber of firms (Dornbusch 1987), the type of exchange rate shock (Krugman 1987; Baldwin 1988a), and the exchange rate regime (Fisher 1989b) will also affect the degree of pass-through.

Although the above studies contributed significantly to the explanation of incomplete exchange rate pass-through, they might not be exhaustive. In this paper, we will provide an alternative explanation, i.e., cost externality, for the phenomenon of incomplete or over pass-through. In practice, exporters often export differentiated goods to different markets. These differentiated goods are of similar quality designed for different markets and thus produced in different product lines under which cost-saving or cost-enhancing externality exists. The existence of cost externality will affect the true marginal cost of exports and therefore affect the degree of exchange rate pass-through. As a matter of fact, negative pass-through, which is somehow not that intuitive but may happen in reality,[1] may be explained by the existence of strong cost-saving externality.

The static model developed in section 10.2 is of a conjectural variation type. Under this model, three types of exchange rate pass-through (i.e., over, incomplete, and negative) can be theoretically derived. The model also shows that cost externality, in addition to market structure, the elasticities of demand curves, and the number of firms, as discussed in various papers (e.g., Feenstra 1987; Dornbusch 1987), will play an important role in determining the degree of exchange rate pass-through. In order to test the theoretical results derived from section 10.2, an econometric model is laid out in section 10.3 for empirical analysis. Section 10.4 presents the empirical results. The conclusions are given in the final section.

10.2 The Model

There are three countries, H, F, and ROW (the rest of the world). Assume that M firms in the country H produce differentiated goods X and Y, while N firms in country F produce good Z. Goods X and Y are exported to countries F and ROW, respectively. For simplicity, we assume that X and Z, sold in country F, are homogeneous goods and compete with each other.[2]

Since X and Y are like products designed for different markets and produced in different product lines, there exists cost-saving or cost-enhancing externality between X and Y. Any change in the production of either good will affect the cost of the other good and hence its level of production. Let $C_x(x,y)$ and $C_y(x,y)$ be the cost function of X and Y expressed in H-currency for a representative firm in country H. When $\partial C_y / \partial x$ or $\partial C_x / \partial y$ is greater than zero, there exists

1. That is, export prices expressed in foreign currency increase even though foreign currency appreciates. See the definition of the degree of pass-through in section 10.2.

2. One rationale for the assumption of homogeneous goods here is that goods sold in the same country (e.g., X and Z in this model) tend to be more homogeneous than those sold in different countries (e.g., X and Y). To simplify the analysis, we therefore assume that X and Y are differentiated goods while X and Z are homogeneous goods.

cost-enhancing externality. On the other hand, if $\partial C_y / \partial x$ or $\partial C_x / \partial y$ is less than zero, there is cost-saving externality.

Let γ be the exchange rate expressed as H-currency per unit of F-currency. Let $P(Q)$, $Q = X + Z$, be the price of X and Z denominated in F-currency, where $X = \sum_{i=1}^{M} x_i$, $Z = \sum_{j=1}^{N} z_j$. $P_y(Y)$ be the price of Y denominated in ROW currency. For simplicity, the exchange rate between the currencies of H and ROW is set to be one. The profit function for a representative firm i in country H can thus be written as

$$\pi = \gamma P(Q)x + P_y(Y)y - C_x(x,y) - C_y(x,y),$$

where subscript i is omitted for notational simplicity.

The profit function for a representative firm in country F can be written as

$$\pi^* = P(Q)z - C_z(z)$$

where C_z is the cost function denominated in F-currency.

Assume that each firm in making its production and sale decisions will take the reaction of other firms into account. Let $\rho_x(\equiv \partial Q / \partial x)$[3] indicate the variation of Q perceived by a representative firm in country H when its exports of x change. Let $\rho_y(\equiv \partial Y / \partial y)$ indicate the conjectural variation of Y perceived by a representative firm when y changes. Similarly, $\rho_z(\equiv \partial Q / \partial z)$ denotes the conjectural variations of Q perceived by a representative firm in country F when its sales of z change.

The optimal choices of x, y, and z for a representative firm in countries H and F must satisfy the following first-order conditions:

$$\gamma P + \gamma x \rho_x P' - C_x' - \alpha = 0, \tag{1}$$

$$P_y + y \rho_y P_y' - C_y' - \beta = 0, \tag{2}$$

$$P + z \rho_z P' - C_z' = 0, \tag{3}$$

where $C_x'(\equiv \partial C_x / \partial x)$, $C_y'(\equiv \partial C_y / \partial y)$, and $C_z'(\equiv \partial C_z / \partial z)$ indicate the marginal cost of X, Y, and Z, respectively; $P'(\equiv \partial P / \partial Q < 0)$ and $P_y'(\equiv \partial P_y / \partial Y < 0)$ are the slope of the demand curves for goods X (or Z) and good Y, respectively; $\alpha \equiv \partial C_y / \partial x$ and $\beta \equiv \partial C_x / \partial y$. A positive α (or β) indicates cost-enhancing externality, while negative α (or β) indicates cost-saving externality.

Equation (1) says that for a representative firm the marginal revenue from exports of x must be equal to the true marginal cost, i.e., the sum of marginal cost C_x and cost externality α. A similar condition holds for good y (eq.[2]).

We assume that firms in the same country are identical. Thus, $X = Mx$, $Y = My$, and $Z = Nz$. We aggregate equation (1) over M firms and divide it by γ to obtain the necessary condition for optimal X:

$$MP + \rho_x XP' = \frac{M(C_x' + \alpha)}{\gamma}, \tag{4}$$

3. $\rho_x \equiv \partial Q / \partial x = \partial X / \partial x + \partial Z / \partial x$.

Similarly, we aggregate equations (2) and (3) over M and N firms, respectively:

$$MP_y + \rho_y YP_y' = M(C_y' + \beta), \tag{5}$$

$$NP + \rho_z ZP' = NC_z'. \tag{6}$$

For simplicity, assume that $\rho_x = \rho_z = \rho$. We then add equations (4) and (6) to derive equation (7):

$$(M + N)\,P + \rho QP' = \frac{M(C_x' + \alpha)}{\gamma} + NC_z'. \tag{7}$$

Equations (5) and (7) are necessary conditions for optimal Y and Q and can be solved simultaneously to derive the reduced-form equations for Y and Q as functions of all exogenous variables, i.e., exchange rate γ, market structures ρ, and demand elasticities.

To examine the effects of a change in exchange rate on total sales when holding other exogenous variables constant, we totally differentiate equations (5) and (7) with respect to Q, Y, and γ to derive the comparative static results:

$$\frac{dQ}{d\gamma} = -\frac{M(C_x' + \alpha)V_y}{\gamma^2 \Delta}, \tag{8}$$

$$\frac{dY}{d\gamma} = \frac{M^2(C_x' + \alpha)}{\gamma^2 \Delta}\frac{\partial \beta}{\partial Q}, \tag{9}$$

in which

$$\Delta \equiv VV_y - \frac{M^2 \partial\alpha\,\partial\beta}{\gamma\,\partial Y \partial Q},$$

$$V \equiv (M + N + \rho)P' = -\frac{(M + N + \rho)P}{\eta Q},$$

$$V_y \equiv (M + \rho_y)P_y' = -\frac{(M + \rho_y)\,P_y}{\eta_y Y}.$$

The stability conditions are $V < 0$, $V_y < 0$, and $\Delta > 0$. The notation $\eta(\equiv -\partial Q/\partial P\ P/Q)$ indicates the elasticity of the demand curve for goods X and Z, and $\eta_y(\equiv -\partial Y/\partial P_y\ P_y/Y)$ for good Y.

It is apparent from equations (8) and (9) that cost externality plays a rather important role in determining the effects of exchange rate on exports of X and Y. When $C_x' + \alpha$ is positive, appreciation of F-currency will increase exports of X, and also exports of Y if $\partial\beta/\partial Q > 0$.

The exchange rate pass-through ratio ε, which is defined to be the negative of the percentage change in export price with respect to a percentage change in exchange rate,[4] can be derived by using the comparative result from equation (8):

4. Usually, $(\gamma/P_x)(\partial P_x/\partial\gamma)$ is negative, because firms tend to lower the export price of X denominated in F-currency when F-currency appreciates.

(10) $$\varepsilon \equiv -\frac{\gamma}{P}\frac{dP}{d\gamma} = -\frac{\gamma}{P}P'\frac{dQ}{d\gamma} = -\frac{M(C'_x + \alpha)V_y}{\gamma\eta Q\Delta}.$$

Thus, the larger ε, the larger a decrease (increase) in export price when F-currency appreciates (depreciates).

Equation (10) implies that the sign of the pass-through ratio will depend on the sign of $C'_x + \alpha$, since $\eta > 0$, $V_y < 0$, and $\Delta > 0$. When $C'_x + \alpha$ is positive, an appreciation of *F*-currency first lowers the true marginal cost of *X* (see eq. [4]) and thus increases the exports of *X* and lowers *P.* This in turn lowers the production of *Z.* As a result, total supply of *X* and *Z* increases (see eq. [8]) and *P* decreases. The pass-through ratio ε is therefore positive. This is the case when cost-enhancing externality (i.e., positive α) exists or cost-saving externality (i.e., negative α) is small. On the other hand, if cost-saving externality is sufficiently large that $C'_x + \alpha$ is negative, an appreciation of F-currency will shift the true marginal cost curve of *X* to the left (see [4]). The export price will therefore increase and negative pass-through will occur. Note that equation (10) implies that positive (negative) $C'_x + \alpha$ is a necessary and sufficient condition for positive (negative) ε.

Moreover, the magnitude of the pass-through ratio depends on the following variables: the magnitude of cost externality α, the conjectural variation indices ρ and ρ_y, the cost share $C'_x/\gamma P$, the elasticities of the demand curves η and η_y, and the number of firms in country *H* relative to that in country *F,* i.e., *M*/*N*.

Let us first look at the effects of α on pass-through ratio:

(11) $$\frac{\partial\varepsilon}{\partial\alpha} > 0.$$

That is, the larger α, the larger the degree of pass-through. The reason for this positive relationship is as follows. A larger α implies larger cost-enhancing externality. The true marginal cost of producing *X* will increase once this externality is taken into consideration. Firms will therefore increase the degree of pass-through as their profit margins decrease.

Equation (11) can be rewritten as (11a) and (11b) by using the definitions of economies and diseconomies of scope and the twice-differentiable property of the cost function:[5]

(11a) $$\frac{\partial\varepsilon}{\partial y} < 0, \text{ if economies of scope exist,}$$

(llb) $$\frac{\partial\varepsilon}{\partial y} > 0, \text{ if diseconomies of scope exist.}$$

5. Economies of scope in the production of *i* and *j* exist if $d(dC_i/di) / dj < 0$ ($i, j = x$ or y, and $i \neq j$). Therefore, an increase in the production of *j* will lower the marginal cost of good *i* and thus increase the production of good *i.* On the other hand, when $d(dC_i/di) / dj > 0$ ($i \neq j$), there are diseconomies of scope. Assume that cost functions are well defined so that $\partial(\partial C_y/\partial x) / \partial y = \partial(\partial C_y/\partial x) / \partial y$. Therefore, α will vary inversely with *Y* if there exist economies of scope because $\partial(\partial C_y/\partial y) / \partial x = \partial\alpha / \partial y < 0$. However, $\partial\alpha / \partial y > 0$ if there are diseconomies of scope. For the definition of economies of scope, see Bulow, Geanakoplos, and Klemperer (1985).

The conjectural variation index, ρ, reflects behavior patterns among competing firms and can thus be used as a measure of market structure for X (or Z). The more collusive the market of X and Z is, the larger ρ will be. From equation (10), we obtain the partial effects of market structure of X (or Z) on ε:

$$(12) \qquad \frac{\partial \varepsilon}{\partial \rho} = -\frac{M(C'_x + \alpha)PV_y^2}{\eta^2 \gamma Q^2 \Delta^2} \begin{cases} < 0, \text{ if } C'_x + \alpha > 0, \\ > 0, \text{ if } C'_x + \alpha < 0, \end{cases} \text{ and}$$

Thus, if cost-saving externality is not too large ($C'_x + \alpha > 0$), the result obtained in Dombusch (1987) will hold. That is, collusive firms will pass through less of the changes in exchange rate to export prices (denominated in foreign currency) than will competitive firms. However, if $C'_x + \alpha < 0$, collusive firms will have a larger pass-through ratio than competitive firms.

Differentiating equation (10) with respect to cost share[6] ($C'_x/\gamma P$) and ε, holding other variables constant, we obtain

$$(13) \qquad \frac{\partial \varepsilon}{\partial (C'_x/\gamma P)} = -\frac{MPV_y}{\eta Q \Delta} > 0.$$

Equation (13) thus implies that the larger the own-cost share relative to its export price, the larger the degree of pass-through.

In addition to γ, ρ, and $C'_x/\gamma P$, the pass-through ratio also depends on demand elasticities (η and η_y) and the number of home firms relative to the number of foreign firms (M/N):

$$(14) \qquad \frac{\partial \varepsilon}{\partial \eta} = \frac{MV_yQ\gamma(C'_x + \alpha)(\Delta - VV_y)}{\gamma^2 \eta^2 Q^2 \Delta^2} \begin{cases} > 0, \text{ if } C'_x + \alpha > 0, \\ < 0, \text{ if } C'_x + \alpha < 0, \end{cases}$$

$$(15) \qquad \frac{\partial \varepsilon}{\partial \eta_y} = \frac{M\eta V_yQ\gamma(C'_x + \alpha)(\Delta - VV_y)}{\eta_y \gamma^2 \eta^2 Q^2 \Delta} \begin{cases} > 0, \text{ if } C'_x + \alpha > 0, \\ < 0, \text{ if } C'_x + \alpha < 0, \end{cases} \text{ and}$$

$$(16) \qquad \frac{\partial \varepsilon}{\partial (M/N)} = \frac{(C'_x + \alpha)PV_y^2N^2}{\gamma \eta^2 Q^2 \Delta^2} \begin{cases} < 0, \text{ if } C'_x + \alpha < 0, \\ > 0, \text{ if } C'_x + \alpha > 0, \end{cases} \text{ and}$$

where $V_y < 0$ and $(\Delta - VV_y) < 0$.[7]

Equations (14), (15), and (16) show that the sign of $C'_x + \alpha$ also plays an important role in determining the effects of η, η_y, and M/N on pass-through ratios. When $C'_x + \alpha > 0$, the effect of η, η_y, or M/N on ε is positive. That is when the demand for Q or Y becomes more elastic or the number of home

6. In the absence of cost externality, own-cost share ($C'_x / \gamma P$) and the behavior pattern among competing firms, ρ, have the same economic implications. However, the existence of cost externality makes these two variables different from each other (see eq. [1]).

7. The assumption of identical firms implies that $\partial X = M\partial x$ and $\partial Y = M\partial y$. This assumption together with $\partial(\partial C_y/\partial y) / \partial x = \partial(\partial C_y/\partial x) / \partial x$ ensure that $(\Delta - VV_y) = -M^2 / \gamma\ \partial\alpha / \partial Y\ \partial\beta / \partial Q < 0$, where $\partial\alpha / \partial Y\ \partial\beta / \partial Q = \partial\alpha / M\partial y\ \partial X / \partial Q\ \partial\beta / M\partial x > 0$.

firms relative to that of foreign firms increases, home firms will respond to an appreciation of F-currency primarily by lowering their prices and increasing their exports.[8]

When η or η_y is sufficiently large and $C'_x + \alpha > 0$, it is likely that the pass-through ratio will exceed one. That is, over pass-through will occur. In such a case, firms will raise export prices more than the extent of the appreciation of F-currency.

10.3 The Empirical Specification

This section presents an empirical framework which will be used to test the theoretical results of equations (11)–(15) in section 10.2, i.e., to test whether cost externality, market structure, cost share, and elasticities of demand curves have significant effects on the pass-through ratio, when other variables are kept constant.[9]

We assume that there are I products exported to J countries. For each product i ($i = 1, 2, \ldots, I$), its exports to different countries are treated as differentiated goods. In order to study the statistical significance of the determinants of pass-through ratios, data consisting of the pass-through ratios ε_i^j for product i ($i = 1, \ldots, I$) exported to country j ($j = 1, \ldots, J$) must first be derived from price equations. The price equation P_i^j, derived in its reduced form in section 10.2, is a function of all exogenous variables, i.e., exchange rate γ^j, market structure ρ_i, and demand elasticities of good i to market j (η_i^j) and to other markets (η_i^y). Since demand elasticities (η_i^j and η_i^y) and market structure (ρ_i) are assumed to be rather stable over the sample period studied here, each reduced-form price equation will thus be a function of exchange rate only. However, in order to capture the effects of inflation and quality changes on the export price over time, we also include the wholesale price index (WP) of that product as a proxy in each price equation (17):

$$\ln P_{it}^j = F(\ln \gamma_t^j, \ln WP_{it}), \tag{17}$$

where subscript t denotes time, P_{it}^j is denominated in j-currency, and γ_t^j is nominal exchange rate expressed as NT dollars per unit of j-currency.[10] A polynomial distributed lag model will be used to run equation (17), as the effects of exchange rates on export prices often exhibit an inverted-V shape (see, e.g., Hooper and Mann 1989; Moffett 1989; Khosla and Teranishi 1989). We will

8. This result is consistent with that from Dornbusch (1987, 97).

9. We will not consider the effect of the number of firms in country H relative to the number in country F on the degree of pass-through because of lack of data and the heterogeneity of firms in reality. In fact, part of the effect of the number of firms is already reflected in the market structure variable.

10. Alternatively, we can use nominal exchange rates adjusted for changes in the price level in the destination market (see e.g., Knetter 1989) to run equation (20). But the result of such an analysis is that more than half (107 out of 186) of the pass-through ratios are negative, which seems unreasonable. We therefore do not report the results here.

use the negative of the sum of the current and lagged coefficients of exchange rates as a proxy for the degree of exchange rate pass-through ε_i^j.

In addition to the derivation of pass-through ratios, the types of cost externality and the demand elasticities have to be identified and derived before proceeding to test the statistical significance of the determinants of pass-through equation (10).

For cost externality, as implied by equations (11a) and (11b), a continuous variable, such as exports to other markets (Y), cannot be used alone to capture cost externality for both cases with economies of scope and those with diseconomies of scope. However, by the definition of scope economies, marginal cost will be a function of exports to other markets. The following cost equation will thus be run over time and across destinations to identify the type of scope economies for each product *i:*

$$(18) \qquad C_{it}^j = G(Y_{it}^j),$$

where C_{it}^j is the marginal cost of good *i* exported to destination *j*[11] and Y_i^j is the total sales of good *i* exported to destinations other than *j*. Therefore, product *i* will have economies of scope if the estimator of the coefficient of Y_i^j is negative, and diseconomies of scope if it is positive. By defining the dummy variable *DY* to be one if economies of scope exist (i.e., if Y_i^j has a negative coefficient) and zero if diseconomies of scope exist (i.e., if Y_i^j has a positive coefficient), we can distinguish two types of cost externalities by including both Y_i^j and the interaction term of Y_i^j with *DY* in the pass-through equation.

As to the derivation of demand elasticities, we will run the following export demand equation in log-linear form:

$$(19) \qquad \ln Q_{it}^j = H(\ln P_{it}^j, \ln I_t^j, \ln AP_{it}^j),$$

where Q is export volume, I^j is importing country *j*'s national income, and AP_i^j is the price of other goods in country *j*. The estimator of the coefficient of $\ln P_i^j$ will be used as demand elasticity η_i^j. The weighted average demand elasticities in all markets other than *j* will be used as the demand elasticity of differentiated goods (i.e., η_i^y).

Moreover as discussed in the previous section, the partial effects of market structure and demand elasticities depend crucially on the sign of $C_x' + \alpha$ (see eqq. [12], [14], and [15]). And from equation (10), positive (or negative) $C_x' + \alpha$ is a necessary and sufficient condition for positive (or negative) ε. Thus, the sign of $C_x' + \alpha$ can be derived from the sign of ε. Define the dummy variable *DS* to be one if ε is positive and zero if ε is negative. Including the interaction of *DS* with market structure and demand elasticities in the pass-through equation will then indicate the additional effects of these variables for the case of positive $C_x' + \alpha$ relative to the case of negative $C_x' + \alpha$.

11. Here, we assume constant marginal cost with respect to its own sales, i.e., $\partial C_i^j/\partial X_i^j = 0$.

After obtaining all the data needed, we run the following pass-through equation to test the statistical significance of the determinants of the degree of pass-through:[12]

$$(20)\ \varepsilon_i^j = \alpha_o + \alpha_1 SY_i^j + \alpha_2\,(SY_i^j * DY) + \alpha_3 DS + \alpha_4 CR_i + \alpha_5(CR_i * DS) + \alpha_6 SC_i + \alpha_7\,\eta_i^j + \alpha_8\,(\eta_i^j * DS) + \alpha_9\eta_i^y + \alpha_{10}(\eta_i^y * DS) + u_i^j.$$

Since equation (20) is run cross-sectionally, we use the export share of good i to markets other than j (i.e., SY_i^j), rather than the export level Y_i^j, because the SY_i^j are comparable across products and destinations. The variable DY is the dummy used to distinguish the type of cost externality, while DS is the dummy used to separate the case of positive ε (or positive $C_x' + \alpha$) from that of negative ε (or negative $C_x' + \alpha$). The variable CR_i indicates the market structure for good i; SC_i indicates the cost share ($C_x'/\gamma P$) for good i; η_i^j and η_i^y indicate the demand elasticities of good i exported to destination j and to destinations other than j, respectively.

The expected signs of coefficients in equation (20) are as follows: a_1 and $a_1 + a_2$ measure the impact of cost externality on the degree of pass-through when there are diseconomies and economies of scope, respectively. By equations (11a) and (11b), we expect a_1 to be positive and $a_1 + a_2$ (if both are statistically significant) to be negative. This implies a negative a_2. From equation (10), a_3 is expected to be positive. Since the direct effect of market structure on pass-through ratios is positive for the case of negative $C_x' + \alpha$ (see eq. [12]), a_4 is expected to be positive. However, the effect will be negative for the case of positive $C_x' + \alpha$, and $a_4 + a_5$ is expected to be negative. Thus, a negative a_5 is expected. Similarly, by (13), a_6, which is the partial effect of cost share on the degree of pass-through, is expected to be positive. For the case of negative $C_x' + \alpha$, demand elasticities to destination j and to the rest of the markets, i.e., η_i^j and η_i^y, have negative impacts on pass-through ratios, thus a_7 and a_9 are expected to be negative (see eqs. [14] and [15]). On the other hand, a_7, a_8, and $a_9 + a_{10}$ are expected to be positive for the case of positive $C_x' + \alpha$.

10.3.1 The Data

Monthly exchange rates for different destinations for the period 1981–88 were obtained from the *Financial Statistics Monthly,* published by the Economic Research Department, Central Bank of Taiwan. Cross-sectional and time-series data on export value and quantity by product category and country of destination are available from the *Monthly Statistics of Exports and Imports of the Republic of China,* published by the Department of Statistics, Ministry of Finance. Export unit value, which equals the quotient of value and quantity,

12. We use structural equation (20) is because equation (10) is structural. For the justification of using this structural equation rather than the reduced-form equation, see the path analysis in Wonnacott and Wonnacott (1990, 417–25).

is used as the export price (P_i^j) in this paper. This may introduce measurement error, as product quality may change over time or across destinations. The measurement error from quality change over time can be reduced by including the wholesale price index in price equation (17). The measurement error from different qualities across destinations will not appear in this paper, as the pass-through ratios of each product are obtained for each country of destination.

Time-series data of wholesale price indices by product used in equation (17) are obtained from the *Commodity-Price Statistics Monthly, Taiwan Area,* published by the Directorate General of Budget, Accounting, and Statistics (DGBAS), Executive Yuan. The wholesale price indices used as a proxy for prices of other goods (*AP*) in equation (19) are drawn from *International Financial Statistics,* published by the International Monetary Fund. The same source is used for national income data.

Data for the cost variable in equation (18) for the period 1981–88 are derived from the *Reports on the Reexamination of Factories*, published by the Department of Statistics, Ministry of Economic Affairs. The cost variable here includes wages, material cost, electricity, and other expenditures. The cost share for equation (20), which is defined as the average cost per dollar of revenue, is calculated from the same source.

Concentration ratios for different products, which are defined as the total sales of the largest four (*CR*4) or eight firms (*CR*8) over industrial sales, are used as proxies for market structure ρ. These ratios are calculated from the *Industrial and Commercial Survey* for 1986, published by DGBAS, Executive Yuan. These ratios are classified by a 4-digit code that is different from the one used for trade data. Thus, the trade data are aggregated to concord with the classification of concentration ratios.

Twenty-one products exported to nine countries are investigated in this paper. These products are listed in table 10.1. The nine countries studied are Australia, Canada, West Germany, Hong Kong, Japan, the Netherlands, Singapore, the United States, and the United Kingdom, the nine largest trading partners for Taiwan.

10.4 The Empirical Results

Monthly data for 1981–88 are used to run equation (17), in which seasonal dummies are also included to capture seasonal fluctuations of prices. Following Kmenta's suggestion (1971, 492–95), we use the highest value of adjusted R^2 as the criteria to choose the length of lags and the degree of the polynomial. The length of lags and degree of polynomial chosen therefore vary across products and destinations. They range from 12 to 36 months for the length of lags, and from two to three for the degree of polynomial. The exchange rate pass-through ratios derived here are thus long-run pass-through ratios.

The total number of pass-through ratios obtained from equation (17) is 186, which is less than the theoretical maximum 189 (ie., 21×9) because data is

Table 10.1 Description of Product Categories

Product Item	Description
2022	Canned foods
2023	Frozen foods
2113	Soft drinks and carbonated water
2201	Cotton textiles
2204	Regenerated and synthetic fiber textiles
2205	Knitting apparel mills
2301	Wearing apparel
2409	Other leather products
2512	Plywood
2706	Synthetic resin and plastic materials
3001	Tires
3409	Other fabricated metal products
3541	Textile and garment-producing machinery
3613	Wires and cables
3619	Electronic products
3623	Electronic parts and components
3711	Ship building and repairing
3751	Bicycles and parts
3804	Watches and clocks
3905	Toys

Source: Industrial and Commercial Survey (Taipei: DGBAS, various issues).
Note: Product 2201 is divided into two parts, 2201A and 2201B, for different measuring units (kilometers and metric tons, respectively).

insufficient to run regression equation (17) in three cases.[13] Table 10.2 reports exchange rate pass-through ratios for Taiwanese exports by product and country. Three types of exchange rate pass-through—over, incomplete, and negative—are observed. Over, incomplete, and negative pass-through occur when the negative of the sum of the current and lagged estimators of exchange rates, respectively, exceeds one, is between zero and one, and is negative. Table 10.2 shows that more than half of the products (13 out of 21) have incomplete average pass-through, and 6 out of 21 products have over pass-through. Products 2113 and 3623 have negative pass-through, which implies that these two products have strong cost-saving externality. The average degree of pass-through also varies across countries of destination. For instance, pass-through is incomplete for Canada, West Germany, Hong Kong, Japan, and the United States, the five largest export markets for Taiwan. For other countries, the degree of pass-through exceeds one by a small margin. It seems that Taiwanese exporters tend to pass through to their export prices less than the full changes in exchange rate in order to maintain their competitiveness, especially in Canada, West Ger-

13. These three cases are product 2023 for Singapore, 2113 for West Germany, and 2201 for the Netherlands.

Table 10.2 Exchange Rate Pass-Through Ratios by Product and Country[a]

Product	Australia	Canada	West Germany	Hong Kong	Japan	Netherlands	Singapore	United States	United Kingdom	Average
2022	0.214	2.424	0.867	0.464	−1.82	0.941	1.965	0.265	−0.67	0.515
2023	1.495	−0.21	1.023	0.960	0.347	1.404	—	0.932	1.279	0.903
2113	0.735	0.150	—	0.429	2.698	−2.15	−0.44	−0.14	−3.19	−0.24
2201A	0.859	0.479	1.670	1.090	0.194	—	0.178	0.89	0.880	0.780
2201B	0.342	0.447	0.418	0.717	0.964	−0.35	1.171	1.372	−0.91	0.462
2204	0.022	−0.55	−3.64	−1.27	1.396	3.639	0.577	0.249	4.416	0.536
2205	0.700	0.057	0.529	0.656	1.544	0.510	2.861	−1.14	0.283	0.666
2301	0.737	0.985	0.350	−0.47	1.408	0.854	4.248	0.640	1.809	1.173
2409	1.052	−0.74	1.454	1.414	−0.63	1.305	0.777	−0.38	2.62	0.762
2512	1.212	1.563	−2.23	1.737	1.696	0.656	0.694	0.352	1.443	0.791
2706	0.831	−0.65	1.730	1.147	0.322	1.228	1.337	0.670	0.418	0.781
3001	1.433	1.070	0.266	1.123	0.912	0.536	2.245	1.161	0.721	1.052
3409	1.210	1.330	1.750	1.654	1.186	1.142	2.163	1.955	1.841	1.581
3541	1.375	1.797	0.815	6.264	1.110	1.853	0.072	−0.34	1.195	1.571
3613	1.266	1.608	0.752	1.021	−0.65	0.261	3.696	1.339	1.960	1.250
3619	5.314	2.050	4.415	−2.15	3.943	4.780	−2.97	2.378	6.407	2.684
3623	3.325	−6.62	−0.11	−2.61	0.790	2.997	−8.17	−0.86	3.345	−1.06
3711	0.730	−2.35	1.268	0.081	1.431	−0.07	5.697	−2.66	0.026	0.460
3751	1.150	0.466	0.018	0.383	0.208	1.162	1.591	2.591	0.228	0.866
3804	−1.09	2.603	−3.76	−1.77	3.138	0.928	5.036	0.953	−2.26	0.417
3905	1.349	−0.21	1.100	1.197	0.757	1.657	1.964	−0.40	1.559	0.996
Average	1.155	0.270	0.433	0.573	0.997	1.163	1.234	0.467	1.113	

[a]Exchange rate pass-through ratios are derived from equation (17).

many, the United States, and Hong Kong. Thus, incomplete pass-through may be one of the factors that cause sluggish adjustment in the trade balance, especially between the United States and Taiwan.

Table 10.3 reports the types of cost externality for each product, obtained from equation (18). Six out of 21 products—2022, 2201A, 2201B, 3619, 3711, and 3804—have diseconomies of scope, while the rest have economies of scope (see table 10.1 for product descriptions). Table 10.4 reports the price elasticities of demand curves (η_i^j) from equation (19).

The empirical results for equation (20) are summarized in table 10.5. In order to test whether pass-through ratios vary across destinations, country dummies are also added, and the United States is used as the base for country dummies. All variables reported in table 10.5 show the signs predicted by the theoretical model in the previous section. In terms of statistical significance, the coefficients of cost externality for the case of economies of scope ($SY * DY$), the dummy variable DS, demand elasticities for the case of positive pass-through ($\eta * DS$), and demand elasticities for other markets (η^y and $\eta^y * DS$) are significantly different from zero at the 5 or 10 percent level. The coefficients for market structure, though correct in sign, are not statistically significant at the 10 percent level for all cases in table 10.5 except case (1) where $CR4$ is used. The above results imply that cost externality does not have significant impact on the degree of pass-through for products with diseconomies of scope, while significant negative impact exists for products with economies of scope. Moreover, the results also imply that for the case of positive pass-through, demand elasticities ($\eta * DS$ and $\eta^y * DS$) play a rather important role in determining the degree of exchange rate pass-through for Taiwanese exports, while for the case of negative pass-through, only demand elasticities for other

Table 10.3 **Types of Cost Externality**[a]

Economies of Scope	Diseconomies of Scope
2023	2022
2113	2201A
2204	2201B
2205	3619
2301	3711
2409	3804
2512	
2706	
3001	
3409	
3541	
3613	
3623	
3751	
3905	

[a]Derived from equation (18).

Table 10.4 Price Elasticities of Demand Curves by Product and Country[a]

Product	Australia	Canada	West Germany	Hong Kong	Japan	Netherlands	Singapore	United States	United Kingdom
2022	−1.43	0.4	−1.00	1.18	1.32	−0.58	0.07	0.26	1.01
2023	0.52	−1.1	0.28	0.07	0.02	−0.93	—	0.52	0.21
2113	0.94	0.31	—	0.63	−0.12	−2.12	0.52	0.94	0.65
2201A	0.67	1.89	−1.21	1.15	0.46	—	−0.43	−1.66	−0.08
2201B	0.76	2.17	0.95	−0.03	0.59	0.14	0.37	1.12	0.77
2204	1.00	0.97	1.04	0.92	1.32	0.99	1.08	1.01	1.02
2205	2.21	0.41	0.44	0.55	0.1	1.24	1.34	1.3	0.44
2301	0.35	0.94	1.26	0.45	0.59	0.37	1.42	0.28	0.64
2409	0.6	0.46	0.84	1.00	0.9	0.38	0.35	0.51	1.12
2512	0.35	0.57	0	−0.29	0.03	0.72	1.17	0.51	−0.05
2706	0.73	−0.1	0.04	0.1	0.53	0.34	1.31	0.12	1.8
3001	−0.49	1.4	0.86	2.32	0.75	0.85	1.63	1.05	−0.06
3409	0.14	1.32	0.62	1.32	1.2	1.96	0.56	−0.01	1.26
3541	0.68	1.5	1.29	1.38	1.17	0.9	0.77	−0.99	−0.06
3613	0.08	0.57	0.7	−0.07	1.18	0.71	0.07	−0.09	1.22
3619	0.63	0.69	0.64	0.97	0.98	0.68	0.96	0.85	0.48
3623	1.26	1.08	0.86	0.74	1.04	0.93	0.37	0.72	0.92
3711	1.33	1.92	1.69	0.41	0.85	0.38	0.62	1.05	1.35
3751	0.02	0.35	−0.08	0.43	0.14	0.91	1.05	0.72	0.71
3804	0.04	0.06	0.02	−0.13	0.14	−0.23	0.66	1.17	1.03
3905	0.86	−0.03	0.42	0.35	0.5	0.45	0.5	−0.14	0.15

[a]Price elasticities are derived from equation (19).

markets (η^y) play an important role. However, market structure is not the main determinant of exchange rate pass-through. Table 10.5 also shows insignificant coefficients for all country dummies, which implies that the degree of pass-through for the other eight markets is not significantly different from that for the U.S. market. This result in turn implies that differences in pass-through ratios across countries stem mainly from different levels of cost externality (SY) and demand elasticities (η and η^y).

One may note that the effects of market structure on the degree of pass-through derived from equation (20) do not include indirect effects through other endogenous variables, e.g., cost externality and cost share. Thus, the insignificant direct effects of market structure from equation (20) may not imply insignificant total effects (the sum of direct effects and indirect effects). In order to find the total effects, we run the pass-through equation in its reduced form. The results are reported in table 10.6, which shows the same conclusions as table 10.5. That is, market structure does not have significant impact on the degree of pass-through even when total effects are considered. One reason for this result is that Taiwanese exporters face stiff competition in international markets and therefore cannot exert monopoly power in setting export prices even when the industrial concentration ratio is high.

So far, we have used long-run pass-through ratios. But what happens if

Table 10.5 **Determinants of Long-run Exchange Rate Pass-Through (from structural form of equation [20])**

	Estimated Coefficient (t-ratio)			
Variable	(1)	(2)	(3)	(4)
Constant	−2.99 (−0.93)	−2.99 (−0.97)	−2.81 (−0.85)	−2.76 (−0.88)
SY	0.78 (1.15)	0.77 (1.13)	0.82 (0.82)	0.82 (0.82)
*SY**DY*	−0.55 (−2.12)	−0.55 (−2.15)	−0.54 (−2.07)	−0.55 (−2.11)
DS	2.49 (4.20)	2.54 (3.77)	2.41 (3.97)	2.42 (3.50)
*CR*4	0.01 (0.56)		0.01 (0.41)	
*CR*8		0.004 (0.36)		0.002 (0.17)
*CR*4**DS*	−0.02 (−1.30)		−0.02 (−1.13)	
*CR*8**DS*		−0.01 (−1.17)		−0.01 (−0.95)
SC	1.81 (0.57)	1.86 (0.62)	1.71 (0.53)	1.76 (0.58)
η	−0.25 (−0.84)	−0.24 (−0.81)	−0.23 (−0.76)	−0.23 (−0.74)
η**DS*	0.48 (1.39)	0.46 (1.34)	0.45 (1.27)	0.44 (1.23)
η_y	−2.45 (−3.09)	−2.45 (−3.08)	−2.51 (−3.06)	−2.52 (−3.06)
η_y**DS*	2.62 (3.12)	2.60 (3.10)	2.70 (3.08)	2.69 (3.07)
Australia			−0.19 (−0.33)	−0.20 (−0.34)
Canada			−0.28 (−0.48)	−0.27 (−0.47)
West Germany			−0.33 (−0.59)	−0.35 (−0.62)
Hong Kong			−0.03 (−0.06)	−0.05 (−0.09)
Japan			−0.19 (−0.36)	−0.20 (−0.37)
Netherlands			0.14 (0.24)	0.14 (0.25)
Singapore			0.22 (0.38)	0.21 (0.37)
United Kingdom			0.17 (0.30)	0.16 (0.27)
R^2	0.5100	0.5115	0.5206	0.5220
Adjusted R^2	0.4820	0.4836	0.4689	0.4705
df	175	175	167	167

short-run pass-through ratios are used? Will they be affected significantly by the same factors as the long-run pass-through ratios? To study this, we derive short-run exchange rate pass-through ratios from equation (17) using lag length 12 and polynomial 3. The results from the pass-through equation are summarized in tables 10.7 and 10.8 for both the structural and reduced-form equations. Table 10.7 shows that cost externality and demand elasticities η are not the main determinants of short-run pass-through. And only the dummy variable *DS* and demand elasticities for other differentiated products ($\eta * DS$ and/or η^y) have significant impact on both the structural and reduced-form equations.

10.5 Concluding Remarks

This paper focuses on the effects of cost externality on the degree of exchange rate pass-through from both theoretical and empirical perspectives. In the theoretical model, we show that the degree of pass-through depends crucially on the extent of cost externality. The larger the cost-enhancing exter-

Table 10.6 Determinants of Long-run Exchange Rate Pass-Through (from reduced form of equation [20])

	Estimated Coefficient (*t*-ratio)			
Variable	(1)	(2)	(3)	(4)
Constant	−0.91 (−1.72)	−0.88 (−1.45)	−0.88 (−1.49)	−0.80 (−1.22)
DS	2.50 (4.25)	2.56 (3.84)	2.40 (3.98)	2.42 (3.53)
*CR*4	0.004 (0.33)		0.003 (0.19)	
*CR*8		0.002 (0.20)		0.0001 (0.01)
*CR*4**DS*	−0.02 (−1.27)		−0.02 (−1.11)	
*CR*8**DS*		−0.01 (−1.17)		−0.01 (−0.94)
η	−0.22 (−0.75)	−0.22 (−0.73)	−0.20 (−0.67)	−0.20 (−0.67)
η**DS*	0.38 (1.12)	0.36 (1.07)	0.35 (0.99)	0.33 (0.95)
η_y	−2.22 (−3.05)	−2.22 (−3.04)	−2.33 (−3.01)	−2.34 (−3.01)
η_y**DS*	2.66 (3.22)	2.63 (3.18)	2.76 (3.19)	2.74 (3.16)
Australia			−0.05 (−0.12)	−0.06 (−0.13)
Canada			−0.12 (−0.29)	−0.11 (−0.26)
West Germany			−0.21 (−0.49)	−0.23 (−0.52)
Hong Kong			−0.09 (0.20)	0.08 (0.18)
Japan			−0.08 (−0.18)	−0.08 (−0.18)
Netherlands			0.27 (0.61)	0.27 (0.62)
Singapore			0.37 (0.86)	0.37 (0.85)
United Kingdom			0.31 (0.74)	0.30 (0.71)
R^2	0.4967	0.4977	0.5079	0.5088
Adjusted R^2	0.4769	0.4780	0.4645	0.4654
df	178	178	170	170

nality, the larger the degree of pass-through. However, when the cost-saving externality is sufficiently large, degree of pass-through may turn out to be negative. Moreover, the partial effects of market structure, elasticities of demand curves, and number of firms on the degree of pass-through will also depend on the extent of cost externality.

By using Taiwan's exports as a case study, we derived, in addition to the usual expected incomplete pass-through, over and negative pass-through from both the theoretical model (section 10.2) and the empirical study (section 10.4). We then tested the statistical significance of the determinants of exchange rate pass-through and found that the theoretical conclusions are supported by the empirical results. To be more specific, we obtained the expected signs for all the variables studied and showed that cost externality, in addition to demand elasticities, has significant impact on the degree of long-run pass-through. However, the determinants of short-run pass-through are somewhat different. That is, demand elasticities for differentiated goods are the main variables which significantly affect short-run pass-through. For both short-run and long-run pass-through, market structure—one of the main focuses of the pass-through literature—was shown not to have significant impact on the degree of pass-through for Taiwanese exports.

Table 10.7 Determinants of Short-run Exchange Rate Pass-Through[a] (from structural form of equation [20])

	Estimated Coefficient (*t*-ratio)			
Variable	(1)	(2)	(3)	(4)
Constant	0.48 (0.10)	0.75 (0.17)	0.28 (0.06)	0.55 (0.13)
SY	0.16 (1.17)	0.15 (0.15)	0.07 (0.05)	0.05 (0.04)
*SY***DY*	0.20 (0.55)	0.23 (0.63)	0.17 (0.47)	0.21 (0.56)
DS	2.36 (3.09)	2.68 (3.03)	2.26 (2.94)	2.54 (2.85)
*CR*4	0.003 (0.27)		0.003 (0.26)	
*CR*8		0.003 (0.32)		0.003 (0.32)
*CR*4**DS*	−0.002 (−0.08)		0.002 (0.10)	
*CR*8**DS*		−0.01 (−0.48)		−0.01 (−0.28)
SC	−2.43 (−0.52)	−2.75 (−0.62)	−2.19 (−0.47)	−2.51 (−0.57)
η	−0.13 (−0.43)	−0.13 (−0.44)	−0.06 (−0.21)	−0.07 (−0.23)
η**DS*	0.50 (1.16)	0.48 (1.11)	0.49 (1.13)	0.47 (1.09)
η_y	−0.80 (−1.16)	−0.79 (−1.15)	−0.87 (−1.26)	−0.86 (−1.25)
η_y**DS*	2.73 (2.63)	2.69 (2.62)	2.84 (2.68)	2.81 (2.67)
Australia			−0.38 (−0.46)	−0.38 (−0.46)
Canada			−0.83 (−1.00)	−0.81 (−0.98)
West Germany			0.79 (0.98)	0.79 (0.98)
Hong Kong			0.13 (0.18)	0.16 (0.21)
Japan			−0.28 (−0.37)	−0.26 (−0.34)
Netherlands			0.32 (0.39)	0.32 (0.40)
Singapore			0.46 (0.55)	0.47 (0.57)
United Kingdom			0.29 (0.34)	0.28 (0.34)
R^2	0.4732	0.4738	0.5056	0.5055
Adjusted R^2	0.4431	0.4437	0.4523	0.4523
df	175	175	167	167

[a]Derived from equation (17) with lag length 12 and polynomial degree 3.

Moreover, from the results of the empirical study it seems that products with incomplete average pass-through tend to be labor-intensive goods, while those with over pass-through tend to be capital-intensive.[14] Thus, factor intensity may also be one possible determinant of exchange rate pass-through and deserves further study.

One final point which might be worth mentioning is that, in addition to the determinants of the degree of pass-through discussed above, other factors not included in this study can also explain the low degree of pass-through for some

14. According to the *Report on the Characteristic Classifications of Tradeable Commodities*, published by the Department of Statistics, Ministry of Finance, the following products have high labor intensity or low capital intensity: canned food (2022), frozen foods (2023), other leather products (2409), synthetic resin and plastic materials (2706), electric parts and components (3623), bicycles and parts (3751), watches and clocks (3804), and toys (3905). While tires (3001), other fabricated metal products (3409), textile and garment producing machinery (3541), and wires and cables (3613) have medium or low labor intensity but medium or high capital intensity.

Table 10.8 **Determinants of Short-run Exchange Rate Pass-Through[a] (from reduced form of equation [20])**

	Estimated Coefficient (*t*-ratio)			
Variable	(1)	(2)	(3)	(4)
Constant	−1.63 (−4.06)	−1.66 (−3.86)	−1.75 (−3.24)	−1.79 (−3.17)
DS	2.30 (3.04)	2.59 (2.96)	2.21 (2.91)	2.46 (2.80)
*CR*4	0.01 (0.58)		0.01 (0.55)	
*CR*8		0.004 (0.57)		0.004 (0.55)
*CR*4**DS*	0.001 (−0.04)		0.003 (0.12)	
*CR*8**DS*		−0.01 (−0.41)		−0.004 (−0.23)
η	−0.10 (−0.31)	−0.08 (−0.29)	−0.03 (−0.10)	−0.02 (−0.08)
η**DS*	0.49 (1.16)	0.47 (1.10)	0.48 (1.13)	0.46 (1.07)
η_y	−0.78 (−1.20)	−0.77 (−1.18)	−0.90 (−1.33)	−0.88 (−1.31)
η_y**DS*	2.79 (2.78)	2.75 (2.75)	2.92 (2.87)	2.88 (2.83)
Australia			−0.30 (−0.50)	−0.30 (−0.50)
Canada			−0.75 (−1.26)	−0.74 (−1.23)
West Germany			0.88 (1.45)	0.88 (1.45)
Hong Kong			0.20 (0.33)	0.22 (0.37)
Japan			−0.22 (−0.37)	−0.20 (−0.34)
Netherlands			0.40 (0.68)	0.41 (0.69)
Singapore			0.53 (0.88)	0.54 (0.90)
United Kingdom			0.36 (0.61)	0.36 (0.60)
R^2	0.4714	0.4712	0.5043	0.5038
Adjusted R^2	0.4506	0.4504	0.4606	0.4600
df	178	178	170	170

[a]Derived from equation (17) with lag length 12 and polynomial degree 3.

major Taiwanese export markets, e.g., the United States. One example, which is rather common in Taiwan, is the high proportion of imported materials used in the production of exports.[15] The other example is transfer pricing by Taiwanese subsidiaries of companies based in the United States and other countries, which may also account for the low degree of exchange rate pass-through. Including these factors in the study may produce a more complete analysis of the determinants of exchange rate pass-through for Taiwan's exports and thus deserves more studies.

References

Aizenman, Joshua. 1989. Market power and exchange rate adjustment in the presence of quotas. *Journal of International Economics* 27:265–82.

Baldwin, Richard. 1988a. Hysteresis in import prices: The beachhead effect. *American Economic Review* 78(4):773–85.

15. See, for example, the study of the Japanese case by Khosla and Teranishi (1989).

———. 1988b. Some empirical evidence on hysteresis in aggregate US import prices. NBER Working Paper no. 2483. Cambridge, Mass.: National Bureau of Economic Research.

Branson, William H. 1989. Exchange rate pass-through in the 1980s: The case of U.S. imports of manufacturers: Comments. *Brookings Papers on Economic Activity,* no. 1:330–33.

Bulow, Jeremy I., John D. Geanakoplos, and Paul D. Klemperer. 1985. Multimarket oligopoly: Strategic substitutes and complements. *Journal of Political Economy* 93(3):488–511.

Dixit, Avinash K. 1988. Anti-dumping and countervailing duties under oligopoly. *European Economic Review* 32:55–68.

———. Hysteresis, import penetration, and exchange rate pass-through. *Quarterly Journal of Economics* 104(2):205–28.

Dornbusch, Rudiger. 1987. Exchange rates and prices. *American Economic Review* 77(1): 93–106.

Feenstra, Robert C. 1987. Symmetric pass-through of tariffs and exchange rates under imperfect competition: An empirical test. NBER Working Paper no. 2453. Cambridge, Mass.: National Bureau of Economic Research.

Fisher, Eric. 1989a. Exchange rate pass-through and the relative concentration of German and Japanese manufacturing industries. *Economics Letters* 31(1):81–85.

———. 1989b. A model of exchange rate pass-through. *Journal of International Economics* 26:119–37.

Froot, Kenneth A., and Paul D. Klemperer. 1989. Exchange rate pass-through when market share matters. *American Economic Review* 79(4):637–54.

Hooper, Peter, and Catherine L. Mann. 1989. Exchange rate pass-through in the 1980s: The case of U.S. imports of manufacturers. *Brookings Papers on Economic Activity,* 297–329.

Jabara, Cathy L., and Nancy E. Schwartz. 1987. Flexible exchange rates and commodity price changes: The case of Japan. *American Journal of Agricultural Economics* 69(3):580–90.

Khosla, Anil, and Juro Teranishi. 1989. Exchange rate pass-through in export prices—An international comparison. *Hitotsubashi Journal of Economics* 3(1):31–48.

Kim, Yoonbai. 1990. Varying parameter estimation of exchange rate pass-through. *Journal of Business and Economic Statistics* 8(3):305–15.

Kmenta, Jan. 1971. *Elements of econometrics.* New York: Macmillan.

Knetter, Michael M. 1989. Price discrimination by U.S. and German exporters. *American Economic Review* 79(1):198–210.

Kravis, Irving B., and Robert E. Lipsey. 1978. Price behavior in the light of balance of payments theories. *Journal of International Economics* 8(2):193–246.

Krugman, Paul. 1987. Pricing to market when the exchange rate changes. In *Real-financial linkages among open economies,* ed. Sven W. Arndt and J. David Richardson. Cambridge: MIT Press.

Mann, Catherine L. 1986. Prices, profit margins, and exchange rates. *Federal Reserve Bulletin* 72:366–79.

Marston, Richard C. 1990. Price behavior in Japanese and U.S. manufacturing. *Journal of International Economics* 29: 217–36.

Moffett, Michael H. 1989. The J-curve revisited: An empirical examination for the United States. *Journal of International Money and Finance* 8(3):425–44.

Ohno, Kenichi. 1990. "Exchange rate fluctuations, pass-through, and market share. *International Monetary Fund Staff Papers* 37(2):294–310.

Wonnacott, Thomas H., and Ronald J. Wonnacott. 1990. *Introductory Statistics for Business and Economics.* New York: Wiley.

Comment Won-Am Park

This paper is interesting and stimulating, as the author calls attention to the effect of cost externality on the pass-through relationship. The paper comprises two parts, one modeling, the other empirical. I will comment on them one at a time.

I have no objections to the setup of the model. However, it is very important to note that the derived model is confined to static pass-through. In the literature, models of pass-through can be grouped into three categories. One contains *hysteresis models,* which explain a structural break after a big movement in exchange rate. The other models try to find reasons for partial pass-through and are divided into two groups. One group is of *dynamic models,* which explain partial pass-through as a short-run response to exchange rate change. The other group contains *strategic interaction models,* which view such interaction as the source of partial pass-through in the static framework. The model presented here is of the last type, which emphasizes strategic interactions. To incorporate dynamics into the model, one must specify expectations formation for exchange rates and short-run adjustment costs.

The empirical part finds more questions than answers about Taiwanese pass-through. This problem is related to the specification of the estimation equation. The empirical investigation was carried out in two stages. The first is estimating the degree of exchange rate pass-through. The second is finding the determinants of exchange rate pass-through.

In the first stage, the author estimates equation (17) instead of equation (7), which is derived from the model, assuming that everything except exchange rate and prices is constant over time and that the effects of exchange rate on export price are reflected in the constant term of equation (17). This assumption is seriously misleading and could distort the final outcome of the paper.

Equation (17) takes the polynomially distributed lag form of exchange rates, in which the length of the lag ranges from 12 to 36 months. This specification can be applied when one wants to obtain rough estimates of pass-through elasticity without specifying the pass-through equation. If a reduced-form equation pass-through, such as equation (7), has been derived, however, it is not sensible to rely on equation (17).

The estimation results for pass-through elasticity by industry are reported in table 10.2. They vary significantly across industries and countries to which goods are exported. Furthermore, the estimated elasticity exceeds one frequently. These results could be avoided if equation (7) were directly estimated with domestic and foreign cost variables in the right-hand side. Then, the lagged coefficients might be less significant and pass-through elasticity might be less than one.

We now turn to the second stage—testing the significance of the determi-

Won-Am Park is a fellow at the Korea Development Institute.

nants of pass-through elasticity. The sample was divided into four groups: first into positive and negative pass-through groups, then each group was subdivided according to economies or diseconomies of scope.

The criteria for the division of the sample play an important role in detecting the impact of cost externality on exchange rate pass-through. If equation (7) is used to obtain the pass-through elasticity, the positive and negative pass-through groups so determined will be different from those in the paper. The criteria for determining economies or diseconomies of scope is crucial. In the paper, economies of scope were represented by negative correlation between marginal cost of good i exported to destination j and export share of good i to markets other than j. It would be better to explain how marginal costs are calculated.

For both the first-stage estimation of equation (17) and the detection of economies of scope on the basis of cost factors, time-series industry-specific cost data are required. If those data are not directly available, one could utilize wage and import price data to construct a cost series. Economies of scope might be better represented by negative correlation between unit cost of a certain industry, which is assumed to be the same across markets, and export share of good i to markets other than j.

Upon reflection, the estimation results are counterintuitive and not always convincing. In table 10.2, the pass-through elasticities of products which have economies of scope are not much larger than those of products which have diseconomies of scope. Also, Taiwan's exports to the United States show low pass-through. If economies or diseconomies of scope play an important role in determining the pass-through rate, there might exist diseconomies of scope for products which are exported to the United States because the United States is the largest export market for Taiwan. In table 10.5, the role of market structure which is represented by the concentration ratio turns out to be insignificant. These results could change if the pass-through is respecified.

I would like to recommend that a pricing-to-market model be used instead of a pass-through model if cost data are not easily available. Changes in costs are likely to be less important in pricing-to-market behavior between domestic and export markets. Furthermore, if the correlation between exchange rates and inflation is strong, the use of relative prices should be seriously considered in work concentrating on estimating pass-through elasticities.

Comment Serguey Braguinsky

The theoretical model of incomplete pass-through in this paper is rather interesting. The main theme can be briefly restated as follows. Ceteris paribus, a

Serguey Braguinsky is associate professor of international economics at Yokohama City University.

firm, enjoying some degree of power in a foreign market, would respond to an appreciation of home currency by raising its export prices less and reducing its volume of exports less than would usually be expected, if in this case it faces cost-saving externality in the production of the export good. Thus, the exchange-rate appreciation would be passed through incompletely (see fig. 10C.1).

Let (P_{x0}, X^0) and (P_{y0}, Y^0) be profit-maximizing prices and quantities in the absence of external effects. In contrast, in the case of favorable external cost effects, the simplest profit-maximizing condition can be written as $P = C_x - P'X + \partial C_y (X,Y)/\partial X$, where $\partial C_y (X,Y)/\partial X < 0$; a similar condition can be specified for P_y. It immediately follows that the price is set lower and the quantity higher than in the absence of externalities. We express it in figure 10C.1 as a shift from point B on the marginal revenue curve to point E to the right of it for both X and Y. Starting from points B on each of the diagrams, increasing production lowers marginal costs in the production of both X and Y, producing a favorable cumulative effect.

Figure 10C.1 can also be used to illustrate incomplete pass-through. An appreciation of home currency relative to the currency of the country where X is marketed can be treated as an upward shift (from FE to BC) in the marginal cost curve of X denominated in foreign currency. If price is raised to P_{x^0} and sales reduced to X^0, this will have an adverse effect on the marginal cost of producing Y. Cutting the production of Y will then feed back to the cost of producing X, etc. An unfavorable chain of events would be set in motion, so it pays to pass through less than what is dictated by the task of maximizing profit in the absence of externalities.

It is likely (and the paper shows this rigorously under its assumptions) that the production of Y will even be increased beyond Y' to offset some of the adverse effects on the marginal cost of X of an appreciating home currency. The extent of the increase (not shown in fig. 10C.1) will be determined by the strength of externalities present, the slope of the respective marginal revenue curves, and the relative sizes of the markets.

Several theoretical problems present themselves, however, at this stage. The most important of them is that, in the case of monopolistic behavior, not all of the increase in cost will be passed through to price in any case. The necessary and sufficient condition under which complete pass-through can be expected in the case of a monopolistic firm is that the demand and marginal revenue curves have the same slope at each X. This is so if the demand function can, for example, be written in the form $P = A - B\log(X)$. Since this cannot be generally expected, a difficult task for the empirical specification of the model in question is to determine, from the market demand function, the degree of pass-through incompleteness which would be observed even in the case where there are no external cost effects.

Since there is no reason to expect that the extent of cost externalities will be correlated in any way to particular forms of demand functions, it is difficult to

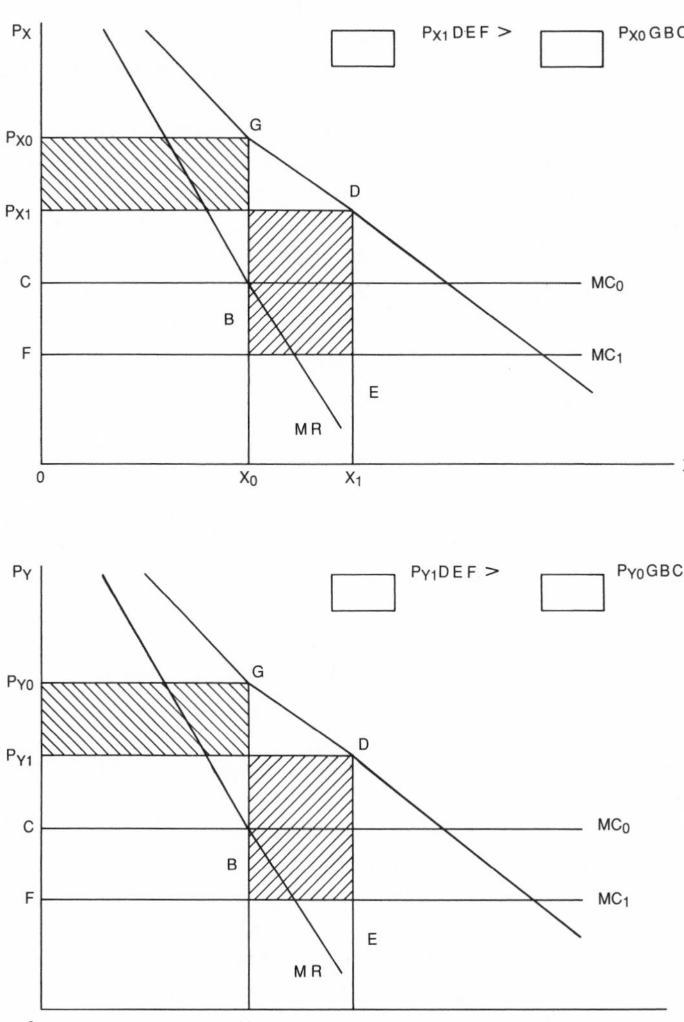

Fig. 10C.1 Cost externalities and the rate of pass-through

see how lower or higher degrees of pass-through among different products can be explained empirically by cost-externalities, as is attempted in the final part of the paper (I will have more to say about this later). In other words, differences between the products' demand functions may more than offset cost externalities in their effects on the degree of pass-through, and this is not taken into account adequately.

To tackle this problem, the author has either to assume linear demand functions for all products (and thus a pass-through ratio of 0.5 in the absence of externalities) or to postulate collusive behavior such that the absence of externalities will imply degree of pass-through equal to one. Neither attempt is made in the paper, indeed, the reaction functions (the ρ's) are left totally unspecified in section 10.2.

This problem can also be brought home by using the very mathematical model presented. Slopes of demand functions enter all the equations describing the reaction to exchange-rate appreciation (see particularly eqq. [8], [9] and [10]). For example, by differentiating equation (10) with respect to P' and P'_y, we see that when $C_x + \alpha$ is negative (strong cost-saving externality) $d\varepsilon/dP'$ and $d\varepsilon/dP'_y$ are less than zero, that is, smaller absolute values of P' and P'_y (more elasticity of demand for X and/or Y) imply smaller ε (less pass-through). In particular, it is clear that, under the same cost externality, Taiwanese firms facing more competitive and larger markets (say, the U.S. market) will pass through less exchange-rate appreciation than those facing smaller markets where demand curves for their products are less elastic.

Also, by differentiating equation (9), we find that, in the case of cost-saving externality and economies of scope, an increase of Y output in response to exchange rate appreciation will be greater, the greater the elasticity of demand for X and Y (that is, $d(dY/d\gamma) / dP' > 0$ when $C'_x + \alpha > 0$ and $d\beta/dQ > 0$, and similarly for $d(dY/d\gamma)/dP'_y$). In words, the more elastic the demand for X and Y, the more it pays to offset an increase in the marginal cost of producing X by expanding production of Y and relying on its favorable external effect. Those demand factors are too important for the empirical part to have real meaning without taking them into account.

Another remark is of a technical nature. In section 10.2, the marginal costs C'_x and C'_y are assumed constant. Taken literally, this means that the cost functions $C_x(x,y)$ and $C_y(x,y)$ are quasi-linear. It is also explicitly assumed that the cost functions are well defined, so that second partial cross-derivatives are equal. Then, $\partial\alpha/\partial y = \partial^2 C_y(x,y)/\partial x\partial y = \partial^2 C_y(x,y)/\partial y\partial x = \partial C'_y/\partial x = 0$, $\partial\beta/\partial x = \partial^2 C_x(x,y)/\partial y\partial x = \partial^2 C_x(x,y)/\partial x\partial y = \partial C'_x/\partial y = 0$, and, by definition, both economies and diseconomies of scope are ruled out. Obviously, the assumption must be changed from constant marginal costs to marginal costs of x and y independent of x and y, respectively.

Finally, it is not clear how market structure in the home country (Taiwan) can directly affect behavior in export markets. The monopolistic producer at home need not be monopolistic when he goes abroad. Thus, apart from its effect on cost share, it is difficult to see how pass-through can depend on internal market structure (thus the rejection of the relevant correlation as statistically insignificant in the empirical discussion appears to be perfectly true from a theoretical point of view as well).

Turning now to the empirical part, the idea of examining the existence of cost externalities indirectly, through the effects of exchange rate appreciation on export volume to other markets, is very neat. There seems to be no intrinsic need, however, to limit attention to export-oriented production alone. If the differentiated product of the same type is produced for the domestic market as well, the existence of externalities would manifest itself in a similar way. Since, it is possible that more information can be obtained about domestic demand functions than about foreign ones, studying the former may help to distinguish externality effects from demand factors, the problem mentioned above.

Generally speaking, though, the empirical section can hardly be regarded as satisfactory. Too many problems remain, notably the already mentioned ambiguity surrounding the key question of what is to be regarded as "proper" pass-through (i.e., disregarding external effects) for each country and each product. The results seem to show that there is some correlation between cost-saving externalities and lower degrees of pass-through. But in view of the overwhelming importance of other factors, this could just be a coincidence, especially if we take into account the very low levels of R^2.

This suspicion is reinforced by differences in the degrees and even the signs of pass-through between products with similar technologies, which one expects to have similar cost externalities—the most striking example being cotton textiles (product 2201). This product is divided into two parts to reflect only different units of measurement, but one part exhibits negative and other rather high positive pass-through. It would have been more helpful, perhaps, if not only product and country averages were presented, but the whole 21×9 matrix of data.

In section 10.3, export shares of good i to markets other than j replace the theoretically correct export levels, obviously for technical reasons. But Liu should be well aware that these are not the same. Namely, if absolute volumes of export and production are falling for other markets, the external cost effects would be adverse even if the share of those other markets was increasing. Thus, the use of shares instead of volumes in determining the type of cost externality cannot be justified.

When dealing with different countries, Liu could also benefit from taking into account the general economic environment, such as price dynamics for competitive products produced in recipient countries relative to exchange rate dynamics. For instance, if the inflation rate in Great Britain was, indeed, higher than the degree of appreciation of the NT dollar against the British pound, this alone could explain a degree of pass-through greater than one. The problem can be addressed, as a first approximation, by using real and not nominal exchange rate appreciation.

It might also be helpful to distinguish between the cases of appreciation and of depreciation of the home currency. For example, in 1986 (the year in question) the NT dollar depreciated, rather than appreciated, against the German mark and the Japanese yen, and it is those countries that exhibit degrees of pass-through almost equal to one.

With the empirical results subject to many unanswered questions, time-series analysis can perhaps be attempted with better results than the cross-sectional approach. In any case, it seems to be absolutely necessary to repeat the calculations for several years and see if the results obtained are really similar for most products and countries (which should be the case unless there were abrupt changes in technology). Only after such evidence relating to at least several points in time is produced, can the study claim any true empirical significance.

11 Tariffs, Quotas, and Inventory Adjustment

Kazumi Asako and Yoshiyasu Ono

11.1 Introduction

The purpose of this paper is twofold. First, we examine the short-run dynamic behavior of a firm that faces both domestic and export markets. We focus on the adjustment process of inventories. Inventories smooth production processes and thereby are productive, and adjustment costs are necessary for the firm to accumulate or decumulate inventories. We want to see how the export decision is related to the short-run dynamics of inventories. Second, by taking into account short-run inventory dynamics, we examine the differential consequences of tariffs and quotas for both exporting and importing countries.

In a static competitive setting, tariffs and quotas exercise equivalent effects on both international and domestic prices and on the welfare of both importing and exporting countries as long as they realize the same import level. However, quotas are more restrictive than tariffs in the sense that the amount of import is completely inflexible under quotas, whereas it is still variable under tariffs. Therefore—in the presence of oligopoly in the importing country, for example—oligopolistic reactions by import-competing firms are very different under tariffs and under quotas.[1] Even without market imperfections, we conjecture that tariffs and quotas would cause critically different effects on the adjustment process if we explicitly consider the dynamic inventory adjustment of firms. In this paper, by considering the inventory adjustment process of a firm, we are able to compare the welfare effects of tariffs and quotas.

Kazumi Asako is professor of economics at Yokohama National University. Yoshiyasu Ono is professor of economics, Institute of Social and Economic Research, Osaka University.

The authors are very much indebted to John Helliwell, Takatoshi Ito, and Kazuo Nishimura for their comments. Any errors, however, are the sole responsibility of the authors.

1. See Itoh and Ono (1982, 1984) for the critical difference between the two trade policies in an oligopolistic setting.

If an import restriction is imposed, the inventory of an exporting firm will gradually decrease and eventually reach a new stationary state. By this process, an exporting firm can control not only domestic supply and employment but also the amount of export if a tariff is imposed. If a quota is imposed, however, there is no room for an exporting firm to control export. It can control only domestic supply and labor employment. This implies that an exporting country cannot help adjusting inventories faster under quotas than under tariffs.

In fact, we show that if a tariff realizes the same stationary-state import level as a quota does, the import level in interim states is always higher under tariffs than under quotas. Since optimal tariff theory implies that a marginal tariff (or quota) always benefits the importing country, a marginal quota benefits the importing country more than a marginal tariff that realizes the same stationary-state import. Since world welfare does not change under a marginal trade restriction, this implies directly that the exporting country prefers tariffs to quotas. This simply restates the well-known property of optimal tariffs and quotas that more restrictive trade policies benefit the importing country more as long as they are marginal.

Recently, trade restrictions have tended to be used as a means of reducing trade deficits rather than as a means of providing long-term protection for an industry, even though trade imbalance as a whole cannot improve through trade restrictions on a particular industry. Then, since a tariff is less restrictive than an equivalent quota, in the above sense, this industry's trade deficits should be higher under a tariff than under the equivalent quota (as long as the marginal revenue of the importing country's demand function is positive). Therefore, if a tariff is imposed to reduce the present value of trade deficits in this industry by the same amount as it would be reduced by a quota, it should be more restrictive than a tariff under which the stationary-state import equals the quota. Then, it is not clear which policy after all more improves the welfare level of the importing country. In this paper, we find that the importing country's welfare is still higher under a quota than under a tariff, even if the two trade policies have the same reduction effect on the present value of an industry's trade deficits.[2]

The rest of the paper consists of three sections. In section 11.2 the basic model of the firm is presented. We focus on two countries that are open to the world. There is a competitive industry whose commodity is traded between the two countries. The representative firm of the industry in question produces output by utilizing labor and inventories of goods in process. Adjustment costs are needed to change inventories, so that adjustments in inventories take place only marginally and continuously. After analyzing the basic features of our model, we consider an autonomous shock to domestic demand. We see that an

2. There are very few works on the welfare analysis of tariffs and quotas in a dynamic setting. Kimbrough (1985) and Ono and Ikeda (1990) are exceptions. The former uses a simulation method, whereas the latter ignores investment in inventory and simply assumes that the output of firms is constant.

initial jump in export occurs when domestic demand autonomously decreases because inventories and thereby output cannot adjust downward immediately. However, in due course, inventories start decreasing. These observations suggest that, depending on the adjustment stage of each industry, the correlation between inventories and exports can either be positive or negative.

In section 11.3, we examine the differential consequences of tariffs and quotas. After analyzing both the long-run and short-run consequences of these trade restrictions for the exporting country, we compare the welfare levels of the importing country under alternative policies. After lengthy calculations, we reach a proposition which, briefly put, states that the importing country prefers quotas to tariffs in order to reduce the trade deficit of an industry. Section 11.4 concludes the paper with several remarks.

11.2 The Basic Model

We focus on two countries that are open to the world. There is a competitive industry whose commodity is traded only between the two countries. Therefore, all prices except that of this industry and the interest rate are given. Furthermore, by assuming that the input of numeraire goods is only labor and that its production technology is linear, the wage rate is also fixed in terms of numeraire goods. In this setting, we can apply a partial-equilibrium analysis to the dynamics of the industry in question.[3]

11.2.1 Optimization by the Representative Firm

The representative firm of the industry in question produces output by utilizing labor and inventories of goods in process. Inventories smooth production processes and thus are productive, but firms must incur adjustment costs to accumulate or decumulate inventories.[4]

The problem for the firm is to maximize the discounted sum of profits:

$$\int_0^\infty (pS + qX - wL)e^{-rt}dt, \tag{1}$$

subject to the constraint

$$F(L,Z) = S + X + \dot{Z} + \Phi(\dot{Z},Z), \tag{2}$$

where S = domestic supply, X = exports, L = labor, Z = inventories, p = domestic price, q = export price, w = wage rate, and r = given world interest rate.

3. If each household's utility is given by $U = y + \Sigma u_i(x_i)$, where we take y as numeraire, then the demand for commodity x_i depends only on its own price p_i. Therefore, by assuming this utility function, we can directly apply a partial-equilibrium analysis of each industry to this general equilibrium model.

4. Uzawa (1986, chap. 2) formulates a model in which inventories enter into the production function. Although we follow his formulation straightforwardly here, the essential feature of the present paper would not change if only inventories yield benefits to the firm.

The adjustment cost function and the production function are assumed homogeneous of degree one, so that $\Phi(\dot{Z},Z) = \phi(a)Z$ and $F(L,Z) = f(\ell)Z$, where $a = \dot{Z}/Z$, and $\ell = L/Z$. We assume the following conditions for the adjustment cost function:

(3) $$\phi(0) = 0,\ \phi'(0) = 0, \text{ and } \phi(a) > 0,\ a\phi'(a) > 0,\ \phi''(a) > 0, \text{ for any } a \neq 0,$$

and the Inada conditions for the production function:

(4) $$f(0) = 0, f'(0) = \infty, \text{ and } f'(\ell) > 0, f''(\ell) < 0, \text{ for any } \ell > 0.$$

Defining H to be the current-value Hamiltonian

(5) $$H = pS + q\,[f(\ell)Z - S - aZ - \phi(a)Z] - \mathrm{w}\ell Z + \theta aZ,$$

the first-order conditions, assuming the interior solution, are (2) and

(6) $$H_s = 0 \text{ or } p = q,$$

(7) $$H_\ell = 0 \text{ or } qf'(\ell) = w,$$

(8) $$H_a = 0 \text{ or } q[1 + \phi'(a)] = \theta,$$

(9) $$\dot{\theta} = r\theta + q\Phi_z(a) - qF_z(\ell),$$

where $\Phi_z(a) = \phi(a) - a\phi'(a)$ and $F_z(\ell) = f(\ell) - \ell f'(\ell)$. The transversality condition must also follow:

(10) $$\lim_{t\to\infty} \theta Ze^{-rt} = 0.$$

Condition (6) is nothing but the "law of one price," which states that the same goods must be priced equally across domestic and foreign markets. Equations (7) and (8) solve l and a, respectively, as functions of price variables with the following derivatives:

(11) $$\ell = \ell(q),\ \ell_q = -f' / qf'' > 0,$$
(12) $$a = a(\theta,q),\ a_\theta = 1/q\phi'' > 0,\ a_q = -\theta/q^2\phi'' < 0.$$

Equation (9) describes the dynamics of the imputed price of inventory.

11.2.2 Industry Equilibrium

We now move from the optimization problem of the representative firm to the determination of the industry equilibrium. To begin with, we postulate that domestic consumption demand, other than that for inventories or lost as adjustment costs, is given by a simple demand function $D(p)$ with the derivative $D_p = D'(p) < 0$. Similarly, the import demand of the foreign country (or the world as a whole) is given by $M(q)$ with $M_q = M'(q) < 0$. For simplicity we assume that there are no import-competing firms. Then the equalities between demand and supply mean that

(13) $$D(p) = S,$$

(14) $$M(q) = X,$$

where $p = q$ from (6).

Second, the firm continuously adjusts investments in inventory by looking at the difference between θ and q to satisfy condition (8). Investment in inventory then alters the accumulated inventory at the next instant.

Third, the equilibrium condition for the goods market as a whole is given by

(15) $$D(q) + M(q) + [a + \phi\,(a)]Z = f(\ell)Z.$$

Equation (15 solves q, for exogenously given w, as a function of Z and θ:

(16) $$q = q\,(Z,\theta),$$

with

(17) $$q_z = \frac{\partial q}{\partial Z} = \frac{f - (a + \phi)}{B} < 0,$$

(18) $$q_\theta = \frac{\partial q}{\partial \theta} = -\frac{(1 + \phi')a_\theta Z}{B} > 0,$$

(19) $$B = D_q + M_q + (1 + \phi')a_q Z - f'\ell_q Z < 0.$$

Fourth, the imputed price of inventory changes according to (9) with the given world interest rate.

11.2.3 Stationary State and Saddle-Point Path

The long-run stationary-state equilibrium is attained when $\dot{Z} = 0$ or $a = 0$ and when the imputed price of inventory remains constant over time, $\dot{\theta} = 0$. In this long-run stationary state (denoted hereafter with an asterisk), we have from (3) and (8)

(20) $$\theta^* = q^*,$$

and from (3), (9), and (20)

(21) $$F_z(\ell^*) = f(\ell^*) - \ell^* f'(\ell^*) = r.$$

Condition (21), which states the equality between the marginal productivity of inventory and the given world interest rate, determines ℓ^* as a function of r alone. Because ℓ^* in turn is a function of q given by (11), q^* is uniquely determined. The long-run inventory stock Z^*, and thereby aggregate supply $f(\ell^*)Z^*$, is determined by (15).

Away from the long-run stationary state, the dynamics of the perfect-foresight economy are regulated by two differential equations:

(22) $$\dot{Z} = J(Z,\theta) = a(\theta,q)Z,$$

(23) $$\dot{\theta} = K(Z,\theta) = r\theta + q\Phi_z\,(a(\theta,q)) - qF_z(\ell(q)).$$

From (22), the $\dot{Z} = 0$ locus is a downward-sloping curve on the (Z,θ) plane, because $J_z = -q_z Z/q\phi'' > 0$ and $J_\theta = (1 - q_\theta)Z/q\phi'' > 0$. Above and to the right of this curve $\dot{Z} > 0$, while below and to the left of it $\dot{Z} < 0$. On the other hand, the $\dot{\theta} = 0$ locus is either a downward-sloping curve or an upward-sloping curve because $K_\theta = r - fq_\theta$ is not definite in sign. However, we have $K_z = -fq_z > 0$ implying that $\dot{\theta} > 0$ to the right of the $\dot{\theta} = 0$ curve, while $\dot{\theta} < 0$ to the left of it.

The phase diagram of figure 11.1 presupposes a downward-sloping $\dot{\theta} = 0$ curve. For this to be the case, we need to assume a sufficiently small q_θ. If q_θ is large enough to approach unity, the $\dot{\theta} = 0$ curve becomes upward-sloping. Nevertheless, for any $0 < q_\theta < 1$, the long-run stationary state exhibits saddle-point stability, because the characteristic equation

(24) $$\eta^2 - (J_z + K_\theta)\eta + (J_z K_\theta - J_\theta K_z) = 0$$

has two roots opposite in sign, which is so because we obtain

(25) $$J_z K_\theta - J_\theta K_z = \ell f' q_z Z/q\phi'' < 0.$$

Thus, for any historically given inventory stock, there is an optimal path, depicted by arrows, pointing to the stationary state, along which inventory eventually reaches the stationary state. Only when the economy is on this optimal saddle-point path is the transversality condition (10) satisfied. Note that, insofar as saddle-point stability exists, the optimal path is definitely downward-sloping whether the slope of the $\dot{\theta} = 0$ curve per se is positive or negative.

11.2.4 Export-Drive Hypothesis

When an autonomous shock occurs which shifts domestic demand downward, inventories become redundant. Then, because the imputed price of in-

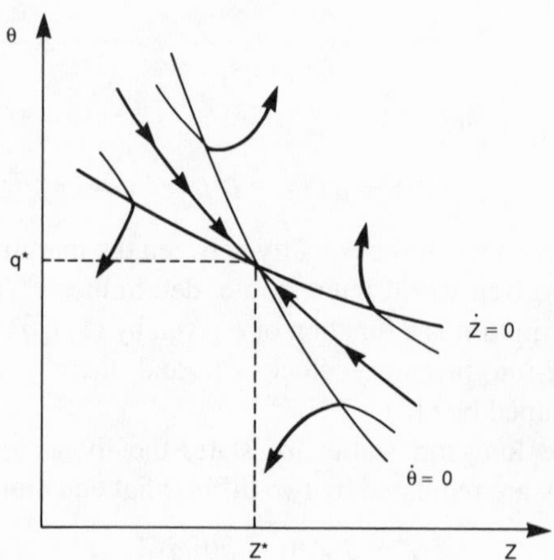

Fig. 11.1 Saddle-point path

ventories jumps down, the export price also jumps down, which in turn brings about an initial upward jump in exports. Throughout this process, inventories cannot decrease immediately, since changing inventories is costly. However, in due course, inventories start decreasing. Then, after the initial increase in exports, both inventories and exports start decreasing as we obtain from (14):

$$\frac{dX}{dZ} = M_q \left(q_z + q_\theta \left. \frac{d\theta}{dZ} \right|_{\text{opt}} \right) > 0, \tag{26}$$

since we have (17) and (18) and we know that θ and Z are inversely related along the optimal path.

Exports keep decreasing to reach the former stationary-state level as the new export price is exactly the same as the former level. This fact is immediate, since we know that ℓ^*, which is a function of q^*, is determined uniquely from (21). Thus, the dynamic effects of a decrease in domestic demand on inventory stock and exports are summarized without any rigorous proof as follows:[5]

Proposition 1: An autonomous decrease in domestic demand causes a gradual reduction in inventories. Exports first increase but later decrease to the former stationary-state level.

In Japan, it is usually pointed out that when the Japanese economy slows down more exports are driven, a presumption known as the export-drive hypothesis. This hypothesis has often been tested by checking whether the correlation between inventory stock and exports is positive. However, from the dynamic optimal behavior presented above, this simple relation may not necessarily hold even when export drive per se is present. In fact, from proposition 1, we find that if domestic demand gradually declines, exports increase because inventories cannot adjust instantaneously, and inventory stock stays too high for a while. In this process, the firm keeps reducing inventories to adjust them to a new stationary state. Thus, there should be a negative correlation between inventories and exports. When domestic demand stops declining, the firm continues to decrease inventories and to reduce exports as well. Thus, in the latter stage, inventories and exports will be correlated positively. Thus, depending on the adjustment stage of each industry, the correlation between inventories and exports can either be positive or negative.[6]

5. A proof of proposition 1 can be established by a phase diagram analysis. The optimal saddle-point path shifts to the left and downward when domestic demand autonomously decreases. This shift is qualitatively the same as the one initiated by the introduction of an import tariff or an import quota by the foreign country. See figure 11.2 of the next section.

6. Asako et al. (1993) examine the determinants of export-output ratios of Japanese manufacturing industries. They find that, whereas there are industries, such as ceramics, metal, and transportation machine manufacturing, for which the correlation between inventory stock and exports is positive, there are also industries, such as foods and textile manufacturing, for which the opposite of this relationship is the case. The implication of proposition 1 is totally consistent with these empirical observations.

11.2.5 Empirical Examination

In this subsection, we conduct an empirical examination utilizing data on Japanese manufacturing firms. The firm's export-output ratio is regressed on two main explanatory variables: inventory-output ratio (INV) and liquidity asset–output ratio (LIQ). The higher the latter ratio, the smaller the expected export-output ratio, because a firm is confronted with less export-drive pressure by the same amount of decrease in autonomous demand. A Tobit model is employed each year from 1964 to 1990 because there are firms each year for which the export-output ratio takes the value zero. The number of firms varies from 869 to 986 depending on the year. All data are taken from the Nikkei NEEDS Company data file.

The estimation results are summarized in table 11.1. The number of samples (SMPL) as well as the number of firms with positive export-output ratios (POS) are indicated in the same table. The SIGMA variable indicates the standard error of the regression of the Tobit model. The inventory-output ratio is

Table 11.1 **Estimation Results**

Year	Constant	INV	LIQ	SIGMA	SMPL	POS
1964	0.0055 (0.31)	0.2824 (4.55)	−0.0227 (3.31)	0.1686 (29.9)	869	509
1965	−0.0140 (0.74)	0.4335 (5.99)	−0.0170 (2.46)	0.1873 (30.8)	880	538
1966	−0.0088 (0.48)	0.4381 (6.40)	−0.0136 (2.03)	0.1770 (31.9)	882	572
1967	0.0026 (0.17)	0.4049 (6.59)	−0.0137 (2.28)	0.1573 (33.8)	885	623
1968	0.0038 (0.25)	0.3842 (6.72)	−0.0083 (1.29)	0.1557 (34.3)	890	640
1969	0.0176 (1.09)	0.3507 (5.89)	−0.0097 (1.47)	0.1595 (35.0)	898	663
1970	0.0218 (1.40)	0.3905 (6.55)	−0.0140 (2.18)	0.1547 (35.7)	912	689
1971	0.0254 (1.68)	0.4027 (6.94)	−0.0098 (1.72)	0.1634 (36.5)	913	710
1972	0.0116 (0.79)	0.2909 (4.86)	0.0048 (0.95)	0.1635 (36.6)	917	717
1973	0.0106 (0.71)	0.3095 (6.06)	−0.0014 (0.24)	0.1579 (36.8)	919	720
1974	0.0409 (2.71)	0.2781 (6.67)	−0.0053 (0.84)	0.1772 (36.9)	922	727
1975	−0.0039 (0.26)	0.3317 (6.96)	0.0126 (2.36)	0.1798 (37.0)	925	730
1976	0.0020 (0.14)	0.3711 (7.83)	0.0105 (1.82)	0.1851 (37.0)	931	731
1977	0.0026 (0.16)	0.3441 (5.40)	0.0161 (2.64)	0.1975 (37.2)	956	744
1978	−0.0023 (0.16)	0.3654 (6.17)	0.0150 (2.77)	0.1893 (37.3)	959	745
1979	−0.0220 (1.52)	0.4207 (6.52)	0.0226 (4.15)	0.1818 (37.5)	962	752
1980	0.0102 (0.78)	0.3251 (5.34)	0.0195 (3.89)	0.1905 (37.7)	967	763
1981	0.0137 (0.97)	0.3772 (5.77)	0.0153 (2.95)	0.1999 (37.9)	971	769
1982	0.0038 (0.28)	0.4358 (7.01)	0.0177 (3.41)	0.1913 (38.5)	977	787
1983	0.0167 (1.27)	0.3574 (5.87)	0.0175 (4.25)	0.1935 (38.6)	981	793
1984	0.0384 (2.98)	0.3814 (5.81)	0.0081 (2.57)	0.1967 (38.9)	984	804
1985	0.0341 (2.69)	0.3618 (5.59)	0.0111 (3.55)	0.1946 (38.9)	986	804
1986	0.0271 (2.35)	0.3526 (5.94)	0.0104 (4.19)	0.1852 (39.0)	986	806
1987	0.0212 (1.75)	0.3510 (5.40)	0.0092 (4.28)	0.1815 (39.0)	986	803
1988	0.0303 (2.62)	0.3212 (5.11)	0.0054 (2.87)	0.1770 (38.7)	986	796
1989	0.0350 (2.97)	0.2571 (4.11)	0.0065 (3.48)	0.1796 (38.7)	986	795
1990	0.0311 (2.48)	0.3296 (4.84)	0.0049 (2.45)	0.1808 (38.6)	986	793

Note: Figures in parentheses are absolute values of *t*-statistics.

estimated with positive sign every year at the 1 percent significance level. This indicates that the initial negative correlation between export and inventory pointed out in proposition 1 is, if it exists, not predominant in the present data set. Thus the larger the inventory-output ratio the higher the export-output ratio.

Meanwhile the LIQ variable takes negative signs only in the early years. From the mid-1970s the export-output ratio is higher, the larger the liquidity asset–output ratio. Since the positive correlation is significant during 1980s, we need a theory which explains this relationship. Although such a topic is interesting, it is beyond the scope of the present paper.

11.2.6 Relative Adjustability of Inventory and Employment

In the argument above we assumed that employment can adjust flexibly whereas inventories adjust only gradually. Even if employment is not perfectly adjustable, proposition 1 holds as long as there is some factor of production, instead of employment, inputs of which can adjust flexibly. However, if there is no flexible factor and employment is not perfectly flexible, a firm cannot instantaneously adjust production. Therefore when domestic demand autonomously declines, exporting firms would first accumulate inventories and increase exports. Then they would gradually reduce inventories, employment, and export. In this way inventory and export may move in parallel. Thus the effect of an exogenous decrease in domestic demand on the movements of inventory and export would differ across countries and across industries, depending on whether employment can adjust flexibly or not.

Messmore (1992), for instance, presents empirical research on the flexibility of employment and inventories. She shows that flexibility of employment differs across countries. Especially in EC countries, such as Belgium, France, Sweden, and Norway, obstacles to the termination of employment contracts are serious, whereas in the United States they are unimportant. Japan and presumably East Asian countries are in between. Proposition 1 may fit the U.S. case more.

11.3 Tariffs and Quotas

In this section, we introduce tariffs and quotas as alternative means of restricting exports of the home country. Namely, the foreign country imposes either a tariff or a quota. A quota does not give any room for exporters to adjust the amount of exports even by reducing prices. Under a tariff, on the other hand, exporters can affect the amount of exports by changing prices. In a static setting, the effects of these two alternative restrictions are the same, as long as the same quantity of export is guaranteed. However, in a dynamic setting, exporters will change the export amount under a tariff in the stage of adjusting inventories since the marginal cost will differ over time. Under a quota the amount of exports is fixed regardless of changes in the marginal cost. Therefore the effect of a tariff on the welfare of an importing country will differ from that of a quota.

Note that the following arguments still hold as long as there is some factor of production, the accumulation of which is costly. Therefore, even if we consider, instead of inventories, real capital accumulation, which is costly, we obtain the same results.

11.3.1 Tariffs

We begin with an import tariff set by the foreign country. The equilibrium condition for the export market of the home country is written, instead of (14), as

$$X = M(q(1 + \tau)), \tag{27}$$

where τ stands for an import tariff. Substituting (27) into (15), we can rewrite the equilibrium condition of the industry as

$$D(q) + [a + \phi(a)]Z = f(\ell)Z - M(q(1 + \tau)). \tag{28}$$

From (28), in response to the marginal introduction of the tariff we have for $\tau = 0$

$$Bdq = -(1 + \phi')\, a_\theta Z d\theta + \{f - (a + \phi)\}dZ - qM_q d\tau. \tag{29}$$

Therefore, besides (17) and (18), we get

$$q_\tau = \frac{\partial q}{\partial \tau} = -\frac{qM_q}{B} < 0. \tag{30}$$

We now discuss the effects of the marginal introduction of a tariff on the long-run stationary state. To begin with, we see from (21) that the labor-inventory ratio ℓ^* depends solely on the interest rate, implying that ℓ^* is unaffected by the tariff. Then, since the marginal productivity of labor is independent of the tariff, the price level q^* stays unaffected by the introduction of the tariff because the wage rate is kept intact in (7) or (11).

When q^* and thereby the imputed price of inventory θ^* are unaffected by the tariff, we obtain from (29) that

$$\frac{dZ^*}{d\tau} = \frac{q^* M_q(q^*)}{f(\ell^*)} < 0. \tag{31}$$

Equation (31) means that the introduction of a tariff by the foreign country decreases the optimal long-run stationary-state inventory stock in the home country. The reduction of inventory should decrease the output supply and thereby exports. Domestic supply is invariant under tariffs as the price level is unaffected.

Next, we examine the short-run transitional impact of the introduction of a tariff. To begin, we observe that the free-trade long-run stationary state now belongs to the region where both Z and θ are increasing over time because we obtain from (22) and (23)

$$\frac{\partial \dot{Z}}{\partial \tau} = a_q q_\tau Z > 0, \tag{32}$$

and

$$\frac{\partial \dot{\theta}}{\partial \tau} = -fq_\tau > 0. \tag{33}$$

This implies that the saddle-point paths shift to the left and downward, as illustrated in figure 11.2.

Figure 11.3 depicts the transitional paths of inventory stock Z, imputed price of inventory θ, export price q, domestic supply S, and exports X. The inventory stock gradually decreases to the new stationary-state level. Price variables θ and q show qualitatively similar variations; i.e., these variables jump down initially and then keep rising until the common old equilibrium level $\theta^* = q^*$ is recovered. The time profile of domestic supply is just the mirror image of that of export price; i.e., it initially jumps up and then decreases gradually until the old equilibrium level is reached. Exports of the home country jumps down initially and then keeps decreasing as the export price keeps rising.

11.3.2 Quotas

Next we consider the effect of an import quota set by the foreign country. Thus we impose the quantity constraint

$$X = \bar{X}, \tag{34}$$

so that we have, in place of (28),

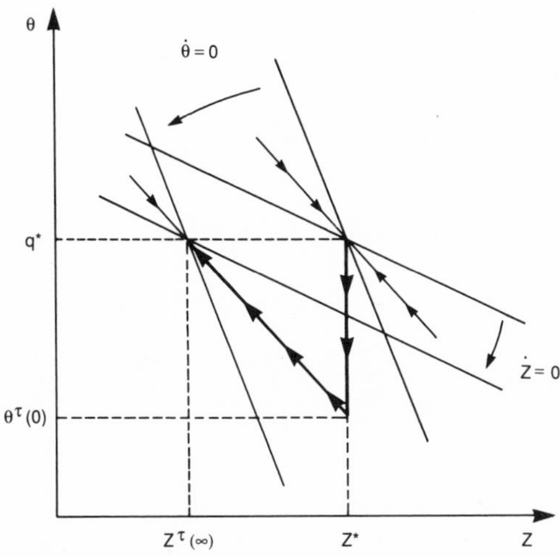

Fig. 11.2 Effect of a tariff

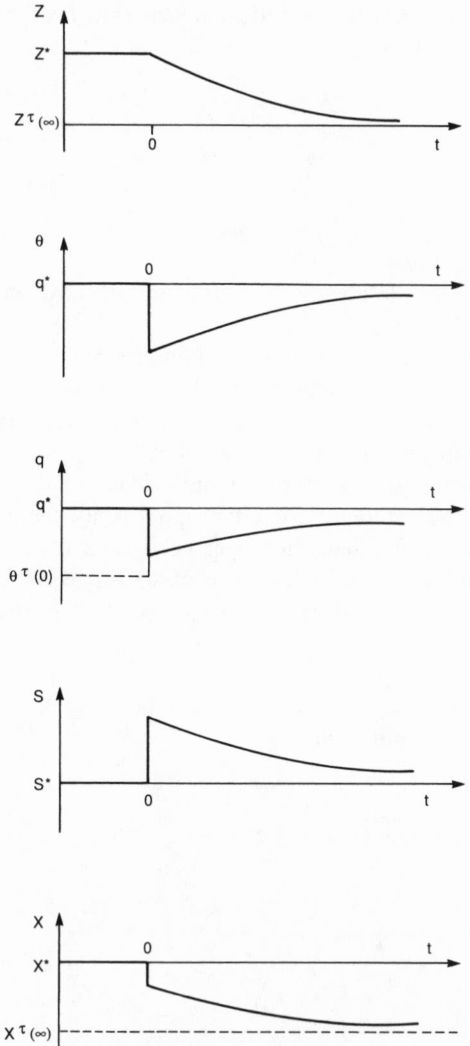

Fig. 11.3 Time profiles of variables under a tariff

(35) $$D(q) + [a + \phi(a)]Z = f(\ell)Z - \bar{X}.$$

The long-run impacts of quotas are qualitatively similar to those of tariffs and, in fact, both policies exert quantitatively the same long-run impact if only

(36) $$D(q^*(1 + \tau)) = \bar{X},$$

holds in the long-run stationary state.

To see the short-run transitional impacts, we first obtain from (35)

(37) $$(B - M_q)\, dq = -a_\theta Z^* d\theta + f dZ - d\bar{X},$$

where derivatives and parameters are evaluated in the stationary state. Comparing (29) and (37), we observe that the short-run dynamics of the transitional paths under quotas are to some extent very similar to those under tariffs, so that we do not depict any particular figure for this case.

However, once we take a closer look at the short-run dynamics, we know that the short-run transitional export price is lower than the long-run stationary level when inventories decumulate. This indicates that

(38) $$M(q^{\tau}(1 + \tau)) > M(q^{\tau *}(1 + \tau)) = \bar{X},$$

holds throughout the transitional path, where q^{τ} denotes the export price under a tariff. Therefore, in the short run exports are greater under tariffs than under quotas. The opposite is the case when inventories accumulate.

11.3.3 Tariffs versus Quotas: Alternative Ways to Reduce Trade Deficits

In this subsection, we compare the welfare effect of a tariff with that of a quota when they decrease the trade deficit of an industry by the same amount.

Suppose that either a marginal tariff or a marginal quota is imposed in a competitive industry where the amount of trade is X^* and price is q^*. We derive from (7) and (21) that in a stationary state q^* is invariant even under trade restrictions. Therefore, we have

(39) $$\Delta q^x(\infty) = q^x(\infty) - q^* = 0,$$

(40) $$\Delta q^{\tau}(\infty) = q^{\tau}(\infty) - q^* = 0,$$

where $q^x(t)$ and $q^{\tau}(t)$, respectively, represent the export price path under the quota and that under the tariff.

If a marginal tariff τ ($\fallingdotseq 0$) and a marginal quota $\bar{X}$ ($\fallingdotseq X^*$) have the same effect on the present value of trade deficit in this industry, we have

(41) $$\int_0^{\infty}(X^*\Delta q^x + q^*\Delta\bar{X})e^{-rt}dt = \int_0^{\infty}[X^*\Delta q^{\tau} + q^*(q^*\Delta\tau + \Delta q^{\tau})M_q]e^{-rt}\,\mathrm{dt},$$

where using (39) and (40) Δq^x and Δq_{τ} are given by

(42) $$\Delta q^x(t) = [\Delta q^x(0) - \Delta q^x(\infty)]e^{\eta^x_t} + \Delta q^x(\infty) = \Delta q^x(0)\mathrm{e}^{\eta^x_t},$$

(43) $$\Delta q^{\tau}(t) = [\Delta q^{\tau}(0) - \Delta q^{\tau}(\infty)]e^{\eta^{\tau}_t} + \Delta q^{\tau}(\infty) = \Delta q^{\tau}(0)e^{\eta^{\tau}_t}.$$

Negative parameters η^x and η^{τ}, respectively, are the solution of characteristic equation (24) under the quota and that under the tariff. Therefore, from (41) we obtain

(44) $$\begin{aligned}&[X^*(\Delta q^x(0)/\Delta\bar{X})/(r - \eta^x) + q^*/r]\Delta\bar{X}\\ &= [(X^* + q^*M_q)(\Delta q^{\tau}(0)/\Delta\tau)/(r - \eta^{\tau}) + (q^*)^2 M_q/r]\Delta\tau.\end{aligned}$$

Since we naturally assume that $\Delta q^x(0)/\Delta \bar{X} > 0$ and $\Delta q^\tau(0)/\Delta\tau < 0$ and that the marginal revenue of the foreign demand function is positive (i.e., $X^* + q^* M_q > 0$),[7] (44) implies that $\Delta\bar{X}/\Delta\tau < 0$ when (41) is satisfied.

Because changes in the importing country's surplus under a quota and under a tariff are given as

$$(45)\quad \Delta W^x/\Delta\bar{X} = -\int_0^\infty X^*[\Delta q^x(t)/\Delta\bar{X}]e^{-rt}dt = -X^*(\Delta q^x(0)/\Delta\bar{X})/(r-\eta^x),$$

$$(46)\quad \Delta W^\tau/\Delta\tau = -\int_0^\infty X^*[\Delta q^\tau(t)/\Delta\tau]e^{-rt}dt = -X^*(\Delta q^\tau(0)/\Delta\tau)/(r-\eta^\tau),$$

we obtain from (44) that

$$(47)\quad \begin{aligned} &[X^*(\Delta q^x(0)/\Delta\bar{X})/(r-\eta^x) + q^*/r][\Delta W^\tau/\Delta\tau - (\Delta W^x/\Delta\bar{X})(\Delta\bar{X}/\Delta\tau)]X^* \\ &= -[X^*(\Delta q^x(0)/\Delta\bar{X})/(r-\eta^x) + q^*/r](\Delta q^\tau(0)/\Delta\tau)/(r-\eta^\tau) \\ &\qquad + [(X^*+q^*M_q)(\Delta q^\tau(0)/\Delta\tau)/(r-\eta^\tau) \\ &\qquad + (q^*)^2 M_q/r](\Delta q^x(0)/\Delta\bar{X})/(r-\eta^x) \\ &= (q^*/r)\{[(\Delta q^x(0)/\Delta\bar{X})/(r-\eta^x)][q^* + r(\Delta q^\tau(0)/\Delta\tau)/(r-\eta^\tau)]M_q \\ &\qquad - (\Delta q^\tau(0)/\Delta\tau)/(r-\eta^\tau)]\}. \end{aligned}$$

Therefore, we have

$$(48)\quad \mathrm{sgn}[\Delta W^\tau/\Delta\tau - (\Delta W^x/\Delta\bar{X})(\Delta\bar{X}/\Delta\tau)] = \mathrm{sgn}(\Omega),$$

where

$$(49)\quad \begin{aligned} \Omega = {} & [(\Delta q^x(0)/\Delta\bar{X})/(r-\eta^x)][q^* + r(\Delta q^\tau(0)/\Delta\tau)/(r-\eta^\tau)]M_q \\ & - (\Delta q^\tau(0)/\Delta\tau)/(r-\eta^\tau). \end{aligned}$$

By calculating Ω, we derive the following property:

Proposition 2: As long as a quota reduces the trade deficit of an industry by the same amount as a tariff does, it is more advantageous for the importing country to impose a quota.

Proof: See appendix.

Thus, the importing country would prefer quotas to tariffs to reduce the trade deficit of an industry.

11.4 Concluding Remarks

In this paper, we have analyzed the dynamic inventory behavior of competitive firms that face both domestic and export markets. We have been especially

7. This can be negative when the marginal cost of the exporting firm is very low. Then, tariffs or quotas even increase trade deficits. Here, we treat the case where trade restrictions reduce trade deficits.

interested in the dynamic interactions between inventory adjustment and exports. The analytical results can be summarized in two theoretical propositions.

Proposition 1 indicates that the correlation between inventories and exports can either be positive or negative, depending on the adjustment stage of each industry. Proposition 2 compares tariffs and quotas in the presence of inventory adjustment. It turned out that an importing country's welfare is higher under a quota than under a tariff when the two trade policies have the same reduction effect on the present value of trade deficits.

Our analytical framework can be utilized to analyze a variety of problems left unanswered in the present paper. These include the incorporation of intertemporal optimization by consumers, consideration of endogenous growth, and extension to a truly standard general equilibrium framework.

Appendix

Proof of Proposition 2

We obtain $\Delta q^x(0)/\Delta\bar{X}$ and $\Delta q^\tau(0)/\Delta\tau$, and derive Ω. At $t = 0$, we obtain from the market equilibrium condition under a quota $\bar{X}$:

$$D(q^x(0)) + \bar{X} = \{f(\ell(q^x(0))) - [a(0) + \phi(a(0))]\}Z(0), \tag{A1}$$

so that

$$D_q(dq^x(0)) + d\bar{X} = -\{[(f')^2/(q^*f'')]dq^x + da(0)\}Z^*, \tag{A2}$$

since $dZ(0) = 0$, $Z(0) = Z^*$, and $\phi'(a(0)) = \phi(0) = 0$. Deriving da from the first-order condition (8) as $da = (d\theta - dq)/(q\phi'')$ and substituting the result into (A2), we obtain

$$-(B^* - M_q)dq^x(0)/d\bar{X} = 1 + [Z^*/(q^*\phi'')]d\theta^x(0)/d\bar{X}, \tag{A3}$$

where B^* equals expression (19) evaluated in the stationary state. Since from the dynamic equation of $\theta^x(t)$ $\theta^x(0)$ is written as

$$\theta^x(0) = q^* + [K^x_z/(\eta^x - K^x_\theta)](Z(0) - Z^x(\infty)), \tag{A4}$$

where $K^x(z, \theta)$ represents (23) under a quota, we get

$$d\theta^x(0)/d\bar{X} = -[K^x_z/(\eta^x - K^x_\theta)]dZ^x(\infty)/d\bar{X}. \tag{A5}$$

In the new stationary state to be reached at $t = \infty$, the equilibrium condition of the industry becomes

$$D(q^x(\infty)) + \bar{X} = f(\ell(q^x(\infty)))Z^x(\infty), \tag{A6}$$

where $q^x(\infty)$ is invariant regardless of trade policies and equals $q^x(0) = q^*$. This implies that we obtain

$$\text{(A7)} \qquad dZ^x(\infty)/d\bar{X} = 1/f(\ell^*).$$

Therefore, we obtain from (A3), (A5), and (A7) that $dq^x(0)/d\bar{X}$ satisfies

$$\text{(A8)} \qquad \begin{aligned} &-(B^* - M_q)dq^x(0)/d\bar{X} \\ &= 1 - [K_z^x/(\eta^x - K_\theta^x)][Z^*/(q^*f\phi'')] \\ &= 1 - \{fZ^*/[(r - \eta^x)(B^* - M_q)q^*\phi'' + fZ^*]\}, \end{aligned}$$

from which we obtain

$$\text{(A9)} \quad -[dq^x(0)/d\bar{X}]/(r - \eta^x) = q^*\phi''/[(r - \eta^x)(B^* - M_q)q^*\phi'' + fZ^*].$$

We next obtain $\Delta q^\tau(0)/\Delta\tau$. The market equilibrium condition under a tariff τ is written as

$$\text{(A10)} \qquad \begin{aligned} D(q^\tau(0)) + M((1 + \tau)q^\tau(0)) = \{&f(\ell(q^\tau(0))) \\ &- [a(0) + \phi(a(0))]\}Z(0), \end{aligned}$$

so that we obtain

$$\text{(A11)} \qquad -B^*dq^\tau(0)/d\tau = q^*M_q + [Z^*/(q^*\phi'')]d\theta^\tau(0)/d\tau.$$

Since from the dynamic equation of $\theta^\tau(t)$ $\theta^\tau(0)$ is written as

$$\text{(A12)} \qquad \theta^\tau(0) = q^* + [K_z^\tau/(\eta^\tau - K_\theta^\tau)](Z(0) - Z^\tau(\infty)),$$

where $K^\tau(z, \theta)$ represents (23) under a tariff, we get

$$\text{(A13)} \qquad d\theta^\tau(0)/d\tau = -[K_z^\tau/(\eta^\tau - K_\theta^\tau)]dZ^\tau(\infty)/d\tau.$$

Letting $t \to \infty$, the equilibrium condition of the industry becomes

$$\text{(A14)} \qquad D(q^\tau(\infty)) + M((1 + \tau)q^\tau(\infty)) = f(\ell(q^\tau(\infty)))Z^\tau(\infty),$$

where $q^\tau(\infty) = q^*$, so that we obtain

$$\text{(A15)} \qquad dZ^\tau(\infty)/d\tau = q^*M_q/f(\ell^*).$$

Therefore, we obtain from (A11), (A13), and (A15) that $dq^\tau(0)/d\tau$ satisfies

$$\text{(A16)} \quad \begin{aligned} -B^*dq^\tau(0)/d\tau &= q^*Mq\{1 - [K_z^\tau/(\eta^\tau - K_\theta^\tau)]\,[Z^*/(q^*f\phi'')]\} \\ &= q^*M_q\{1 - fZ^*/[(r - \eta^\tau)B^*q^*\phi'' + fZ^*]\}, \end{aligned}$$

from which we obtain

$$\text{(A17)} \quad -[dq^\tau(0)/d\tau]/(r - \eta^\tau) = (q^*)^2M_q\phi''/[(r - \eta^\tau)B^*q^*\phi'' + fZ^*].$$

Now, applying (A9) and (A17) to (49), we derive

(A18) $$[(B^* - M_q)(r - \eta^x) + fZ^*/(q^*\phi'')][B^*(r - \eta^\tau) + fZ^*/(q^*\phi'')]\Omega/(q^*M_q) = B^*\eta^\tau - (B^* - M_q)\eta^x,$$

which implies that

(A19) $$\mathrm{sgn}(\Omega) = \mathrm{sgn}[(B^* - M_q)\eta^x - B^*\eta^\tau].$$

But, η^τ and η^x are, respectively, negative roots of the following characteristic equations:

(A20) $$(\eta^\tau)^2 - r\eta^\tau + [fZ^*(f - r)/(B^*q^*\phi'')] = 0, \text{ and}$$

(A21) $$(\eta^x)^2 - r\eta^x + [fZ^*(f - r)]/[(B^* - M_q)q^*\phi''] = 0.$$

Then, because we know $B^* < B^* - M_q < 0$ and because it is easy for us to derive $\partial(\eta^\tau B^*)/\partial B^* < 0$, by comparing (A20) and (A21) we get $(B^* - M_q)\eta^x < B^*\eta^\tau$. This implies that (A19) is negative, which in turn implies that

(A22) $$\Delta W^\tau/\Delta\tau < (\Delta W^x/\Delta\bar{X})(\Delta\bar{X}/\Delta\tau).$$

Inequality (A22) proves proposition 2. Q.E.D.

References

Asako, K., H. Izawa, A. Kawaguchi, and N. Tomita. 1993. Yusyutsu Hiritsu no Kettei Youin (Determinants of export ratio). Mimeograph.

Itoh, M., and Y. Ono. 1982. Tariffs, quotas and market structure. *Quarterly Journal of Economics* 96 (May): 295–305.

———. 1984. Tariffs vs. quotas under duopoly of heterogeneous goods. *Journal of International Economics* 17 (November): 359–73.

Kimbrough, Kent P. 1985. Tariffs, quotas and welfare in a monetary economy. *Journal of International Economics* 19: 257–277.

Messmore, Lauren B. 1992. *The effect of labor turnover costs on inventory investment: A cross-country analysis.* Ph.D. thesis, Department of Economics, Harvard University.

Ono, Yoshiyasu, and Shinsuke Ikeda. 1990. International welfare effects of saving controls and trade restrictions. ISER Discussion Paper no. 235, Osaka University, October.

Uzawa, Hirofumi. 1986. *Keizai Dogaku no Riron (A theory of economic dynamics).* Tokyo: University of Tokyo Press.

Comment Kazuo Nishimura

Asako and Ono present a dynamic trade model with inventory adjustment. Two main results are reported in this paper. I will discuss them in order.

The first result concerns the export-drive hypothesis, which says that a decrease in domestic demand leads to inventory accumulation, which drives a country to export more. Asako and Ono say that there is not necessarily a positive correlation between inventories and exports, which is contrary to the export-drive hypothesis. However I do not fully agree with their interpretation of proposition 1. The level of inventory Z is a state variable in the model. All other variables are functions of inventory. If there is exogenous shock (autonomous decline in demand), the domestic demand function $D(p)$ shifts downward. This will change the values of the shadow price of inventory θ, goods prices $p = g$, and the other variables a and l and also the amount of export associated with the given initial level of inventory. This is the only case when export increases. However inventory stays at the initial level in this case. Then, a decline in demand causes a change of stationary state, and inventory and export start to move toward a new stationary state. As inventory decreases, export will also decrease. Therefore, whenever inventory changes, we observe a positive correlation between inventory and export. In conclusion there is nonnegative correlation between inventory and export and thus effect in the adjustment process contradicting the export-drive hypothesis.

The second result states that a quota is more advantageous than a tariff for the importing country, given the condition that the trade deficits under both policies are the same. Trade deficit here is restricted to mean the trade deficit of the imported good industry. Hence it is equivalent to the total value of the import. And by total value Asako and Ono mean the discounted present value of the import. The advantage of the importing country is measured by its welfare change. Welfare is measured by consumer surplus. Because the demand curve for the imported good by importing country is fixed, there is no substitute good for the imported good.

Since the model of this paper is formulated to explain the dynamics of the exporting country, proposition 2 should be a result on the welfare of the exporting country. The welfare implication for the importing country may be given as a corollary or in a remark after proposition 2. The import function $M(q)$ is the only place in this model where the importing country plays a part. Therefore the welfare implication for the importing country given in proposition 2 should not be counted as a main result.

My comments above are only on the interpretation or statement of the results. Reading through the paper, I must say that Asako and Ono derive the comparative dynamics in a very clever way. I think that comparative *dynamics*

Kazuo Nishimura is a professor of economics at the Institute of Economic Research, Kyoto University.

are much more difficult than comparative statics in most cases. Their contribution is certainly an important addition to the literature.

Comment John F. Helliwell

This paper provides an imaginative use of costly inventory adjustment as a means of modeling differentially the effects of tariffs and quotas and of analyzing the movements of exports and inventories following an unexpected drop in domestic demand. The two main parts of the paper focus on separate issues and depend for their results on different features of the model setup, so they should be considered separately.

Inventories and Exports

The authors' main conclusion in this section is that the correlation between inventories and exports can be either positive or negative, depending on the stage of an industry's response to an unexpected change in tariffs or quotas. In the first stage of response to an unexpected drop in domestic sales, inventories will be dropping gradually while exports will be rising. This, they argue, upsets the commonly held presumption, known as the export-drive hypothesis, whereby a positive relation is to be expected. The fact that their model upsets the export-drive hypothesis depends on very special features of their model setup, and in particular on assumptions that are contrary to those that underlie the export-drive hypothesis. I think that their assumption may be less plausible than an alternative setup that would be more compatible with the export-drive hypothesis. To focus more clearly on the issue, I shall first outline what I take to be the logic of the export-drive hypothesis and then spell out how that hypothesis assumes a quite different set of assumptions about inventory and factor adjustment costs than is employed by Asako and Ono.

The export-drive hypothesis starts with the notion that inventories accumulate in the wake of an unexpected drop in domestic sales, and producers then make a drive to expand export markets in order to help eliminate their excess inventories. Thus periods with high inventories tend to be associated with high exports as well, at least in those instances where the high inventories are due to an unexpected drop in domestic sales. Obviously, if the sales surprise took the form of an unexpected increase in export demand, then high exports would be associated with low inventories, following the same logic about the buffer stock use of inventories. Hence, the correlations that are being talked about in

John F. Helliwell is Mackenzie King Visiting Professor of Canadian Studies at Harvard University, professor of economics at the University of British Columbia, and a research associate of the National Bureau of Economic Research.

the export-drive hypothesis are specific to a particular shock and cannot be tested by simple correlations.

By contrast, when the Asako-Ono model is confronted with unexpectedly low domestic demand, inventories are gradually reduced, while exports are increased at first, before eventually returning to the former stationary-state level. Both models show an increase in exports, above the path that otherwise would have taken place, but some of the implications for inventory stocks are strikingly different. In the Asako-Ono setup and in the model implicitly underlying the export-drive hypothesis, long-run target inventories are reduced in response to any reduction in long-run expected sales. What distinguishes the two approaches is the nature of the short-run inventory adjustment. In the Asako-Ono setup, inventories drop right from the outset. Inventory stocks do not drop immediately to the new target level, since they are subject to adjustment costs that increase with the speed of adjustment. However, inventories cannot increase in response to an unexpected drop in sales since there are assumed to be no costs of adjusting other factor inputs. Hence output immediately falls by more than the unexpected drop in sales, by an extra amount equal to the partial adjustment of inventories toward their new target level.

In the model implicitly underlying the export-drive hypothesis, by contrast, there is room for inventories to act as an optimal buffer between unexpected sales changes and a stabilized production level because there are assumed to be costs entailed by changing the level of output and none to changing the level of inventories, beyond those that might flow from the fact that factor inputs, and hence output, are costly to adjust.

Thus the Asako-Ono conclusion about the movement of inventories in response to an unexpected drop in domestic sales differs from the export-drive hypothesis because of fundamentally different assumptions about adjustment costs. A judgment about the relative plausibility of the two results requires us to choose between the two conflicting sets of assumptions about adjustment costs.

Which is the more likely assumption about adjustment costs? I would be inclined to cast my vote for assuming that output is costly to adjust, which amounts to assuming that all measured factor inputs are costly to adjust, and that abnormal rates of factor utilization, while possible, are not costless. With these assumptions about adjustment costs, it is not necessary to assume any further adjustment costs in the level of inventories, and the door is opened for inventory stocks to play a buffering role between uncertain changes in sales and costly-to-adjust production levels.[1] Indeed, I am inclined to think that something of this sort probably underlies Asako and Ono's initial argument that inventories are productive because they smooth production processes. This would in turn seem to imply that there are cost advantages to a smooth produc-

1. Some evidence favoring such a buffer-stock role for inventories in the industrial countries is presented in Helliwell and Chung (1981).

tion process, and if inventories are to play such a role, it is presumably because they are available to be run up or run down to help buffer unexpected changes in demand or cost conditions.

Tariffs and Quotas

On the tariffs versus quotas issue, the main point the authors emphasize is that costly adjustment alters the relative present values of the costs of using tariffs and quotas in favor of using quotas to achieve any given target reduction in the present value of trade deficits. I conjecture that this result is quite general and is likely to hold for a variety of specifications of costs of adjustment. This is likely because the result depends on the central distinction between tariffs and quotas, that the latter bite immediately on quantities and hence have a larger ratio of short-term to long-term trade balance effects in the presence of adjustment costs. To illustrate the generality of this result and its independence from the specific role of inventories, I think it would be possible to relabel inventories as plant and equipment and the analysis would carry through just as it does now, providing we continue to make the assumption that capital goods are an undifferentiated part of the homogeneous output of the representative firm.

Given the practical importance of the choice between tariffs and quotas and the likelihood that the result does not depend on the authors' specific assumptions about the role and costliness of inventory adjustment, it would be helpful to provide some indication of how it might be possible to assess the likely magnitude of the partial preference of quotas over tariffs. If the likely effect is small, then it can safely be treated as a secondary member of the larger set of efficiency issues surrounding the revenue, distribution, and political consequences of the use of tariffs and quotas. In any event, fine-tuning the choice between tariffs and quotas, as applied by one country acting on its own, ought to be subservient to the larger questions of the likelihood of retaliation of others and of the systemic effects of making industry-specific tariffs and quotas a feasible goal for firms that might better be spending their scarce entrepreneurial talents finding new products, improving production techniques, and developing new markets.

Although I regard the comparison of tariffs and quotas to be more convincing than the arguments about the short-run dynamic linkages between inventories and exports, the quality of the analysis is high throughout the paper, reflecting the sensible application of sharp tools to interesting issues.

Reference

Helliwell, J. F., and A. Chung. 1981. Aggregate output with variable rates of utilization of employed factors. *Journal of Econometries* 19:597–625.

12 Yen Bloc or Dollar Bloc? Exchange Rate Policies of the East Asian Economies

Jeffrey A. Frankel and Shang-Jin Wei

12.1 Introduction

One hears increasingly of a yen bloc forming in East Asia, of a switch on the part of the countries in this region in economic allegiance from the United States to Japan. This bloc is said to be forming in parallel with, and perhaps in response to, the formation of blocs in the Western Hemisphere and Europe.

In the case of Europe, the policy elements of a likely bloc are self-evident. The European Community agreed in the 1980s to strengthen its economic integration, most notably with the Single Market Act of 1985 and the other initiatives associated with the year 1992. Leading the way have been attempts to stabilize the values of the European currencies vis-à-vis each other—beginning with the Snake of the 1970s and followed by the more successful European Monetary System founded in 1979—and the more ambitious plans for European Monetary Union agreed upon at Maastricht in December 1991. In the case of the Western Hemisphere, the policy elements are almost as self-evident. On the trade front they consist most notably of the Canadian–U.S. Free Trade Area, followed by the addition of Mexico to a North American Free Trade Area currently under negotiation and future plans for other Latin American countries to join in. Integration on the currency front is not as strong a trend in the Western Hemisphere as in Europe. But most Latin American countries remained pegged to the dollar in the mid-1970s (following it in the

Jeffrey A. Frankel is professor of economics at the University of California at Berkeley and a research associate of the National Bureau of Economic Research. Shang-Jin Wei is assistant professor at the Kennedy School of Government, Harvard University.

The authors thank Warwick McKibbin for data, Koichi Hamada, Takatoshi Ito, Sung-Hee Jwa, Masahiro Kawai, Anne Krueger, and Alan Winters for useful comments, and Benjamin Chui for research assistance. They also thank the Center for International and Development Economics Research (funded at U.C. Berkeley by the Ford Foundation) and the Japan–United States Friendship Commission (an agency of the U.S. government) for research support.

devaluations of 1971 and 1973, for example). Fifteen years later, having first lost their monetary virginity and then having fought their way back most of the way to price stability, a few Latin American countries are considering whether to repeg their currencies to the dollar.[1] Argentina has already done so.

In East Asia, explicit policy initiatives are missing. The phrase "yen bloc" connotes to some a concentration of trade and direct investment relations on the part of East Asian countries, to others a heightened role in the region for the Japanese currency. These two possible interpretations of "yen bloc" are not necessarily in competition, because one could be a contributing cause of the other.

Not only have currency links and bilateral trade links been less often the subject of policy initiatives in East Asia than in other regions, but they have also been less extensively studied. We consider in this paper three possible components of a yen bloc hypothesis: (1) The role of the yen is increasing over time in the exchange rate policies of the East Asian economies. Actions are taken by the countries in the region to stabilize bilateral exchange rates vis-à-vis Japan (and thereby vis-à-vis each other). (2) A regional trading bloc centered on Japan is emerging. Trade between Japan and other East Asian economies has been increasing more rapidly than what would be predicted based on such factors as bilateral GNPs and transportation costs. (3) Stabilization of exchange rates vis-à-vis the yen, item 1 above, is one of the causes of increased intraregional trade, item 2.[2]

This paper examines relevant statistics on all three aspects of a de facto yen bloc. Even if these hypotheses clearly held, there would still be a fourth question to consider: To what extent is the increased role of the yen orchestrated by the Japanese government, or deliberately enhanced by other governments in the region? Throughout, we will concurrently investigate an alternative hypothesis, that East Asia remains part of a U.S. dollar bloc. Our conclusions, to anticipate, are that the yen bloc hypothesis and its constituent propositions stated above do not hold up as empirical characterizations of the 1980s. Rather, East Asia remains more closely affiliated with the dollar bloc.

12.2 The Yen versus the Dollar in East Asia

The theory of optimum currency areas suggests that relatively small trade-oriented countries might want to stabilize the foreign exchange value of their currencies. In the case of the East Asian countries, though they tend to be trade-oriented, it is not clear *which* major foreign currency should be the one to link to.

1. Dornbusch (1992) has suggested that Mexico might repeg its peso. Mancera (1991), however, thinks this unlikely.

2. This paper thus extends the results on bilateral trade in Frankel (1992a) by focusing on the role of links between East Asian currencies and the yen and dollar.

12.2.1 Weights in the Exchange Rate Baskets of East Asian Currencies

We begin by examining the relative importance of the Japanese yen and U.S. dollar in the exchange rate policies of nine East Asian developing countries. We will argue that in the sphere of exchange rate policies, the evidence of an increasing role of the yen is relatively faint, and the U.S. dollar continues to dwarf all other currencies.

Only a few Asian currencies are pegged to the dollar, and none is to the yen.[3] Many are officially or de facto linked to a basket of major currencies. Typically, the weights assigned to various currencies are not announced, but the U.S. dollar and Japanese yen are clearly on the list of candidates. One possible piece of evidence for the formation of a yen bloc in East Asia would be an increasing weight assigned to the yen in these countries' baskets. Since the weights are generally secret, it is particularly important to infer policies by observing actual behavior, rather than relying on official pronouncements.[4] We estimate the implicit weights econometrically.

We use weekly data (Friday close of the London market, from Data Resource Inc.) from the beginning of 1979 to the second week of May of 1992. The test is a regression of the changes in the value of the domestic currency against the changes in the values of foreign currencies.

In the case of a perfect basket peg, ordinary least squares (OLS) regression will uncover the correct weights regardless of the choice of numeraire used to measure "the values" of currencies (assuming only that the list of currencies used to try to explain the exchange rate includes all relevant candidates). When the currency is not perfectly pegged to any basket, the choice of numeraire affects the interpretation of the error term. Frankel (1992a) chooses the inverse of domestic CPI as the numeraire, so as to interpret changes in the values of currencies as the changes in the purchasing power of the currency in question. The CPI data are only available on a monthly basis. We choose here to express the values of all currencies in terms of the Swiss franc. We use the bilateral exchange rate data in our regressions because we want to take advantage of weekly data. (We have tried the same tests using the special drawing right [SDR] as the numeraire, for several of the countries, including Korea, and find very similar results. These results are not reported here.)

3. Reisen and Trotsenburg (1988) discuss the pros and cons of the Four Dragons pegging to the yen. Park and Park (1991) emphasize the problems that fluctuations in the yen/dollar rate create for these four countries. Kwan (1992) argues that the Four, who compete with Japan in third markets, are relatively better candidates to peg to the yen, while the ASEAN countries, who import manufactures from Japan and export commodities, are relatively worse candidates to peg to the yen.

4. Indeed, many countries that claim to follow a basket peg do not in fact do so. For a possible explanation of why countries keep the weights secret, see Lowell (1992) and Takagi (1988). The basic idea is that secret weights allow the governments to devalue their currencies secretly when they so desire. But secret weights undermine the governments' ability to commit credibly to a low-inflation monetary policy.

Two kinds of regressions are reported here for each currency and each sample period. The first one uses the U.S. dollar and Japanese yen as the only regressors (plus a constant to pick up any trend appreciation or depreciation). The second also includes the deutschemark (DM), Australian dollar, and New Zealand dollar in the list. Other European currencies are not used, in part because they are highly correlated with the movement of the DM.

The main findings are as follows: (1) All nine currencies assign heavy weight to the U.S. dollar during each two-year period in the sample. (2) Only one East Asian currency, the Singapore dollar, has throughout the period assigned weight to the yen in addition to the dollar. (3) Several currencies gave a bit of increased weight to the yen during the period 1981–84, when the dollar was strongly appreciating (the Singapore dollar), in 1985–86, as the dollar hit its peak and began to depreciate (the Hong Kong dollar, Indonesian rupiah, Thai baht), or in 1987–88, after the dollar had completed most of its depreciation (the New Taiwan [NT] dollar). (4) The only currencies to place a significant weight on the yen in the most recent subperiod (1991–92), besides the Singapore dollar, are the Malaysian ringgit and the Thai baht.

In summary, the observed role of the yen in the mid-1980s is likely to have been the result of a temporary overvaluation of the U.S. dollar. As far as exchange rate policies are concerned, a more permanent role for the yen is yet to be seen.

We now turn to details of exchange rate targeting for individual currencies. Detailed regression results are reported in tables 12.1–12.9.

Korean Won

The Korean won has been linked more or less solely to the U.S. dollar according to these estimates. The average weight assigned to the dollar in the entire 1979–92 sample is about 0.96.

In the 1979–80 period, the won had an implicit weight of 0.93 on the dollar. The dollar weight was even higher in the 1981–88 period, even though Korea supposedly abandoned its official dollar peg in January 1980 in favor of a basket. No positive weight is found assigned to the Japanese yen in these estimates (except for some faint signs in the 1981–82 and 1987–88 periods), nor to the DM or other currencies. Throughout the sample, the won systematically and statistically significantly depreciated against the numeraire currency (the Swiss franc) for every two-year period, except for the brief period of 1987–88, when the won appreciated.

In the most recent subperiods, 1989–90 and from 1991 to the second week of May of 1992, the weight on the dollar is statistically not different from one (and the adjusted R^2 is about 0.98 in both periods). This finding is particularly interesting in light of the "market average rate" (MAR) system of setting the exchange rate of the won adopted by the Korean authorities. The MAR system was instituted in March 1990, in response to American political pressure, and supposedly allows a greater role for the market in determining the won/dollar

Table 12.1 **Weights Assigned to Foreign Currencies in Determining Changes in Value of Korean Won (January 1, 1979–May 8, 1992)**

Years	Constant	Dollar	Yen	DM	Aus$	NZ$	R^2/D-W	Chow/White
1979–80	−.0030##	.93**	−.10				.31/2.03	.79/1.52
	.0017	.14	.13					
	−.0030	.87*	−.11	−.23	.11	.02	.30/2.02	.74/6.18
	.0018	.35	.13	.37	.41	.29		
1981–82	−.0012**	.98**	.04				.96/2.24	.49/3.00
	.0004	.02	.03					
	−.0012**	1.03**	.06#	.07	−.11	.00	.96/2.19	1.21/6.33
	.0004	.07	.04	.05	.10	.02		
1983–84	−.0008*	.94**	−.00				.94/2.34	1.54/1.03
	.0003	.03	.05					
	−.0008*	.93**	−.00	.01	.00	.00	.93/2.35	.75/12.06
	.0003	.03	.05	.06	.02	.02		
1985–86	−.0007**	.94**	.01				.99/1.45	11.51**/7.24
	.0002	.01	.02					
	−.0007**	.95**	.01	−.01	−.00	−.01	.99/1.45	5.72**/18.12
	.0002	.02	.02	.04	.01	.01		
1987–88	.0021**	.94**	.05##				.98/.97	8.21/7.25
	.0002	.02	.03					
	.0020**	.90**	.02	.04	.05**	−.01	.98/.93	3.36**/14.96
	.0002	.02	.03	.07	.02	.01		
1989–90	−.0004*	1.00**	.01				.98/1.38	3.70/2.81
	.0002	.02	.02					
	−.0005*	1.01**	.00	.03	−.01	−.01	.98/1.39	2.30*/16.67
	.0002	.02	.02	.04	.02	.02		
1991–92	−.0010**	1.03**	−.10*				.98/2.26	1.55/6.43
	.0004	.03	.04					
	−.0009*	.98**	−.10*	−.09##	−.01	.07##	.98/2.24	.84/30.43
	.0004	.05	.04	.06	.03	.05		
1979–92	−.0007*	.96**	−.01				.82/1.94	4.65**/1.76
	.0003	.02	.03					
	−.0007*	.95**	−.01	−.00	.01	.01	.82/1.94	2.29*/4.02
	.0003	.03	.03	.05	.02	.02		

Notes: "R^2" refers to "R^2 adjusted for degrees of freedom." Numbers reported below coefficients are standard errors. All currencies are in terms of units of Swiss francs.

**Statistically significant at the 99 percent level.

*Statistically significant at the 95 percent level.

#Statistically significant at the 90 percent level.

##Statistically significant at the 85 percent level.

rate.[5] But the absence of any fall in the R^2 or dollar coefficient in these estimates suggests that the won is as closely pegged to the dollar as it ever was. We consider the case of the won in detail in the last section of this paper,

5. Monthly estimates of the determination of the won in Frankel (1992b) assign a significant weight to the yen during the period April 1988–March 1990 when currency values are measured in terms of purchasing power, but not when they are measured in terms of the SDR.

Table 12.2 **Weights Assigned to Foreign Currencies in Determining Changes in Value of Singapore Dollar (January 1, 1979–May 8, 1992)**

Years	Constant	Dollar	Yen	DM	Aus$	NZ$	R^2/D-W	Chow/White
1979–80	.0005	.80**	.09*				.82/2.37	.32/3.35
	.0006	.05	.04					
	.0005	.19*	.05##	.21*	.45**	.20**	.89/2.50	4.50**/36.30*
	.0004	.09	.03	.09	.10	.07		
1981–82	.0002	.73**	.18**				.89/2.32	.97/3.19
	.0005	.03	.04					
	.0006	.51**	.10*	.05	.31*	−.00	.90/2.30	2.19/50.16**
	.0005	.09	.05	.08	.14	.03		
1983–84	.0000	.75**	.18**				.91/2.00	3.17*/4.13
	.0003	.03	.05					
	.0001	.73**	.17**	.00	.03	.01	.91/1.99	2.06/12.60
	.0003	.03	.05	.06	.03	.02		
1985–86	−.0015*	.66**	.09				.80/2.28	8.15**/33.99**
	.0007	.05	.07					
	−.0016*	.62**	.10##	.17	.00	.02	.79/2.28	4.66**/43.49**
	.0008	.06	.07	.14	.03	.03		
1987–88	.0008**	.78**	.08#				.94/2.08	.97/9.62
	.0003	.02	.04					
	.0008*	.76**	.08#	.14	−.01	.02	.94/2.03	.70/18.97
	.0003	.03	.04	.10	.03	.02		
1989–90	.0013**	.80**	.17**				.89/2.42	.39/6.22
	.0004	.03	.03					
	.0011**	.86**	.15**	.12##	−.06##	−.04	.90/2.31	.94/28.43
	.0004	.05	.03	.07	.04	.05		
1991–92	.0008	.74**	.15				.81/2.26	2.21/.77
	.0009	.07	.11					
	.0005	.72**	.16##	.31*	−.08	.08	.82/2.36	1.54/14.09
	.0009	.12	.11	.15	.08	.11		
1979–92	.0003##	.75**	.13**				.86/2.28	.55/46.80**
	.0002	.01	.02					
	.0003##	.71**	.12**	.14**	.01	.02##	.86/2.28	1.97/87.20**
	.0002	.02	.02	.04	.02	.01		

Notes: "R^2" refers to "R^2 adjusted for degrees of freedom." Numbers reported below coefficients are standard errors. All currencies are in terms of units of Swiss francs.

**Statistically significant at the 99 percent level.

*Statistically significant at the 95 percent level.

#Statistically significant at the 90 percent level.

##Statistically significant at the 85 percent level.

in light of the special role played by Korea's political relationship with the United States.

Singapore Dollar

The Singapore dollar is the only currency among the nine examined here that assigns weights to both the yen and dollar during the entire sample period (1979–92).

At the beginning of the 1980s, the Singapore dollar moved with a basket of at least five currencies: U.S. dollar, yen, DM, Australian dollar, and New Zealand dollar, with estimated weights of .19, .05, .21, .45, and .20.[6] The weight on the yen was among the lowest, a mere 5 percent, and only marginally significant at the 85 percent level. The Australian dollar had the highest apparent weight (45 percent), but it may be picking up some of the weight that should properly be assigned to the U.S. dollar.

In the early 1980s, the weight on the yen doubled, the weight on the dollar fell slightly, and the weights on other currencies fell sharply. For example, during the 1983–84 period the weights on the U.S. dollar and yen are statistically significant (0.73 and 0.18, respectively), while weights on all the other currencies are statistically not different from zero (these are similar to the results in Frankel [1992a]).

Relative to the numeraire currency, the Singapore dollar depreciated by about 0.15 percent during 1985–86, after controlling for the movement of the U.S. dollar and other currencies relative to the numeraire. But the Singapore dollar appreciated during the subsequent 1987–90 period to more than offset the earlier depreciation.

Hong Kong Dollar

The Hong Kong dollar gives very heavy weight to the U.S. dollar. In the early 1980s the peg was nevertheless somewhat loose. During the period 1987–92, the U.S. dollar peg is close to perfect: a coefficient and R^2 virtually equal to 1.0 and a constant term of zero. The only subperiod when significant weight is granted the yen is 1985–86, when Hong Kong appeared to experiment with a peg to a basket of the two major currencies, presumably to avoid overvaluation from pegging solely to the U.S. dollar during a period when the American currency was very strong.

New Taiwan Dollar

The NT dollar was apparently rigidly pegged to the U.S. dollar with very narrow margin before 1981. The point estimate of the dollar weight during 1979–80 was one, and the R^2 was 1.0. The fluctuation margin widened after 1981. The dollar weight was not statistically different from one during the 1983–84 and 1985–86 periods (and R^2s were above .97), though the value of the NT dollar could deviate somewhat more from that of the U.S. dollar at any given point in time. Prior to 1986, the U.S. dollar was clearly the only currency to which the NT dollar was pegged.

During 1987–88, the yen did receive significant weight (an estimated 13 percent). Why did the yen weight suddenly rise? Since 1986 the U.S. Treasury had been applying pressure to Taiwan and the other newly industrialized countries (NICs) to allow their currencies to appreciate against the dollar; the Amer-

6. The weights do not necessarily add up to one because no such constraint is imposed in the regressions.

Table 12.3 **Weights Assigned to Foreign Currencies in Determining Changes in Value of Hong Kong Dollar (January 1, 1979–May 8, 1992)**

Years	Constant	Dollar	Yen	DM	Aus$	NZ$	R^2/D-W	Chow/White
1979–80	−.0006	.90**	−.01				.71/2.00	1.04/4.10
	.0008	.06	.06					
	.0008	.37**	−.04	.09	.64**	−.04	.71/2.00	1.04/4.10
	.0008	.15	.05	.15	.17	.12		
1981–82	−.0020##	.77**	−.03				.50/2.30	.60/6.14
	.0014	.09	.11					
	−.0016	.59*	−.09	.03	.20	.05	.49/2.26	3.11**/26.47
	.0015	.26	.14	.21	.38	.09		
1983–84	−.0014	.91**	−.13				.39/1.79	1.55/2.59
	.0014	.13	.22					
	−.0013	.92**	−.12	.06	−.05	.02	.37/1.80	.97/12.32
	.0015	.15	.23	.24	.11	.07		
1985–86	−.0002	.95**	.06**				.99/2.78	3.39*/69.39**
	.0002	.01	.02					
	−.0001	.96**	.06**	−.01	.00	−.01	.99/2.77	2.22*/74.76**
	.0002	.02	.02	.04	.01	.01		
1987–88	.0000	.98**	.01				1.00/2.25	.14/.78
	.0000	.01	.01					
−.0000	.98**	.01	−.02	.00	.00.	00	1.00/2.24	.18/4.88
	.0000	.01	.01	.03	.01	.01		
1989–90	−.0000	.99**	.00				.99/2.04	.88/1.55
	.0001	.01	.01					
	−.0000	.99**	.01	−.01	.016#	−.01	.99/2.09	.50/6.10
	.0001	.01	.01	.02	.009	.01		
1991–92	.0000	1.01**	−.01				.99/2.49	.31/2.71
	.0002	.02	.02					
	.0001	1.00**	.01	.01	.02	.04	.99/2.50	1.06/8.31
	.0002	.03	.02	.03	.02	.03		
1979–92	−.0007*	.92**	−.00				.76/2.04	6.37**/3.26
	.0003	.02	.03					
	−.0007*	.89**	−.01	.02	.01	.02	.76/2.03	3.22**/9.51
	.0003	.03	.03	.06	.03	.02		

Notes: "R^2" refers to "R^2 adjusted for degrees of freedom." Numbers reported below coefficients are standard errors. All currencies are in terms of units of Swiss francs.

**Statistically significant at the 99 percent level.

*Statistically significant at the 95 percent level.

#Statistically significant at the 90 percent level.

##Statistically significant at the 85 percent level.

ican government was disappointed that its trade balance had not yet responded to the 1985–86 Plaza-induced depreciation of the dollar against the yen and European currencies and thought that part of the explanation might lie in the choice of the NICs and other countries to follow the dollar down. Taiwan, with a visible stockpiling of international reserves that was close to a world record, was a particular target. The Taiwanese apparently responded to the pressure to

Table 12.4 **Weights Assigned to Foreign Currencies in Determining Changes in Value of Taiwan Dollar (January 1, 1979–May 8, 1992)**

Years	Constant	Dollar	Yen	DM	Aus$	NZ$	R^2/D-W	Chow/White
1979–80	.0000	1.00**	.00				1.00/2.83	.25/103.0*
	.0000	.00	.00					
	.0000	1.00**	.00	.00	.00	.00	1.00/2.83	.35/103.0**
	.0000	.00	.00	.00	.00	.00		
1981–82	−.0008	.94**	.04				.82/1.92	.44/9.89
	.0008	.05	.07					
	−.0004	.74**	−.03	−.01	.29	.01	.82/1.93	.39/17.45
	.0008	.15	.09	.12	.23	.05		
1983–84	.0000	1.01**	−.01				.97/1.62	1.52/3.19
	.0002	.02	.04					
	.0000	1.01**	−.01	.02	−.00	.00	.97/1.63	.95/7.28
	.0002	.02	.04	.04	.02	.01		
1985–86	.0009**	.99**	.01				.98/1.14	8.57**/2.95
	.0003	.02	.02					
	.0009**	.99**	.02	.04	.00	−.01	.98/1.17	4.89**/12.17
	.0003	.02	.03	.05	.01	.01		
1987–88	.0020**	.94**	.13*				.92/.85	10.36**/5.79
	.0004	.03	.06					
	.0020**	.97**	.13*	−.19	−.01	.01	.92/.86	5.06**/20.12
	.0004	.04	.06	.15	.04	.03		
1989–90	.0006	.99**	.09				.65/2.41	3.15*/7.04
	.0011	.08	.08					
	.0006	.83**	.05	.06	.01	.18	.65/2.45	1.33/25.77
	.0011	.12	.08	.19	.10	.13		
1991–92	.0011*	.94**	.08				.94/1.93	.63/3.19
	.0005	.04	.07					
	.0009#	.94**	.10##	.15#	−.09*	.08	.95/1.92	1.02/51.47**
	.0005	.07	.06	.09	.05	.07		
1979–92	.0005*	.96**	.05*				.88/2.07	5.03**/2.96
	.0002	.02	.02					
	.0005*	.94**	.04*	.05	.01	.01	.88/2.07	2.55*/16.37
	.0002	.02	.02	.04	.02	.01		

Notes: "R^2" refers to "R^2 adjusted for degrees of freedom." Numbers reported below coefficients are standard errors. All currencies are in terms of units of Swiss francs.

**Statistically significant at the 99 percent level.

*Statistically significant at the 95 percent level.

#Statistically significant at the 90 percent level.

##Statistically significant at the 85 percent level.

appreciate their currency by putting some weight in their basket on the appreciating yen, as well as by appreciating steadily against the basket overall.

Malaysian Ringgit

At the beginning of the 1980s, Malaysia had a diversified basket for the ringgit. The yen was clearly included in this basket during 1981–82. The large weight on the dollar fluctuates during the eighties, between .64 and .90. The

Table 12.5 **Weights Assigned to Foreign Currencies in Determining Changes in Value of Malaysian Ringgit (January 1, 1979–May 8, 1992)**

Years	Constant	Dollar	Yen	DM	Aus$	NZ$	R^2/D-W	Chow/White
1979–80	.0001	.87**	.07##				.80/2.02	.38/2.95
	.0006	.05	.05					
	.0001	.11	.02	.23*	.64**	.18*	.88/2.00	3.90**/57.07**
	.0005	.09	.04	.10	.11	.08		
1981–82	−.0002	.75**	.15**				.90/1.95	.20/.99
	.0005	.03	.04					
	−.0000	.65**	.11*	.08	.12	.01	.90/1.92	1.99/16.29
	.0005	.09	.05	.07	.14	.03		
1983–84	.0008	.64**	−.16				.25/2.44	6.68**/10.43
	.0012	.12	.21					
	.0009	.64**	−.18	−.12	−.55	.02	.23/2.43	3.59**/24.63
	.0014	.14	.21	.23	.11	.06		
1985–86	−.0017**	.76**	−.04#				.86/2.04	2.09/6.17
	.0006	.04	.06					
	−.0020**	.77**	−.04#	−.20	−.06	.02	.86/1.96	.86*/33.03*
	.0006	.05	.06	.12	.03*	.03		
1987–88	−.0008*	.74**	.11*				.90/1.92	.43/2.44
	.0004	.03	.05					
	−.0008*	.71**	.06	−.16	.08*	−.01	.90/1.95	.37/7.17
	.0004	.04	.06	.13	.03	.02		
1989–90	−.0000	.90**	.07**				.96/1.84	.77/.84
	.0003	.02	.02					
	−.0001	.88**	.04*	.09#	−.02	.04	.96/1.86	.76/17.90
	.0003	.03	.02	.05	.02	.03		
1991–92	.0012*	.80**	.14*				.94/1.45	6.29**/6.18
	.0005	.04	.06					
	.0010*	.77**	.14*	.16#	−.02	.04	.94/1.41	3.40/20.34
	.0005	.07	.06	.09	.05	.07		
1979–92	−.0003	.78**	.07**				.79/2.19	2.70*/2.29
	.0003	.02	.02					
	−.0002	.73**	.06*	.12*	.01	.03##	.79/2.19	1.87/4.38
	.0003	.03	.02	.05	.02	.02		

Notes: "R^2" refers to "R^2 adjusted for degrees of freedom." Numbers reported below coefficients are standard errors. All currencies are in terms of units of Swiss francs.

**Statistically significant at the 99 percent level.

*Statistically significant at the 95 percent level.

#Statistically significant at the 90 percent level.

##Statistically significant at the 85 percent level.

yen, though significant in the early 1980s, lost its influence in the period 1983–86, and then reemerged with a statistically significant weight later in the decade, reaching .14 in 1991–92.

Indonesian Rupiah

Up to 1982, the rupiah was tightly pegged to the U.S. dollar, which accounted for 97 percent of fluctuations. Beginning in 1983, the peg became

Table 12.6 **Weights Assigned to Foreign Currencies in Determining Changes in Value of Indonesian Rupiah (January 1, 1979–May 8, 1992)**

Years	Constant	Dollar	Yen	DM	Aus$	NZ$	R^2/D-W	Chow/White
1979–80	.0000	1.00**	−.00				1.00/2.99	.22/1.70
	.0000	.00	.00					
	.0000	.99**	−.00	−.00	−.01**	.02**	1.00/2.49	5.38**/33.48*
	.0000	.00	.00	.00	.00	.00		
1981–82	−.0010**	.99**	.00				.98/1.65	3.10*/4.10
	.0003	.02	.02					
	−.0010**	1.01**	.01	−.03	−.01	.00	.98/1.62	1.88/11.73
	.0003	.05	.03	.04	.08	.02		
1983–84	−.0044	.86**	.32				.13/1.99	.51/.96
	.0032	.03	.50					
	−.0044	.84**	.31	.03	.04	−.00	.10/2.00	.37/3.19
	.0033	.33	.51	.55	.26	.15		
1985–86	−.0050	.76**	.91**				.30/1.97	.77/9.60
	.0034	.23	.34					
	−.0062##	.81**	.97**	.61	−.19	−.02	.29/1.97	1.68/25.84
	.0039	.30	.35	.73	.17	.17		
1987–88	−.0007**	.92**	.08**				.99/2.11	1.82/19.78*
	.0002	.01	.02					
	−.0007**	.93**	.08**	.02	−.01	−.00	.99/2.17	.92/25.67
	.0002	.02	.02	.05	.01	.01		
1989–90	−.0008**	.94**	.06**				.97/2.93	.57/5.08
	.0003	.02	.02					
	−.0008**	.92**	.06**	.05	.02	−.01	.97/2.89	.73/12.43
	.0003	.03	.02	.04	.02	.03		
1991–92	−.0009**	.97**	.01				.99/2.30	2.33/1.40
	.0002	.01	.02					
	−.0009**	.98**	.01	−.04	.01	−.01	.99/2.30	2.06/13.12
	.0002	.02	.02	.03	.02	.02		
1979–92	−.0018*	.95**	.16*				.44/2.04	1.97/4.44
	.0007	.05	.07					
	−.0018*	1.01**	.17*	−.00	−.07	.01	.44/2.04	1.30/12.93
	.0008	.07	.07	.13	.06	.05		

Notes: "R^2" refers to "R^2 adjusted for degrees of freedom." Numbers reported below coefficients are standard errors. All currencies are in terms of units of Swiss francs.

**Statistically significant at the 99 percent level.

*Statistically significant at the 95 percent level.

#Statistically significant at the 90 percent level.

##Statistically significant at the 85 percent level.

much looser, though the dollar still had the predominant role. Around 1985, a dramatic change occurred in Indonesian exchange rate policy: the yen suddenly received significant weight. In fact, the point estimate on the yen is actually bigger than that on the dollar for the subperiod 1985–86. This is the period when Indonesia substantially increased the share of its international debt denominated in yen (see table 12.11). Subsequently the yen weight declined, disappearing altogether during the most recent subsample (1991–92).

Philippine Peso

The peso has been firmly pegged or closely linked to the U.S. dollar. At the same time, against the numeraire currency (Swiss franc), the central par value of the peso has also been steadily devalued more than the dollar. So far, it has shown absolutely no sign of following the movement of the yen.

Table 12.7 **Weights Assigned to Foreign Currencies in Determining Changes in Value of Philippine Peso (January 1, 1979–May 8, 1992)**

Years	Constant	Dollar	Yen	DM	Aus$	NZ$	R^2/D-W	Chow/White
1979–80	−.0003	1.01**	−.02				.83/2.81	.26/.95
	.0006	.05	.04					
	−.0003	1.15**	.00	.12	−.12	−.08	.83/2.82	1.12/12.67
	.0006	.12	.05	.13	.14	.09		
1981–82	−.0018**	1.01**	.02				.97/1.93	1.75/1.67
	.0003	.02	.03					
	−.0019**	1.09**	.05	.10	−.14	−.00	.97/1.97	2.60*/20.90
	.0003	.06	.03	.05	.09	.02		
1983–84	−.0083*	1.33**	.05				.19/2.07	.29/3.19
	.0036	.33	.56					
	−.0085*	1.37**	−.03	−.76	.00	−.02	.18/2.06	.25/13.38
	.0036	.37	.57	.61	.28	.16		
1985–86	.0004	1.18**	−.18				.69/2.01	.86/7.47
	.0015	.09	.14					
	−.0002	1.11**	−.19	.45	−.09	.12	.70/1.99	1.04/57.11**
	.0015	.12	.14	.29	.07	.07		
1987–88	−.0003	.99**	−.04				.92/2.34	.03/4.48
	.0004	.03	.06					
	−.0003	.93**	−.09	.00	.06	.01	.92/2.34	.48/23.11
	.0004	.04	.06	.15	.04	.03		
1989–90	−.0024*	1.11**	.05				.75/2.22	1.39/1.67
	.0010	.07	.07					
	−.0023*	1.16**	.08	−.08	.02	−.06	.75/2.23	.83/4.57
	.0010	.11	.08	.17	.09	.11		
1991–92	.0007	1.03**	.01				.71/2.56	.52/2.34
	.0015	.12	.18					
	.0007	1.19**	.05	−.06	−.23#	.05	.71/2.27	.80/20.61
	.0015	.21	.18	.26	.14	.19		
1979–92	−.0018**	1.07**	−.01				.54/2.06	.75/3.00
	.0006	.04	.06					
	−.0018**	1.09**	−.01	−.05	−.05	.03	.54/2.05	.68/10.42
	.0006	.06	.06	.11	.05	.04		

Notes: "R^2" refers to "R^2 adjusted for degrees of freedom." Numbers reported below coefficients are standrard errors. All currencies are in terms of units of Swiss francs.

**Statistically significant at the 99 percent level.

*Statistically significant at the 95 percent level.

#Statistically significant at the 90 percent level.

##Statistically significant at the 85 percent level.

Thai Baht

The baht too has followed relatively closely the movement of the dollar. There was no clear role of the yen in Thai exchange rate policy prior to 1984. But the yen received a statistically significant weight of 0.10 during 1985–86, while the dollar weight declined to 0.71, from 0.91 at the beginning of the

Table 12.8 Weights Assigned to Foreign Currencies in Determining Changes in Value of Tahi Baht (January 1, 1979–May 8, 1992)

Years	Constant	Dollar	Yen	DM	Aus$	NZ$	R^2/D-W	Chow/White
1979–80	−.0001##	1.01**	.00				1.00/2.03	3.30/12.44
	.0000	.01	.01					
	−.0002##	1.02**	.01	.00	−.00	−.01	.99/1.94	2.30*/32.07*
	.0001	.02	.01	.02	.02	.02		
1981–82	−.0010	.95**	.05				.76/2.04	.79/1.04
	.0010	.06	.08					
	−..014	1.16**	.13	.17	−.37	.00	.76/1.99	.61/7.40
	.0011	.19	.10	.15	.27	.06		
1983–84	−.0028##	1.31**	.26				.57/2.17	2.92*/44.74**
	.0016	.15	.25					
	−.0029##	1.32**	.26	−.03	.01	−.03	.56/2.18	1.60/60.08**
	.0017	.17	.26	.28	.13	.07		
1985–86	.0008#	.73**	.10*				.93/2.31	6.95**/9.47
	.0004	.03	.04					
	−.0009	.71**	.10*	.08	−.01	.02	.93/2.24	4.04**/34.31*
	.0004	.03	.04	.08	.02	.02		
1987–88	.0002	.84**	−.00				.69/2.53	.35/2.25
	.0009	.06	.12					
	.0003	.90**	.08	.33	−.07	−.05	.69/2.47	1.54/20.39
	.0009	.09	.13	.30	.07	.05		
1989–90	−.0001	.89**	.04				.86/2.99	1.00/1.98
	.0001	.04	.04					
	−.0000	.74**	.02	.11	.12**	.04	.88/2.91	2.50*/41.02**
	.0005	.06	.04	.09	.04	.06		
1991–92	−.0001	.82**	.12**				.99/2.61	.38/4.90
	.0002	.01	.02					
	−.0002	.81**	.12**	.07**	−.01	.01	.99/2.70	.55/26.35
	.0002	.02	.02	.03	.02	.02		
1979–92	−.0004	.91**	.05##				.75/2.24	5.45**/7.33
	.0003	.02	.03					
	−.0004	.92**	.05##	.03	−.01	−.00	.75/2.24	3.14**/17.81
	.0003	.03	.03	.06	.03	.02		

Notes: "R^2" refers to "R^2 adjusted for degrees of freedom." Numbers reported below coefficients are standard errors. All currencies are in terms of units of Swiss francs.

**Statistically significant at the 99 percent level.

*Statistically significant at the 95 percent level.

#Statistically significant at the 90 percent level.

##Statistically significant at the 85 percent level.

sample. Evidently Thailand—like Singapore, Hong Kong, and Indonesia—shifted a bit from the dollar to the yen in the mid-1980s, when the dollar was near its peak. During 1987–90, this shift was reversed. And then from 1991 to May 1992, the yen weight rose again to 0.12 (significant at the 99 percent level), with the remaining weight divided between the U.S. dollar and DM (0.81 and 0.07, respectively). As with the other East Asian currencies studied, the U.S. dollar currently remains more important than the yen.

Chinese Yuan

China claims to be on a basket peg. But the U.S. dollar is the only currency with whose value the yuan is highly correlated. From 1987 onward, the yuan has been relatively rigidly pegged to the dollar, although devaluations of the par have also been frequent, particularly toward the end of the sample period. Neither the yen nor any other non–U.S. dollar currency seems to play a role in the external value of the yuan.

To summarize, to date the U.S. dollar has remained the dominant currency to which all the East Asian economies pay attention in their exchange rate policies. The Japanese yen occupies some weight in some countries, but is still far from replacing the U.S. dollar in the region. We now briefly consider other measures of international currency use, before turning to trade.

12.2.2 The Use of the Dollar and Yen in Invoicing

It is interesting to observe that, even though the share of the Japanese economy in the world economy has risen substantially, the internationalization of the yen has not tempted East Asian governments to link their currencies more strongly with the yen. Despite the fact that trading with Japan has become increasingly important for the East Asian developing countries, and reducing exchange rate volatility is thought to help trade in goods and services, the yen remains in low profile. Why? Developing and developed countries alike are known to invoice their trade in U.S. dollars, rather than in their own or trading partners' currencies. Given trade invoiced in dollars, pegging to the dollar creates less exchange rate risk than pegging to the yen. But then the question becomes, Why is the dollar still the dominant currency in invoicing even for trade with Japan?

There is some evidence that the yen is being used more widely to invoice lending and trade in Asia. The countries that incurred large international debts in the 1970s and early 1980s subsequently shifted the composition away from dollar-denominated debt and toward yen-denominated debt. Table 12.10 shows that the share of trade denominated in yen is greater in Southeast Asia than in other regions and that there was an especially rapid increase from 1983 to 1990 in the share of Southeast Asian imports denominated in yen. Table 12.11 shows that the yen share among five major Asian debtors nearly doubled between 1980 and 1988, entirely at the expense of the dollar (Tavlas and Ozeki [1991, 1992] give further statistics and discussion). It is too early to tell whether this

Table 12.9 **Weights Assigned to Foreign Currencies in Determining Changes in Value of Chinese Yuan (January 1, 1979–May 8, 1992)**

Years	Constant	Dollar	Yen	DM	Aus$	NZ$	R^2/D-W	Chow/White
1979–80	.0007	1.09**	.02				.76/2.53	.46/10.41
	.0009	.07	.06					
	.0008	1.00**	.02	.02	.05	.05	.75/2.55	.39/33.72
	.0009	.17	.06	.18	.20	.14		
1981–82	−.0020**	.05**	.14*				.65/1.99	1.36/4.73
	.0008	.05	.06					
	−.0009	.10	.01	.28**	.38*	.12**	.72/1.89	1.70/13.16
	.0007	.13	.07	.10	.19	.04		
1983–84	−.0023**	.53**	−.07				.42/1.95	7.81**/4.90
	.0008	.07	.12					
	−.0022**	.53**	−.04	.25#	−.05	.02	.44/1.97	4.38**/20.79
	.0008	.08	.12	.13	.06	.03		
1985–86	−.0027#	1.02**	−.26#				.60/2.05	.58/4.47
	.0015	.09	.14					
	−.0023##	.94**	−.28#	−.07	.09	.05	.60/2.08	1.34/33.03*
	.0016	.12	.14	.30	.07	.07		
1987–88	.0000	1.00**	.006				1.00/3.10	1.73/11.39*
	.0000	.00	.004					
	−.0000	1.00**	.005	−.01	.00	.00	1.00/3.09	1.00/20.48
	.0000	.00	.005	.01	.00	.00		
1989–90	−.0036##	1.04**	−.20				.24/2.09	.11/1.36
	.0025	.19	.18					
	−.0034	1.20**	−.10	−.49	−.03	−.08	.22/2.15	.68/11.41
	.0026	.28	.20	.43	.22	.30		
1991–92	−.0007**	.98**	−.03				.99/2.15	.69/5.79
	.0002	.02	.03					
	−.0006**	.98**	−.02	−.55	−.05**	.05#	.99/1.78	1.34/29.7
	.0002	.03	.03	.04	.02	.03		
1979–92	−.0018**	.87**	−.04				.54/2.05	8.99**/2.14
	.0005	.04	.05					
	−.0017**	.79**	−.06	.05	.06##	.04	.54/2.06	5.71**/10.97
	.0005	.05	.05	.09	.04	.03		

Notes: "R^2" refers to "R^2 adjusted for degrees of freedom." Numbers reported below coefficients are standard errors. All currencies are in terms of units of Swiss francs.

**Statistically significant at the 99 percent level.

*Statistically significant at the 95 percent level.

#Statistically significant at the 90 percent level.

##Statistically significant at the 85 percent level.

increase of the role of the yen is a permanent trend. But for present purposes, the key point is that the share of the yen in the denomination of trade and finance has not increased anywhere nearly as rapidly as has Japan's share in East Asian trade.

Why should the dollar rather than the yen continue to be the preferred invoicing currency? Several explanations are generally given. First, short-term

Table 12.10 Share of the Yen in Denomination of Foreign Trade (%)

	Denomination of Exports		Denomination of Imports	
	Southeast Asia	All Regions	Southeast Asia	All Regions
1983	48.0	40.4	2.0	3.0
1986	37.5	35.5	9.2	9.7
1987	36.3	34.7	13.9	11.6
1988	41.2	34.3	17.5	13.3
1989	43.5	34.7	19.5	14.1
1990	48.9	37.5	19.4	14.4

Source: Japanese Ministry of Finance, *Annual Report,* as reported in Tavlas and Ozeki (1992, 33).

Table 12.11 Yen Share in Debt Denomination and Official Reserve Holdings (%)

	Yen Share in External Debt						Yen Share in Official Holdings	
Year	Indonesia	Korea	Malaysia	Philippines	Thailand	Total	Asia*	World
1980	20.0	16.6	19.0	22.0	25.5	19.5	13.9	4.4
1981	19.3	14.1	16.9	20.6	23.2	17.8	15.5	4.2
1982	21.0	12.3	13.3	19.2	24.0	17.2	17.6	4.7
1983	23.3	12.5	14.2	20.0	27.3	18.5	15.5	5.0
1984	25.0	12.8	21.2	20.0	29.2	20.3	16.3	5.8
1985	31.7	16.7	26.4	24.9	36.1	25.8	26.9	8.0
1986	33.9	22.0	30.4	25.5	39.9	29.3	22.9	7.9
1987	39.4	27.2	35.7	35.2	43.1	36.0	30.0	7.5
1988	39.3	29.5	37.1	40.5	43.5	37.9	26.7	7.7
1989	35.2	26.6	36.6	32.6	40.9	35.7	17.5	7.9
1990							17.1	9.1

Source: Tavlas and Ozeki (1992, 39).
*Selected Asian countries (not including Japan).

financial markets, particularly bankers' acceptances, are not as well-developed in Japan as in, for example, New York or London, so that the yen is a less convenient currency in which to finance trade. One possibility is that Japan itself resists the internationalization of the yen in order to avoid large fluctuations of its reserves, or to avoid destabilizing effects on its domestic price level, and thus that the slow internationalization of Japanese financial markets is government policy.[7] Second, a large percentage of Japanese trade is conducted by the huge trading firms called *sogo shosha;* they are more able to diversify and

7. At the time of the yen/dollar talks in 1984, the Japanese government was not enthusiastic about internationalizing the yen (Frankel 1984). More recently, some Japanese have come to favor it. Suzuki (1991, 26–30) thinks that internationalizing the yen in East Asia would be a good idea.

hedge claims and liabilities in a foreign currency than would be a small exporter or importer. Third, oil, minerals, and other raw materials and basic commodities occupy a large share of trade in East Asia, because Japan must import so much and Southeast Asia exports so much; such commodities tend everywhere to be invoiced in dollars. Fourth, a high percentage of East Asian trade is with the United States and the rest of the Western Hemisphere, where the dollar is the dominant international currency. Fifth, Japanese firms are believed to undertake "pricing to market," especially in the U.S. export market, because they are readier than U.S. firms to suffer short-run fluctuations in their profits for the sake of maintaining market share.[8]

There is a strong "multiple equilibrium" or "coordination" aspect to the international currency problem. Krugman (1980, 1984) modeled the worldwide economies of scale in the choice of international currency. Any country expecting to use the dollar as the invoicing currency for the next transaction prefers to use the dollar as the invoicing currency in this round. The result is that there are multiple (locally stable) equilibria in the choice of international currency, and the dollar (or the pound before it) could remain the dominant currency even after the patterns of trade and production have shifted.

As long as the dollar remains the dominant invoicing currency in international trade and lending, it makes sense for the East Asian economies to continue to assign heavy weights to the dollar. Of course, the economies-of-scale analysis that applies to the choice of an international currency for invoicing trade also applies to the choice of an international currency for pegging and other uses.

An analogy with the English language can be, and has been, made. A foreign visitor to China is likely to encounter on the street two requests more than any others: a request for dollars (in exchange for local currency) and a request to speak English (so that the person can practice). It is not the superior intrinsic qualities of the language, or the currency, that they are after, nor is it especially the prestige of the United States. Rather, English is rapidly becoming the lingua franca of Asia, as it is of the world, simply because the world needs a lingua franca, and there is no other obvious choice. The same may be true of the dollar.

12.3 Is There a Regional Trade Bloc Centered on Japan?

There is no standard definition of a "trade bloc." A useful definition might be a group of countries who are concentrating their trading relationships with each other, in preference to the rest of the world. One might wish to add to the definition the criterion that this concentration is the outcome of government

8. Reasons for the disproportionately low use of the yen in invoicing are given in Frankel (1984), Ito (1992), and Tavlas and Ozeki (1992). Frankel (1991c) considers the international currency question and gives further references.

policy, or perhaps of factors that are noneconomic in origin, such as a common language or culture. In two out of the three parts of the world, there have clearly been recent deliberate political steps toward economic integration, as noted at the outset of this paper.

In East Asia, by contrast, overt preferential trading arrangements or other political moves to promote regional economic integration are lacking. The Association of Southeast Asian Nations (ASEAN) countries, to be sure, are taking steps in the direction of turning what used to be a regional security group into a free trade area of sorts. But when Americans worry, as they are wont to do, about a trading bloc forming in Asia, it is generally not ASEAN that concerns them. Rather it is the possibility of an East Asian bloc dominated by Japan.

In fact, Japan is unusual among major countries in *not* having preferential trading arrangements with smaller neighboring countries. But the hypothesis that has been put forward is that Japan is forming an economic bloc in the same way that it runs its economy: by means of policies that are implicit, indirect, and invisible. Specifically, the hypothesis is that Japan operates, by means of such instruments as flows of aid, foreign direct investment, and other forms of finance, to influence its neighbors' trade toward itself (for one of many examples, see Dornbusch 1989). This is a hypothesis that should not be accepted uncritically, but rather needs to be examined empirically.

We must begin by acknowledging the obvious: the greatly increased economic weight of East Asian countries in the world economy. The rapid outward-oriented growth of Japan, followed by the four East Asian NICs and more recently by some of the other ASEAN countries, is one of the most remarkable and widely remarked trends in the world economy over the last three decades. But when one asks whether a yen bloc is forming in East Asia, one is presumably asking something more than whether the economies are getting larger, or even whether economic flows among them are increasing. One must ask whether the share of intraregional trade is higher, or increasing more rapidly, than would be predicted based on such standard economic factors as the GNP or growth rates of the countries involved.

12.3.1 Adjusting Intraregional Trade for Growth

Table 12.12 reports three alternative ways of computing intraregional trade bias. The first part of the table is based on a simple breakdown of trade (exports plus imports) undertaken by countries in East Asia, into trade with other members of the same regional grouping versus trade with other parts of the world.[9] For comparison, the analogous statistics are reported for Western Europe (the EC12) and for North America (the United States, Canada, and Mexico).

The share of intraregional trade in East Asia increased from 33 percent in 1980 to 37 percent in 1989. Pronouncements that a clubbish trade bloc is form-

9. These statistics are presented in more detail in table 1 in Frankel (1991a).

Table 12.12 **Summary Measures of Intraregional Trade Biases**

	Year	Pacific Asia	North America	European Community
1. Intraregional trade/total trade	1980	.33	.32	.51
	1986	.32	.35	.57
	1989	.37	.36	.59
2. Intraregional bias holding constant for size of exports	1980	2.2	1.9	1.3
	1989	1.9	1.9	1.5
		Pacific Asia	Western Hemisphere	European Community
3. Intraregional bias holding constant for GNP, population, distance, etc.	1980	.70	.53	.23
	1985	.40	.34	.44
	1990	.60	.97	.46

Sources: 1, Schott (1991); *Direction of Trade,* (Washington, D.C.: International Monetary Fund, various issues), as computed in Frankel (1991c). 2, computed as the ratio of line 1 to shares of world trade, as in Frankel (1991a). 3, gravity regressions, reported in tables 2, 3, and 4, respectively, Frankel (1992a). They include also significant coefficients on the APEC bloc, among other variables.

ing in the region are usually based on figures such as these. But the numbers are deceptive. It is easy to be misled by intraregional trade shares such as those reported in table 12.12. If one allows for the phenomenon that most of the East Asian countries in the 1980s experienced rapid growth in *total* output and trade, then in fact there has been no movement toward intraregional bias in the evolving pattern of trade. The increase in the intraregional share of trade that is observed in table 12.12 could be entirely due to the increase in the economic size of the countries. A simple back-of-the-envelope calculation that corrects trade shares for the size of the partner countries, reported in table 12.12, item 2, shows that this is indeed the case.[10] The East Asian bias toward within-region trade, far from rising, actually diminished slightly in the 1980s!

12.3.2 A Test on Bilateral Trade Flows

The analysis should be elaborated by use of a systematic framework for measuring what patterns of bilateral trade are normal around the world: the so-called gravity model.[11] A dummy variable can then be added to represent when both countries in a given pair belong to the same regional grouping, and one

10. Frankel (1992a). This conclusion also emerges for time-spans stretching farther back in history. Economists such as Drysdale and Garnaut (1992), Anderson and Norheim (1992), and Petri (1992a) have been reporting this for some time, based on similar calculations of "intensity of trade indexes" or "double-relative measures."

11. Wang and Winters (1991) and Hamilton and Winters (1992) have recently applied the gravity model to the question of potential Eastern European trade patterns, and Wang (1992) to China's trade. They and Frankel (1992a) give references on the gravity model.

can check whether the level and trend in the East Asia/Pacific grouping exceeds that in other groupings. We do not currently have measures of historical, political, cultural, and linguistic ties. Thus it will be possible to interpret the dummy variables as reflecting these factors, rather than necessarily as reflecting discriminatory trade policies. Perhaps we should not regret the merging of these different factors in one term, because as noted there are in any case no overt preferential trading arrangements on which theories of a Japanese trading bloc could rely.

The dependent variable is trade (exports plus imports), in log form, between pairs of countries in a given year. We have 63 countries in our data set, so that there are 1,953 data points (= 63 × 62/2) for a given year. The goal, again, is to see how much of the high level of trade within the East Asian region can be explained by simple economic factors common to bilateral trade throughout the world and how much is left over to be attributed to a special regional effect.[12]

One would expect the two most important factors in explaining bilateral trade flows to be the geographical distance between the two countries and their economic sizes. These factors are the essence of the gravity model. A large part of the apparent bias toward intraregional trade is certainly due to simple geographical proximity. Indeed Krugman (1991b) suggests that most of it may be due to proximity, so that the three trading blocs are welfare-improving "natural" groupings (as distinct from "unnatural" trading arrangements between distant trading partners such as the United States and Israel). Although the importance of distance and transportation costs is clear, there is not a lot of theoretical guidance on precisely how they should enter. A bit of experimentation with functional forms is described in Frankel (1992a). We also add a dummy ADJACENT variable to indicate when two countries share a common land border.

The equation to be estimated is:

$$\begin{aligned}\log(T_{ij}) = {} & \alpha + \beta_1 \log(GNP_i GNP_j) + \beta_2 \log[(GNP/pop)_i (GNP/pop)_j] \\ & + \beta_3 \log(\text{DISTANCE}) + \beta_4(\text{ADJACENT}) + \gamma_1(\text{EEC}_{ij}) \\ & + \gamma_2(\text{WH}_{ij}) + \gamma_3(\text{ASIA}_{ij}) + u_{ij}.\end{aligned}$$

The last four explanatory factors are dummy variables.

Entering GNPs in product form can be easily justified by the modern theory of trade under imperfect competition.[13] In addition there is reason to believe that GNP per capita has a positive effect, for a given size: as countries become

12. The list of countries, regional groupings, and cities used to compute distances, is given in an appendix to Frankel (1992a).

13. The specification implies that trade between two equal-sized countries (say, of size .5) will be greater than trade between a large and a small country (say, of sizes .9 and .1). This property of models with imperfect competition is not a property of the classical Heckscher-Ohlin theory of comparative advantage. See Helpman (1987) and Helpman and Krugman (1985, section 1.5). Foundations for the gravity model are also offered by Anderson (1979) and other papers surveyed by Deardorff (1984, 503–6).

more developed, they tend to specialize more and to trade more. Other gravity model studies often estimate separate equations for exports and imports and allow the coefficients on GNP and GNP per capita (or, equivalently, population) to differ between the importing and exporting country. When we aggregated exports and imports, we implicitly assumed that these elasticities were symmetric. Our motivation in estimating the equation in terms of exports *plus* imports is to eliminate the macroeconomic factors, such as real exchange rate fluctuations and relative positions in the business cycle, that necessarily influence the level of exports and the level of imports considered individually.[14]

The results are reported in tables 2, 3, and 4 of Frankel (1992a). We found all three standard variables to be highly significant statistically (> 99 percent level). The coefficient on the log of distance was about −.56, when the adjacency variable (which is also highly significant statistically) is included at the same time. This means that when the distance between two nonadjacent countries is higher by 1 percent, the trade between them falls by about .56 percent.

The estimated coefficient on GNP per capita is about .29 as of 1980, indicating that richer countries do indeed trade more, though this term declines during the 1980s, reaching .08 in 1990. The estimated coefficient for the log of the product of the two countries' GNPs is about .75, indicating that, though trade increases with size, it increases less than proportionately (holding GNP per capita constant). This presumably reflects the widely known pattern that small economies tend to be more open to international trade than larger, more diversified, economies.

If there were nothing to the notion of trading blocs, then these basic variables would soak up most of the explanatory power. There would be little left to attribute to a dummy variable representing whether two trading partners are both located in the same region. In this case, the level and trend in intraregional trade would be due solely to the proximity of the countries and their rapid rate of overall economic growth. But we found that dummy variables for intraregional trade *are* statistically significant, both in East Asia and elsewhere in the world. If two countries are both located in the Western Hemisphere for example, they will trade with each other by an estimated 70 percent more than they would otherwise, even after taking into account distance and the other gravity variables (exp(.53) = 1.70). Intraregional trade goes beyond what can be explained naturally by proximity.

It is as yet difficult to draw conclusions regarding economic welfare, because the empirical equation is too far removed from theoretical foundations. But it seems possible that the amount of intraregional bias explained by proximity, as compared to explicit or implicit regional trading arrangements, is small enough in our results that those arrangements are welfare-reducing. This

14. The results in Wang and Winters (1991) and Hamilton and Winters (1992) show coefficient estimates for importing and exporting countries that are fairly close, but nonetheless show nonoverlapping confidence intervals. Our estimates are extremely close to theirs for the importing country, which are slightly smaller than theirs for the exporting country.

could be the case if trade-diversion outweighs trade creation. Inspired by Krugman's (1991a, 1991b) "natural trading bloc" terminology, we might then refer to the observed intraregional trade bias as evidence of "supernatural" trading blocs.

When the boundaries of the Asian bloc are drawn along the lines of those suggested by Malaysian Prime Minister Mahatir in his proposed East Asian Economic Caucus (EAEC), which excludes Australia and New Zealand, the coefficient on the Asian bloc appears to be stronger than that on the European or Western Hemisphere blocs. Even when the boundaries are drawn in this way, however, there is no evidence of an *increase* in the intraregional bias of Asian trade during the 1980s: the estimated coefficient actually decreases somewhat from 1980 to 1990. Thus the gravity results corroborate the back-of-the-envelope calculation noted in section 12.3.1. The precise pattern is a decrease in the first half of the decade, followed by a very slight increase in the second half, matching the results of Petri (1991).[15] None of these changes over time is statistically significant.

It is perhaps surprising that the estimated *level* of intraregional trade bias was higher in East Asia as of 1980 than in the other two regions. One possible explanation is that there has historically been a sort of "trading culture" in Asia. To the extent that such a culture exists and can be identified with a particular nation or ethnic group, we find the overseas Chinese to be a more plausible factor than the Japanese.

Of the three trading blocs, the European Economic Community (EEC) and the Western Hemisphere are the two that show rapid intensification in the course of the 1980s. Both show an approximate doubling of their estimated intraregional bias coefficients. As of 1980, trade within the EEC is not strong enough—after holding constant for the close geographical proximity and high incomes per capita of European countries—for the bias coefficient of .2 to appear statistically significant. The EEC coefficient increased rapidly in level and significance in the first half of the 1980s, reaching about .4 by 1985, and continued to increase a bit in the second half. The effect of two countries being located in Europe per se, when tested, does not show up as being nearly as strong in magnitude or significance as the effect of membership in the EEC.

The Western Hemisphere coefficient experienced all its increase in the second half of the decade, exceeding .9 by 1990. The rapid increase in Western Hemisphere intraregional bias in the second half of the 1980s is in itself an important new finding. The recovery of Latin American imports from the United States after the compression that followed the 1982 debt crisis must be part of this phenomenon. The Canada–U.S. Free Trade Agreement signed in 1988 may also be part of the explanation.

We consider a sequence of nested candidates for trading blocs in the Pacific.

15. Petri infers, from the data on intraregional trade shares, a decrease in East Asian interdependence in the early 1980s, followed by a reversal in the second half of the decade.

The significance of a given bloc effect turns out to depend on what other blocs are tested at the same time. One logical way to draw the boundaries is to include all the countries with eastern coasts on the Pacific.[16] We call this grouping "Asian Pacific" in the tables. Its coefficient and significance level both appear higher than the EAEC dummy. But when we broaden the bloc search and test for an effect of the Asian Pacific Economic Cooperation group (APEC), which includes the United States and Canada in with the others, it is highly significant. The significance of the Asian Pacific dummy completely disappears, and that of the EAEC dummy returns.

It appears that APEC is the correct place to draw the boundary. The APEC effect is striking: the United States and Canada appear to be full partners in the Pacific bloc, even while simultaneously belonging to the significant but distinct Western Hemisphere bloc. The APEC coefficient is the strongest of any. Its estimate holds relatively steady at 1.5 (1980), 1.3 (1985), and 1.4 (1990).[17]

One possible explanation for the apparent intraregional trade biases within East Asia and within the APEC grouping is that transportation between Pacific Asian countries is mostly by water, while transportation among European or Western Hemisphere countries is more often over land, and that ocean shipping is less expensive than shipping by rail or road.[18] This issue bears further investigation. The issue of water versus land transport should not affect results regarding *changes* in intraregional trade bias in the 1980s, however, given that the nature of shipping costs does not appear to have changed over as short a time span as five or ten years.

Several further questions naturally arise. In 1977, ASEAN negotiated a preferential trading arrangement within its membership (although serious progress in removal of barriers did not get underway until 1987). In early 1992, the members proclaimed plans for an ASEAN Free Trade Area, albeit with exemptions for many sectors. Does this grouping constitute a small bloc nested within the others? We include in our model a dummy variable for common membership in ASEAN. It turns out to have a significant coefficient only if none of the broader Asian blocs are included. The conclusion seems to be that ASEAN is not in fact functioning as a trade bloc.[19]

16. This is the grouping used in table 12.12.

17. Others have reported the high volume of trans-Pacific trade. But it has been difficult to evaluate such statistics when no account is taken of these countries' collective size. A higher percentage of economic activity in a larger region will consist of intraregional trade than in a smaller region, even when there is no intraregional bias, merely because smaller regions tend by their nature to trade across their boundaries more than larger ones. In the limit, when the unit is the world, 100 percent of trade is intra-"regional."

18. Wang (1992) enters land distance and water distance separately in a gravity model. She finds a small, though statistically significant, difference in coefficients.

19. In tests similar to ours, Hamilton and Winters (1992), Wang (1992), and Wang and Winters (1991) found the ASEAN dummy to reflect one of the most significant trading areas in the world. That they did not include a broader dummy variable for intra-Asian trade may explain the difference in results.

We have carried out some other extensions elsewhere. In Frankel (1992a), we allow for the greater openness of East Asian countries generally, and of Hong Kong and Singapore in particular. These dummy variables are highly significant. The inclusion of each variable has relatively little effect on the coefficients of the original variables in the equation (with a coefficient of .9) when it is included, but the net effect of all of them (particularly the simultaneous presence of the APEC bloc variable and Asian openness variable) is to diminish the East Asian bloc variable to borderline significance. We also disaggregated trade into manufactured goods, agricultural products, fuels, and other raw materials. In Frankel and Wei (1993), we undertake still more extensions, such as including factor endowment terms, estimating openness or trade-diversion effects in other parts of the world, and checking for robustness with respect to heteroscedasticity and the omission of zero-trade points. In each case, the results changed little.

To summarize the most relevant effects, if two countries both lie within the boundaries of APEC, they trade with each other 100 percent more than they otherwise would. The nested EAEC bloc is less strong, and has declined slightly in magnitude and significance during the course of the 1980s. The Western Hemisphere and EC blocs, by contrast, intensified rapidly during the decade. Indeed, by 1990, the Western Hemisphere bloc was stronger than the EAEC bloc, if one takes into account the existence of the APEC effect. There was never a special Japan effect within Pacific Asia.

In short, beyond the evident facts that countries near each other trade more with each other, and that East Asian countries are growing rapidly, there is no evidence that they are collectively moving toward a trade bloc in the way that Western Europe and the Western Hemisphere appear to be.

12.4 The Correlation between Bilateral Exchange Rate Variability and Bilateral Trade Flows

12.4.1 The Role of Exchange Rate Stabilization

One rationale for assigning weight to a particular currency in determining one's exchange rate is the assumption that a more stable bilateral exchange rate will help promote bilateral trade with the partner in question. This is a major motivation for exchange rate stabilization in Europe. There have been quite a few time-series studies of the effect of exchange rate uncertainty on trade overall,[20] but fewer cross-sectional studies of bilateral trade.

One exception is De Grauwe (1988), which looks at only ten industrialized countries (and is motivated in part by the European experience). Two others

20. For example, Hooper and Kohlhagen (1978), Kenen and Rodrik (1986), and Akhtar and Hilton (1984). The literature is surveyed in IMF (1983).

are Abrams (1980) and Brada and Mendez (1988). We will reexamine the question here using a data set that is more recent as well as broader, covering 63 countries. A problem of simultaneous causality should be noted at the outset: if exchange rate variability shows up with an apparent negative effect on the volume of bilateral trade, it could be due to the government's efforts to stabilize the currency vis-à-vis a valued trading partner as easily as the reverse. With this consideration, we will also use the method of instrumental variable estimation to tackle the possible simultaneity bias.

Volatility is defined to be the variance of the first difference of the logarithmic exchange rate. We start with the volatility of nominal exchange rates and embed this term in our gravity equation for 1980, 1985, and 1990. The results are reported in table 12.13. Most coefficients are similar to those reported in the earlier results without exchange rate variability, though the majority of the bloc dummy variables appear with slightly lower coefficients, suggesting that a bit of the bloc effect may have been attributable to exchange rate links. In 1980, the coefficient for the volatility term is indeed negative and statistically significant at the 99 percent level. The magnitude is moderately small. On average, a one percent increase in the standard deviation reduces bilateral trade by 0.046 percent, holding constant all other variables. In 1985, the volatility parameter is no longer significant (with the point estimate turning positive). In 1990, the volatility coefficient becomes positive and statistically significant at the 99 percent level.

These puzzling results need not be taken at face value, since a presumably more relevant measure of exchange rate uncertainty is the volatility of real exchange rates, which takes into account the differential inflation rates in the two countries in addition to movements in nominal exchange rates. Regressions with the volatility of real exchange rates are also presented in table 12.13. In 1980, the volatility parameter is still negative (−0.66) and statistically significant. The parameter for 1985 is negative, though still insignificant. In sharp contrast to the regression with the volatility of nominal rates, the volatility parameter for 1990 is a statistically significant negative number (−0.48). In short, these results are consistent with one's prior expectation that real exchange rate volatility depresses bilateral trade. The change in the intraregional bias coefficients when exchange rate volatility is included in the equation also suggest that part of the regional trade bloc effects reported above for Europe and the Western Hemisphere were attributable to patterns of exchange rate variability. This would appear to be a piece of evidence that the stabilization of exchange rates within Europe has helped to promote intra-European trade.

Even part of the Pacific term appears to be attributable to exchange rate patterns, which one could interpret as the effect of the strong role played by the dollar throughout the region. The East Asian coefficient, on the other hand, is not at all reduced by the presence of the exchange rate volatility term. This

Table 12.13 **Exchange Rate Volatility and Bilateral Trade (OLS estimation)**

	Volatility	GNP	GNP/pop	DISTANCE	ADJACENT	WH	EEC	EAEC	APEC	Adjusted R^2	SEE
1980											
		.74**	.29**	−.56**	.72**	.52**	.23	.88**	1.51**	.71	1.20
		.02	.02	.04	.18	.15	.18	.27	.17		
Nominal exchange rate	−.046*	.76**	.26**	−.68**	.27	.16	.03	1.04**	1.35**	.73	1.20
	.023	.02	.02	.05	.21	.23	.18	.37	.20		
Real exchange rate	−.066*	.74**	.27**	−.67**	.43#	.18	.04	.96**	1.38**	.76	1.14
	.029	.02	.02	.05	.22	.20	.20	.37	.22		
1985											
		.76**	.25**	−.70**	.75**	.33**	.44*	.59*	1.28**	.74	1.17
		.02	.02	.04	.18	.16	.17	.26	.17		
Nominal exchange rate	.015	.77**	.24**	−.74**	.61**	.23	.43*	.79*	1.18**	.75	1.16
	.021	.02	.02	.05	.19	.18	.17	.36	.19		
Real exchange rate	−.026	.76**	.24**	−.75**	.45*	.01	.26##	.72*	1.12**	.78	1.12
	.028	.02	.02	.05	.22	.20	.17	.36	.21		
1990											
		.75**	.09**	−.56**	.79**	.92**	.47**	.69*	1.36**	.77	1.07
		.02	.02	.04	.16	.14	.16	.24	.15		
Nominal exchange rate	.076**	.77**	.09**	−.66**	.61**	.82**	.54**	.75*	1.36**	.79	1.04
	.014	.02	.02	.04	.16	.14	.16	.33	.17		
Real exchange rate	−.048**	.79**	.11**	−.60**	.31##	.51**	.27##	.95*	1.06**	.83	.97
	.023	.02	.02	.04	.20	.17	.17	.38	.28		

Notes: All the variables except the dummies are in logarithm. All the regressions have an intercept for which the estimate is not reported here. Standard errors are below the coefficient estimates.

**Statistically significant at the 99 percent level.

*Statistically significant at the 95 percent level.

#Statistically significant at the 90 percent level.

##Statistically significant at the 85 percent level.

result is what we would expect, in light of our findings in the first part of the paper that most of the East Asian currencies still give much less weight (if any at all) to the yen than to the dollar.

All such interpretations are threatened however, by the likelihood of simultaneity bias in the above regressions. Governments may choose deliberately to stabilize bilateral exchange rates with their major trading partners. This has certainly been the case in Europe, for example. Hence, there could be a strong correlation between trade patterns and currency linkages even if exchange rate volatility does not depress trade. To address this problem, we use the method of instrumental variable estimation, with the standard deviation of relative money supply as our instrument for the volatility of exchange rates.[21] The results are reported in table 12.14.

Let us concentrate our discussion on the regressions involving real exchange rates. In 1980, the volatility parameter is still negative and significant at the 90 percent level. But the magnitude (−0.10) is smaller than without using the instrument, suggesting that part of the apparent depressing effect of volatility was indeed due to the simultaneity bias. (Also, the presence of the volatility term no longer produces a clear drop in the EC and WH bloc terms.) Similarly in 1985, the volatility parameter has a correspondingly smaller point estimate and is statistically indistinguishable from zero. Finally, in 1990, the volatility parameter turns again into a positive number (0.32) which is significant at the 99 percent level.

These results suggest that if exchange rate volatility did depress bilateral trade, its negative effect appears to have diminished over the course of the 1980s. This sharp change is somewhat surprising. One possible explanation is the rapid development of exchange-risk hedging instruments. In particular, futures and forward markets for a broad range of currencies came into much wider use in the 1980s. Currency options were introduced in the United States at the end of 1982 on the pound/dollar, yen/dollar, and DM/dollar rates and soon spread to cover virtually all major currencies by late 1980s. The use of currency swaps was also on the rise. The market in financial instruments to hedge against exchange rate fluctuations, in addition to expanding in scope, has also become more efficient, lowering costs to hedgers.[22]

If exchange rate volatility no longer seriously depresses bilateral trade, then whether East Asian countries stabilize their currencies against the yen will not directly affect their trading volume with Japan and with each other. The gravity

21. The argument in favor of this choice of instrument is that relative money supplies and bilateral exchange rates are highly correlated, in theory (they are directly linked under the monetary theory of exchange rate determination), and in our data as well, but monetary policies are less likely than exchange rate policies to respond to bilateral trade.

22. The costs of doing foreign exchange transactions are themselves related to the volatility of the exchange rate. For a recent theoretic and empirical study on the relationship between bid-ask spreads and volatility, see Wei (1991). After controlling for volatility, Glassman (1987) finds some evidence that transaction costs in the foreign exchange market have decreased over time.

Table 12.14 **Exchange Rate Volatility and Bilateral Trade (instrumental variable estimation)**

	Volatility	GNP	GNP/pop	DISTANCE	ADJACENT	WH	EEC	EAEC	APEC	Adjusted R^2	SEE
1980											
Nominal exchange rate	−.008##	.73**	.27**	−.56**	.74**	.54**	.20	.93**	1.48**	.71	1.20
	.005	.02	.02	.04	.18	.15	.18	.27	.17		
Real exchange rate	−.010*	.73**	.26**	−.56**	.75**	.56**	.22	.94**	1.48**	.71	1.20
	.005	.02	.02	.05	.18	.15	.18	.27	.17		
1985											
Nominal exchange rate	−.001	.76**	.24**	−.70**	.76**	.34*	.43*	.59*	1.28**	.74	1.17
	.005	.02	.02	.04	.18	.16	.17	.26	.17		
Real exchange rate	−.000	.76**	.25**	−.70**	.75**	.33*	.43*	.59*	1.28**	.74	1.17
	.005	.02	.02	.04	.18	.16	.17	.26	.17		
1990											
Nominal exchange rate	.029**	.77**	.15**	−.57**	.71**	.88**	.44**	.47*	1.40**	.77	1.06
	.005	.02	.02	.04	.16	.14	.16	.24	.15		
Real exchange rate	.032**	.77**	.15**	−.57**	.71**	.87**	.43**	.45#	1.39**	.78	1.06
	.005	.02	.02	.04	.16	.14	.16	.24	.15		

Notes: All the variables except the dummies are in logarithm. All the regressions have an intercept for which the estimate is not reported here. Standard errors are below the coefficient estimates.

**Statistically significant at the 99 percent level.

*Statistically significant at the 95 percent level.

#Statistically significant at the 90 percent level.

##Statistically significant at the 85 percent level.

regressions reported here bear further investigation to test the robustness of the relationships.[23]

12.5 Is It Japan or the United States That Wants the Yen to Play a Greater Role in East Asia?

An important question related to the issue of yen bloc has thus far been left unanswered. Are the financial and monetary trends of the increased importance of the yen, to the extent they exist at all, the outcome of deliberate policy measures on the part of Japan? Gradually increasing use of the yen internationally is primarily the outcome of private decisions by importers, exporters, borrowers, and lenders. It is difficult to see signs of deliberate policy actions taken by the Japanese government to increase its financial and monetary influence in Asia. On the contrary, at least until recently, the Japanese government was inclined to resist whatever tendency there was for the yen to become an international currency in competition with the dollar.

It has been the U.S. government, in the Yen/Dollar Agreement of 1984 and in subsequent negotiations, that has been pushing Japan to internationalize the yen, to promote its worldwide use in trade, finance, and central bank policies (Frankel 1984). It has also been the U.S. government that has been pushing Korea and the other East Asian NICs to open up their financial markets, thereby allowing Japanese capital and Japanese financial institutions to enter these countries. It has again been the U.S. government that has been pushing Korea and Taiwan to move away from policies to stabilize the value of their currencies against the dollar.[24] An increasing role for the yen in Pacific Asia may or may not be a good idea. But it is an idea that originated in Washington, not in Tokyo.

12.5.1 Negotiations on the Korean Won

Korea and Taiwan were singled out by the U.S. Treasury in 1989, to "liberalize" their foreign exchange rate policies, with the implied outcome of being delinked from the dollar. Here, we study the case of Korea to illustrate the role of U.S. pressure in East Asian exchange rate policies.

Korea maintained a fixed exchange rate against the dollar in the late 1970s. As the inflation rate was higher at home than abroad, the won became progressively more overvalued in real terms, and exports suffered as a result. In 1979 the government enacted an important and needed program of macroeconomic stabilization and microeconomic reform. In January 1980 the won devalued by 20 percent. This devaluation, and the contractionary macroeconomic measures

23. We plan, for example, to include terms for factor endowments, levels of trade barriers, and political and linguistic associations.

24. Balassa and Williamson (1990), Noland (1990), and Frankel (1989). Financial negotiations between the U.S. Treasury and the governments of Korea and Taiwan were a response to congressional passage of the 1988 Omnibus Trade Bill.

taken in the preceding year, succeeded in stimulating rapid export growth and reducing the current account deficit. This left Korea as one of the few major debtors that was well positioned when the 1982 international debt crisis hit (Balassa and Williamson 1990; Collins and Park 1989; Kim 1990).

The official exchange rate policy in 1980 became one of defining the won's value in terms of a basket of five foreign currencies, rather than just the dollar.[25] Korea, as many other countries on a basket peg do, does not publicly announce what the currency weights are. The IMF was perceptive enough to classify Korea as a "managed floater" rather than a "basket-pegger." Test like those reported in section 12.2 (table 12.1) confirm that nondollar currencies in fact played very little role in this "basket."

The phase of dollar depreciation that began in 1985, as represented by the Plaza Accord, was welcomed in Korea as one of "three blessings" in the world economic environment: low dollar, low interest rates, and low oil prices. For two years Korea kept the won close to the dollar, which meant a substantial depreciation against the yen and other currencies, and basked in the stimulus to its exports. But the country responded to U.S. pressure by appreciating the won against the dollar in 1987 and 1988.

The U.S. government has continued to press Korea to delink the won from the dollar. The U.S. Treasury's October 1989 report announced: "Recently, the Treasury and the Korean Ministry of Finance have agreed to initiate talks on financial policies, including the exchange rate system and capital market issues. We hope to encourage a more market-oriented exchange rate system in Korea within the framework of these talks" (U.S. Department of the Treasury 1989, 29). Two rounds of financial policy talks took place in February and November 1990. Those talks did not explicitly focus on the level of the won/dollar rate per se. Rather, the United States sought to "encourage the liberalization of Korea's exchange rate system and of the capital and interest rate controls that impede the full operation of market forces." Just what is meant by "market-oriented exchange rate system" or "liberalization"? Given that the won had been rigidly targeted to the dollar, a liberalization implies a delinking. It was expected by the U.S. government that the won would appreciate against the dollar as a consequence of the "liberalization." Since bilateral trade and investment between Korea and Japan are large and increasingly important, another natural outcome would be a new degree of linkage between the won and the yen.

On March 2, 1990, the Korean authorities adopted a "market average rate" (MAR) system of setting the exchange rate each week (Hwang 1990, 15). This reform led the U.S. Treasury to drop charges of exchange rate manipulation in its April 1990 report, where the earlier won appreciation was apparently not sufficient to convince it to do so. The U.S. Treasury in its May 1991 report

25. Supposedly, according to Lindner (1991, 5) and Wang (1991, 3), the basket includes the U.S. dollar, yen, DM, pound, and Canadian dollar.

found: "During the first thirteen months of the MAR system (through April 12, 1991), the won depreciated 4.4 in nominal terms against the dollar. . . . Foreign banks accounted for a large share of transactions in the inter-bank market, generally 40–60 percent of the total. The Bank of Korea (BOK) was not a direct participant in the market, and other government-owned banks accounted for only a small share of inter-bank activity" (1991, 15). This sounds like a genuinely market-oriented system.

The U.S. Treasury notes in the same 1991 report, however, that "the Korean authorities maintain a comprehensive array of controls on foreign exchange and capital flows." Our regression result in section 12.2 actually provides a suggestive indication of continued heavy government intervention. The coefficient on the dollar and the R^2 term suggest that the link to the dollar was as strong during the period 1991 to May 1992 as in the preceding two to four years.

12.6 Concluding Remarks

This paper reaches several conclusions. (1) The U.S. dollar continues to be the dominant international currency in East Asian exchange rate policies. All nine East Asian countries have assigned heavy weight to the dollar, and many of them to the dollar alone. (2) Some currencies increased their weight on the yen during the mid-1980s. This may have been associated with the overvaluation of the dollar, instead of a genuine and steady increase in the role of the yen. Only two or three currencies actually showed a sign of increased yen weight at the end of the sample. Overall, the evidence does not suggest a substantial trend of an increased role for the yen in East Asian exchange rate policies.

(3) The level of trade in East Asia, like trade within the European Community and within the Western Hemisphere, is biased toward intraregional trade, to a greater extent that can be explained by distance, GNPs, and other gravity variables. However, (4) there is no evidence of any trend increase in the intra-Asian trade bias, (5) the intra-Asia trade bias is not centered on Japan, (6) the strongest "bloc" of any is the trans-Pacific one (APEC), including the United States and Canada along with the East Asian countries, and (7) the East Asian bloc effect diminishes when we include terms for APEC and for the general openness of Asian countries.

(8) Adding bilateral real exchange rate variability to the equation explaining bilateral trade flows, we find a significant effect in 1980, decreasing subsequently. Such cross-sectional evidence is an important addition to the time-series evidence on the effect of exchange rate uncertainty on trade. An important caveat is that an attempt to correct for likely simultaneity bias eliminated any negative effect of exchange rate volatility on trade in 1990 (though some remains in 1980). (9) The effect of exchange rate variability is relatively small. Even in the European Community, which did in some sense become a

currency bloc in the 1980s, the stabilization of exchange rates explains only a small part of our estimated trade-bloc effects.

Overall, the evidence with respect to both trade and currency links suggests little support for the formation of a yen bloc. On the contrary, East Asian countries continue to be strongly linked to the United States. Why does the yen not play a larger role in East Asian exchange rate policies? The U.S. dollar remains the preferred invoicing currency in international trade and lending, even within Asia, presumably for reasons of scale economies and history. Perhaps the even smaller role for the yen in exchange rate policies can be attributed to the same causes.

References

Abrams, Richard. 1980. International trade flows under flexible exchange rates. *Economic Review* (Federal Reserve Bank of Kansas City), March 3–10.

Akhtar, M. Akbar, and Spence Hilton. 1984. Effects of exchange rate uncertainty on German and U.S. trade. *Federal Reserve Bank of New York Quarterly Review* 9, no. 1 (Spring): 7–16.

Anderson, James. 1979. A theoretical foundation for the gravity equation. *American Economic Review* 69, no. 1 (March): 106–16.

Anderson, Kym, and Hege Norheim. 1992. History, geography and regional economic integration. Workshop on Regionalism and the Global Trading System, September 3–5.

Balassa, Bela, and John Williamson. 1990. *Adjusting to success: Balance of payments policy in the East Asian NICs.* Policy Analyses in International Economics, no. 17. Rev. ed. Washington, D.C.: Institute for International Economics, April.

Bergsten, C. Fred. 1991. Comment on Krugman. In *Policy implications of trade and currency zones.* 43–57. Symposium Sponsored by the Federal Reserve Bank of Kansas City, Jackson Hole, Wyo., August.

Bhagwati, Jagdish. 1990. Regional accords be-GATT trouble for free trade. *Wall Street Journal,* December 5.

———. 1992. Regionalism vs. multilateralism: An overview. Conference on New Dimensions in Regional Integration, World Bank, Washington, D.C., April 2–3.

Brada, Josef, and Jose Mendez. 1988. Exchange rate risk, exchange rate regimes and the level of international trade. *Kyklos* 41 (2): 198.

Collins, Susan, and Won-Am Park. 1989. External debt and macroeconomic performance in South Korea. In *Developing country debt and macroeconomic performance,* ed. Jeffrey Sachs. Chicago: University of Chicago Press.

Deardorff, Alan. 1984. Testing trade theories and predicting trade flows. In *Handbook of international economics,* ed. R. Jones and P. Kenen, vol. 1, 467–517. Amsterdam: Elsevier Science Publishers.

De Grauwe, Paul. 1988. Exchange rate variability and the slowdown in growth of international trade. *IMF Staff Papers* 35:63–84.

Dornbusch, Rudiger. 1989. The dollar in the 1990s: Competitiveness and the challenges of new economic blocs. In *Monetary policy issues in the 1990s.* Kansas City: Federal Reserve Bank of Kansas City.

———. 1992. What now, Mexico? *The International Economy,* March/April: 26–28.

Drysdale, Peter, and Ross Garnaut. 1992. "The Pacific: An application of a general theory of economic integration. Twentieth Pacific Trade and Development Conference, Washington, D.C., September 10–12.

Frankel, Jeffrey. 1984. *The Yen/Dollar Agreement: Liberalizing Japanese capital markets.* Policy Analyses in International Economics, no. 9. Washington, D.C.: Institute for International Economics.

———. 1989. And now won/dollar negotiations? Lessons from the yen/dollar agreement of 1984. In *Korea's Macroeconomic and Financial Policies.* Seoul: Korea Development Institute, December.

———. 1991a. Is a yen bloc forming in Pacific Asia? In *Finance and the International Economy: The AMEX Bank Review prize essays,* ed. R. O'Brien. London: Oxford University Press.

———. 1991b. The Japanese cost of finance: A survey. *Financial Management* (Spring): 95–127.

———. 1991c. On the dollar. Pacific Basin Working Paper no. PB91-04. (In *The new Palgrave dictionary of money and finance.* London: Macmillan Press Reference Books, 1992.)

———. 1991d. Quantifying international capital mobility in the 1980s. In *National saving and economic performance,* ed. D. Bernheim and J. Shoven, 227–60. Chicago, University of Chicago Press.

———. 1992a. Is Japan creating a yen bloc in East Asia and the Pacific? NBER Working Paper no. 4050. Cambridge, Mass.: National Bureau of Economic Research. (In *Regionalism and rivalry: Japan and the U.S. in Pacific Asia,* ed. Jeffrey Frankel and Miles Kahler. Chicago: University of Chicago Press, 1993.)

———. 1992b. Liberalization of Korea's foreign exchange markets, and tests of U.S. versus Japanese influence. *Seoul Journal of Economics* 5, no. 1 (Spring): 1–29. (An earlier version was presented at a conference on U.S.-Korea Economic Relations, December 5–6, 1991, and is forthcoming in *Building a new economic relationship: Republic of Korea and United States economic relations,* ed. J. Mo and R. Myers. Stanford, Calif.: Hoover Institution Press.)

Frankel, Jeffrey, and Shang-Jin Wei. 1993. Trade blocs and currency blocs. NBER Working Paper no. 4335. Cambridge, Mass.: National Bureau of Economic Research.

Froot, Kenneth, and David Yoffie. 1991. Strategic trade policies in a tripolar world. Working Paper no. 91-030, Harvard Business School. Revised.

Glassman, Debra. 1987. Exchange rate risk and transactions costs: Evidence from bid-ask spread. *Journal of International Money and Finance* 6 (June).

Hamilton, Carl, and L. Alan Winters. 1992. Opening up international trade in Eastern Europe. *Economic Policy* (April).

Helpman, Elhanan. 1987. Imperfect competition and international trade: Evidence from fourteen industrial countries. *Journal of the Japanese and International Economies* 1:62–81.

Helpman, Elhanan, and Paul Krugman. 1985. *Market structure and foreign trade,* Cambridge: MIT Press.

Hooper, Peter, and Steven Kohlhagen. 1978. The effect of exchange rate uncertainty on prices and volume of international trade. *Journal of International Economics* 8 (November): 483–511.

Hwang, Eui-Gak. 1990. Trade policy issues between South Korea and the United States, with some emphasis on Korea's position. Symposium on the Impact of Recent Economic Developments on US/Korean Relations and the Pacific Basin, University of California, San Diego, November 9–10.

IMF (International Monetary Fund). 1983. Exchange rate volatility and trade. Research Department, December 9.

Ito, Takatoshi. 1992. The yen and the international monetary system. Twentieth Pacific Trade and Development Conference, Washington, D.C., September 10–12. Revised, October.

Kenen, Peter, and Dani Rodrik. 1986. Measuring and analyzing the effects of short-term volatility in real exchange rates. *Review of Economics and Statistics* 68 (May): 311–15.

Kim, Kihwan. 1990. Deregulating the domestic economy: Korea's experience in the 1980s. Paper presented at Senior Policy Seminar, Caracas. Revised December.

Krugman, Paul. 1980. Vehicle currencies and the structure of international exchange. *Journal of Money, Credit and Banking* 12:513–26.

———. 1984. The international role of the dollar: Theory and prospect. In *Exchange rate theory and practice,* ed. John F. O. Bilson and Richard Marston, 261–78. Chicago: University of Chicago Press.

———. 1991a. Is bilateralism bad? In *International trade and trade policy,* ed. E. Helpman and A. Razin. Cambridge: MIT Press.

———. 1991b. The move toward free trade zones. In *Policy implications of trade and currency zones,* 7–42. Symposium Sponsored by the Federal Reserve Bank of Kansas City, Jackson Hole, Wyo., August.

Kwan, C. H. 1992. An optimal peg for the Asian currencies and an Asian perspective of a yen bloc. *Nomura Asian Perspectives* 9, no. 2 (April). (Forthcoming in *Exchange rate policy and interdependence: Perspectives from the Pacific Basin,* ed. R. Glick and M. Hutchison. New York: Cambridge University Press.)

Lindner, Deborah. 1991. The political economy of the won: U.S.-Korean bilateral negotiations on exchange rates. Forthcoming in *Building a new economic relationship: Republic of Korea and United States economic relations,* ed. J. Mo and R. Myers. Stanford, Calif.: Hoover Institution Press.

Lowell, Julia. 1992. Do governments do what they say (and do we believe them)? Two essays on national debt and exchange regime policies. Ph.D. dissertation, Department of Economics, University of California, Berkeley.

Mancera, Miguel. 1991. Characteristics and implications of different types of currency areas. In *Policy implications of trade and currency zones,* 95–101. Symposium Sponsored by the Federal Reserve Bank of Kansas City, Jackson Hole, Wyo., August.

Moreno, Ramon. 1988. Exchange rates and monetary policy in Singapore and Taiwan. In *Monetary Policy in Pacific Basin Countries,* ed. Hanson Cheng. Boston: Kluwer Press.

Noland, Marcus. 1990. *Pacific basin developing countries: Prospects for the future.* Washington, D.C.: Institute for International Economics.

Oum, Bongsung. 1991. Liberalization of Korea's financial and capital markets. Paper presented at New Economic Order: A U.S.-Korea Forum, Washington, D.C., June 25.

Park, Yung Chul, and Won-Am Park. 1991. Exchange rate policies for the East Asian newly industrialized countries. In *Exchange rate policies in developing and post-socialist countries,* ed. Emil-Maria Claasen. San Francisco: ICS Press.

Petri, Peter. 1991. Market structure, comparative advantage and Japanese trade under the strong yen. In *Trade with Japan: Has the door opened wider?,* ed. Paul Krugman, 51–84. Chicago: University of Chicago Press.

———. 1992a. The East Asian trading bloc: An analytical history. Paper presented at an NBER conference, Del Mar, Calif., April 3–5. (In *Regionalism and rivalry: Japan and the U.S. in Pacific Asia,* ed. Jeffrey Frankel and Miles Kahler. Chicago: University of Chicago Press, 1993.)

———. 1992b. One bloc, two blocs or none? Political-economic factors in Pacific trade policy. In *The U.S.-Japan economic relationship in East and Southeast Asia: A policy framework for Asia-Pacific economic cooperation,* Significant Issues Series, vol. 14, no. 1, ed. Kaoru Okuzumi, Kent Calder, and Gerrit Gong, 39–70. Washington, D.C.: Center for Strategic and International Studies.

Reisen, Helmut, and Axel van Trotsenburg. 1988. Should the Asian NICs peg to the yen? *Intereconomics,* July/August: 172–77.

Schott, Jeffrey. 1991. Trading blocs and the world trading system. *The World Economy* 14, no. 1 (March).

Suzuki, Yoshio. 1991. Japan in the world economic scene. Tokyo: Nomura Research Institute, Ltd., June.

Takagi, Shinji. 1988. A basket policy: Operational issues for developing countries. *World Development* 16(2): 271–79.

Tavlas, George, and Yuzuru Ozeki. 1991. The Japanese yen as an international currency. IMF Working Paper WP/91/2. Washington, D.C.: International Monetary Fund, January.

———. 1992. The internationalization of currencies: An appraisal of the Japanese yen, Occasional Paper 90. Washington, D.C.: International Monetary Fund, January.

U.S. Department of the Treasury. 1989. Report to the Congress on international economic and exchange rate policy. October.

———. 1990. Report to the Congress on international economic and exchange rate policy. December.

———. 1991. Report to the Congress on international economic and exchange rate policy. May.

Wang, Yen Kyun. 1991. Exchange rate and current account balance of Korea and U.S.-Korea negotiations on the exchange rate policy. Forthcoming in *Building a new economic relationship: Republic of Korea and United States economic relations,* ed. J. Mo and R. Myers. Stanford, Calif.: Hoover Institution Press.

Wang, Zhen Kun. 1992. China's potential trade: An analysis based on the gravity model. Department of Economics, University of Birmingham, UK.

Wang, Zhen Kun, and L. Alan Winters. 1991. The trading potential of Eastern Europe. CEPR Discussion Paper no. 610. London: Centre for Economic Policy Research, November.

Wei, Shang-Jin. 1991. Anticipations of foreign exchange volatility and bid-ask spreads. *International Finance Discussion Papers,* no. 409. Washington, D.C.: Board of Governors of the Federal Reserve System, August.

Comment Koichi Hamada

In this paper questions are clearly stated, analysis thoroughly carried out, and interpretations articulately given. I have no strong arguments against most of the authors' findings and conclusions. I differ only in the emphasis I would put on the findings and in the nuance of my interpretation. Let me summarize here the authors' main statements and my reactions to them.

"All nine East Asian countries have assigned heavy weights to the dollar, even though some countries have assigned increasing weights to the yen in recent years."

Koichi Hamada is professor of economics at Yale University and a research associate at the National Bureau of Economic Research.

There would be a gap in the logic if one concluded from this statement that East Asia should be in the dollar bloc. The missing link, a hidden assumption, is that each country was driven by a purely economic rationale in its exchange-rate policy. In practice, however, political considerations may have motivated the pegging policy.

I would not carry this argument much further because I do not mean that putting more weight on the yen would be more rational. Due to the public-good nature of an international currency, which is well described in this paper, it is natural that many countries put heavy weight on the currency that is dominantly used as the international medium of exchange.

"Though the *level* of trade in East Asia is biased toward intraregional trade to a greater extent than can be explained by distance, GNPs, etc., there is no evidence of any *increasing trend* in intra-Asia trade, and the intra-Asia trade bias is not centered on Japan."

The absence of trend coincides with our findings (Goto and Hamada, chap. 14 in this volume). But is the level not as important as the pace of changes in the discussion of a currency union? It was quite natural for European countries to increase the intraregional bias in recent years when they were moving toward economic integration. Is it not important to point out that the degree of interrelatedness in trade among Asian countries have been high in spite of the absence of such a movement toward economic integration?

Geographical distance is important and the gravity model is a useful way to take account of geographical considerations. The authors seem to imply that the intraregional trade bias due to proximity is not grounds for the formation of a currency bloc. But if intraregional trade bias is strong because of the affinity of locations, it will not preclude the desirability of creating an integrated market within a region. If Asian nations are trading much with each other because of the geographical affinity among them—indeed, an understandable phenomenon—it will not weaken the case for creating a unified currency area among them.

There is one inaccurate statement in the paper: In section 12.5, the authors write, "at least until recently, the Japanese government was inclined to resist *whatever* tendency there was for the yen to become an international currency in competition with the dollar" (emphasis mine). Indeed, the Japanese monetary authorities retained until recently many regulations to protect domestic financial institutions. They did not encourage sufficiently the rapid creation of a full-fledged domestic short-term capital market. Those regulations and policies sometimes worked against the more extensive use of the yen as an international currency. They regulated, however, for the sake of protecting domestic financial institutions. They did not have a consistent policy of resisting all tendencies toward the internationalization of the yen. Even within the Ministry of Finance, as in other bureaus like the Ministry of International Trade and Industry (MITI), there was tension between the internationalists who advocated internationally oriented policy and the traditionalists who defended the policy of protecting domestic markets. The statement in this paper is much too strong.

In summary, this paper presents coherent documentation of facts and quantitative tests. The conclusions should be taken with a grain of salt, however. Alternative interpretations are possible. As the authors convincingly argue, the statistics do not support the immediate need for a currency bloc centering on the yen. But neither do they preclude the desirability of a currency area of Asian nations by themselves, nor do they present grounds for creating one in Asia based on the dollar.

Finally, I had difficulty identifying any advocates of "the three *possible* components of a yen bloc hypothesis" (emphasis mine). Presumably this straw man was created as well as shot down in Berkeley.

Comment Sung Hee Jwa

The authors seem to have succeeded in dispelling a myth about the yen bloc so clearly and forcefully that one cannot quarrel with their conclusion in any seriously critical manner.

Frankel and Wei's main findings are: (1) compared with the dollar, the yen has had a relatively small role in exchange rate determination in the East Asian economies, and its role as an invoicing currency in trade and finance has not increased as rapidly as the share of Japanese trade within the region. Therefore, the concept of the yen bloc can not be substantiated. (2) there is no strong, convincing evidence that trade activities in the East Asian economies have been concentrated within the region and centered on Japan to a "supernatural" extent, beyond what can be explained by "normal" economic forces, such as the growth of economies in the area and short distances between them, within the context of the standard gravity model. (3) there is no genuine incentive for East Asian economies to maintain the stability of their currencies vis-à-vis the yen except to the extent that Japan happens to be their major trading partner. (4) the authors observe that it is the United States rather than Japan that wants the yen to play a larger role in East Asia. I will address each of these issues in the order they were presented.

The Role of the Yen

The rise to dominance of an international currency is analogous to that of a common language in which increasing the number of people who use the language consequently increases its utility, thereby allowing the language to assume the dominant role as a common tongue and to inhibit any newcomers

Sung Hee Jwa is a fellow at the Korea Development Institute.

from assuming its role. Therefore, if the yen were to emerge as the dominant currency over the dollar, it would happen discretely—as a regime change when the environment (including noneconomic aspects) ripens to support it—rather than as a gradual process. Where the proportion of yen usage in trade and finance passes a certain threshold and is large enough to exploit the inherent external effect, the yen, which now plays only a minor role, will begin to assume a disproportionately and accumulatively larger role as the dominant currency.

How high the threshold must be is a challenging question, to be resolved in future research, but one should not expect any noticeable increase in the role of the yen until the threshold is reached. Therefore, the authors' findings about the lower than expected role of the yen in exchange rate determination and as an invoicing currency should not be a surprise or a disappointment. Rather, it seems that the Japanese share in the world economy still falls short of the threshold even if the authors believe it is very high and rising substantially.

In this context, it may be interesting to compare the importance of the currencies of major economies as invoicing currencies relative to the shares of those economies in the world economy and see if the importance of the yen is disproportionately greater or less than other major currencies.

A Normal versus a Supernatural Trading Bloc in East Asia

Frankel and Wei were interested in and searched for noneconomic forces, such as historical, political, cultural, and linguistic ties, leading to a possible supernatural trading bloc in the East Asian economies but failed to find supporting evidence. However, to anyone who hopes for or worries about the economic effects of a trading bloc centered on Japan, it is the simple fact of the bloc actually being formed regardless of the events causing the bloc that is the concern. For this reason, it is also equally important to note that the authors have clearly and systematically shown the emergence of a normal or natural trading bloc among the East Asian economies, as the Japanese and other economies in the region have grown so rapidly in recent years.

In addition, their finding that no "supernatural" forces play a role in promoting a trading bloc among the East Asian economies is not at all surprising, because it seems natural to think that the East Asian region shares relatively fewer common noneconomic factors than Europe or North America. But in spite of their argument that there was no evidence that Japan had established or come to dominate a trading bloc in Asia, implicitly, indirectly, or openly, one should not be ignorant of the fact that Japan is investing a lot to improve the level of East Asian understanding of Japan, which may be conducive to forming a supernatural trading bloc in the future.

Concerning Frankel and Wei's regression equation based on the gravity model, it would be interesting to investigate whether there are any mutually enhancing and cumulative effects among the GNP or GNP per capita variable and other variables by adding cross-product terms of those variables.

Who Is Interested in a Larger Role for the Yen?

While the authors argue that it is not Japan but the United States that is interested in a larger role for the yen, it seems that this question can not be readily or easily answered. As mentioned earlier, even if Japan is eager to form and lead a trading bloc, as well as a yen bloc, and is taking action in this direction, the special Japan factor may not be visibly detected in Frankel and Wei's approach. This may be because their approach may only be applicable to continuous cases and not to the discrete case of a shift of the natural monopolist from the dollar, the existing dominant international currency, to the yen, the new competitor.

13 On the Internationalization of the Japanese Yen

Hiroo Taguchi

The internationalization of the yen is a widely discussed topic, among not only economists but also journalists and even politicians. Although various ideas are discussed under this heading, three are the focus of attention: First, and the most narrow, is the use of yen by nonresidents. Second is the possibility of Asian economies forming an economic bloc with Japan and the yen at the center. Third, is the possibility that the yen could serve as a nominal anchor for Asian countries, resembling the role played by the deutsche mark in the European Monetary System (EMS).

Sections 13.1–13.3 of this paper try to give a broad overview of the key facts concerning the three topics, above. The remaining sections discuss the international role the yen could play, particularly in Asia.

13.1 The Yen as an Invoicing Currency

Following the transition to a floating exchange rate regime, the percentage of Japan's exports denominated in yen rose sharply in the early 1970s and continued to rise to reach nearly 40 percent in the mid-1980s, a level since maintained (table 13.1). There is a marked difference according to export destination—while yen is rarely used vis-à-vis exports to the United States, nearly half of all exports to Asian countries are invoiced in yen.

The yen is even less used for invoicing imports into Japan. However, the

Hiroo Taguchi is chief manager of Research Division I of the Institute for Monetary and Economic Studies of the Bank of Japan.

The author benefited greatly from discussions with, and suggestions from, Kunio Okina and Kazuo Momma, as well as the valuable comments of the participants in the Third Annual East Asia Seminar on Economics, in particular Anne Krueger and Kazuo Ueda. He also thanks Yuko Nishijima, Michiko Matsumoto, and Atsushi Inoue for their help in preparing the tables. Views expressed herein are those of the author and do not necessarily reflect those of the Bank of Japan.

Table 13.1 Use of Yen as Invoicing Currency in Japan's Trade (% of value)

	1970	1975	1980	1985	1987	1990
Exports to:						
World	0.9	17.5	29.4	39.3	33.4	37.5
United States	—	—	—	19.7[a]	15.0	16.2
European Community	—	—	—	51.3[a]	44.0	42.1
Southeast Asia	—	—	—	47.3[a]	41.1	48.9
Imports from:						
World	0.3	0.9	2.4	7.3[b]	10.6	14.5
United States	—	—	—	—	9.2	11.6
European Community	—	—	—	—	27.3	26.9
Southeast Asia	—	—	—	—	11.5	19.4

Sources: Ministry of International Trade and Industry (MITI), *Statistics on Export Confirmation (Yushutu Kakuninn Toukei)* and *Statistics on Import Report (Yunyuu Houkoku Toukei)* (Tokyo, various issues).

[a]Based on number of export confirmations.

[b]As of FY 1985.

percentage of yen-denominated imports has been rising steadily since the 1980s, especially from Asian countries. In trade among third countries ("vehicle currency"), the use of the yen is almost negligible.

The limited utilization of domestic currency in invoicing Japan's trade is in sharp contrast with the situation in other major industrial countries (table 13.2). There are a number of reasons for this.[1] First, and perhaps most important, there is a significant historical (or "hysteresis") element involved in selecting a transaction currency, which works naturally for "old" international currencies like the U.S. dollar and the pound sterling. However, there are also several other reasons.

If the level of expected profit from trade is given, both exporters and importers will seek the smallest possible fluctuation in trading profits, assuming they are risk-averse. However, they should be willing to accept greater profit fluctuation if the expected profit is also higher. Therefore, the choice of which currency to use should depend primarily on whether the cost of hedging exchange rate risk is lower for the exporter or the importer.

One way to manage exchange rate risk is to pass through exchange rate fluctuations to input and output prices. With regard to input prices, the larger the share of imports in total production costs and the more dependent the home country is on trade, the easier it is to mitigate the impact of exchange rate movements through changes in input costs like wages and material prices. With regard to output prices, it should be easier to pass through increases to the consumer if there are few or no domestic substitutes in the importing country.

1. For discussions on the invoicing currency role of the Japanese yen, see also Taguchi (1982), Tavlas and Ozeki (1991), Kawai (1992), and Takeda and Turner (1992).

To a considerable extent these factors explain the relatively high utilization of domestic currency for invoicing the exports of major developed countries, and vice versa with respect to imports, since they tend to export industrial goods with a high degree of differentiation and import primary products for which there are few domestic substitutes. The small use of the yen for Japanese imports seems to be consistent with the very high proportion of food, fuel, and raw materials in Japan's total import composition, e.g., 53 percent in 1988, as compared to 25 percent in the case of Germany.

Another factor that also seems to help explain the tendency to invoice Japan's trade in foreign currencies is the existence of large trading companies in Japan. These companies, which handle the bulk of both Japan's exports and imports, have a relative advantage in managing foreign exchange risk compared with their trading counterparts. They enjoy economies of scale in terms of risk management; moreover, they are able to offset a considerable portion of their risk exposure stemming from their export business with that from imports.

Another possible factor is the strong preference of Japanese manufacturers, relative to their trading partners, for stable production levels, which perhaps reflects Japan's life-long employment system. Thus, to minimize fluctuations in foreign demand occasioned by exchange rate movements, they tend to have their exports denominated in the currency of the importer.

The explanations provided above seem to be broadly consistent with several important observations: (i) the proportion of exports invoiced in yen has risen as Japanese export goods have become more differentiated; (ii) invoicing in yen is not common for exports to the United States (which is the single largest export market for Japan and where importers are less experienced in managing foreign exchange risk), while it is relatively common for exports to Southeast Asia (which is a more marginal market than the United States and where traders are more familiar with handling exchange rate risk); and (iii) the increase in yen-invoiced imports from Southeast Asia reflects the growth in imports from Japanese implants (whose cost structure has a high yen component).

Table 13.2 **Share of Trade Denominated in Domestic Currency of Selected Industrial Countries (% of value)**

	Exports		Imports	
Country	1980	1988	1980	1988
United States	97.0	96.0	85.0	85.0
Germany	82.3	81.5[a]	43.0	52.6
France	62.5	58.5	33.1	48.9
United Kingdom	76.0	57.0	38.0	40.0
Italy	36.0	38.0[a]	18.0	27.0[a]
Japan	29.4	34.3	2.4	14.1

Source: Tavlas and Ozeki (1991).

[a]As of 1987.

13.2 Use of Yen in International Finance

13.2.1 Capital Market

Until the mid-1980s, the bulk of international bonds (Euro-bonds plus foreign currency bonds) was denominated in U.S. dollars, followed by deutsche marks and Swiss francs. In fact, around 80 percent of newly placed international bonds were denominated in these three currencies (table 13.3). Following a series of liberalization measures, the share of yen-denominated bonds started to rise in the second half of the 1980s and now accounts for about 13 percent of total new issues. However, it should be noted that this recent increase reflects, in addition to basic factors such as lower issue fees and fewer regulatory encumbrances in the overseas markets, partly a temporary situation whereby many Japanese companies had difficulty raising funds in the stock market due to the drastic fall in stock prices and thus tried to raise funds abroad. A great share of those bonds were apparently purchased by affiliates of Japanese companies and thus in that sense could be considered de facto domestic issue.

13.2.2 International Bank Loans

The proportion of yen-denominated loans was negligible in the 1970s, but rose sharply in the 1980s when Japanese banks tried to establish themselves overseas (table 13.4). However, it has leveled off recently, reflecting mainly the increasingly cautious behavior of Japanese banks abroad, influenced by the Bank for International Settlements (BIS) capital adequacy ratio and problems involving sovereign loans to some developing countries.

Although yen loans still play only a modest role globally, they are becoming common in Asian countries. Table 13.5 gives a currency breakdown of the total foreign debt of selected Asian countries (Korea, Thailand, Malaysia, Indonesia, and the Philippines). The proportion of yen-denominated debt in the total borrowing of these countries doubled from 19.5 percent at the end of 1980 to

Table 13.3 **Currency Composition of International Bonds (% of new issues)**

Currency	1975	1980	1985	1990	1991
U.S. dollar	50.6	42.7	60.6	33.3	28.5
Japanese yen	0.4	4.8	7.7	13.5	12.9
Pound sterling	0.2	3.0	4.2	9.5	9.1
Swiss franc	17.1	19.5	8.9	10.5	7.3
Deutsche mark	16.4	21.9	6.7	8.3	7.1
ECU	—	—	4.1	8.1	11.1
Other	15.3	8.1	7.8	16.8	24.0
Total	100.0	100.0	100.0	100.0	100.0
(billion $ U.S.)	(20.0)	(38.3)	(167.8)	(240.2)	(311.4)

Source: OECD, *Financial Market Trends* (Paris, various issues).

Table 13.4 **Currency Composition of International Bank Lending (% of amount outstanding)**

	1980	1985	1990	1991[a]
U.S. dollar	66.3	64.6	49.8	49.6
Pound sterling	2.7	2.7	4.5	4.0
Japanese yen	2.2	5.7	11.2	11.6
Deutsche mark	14.4	11.3	14.5	13.2
Swiss franc	7.0	6.4	5.5	5.0
ECU	0.0	2.2	3.3	3.8
Other	7.4	7.1	11.2	12.8
Total	100.0	100.0	100.0	100.0
(billion $ U.S.)	(1,500.1)	(2,557.2)	(6,132.4)	(5,735.4)

Source: BIS, "International Banking and Financial Market Developments" (Basle, various issues).
[a]First nine months of 1991.

Table 13.5 **Currency Composition of External Debt in Southeast Asian Countries (%)**

	1980		1985		1990	
	Yen	Dollar	Yen	Dollar	Yen	Dollar
Korea	16.6	53.5	16.7	60.3	29.5	32.4
Thailand	25.5	39.7	36.1	25.5	43.5	20.8
Malaysia	19.0	38.0	26.4	50.6	37.1	35.6
Indonesia	20.0	43.5	31.7	30.7	39.3	18.5
Philippines	22.0	51.6	24.9	47.8	40.5	34.7
Total of above	19.5	47.3	25.8	44.7	37.9	27.0
(billion $ U.S.)	(45.2)		(93.5)		(115.6)	

Source: Tavlas and Ozeki (1991).

37.9 percent at the end of 1990. This rapid increase owes partly to currency revaluation occasioned by the appreciation of the yen in the second half of the 1980s, as well as to an increase in official yen loans which reflects efforts to increase official development aid (ODA).

13.2.3 Yen as a Reserve Currency

To obtain a broad idea of the use of the yen as a reserve currency in the private sector, it should be noted that the proportion of yen in total Euro-deposits is growing steadily, but was still only 5.0 percent at the end of 1990, compared with 55.2 percent for the U.S. dollar and 13.8 percent for the deutsche mark (table 13.6). The yen's share is about the same as that of the Swiss franc. However, Japan's GDP is 13 times larger than Switzerland's, so it is fair to say that the yen is playing only a very modest role in the Euro-deposit market.

Table 13.6 **Currency Composition of Euro-currency Market (deposits outstanding; %)**

	1980	1985	1990	1991[a]
U.S. dollar	71.8	68.7	55.2	55.2
Deutsche mark	13.5	8.9	14.9	13.8
Swiss franc	6.0	6.3	5.2	4.8
Japanese yen	1.5	3.7	5.0	5.0
Pound sterling	2.4	1.7	4.0	3.7
ECU	—	2.7	4.3	5.1
Other	4.8	8.0	11.4	12.4
Total	100.0	100.0	100.0	100.0
(billion $ U.S.)	(1,168)	(1,862)	(4,628)	(4,358)

Source: BIS, "International Banking and Financial Market Developments (Basle, various issues).
Note: Foreign currency–denominated debt outstanding by BIS reporting banks.
[a]First nine months of 1991.

As an official reserve asset, the presence of yen is somewhat greater. The share of yen assets in total official reserves of IMF member countries grew gradually in the 1980s, and reached 9.1 percent at the end of 1990 (table 13.7). In particular, in the portfolios of the official monetary institutions of Asian countries the proportion held in yen is relatively high—17.5 percent at the end of 1990. The fact that the yen is relatively important as an official reserve asset in Asia seems to reflect the growing interdependence between Japan and the Asian countries and the increased (official) yen debts of the latter. The figure was even higher in the second half of the 1980s. However, after having recorded a high of 30.0 percent at the end of 1987 and thus coming quite close to the figure for the U.S. dollar (41.2 percent), the share has since declined.

The rise in the yen's share in the mid-1980s seems to reflect the yen's appreciation, greater desire on the part of Asian authorities to hedge against exchange rate risk in light of increased official borrowing in yen, and undoubtedly some speculative elements seeking capital gains from the further appreciation of the yen.

The background to the subsequent decline is not that obvious. However, it is likely that Asian authorities sought higher interest income by moving out of yen as exchange rate fluctuations moderated at around 120–140 yen/dollar. The fact that the yen's weight in the official reserve portfolios of Asian countries displayed large swings in a relatively short period suggests that the yen still remains a kind of secondary reserve asset for them in the sense that profitability, in addition to liquidity, is a significant motive for holding the currency.

13.2.4 Foreign Exchange Market

Looking at the volume of yen transactions on foreign exchange markets, in 1980 in the New York market, for example, U.S. dollar/yen transactions accounted for only 10.2 percent of total transactions; however, by 1989 this figure had grown to 25.2 percent, closer to the 32.9 percent for U.S. dollar/deutsche mark transactions (table 13.8). In the world's major markets as a whole (table 13.9), transactions involving yen account for 27 percent of total transactions and, together with the deutsche mark, the yen is the second most traded currency after the U.S. dollar. In table 13.9, both currencies involved in a transaction are counted and therefore the total adds up to 200 percent, not 100 percent. Note also that the share of the deutsche mark is somewhat underestimated since transactions in German foreign exchange markets are not included.

It is worthwhile to mention that the yen is the second most traded currency in the Hong Kong and Singapore markets, which have considerable trading volumes even if smaller than those of the three biggest markets, namely, New York, London, and Tokyo. In contrast, the volume of yen-related transactions is still small in the Australian foreign exchange market.

There is no reliable data on international use of the yen in its most direct sense, that is use of yen notes abroad. Anecdotal evidence, however, suggests that although the use of yen notes abroad by Japanese tourists is growing, they are only rarely used for transactions among non-Japanese. The return of yen notes to Japan from abroad amounts to about ¥1 trillion per year. Assuming that the notes remain abroad for an average of three months (piecemeal information suggests that the actual stay is shorter), the outstanding amount of yen

Table 13.7 **Currency Composition of Identified Official Foreign Exchange Holdings of IMF Member Countries (%; year-end data)**

Countries	1970	1975	1980	1985	1990
All					
U.S. dollar	77.2	79.5	68.6	65.0	56.4
Japanese yen	0.0	0.5	4.4	8.0	9.1
Deutsche mark	1.9	6.3	14.9	15.2	19.7
Pound sterling	10.4	3.9	2.9	3.0	3.2
French franc	1.1	1.2	1.7	0.9	2.1
Swiss franc	0.7	1.6	3.2	2.3	1.5
Other	8.8	7.1	4.3	5.6	8.0
Total	100.0	100.0	100.0	100.0	100.0
Asian					
U.S. dollar			48.6	44.8	56.4
Japanese yen			13.9	26.9	17.5
Deutsche mark			20.6	16.4	15.2
Pound sterling			3.0	4.1	6.4
French franc			0.6	0.9	0.5
Swiss franc			10.6	4.9	3.0
Other			4.7	2.1	1.0
Total			100.0	100.0	100.0

Source: IMF, *Annual Report* (Washington, D.C., various issues).

Table 13.8 Currency Composition of Transactions on the New York Foreign Exchange Market (average of daily transaction value; %)

	March 1980	April 1983	March 1986	April 1989
U.S. dollar/Japanese yen	10.2	22.0	23.0	25.2
U.S. dollar/deutsche mark	31.7	32.5	34.2	32.9
U.S. dollar/pound sterling	22.8	16.6	18.6	14.6
U.S. dollar/Swiss franc	10.1	12.2	9.7	11.8
Cross transactions	—	0.2	—	3.6
Total[a]	100.0	100.0	100.0	100.0
(billion $ U.S.)	(18.0)	(26.0)	(58.5)	(128.9)

Sources: BIS, "Survey of Foreign Exchange Market Activity" (Basle, various issues); and other sources.

[a]Total includes transactions involving currencies other than those listed above and so is not the sum of numbers above.

notes overseas would be less than 1 percent of total notes outstanding. This is in sharp contrast with U.S. dollar notes, which are widely used as a "parallel currency" in many developing countries and recently in Eastern Europe: according to some unpublished sources, a variety of evidence suggests that more than half of all U.S. currency outstanding is held abroad.

13.3 Background to the Increase in the International Use of Yen

To summarize developments reviewed in the previous section: the yen emerged as an international currency in 1970, a trend which grew rapidly in the mid-1980s. This growth owed much to the greater international presence of the Japanese economy and also partly to the revision of the Foreign Exchange and Foreign Trade Control Law in 1980, which saw a major change in principle, from "prohibited if not explicitly allowed" to "allowed if not explicitly prohibited." Growth has decelerated considerably since the late 1980s, principally because potential demand for yen had already been satisfied to a large extent.

However, it is premature to draw the conclusion that the international use of yen is likely to grow only pari passu with the growth of the Japanese economy. For a currency to become widely used as an international currency, there must be (see, e.g., Tavlas and Ozeki 1992; Black 1990): (i) confidence that its value will be stable, which means not only low inflation with little fluctuation but also political stability in the home country, and (ii) the existence of stable financial markets in the home country where a wide range of instruments are traded freely in considerable volume.

13.3.1 Inflation

Table 13.10 compares both the level and fluctuation of inflation in selected industrial countries and Asian economies. Together with Germany, Japan has

Table 13.9 **Currency Composition of Transactions on Major Foreign Exchange Markets (billion $ U.S.)**

Market	U.S. Dollar	Deutsche mark	Japanese Yen	Pound Sterling	ECU	Other	Total
United Kingdom	216 (90)	70 (29)	42 (17)	74 (31)	4.0 (1.7)	77 (32)	241 (200)
United States	167 (96)	58 (33)	48 (28)	25 (14)	0.5 (0.3)	49 (28)	174 (200)
Japan	138 (95)	14 (10)	116 (80)	5.4 (4)	—	17 (12)	145 (200)
Singapore	60 (95)	18 (29)	18 (29)	11 (17)	—	20 (32)	63 (200)
Hong Kong	56 (93)	12 (20)	15 (25)	7.7 (13)	0.1 (0.2)	29 (48)	60 (200)
Australia	36 (97)	5.6 (15)	3.7 (10)	3.1 (8)	—	26 (70)	37 (200)
Total of major 21 markets	838 (90)	247 (27)	253 (27)	138 (15)	8 (1)	382 (41)	932 (200)

Source: BIS, "Survey of Foreign Exchange Market Activity" (Basle, February 1990).

Notes: Daily average in April 1989. Number in parentheses is currency's share as a percentage of total transactions.

Table 13.10 **Inflation Rate in Selected Countries (%)**

	Average		Standard Deviation	
Country	1/80–12/85	1/86–10/91	1/80–12/85	1/86–10/91
Japan	3.6	1.6	2.2	1.4
United States	6.9	4.0	3.9	1.3
Germany	4.1	1.6	1.7	1.4
France	10.3	3.1	3.0	0.5
Italy	15.3	5.8	4.4	0.9
Belgium	7.0	2.3	1.4	1.1
Korea	11.0	6.1	10.8	2.8
Hong Kong	10.2	7.7	4.0	2.8
Taiwan	6.6	2.4	8.4	2.0
Philippines	21.1	8.9	16.0	6.0
Singapore	4.2	1.6	3.6	1.9
Indonesia	11.2	7.7	4.5	1.8
Malaysia	5.0	2.2	3.0	1.4
Thailand	7.5	4.0	6.9	1.8
Australia	8.7	7.4	2.8	1.7
New Zealand	13.0	8.6	4.9	5.2

Source: IMF, "International Financial Statistics" (Washington, D.C.).

recorded the best performance in terms of both measures in the last decade, although the difference among countries has been narrowing in recent years.

13.3.2 Political Stability

Price stability alone is not sufficient to assure confidence in a currency: political instability in an issuing country may undermine confidence in its currency even if inflation is not a problem. This is a major reason that the U.S. dollar has maintained its role as the dominant international currency. It could be argued that in light of recent regime changes in Eastern Europe and the former Soviet Union, the importance of this "safe haven" function of the U.S. dollar is diminishing in favor of the yen. However, in Asia, geopolitical instability still persists, most notably in the form of North Korea and Indochina. In addition, trade and social friction between Japan and the United States may also work against the wider use of the yen worldwide and in Asia in particular.

13.3.3 Current Account Surplus

At least in the early phase of "internationalization," a (large) current account surplus is considered important. Indeed, it cannot be denied that the fact that Japan has consistently recorded a large current account surplus since the early 1980s has been conducive to wider use of the yen outside Japan. For one thing, Japanese financial institutions were in an advantageous position in recycling that surplus to deficit countries. Perhaps more important, this large accumu-

Table 13.11 **Size of Short-term Money Markets in Japan, the United States, and Germany (billion $ U.S.)**

	1981 (year-end)	1985	1990
Japan	84.8 (7.3)	182.3 (13.5)	676.2 (22.8)
United States	964.3 (31.6)	1260.6 (31.4)	1760.8 (32.2)
Germany	101.8 (14.9)	128.8 (20.7)	497.9 (33.2)

Source: Bank of Japan, *Comparative Economic and Financial Statistics—Japan and Other Major Countries* (Tokyo, various issues).
Note: Figures in parentheses are ratio to GNP.

lated surplus, which exceeded $530 billion during 1980–91, has certainly helped foster the credibility of Japan's financial institutions, markets, and currency.

13.3.4 Financial Markets

The size of Japan's money markets grew considerably in the 1980s (table 13.11) and, taking into account the recent progress of interest rate deregulation, as well as the size of capital markets, it is fair to say that the condition of having "wide, deep, and free financial markets" is already met to a large extent. However, it is also true that there is still significant room for improvement in many respects, inter alia, with regard to the transparency of financial institutions and their transactions, freedom concerning the placement of new instruments, and taxation on financial and capital transactions.

13.4 The Potential Role of the Yen as a "Nominal Anchor" for Asia

In sum, the conditions necessary for the yen to assume a greater role than it currently plays are already broadly met, even if there is some room for improvement. What role, then, should the yen play? This section discusses the possibility of a "yen bloc" in Asia.

A brief look at trade figures shows that intraregional trade among major economies in Asia and Oceania[2] (hereafter referred to as Asia) is growing steadily, accounting for about 40 percent of the total trade of the economies in the region (table 13.12). However, it should also be noted that trade with the United States accounts for about 20 percent. The fact that the United States is still by far the single most important trading partner for Asian economies no doubt explains why the U.S. dollar plays an important role in the region.

Japan's direct investments in the region grew considerably in the second half of the 1980s (table 13.13). It is true that as a proportion of total investments, they are still not very large; in fact, the proportion was much larger in the

2. Japan, Korea, Hong Kong, Taiwan, Singapore, Malaysia, Philippines, Indonesia, Thailand, Australia, New Zealand, and China.

Table 13.12 **Country Composition of Trade in Asian Countries (%)**

	1975	1980	1985	1990
United States	19.58	19.28	25.12	22.55
Asia (A)	33.35	34.69	36.37 (39.16)	39.13 (43.47)
Japan	11.03	10.73	10.32	11.09
Ratio of trade in Asian countries to world trade (B)	12.33	14.26	17.06 (19.17)	18.69 (20.76)
A/B	2.71	2.43	2.13 (2.04)	2.09 (2.09)

Sources: IMF, *Direction of Trade* (Washington, D.C., various issues); other sources.
Notes: Trade with Taiwan is included only in figures in parentheses.
Annual growth rates of world trade were 18.5, −0.6, and 12.9 percent for the periods 1975–80, 1980–85, and 1985–90, respectively. Annual growth rates of Asian trade (excluding trade with Taiwan) were 22.0 and 3.9 percent for the first two periods and (including trade with Taiwan) was 14.7 percent for the last period.

Table 13.13 **Japan's Outward Direct Investment by Country**

	1975	1980	1985	1990	Total from 1951
Total (billion $ U.S.)	32.8	46.9	122.2	569.1	3,108.1
Country share (%)					
United States	26.8	31.6	44.2	45.9	42.0
Europe	10.2	12.3	15.8	25.1	19.1
Southeast Asia[a] (A)	32.8	24.8	10.8	11.6	14.2
China (B)	0.0	0.3	0.8	0.6	0.9
Australia (C)	4.8	9.3	3.8	6.5	5.2
New Zealand (D)	0.1	0.2	0.2	0.4	0.3
A+B+C+D	37.7	34.7	16.4	19.7	20.5

Source: Ministry of Finance (Tokyo).
Note: Years are fiscal years.
[a]Includes Korea, Hong Kong, Taiwan, Singapore, Malaysia, the Philippines, Indonesia, and Thailand.

1970s. However, while investments in the 1970s were concentrated in a few countries like Indonesia and the Philippines, they are now much more widespread geographically.

Another fact that stands out is the recent growth in direct investment between the so-called newly industrialized economies (NIEs) and Association of Southeast Asian Nations (ASEAN) countries. Tables 13.14 and 13.15 give a breakdown of direct investments in Indonesia and Thailand by investor country. In the case of Thailand, Japan is the largest investor, accounting for 37.2 percent of total investments in the 1970–89 period, followed by Hong Kong,

Singapore, and Taiwan together at 22.7 percent (which exceeds the U.S. figure of 20.7 percent). The importance of the NIEs as investors is becoming even more pronounced. In Indonesia, NIEs account for more than half of nonpetrol direct investment projects.

Such trade and investment data suggest that economic interdependence is growing rapidly among Asian economies. However, since growth in intraregional trade and investments is partly a reflection of the higher growth of the region compared to that of the rest of the world, one cannot go so far as to say that Asia is on the way to forming an economic bloc. As shown in Frankel (1992), the intraregional trade bias index (defined as the share of intraregional trade in the total trade of a region divided by the share of trade of that region

Table 13.14 Direct Investment in Nonpetrol Projects to Indonesia

	1986	1987	1988	1989	Total 1986–89
Total (million $ U.S.)	245	498	2,498	4,328	7,569
Country share (%)					
Japan	8.0	25.9	6.8	31.1	22.0
United States	8.3	5.3	8.1	1.2	4.0
Europe	27.0	13.1	9.6	6.0	8.4
NIES	33.5	33.4	67.5	50.2	54.2
Hong Kong	4.0	16.9	10.6	9.7	10.3
Korea	7.7	9.8	15.9	21.6	18.5
Singapore	11.7	4.5	3.9	6.3	5.5
Taiwan	10.1	2.3	37.1	12.5	19.9
Other Asia	14.7	1.4	1.1	2.4	2.3
Other	8.5	20.9	6.9	9.1	9.1

Source: Pangestu (1991).

Table 13.15 Direct Investment to Thailand by Country (cumulative investment since 1970)

	1974	1981	1986	1989
Total amount received (million $ U.S.)	416	1,282	2,662	5,871
Country share (%)				
Japan	27.9	27.4	29.5	37.2
United States	38.5	33.9	30.8	20.7
Other OECD countries	11.8	14.0	15.7	13.2
Three NIEs	16.6	18.8	15.9	22.7
Hong Kong	11.1	10.5	10.3	11.1
Singapore	5.3	8.1	5.0	5.4
Taiwan	0.5	0.2	0.6	6.2
Four ASEAN countries	1.7	1.2	0.9	0.5
Other	3.6	4.8	7.2	5.8

Source: Tambunlertchai and Ramstetter (1991).

in world trade) declined for Asia from 2.2 in 1980 to 1.9 in 1989, in contrast to a rise in EC countries from 1.3 to 1.5. Even taking into account that Frankel's estimate does not include Taiwan and that trade figures in Asia for 1989 were negatively influenced by the Tienanmen Square incident, this estimate persuasively suggests that Asian countries are not moving toward a "Fortress Asia"–type bloc.

These trends seem to suggest that the yen is not likely to replace (at least not in the foreseeable future) the U.S. dollar as the key currency, even in Asia, with respect to the three traditional functions of money: as a unit of account (invoicing currency), as a means of transaction, and as a store of value (international financial asset).

A more meaningful role for the yen in a potential "yen zone" in Asia would be one resembling that of the deutsche mark in Europe.

The EMS is generally viewed as a de facto deutsche mark bloc. However, that does not mean that the deutsche mark is in every respect the most important foreign currency for non-German EMS member countries. For example, deutsche marks constitute only about 23.4 percent of the total foreign reserves of EMS countries. Although this is considerable, it is well below the 57.9 percent held in U.S. dollars. To give another example, 43.8 percent of transactions in French foreign exchange markets involve the deutsche mark, compared with 71.9 percent involving the U.S. dollar (note that the currency breakdown total adds up to 200 percent). Similar trends are observed in other EMS countries.

The reason that the EMS countries are nevertheless considered a deutsche mark bloc is that the deutsche mark is playing the important role of "nominal anchor" in maintaining price stability in EMS member countries.

A currency may serve as a nominal anchor for other countries in various ways. In its most rigid form, it is the currency against which exchange rates are pegged. This is the role the deutsche mark presently plays within the EMS. However, a currency can also serve as an anchor for price stability in a less formal way, if other countries attempt to keep their respective inflation rates in line with that of the nominal anchor country, or if monetary authorities, in conducting monetary policy, pay due attention to developments in that country.

It is this kind of mild nominal anchor role that the yen might play in the future. However, before examining that possibility in detail, we should first briefly review foreign exchange arrangements in Asian and Pacific region countries.

While Hong Kong links its currency to the U.S. dollar and Australia and New Zealand let their currencies float, other Asian countries officially link their currencies to a basket which includes, inter alia, the U.S. dollar and Japanese yen. However, the composition of these baskets is not officially announced and, in practice, they could be considered de facto "managed floating," with the main focus on the exchange rate against the U.S. dollar.

Accordingly, fluctuations in the exchange rates of their respective currencies vis-à-vis the U.S. dollar, measured in terms of variation coefficients, tend to be smaller than in those against the yen (table 13.16). However, these fluctuations tended to be generally smaller in the second half of the 1980s than in the first. Moreover, in the case of the Korean won, volatility vis-à-vis the yen was in fact slightly smaller than vis-à-vis the U.S. dollar, and in the case of the Singapore dollar, the difference was only very marginal.

In fact, it seems that in forming their monetary and foreign exchange policy, Asian authorities are becoming increasingly more sensitive to developments in Japan. This seems to be quite natural since these economies are competing more and more with Japan in world export markets and therefore have an interest in keeping their inflation rate in line with Japan's.

In the previous sections and the first part of this section, we reviewed the linkage between Japan and Asian countries in terms of the scale of trade, direct investment, and financial transactions. In considering the potential role of the yen as a nominal anchor currency as explained above, however, it is not sufficient to look at these quantitative variables. In fact, the relationship between Asian countries and Japan from the viewpoint of linkage of prices, e.g., interest rates and the prices of goods, is perhaps more relevant. To obtain a broad view of this context, the correlation coefficients of movements in several key variables in Asian countries and those in Japan were estimated and compared with coefficients between the former and those of the United States.

There are several reasons for not employing more sophisticated methods. For one, there are differences in the quality of data among countries. Moreover, in light of the difference in the depth and structure of financial markets, some reservations are in order about the international comparability of data. In addi-

Table 13.16 Coefficient of Variation of Selected Exchange Rates vis-à-vis U.S. Dollar and Japanese Yen (coefficient variable to dollar and yen rate)[a]

	1980–85		1986–91	
	Dollar	Yen	Dollar	Yen
Korea	0.116	0.125	0.096	0.085
Singapore	0.023	0.062	0.085	0.089
Malaysia	0.041	0.066	0.033	0.111
Thailand	0.094	0.099	0.014	0.082
Philippines	0.389	0.386	0.119	0.171
Australia	0.169	0.217	0.077	0.160
New Zealand	0.236	0.266	0.075	0.169
Indonesia	0.248	0.248	0.136	0.193

Note: Countries in Asia and Oceania use the following exchange rate systems: Korea, market average rate (allows certain amount of fluctuation centering on market average rate the previous day); Australia, New Zealand, and Taiwan, floating exchange rate; Hong Kong, dollar-pegged (HK$7.8 = $1 U.S.); Malaysia, Singapore, and Thailand, currency basket (basket not publicized); Indonesia and the Philippines, managed floating exchange rate.

[a]Standard deviation/average.

tion, since the definition of "nominal anchor" is, by nature, rather vague, it might be too much to investigate causal relationships in different countries.

Table 13.17 shows the correlation coefficients of movements in Asian short-term interest rates with those of Japan and the United States. The coefficients were low in the case of Japanese versus Asian interest rates; in fact, negative coefficients were obtained in many cases.

However, these low coefficients might not be sufficient justification to come to any decision. Using a simple interest rate function and concentrating on more recent data, Frankel (1992) obtained results suggesting that the influence of Japan's short-term interest rates (relative to interest rates of the United States and Germany) on rates in Hong Kong and Singapore was rising (table 13.18). Moreover, if two countries are influenced by different real shocks, efforts by either to bring its inflation rate in line with the other's may widen, rather than narrow, the difference between nominal interest rate movements in the two countries. From a theoretical point of view, it would also be interesting to examine the relationship among long-term interest rates, especially real interest rates. However, the lack of free and deep trading markets for long-term instruments in most Asian countries prevent any meaningful analysis in this direction.

Similar exercises were conducted with regard to prices of goods. There remains the problem of which price index to choose. Needless to say, the choice hinges crucially upon the aim of the analysis. If one wants to focus on relative competitiveness in the world market, analysis based on domestic manufactured goods or export goods may be most relevant. On the other hand, to investigate the existence and strength of common external shocks, it would be worthwhile to look at the comovements of import prices. Or, if one is interested in causal relationships, one may try to relate one country's import prices to the export prices of another. However, because the focus here is in the potential of the

Table 13.17 **International Linkage of Short-term Interest Rate Fluctuation (correlation coefficient based on changes from the previous month)**

	1980–85		1986–91	
	United States	Japan	United States	Japan
Korea	0.022	0.077	0.038	0.003
Taiwan	0.201	−0.146	0.053	−0.054
Hong Kong	0.168	0.280	0.087	−0.179
Singapore	0.350	0.153	0.583	0.008
Malaysia	−0.065	−0.076	−0.119	−0.031
Thailand	0.495	0.112	0.138	0.198
Philippines	0.054	0.016	0.081	−0.080
Australia	−0.002	−0.180	0.013	0.270
New Zealand	0.114	−0.444	0.216	0.044

Table 13.18 **Japanese and U.S. Interest Rate Effects in Five Pacific Countries**

	Constant Term	Tokyo Effect	New York Effect	R^2	D-W
Singapore					
A	−2.29**	0.82**	0.43**	.85	0.53
	(0.84)	(0.07)	(0.09)		
B	3.30**	−0.01	0.27**	.71	0.43
	(0.39)	(0.03)	(0.05)		
C	1.47**	0.29**	0.41**	.72	1.41
	(0.45)	(0.05)	(0.06)		
Australia					
A	−6.66**	0.74**	2.11**	.73	0.19
	(2.32)	(0.18)	(0.26)		
B	13.90**	0.10*	−0.07	.03	0.20
	(1.40)	(0.06)	(0.12)		
C	3.83**	0.07	0.67**	.76	1.36
	(1.13)	(0.21)	(0.20)		
Taiwan					
A	−4.93	1.91**	0.32	.53	1.17
	(4.04)	(0.32)	(0.45)		
B	7.14	0.07	0.10	.05	0.82
	(0.67)	(0.08)	(0.12)		
Korea					
A	−4.08*	1.29**	1.16**	.69	0.78
	(2.33)	(0.19)	(0.26)		
B	11.65**	0.04	0.27**	.55	1.28
	(0.32)	(0.04)	(0.07)		
Hong Kong					
A	−6.40**	0.25*	1.66**	.79	0.59
	(1.51)	(0.15)	(0.17)		

Source: Frankel (1992).

Notes: Table reports regressions of local interest rate against: A—Japanese and U.S. interest rates (1988–91 monthly data), B—Japanese and U.S. interest rates adjusted for expectations of exchange rate changes (reflected in *Currency Forecasters' Digest*), and C—Japanese and U.S. interest rates adjusted for forward discount.

Numbers in parentheses are standard errors.

*Statistically different from 0 at the 90 percent level.

**Statistically different from 0 at the 99 percent level.

yen as a nominal anchor in the conduct of monetary policy, I have decided to concentrate on the consumer price index (CPI), which is the most relevant variable in discussing the main objective of monetary policy, that is, overall price stability. The results are reported in table 13.19.[3]

3. Although the comovement of CPI inflation would be a useful criterion for assessing the role of a currency as a nominal anchor in an informal way, it may not be for assessing the possibility of a fixed exchange rate regime. As De Grauwe (1992) argues, it would be difficult to achieve both convergence on inflation and fixed exchange rates if the differential in productivity growth between tradables and nontradables varies among countries.

Table 13.19 **International Linkage of Price Fluctuation (correlation coefficient based on changes in year-on-year CPI inflation rate; monthly data)**

	1980–85		1986–91	
	United States	Japan	United States	Japan
Korea	0.295	0.004	0.019	0.058
Taiwan	0.015	0.175	0.018	0.176
Hong Kong	−0.119	−0.008	0.055	0.038
Singapore	0.303	0.034	0.440	0.122
Malaysia	0.042	0.027	0.101	0.302
Thailand	0.261	0.211	0.046	−0.036
Philippines	0.175	0.052	−0.156	0.146
Australia[a]	−0.182	0.064	0.128	0.279
New Zealand	0.183	0.071	−0.081	−0.076
Indonesia	0.055	−0.127	0.088	0.052

[a]Based on quarterly data.

It is interesting that, compared to the first half, coefficients tended to be higher in the second half of the 1980s; moreover, the comovement of inflation in Asian countries and Japan, relative to that in the United States, is more pronounced in the latter period. These tendencies are most noticeable between Japan on one hand and Taiwan, Singapore, Malaysia, and Australia on the other.

It is not surprising that the coefficients are not very high, if one considers that it is the second derivative of price level which is examined.[4] Even within Japan, the correlation coefficients between changes in inflation rates vary significantly among different cities. The correlation coefficient between Tokyo and Naha, Okinawa, is not very much higher than that between Japan and Malaysia, for instance.[5]

Not many will deny that the European economies are much more homogeneous with each other than are Asian economies. However, there was little similarity in price movement among European countries in the 1970s, and it was not until the second half of the 1980s that the linkage became obvious.[6]

Table 13.20 shows the correlation coefficients of stock price movements. Here, the similarity of movement becomes more significant, at least in the second half of the 1980s. The linkage between price movements in Asian stock

4. I also calculated correlation coefficients based on the first derivative of CPI, that is, the level of inflation. Naturally, the coefficients were higher than those reported in the paper; however, the general tendency was much the same.

5. During 1980–85, the Naha/Tokyo and Naha/Sapporo correlation coefficients were 0.409 and 0.441, respectively. During 1986–91, these coefficients were 0.377 and 0.717.

6. The Belgium/Germany correlation coefficients for the periods 1970–75, 1976–80, 1981–85, and 1986–91 were −0.013, 0.213, 0.458, and 0.691, respectively. The France/Germany coefficients for these periods were 0.029, 0.102, 0.109, and 0.573.

markets and in Japan's market is almost as close as that between the former and the U.S. stock market. Although these results should be interpreted with caution, not least since the high coefficients are to some extent due to the 1987 stock market crash, they are nevertheless suggestive of the growing interdependence of these markets.

Finally, to summarize these exercises, and also to focus on more recent periods, canonical correlation coefficients were estimated using inflation rates, stock prices, short-term interest rates, and, where reliable data was available, long-term interest rates for the periods 1980–87 and 1988–91 (table 13.21). It is interesting that coefficients in the case of Asian countries vis-à-vis Japan were higher, without exception, for 1988–91 than for 1980–87. Moreover, in many cases, they were higher than, or very close to, coefficients for Asia vis-à-vis the United States. Admittedly, the estimation period may be too short to make too much out of this result. Nevertheless, it also seems to illustrate that the interdependence of Japan and Asian economies has grown remarkably in recent years.

13.5 Tentative Conclusion

It is not easy to draw any firm implication from the facts and results discussed in the previous sections: they provide only piecemeal information, which is sometimes contradictory. Moreover, analysis is simplistic: for example, a relatively high correlation coefficient may only be a coincidence.

Nevertheless, to me at any rate, they seem to suggest that the Japanese yen has the potential to serve as a nominal anchor for Asian countries, though not as formally as the deutsche mark does for Europe now. One may even venture to argue that the Japanese yen is already playing such a role, albeit in a very

Table 13.20 International Linkage of Stock Price Fluctuation (correlation coefficient based on year-on-year changes; monthly data)

	1980–85		1986–91	
	United States	Japan	United States	Japan
Korea	−0.202	0.093	0.316	0.381
Taiwan	0.146	0.135	0.253	0.259
Hong Kong	0.281	0.383	0.445	0.211
Singapore	0.251	0.217	0.560	0.334
Malaysia	0.344	0.412	0.530	0.390
Thailand	0.078	−0.016	0.507	0.468
Philippines	0.043	0.162	0.093	0.061
Australia	0.614	0.393	0.649	0.413
New Zealand	0.026	0.147	0.537	0.288

Table 13.21 Canonical Correlation Coefficients using Changes in Interest Rates, Inflation Rates, and Stock Prices

	Japan		United States	
	1980–87	1988–91	1980–87	1988–91
Korea	0.451	0.562	0.558	0.584
Taiwan	0.284	0.416	0.417	0.411
Hong Kong	0.354	0.538	0.404	0.584
Singapore	0.392	0.609	0.604	0.704
Malaysia	0.515	0.705	0.603	0.582
Thailand	0.578	0.758	0.618	0.803
Philippines	0.306	0.478	0.393	0.562
Australia	0.554	0.683	0.682	0.699
New Zealand	0.311	0.537	0.372	0.614
Indonesia	0.266	0.361	0.450	0.367

weak sense, since Asian authorities, in formulating their macroeconomic policies, pay attention to Japan's low inflation record.

To what extent, and at what pace, the Japanese yen will become an anchor currency in Asia hinges on many economic and noneconomic factors: e.g., how intraregional trade and investment will develop, the future military presence of the United States in this region, whether political ties among Asian countries become closer, and the development of the U.S. economy.

The development of the U.S. economy is particularly important. As discussed earlier, the U.S. dollar is now by far the dominant currency in Asia. As long as the U.S. economy remains sound and its inflation rate low, the incentive for Asian authorities to pay greater attention to the yen and the Japanese economy in forming their monetary policy may not strengthen significantly. However, if for some reason the performance of the U.S. economy becomes less satisfactory to them, the increase in the importance of the yen may accelerate.

Finally, a greater role for the yen as a nominal anchor for Asian countries is a tendency that should neither be encouraged nor discouraged from the Japanese viewpoint. The decision whether to have the yen serve such a function should be made by the Asian countries themselves. Japan's responsibility is to make sure its financial and capital markets are more convenient and safe for Asian areas, as well as for the rest of the world. Moreover, it is crucial that Japan make every effort to maintain price stability so that Asian countries could use the yen as a nominal anchor if they so decided.

References

BIS (Bank for International Settlements). 1990. Survey of foreign exchange market activity. Basle: Bank for International Settlements, February.

Black, Stanley W. 1990. The international use of currencies. In *The evolution of the international monetary system: How can efficiency and stability be attained?* ed. Yoshio Suzuki, Junichi Miyake, and Mitsuaki Okabe, 175–94. Tokyo: University of Tokyo Press.

De Grauwe, Paul. 1992. Inflation convergence during the transition to EMU. CEPR Discussion Paper no. 658. London: Centre for Economic Policy Research, June.

Frankel, Jeffrey A. 1991. Is a yen bloc forming in Pacific Asia? In *Finance and the international economy,* ed. R. O'Brien and S. Hewin. New York: Oxford University Press.

———. 1992. Is Japan creating a yen bloc in East Asia and the Pacific? NBER Working Paper no. 4050. Cambridge, Mass.: National Bureau of Economic Research.

Kawai, Masahiro. 1992. Yen no Kokusaika (Internationalization of the yen). In *Kokusai Kinyu no Genjo (International finance),* ed. Takatoshi Ito, 275–326. Tokyo: Yuhikaku.

Pangestu, Mari. 1991. Foreign firms and structural changes in the Indonesian manufacturing sector. In *Direct foreign investment in Asia's developing economies and structural change in the Asia-Pacific Region,* ed. Eric D. Ramstetter, 35–64. Boulder, Colo.: Westview.

Taguchi, Hiroo. 1982. A survey on the international use of the yen. BIS Working Paper no. 6. Basle: Bank for International Settlements, July.

Takeda, Masahiko, and Philip Turner. 1992. The liberalization of Japan's financial markets: some major themes. BIS Economic Papers. Basle: Bank for International Settlements, November.

Tambunlertchai, Somsak, and Eric D. Ramstetter. 1991. Foreign firms in promoted industries and structural change in Thailand. In *Direct foreign investment in Asia's developing economies and structural change in the Asia-Pacific region,* ed. Eric D. Ramstetter, 65–102. Boulder, Colo.: Westview.

Tavlas, George S., and Yuzuru Ozeki. 1991. The Japanese yen as an international currency. IMF Working Paper WP/91/2. Washington, D.C.: International Monetary Fund, January.

———. 1992. The internationalization of currencies: An appraisal of the Japanese yen. Occasional Paper 90. Washington, D.C.: International Monetary Fund, January.

Comment Kazuo Ueda

This paper provides a well-balanced assessment of the current degree of internationalization of the yen and a quite reasonable speculation about what is likely to happen in the near future. Taguchi supports his argument by using interesting statistics, some of which I see for the first time. I am afraid I do not have much to disagree with.

Taguchi, quite appropriately, differentiates two types of internationalization of a currency: one, playing the role of a key or vehicle currency and, the other, becoming a currency against which other central banks try to peg their currencies. In the world today, the first role is clearly played by the dollar. The deutsche mark is partly playing the second role. I quite agree with Taguchi that

Kazuo Ueda is professor of economics at the University of Tokyo.

the two aspects of internationalization can be separate issues and that the yen could increasingly play the second role, especially in Asia.

First, I will argue that the yen is not likely to play the first role in the near future, largely because Japanese money and financial markets are not fully deregulated. Deregulation of the extent that we see in New York or London is certainly a necessary condition for the yen to become a key currency. Thus, we do not have a large scale treasury bond (TB) market. Because of this, the Bank of Japan is having trouble carrying out its daily operations. There are strange taxes—for example, the transactions tax—which have had a serious negative impact on the repurchase agreement (*gensaki*) market for Japanese government bonds (JGBs). And there is nontransparent moral suasion and administrative guidance (*gyouseishido*) everywhere.

Second, I would like to point out a problem with other Asian countries pegging to the yen. Suppose this happened and the Bank of Japan successfully stabilized Japan's CPI at 0–2 percent, as it did in the 1980s. Over the last couple of decades Japanese export prices have been falling steadily relative to the CPI. Hence, zero percent inflation in the Japanese CPI implies a negative inflation rate for Japanese export prices, creating strong deflationary pressure on other countries.

Comment Anne O. Krueger

At a time when there is discussion of Maastricht in connection with the European Single Market and of a Western Hemisphere Free Trade Agreement with the dollar already the regional currency, it is natural that many are discussing the trading and exchange relationships among Asian countries. In this connection, Hiroo Taguchi has performed a valuable service in considering the Japanese yen's potential as the nominal anchor for the exchange rates of the region.

I found his analysis insightful and to the point. I also agree with him that the factors conducive to the use of the yen as an international currency are substantially weaker than those affecting the dollar or the deutsche mark. It was only in the mid-1980s that Japan liberalized the regulations governing yen transactions on capital account. Until that had happened, it was not conceivable that the yen could be an international currency. Even now, although liberalization has proceeded a considerable distance, I suspect that there are still constraints on yen capital account convertibility. The fact that liberalization has only been recent and still may not be complete will limit the yen's role for some time.

Because I am so much in accord with the basic thrust of the paper, I shall use my time to extend his analysis, rather than to comment directly on it. A

Anne O. Krueger is professor of Economics at Stanford University and a research associate at the National Bureau of Economic Research.

useful starting point, it seems to me, is the old "optimum currency area" discussion pioneered by Mundell (1961). There, Mundell noted that the currency of a country producing only a single commodity (such as bananas or tin) would be of little use as a store of value, since its purchasing power (assuming domestic price stability) reflected nothing more than the price of other commodities in terms of that single commodity.

However, when domestic prices are nominally sticky, exchange rate changes can serve to bring about the necessary relative price adjustments. To make his point, Mundell questioned whether western Canada and the western United States might not form an optimum currency area relative to the eastern parts of both countries, since the West was mineral- and agriculture-rich and the East was more manufacturing-intensive.

Mundell's analysis intentionally neglected the role of public policy in smoothing the resource reallocations that terms of trade changes bring about. Therefore, a second aspect of an optimum currency area—the area within which mechanisms are in place through internal transfers to smooth adjustments that are needed—was not considered.

In many regards, this second aspect is dominant when we consider the yen as a nominal anchor for Asian countries: as of 1992, inflation rates had not converged, and the commodity composition of output and trade differed greatly between Japan and other East Asian countries. By contrast, EC members' commodity composition of output was, while not identical, sufficiently similar so that a movement of the ECU against the dollar was meaningful in facilitating a terms of trade change. A simultaneous movement of the yen, ringgit, and rupiah would do nothing to assist in adjusting to terms of trade changes, be they of petroleum, agricultural commodities, or other goods. Japan imports primary commodities from Southeast Asia and exports manufactures to it: if Malaysia, Indonesia, or Thailand used the yen as a nominal anchor, those countries would need to achieve a degree of price-level stability similar to that of Japan and simultaneously find other mechanisms for adjusting to terms of trade shocks.

Hence, I conclude that the use of the yen as a nominal anchor for Asian currencies will probably be weak for the foreseeable future. I do agree that price-level stability in Japan increases resistance to inflation in other countries, but not sufficiently to bring about convergence in inflation rates.

At any event, integration of trade need not mean currency integration, at least for the next decade. To the extent that the Southeast and East Asian countries continue their rapid growth, convergence in living standards, economic structures, and inflation rates may begin to occur. As that happens, there may be more scope in the future for an Asian currency area.

Reference

Mundell, Robert A. 1961. A theory of optimum currency areas. *American Economic Review* 51 (September): 657–65.

14 Economic Preconditions for Asian Regional Integration

Junichi Goto and Koichi Hamada

14.1 Introduction

The United Europe of 1992 and the attempt to form the North American Free Trade Area (NAFTA) tell us that the world is under a new tide of regionalism. We hope that the tidal wave will not result in the formation of highly protective regional blocs, as the phrase "Fortress Europe" might suggest, but that these are moves toward an integrated world economy with free trade. In any case, a series of questions arises: Will Asian countries form an economic bloc in the near future? Will the Association of South East Asian Nations (ASEAN) create a more integrated economic community? Will the plan to form the East Asian Economic Caucus (EAEC) or Group (EAEG) be realized? Is it practical to conceive of a currency union in East Asia?

In fact, Asian nations have now begun to move toward the creation of a free trade area (FTA). For example, in November 1991, the Asian-Pacific Economic Cooperation (APEC) Minister Conference agreed that it would promote free trade within the region; in January 1992, the summit meeting of ASEAN decided to create an FTA. Are these steps toward Asian economic integration desirable for Asia?

The political aspects of these questions are far from simple. First, the United States may oppose the creation of an FTA in Asia that would restrict export flows from the United States to this area, as it has already indicated by its

Junichi Goto is associate professor of economics at Kobe University. Koichi Hamada is professor of economics at Yale University and a research associate of the National Bureau of Economic Research.

The authors thank Shigeyuki Abe, Tetsushi Honda, and T. N. Srinivasan for valuable discussions and Megan Weiler for editorial assistance.

response to the plan for the EAEC or EAEG. Second, the idea of including Japan in an Asian bloc may invoke complex and ambivalent, if not entirely hostile, reactions by many nations in the region, because it triggers memories of the infamous "co-prosperity area" formed under Japan's lead during World War II.

In his prize-winning essay, Jeffrey Frankel (1991) notes that the Japanese government is not necessarily taking a positive stance toward the formation of a yen bloc in Asia or East Asia. This reluctance reflects Japan's delicate political position, a legacy of the past. It corresponds to the low political profile maintained by Germany, despite its economic affluence.

This paper does not address the political feasibility of any form of Asian economic integration, nor does it intend to advocate any. Rather, we present a general assessment of economic conditions in Asia as a preliminary step to a discussion of the issues involved in such an integration. While Frankel (1991) focused on the question of Japan's influence in the region, we shall examine various statistical indicators in order to assess how closely the Asian national economies are interrelated. We shall attempt to discover whether conditions in the Asian economies are favorable or unfavorable for the creation of an FTA or a common currency area and, specifically, whether the Asian economies are more or less homogeneous than those of the European Community, which are moving toward economic unification.

In section 14.2, we will review selected macroeconomic indicators for the East Asian nations, trace how closely their movements coincide, and examine how closely they are interrelated. In other words, we will assess the degree of homogeneity and the degree of economic proximity in Asia. Then we will compare them with those in Europe.

In section 14.3, we will study whether the region meets preconditions for an FTA or FTAs by examining trade intensity indices among Asian nations. Since the conventional trade intensity index captures the degree of closeness in terms of trade only relative to the size of its trading partner and not the absolute degree of dependence of a country on trade with its partner, we will supplement the trade intensity index with an alternative measure, the *trade dependence index,* which indicates the importance of a trading partner.

In order to assess conditions for creating an FTA, we have to know not only how closely nations are interwoven by trade, but also how their import-competing industries are protected by tariffs and other barriers. We will study the degree of protection. The more nations protect their import-competing industries, the greater the trade-creating effect of the formation of an FTA.

In section 14.4, we will review conditions for creating a currency union in Asia. Thanks to the theory of an optimal currency area initiated by Mundell (1961), we have more criteria by which to judge the appropriateness of the formation of a common currency area than we do to judge that of an FTA. We will review the similarity or the diversity of macroeconomic disturbances, both real and nominal, and the ease of factor movements among nations within the region.

In section 14.5, we will summarize the results and possible policy implications. As a tentative conclusion, we may say that the degree of interdependence among Asian nation is high, even higher in some respects than among EC countries. Preconditions for an FTA in this region are satisfied. However, since Asian countries depend heavily on trade with the United States and Japan, an FTA that hinders trade with these countries would not be practical. Preconditions for a currency union in Asia are also met. In such a currency union, it is not clear whether the Asian countries would benefit from linking their common currency to a major currency such as the dollar or the yen.

14.2 Confluence in Macroeconomic Variables in Asia

As a prelude to a discussion of the feasibility of economic integration in Asia, let us review key macroeconomic indicators in East Asian countries, including both the Asian newly industrialized economies (NIEs) and ASEAN countries and then compare them with corresponding indicators in other regions. Table 14.1 summarizes the main economic indicators for selected countries. From a quick glance at this table, one sees that an East Asian nation can be characterized as a high-income, rapidly growing economy with a relatively stable price level (especially in the 1980s). The Philippines in the mid-1980s

Table 14.1 Main Economic Indicators for Selected Countries

Country	Population (million)	GNP per Capita (U.S. $) (1988)	Growth Rate (%) (1965–88)	Inflation Rate (%) (1965–80)	Inflation Rate (%) (1980–88)
Hong Kong	5.7	9,220	6.3	8.1	6.7
Korea	42.0	3,600	6.8	18.7	5.0
Singapore	2.6	9,070	7.2	4.9	1.2
Taiwan	20.1	6,333	8.9[a]	10.4[b]	4.7
Indonesia	174.8	440	4.3	34.2	8.5
Malaysia	16.9	1,940	4.0	4.9	1.3
Philippines	59.9	630	1.6	11.7	15.6
Thailand	54.5	1,000	4.0	6.3	3.1
United States	246.3	19,840	1.6	6.5	4.0
Japan	122.6	21,020	4.3	7.7	1.3
World[c]	4,736.2	3,470[d]	1.5[d]	9.8[d]	14.1[d]

Sources: World Bank, *World Development Report 1990* (Washington, D.C.); *Taiwan Kenkyu Sho, Taiwan Soran (Taiwan Statistical Data Book),* 1991.

[a]1970–90.

[b]1970–80.

[c]Total countries reporting data to the World Bank.

[d]Weighted average.

is a notable exception. In 1984 and 1985, the consumer price level in the Philippines increased by 50.3 and 23.1 percent, respectively. In the same period, during which the country experienced severe political unrest, real GNP *declined* by almost 10 percent in the annual average rate. All other East Asian nations enjoyed good economic performance throughout the 1970s and 1980s.

In order to elaborate the above statement somewhat more rigorously, we conducted *t*-tests on three macroeconomic indicators: inflation, growth, and investment. We compared the sample mean of each variable in eight East Asian countries with those in 15 developed countries as well as with those in 20 developing countries. Table 14.2 compares the sample means of the three variables in East Asian countries with those in 20 developing countries. The East Asian countries in the following discussion include both the Asian NIEs and ASEAN countries: Hong Kong, Korea, Taiwan, Singapore, Indonesia, Malaysia, the Philippines, and Thailand. A second, control, group of less-developed countries (LDCs) includes Mexico, Algeria, Côte d'Ivoire, Ghana, Morocco, Nigeria, Zaire, Egypt, Turkey, Yugoslavia, Argentina, Brazil, Chile, Colombia, Peru, Uruguay, Venezuela, India, Pakistan, and Sri Lanka.

Table 14.2 shows the sample means and the standard errors of difference in means of the three variables during 1970–90. The table indicates that the East Asian countries enjoyed significantly lower inflation, higher economic growth, and more active investment than the 20 control-group LDCs. While many Latin American countries suffered from hyperinflation, as high as 500–1000 percent per annum during the 1980s, annual rates of increase in consumer prices in East Asia were in most cases less than 10 percent, with the aforementioned exception of the Philippines. With this price stability, real GNP grew rapidly. While the average economic growth rate in the control-group LDCs was 3.4 percent, in the East Asian countries it was 7.4 percent, more than twice as high. This rapid growth was not limited to the NIEs (i.e., Hong Kong, Korea, Tai-

Table 14.2 Sample Means for Selected Macroeconomic Variables: Asia versus Control-Group Less-Developed Countries

Variable	Asia[a]	Control LDC[b]	Difference	Standard Error
Inflation[c]	8.829	96.299	−87.470*	36.818
Growth[d]	7.421	3.352	4.069**	0.467
Investment[e]	26.841	20.234	6.607**	0.714

Source: IMF, *International Financial Statistics* (Washington, D.C., various issues).

[a]Hong Kong, Korea, Taiwan, Singapore, Indonesia, Malaysia, the Philippines, Thailand.

[b]Mexico, Algeria, Côte d'Ivoire, Ghana, Morocco, Nigeria, Zaire, Egypt, Turkey, Yugoslavia, Argentina, Brazil, Chile, Colombia, Peru, Uruguay, Venezuela, India, Pakistan, Sri Lanka.

[c]Change in consumer price index (%).

[d]Change in real GDP (GNP) (%).

[e]Ratio of investment to GDP (GNP) (%).

*Significant at 95 percent level.

**Significant at 99 percent level.

Table 14.3 **Sample Means for Selected Macroeconomic Variables: Asia versus Developed Countries**

Variable	Asia[a]	Developed	Difference	Standard Error
Inflation[c]	8.829	8.813	0.016	0.674
Growth[d]	7.421	3.078	4.343**	0.309
Investment[e]	26.841	22.081	4.760**	0.520

Source: IMF, *International Financial Statistics* (Washington, D.C., various issues).
[a]Hong Kong, Korea, Taiwan, Singapore, Indonesia, Malaysia, the Philippines, Thailand.
[b]United States, Japan, Canada, and 12 EC countries.
[c]Change in consumer price index (%).
[d]Change in real GDP (GNP) (%).
[e]Ratio of investment to GDP (GNP) (%).
**Significant at 99 percent level.

wan, and Singapore). For example, economic growth rates in Malaysia and Thailand in 1990 exceeded 10 percent.

The third row of the table shows the degree of investment activity (the ratio of fixed capital formation to total GDP). While investment activities were stagnant in the control-group LDCs during the 1980s, investment in East Asia accelerated in that period, and it has shown no sign of slowdown in recent years. Active investment in East Asia suggests that even faster economic growth may be realized in this region in the future.

Since the 20 LDC countries in the control group were suffering to varying degrees from recent economic difficulties, a comparison with these LDCs may not necessarily prove the good economic performance of East Asian nations. Hence, we also compared the same macroeconomic indicators for East Asia with those for developed countries including the United States, Japan, Canada, and 12 EC countries (see table 14.3). The comparison with developed countries, however, shows again the East Asia was growing dynamically under stable prices. Economic performance in East Asia was generally better, not only than other developing countries, but also than our group of developed countries, which includes such economic superstars as Germany and Japan.

Although there is no significant difference in the inflation rates in the two groups, economic growth rates were significantly higher and investment significantly more active in East Asia than in developed countries. Thus, from their economic performance during the 1970s and 1980s, the East Asian nations can be characterized as a group of dynamically growing economies with stable price levels.

Let us now ask how homogeneous macroeconomic variables are in the East Asian region and by what standard one can judge whether the Asian nations have similar economic structures. If we were interested in the degree of interdependence between a pair of variables, we would naturally be interested in the correlation coefficient between them. However, in studying the degree of coherence in a group of more than two variables, the correlation coefficient does not help much. The canonical correlation between groups of variables gives a measure of correlation between the groups, but not the degree of confluence within a single group. Neither does regression analysis among variables make much sense.

There are alternative methods of measuring the degree of confluence. For example, the dissimilarity index (Kaufman and Rousseeuw 1990) and the Mahalanobis D^2 (Mahalanobis 1936) could be useful devices. In this paper we apply principal component analysis to measure the degree of confluence in macroeconomic time series in the Asian countries. The principal components of a set of m variables are a set of m artificially constructed variables that are mutually orthogonal linear combinations of the original variables. The first component explains as much as possible of the total variance of the original variables, the second explains as much as possible of the variance that is left unexplained by the first, and so forth. We propose to measure the degree of confluence in variables by the ratio of the variance explained by the first component to the total variance.

The rationale is as follows: If a set of variables is perfectly correlated, the first (or any) component explains all of the variance. If they are mutually independent and have identical variance, the first component explains $1/m$ of the total variance. In general, the ratio of the variance explained by a principal component to the total variance is equal to the value of the characteristic root of the correlation matrix corresponding to the component divided by m.

As is well known, possible problems remain in this approach. The principal components are not independent of the scaling of the variables; it is hard to interpret principal components in economic terms, even though factor analysis, which is closely related to the principal component method, provides a way to interpret them. In spite of these potential problems, the principal component method seems to be a useful tool that effectively serves our objectives. In fact, Stone (1945) utilized principal component analysis to clarify the structure of income and outlay in the United States by economizing on the number of variables, and Adelman and Morris (1967) used factor analysis to classify developing countries by the similarity of their social, economic, and political characteristics.

We apply principal component analysis to five key macroeconomic variables in the East Asian countries—change in money supply (M_1), interest rate, inflation rate, economic growth rate, and investment activity—in order to evaluate the degree of confluence of these variables within the region. We solve the characteristic equation of the correlation matrix of macroeconomic variables. The principal components are normalized in such a way that they have zero mean and unitary variance.

Table 14.4 summarizes for each macroeconomic variable the proportion of its total variation among the eight East Asian countries (exactly speaking, seven for money supply and interest rate because the data for Hong Kong were

Table 14.4 Principal Component (P.C.) Analysis of Selected Macroeconomic Variables (cumulative R^2)

Variable and Component	Asia[a]	Larger EC[b]	Smaller EC[c]
Change in money supply			
First P.C.	0.522	0.423	0.321
Second P.C.	0.690	0.677	0.512
Third P.C.	0.843	0.811	0.686
Interest rate			
First P.C.	0.487	0.578	0.492
Second P.C.	0.840	0.760	0.756
Third P.C.	0.932	0.899	0.916
Change in consumer price			
First P.C.	0.672	0.767	0.656
Second P.C.	0.806	0.875	0.826
Third P.C.	0.903	0.925	0.911
Change in real GDP			
First P.C.	0.401	0.495	0.456
Second P.C.	0.623	0.711	0.676
Third P.C.	0.821	0.839	0.821
Ratio of investment in GDP			
First P.C.	0.423	0.504	0.443
Second P.C.	0.725	0.790	0.704
Third P.C.	0.878	0.949	0.935

[a]For change in money supply and interest rate: Korea, Taiwan, Singapore, Indonesia, Malaysia, Philippines, and Thailand. For change in consumer price, change in real GDP, and ratio of investment in GDP: Hong Kong, Korea, Taiwan, Singapore, Indonesia, Malaysia, Philippines, and Thailand.

[b]For change in money supply and interest rate: Germany, France, Italy, United Kingdom, Spain, the Netherlands, and Belgium. For change in consumer price, change in real GDP, and ratio of investment in GDP: Germany, France, Italy, United Kingdom, Spain, the Netherlands, Belgium, and Denmark.

[c]For change in money supply and interest rate: Luxembourg, Ireland, Portugal, Greece, Denmark, Belgium, and the Netherlands. For change in consumer price, change in real GDP, and ratio of investment in GDP: Luxembourg, Ireland, Portugal, Greece, Denmark, Belgium, the Netherlands, and Spain.

unavailable) that is accounted for by the first three principal components. Thus, for example, with regard to the change in money supply, the first principal component accounts for 52.2 percent of the total variation of the seven Asian variables, the second for 16.8 percent (or 69.0 percent cumulatively), and the third for an additional 15.3 percent.

In an attempt to grasp intuitively the degree of confluence of macroeconomic activities among Asian countries, we compare these values for Asia with those for two sets of EC countries: the larger EC countries and the smaller EC countries (divided in terms of their GNP). In order to avoid a misleading impression due to the difference in the number of countries in each group, or in the degree of freedom, the number of countries in each group is set to be the same for each comparison.

As can be seen in table 14.4, changes in money supply are more homogeneous by far in the Asian countries than in the EC countries, which are expected to form a single currency area in the near future. While the first principal component accounts for more than half of the total variation of the Asian variables, it explains only a little more than 40 percent among variables for the larger EC countries and less than one third among variables for the smaller EC countries.

For the remaining four variables, too, the Asian variables are found to be fairly homogeneous. Although the ratio of the variance explained by the first component to the total variance in Asia is generally smaller than that among the larger EC countries, there is little difference between the ratio in Asia and that among the smaller EC countries. Thus in terms of these macroeconomic variables, East Asia is a group as homogeneous as the European Community.

It is also interesting to consider the contribution of each additional variable to the principal components. For that purpose, we examine the "loading factor." The loading factor equals the correlation coefficient between a principal component and the original variable. The sum of the squares of loading factors of a component equals its characteristic root.

Table 14.5 indicates the loading factors for the first three principal components for five macroeconomic variables: change in money supply, interest rate, change in CPI, change in real GNP, and ratio of investment to GNP. Loading factors are also interpreted as the correlation coefficient between the principal component and the corresponding country variable. In order to find the affinity of each principal component to two large economies, the correlation coefficient between a principal component and the United States and Japan variables are reported. Needless to say, the United States and Japan are not included in the variable set that yields the principal component; the last two rows are reported only for reference.

We can give the following interpretation to the loading factors of major principal components. Like the interpretation of factors in factor analysis, its value is heuristic rather than definitive. However, a close look at loading factors yields various clues as to the homogeneity as well as the diversity of macroeconomic activities in the region.

1. Change in money supply: The first principal component, which explains about one-half of the total variance, indicates that this series consists of variables that are rather homogeneous across the countries studied, with the possible exception of Taiwan. This common trend shows a pattern similar to Japan's changes in money supply. The second principal component seems to be related to the difference between the money supply pattern in Indonesia, on one hand, and in the Philippines and Thailand, on the other.

2. Interest rate: Loading factors of the first components seem to suggest that NIEs such as Korea, Singapore, and Taiwan behave differently from other countries in the region, and the difference between them explains a substantial part of the total variance.

Table 14.5 Loading Factor of Each Principal Component

Variable and Country	Principal Component 1	2	3
Change in money supply			
Korea	0.812	0.243	0.277
Indonesia	0.656	0.587	−0.160
Malaysia	0.877	0.094	−0.295
Philippines	0.715	−0.591	−0.100
Singapore	0.779	0.293	0.170
Thailand	0.719	−0.499	−0.364
Taiwan	0.402	−0.280	0.844
(USA)[a]	−0.238	−0.191	0.634
(Japan)[a]	0.579	0.129	0.385
Interest rate			
Korea	0.926	0.012	0.205
Indonesia	−0.761	0.359	0.522
Malaysia	−0.696	−0.480	−0.430
Philippines	−0.626	−0.660	0.351
Singapore	0.528	−0.821	0.119
Thailand	−0.420	−0.857	0.023
Taiwan	0.802	−0.514	0.092
(USA)[a]	0.404	−0.764	0.142
(Japan)[a]	0.383	−0.799	0.064
Change in consumer price			
Korea	0.572	0.689	0.365
Indonesia	0.887	−0.003	−0.038
Malaysia	0.960	−0.034	−0.038
Philippines	0.393	−0.638	0.656
Singapore	0.895	−0.244	−0.256
Thailand	0.956	0.168	−0.090
Taiwan	0.912	0.179	0.189
Hong Kong	0.799	−0.265	−0.318
(USA)[a]	0.739	0.416	0.204
(Japan)[a]	0.812	0.183	0.191
Change in real GDP			
Korea	0.075	0.539	0.786
Indonesia	0.531	0.260	−0.740
Malaysia	0.783	−0.507	0.055
Philippines	0.665	−0.196	0.091
Singapore	0.886	−0.372	0.043
Thailand	0.648	−0.096	0.563
Taiwan	0.453	0.821	0.058
Hong Kong	0.673	0.549	−0.297
(USA)[a]	0.190	0.539	0.363
(Japan)[a]	0.169	−0.199	0.435
Ratio of investment in GDP			
Korea	0.368	0.703	0.212
Indonesia	−0.447	−0.463	0.676
Malaysia	0.738	−0.615	0.219

(continued)

Table 14.5 (continued)

Variable and Country	Principal Component 1	2	3
Philippines	0.944	−0.241	0.131
Singapore	0.524	−0.810	0.063
Thailand	−0.026	0.517	0.805
Taiwan	0.870	0.412	−0.090
Hong Kong	0.784	0.377	0.006
(USA)[a]	0.445	0.502	−0.527
(Japan)[a]	0.549	0.742	0.255

Source: See main text for detail.

[a]Correlation coefficients with macroeconomic variables for the United States and Japan are given for reference.

3. Change in CPI: The first component indicates a generic movement that is at the same time closely related to movements in CPI in the United States and Japan.

4. Change in real GNP: Here also Korea shows a different movement from other countries, as indicated by the first component.

5. Ratio of investment to GNP: Here the NIEs and the Philippines somehow move together, and Indonesia and Thailand have something in common.[1]

We have seen by principal component analysis that the degree of confluence in macroeconomic variables in eight East Asian nations is comparable to that in the European Community where momentum is toward market integration and currency unification.

14.3 The Degree of Trade Intensity and the Rate of Protection in Asia

In this section we will examine to what extent Asian nations satisfy the preconditions for an FTA or FTAs. Let us review first how closely Asian nations are interrelated by trade. Frankel (1991) doubts the existence of a trend of increasing intraregional trade intensity. According to him, the share (37.4 percent) of intraregional trade among Asian nations in 1989 was smaller than that among EC countries (59.9 percent), and there is very little difference from that in North America (36.0 percent). The reason for the increase in the share from 33 percent in 1980 to 37 percent in 1989 was merely the increase of the Asian share in the total trade volume in the world. He concludes, "it is likely that there has in fact been no movement toward intra-regional bias in the evolv-

1. It is interesting to see from a similar observation that in EC countries we suspect different patterns between Germany, on one hand, and Romance countries such as France, Italy, and Spain, on the other.

ing pattern of trade." We will examine whether this statement reflects the Asian trade situation.

In order to assess their degree of interconnectedness in trade, let us compare Asian nations with EC nations by the trade intensity index which Yamazawa, Hirata, and Yokota (1991) have developed extensively. The trade intensity index between country *i* and country *j* ($I_{i,j}$) is defined as

(1) $$I_{i,j} = (T_{i,j}/T_i) / (T_{W,j} / T_W) \text{ where}$$

$T_{i,j}$ = trade volume of country *i* with country *j*,
T_i = the total trade volume of country *i*,
$T_{W,j}$ = trade volume of the world with country *j*, and
T_W = the total trade volume of the world.

Accordingly, the index is the ratio of the share of trade with country *j* in the total trade of country *i* to the share of country *j*'s trade in total world trade. The index is normalized by dividing by the relative share of the country in total world trade so that mere size effects are eliminated. If the degree of trade interaction between country *i* and country *j* is equal to that between the world and country *j*, then the index is equal to unity. The higher the index, the more closely the two countries are interrelated by trade.

The rationale of using a trade intensity index to evaluate the existence of preconditions for the creation of an FTA is as follows: (i) an FTA is more likely to be created among countries which are "natural trading partners" to each other, because an FTA consisting of natural trading partners is likely to be trade-creating rather than trade-diverting, and because an economic incentive to create one is stronger than otherwise; (ii) if countries are natural trading partners to each other, they must be already closely interrelated by trade (i.e., the trade intensity indices among these countries should be high); (iii) hence (from [i] and [ii]), if trade intensity indices are high among a group of countries, an FTA is more likely to be formed among these countries than otherwise when some political move is initiated.

Tables 14.6 and 14.7 depict the trade intensity indices among Asian countries and among EC countries, respectively. As is easily seen, those indices that adjust for the size effect of trading partners show in many cases higher values than those in the EC. For example, in the European Community those indices exceed three only in three cases, i.e., United Kingdom–Ireland, Belgium-Luxembourg–Netherlands, and Italy-Greece; in East Asia they exceed three in nine cases, despite the fact that the number of countries in Asia (9) is smaller than that in the European Community (11). In particular, trade intensity among Malaysia, Singapore, and Thailand is extremely strong. In general, Singapore is interrelated strongly with other East Asian countries. Furthermore, the high values of the trade intensity indices with Japan indicate that Japan plays an important role in Asia. As far as we can tell from the levels of the trade intensity index, we may say that, contrary to the impression given by Frankel

Table 14.6 Trade Intensity Indices among Asian Countries, 1990

	United States	Japan	Hong Kong	Korea	Taiwan	Brunei	Indonesia	Malaysia	Philippines	Singapore	Thailand
United States		2.10	1.23	2.15	2.13	0.44	0.90	1.15	1.95	1.33	1.15
Japan	2.10		1.46	3.43	2.63	4.41	4.88	2.44	2.57	1.89	3.30
Hong Kong	1.23	1.46		1.84	3.43	0.16	1.28	1.12	2.27	2.27	1.62
Korea	2.15	3.43	1.84		1.18	3.11	2.85	2.02	1.84	1.41	1.30
Taiwan	2.13	2.63	3.43	1.18		1.29	2.71	2.09	2.71	1.82	1.95
Brunei	0.44	4.41	0.16	3.11	1.29		0.48	2.76	8.47	10.68	6.25
Indonesia	0.90	4.88	1.28	2.85	2.71	0.48		1.65	1.57	4.35	1.02
Malaysia	1.15	2.44	1.12	2.02	2.09	2.76	1.65		2.94	15.18	3.68
Philippines	1.95	2.57	2.27	1.84	2.71	8.47	1.57	2.94		2.60	1.90
Singapore	1.33	1.89	2.27	1.41	1.82	10.68	4.35	15.18	2.60		5.95
Thailand	1.15	3.30	1.62	1.30	1.95	6.25	1.02	3.68	1.90	5.95	

Source: IMF, *Directions of Trade Statistics* (Washington, D.C., 1991).

Table 14.7 **Trade Intensity Indices among EC Countries, 1990**

	United States	Japan	United Kingdom	Belgium-Luxembourg	Denmark	France	Germany	Italy	Netherlands	Greece	Ireland	Portugal	Spain
United States		2.10	0.91	0.48	0.35	0.45	0.49	0.47	0.50	0.34	0.78	0.33	0.47
Japan	2.10		0.54	0.30	0.43	0.31	0.53	0.30	0.35	0.45	0.42	0.25	0.30
United Kingdom	0.91	0.54		1.44	1.64	1.51	1.36	1.14	1.67	1.15	6.95	1.68	1.52
Belgium-Luxembourg	0.48	0.30	1.44		0.75	2.68	2.07	1.11	3.49	0.89	0.94	0.93	0.91
Denmark	0.35	0.43	1.64	0.75		0.86	2.00	0.92	1.42	1.28	1.00	1.48	0.69
France	0.45	0.31	1.51	2.68	0.86		1.82	2.32	1.44	1.34	1.17	2.01	2.79
Germany	0.49	0.53	1.36	2.07	2.00	1.82		1.91	2.33	1.94	0.94	1.50	1.50
Italy	0.47	0.30	1.14	1.11	0.92	2.32	1.91		1.02	3.25	0.70	1.58	2.16
Netherlands	0.50	0.35	1.67	3.49	1.42	1.44	2.33	1.02		1.38	1.20	1.18	1.09
Greece	0.34	0.45	1.15	0.89	1.28	1.34	1.94	3.25	1.38		0.74	0.64	0.99
Ireland	0.78	0.42	6.95	0.94	1.00	1.17	0.94	0.70	1.20	0.74		0.76	0.83
Portugal	0.33	0.25	1.68	0.93	1.48	2.01	1.50	1.58	1.18	0.64	0.76		7.07
Spain	0.47	0.30	1.52	0.91	0.69	2.79	1.50	2.16	1.09	0.99	0.83	7.07	

Source: IMF, *Direction of Trade Statistics* (Washington, D.C., 1991).

(1991), the degree of trade interdependence is quite strong among Asian nations. (In fact his other study using the gravity model [Frankel 1992] confirms our findings.)

Let us now turn to changes in the trade intensity indices during the 1980s. Table 14.8, which is cited from Yamazawa et al. (1991), indicates changes in trade intensity indices of exports from 1980 to 1987. The entry in the *i*th row and *j*th column indicates exports from country *i* to country *j*. The index rose slightly from 1.598 to 1.711 among EC countries. Some of the indices among Asian nations increased, but some decreased. Therefore it is hard to say whether Asian trade intensity indices increased. As far as the trend is concerned, the trade intensity indices confirm the argument of Frankel (1991).

In summary, though we found the level of trade intensity among Asian nations to be even higher than in the European Community, we could not necessarily detect a distinct increasing trend. This seems to reflect the fact that, while in the European Community several programs aimed toward market integration were realized during the 1980s, in Asia the push toward an FTA became active only recently. In light of recent political developments toward an FTA mentioned in the introduction, intraregional trade intensity can be expected to increase in Asia in the 1990s, as it did in Europe in the 1980s.

Table 14.6 appears to indicate that trade intensity between the United States and Asian countries is not particularly strong. The indices exceed two only with respect to Japan, Korea, and Taiwan. This hardly means, however, that the United States is not an important trading partner of Asian nations. This misleading impression comes from the nature of the trade intensity index, which captures the degree of closeness in terms of trade only *relative* to the size of a country's trading partner. It does not capture the absolute degree of a country's dependence on trade with a particular partner. For example, if a small Asian nation has a low trade intensity index with the United States, this may just imply that the share of trade with the small nation in the trade volume of the United States is relatively small. The United States may well be an important trading partner of the Asian nation. Thus we have to provide an alternative index that indicates the degree of one nation's dependence on trade with another.

Table 14.9 summarizes our attempt to provide such an index. It tabulates the amount of exports and imports of a country with a particular trading partner as a percentage of the country's GNP. For example, the third entry of the first row (14.86) shows that the amount of Korea's trade with the United States ($35.6 billion) is 14.86 percent of Korea's GNP ($239.8 billion). We may call it a *trade dependence index,* because it shows the degree to which a country depends on trade with a specific partner, or the degree to which a country would be jeopardized by a trade embargo (export or import) by a particular trading partner.

Table 14.9 reveals that East Asian nations depend heavily on trade with the United States and with Japan. Therefore, it would be infeasible as well as un-

Table 14.8 **Matrix of Trade Intensity Indices, 1980 and 1987**

		Importer									
Exporter		Japan	United States	Malaysia	Philippines	Singapore	Thailand	Korea	Taiwan	Hong Kong	EC12
Japan	1980		2.028	3.278	3.461	2.755	3.464	4.125	4.470	3.681	0.401
	1987		2.411	1.859	2.217	2.207	2.468	3.893	3.937	2.209	0.482
United States	1980	1.552		1.244	2.477	1.275	1.193	2.060	2.212	1.207	0.754
	1987	2.093		1.498	2.305	1.347	1.148	2.072	2.121	0.874	0.680
Malaysia	1980	3.688	1.356		4.053	17.641	3.406	2.014	3.325	1.889	0.507
	1987	3.703	1.086		6.486	15.470	5.459	3.582	2.896	1.610	0.413
Philippines	1980	4.208	2.286	3.361		1.795	2.547	3.487	2.043	3.329	0.504
	1987	3.261	2.371	4.104		2.925	4.204	1.161	2.402	2.775	0.553
Singapore	1980	1.301	1.056	30.949	3.775		10.229	1.494	1.157	7.752	0.369
	1987	1.713	1.598	27.905	5.228		8.118	1.114	1.293	3.612	0.355
Thailand	1980	2.437	1.050	9.279	0.963	7.130		0.754	1.402	5.098	0.749
	1987	2.838	1.226	6.592	2.205	7.713		0.892	1.245	2.408	0.645
Korea	1980	2.800	2.194	2.155	2.298	1.405	2.198		1.204	4.735	0.448
	1987	3.381	2.550	1.247	1.675	1.669	1.105		0.801	2.662	0.407
Taiwan	1980	1.775	2.850	1.769	2.631	2.539	2.088	1.341		7.837	0.421
	1987	2.459	2.909	0.995	3.082	2.141	1.513	0.802		4.382	0.398
Hong Kong	1980	0.744	2.170	1.836	4.440	4.039	2.536	1.145	1.257		0.668
	1987	0.965	1.826	1.245	3.685	2.332	1.763	1.767	1.098		0.468
EC12	1980	0.155	0.452	0.423	0.307	0.322	0.342	0.193	0.201	0.431	1.598
	1987	0.310	0.568	0.277	0.352	0.326	0.379	0.295	0.330	0.325	1.711

Source: Yamazawa et al. (1991).

Table 14.9 **Trade Dependence Indices: Ratio of the Amount of Trade (export plus import) to GNP, 1990 (%)**

	Partner				
Country	NIEs[a]	ASEAN[b]	United States	Japan	World
Korea	4.07	3.90 (1.08)	14.86	13.57	53.60
Hong Kong	31.45	17.51 (8.53)	37.82	25.64	235.18
Singapore	34.48	68.46	60.74	48.79	328.64
Taiwan	9.99	6.74 (2.23)	21.24	15.05	75.78
Brunei[c]	26.24	27.98 (17.50)	4.30	32.39	103.42
Indonesia	8.05	4.04 (2.97)	5.48	15.26	44.37
Malaysia	39.42	33.11 (25.99)	23.34	27.17	137.89
Philippines	7.92	4.19 (1.70)	12.86	9.16	48.25
Thailand	11.42	8.48 (5.33)	10.96	17.81	70.57
United States	1.91	0.86 (0.33)	—	2.61	16.98
Japan	2.81	1.64 (0.49)	4.90	—	17.79

[a]Singapore is included in both NIEs and ASEAN.
[b]Singapore figure is shown in parentheses.
[c]Figures for 1989.

profitable for East Asian nations to form an FTA without the United States and Japan.

Let us now examine the degree of protection in East Asian countries, because, in order to assess the conditions for creating an FTA, we have to know not only how closely nations are interwoven by trade, but also how much their import-competing industries are protected by tariff and nontariff barriers (NTBs). Figure 14.1 compares trade-weighted average most-favored-nation (MFN) tariffs of six Asian nations with those of Japan and the United States. Except for Singapore, where the trade-weighted average tariff is very low (i.e., about one percent), tariffs in East Asian countries are substantially higher than in Japan and the United States. In particular, those in Indonesia and the Philippines are high at around 20 percent, while those in Japan and the United States are less than 4 percent. Thus, as is the case in most developing countries, the degree of tariff protection in East Asia is fairly high.

Table 14.10 summarizes the (simple) average of tariff rates by commodities in East Asia. Note that the numbers in figure 14.1 are *trade-weighted* average

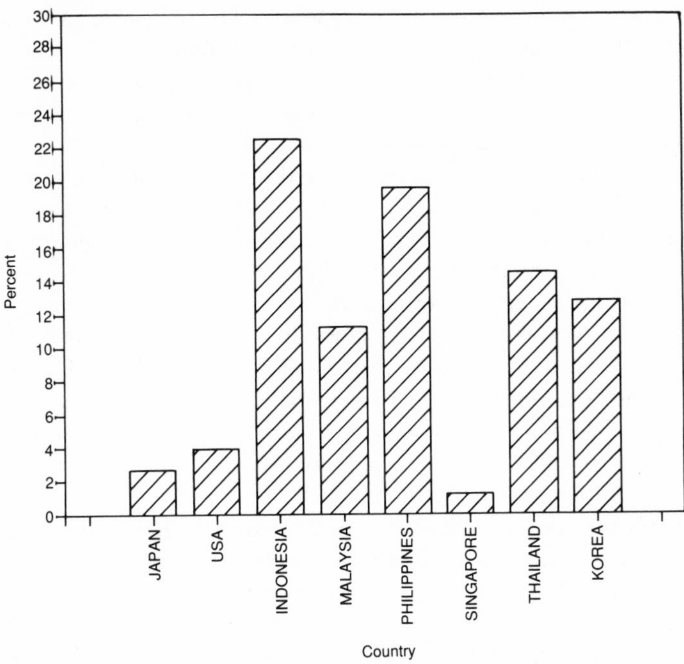

Fig. 14.1 Trade-weighted average most-favored-nation (MFN) tariff

Table 14.10 Average Tariff Rate by Broad Tariff Categories

Category	Indonesia (1980)	Malaysia (1982)	Philippines (1982)	Singapore (1983)	Thailand (1983)	ASEAN
Primary goods	14.86	3.46	23.56	0.11	19.76	12.35
Intermediate goods	24.94	17.04	26.65	8.62	26.96	20.84
Capital goods (including parts, excluding transport equipment)	20.05	6.50	21.97	0.28	23.72	14.50
Consumer goods	65.57	63.85	42.21	9.46	49.40	46.10
Transport equipment (excluding passenger motor cars, including parts)	27.39	19.26	20.92	2.00	22.41	18.40
Other	17.16	10.64	27.66	0.00	13.12	13.72
Total	32.59	24.99	29.18	6.41	30.66	24.77

Source: Naya and Plummer, (1989).

tariff rates, which cannot be directly compared with those in table 14.10. Table 14.10 shows that the tariff rate increases according to the degree of processing: consumer goods have the highest tariff rate, and primary goods the lowest. It should be noted that in Indonesia and Malaysia the average tariff rates for consumer goods are as high as 60 percent.

In addition to tariffs, import-competing industries in East Asian countries are heavily protected by NTBs, such as quotas, restrictive licensing, and import prohibition. Table 14.11, cited from Naya and Plummer (1989), indicates the number of NTBs by broad commodity categories in East Asia. Due to the limitation of data, we are not able to provide here comparison with countries in other regions. However, table 14.11 shows that quite a few products are restricted by NTBs in these countries. In particular, the number of NTBs in Indonesia (799) and the Philippines (497) is remarkable. As is the case for tariff protection, NTBs seem to rise along with the degree of processing. In all countries listed in table 14.11, the number of NTBs on manufactures is substantially larger than that on primary goods.

The numbers above show that trade in East Asia, especially trade in the manufacturing sector, is heavily protected by both tariffs and NTBs at present. Therefore, if an FTA is formed among these countries, the manufacturing trade in the area is likely to increase substantially. The magnitude of the possible gains from trade liberalization among Asian countries, along with their already high degree of economic interrelatedness, would seem to constitute a strong incentive for these nations to create an FTA (or FTAs) in East Asia.

14.4 Conditions for a Currency Union

Are the Asian nations or some subset of them an appropriate group of economies for the use of a single currency, or at least for the fixing of exchange rates among their currencies? It seems appropriate here to recall how Mundell (1961) started to analyze this question. If there is neither wage-price rigidity nor transaction costs, the exchange rate regime may not make a substantial difference because money would be neutral. This seems to be the main message of the cash-in-advance model applied to the problem of exchange-rate regime choice (e.g., Helpman and Razin 1979; Lucas 1982). However, if there

Table 14.11 ASEAN Nontariff Barriers (in numbers of six-digit CCCN products affected)

Category	Brunei	Indonesia (1980)	Malaysia (1981)	Philippines (1983)	Singapore (1983)	Thailand (1983)
Primary goods	62	319	103	147	70	65
Manufactures	77	480	70	350	91	118
Total	139	799	173	497	161	184

Source: Naya and Plummer (1989).

is price rigidity or transaction costs, regions that have different real exogenous shocks should be within different currency areas, because prices do not adjust enough if they are closely linked by fixed exchange rates. If, for instance, the Japanese island of Hokkaido and the mainland Honshu are under different real shocks and wages are rigid, then it is better for the two regions to have different monetary policies.

McKinnon (1963) emphasized the role of the degree of openness as a criterion for the feasibility of the floating regime. Autonomy in conducting monetary policy is the main merit of floating exchange rates. If a country is too open and the role of nontraded goods is minimal, then the merit of an autonomous monetary policy will be small because the wage level will immediately adjust to the international level.

Mundell and others (e.g., Ingram 1973) also emphasized the role of factor movements. If labor can move quickly from Hokkaido to Honshu, then unemployment in Hokkaido is a lesser concern because workers can move to Honshu. If funds are easily moved from one place to other, it reduces the problem of balance of payments constraints, which could be a limiting factor for macroeconomic stabilization between regions with sticky wages and prices.

We shall examine these three conditions in turn. The first aspect, the importance of the synchronization or the dissynchronization of real disturbances for the choice of a currency area, is developed by Fukuda and Hamada (1988) in the context of a two-country version of the Dornbusch model of exchange rate determination. They showed that Poole's (1970) familiar argument for the choice of targets for stabilization in the IS-LM model can be extended to the discussion of optimal interventions in the exchange market.

In a two-country model positing symmetric economic structures, Fukuda and Hamada showed, using the technique of Aoki (1981), that the system can be decomposed into the system of average variables and difference variables. In the system of average variables, that is, in the whole system, Poole's results hold: worldwide demand shocks on IS can be more effectively handled by controlling the average money supply of the world as in McKinnon's proposal for controlling the total money supply of the world. Worldwide shocks on the LM curve, on the other hand, can be more effectively handled by controlling the average interest rate.

In the system of difference variables the following results have direct implication on the choice of a monetary regime: no or little intervention is needed when country-specific disturbances are mainly on the IS curve, including disturbances due to changing competitiveness in trade; extensive intervention in order to slow down the movements of exchange rate, or pegging the exchange rate, is desirable when country-specific disturbances are mainly on the LM curve.

The results corresponding to country-specific disturbances can be reinterpreted in the context of the choice of a currency area. Consider a region, a group of nations. Economic interactions with the rest of the world can be regarded as regionwide shocks to the system consisting of these economies. The basic economic difference between a currency union with fixed exchange rates and a floating exchange-rate regime within the region rests on the absence or presence of autonomy in macroeconomic policy. By forming a currency union these countries indirectly align their price levels with each other. With the floating exchange-rate regime, on the other hand, a country can essentially choose its own price level.

Suppose country-specific monetary disturbances affect these countries differently, but country-specific real disturbances hardly affect them, then keeping price levels aligned among these countries will promote economic stabilization. If, on the other hand, country-specific real disturbances affect these countries differently, but country-specific monetary disturbances hardly affect them, then it will be desirable that each country be allowed to conduct independent monetary policy provided that some degree of wage-price rigidity exists. It is at least clear from this reasoning that a group of nations will be better off not forming a currency union if country-specific real disturbances are prevalent. The reader will see that this is a rather straightforward extension of Mundell's argument.

In the following, we will measure the degree of synchronization of real as well as monetary disturbances among Asian countries and compare the degree of synchronization with that among EC countries. Here again, we rely on the principal component method. We will show that the degree of confluence in real disturbances is quite high among Asian nations. A brief explanation of our method follows:

With regard to real disturbances, we concentrate on disturbances of investment behavior because we found that consumption behavior is much more stable and that the magnitude of net export is much smaller. We estimated the following investment function first:

$$\text{(2)} \qquad \ln I_t^i = \alpha_0^i + \alpha_1^i \ln r_{t-1}^i + \alpha_2^i \ln Y_{t-1}^i + \alpha_3^i T + \varepsilon_t^i, \text{ where}$$

I_t^i = investment (in real terms) in country i at time t,
r_{t-1}^i = interest rate in country i at time $t-1$,
Y_{t-1}^i = real GNP in country i at time $t-1$,
T = time trend, and
ε_t^i = error term.

Since data for interest rates in Hong Kong were unavailable, we ran ordinary least squares (OLS) regressions on annual data (1978–90) from the remaining seven Asian countries: Korea, Singapore, Taiwan, Indonesia, Malaysia, the Philippines, and Thailand. We obtained fairly satisfactory results for most countries, with expected signs of coefficients (i.e., $\alpha_1^i < 0$ and $\alpha_2^i > 0$) and with statistical significance. Then, we used the obtained error term (ε) as a proxy variable for real disturbances in each country.

For monetary disturbances, we estimated the following money demand function:

(3) $$\ln M_t^i = \beta_0^i + \beta_1^i \ln r_t^i + \beta_2^i \ln Y_t^i + \beta_3^i T + \eta_t^i, \text{ where}$$

M_t^i = real money supply (M_1) in country i at time t and
η_t^i = error term,

and the remaining notations are the same as those in equation (2). We again ran OLS regressions on annual data (1977–89) from the seven countries mentioned above. Again, for most countries we obtained coefficient estimates with correct signs (i.e., $\beta_1{}^i < 0$ and $\beta_2{}^i > 0$) and with statistical significance. We used the error term (η) as a proxy variable for monetary disturbances.

Then, we performed principal component analysis for the above residuals as proxies for real and monetary disturbances. For the purpose of comparison, we made similar estimates for the two sets of EC countries (see section 14.2 above) and for the Summit countries (the United States, Japan, Germany, France, Italy the United Kingdom, and Canada).

Table 14.12 shows the contribution of the first three principal components to explaining the variance of real and monetary disturbances. In the case of real or IS disturbances, the first principal component explains 46.1 percent of the total variance in Asia, whereas it explains less than one-third of the total variance in other groups. In particular, in the larger EC countries it explains only one-quarter. This shows that investment equations in Asian economies are subject to disturbances that are more synchronized than in other regions.

For monetary shocks, on the other hand, there does not seem to exist a significant difference in the accounting power of the first principal component. The theoretical analysis of Fukuda and Hamada (1988) concludes that synchronized real disturbances are a good reason to form a currency union. Thus our analysis seems to suggest that there are grounds to form a currency union in East Asia and that they are at least as good as the reasons for forming one

Table 14.12 Principal Components (P.C.) Analysis of Macroeconomic Disturbances (cumulative R^2)

Disturbance	Asia[a]	Larger EC[b]	Smaller EC[c]	Summit[d]
Real disturbance (ε)				
First P.C.	0.461	0.259	0.303	0.323
Second P.C.	0.657	0.491	0.575	0.557
Third P.C.	0.809	0.678	0.747	0.721
Monetary disturbance (η)				
First P.C.	0.410	0.320	0.385	0.331
Second P.C.	0.634	0.529	0.593	0.543
Third P.C.	0.772	0.686	0.755	0.724

Source: See main text for details.

[a]Korea, Taiwan, Singapore, Indonesia, Malaysia, Philippines, and Thailand.

[b]Germany, France, Italy, United Kingdom, Spain, Netherlands, and Belgium.

[c]Luxembourg, Ireland, Portugal, Greece, Denmark, Belgium, and Netherlands.

[d]United States, Japan, Germany, France, Italy, United Kingdom, and Canada.

in Europe. The negative correlations between U.S. and Japanese real disturbances and the first principal component in table 14.13 suggest that linking a common East Asian currency to the U.S. dollar and the yen may not be necessary.

We add the following heuristic remarks on loading factors of principal components of these residuals (see table 14.13):

1. IS residuals: The first factor may be interpreted as the average part of the macroeconomic time series. Every East Asian nation except Korea contributes to this factor. This seems to indicate that Korea was subject to different kinds of real shocks during this period. (As far as the numbers tell, this might give some economic rationale for creating a currency union excluding Korea. We are by no means suggesting such a union from this casual finding. Moreover, we have to take into account many other aspects, geographical, political, and so forth, before proposing a concrete currency union.) The second factor is associated with the Philippines and Indonesia. The third principal component is dominated by the influence of Korea.

2. LM residuals: Loading factors of the first principal component of LM

Table 14.13 Loading Factors of Each Principal Component

	Principal component		
Disturbance and Country	1	2	3
Real disturbance			
Korea	0.096	0.025	0.992
Indonesia	0.388	0.662	−0.127
Malaysia	0.950	0.050	0.043
Philippines	0.462	0.775	0.090
Singapore	0.830	−0.467	−0.031
Thailand	0.668	−0.330	0.119
Taiwan	0.902	−0.063	−0.201
(USA)[a]	−0.548	−0.137	−0.146
(Japan)[a]	−0.067	−0.395	0.278
Monetary disturbance			
Korea	0.553	0.534	0.466
Indonesia	0.654	0.060	0.354
Malaysia	0.853	−0.318	−0.134
Philippines	0.573	0.563	0.037
Singapore	0.569	−0.715	−0.098
Thailand	−0.115	−0.587	0.714
Taiwan	0.862	−0.053	−0.300
(USA)[a]	0.042	−0.468	0.262
(Japan)[a]	0.370	−0.186	−0.464

Source: See main text for details.

[a]Correlation coefficients with real and monetary disturbances for the United States and Japan are given for reference.

residuals tell that monetary disturbances in Thailand move differently from those in other East Asian countries.

Before going into the discussion of the degree of factor mobility, let us look briefly at McKinnon's argument on openness of national economies. The last column of table 14.9 indicates that some Asian countries have an extremely high degree of openness. This implies that, for example, to make Hong Kong, Singapore, and Malaysia each a single currency union with a floating rate may not be an appropriate choice of monetary regime. Incidentally, the corresponding figures for EC countries range from very open countries (Ireland, 141.9 percent; Belgium-Luxembourg, 141.4 percent; and the Netherlands, 106.6 percent) to fairly closed countries (Spain, 29.3 percent; Italy, 37.1 percent; and France, 38.3 percent).

Now let us examine the degree of factor mobility, both capital and labor, among East Asian nations. As Ingram (1969) pointed out, high mobility of production factors is another reason for the formation of a common currency area.

Comprehensive data on labor mobility in East Asia are hard to obtain. Available data suggest, however, that there is a high degree of labor mobility among East Asian nations, mostly from less-developed ASEAN nations to the more industrialized and capital-abundant NIEs. Table 14.14 shows the degree of labor inflow in selected countries. In Singapore, one of the largest labor recipient countries in East Asia, the level of inflow of foreign workers was 128,000, and the share of foreign labor in the total labor force was about 10 percent. As the table shows, the share of labor inflow in the total labor force in Singapore was generally higher than those in Europe and Japan. Except for Switzerland, where the share was as high as 17.48 percent, the share for Singapore was higher than any other country in the table, that is, even higher than Germany, a major recipient of "guest workers" for many years. Singapore receives many foreign workers from neighboring ASEAN countries: Malaysia, Indonesia, the Philippines, and Thailand. In 1989, the share of workers coming from these four countries in the total labor inflow into Singapore was as high as 83.1 percent.

To some East Asian countries, the outflow of labor to foreign countries is also important. For example, in 1987, the Philippines sent about 400,000 workers to foreign countries, according to the official statistics which generally underestimate the degree of labor mobility. The outflow of labor amounted to about 2 percent of the total labor force in the Philippines. While most of these workers were directed to the Middle East, about 100,000 (or one-fourth of the labor outflow) went to Asian countries.

The degree of capital mobility is also high among East Asian countries. Table 14.15 compares the ratio of the inflow of foreign direct investment (FDI) to GNP in ASEAN countries with ratios for major developed countries. Except for the Philippines, which has been suffering from economic difficulties since the middle of the 1980s, the ratio of FDI inflow to GNP is higher in the

Table 14.14 Share of Foreign Workers in Labor Force, 1986

	Number (thousands)	Share (%)
Singapore[a]	127.6	9.99
Austria	146.0	4.31
France	1,658.2	7.12
Germany	1,833.8	6.77
Netherlands	168.6	2.91
Sweden	214.9	4.88
Switzerland	566.9	17.48
Japan	30.6	0.05

Sources: Goto (1990); Japanese Ministry of Labor, *Kaigai Rodo Josei (Annual Report of Overseas Economy),* 1991.

[a]For Singapore, figure used is for 1989.

Table 14.15 Ratio of Inflow of Foreign Direct Investment to GNP, 1989[a] (%)

Country	Ratio
Indonesia	5.28
Malaysia	8.97
Philippines	1.92
Thailand	11.73
United States	8.14
Japan	0.28
France	4.47
Germany	5.22

Sources: Asian Development Bank, *Asian Development Outlook,* 1991; U.S. Department of Commerce, *Survey of Current Business* (Washington, D.C., various issues); IMF, *International Financial Statistics* (Washington, D.C., various issues).

[a]For developed countries, data used is for 1988.

ASEAN countries than in major developed countries. The figures for Malaysia (8.97 percent) and Thailand (11.73 percent) are especially high. Furthermore, it should be noted that the major part of FDI inflow to these countries comes from neighboring Asian countries. The shares of FDI from Asian countries (from Japan in parentheses) in Indonesia, Malaysia, the Philippines, and Thailand, are 41.7 (16.3) percent, 72.9 (31.1) percent, 59.8 (19.7) percent, and 69.2 (44.1) percent, respectively.

Thus, although the data are fairly limited, the above examples suggest a high degree of factor mobility among East Asian countries. This could be another rationale for creating a common currency area in East Asia.

14.5 Concluding Remarks

We have offered an overview of the conditions that are favorable or unfavorable for the formation of an FTA and of a currency union in Asia. Our method is descriptive and our finding suggestive rather than decisive. By referring to many statistical indicators from various angles, however, we hope we have provided a fairly comprehensive view of the conditions for economic integration in Asia. We can summarize our findings as follows:

The degree of interdependence among Asian nations through trade and factor movements is substantial. It might not have progressed much in recent years, as Frankel (1991) points out. However, some indicators show a higher degree of interdependence among Asian countries than among the EC countries that are about to form an integrated market. Thus, preconditions for an FTA seem to be met among Asian countries. At the same time, our study of the trade dependence index reveals that it is not advisable to allow the formation of an FTA that would hinder trade with the United States or Japan, as Asian nations are highly dependent upon these two countries. One of the reasons the Mahathir plan to create an FTA without the participation of the United States was brought to a deadlock could be the high degree of Asian economic dependence on the American economy. From this angle, some justification may be found for the seemingly premature and self-centered reaction of the United States in strongly opposing the EAEG plan despite its own move toward the NAFTA.

As for the desirability of a common currency area, we have studied several indicators: the synchronization of real disturbances emphasized by Mundell (1961) and Fukuda and Hamada (1988), the openness of Asian countries emphasized by McKinnon (1963), and the degree of capital and labor mobility emphasized by Ingram (1973) and Mundell (1961). All of these indicators seem to suggest that a case can be made for a currency union in Asia, even though it is not clear whether the common currency should be linked to a major currency such as the dollar or the yen.

We can extend the present research in various directions. For example, we may ask what the consequences of the European integration will be for the Asian economy, and what the consequences of Asian economic integration would be for the rest of the world. We may also examine the way in which Asian nations can exploit their possible strategic positions in this world where movements toward economic blocs are gaining momentum. Our findings indicate that conditions in Asia are at least as favorable to economic integration as those in already-unifying Europe.

During its notorious formation of the Greater East Asia Co-prosperity sphere that ended in the Second World War, Japan attempted to implement a scheme of mobilizing goods and resources within the region. At the same time, it attempted to create a yen bloc in East Asia in two ways. In one form, Japan issued military scrip—for example, in the Philippines, Singapore, Indonesia, and Burma—from the Southern Development Credit Vault, a kind of overseas military bank. This process implied direct economic confiscation from Asian nations of the seigniorage right. In the other form, Japan created central banks—for example, in Manchuria and North and South China—that issued

Table 14.16 Money Supply and Price Indices of Territories Occupied by Japan during World War II

	Money Supply (million)						
	Central Bank Note			Military Scrip			
Year and Month	Manchuria (yuan)	North China (yuan)	South China (yuan)	Singapore (dollar)	Philippines (peso)	Indonesia (guilder)	Burma (lupee)
1941.12	1,262	956	280				
1942.12	1,669	1,593	3,696				
1943.9	2,121	2,552	11,798	385	348	537	497
1943.12	3,011	3,762	19,150	482	513	674	685
1944.12	5,877	15,841	139,699	1,512	4,874	1,976	2,832
1945.8	8,158	93,585	2,277,179	5,650	6,150	3,880	5,654
	Price Index (1941.12 = 100)						
	Changchun	Beijing	Shanghai	Singapore	Manila	Jakarta	Rangoon
1942.12	112	158	206	352	200	134	705
1943.12	122	267	671	1,201	1,196	227	1,718
1944.12	162	892	5,707	10,766	14,285	1,279	8,707
1945.8	—	17,273	7,189	35,000	14,285	3,197	185,647

Source: Nakamura (1989, 31).

regional currencies that were pegged at par with the yen. Through the monetary expansion by these central banks, these regions suffered tremendous inflation. Japanese war merchants exporting goods to these areas earned profits from the inflation, and by their privilege they could convert their regional profits into the yen at par. Table 14.16 illustrates this.

This clearly tells us that there is a great distance between designating one region a suitable common currency area and actually implementing a common currency union. The question of seigniorage should be cleared, and the political-economy aspect cannot be neglected. This paper will be merely a modest, preliminary step to these goals, if a currency union is ever to be contrived in Asia.

References

Adelman, I., and C. T. Morris. 1967. *Society, politics, and economic development: A quantitative approach.* Baltimore, Md.: Johns Hopkins University Press.

Aoki, M. 1981. *Dynamic analysis of open economies.* New York: Academic Press.

Frankel, J. 1991. Is a yen bloc forming in Pacific Asia. In *Finance and the international economy: The AMEX Bank Review prize essays,* ed. R. O'Brien. London: Oxford University Press.

———. 1992. Is Japan creating a yen bloc in East Asia and the Pacific? Paper prepared for the NBER conference on Japan and the U.S. in Pacific Area.

Fukuda, S., and K. Hamada. 1988. Towards the implementation of desirable rules of monetary coordination and intervention. Economic Growth Center Paper no. 411, Yale University.

Goto, J. 1990. *Gaikokujin Rodo no Keizaigaku (An economic analysis of migrant workers).* (In Japanese.) Tokyo: The Oriental Economist, Ltd.

Helpman, E., and A. Razin. 1979. Towards a consistent comparison of alternative exchange rate systems. *Canadian Journal of Economics* 12:394–409.

Ingram, J. C. 1969. Some implications of Puerto Rican experience. In *International Finance,* ed. R. N. Cooper. Middlesex: Penguin Books.

———. 1973. *The case for European monetary integration.* Essays in International Finance, no. 98. Princeton, N.J.: Princeton University Press.

Kaufman, L. and P. Rousseeuw. 1990. *Finding groups in data: An introduction to cluster analysis.* New York: Wiley.

Lucas, R. E., Jr. 1982. Interest rates and currency prices in a two-country world. *Journal of Monetary Economics* 10:335–59.

Mahalanobis P. C. 1936. On the generalized distance in statistics. *Proceedings of National Institute of Science of India* 12:49–55.

McKinnon, R. 1963. Optimum currency area. *American Economic Review* 53:717–24.

Mundell, R. 1961. The theory of optimum currency areas. *American Economic Review* 51:657–64.

Nakamura, T. 1989. *Keikakuka to Minshuka (Planning and democratization).* Tokyo: Iwanami Shoten.

Naya, S., and M. Plummer. 1989. *AUI background papers: Research contributions to the ASEAN-U.S. initiative.* Honolulu: East-West Center.

Poole, W. 1970. Optimal choice of monetary policy instruments in a simple stochastic macro model. *Quarterly Journal of Economics* 84.

Stone, R. 1945. The analysis of market demand. *Journal of the Royal Statistical Society,* ser. A, 108:286–382.

Yamazawa, I., A. Hirata, and K. Yokota, 1991. Evolving pattern of comparative advantage in the Pacific economies. In *The Pacific economy: Growth and external stability,* ed. M. Ariff. New York: Allen & Unwin.

Comment Masao Satake

Goto and Hamada's paper provides not only a useful empirical fact but also a stimulating discussion of economic integration for East Asia. The economic feasibility of integration for this region urgently requires analysis, so this paper can be regarded as one of the early and important contributions in this field.

The authors' main findings can be summarized as follows: First, East Asian countries are very closely interrelated, in some respects more closely than are the EC countries; second, in terms of macroeconomic variables, East Asian countries have similar economic structures, in some cases more similar than

Masao Satake is professor of economics at Otaru University of Commerce.

those of EC countries. From these observations the authors hypothesize that the preconditions for Asian economic integration are met.

Two types of integration are considered in this paper: the creation of a free trade area (FTA) and of an optimum currency area. My comment concerns only the problems involved in the FTA idea for this region because my comparative advantage lies there.

The authors make three remarks based on the analysis of trade intensity in tables 14.6–14.8 in section 14.3. First, East Asian nations are more closely related than EC nations. This is obtained from tables 14.6 and 14.7, where the trade intensity indices among the East Asian countries are higher on average than that in the European Community. Second, it is not clear from table 14.8 whether the degree of interdependence among East Asian nations has increased throughout the 1980s. Third, it is expected that the interrelationship in this area will become stronger in the 1990s because of political developments toward an FTA.

The first claim, as the authors note, contrasts with the assertion by Frankel and Wei's paper in this volume (chap. 12). According to table 12.12 in the paper by Frankel and Wei, the ratio of intraregional trade to total trade among East Asian nations is much lower than that among EC nations. And even the rise in the 1980s from 33 to 37 percent is due only to economic expansion, rather than to real integration. How do we explain these different results, and which region can we say is more closely intrarelated? There are some obvious differences in the two indexes.

In particular, the trade intensity index presents a bilateral relationship, while the intraregional trade to total trade ratio is obtained from aggregate data of trade in the region. However, it must be noted that, besides this difference, the nature of trade intensity tends to make each East Asian country's index higher than that in the European Community. The denominator of the trade intensity index T_j/T_w is country j's share of world trade. This denominator may be lower in East Asia than in the European Community, because the value of trade in the former may be smaller than in the latter. Unless the numerator $T_{i,j}/T_j$ differs significantly between the two regions, trade intensity is likely to be higher among the East Asian countries. Considering the nature of trade intensity, we must be careful when using it to compare the degree of interrelationship among regions or countries of different regions.

As for the future of intraregional trade among East Asian countries, I have a different view from the authors. We can see from table 12.12 in the paper by Frankel and Wei that in the 1980s East Asia's interregional trade with the European Community and North America expanded faster than intraregional trade. I think that this diversification of trading partners will continue because of the rapid industrialization of East Asia, unless the other two regions—the European Community and North America—become "a strong fortress."

In the latter part of section 14.3, Goto and Hamada show that the rate of protection of ASEAN countries is quite high. And so the formation of an FTA will be an enormous boon to this region. I agree with this point, but an FTA is not the only policy option for trade liberalization. It is important to compare it with the nondiscriminatory form of liberalization. If it is true that this region is very closely intrarelated, liberalization on a nondiscriminatory basis will not increase imports from outside, and therefore it may be a better policy alternative than an FTA (Drysdale and Garnaut 1989, 230–31).

My last comment relates to the question of whether the FTA proposal includes the United States and Japan. I agree with the authors' assertion that it would be infeasible as well as unprofitable for East Asian nations to form an FTA without the United States and Japan. But can an expanded region that includes the United States and Japan still keep the close relationships, as well as the homogeneity in terms of macroeconomic variables, analyzed in the first part of the paper?

In conclusion, it may be true that the East Asian countries are very closely interrelated, like those of the European Community. But I think that this does not necessarily lead to an economic justification of an East Asian free trade area.

Reference

Drysdale, Peter, and Ross Garnaut. 1989. A Pacific free trade area? In *Free trade areas and U.S. trade policy,* ed. Jeffrey J. Schott. Washington, D.C.: Institute for International Economics.

Comment Toshiaki Tachibanaki

Goto and Hamada's paper is interesting and useful because it reveals the possibility of Asian regional integration in economic activities. The basic reason for proposing such an integration is that the degree of interdependence among Asian nations is high, and even higher in some respects than among EC countries. I would like to offer two major comments and several minor comments. The two major comments are as follows.

First, I find that Goto and Hamada's empirical work is not convincing enough to conclude that the degree of interdependence among Asian nations is high. I am concerned with the definition of the East Asian countries. Goto and Hamada consider only Hong Kong, South Korea, Taiwan, Singapore, Indonesia, Malaysia, the Philippines, and Thailand. Those countries are chosen, according to the authors' statement, because data reliability in those countries is high. We see many Asian countries missing—for example, mainland China,

Toshiaki Tachibanaki is professor of economics at the Kyoto Institute of Economic Research at Kyoto University.

North Korea, Mongolia, Vietnam, Cambodia, Laos, Brunei, and some others—in all, about ten countries. Some countries are socialist, others are developing countries. However, there are no strong reasons for excluding these countries from their statistical examination.

This causes a sample selection bias. It may be possible to show that the authors chose the countries which already have a high degree of interdependence. In other words, the countries where reasonably reliable data are available are already semideveloped and are already interdependent. If all countries in East Asia were included in the sample, the degree of interdependence might not be so high. In fact, Jeffrey Frankel's (1991) paper suggested a low degree of interdependence, as mentioned by Goto and Hamada. Therefore, the choice of countries is crucial for the examination of interdependence in any region.

The second major comment concerns the role of Japan in Asian regional integration. Japan might be relatively too strong, if Asia were integrated economically. My guess is that if one country in any regional integration is too strong, the integration will not work very well. We can see an example in the role of the United States in the Central, and possibly South, American regions, where regional integration does not work well. Even in Europe, where economic integration is anticipated, several smaller countries such as Denmark are somewhat reluctant to integrate and may prefer independence rather than regional integration for fear of the power of big countries.

Another reason Asian regional integration, embracing Japan, is not desirable at this stage is that the memory of the Second World War has not yet disappeared in Asia, in particular the memory of Japanese military aggression. This memory will fade when the generation changes, though it is impossible to expect it to disappear entirely. Now, however, it is too early to argue for Asian regional integration. Japan may also be unwelcome in Asia because of its current status of economic superpower. In sum, we need more careful discussion about Asian regional integration if Japan is to be included.

I add several minor comments. First, the authors chose five key macroeconomic variables to conduct the principal component analysis. I would prefer more detail about the reasons these five variables were chosen. Second, in section 14.4 there is a proposition that factor mobility in labor and capital in Asia is high. However, only Singapore is picked up as an example of labor mobility. The degree of factor mobility must be evaluated by considering many countries in Asia.

Reference

Frankel, J. 1991. Is a yen bloc forming in Pacific Asia? In *Finance and the international economy: The AMEX Bank review prize essays,* ed. R. O'Brien. London: Oxford University Press.

Contributors

Kazumi Asako
Faculty of Economics
Yokohama National University
156 Tokiwadai Hodogaya-ku
Yokohama 240
Japan

Serguey Braguinsky
Department of Economics and Business Administration
Yokohama City University
22-2 Seto, Kanazawa-ku
Yokohama 236
Japan

Pochih Chen
Department of Economics
National Taiwan University
21 Hsu-Chou Road
Taipei 10020, Taiwan
The Republic of China

Cheng-Chung Chu
Taiwan Institute of Economic Research
178 Nanking E. Rd. Sec 2
Taipei, Taiwan
The Republic of China

Jeffrey A. Frankel
Department of Economics
797 Evans Hall
University of California
Berkeley, CA 94720

Shin-ichi Fukuda
The Institute of Economic Research
Hitotsubashi University
2-1 Naka Kunitachi
Tokyo 186
Japan

Hideki Funatsu
Otaru University of Commerce
Otaru 047
Japan

Maria S. Gochoco
School of Economics
University of the Philippines
Diliman
Quezon City 1101
The Philippines 3004

Junichi Goto
Research Institute for Economics and Business Administration
Kobe University
2-1 Rokkodai-cho
Nada-ku, Kobe 657
Japan

Koichi Hamada
Economic Growth Center
Yale University
27 Hillhouse Avenue
New Haven, CT 06520

John F. Helliwell
Department of Economics
University of British Columbia
1873 East Mall
Vancouver BC V6T 1W5

Takatoshi Ito
Hitotsubashi University
Kunitachi, Tokyo 186
Japan

Sung Hee Jwa
Korea Development Institute
P.O. Box 113, Chungnyang
Seoul 130-012
Korea

Bon Ho Koo
Department of Economics
Hanyang University
17, Haengdang-Dong, Sungdong-Gu
Seoul 133-791, Korea

Anne O. Krueger
Department of Economics
Stanford University
Stanford, CA 94305–6072

Jin-Lung Lin
Institute of Economics
Academia Sinica
Nankang, Taipei, Taiwan
Republic of China

Bih Jane Liu
Department of Economics
National Taiwan University
21 Hsu-Chou Road
Taipei 10020, Taiwan
The Republic of China

Rachel McCulloch
Department of Economics
Brandeis University
Waltham, MA 02254

Chong-Hyun Nam
Department of Economics
Korea University
1, 5-Ga, Anam-dong, Sungbuk-ku
Seoul 136-701
Korea

Kazuo Nishimura
Institute of Economic Research
Kyoto University
Sakyo-ku
Kyoto 606
Japan

Michihiro Ohyama
Department of Economics
Keio University
2-15-45 Mita, Minato-ku,
Tokyo 108
Japan

Yoshiyasu Ono
Institute of Social and Economic Research
Osaka University
Mihogaoka, Ibaraki
Osaka 567
Japan

Won-Am Park
Korea Development Institute
P.O. Box 113, Chungnyang
Seoul 130-012
Korea

San Gee
Graduate Institute of Industrial Economics
National Central University
Chung-li, Taiwan
Republic of China

Masao Satake
Otaru University of Commerce
Otaru 047
Japan

Chi Schive
National Taiwan University
21 Hsu-Chou Road
Taipei 10020, Taiwan
The Republic of China

Toshiaki Tachibanaki
Kyoto Institute of Economic Research
Kyoto University
Yoshida-honmachi, Sakyo-ku, Kyoto 606
Japan

Hiroo Taguchi
Institute of Monetary and Economic Studies
Bank of Japan
Hongoku-cho Nihonbashi Chuo-ku
Tokyo 103
Japan

Kazuo Ueda
Department of Economics
University of Tokyo
Bunkyo-ku
Tokyo 113
Japan

Shang-Jin Wei
Kennedy School of Government
79 JFK Street
Harvard University
Cambridge, MA 02138

Chung-Shu Wu
Research Fellow
The Institute of Economics
Academia Sinica
Nankang, Taipei, Taiwan
Republic of China

Naohiro Yashiro
Sophia University and Japan Center for Economic Research
2-6-1, Kayabacho, Nihonbashi
Chuo-ku, Tokyo 103
Japan

Author Index

Subject Index